Dictionary of

Computer and

Internet Terms

Seventh Edition

Douglas A. Downing, Ph.D.
School of Business and Economics
Seattle Pacific University

Michael A. Covington, Ph.D.
Artificial Intelligence Center
The University of Georgia

Melody Mauldin Covington
Covington Innovations
Athens, Georgia

BARRON'S

ABOUT THE AUTHORS

Douglas Downing teaches economics and quantitative methods and is undergraduate program director for the School of Business and Economics at Seattle Pacific University. He is the author of several books in both Barron's Easy Way and Business Review series. He is also the author of *Java Programming the Easy Way* and *Dictionary of Mathematics Terms*, published by Barron's Educational Series, Inc. He holds the Ph.D. degree in economics from Yale University.

Michael Covington is Associate Director of the Artificial Intelligence Center at the University of Georgia. He is a contributing editor for *Poptronics* magazine and is the author of *Computer Science Study Keys* (published by Barron's). He holds the Ph.D. degree in linguistics from Yale University.

Melody Mauldin Covington is a graphic designer living in Athens, Georgia. She is the author of *Dictionary of Desktop Publishing* (published by Barron's).

All inquiries should be addressed to:
Barron's Educational Series, Inc.
250 Wireless Boulevard
Hauppauge, New York 11788
http://www.barronseduc.com

Library of Congress Catalog Card No. 99-35913

International Standard Book No. 0-7641-1265-1

Library of Congress Cataloging-in-Publication Data

Downing, Douglas.
    Dictionary of computer and Internet terms / Douglas A. Downing,
  Michael A. Covington, Melody Mauldin Covington—7th ed.
        p.   cm.
    First-4th eds. published under title: Dictionary of computer
  terms.
    ISBN 0-7641-1265-1
    1. Computers—Dictionaries.   2. Internet (Computer network)—
Dictionaries.   I. Covington, Michael A., 1957–   .   II. Covington,
Melody Mauldin.   III. Downing, Douglas. Dictionary of computer
terms.   IV. Title.
QA76.15.D667   2000
004′.03—dc21   99-35913
                                                                CIP

PRINTED IN THE UNITED STATES OF AMERICA

87654321

CONTENTS

TO THE READER

Our goal in writing this book is to *explain,* not just *define.* We feel you have a right to know how your computer works, not just how to use it. Thus we cover not only business software, personal computers, and the Internet, but also fundamentals such as computer architecture and binary arithmetic.

Terms are marked *slang* or *humorous* if they are seldom used in serious writing. They are marked *jargon* if, in our estimation, they are somewhat pretentious new names for old concepts and are unlikely to remain in wide use. We provide occasional *Usage notes* to explain grammar, spelling, and proper use of words.

In recent years, several manufacturers have redefined the meaning of existing abbreviations. For example, *DVD* originally stood for *digital video disc* and is now said to stand for *digital versatile disc.* The new names do not always catch on. We are more concerned with the actual origins and meanings of terms than with the wishes of marketing departments.

Throughout, we use SMALL CAPITALS to mark important words that are defined elsewhere in this book. By following cross-references, you can quickly find all the entries that pertain to whatever interests you. For example, to learn how a computer works, look up COMPUTER ARCHITECTURE and follow the references.

Be sure to notice the visual dictionary of symbols at the end of the book. If you don't know what Σ or $\approx$ or $\bullet$ is called, don't worry; you can look it up there.

This edition adds over 200 new entries, including new coverage of Windows 2000 and substantially increased coverage of UNIX, networking, and Internet commerce, as well as a dozen new illustrations. All three of us want to thank the University of Georgia and Seattle Pacific University for access to facilities and for accommodating us as we worked on this project. Also, we'd like to thank Robert Downing for his help with 1960's data processing concepts. Many thanks also to Cathy and Sharon Covington.

We will maintain a web page with links to many of the sites mentioned in this book at:

http://www.spu.edu/~ddowning/dcitlinks.html

Many of the words used in this book are registered trademarks. We have made no attempt to determine or report their legal status. For further information about any particular product name, consult the manufacturer's literature.

NUMBERS

3COM a leading producer of networking hardware, mainly focusing on residential and small to medium businesses. In recent years the company has sharpened its focus in this area by acquiring U.S. Robotics but selling off Palm (see PALM PILOT). Their web address is www.3com.com.

3D *see* THREE-DIMENSIONAL GRAPHICS.

7-layer model *see* DATA COMMUNICATION.

8.3 filename a filename consisting of up to 8 letters or digits, a dot (period), and up to three more letters or digits, as in MS-DOS and Windows 3. *Contrast* LONG FILENAME.

10base-2 thinwire Ethernet; a type of Ethernet connection using thin coaxial cable with BNC T-connectors, a bus topology, and a maximum data rate of 10 megabits per second. Cable segments can range from 2 feet (0.6 m) to 607 feet (185 m) in length. *See* THINWIRE.
 Usage note: In this and similar terms, *10* stands for the data rate in megabits per second; *base* means *baseband* (not modulated on a higher-frequency carrier); and *2* is the approximate maximum cable length in hundreds of meters. The hyphen is often left out.

10base-5 thickwire Ethernet; a type of Ethernet connection using thick coaxial cable with special cable-piercing taps, a bus topology, and a maximum data rate of 10 megabits per second. Cable segments can range from 8.2 feet (2.5 m) to 1640 feet (500 m) in length. *See* ETHERNET; THICKWIRE.

10base-F fiber-optic Ethernet; a type of Ethernet connection using fiber-optic cable and a maximum data rate of 10 megabits per second. Cables can be as long as 1.2 miles (2 km). *See* ETHERNET; FIBER OPTICS.

10base-T twisted-pair Ethernet using Category 3 or Category 5 cable and RJ-45 modular connectors, a star topology with hubs, and a maximum data rate of 10 megabits per second. Each cable can be up to 328 feet (100 m) long. However, because they are unshielded, these cables are somewhat subject to electrical noise if placed close to motors or fluorescent lights. *See* ETHERNET; CROSSOVER CABLE; CATEGORY 5 CABLE.

16-bit program a program that runs on Intel microprocessors using only the features of the 8088 or 80286, with 16-bit internal registers. Most DOS applications and many Windows 3.1 applications are 16-bit programs. *Contrast* 32-BIT PROGRAM.

24-bit graphics graphical images that use 24 bits to represent each color, so that each color is made by mixing red, green, and blue, each of which is measured on a scale of 0 to 255, and a total of 16,777,216 colors is available. Often called "millions of colors."

24 × 7 available 24 hours a day, 7 days a week.

32-bit program a program that uses the 32-bit internal registers and large memory capacity of the Intel 386, 486, Pentium, or other compatible microprocessor; generally faster than a 16-bit program doing the same computation on the same CPU. *Contrast* 16-BIT PROGRAM. *See also* WIN32S.

100base-F fast fiber-optic Ethernet, like 10base-F but with a maximum data rate of 100 megabits per second.

100base-T fast twisted-pair Ethernet using Category 5 cable and RJ-45 modular connectors; like 10base-T but with a maximum data rate of 100 megabits per second. Many network cards and hubs are compatible with both 10base-T and 100base-T transmission. Thus, you can convert a 10base-T network to 100base-T component-by-component and switch to the higher speed when all the components have been modernized.

386 the first Intel microprocessor with 32-bit internal registers and good support for multitasking and extended memory; able to run Windows 95, but too slow for most present-day software. *See* MICROPROCESSOR; SX; DX.

403 FORBIDDEN HTTP error message indicating that the HTTP server is not permitted to read a file. This usually means that the owner of the web page has not set the correct permissions on the file. *See* PERMISSION.

404 NOT FOUND HTTP error message indicating that a web address is invalid. *See* DEAD LINK.

486 an Intel microprocessor similar to the 386 but faster; predecessor of the Pentium. *See* MICROPROCESSOR; SX; DX.

640K limit *see* DOS 640K LIMIT.

2000 *see* YEAR 2000 PROBLEM.

8088 the Intel microprocessor used in the original IBM PC (1981). It has 16-bit registers and an 8-bit external bus. *See* MICROPROCESSOR.

68000 the series of Motorola microprocessors used in the Apple Macintosh. *See* MICROPROCESSOR.

80286 the Intel microprocessor used in the IBM PC AT (1984). It is faster than the 8088 and supports extended memory but does not have 32-bit registers or the built-in ability to emulate multiple 8088s; for that reason, multitasking operating systems did not become common until the 386 was introduced. *See* MICROPROCESSOR.

80386, 80486 unofficial names for the Intel 386 and 486 microprocessors. *See* 386, 486 and references there.

GREEK LETTERS

For the complete Greek alphabet see page 554.

α (alpha) the opacity of a layer in a graphical image. *See* ALPHA.

γ (gamma) a measure of the contrast of photographic film or the nonlinearity of an electronically obtained image. *See* GAMMA.

μ (mu) abbreviation for *micro-* (one-millionth). *See* METRIC PREFIXES.

μC abbreviation for *microcontroller*.

μP abbreviation for *microprocessor*.

π (pi) the ratio of the circumference of a circle to its diameter, approximately 3.14159. *See* PI.

A

A abbreviation used in HTML to indicate an anchor, a link to another location. For an example, *see* HTML.

FIGURE 1. A4 PAPER IS LONGER AND NARROWER
THAN LETTER SIZE

A4 the standard size of typing paper everywhere except the United States, 210 × 297 mm, about $8\frac{1}{4} \times 11\frac{3}{4}$ inches. American typing paper is $8\frac{1}{2} \times 11$ inches.

A4 is part of an ISO standard for paper sizes, chosen so that A0 paper (840 ×1189 mm) has an area of 1 square meter and each size can be cut in half to make the next smaller one. Thus, the area of a sheet of A4 paper is $\frac{1}{16}$ m². For table, see PAPER SIZES (ISO).

A/B switch a two-way switch for parallel or serial port cables. It can be used to connect two printers or modems to one computer, or two computers to one printer or modem. Using an A/B switch requires some care because the computer does not know when the switch has been flipped; it is usually necessary to set the software to use the devices that are actually connected at any particular time.

ABEND (**ab**normal **end**) abnormal termination of a program due to an error condition, such as running out of memory or dividing by zero. The term is used only on IBM mainframes.

ABOI abbreviation for alt.best.of.internet, a newsgroup intended to contain interesting items that were originally posted on other newgroups. Nowadays, ABOI contains large amounts of unwanted advertising material (spam). *See* NEWSGROUP; SPAM.

abort to cancel an action or command.

Abort, Retry, Fail? an error message displayed by DOS and similar operating systems when a disk is unreadable or some other input or output operation is physically impossible. An earlier version said, "Abort, Retry, Ignore?"

The user should press a to abort (cancel) the operation, r to retry the operation (usually the best choice if it's a disk problem), or f to make the operation fail, i.e., let the program continue running but notify it that the operation was not performed. Pressing f is usually a risky move because not all programs behave correctly after a failed operation. *See also* GENERAL FAILURE, INVALID MEDIA.

ABS the function that calculates absolute value in BASIC and other programming languages. It converts negative numbers to positive while leaving positive numbers and zero unchanged. For example, ABS(37) = 37; ABS(-37) = 37; ABS(-2.5) = 2.5; ABS(1985) = 1985; ABS(0) = 0.

absolute address

1. a fixed location in the computer's memory. *See* COMPUTER ARCHITECTURE; SEGMENT; OFFSET.

2. in a spreadsheet program, a cell address that refers to a fixed location that will not change when a formula is copied to another location. In Lotus 1-2-3 and Excel, absolute addresses are indicated by placing a dollar sign before the column and row indicator. For example, if the formula 2*D7 is entered into a cell, then D7 is an absolute address. If this formula is copied to another cell, the address D7 will not change. *Contrast* RELATIVE ADDRESS.

absolute URL

a URL that contains the full address, identifying the machine, directory, and file. For example, if a web page contains the link:

```
<a href="http://www.tcoll.edu/~kstanwell/doc1.html">
```

it will find doc1 in the public directory of user kstanwell at the computer labeled www.tcoll.edu. *Contrast* RELATIVE URL.

abstract

1. a summary of a document or file. For example, in Java programming, a JAR file contains class files together with an encrypted abstract (summary) calculated with a kind of hash function. If one of the class files is tampered with, the hash function calculated from the downloaded files will not match the hash function in the abstract, so the verifier will not allow the class to load. *See also* MANIFEST.

2. not tied to a specific pre-existing example. For example, an abstract data type is one that does not correspond exactly to anything in the architecture of the computer; instead, it is declared by the programmer to suit the purposes of the program.

In Java, a class is declared abstract if there will not be any data or methods specific to that class; instead, it is to be used as a superclass for other classes that will have specific data. An abstract class cannot be instantiated, but other classes can extend it.

accelerator a device that makes an operation run faster. For example, a graphics accelerator is a card that contains built-in circuits for performing graphics operations, allowing the system to render graphics more quickly than would be the case if the microprocessor bore the entire load. *See* PC CARD.

accents marks added to letters (as in *é è ê ë*) to indicate differences of pronunciation; said to have been introduced by Aristophanes of Byzantium c. 200 B.C. to preserve the pitch accent of ancient Greek, which was dying out. The only major languages that do not require accents are English and Latin.

Most computer software treats a letter with an accent as a single character. More sophisticated systems represent the accent and the letter separately, so that any accent can be put on any letter. *See* ANSI.

acceptable-use policy a policy established by the owner of a computer system, or by an Internet service provider, concerning acceptable use of the computer and network facilities. Acceptable-use policies should generally include the following points:

1. Users are accountable for what they do. Deliberate snooping, harassment, or interference with other users will not be tolerated, nor will any deliberate unauthorized activity.

2. The computer shall be used only for its intended purposes. For example, you generally can't use your employer's computer to run another business on the side; nor can you run private money-making schemes on a computer owned by a state university. Employees are accountable for how they use their time at work.

3. Passwords must be kept secret. (*See* PASSWORD.)

4. The service provider has the right to suspend accounts that are being misused. People accused of misconduct have the right to a fair hearing.

5. Users must abide by the acceptable-use policies of newsgroups and other electronic discussion forums, which are mostly paid for by other people. On the Internet you are always someone's guest.

6. Chain letters and mass e-mailing are expensive, unwelcome, and generally not permitted. The correct way to reach a wide audience is to use an appropriate newsgroup.

7. Cyberspace is not above the law. Practices that are illegal in the real world, such as forgery, gambling, obscenity, and threatening or inciting violence, are still illegal when you do them on the computer.

8. Losing an account is not necessarily the only penalty for misconduct. The service provider cannot shield users from criminal or civil liability when they break laws or deliberately harm others. Really destructive computer abusers generally have several accounts and must be stopped by other means.

access provider (**Internet service provider**) a company that provides its customers with access to the INTERNET, typically through DIAL-UP NETWORKING. Major access providers in the United States include Microsoft, Netcom, Earthlink, and America Online. CompuServe and Prodigy provide Internet access among their other services.

Typically, the customer pays a monthly fee, and the access provider supplies software that enables the customer to connect to the Internet by modem. Some access providers also provide file space for pages on the WORLD WIDE WEB and FTP file storage.

access time the amount of time needed by a memory device to transfer data to the CPU. It is measured from the instant that the CPU requests data until the instant that the CPU receives the data. The fastest access times are those of RAM chips (typically 70 nanoseconds = 7×10^{-8} second); video RAM is somewhat slower, and disk drives are slower yet. For example, the access time of a hard disk is typically between 10 and 20 milliseconds, and that of a CD-ROM drive is more like 200 milliseconds. The access time of a CD-ROM drive sets a limit on the speed with which video or other complex data stored on the CD can be displayed.

accounts payable bills that need to be paid.

accounts receivable money that is owed to a business and can be counted as a financial asset.

accumulator the register where a computer stores the result of an arithmetic operation. For example, in 8086 assembly language, the instruction ADD AX,10 means "Add 10 to the number in the accumulator, and leave the result there." Some computers can use more than one register as an accumulator. *See* COMPUTER ARCHITECTURE; ASSEMBLY LANGUAGE.

ack an abbreviation for ASCII code 6, which stands for "acknowledged" in older teletype systems and in XMODEM and some other protocols. ACK is sent when a data packet has been received correctly and the receiving computer is ready for the next one. *Contrast* NAK.

ACM (**A**ssociation for **C**omputing **M**achinery) a worldwide association of computer professionals headquartered in the United States. Their web address is www.acm.org.

ACPI (**A**dvanced **C**onfiguration and **P**ower **I**nterface) a set of standard hardware/software interactions that give the operating system the ability to direct power management of hardware devices. For example, a computer with ACPI can turn itself off under software control as the last step in shutting down the operating system.

acquire to obtain a file (for editing) from an ANALOG source, such as a SCANNER or video input (*see* FRAME GRABBER). Similar to IMPORT, except that the image is not coming from a file.

Acrobat software from ADOBE SYSTEMS, INC. for creating and reading PDF (**P**ortable **D**ocument **F**ormat) files. Acrobat Reader enables users to view and print PDF files that they receive from others; it is distributed free from http://www.adobe.com. Acrobat Distiller, a commercial product, creates PDF files by "distilling" (converting) existing PostScript files and by functioning as a printer driver so that any application can "print" to a PDF file. *See* PDF.

acronym a word formed from the initial parts of other words. For example, BASIC stands for **B**eginner's **A**ll-Purpose **S**ymbolic **I**nstruction **C**ode. *See* TLA.

activate
1. to choose a window in which you want to type. This is done by moving the mouse pointer into the window and clicking one button. In some operating systems you must click on the window's title bar. *See* WINDOW.

2. to start a piece of software by double-clicking on its name or icon. *See* CLICK; ICON.

active color the color currently selected (in a painting or drawing program). Whatever tool is being used will paint or draw in the active color.

Active Desktop in Windows 98 and its derivatives, the ability to use a WEB PAGE as the desktop, i.e., the screen itself, not just as one of the programs running on it. This makes it easy to display a web page that is constantly updated, such as weather or stock price information, without having to start and run a BROWSER. *See also* DESKTOP; WORLD WIDE WEB.

active matrix a type of liquid crystal display (LCD) that produces higher contrast than earlier passive-matrix displays by incorporating transistors into the LCD matrix.

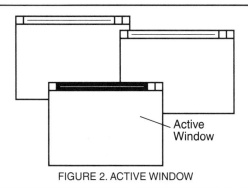

Active
Window

FIGURE 2. ACTIVE WINDOW

active window the window currently in use, the one in which the user is typing, drawing, or making menu choices (*see* Figure 2). There can only be one active window at a time. *See* WINDOW; ACTIVATE.

ActiveX a Microsoft system for component software for Windows that is an updated version of OLE (*see* OBJECT LINKING AND EMBEDDING). ActiveX allows executable code to be included in a document such as a word processing document or a web page. An ActiveX control can be written in a programming language such as C++ or Visual Basic. An advantage of ActiveX is the ability to re-use software components. For an alternate way to include executable code in a web page, *see* JAVA; for an alternate software component system, *see* JAVABEAN.

actor (animation program) an object that moves in a specified manner along a PATH.

actual parameter the value actually passed to a function or procedure in a programming language. For example, if you compute ABS(X) and the value of X is −2.5, then −2.5 is the actual parameter of ABS. Contrast FORMAL PARAMETER. For an example *see* PARAMETER.

FIGURE 3. AUGUSTA ADA BYRON (1815–1852)

Ada a programming language developed in the late 1970s for the U.S. Department of Defense. It is named for Augusta Ada Byron, Countess of Lovelace, who worked with Babbage's mechanical calculator in the nineteenth century.

Ada is based on Pascal, with some influence from PL/I and ALGOL 68. Comments begin with two hyphens and continue to the end of the line. Every statement ends with a semicolon even if it is embedded within another statement (such as an if-then or loop-end loop structure); in this respect Ada is like PL/I and C and unlike Pascal.

Ada subprograms can be compiled separately and linked together before execution. In the sample program, the with and use statements specify that this program uses a library of precompiled subroutines called I_O_PACKAGE.

Much of the original motivation for designing Ada was the need for a better language for real-time programming, that is, programming

```
with I_O_PACKAGE;
procedure FACTORIAL is
  use I_O_PACKAGE;
  -- This program reads a number and
  -- computes its factorial.
  NUM, FACT, COUNT: INTEGER;
begin
  GET(NUM);
  FACT := 1;
  for COUNT in 2..NUM loop
    FACT := FACT * COUNT;
  end loop;
  PUT("The factorial of ");
  PUT(NUM);
  PUT(" is ");
 PUT(FACT);
end;
```

FIGURE 4. AN ADA PROGRAM

computers to control automatic or semiautomatic equipment. Toward this end, Ada allows the programmer to create multiple tasks that run concurrently (*see* TIMESHARING), to pass signals from one task to another, and to introduce controlled time delays.

adaptive technology technology that helps people work around physical limitations. Computer-related examples include magnified screen displays, speech recognition devices, and keyboards with latching shift and control keys for people who can press only one key at a time.

ADC *see* ANALOG-TO-DIGITAL CONVERTER.

A/D converter *see* ANALOG-TO-DIGITAL CONVERTER.

FIGURE 5. ADD NOISE FILTER ADDS TEXTURE TO IMAGE

add noise a photopaint filter that adds texture to a picture. Since the overall effect is rather unpredictable, it may be wise to save a copy of the image before applying this filter.

address

    1.   a number or bit pattern that uniquely identifies a location in a computer memory. Every location has a distinct address.

    2.   a letter and number identifying the column and row of a cell in a spreadsheet. *See* RELATIVE ADDRESS; ABSOLUTE ADDRESS.

    3.   a set of numbers identifying a machine on the Internet; *see* IP ADDRESS.

    4.   an electronic mail address. *See* ELECTRONIC MAIL; INTERNET.

    5.   a URL identifying a web page. *See* URL.

ADM-3A a type of computer terminal marketed by Lear Siegler in the early 1980s. Its codes for controlling the screen were adopted on a few other terminals and early microcomputers.

Administrator the account name used by the system administrator under Windows NT and 2000. *Compare* ROOT.

Adobe Systems, Inc. (San Jose, California) the software company that pioneered the PostScript command language for output devices. Adobe is also a leader in producing high-quality fonts and graphics software, including Adobe Type Manager (ATM), Photoshop, Illustrator, and PageMaker (for both Macintosh and PC platforms). For digital video production Adobe markets Premiere and After Effects. Also of interest is Adobe Acrobat—a program which allows electronic distribution of formatted documents. (*See* PDF.)

    For further information about Adobe and their products, you can reach their web site at http://www.adobe.com. *See also* POSTSCRIPT; ATM; DESKTOP PUBLISHING; PORTABLE DIGITAL DOCUMENT; TYPE I FONTS.

Adobe Type Manager *see* ATM (definition 1).

ADSL (**A**symmetric **D**igital **S**ubscriber **L**ine) a type of high-speed digital telephone connection used mainly for systems that involve digital video. It supports data rates of 6 million bits per second in one direction and 576 kilobits per second in the other direction. *Contrast* ISDN; T1 LINE; CABLE MODEM; DSL.

adventure game a computer game in which the user finds a path through a set of "rooms" that are described verbally or graphically, manipulating objects along the way (Fig. 6). The computer responds to simple commands in English. The first adventure game is said to have been invented by Will Crowther in the 1970s.

    Adventure games provided the foundation for MUD and other sophisticated user interfaces. *See also* VIRTUAL REALITY.

adware software that is distributed free in order to advertise a product. *Compare* SHAREWARE, FREE SOFTWARE.

AF (**a**udio **f**requency) a frequency within the range of human hearing, 20 to 20,000 hertz. *Contrast* RF.

```
You are in a maze of twisting passages, all alike.

> go north

You are in a dimly lit room.  Paths lead to the
south and west.  A lamp is on the floor.

> pick up the lamp

Done.

> rub the lamp

A genie appears...
```

FIGURE 6. AN ADVENTURE GAME

AFAIK e-mail abbreviation for "**as far as I** know."

AFAIR e-mail abbreviation for "**as far as I** remember."

agent a piece of software that performs a service for someone, usually silently and automatically. For example, an agent might run on a CLIENT computer to keep the SERVER informed of its needs.

AGP (**A**ccelerated **G**raphics **P**ort) a fast bus connection that allows the graphics adapter to communicate with the CPU at a higher speed than the conventional ISA, EISA, or PCI bus. AGP was introduced with Intel's Pentium II processor.

ai file extension for Adobe Illustrator's native file format. These files use a subset of the PostScript language. Many DRAW PROGRAMS can use .ai files as well as their own, thus providing a method of exchanging drawings between different programs. *See* EXTENSION; FILE FORMAT.

AI *see* ARTIFICIAL INTELLIGENCE.

FIGURE 7. AIRBRUSH

airbrush a tool available in some paint and photopaint programs that simulates the effect of an airbrush; the edges are soft and the colors are translucent. The softness of the edge, size of the spray pattern, and the degree of opaqueness can be controlled (*see* Figure 7).

    In bitmap-editing programs that do not offer an airbrush tool, there is usually a SPRAY CAN, which is basically a coarser version of the airbrush.

alert box *see* MESSAGE BOX.

ALGOL (**Algo**rithmic **L**anguage) a pair of programming languages that had a strong impact on programming language design. The first, ALGOL 60 (developed by an international committee around 1960), was an immediate ancestor of Pascal and introduced many Pascal-like features that have been adopted by numerous other languages, including:

- recursion;

- begin and end keywords to allow grouping statements into blocks;

- the "block if" statement, of the form:
  ```
  if condition then
      begin
          statements
      end
  else
      begin
          statements
      end
  ```

- the symbol := for arithmetic assignment;

- semicolons between statements, leaving the programmer free to arrange statements in any convenient layout rather than putting one statement on each line.

The key idea is that whereas a BASIC or FORTRAN program is a list of numbered instructions, an ALGOL program is a set of blocks of statements embedded within larger blocks. Thus, hierarchical design is easier to establish and follow.

    But the ALGOL 60 standard did not specify statements for input and output, since these were considered machine-specific, and as a result, although much admired for its design, ALGOL 60 was not widely used in practice.

    ALGOL 68 (released in 1968) is a much more abstract language with a reputation for being powerful but hard to learn. It introduced widespread use of pointer variables (called *refs*) and variant types (called *unions*). An important principle of ALGOL 68 is *orthogonality*,

algorithm   **14**

which means that all meaningful combinations of features are allowed. (In geometry, two things are orthogonal if they meet at right angles.)

Discontent with the complexity of ALGOL 68 led Niklaus Wirth to design first ALGOL W and then Pascal (*see* PASCAL), which has almost completely replaced ALGOL in practical use today. *See also* RECURSION; STRUCTURED PROGRAMMING; POINTER; VARIANT.

algorithm a sequence of instructions that tell how to solve a particular problem. An algorithm must be specified exactly, so that there can be no doubt about what to do next, and it must have a finite number of steps. A computer program is an algorithm written in a language that a computer can understand, but the same algorithm can be written in several different languages. An algorithm can also be a set of instructions for a person to follow.

A set of instructions is not an algorithm if it does not have a definite stopping place, or if the instructions are too vague to be followed clearly. The stopping place may be at variable points in the general procedure, but something in the procedure must determine precisely where the stopping place is for a particular case.

If you study the game of tic-tac-toe long enough, you will be able to develop an algorithm that tells you how to play an unbeatable game. However, some problems are so complicated that there is no known algorithm to solve them, and in other cases, the only known algorithm takes impossibly large amounts of time. *See* HEURISTIC; LIMITS OF COMPUTER POWER.

alias

    1. (Macintosh) a copy of a file icon that provides an alternate way of starting an application program or opening a file, folder, or disk. You can place the alias anywhere that's convenient — the desktop, the Apple menu, or a special folder. The title of an alias icon is in italics. In OS/2 and Windows 95 and its successors, an alias is called a SHORTCUT.

    2. (UNIX) an alternative way of typing a command. The `alias` command creates aliases. For example, if you execute the command

```
alias dir ls -al
```

then from then on, `dir` will mean `ls -al` (the complete file listing command).

Stairsteps

FIGURE 8. ALIASING CREATES A "STAIRSTEP"
APPEARANCE

aliasing the appearance of false stairsteps or bands in an image, or false
frequencies in digitized sound, due to interaction of the original signal
with the sampling rate. *See* ANTIALIASING; SAMPLING RATE.

FIGURE 9. ALIGN

align to make things line up, either horizontally or vertically. Most drawing programs and page layout programs have specific commands to help
you align objects and text.

allocation unit the units of disk space that can be allocated to a file.
For example, if a disk drive uses 4096-byte allocation units, the space
occupied by every file will be a multiple of 4096 bytes, regardless of
how small the file is. Also called CLUSTER. *See* FAT32.

alpha (α) a measure of the opacity, or visibility, of an object in a graphical
image. A transparent object has an alpha of 0 and is invisible; most
objects have an alpha of 1 and completely cover the objects behind
them.

Alpha a fast 64-bit microprocessor originally made by Digital Equipment Corporation, which has now merged with Compaq. As of 2000,
the Alpha was available with clock speeds greater than 1 GHz (1000
MHz) and was the fastest microprocessor. Alpha-based computers run
UNIX, VAX/VMS, Windows NT or Windows 2000; the Alpha can also
emulate a 386 to run PC software.

alpha channel (photopaint program) a CHANNEL that defines a selection. Instead of specifying a color of ink to print, the alpha channel marks part of the image for special treatment. An image may have multiple alpha channels. *See* SELECTION TOOL.

alphanumeric characters letters and digits (but not punctuation marks, mathematical symbols, or control codes).

On large IBM computers, the characters @, #, and $ count as alphabetic, and hence as alphanumeric. They are called *national characters* because they print differently on computers designed for use in different countries.

alpha testing the first stage of testing of a new software product, carried out by the manufacturer's own staff. *Contrast* BETA TESTING; GAMMA TESTING.

alt prefix identifying "alternative" Usenet newsgroups, those that have not been voted on by the members, such as alt.folklore.urban. *See* NEWSGROUP.

Alt a key on a computer keyboard that is used to give an alternate meaning to other keys. It is used like a shift key; that is, you hold it down while pressing the other key. For example, to type Alt-P, type P while holding down Alt.

The effect of the Alt key depends on the software being used. For example, in WordPerfect and Lotus 1-2-3, the Alt key is used in combination with various letters to call up macros (*see* MACRO).

Another use of the Alt key on PC-compatible computers is to type special characters. For example, under DOS or OS/2, or in a Windows DOS-mode window, you can type the character *ä*, whose extended ASCII code is 132, by holding down Alt while you type 132 on the numeric keypad at the right-hand side of the keyboard. Under Windows, which uses the ANSI extended character set, the codes are different and you must precede the code number with 0. For example, to type *ä* (ANSI code 228), hold down Alt while typing 0228 on the numeric keypad. *See* ASCII; ANSI; MODIFIER KEY.

Altair a pioneering microcomputer marketed to hobbyists in 1975, significant because the version of BASIC for this machine was the first Microsoft product.

AltaVista a popular World Wide Web SEARCH ENGINE originally developed by Digital Equipment Corporation. Their web address is www.altavista.com.

Amazon.com a pioneering on-line bookstore established in 1995 in Seattle, Washington, with branches in Britain (amazon.co.uk) and Germany (amazon.de). By 1999, it was one of the world's largest booksellers. Customers buy books and other merchandise through the World Wide Web using credit cards; secure communication protocols protect credit card numbers from theft. Amazon.com was the first prominent E-TAIL merchant. Competitors quickly sprang up, such as `www.bn.com` and `www.blackwells.co.uk` (both of which are on-line branches of large, preexisting book retailers). Today, Amazon.com also sells consumer electronic goods and other merchandise, and it also operates an auction service. *See* E-TAIL; ELECTRONIC COMMERCE.

ambient lighting (in three-dimensional computer graphics) the overall lighting of a scene. Ambient lighting in a computer scene appears to have no specific source.

AMD (**A**dvanced **M**icro **D**evices) a manufacturer of digital integrated circuits, including the K5 and K6 microprocessors, which are compatible substitutes for Intel's Pentium. AMD is headquartered in Sunnyvale, California, and can be reached on the Web at `http://www.amd.com`. *See also* MICROPROCESSOR; PENTIUM.

America Online (AOL) an on-line information service based in Dulles, Virginia, and accessible by modem from anywhere in the United States. (*See* MODEM.) America Online offers its subscribers e-mail, conferencing, software, computing support, interactive magazines and newspapers, on-line classes, and Internet access. In 2000, AOL merged with Time Warner. Web address: `http://www.aol.com`. *See* INTERNET; ON LINE (usage note).

AMI (**A**merican **M**egatrends, **I**nc.) the leading supplier of the BIOS software built into PC motherboards (*see* BIOS). AMI also makes diagnostic software, RAID disk array controllers, and other products. The company is headquartered in Norcross, Georgia (a suburb of Atlanta), and can be reached on the Web at `http://www.ami.com`.

Amiga a computer marketed by Commodore Business Machines in the 1980s. Similar in size and cost to the IBM PC, it had a quite different architecture and was ahead of its time in many ways, offering multitasking, windowing, an advanced graphics system, and MIDI music. Like the Macintosh, it used Motorola 68000-series microprocessors.

Though much admired by knowledgeable programmers, the Amiga never achieved the popularity of the PC or Macintosh, and application software was not abundant.

ampere (amp) a unit for measuring electric current. A current of 1 ampere means that 6.25×10^{18} electrons are flowing by a point each second. A group of 6.25×10^{18} electrons has a charge of 1 coulomb, so 1 ampere = 1 coulomb per second.

FIGURE 10. AMPERSANDS

ampersand the character &, which stands for the word *and*. For an illustration of ampersands in various typefaces, *see* Figure 10.

amplified speaker a speaker that includes its own amplifier to produce louder sound and stronger bass. *See* SOUNDCARD; MULTIMEDIA.

analog representing data in a form other than binary bits. The image picked up by a conventional camera or scanner and the sound picked up by a microphone are examples of analog data that must be digitized (converted into the computer's internal representation) in order to be stored in a computer. *See also* ANALOG COMPUTER; ANALOG-TO-DIGITAL CONVERTER. *Contrast* DIGITAL.

analog computer a computer that represents information in a form that can vary smoothly between certain limits rather than having discrete values. (*Contrast* DIGITAL COMPUTER.) A slide rule is an example of an analog computer because it represents numbers as distances along a scale.

All modern, programmable computers are digital. Analog computer circuits are used in certain kinds of automatic machinery, such as automotive cruise controls and guided missiles. Also, a fundamental analog computer circuit called an *operational amplifier* is used extensively in audio, radio, and TV equipment.

analog monitor a video screen that can display an unlimited range of brightnesses for each primary color, from fully on to fully off. As a result, the monitor can display any color that the computer can generate. *See* RGB MONITOR; COLOR.

analog-to-digital converter (ADC) a device that changes data from analog to digital form. For example, a sound card uses an analog-to-digital converter to convert audio waveforms into digital representations. Laptop computers use analog-to-digital converters to measure the voltages of their batteries. *See* ANALOG COMPUTER; SOUND CARD; CODEC.

Analytical Engine *see* COMPUTERS, HISTORY OF.

anchor a marked position in an HTML document (web page), to which the user can jump from elsewhere. For example, the HTML command

```
<A NAME="Elephants">All about Elephants</A>
```

marks its position as an anchor named "Elephants," and if it resides in file `http://www.vet.uga.edu/animals.html`, then the full address of the anchor is:

```
http://www.vet.uga.edu/animals.html#Elephants
```

See HTML; WORLD WIDE WEB.

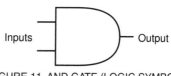

FIGURE 11. AND GATE (LOGIC SYMBOL)

AND gate a logic gate that produces an output of 1 only when all of its inputs are 1, thus:

Inputs		Output
0	0	0
0	1	0
1	0	0
1	1	1

The symbol for an AND gate is shown in Fig. 11.

AND gates are used in computer arithmetic. In addition, AND gates with more than two inputs are used to recognize signals coming in simultaneously on several wires, such as memory addresses. (*See* BINARY ADDITION; DECODER; LOGIC CIRCUITS.)

angle brackets the characters < >.

FIGURE 12. ANIMATION

animation the use of motion in images on a computer screen.

Moving images are actually fixed images redrawn many times per second. Thus, even a few seconds of moving video require as much storage (on disk or CD-ROM) as dozens or hundreds of still pictures, and it is necessary to retrieve the data and put it on screen at full speed. That is why the access time of a CD-ROM drive is important for animation. A slow CD-ROM drive will cause pauses in the motion.

Software designers can cut down data storage requirements by animating only part of the screen or by reducing the amount of drawing required for each image (e.g., by moving only one small object against a fixed background, as is commonly done in video games).

anonymous FTP *see* FTP.

anonymous variable in Prolog, a variable (written _) that does not retain a value. If several anonymous variables occur in the same fact or rule, they are not the same variable. In pattern matching, anonymous variables match anything. *See* PROLOG.

ANSI (**A**merican **N**ational **S**tandards **I**nstitute) the main industrial standardization organization in the United States. There are official ANSI standards in almost all industries, and many of them have to do with computers. In computer programming, ANSI most often refers to one of the following:

    1. ANSI standard versions of C, FORTRAN, COBOL, or other programming languages. Typically, a particular manufacturer's version of a language will include all of the features defined in the ANSI standard, plus additional features devised by the manufacturer. To be easily transportable from one computer to another, a program should not use any features that are not in the ANSI standard. The programmer can then produce executable versions of it for different types of computers by compiling the same program with different compilers.

    2. ANSI standard *escape sequences* for controlling the screen of a computer terminal or microcomputer. An escape sequence is a series of character codes which, when sent to the screen, causes the screen to do something other than simply display the characters to which the codes correspond. The ANSI escape sequences all begin with the ASCII Escape character (code 27). *See* ANSI SCREEN CONTROL.

    3. The ANSI extended character set used in Microsoft Windows, and shown in Table 1. It includes all the ASCII characters plus many others. *See* ASCII; WINDOWS (MICROSOFT); IBM PC; UNICODE.

    To type any ANSI character in Microsoft Windows, hold down the Alt key while typing 0 followed by the character code number on the numeric keypad at the right-hand side of the keyboard. For example, to type *é*, hold down Alt and type 0233. You may prefer to use the Character Map utility to select characters and copy them to the Clipboard, then paste them into your application.

ANSI C a standard version of the C programming language defined by the American National Standards Institute (ANSI) in 1989. Unlike the older language (defined by Kernighan and Ritchie), ANSI C includes a "void" declaration for functions that do not return values, as well as additional error checking features and other extensions. *See* C.

ANSI escape sequences *see* ANSI SCREEN CONTROL.

ANSI graphics a colloquial term for a technique of drawing pictures and other special effects by sending ANSI escape sequences and IBM PC special characters to the screen of a computer. Strictly speaking, the term is inappropriate because the computer is not in graphics mode and the special characters are not covered by an ANSI standard. *See also* ASCII GRAPHICS.

TABLE 1
ANSI CHARACTER SET USED IN MICROSOFT WINDOWS

0128	€	0160		0192	À	0224	à
0129		0161	¡	0193	Á	0225	á
0130	,	0162	¢	0194	Â	0226	â
0131	ƒ	0163	£	0195	Ã	0227	ã
0132	„	0164	¤	0196	Ä	0228	ä
0133	…	0165	¥	0197	Å	0229	å
0134	†	0166	¦	0198	Æ	0230	æ
0135	‡	0167	§	0199	Ç	0231	ç
0136	ˆ	0168	¨	0200	È	0232	è
0137	‰	0169	©	0201	É	0233	é
0138	Š	0170	ª	0202	Ê	0234	ê
0139	‹	0171	«	0203	Ë	0235	ë
0140	Œ	0172	¬	0204	Ì	0236	ì
0141		0173	-	0205	Í	0237	í
0142		0174	®	0206	Î	0238	î
0143		0175	¯	0207	Ï	0239	ï
0144		0176	°	0208	Ð	0240	ð
0145	'	0177	±	0209	Ñ	0241	ñ
0146	'	0178	²	0210	Ò	0242	ò
0147	"	0179	³	0211	Ó	0243	ó
0148	"	0180	´	0212	Ô	0244	ô
0149	–	0181	µ	0213	Õ	0245	õ
0150	–	0182	¶	0214	Ö	0246	ö
0151	—	0183	·	0215	×	0247	÷
0152	˜	0184	¸	0216	Ø	0248	ø
0153	™	0185	¹	0217	Ù	0249	ù
0154	š	0186	º	0218	Ú	0250	ú
0155	›	0187	»	0219	Û	0251	û
0156	œ	0188	¼	0220	Ü	0252	ü
0157		0189	½	0221	Ý	0253	ý
0158		0190	¾	0222	Þ	0254	þ
0159	Ÿ	0191	¿	0223	ß	0255	ÿ

ANSI screen control the use of ANSI standard sequences of characters (*escape sequences*) that, when sent to the screen of a computer, make it perform actions such as clearing the screen. Some computers obey these codes at all times. These include all DEC VT-100-compatible terminals. PC-compatible computers running DOS obey ANSI screen control codes only if the CONFIG.SYS file contains a line of the form

```
DEVICE=ANSI.SYS
```

and the codes are sent to the screen using DOS services rather than BIOS services. (On PC-compatibles, ANSI control codes can also be used to redefine keys; see the DOS Technical Reference Manual for details.)

All ANSI control sequences begin with Esc (code 27) followed by a left square bracket; many of them contain numbers that specify how far the cursor is to be moved or where it is to be placed. For example, Esc [2 J clears the screen, Esc [1 5 C moves the cursor 15 spaces to the right, and Esc [3 C moves it only 3 spaces to the right.

FIGURE 13. ANTIALIASING OF DIAGONAL BORDERS

antialiasing

1. a technique for eliminating the stairstep appearance of slanted and curved lines on computer displays by partly illuminating some of the pixels adjacent to the line. See Figure 13.

2. a technique for eliminating spurious tones in digitized sound by filtering out all frequencies above, or too close to, the sampling rate. *See* ALIASING.

antitrust law laws that are designed to keep markets competitive, rather than allowing them to be dominated by monoplists. The main U.S. antitrust law is the Sherman Antitrust Act. Section 1 of this law makes it illegal for sellers of a product to join together to raise the price of the product. Section 2 makes monopolizing acts illegal. However, it does not automatically make having a monopoly illegal, since an inventor with a patent has a legal monopoly on that invention. It is illegal to acquire a monopoly through anticompetitive means, but the exact meaning of the law depends on how the courts interpret it. An antitrust case was filed against IBM in 1969 because of its dominance of the mainframe computer market in the 1960s. The case dragged on until 1982 when it was finally dropped because the technology had changed so much that it was no longer relevant. *See also* MICROSOFT ANTITRUST CHARGES.

antivirus software software that protects a computer from viruses (secretly destructive software modifications), either by blocking the modifications that a virus tries to make, or by detecting a virus as soon as possible after it enters the machine. *See also* VIRUS.

AOL *see* AMERICA ONLINE.

Apache a web (HTTP) server program used by many web sites on a variety of computers. It is an example of open-source software, where the source code is published and a variety of people make contributions. The first version was released in 1995. Within a year, it became the leading web server software. Apache is available from the Apache Software Foundation at www.apache.org.

API (**A**pplication **P**rogram **I**nterface) the set of services that an operating system makes available to programs that run under it. For example, the Windows API consists of a large number of procedures and data areas that can be used by programs running under Windows. With modern operating systems, it is important for programs to use the operating system API, as far as possible, rather than manipulating hardware directly, because direct manipulation of hardware can interfere with other programs that are running concurrently.

APL a programming language invented by Ken Iverson in the early 1960s and still used for some kinds of mathematical work. APL stands for *A Programming Language,* the title of Iverson's 1962 book.

APL has its own character set, so that most operations are represented by special characters rather than keywords. Additionally, in APL, arrays rather than single numbers are considered the basic data type; a single number is merely a one-element array. Here is an APL program that reads a series of numbers into an array and computes their average:

$$\nabla\ AVG$$
$$[1]\ X \leftarrow \square$$
$$[2]\ K \leftarrow \rho X$$
$$[3]\ (+/X) \div K$$
$$\nabla$$

Here $X \leftarrow \square$ means "read something from the keyboard into X," and X becomes an array if the user types a series of numbers rather than just one. Then ρX is the number of elements in X, and $(+/X)$ is the operation of addition distributed over X, i.e., the sum of all the elements. The last line of the program is an expression that defines the result.

app *(slang) see* APPLICATION PROGRAM.

append to put something at the end of something else, for example, to append information at the end of a file, or append additional files at the end of a tape.

Apple one of the largest personal computer manufacturers. The Apple II, introduced in 1977, was one of the earliest popular microcomputers. It was based on the 8-bit MOS technology 6502 microprocessor. A wide range of software was written for the Apple II and its followers. In particular, the Apple II was widely used in educational institutions, and the first microcomputer spreadsheet program (VisiCalc) ran on the Apple II.

In 1984 Apple introduced the Macintosh, which was the first widely-used computer with a graphical user interface (GUI), based on a mouse that moves a pointer around the screen and icons that identify commands. The Macintosh became widely used for desktop publishing and artistic applications, and it became one of the two main standards for microcomputers (the other being the IBM PC). *See* MACINTOSH.

In 1994 Apple introduced the PowerMac, based on the PowerPC chip jointly developed by Apple, IBM, and Motorola. *See* POWERPC. Apple has continued the Macintosh line of computers with the iMac. The iMac, introduced in 1998, is a fully featured G3-based Macintosh built within an unconventional, brightly colored, one-piece enclosure. (The *i* in iMac stands for *Internet.*) One of the more controversial points of the iMac's design is its lack of an internal diskette drive, although easy access to peripheral devices (e.g., a Zip drive) through USB ports should make this a moot point.

For a picture, see the entry at IMAC.

Apple also offers laptop computers based on their Power Macintosh and iMac desktop counterparts.

The company, located in Cupertino, California, was founded by Steve Jobs and Steve Wozniak, who began work in a garage. For further information, see http://www.apple.com.

Apple menu (Macintosh) the menu at the far left of the menu bar that holds desk accessories (DAs), control panels, and aliases of frequently used software. *See* ALIAS.

applet
   1. a small application program that is inexpensive and designed to do a small, specific job. Most operating systems come with several applets, such as a calculator, a calendar, and a note editor.
   2. an application program that is downloaded automatically through a World Wide Web browser and executed on the recipient's machine. Applets are normally written in Java. *See* WORLD WIDE WEB; BROWSER; JAVA.

AppleTalk the network communication protocol built into Macintosh computers.

application *see* APPLICATION PROGRAM.

application framework a set of predefined procedures or classes that saves the programmer much of the work of writing a program with a sophisticated user interface. Using an application framework, the programmer need not write code to handle menu choices, mouse movements, etc., because that work has already been done.

Examples of application frameworks are MacApp for Macintosh, Turbo Vision for DOS, and various Windows application frameworks provided with Borland and Microsoft compilers. Newer programming languages such as Java, Borland Delphi for Windows, Microsoft Visual Basic for DOS and Windows, and CA-Realizer for OS/2 have application frameworks built in.

Application Menu (Macintosh) the menu at the far right end of a window's title bar that allows you to quickly switch between open application programs. The icon for the Application menu changes to show the active program.

A similar Windows 3.1 feature is the TASK LIST; for Windows 95 and its successors, the TASKBAR is analogous to the Macintosh Application Menu.

application program a computer program that performs useful work not related to the computer itself. Examples include word processors, spreadsheets, accounting systems, and engineering programs. *Contrast* UTILITY; OPERATING SYSTEM.

applications programmer a person who writes programs that use the computer as a tool to solve particular problems, rather than just to manage the computer itself. *Contrast* SYSTEMS PROGRAMMER.

arc

1. part of a circle.
2. a data compression program for the IBM PC formerly produced by System Enhancement Associates in the mid-1980s, a precursor of ZIP. *See* ZIP FILE.

arccos *see* ARC COSINE.

arc cosine the inverse of the trigonometric cosine function. If $x = \cos y$ then $y = \arccos x$. Many computer languages provide the arc tangent function but not the arc cosine function. You can work around this by using the relation:

$$\arccos x = \arctan \frac{\sqrt{1 - x^2}}{x}$$

where x is positive and angles are expressed in radians. *See also* TRIGONOMETRIC FUNCTIONS.

archival storage storage for data that must be kept for a long time but will seldom be used, such as backup copies of working programs. Microcomputers often use diskettes, tape cartridges, Zip drives, CD-R, or Jaz drives for archival storage. Magnetic tape is usually the cheapest form of archival storage, but the tapes should be copied every 2 or 3 years if their contents are still needed, since tapes can become demagnetized with age. *See also* GRANDFATHER TAPE.

archive

1. a filing system for information designed to be kept for a long time. *See* ARCHIVAL STORAGE.

2. a file containing the compressed contents of other files. The original files can be reconstructed from it. *See* ARC; ZIP FILE; TAR FILE; DATA COMPRESSION.

3. in DOS, OS/2, and Windows, every file has an archive bit that says whether or not it has been backed up by copying to another disk or tape. The `attrib` command can be used to examine or change archive bits. The archive bit makes it possible to back up only the files that have not already been backed up.

ARCNET a type of local area network that works like a token-ring network except that the connections between computers need not be in the shape of a ring. A special message, the token, is passed from computer to computer and only the computer holding the token is allowed to transmit. ARCNET usually uses Ethernet hardware. *See* TOKEN RING; LOCAL-AREA NETWORK; ETHERNET.

arcsin *see* ARC SINE.

arc sine the inverse of the trigonometric sine function. If $x = \sin y$, then $y = \arcsin x$. Many computer languages provide the arc tangent function but not the arc sine function. You can work around this by using the relation:

$$\arcsin x = \arctan \frac{x}{\sqrt{1 - x^2}}$$

in which all angles are expressed in radians. *See* TRIGONOMETRIC FUNCTIONS.

arctan *see* ARC TANGENT.

arc tangent the inverse of the trigonometric tangent function. If $x = \tan y$, then $y = \arctan x$. In BASIC, the arc tangent function is called `ATN`. *See* TRIGONOMETRIC FUNCTIONS.

arguments (**actual parameters**) values passed to a function or procedure by the calling program. *See* ACTUAL PARAMETER.

ARPANET a computer network originally developed for the U.S. Defense Advanced Research Projects Agency (ARPA, now known as DARPA) to link research institutions. ARPANET introduced the TCP/IP protocols and eventually developed into the Internet. *See* INTERNET; WIDE AREA NETWORK; TCP/IP.

arrange

1. to place the icons on the screen in neat rows and columns, retrieving any that have been moved off the edge of the screen (Fig. 14).

FIGURE 14. "ARRANGE ICONS"

In Windows 95 and later, "Arrange Icons" is on the menu that pops up when you right-click on an empty area of the desktop; it is also on the "View" menu of individual windows. In Windows 3.1, it is usually on a menu titled "Windows" or "View."

If you want the computer to keep the icons arranged automatically, turn on the "Auto arrange" feature; a check mark shows that it is selected. *See also* CASCADE; TILE.

2. to place an item in relation to other items. In drawing programs, there is usually an Arrange menu that contains commands (ALIGN, SEND TO FRONT, BACK ONE, etc.) relating to the placement of selected objects. Objects are layered as if they were opaque pieces of paper.

array a collection of data items that are given a single name and distinguished by numbers (subscripts). For example, in BASIC, the declaration

```
DIM X(5)
```

creates an array of five elements that can be referred to as $X(1)$, $X(2)$, $X(3)$, $X(4)$, and $X(5)$.

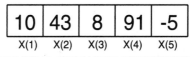

FIGURE 15. ARRAY (ONE-DIMENSIONAL)

You can store numbers in these elements with statements such as:

```
X(1) = 10
X(2) = 43
X(3) = 8
X(4) = 91
X(5) = -5
```

just as if each element were a separate variable. You can also use INPUT and READ statements on array elements just as if they were ordinary variables.

Arrays are useful because they let you use arithmetic to decide which element to use at any particular moment. For example, you can find the total of the numbers in the five-element array X by executing the statements:

```
TOTAL = 0
FOR I = 1 TO 5
  TOTAL = TOTAL + X(I)
NEXT I
PRINT TOTAL
```

Here TOTAL starts out as 0 and then gets each element of X added to it.

Arrays can have more than one dimension. For example, the declaration DIM Y(3,5) creates a 3 × 5 array whose elements are:

```
Y(1,1)    Y(1,2)    Y(1,3)    Y(1,4)    Y(1,5)
Y(2,1)    Y(2,2)    Y(2,3)    Y(2,4)    Y(2,5)
Y(3,1)    Y(3,2)    Y(3,3)    Y(3,4)    Y(3,5)
```

31	17	95	43	60
32	95	86	72	40
27	45	93	43	81

FIGURE 16. ARRAY (TWO-DIMENSIONAL, 3×5)

Multidimensional arrays are useful for storing tables of data, such as three test grades for each of five students. *See also* DATA STRUCTURES; SORT.

arrow keys keys that move the cursor up, down, or to the left or right. The effect of these keys depends on the software being used. In a GUI environment, the arrow keys are basically an alternative to a mouse. Some drawing environments let you NUDGE the selected object with the arrow keys, giving you greater precision. Touch typists sometimes prefer the arrow keys to a mouse because it allows them to keep their hands on the keyboard. *See* NUDGE; KEYBOARD; MOUSE.

artificial intelligence (**AI**) the use of computers to simulate human thinking. Artificial intelligence is concerned with building computer programs that can solve problems creatively, rather than simply working through the steps of a solution designed by the programmer.

For example, consider computer game playing. Some games, such as tic-tac-toe, are so simple that the programmer can specify in advance a procedure that guarantees that the computer will play a perfect game. With a game such as chess, however, no such procedure is known; the computer must instead use a *heuristic,* that is, a procedure for discovering and evaluating good moves.

One possible heuristic for chess would be for the computer to identify every possible move from a given position and then evaluate the moves by calculating, for each one, all the possible ways the game could proceed. Chess is so complicated that this would take an impossibly long time (millions of years with present-day computers).

A better strategy would be to take shortcuts. Calculating only five or six moves into the future is sufficient to eliminate most of the possible moves as not worth pursuing. The rest can be evaluated on the basis of general principles about board positions. In fact, an ideal heuristic chess-playing machine would be able to modify its own strategy on the basis of experience. Like a human chess player, it would realize that its opponent is also following a heuristic and would try to predict her behavior.

One of the main problems of AI is how to represent knowledge in the computer in a form that can be *used* rather than merely reproduced. In fact, some workers define AI as the construction of computer programs that utilize a knowledge base. A computer that gives the call number of a library book is not displaying artificial intelligence; it is merely echoing back what was put into it. Artificial intelligence would come into play if the computer used its knowledge base to make generalizations about the library's holdings or construct bibliographies on selected subjects. (*See* EXPERT SYSTEM.)

Computer vision and *robotics* are important areas of AI. Although it is easy to take the image from a TV camera and store it in a computer's memory, it is hard to devise ways to make the computer recognize the objects it "sees." Likewise, there are many unsolved problems associated with getting robots to move about in three-dimensional space — to walk, for instance, and to find and grasp objects — even though human beings do these things naturally.

Another unsolved problem is *natural language processing* — getting computers to understand speech, or at least typewritten input, in a language such as English. In the late 1950s it was expected that computers would soon be programmed to accept natural-language input, translate Russian into English, and the like. But human languages have proved to be more complex than was expected, and progress has been slow. The English speaking computers of *Star Wars* and *2001* are still some years away. *See* NATURAL LANGUAGE PROCESSING.

The important philosophical question remains: Do computers really think? Artificial intelligence theorist Alan Turing proposed a criterion that has since become known as the Turing test: A computer is manifesting human-like intelligence if a person communicating with it by teletype, cannot distinguish it from a human being. Critics have pointed out that it makes little sense to build a machine whose purpose is to deceive its makers. Increasing numbers of AI workers are taking the position that computers are not artificial minds, but merely tools to assist the human mind, and that this is true no matter how closely they can be made to imitate human behavior. *See also* ELIZA.

ASC the function, in BASIC, that finds the ASCII code number associated with a given character. (*See* ASCII.) For example, `ASC("A")` is 65 because the ASCII code of the character *A* is 65 (expressed in decimal).

FIGURE 17. ASCENDERS

ascender the part of a printed character that rises above the body of the letter. For instance, the letter *d* has an ascender and the letter *o* does not. *See* DESCENDER; TYPEFACE; X-HEIGHT.

ASCII (**A**merican **S**tandard **C**ode for **I**nformation **I**nterchange) a standard code for representing characters as numbers that is used on most microcomputers, computer terminals, and printers. In addition to printable characters, the ASCII code includes control characters to indicate carriage return, backspace, etc. Table 2 shows all the ASCII character codes as decimal numbers. For two popular extensions of ASCII, *see* IBM PC (character set chart) and ANSI character set (Table 1, page 21). For alternatives to ASCII, *see* EBCDIC and UNICODE.

ASCII file a text file on a machine that uses the ASCII character set. (*See* TEXT FILE.) In DOS, Windows, and OS/2, each line ends with a carriage return and line feed (code 13 and 10).

ASCII graphics A colloquial term for a technique of drawing pictures using the standard keyboard characters (*see* Figure 18). By making use of the intrinsic shapes of the characters, or of their relative densities, the artist can render surprisingly realistic graphics. These pictures are best when designed and displayed in a fixed-pitch font. (*See* FIXED-PITCH TYPE.) Because ASCII graphics uses only standard characters, these pictures can easily be transmitted by e-mail or in newsgroup postings and are popular in SIGNATURE FILES.

TABLE 2
ASCII CHARACTER CODES (DECIMAL)

0	Ctrl-@	32	Space	64	@	96	'
1	Ctrl-A	33	!	65	A	97	a
2	Ctrl-B	34	"	66	B	98	b
3	Ctrl-C	35	#	67	C	99	c
4	Ctrl-D	36	$	68	D	100	d
5	Ctrl-E	37	%	69	E	101	e
6	Ctrl-F	38	&	70	F	102	f
7	Ctrl-G	39	'	71	G	103	g
8	Backspace	40	(	72	H	104	h
9	Tab	41	)	73	I	105	i
10	Ctrl-J	42	*	74	J	106	j
11	Ctrl-K	43	+	75	K	107	k
12	Ctrl-L	44	,	76	L	108	l
13	Return	45	–	77	M	109	m
14	Ctrl-N	46	.	78	N	110	n
15	Ctrl-O	47	/	79	O	111	o
16	Ctrl-P	48	0	80	P	112	p
17	Ctrl-Q	49	1	81	Q	113	q
18	Ctrl-R	50	2	82	R	114	r
19	Ctrl-S	51	3	83	S	115	s
20	Ctrl-T	52	4	84	T	116	t
21	Ctrl-U	53	5	85	U	117	u
22	Ctrl-V	54	6	86	V	118	v
23	Ctrl-W	55	7	87	W	119	w
24	Ctrl-X	56	8	88	X	120	x
25	Ctrl-Y	57	9	89	Y	121	y
26	Ctrl-Z	58	:	90	Z	122	z
27	Escape	59	;	91	[	123	{
28	Ctrl-\	60	<	92	\	124		
29	Ctrl-]	61	=	93	]	125	}
30	Ctrl-^	62	>	94	^	126	~
31	Ctrl-_	63	?	95	_	127	Delete

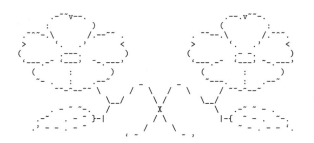

FIGURE 18. ASCII GRAPHICS

ASIC (**A**pplication **S**pecific **I**ntegrated **C**ircuit) an integrated circuit (silicon chip) specifically made for a particular complete piece of electronic equipment. For example, the video controller in a typical PC is an ASIC designed specifically for use on that particular make and model of video card, whereas the memory chips are standard ICs also used in other types of computers.

ASP

1. (**A**ctive **S**erver **P**ages) a Microsoft system for developing Web pages that can dynamically change in response to user input. For information on how a web page can store information on the browser's computer, *see* COOKIE.

2. (**A**pplication **S**ervice **P**rovider) a network service provider that also provides application software, such as networked database programs. *Compare* INTERNET SERVICE PROVIDER, CONTENT PROVIDER.

aspect ratio the ratio of height to width.

ASPI (**A**dvanced **SCSI P**rogramming **I**nterface) a standard way for application programs to access SCSI hardware. *See* SCSI.

assembler a computer program that translates assembly language into machine language. *See* ASSEMBLY LANGUAGE; MACHINE LANGUAGE; COMPILER.

assembly language a computer language in which each statement corresponds to one of the binary instructions recognized by the CPU. Assembly-language programs are translated into machine code by an *assembler.*

Assembly languages are more cumbersome to use than regular (or high-level) programming languages, but they are much easier to use than pure machine languages, which require that all instructions be written in binary code.

```
; Example of IBM PC assembly language
; Accepts a number in register AX;
; subtracts 32 if it is in the range 97-122;
; otherwise leaves it unchanged.

SUB32   PROC           ; procedure begins here
        CMP   AX,97    ; compare AX to 97
        JL    DONE     ; if less, jump to DONE
        CMP   AX,122   ; compare AX to 122
        JG    DONE     ; if greater, jump to DONE
        SUB   AX,32    ; subtract 32 from AX
DONE:   RET            ; return to main program
SUB32   ENDP           ; procedure ends here
```

FIGURE 19. ASSEMBLY LANGUAGE

Complete computer programs are seldom written in assembly language. Instead, assembly language is used for short procedures that must run as fast as possible or must do special things to the computer hardware. For example, Figure 19 shows a short routine that takes a number, checks whether it is in the range 97 to 122 inclusive, and subtracts 32 if so, otherwise leaving the number unchanged. (That particular subtraction happens to convert all lowercase ASCII codes to their uppercase equivalents.)

This particular assembly language is for the Intel 8086 family of processors (which includes all PC-compatible computers); assembly languages for other processors are different. Everything after the semicolon in each line is a comment, ignored by the computer. Two lines (PROC and ENDP) are *pseudo instructions*; they tell the assembler how the program is organized. All the other lines translate directly into binary codes for the CPU.

Many of the most common operations in computer programming are hard to implement in assembly language. For example, there are no assembly language statements to open a file, print a number, or compute a square root. For these functions the programmer must write complicated routines from scratch, use services provided by the operating system, or call routines in a previously written library.

assignment statement a statement in a computer language that calculates the value of an expression and stores that value in a variable.

For example, this is an assignment statement in BASIC:

```
10 LET Y = (A*X^2 + B*X + C)^0.5
```

This statement calculates the value of $\sqrt{AX^2 + BX + C}$ and then gives that value to the variable Y. Another example is

```
20 LET I = I + 1
```

which makes I take on a value 1 greater than its previous value. In newer versions of BASIC, the line number and the keyword LET are optional.

associate to tell a computer that a particular file should always be processed by a particular program, so that the next time the user opens the file, that program will automatically start.

Under Windows 3, Windows 95 and its successors, associations are largely based on filename extensions. (*See* EXTENSION, definition 2.) To change the association of a file extension, open any directory (folder), then select View, Folder Options, File Types. Associations can also be changed by editing the registry.

FIGURE 20. ASTERISKS

asterisk the star-shaped character ∗. An asterisk is usually used to mark a footnote.

In DOS, Windows, OS/2, UNIX, and other operating systems, an asterisk is used as a wild card character, to match any characters occurring in a particular place in a filename. For example, if you type `dir *.exe` you will get a list of all files whose names end in `exe`.

asynchronous not synchronized. For example, most computer terminals use asynchronous data transmission, in which the terminal or the computer is free to transmit any number of characters at any time. (The bits constituting each character are transmitted at a fixed rate, but the pauses between characters can be of any duration.)

Synchronous terminals, by contrast, transmit data in packets of more than one character. This is faster than asynchronous communication because there is no need for a start bit or stop bit on each individual character.

asynchronous discussion a discussion where the participants do not all have to be present at the same time. For example, in a newsgroup, participants can read comments about a particular topic that have been previously posted by other participants and then add to them. *See* NEWSGROUP.

AT (**A**dvanced **T**echnology) the class of IBM PCs originally introduced in 1984 using the 80286 microprocessor and a 16-bit bus. *See* IBM PC. *Contrast* XT.

ATA (**AT** **A**ttachment, where *AT* means *PC AT*) the interface used by IDE hard disks, essentially a buffered connection to the system bus. *See also* IDE.

ATAPI (**AT** **A**ttachment **P**acket **I**nterface) the interface used by CD-ROM drives and other devices other than hard disks that are connected to an IDE hard disk controller.

AT command set the set of commands used to control Hayes modems; they all begin with the letters AT. *See* MODEM.

Athlon a high-speed Pentium-compatible microprocessor made by AMD. *See* MICROPROCESSOR.

ATM

    1. Adobe **T**ype **M**anager, a font management utility that allows Windows systems to use Type 1 as well as TrueType fonts. Version 4.0

allows the user to group fonts in categories, print samples, and define *instances* of MULTIPLE-MASTER FONTS. *See* TRUETYPE FONT; TYPE I FONT.

2. in banking, abbreviation for **au**tomatic **t**eller **m**achine.

3. in networking, abbreviation for **a**synchronous **t**ransfer **m**ode, a set of high-speed data transmission protocols. *See* PROTOCOL. *Contrast* TCP/IP; NETBEUI; IPX/SPX.

ATN the function, in BASIC, that computes the trigonometric arc tangent. *See* ARC TANGENT; TRIGONOMETRIC FUNCTIONS.

FIGURE 21. AT SIGN

at sign the symbol @, which stands for "at" and was originally used in price quotes (e.g., 4 items @ $3 each) and is now used in e-mail addresses (mcovingt@ai.uga.edu). Some colorful nicknames for @ include "elephant's ear" and "cinnamon bun."

In DOS .bat files and OS/2 .cmd files, commands beginning with @ are not displayed on the screen.

attachment a file transmitted as part of a piece of electronic mail. *See* ELECTRONIC MAIL.

atto- metric prefix meaning ÷1,000,000,000,000,000,000. *Atto-* is derived from the Danish word for "eighteen" (because it signifies 10^{-18}). *See* METRIC PREFIXES.

attributes the properties of files in DOS and similar operating systems. Files can be marked as hidden, system, read-only, and archive (which means that they have changed since last backed up to tape). The attrib command displays and changes file attributes.

auction a sale in which buyers make bids (offers) and the highest offer is accepted. For information about on-line auctions *see* EBAY. *See also* DUTCH AUCTION; RESERVE PRICE; BID.

FIGURE 22. AUDIO (SOUND) WAVEFORM
DISPLAYED GRAPHICALLY

audio sound, represented by means of electronic signals. *See also* SOUND CARD; FM SYNTHESIS; WAVETABLE SYNTHESIS; MIDI. *Contrast* VIDEO.

audit trail a record kept by a computer program that shows how data was entered into the computer. These records are essential for ensuring the reliability of financial data processing systems.

AUP *see* ACCEPTABLE-USE POLICY.

authoring software software packages used to produce multimedia or HYPERTEXT presentations (web pages, multimedia encyclopedias, interactive displays). The authoring software provides ways of linking sounds, music, visuals, and text. An interactive presentation may have highlighted keywords, which will lead the reader to another section of the presentation. Authoring software gives the developer the necessary tools to create these hypertext links. The possibility of creating different paths through the material is what sets authoring software apart from presentation software.

Many of the layout and graphic design skills necessary for good desktop publishing carry over to these new media. The common thread is good communication skills. *See* ELECTRONIC PUBLISHING; WORLD WIDE WEB; WEB PAGE; HTML; PRESENTATION GRAPHICS.

authorware software designed to aid in the production of multimedia presentations and WEB PAGES. *See* AUTHORING SOFTWARE.

autodimensioning a CAD feature that keeps imported graphics correctly scaled as the drawing or diagram is completed.

AUTOEXEC.BAT in DOS and Windows, the name of a file that contains commands to be executed automatically whenever the computer boots up. For example, an AUTOEXEC.BAT file containing the following lines will tell the computer to look for commands in directories C:\DOS and C:\UTIL in that order, and then will check disk drive C for lost clusters:

```
PATH C:\DOS;C:\UTIL
CHKDSK C:/F
```

Many pieces of software automatically add their directories to the path command and make other changes in AUTOEXEC.BAT when you install them. (*See also* PATH.)

Under Windows 95 and its successors, AUTOEXEC.BAT executes upon startup if it exists, but is usually not needed.

Under OS/2, AUTOEXEC.BAT is executed by each DOS process that does not have a different startup file specified. The startup of OS/2 itself is controlled by CONFIG.SYS. Under DOS, CONFIG.SYS loads device drivers and makes other settings prior to executing AUTO-EXEC.BAT. *See also* CONFIG.SYS.

autojoin a feature of drawing programs that automatically joins endpoints that are within a certain distance of each other, so that you can draw a closed curve without having to come back to the exact pixel where the curve started. If you are having trouble getting curves to close so you can fill them, try increasing the autojoin setting. See your software manual for details.

FIGURE 23. AUTOTRACING A BITMAP

autotrace (DRAW PROGRAM) a command that instructs the computer to fit a curve to the outline of a bitmap. When the bitmap is traced (converted into VECTOR GRAPHICS), it is more easily manipulated in the drawing program.

AVI file (Audio-Video Interleave) a file containing video and audio (i.e., moving pictures with sound) in Video for Windows format, identified by a filename ending in .avi. *Compare* QUICKTIME.

```
# Sample program in AWK -- M. Covington 1995

# Code to execute at beginning of program
BEGIN   { printf("Program starting...\n") }

# Code to execute when line begins with U
/^U/    { printf("%10s %5d\n",$2,$3)
          utotal = utotal + $3
        }

# Code to execute when line begins with C
/^C/    { ctotal = ctotal + $3 }

# Code to execute at end of program
END     { print "USA total", utotal
          print "Canada total", ctotal
        }
```

FIGURE 24. AWK PROGRAM.

AWK a programming language for scanning text files and processing lines or strings that match particular patterns. It is widely used to write utilities under UNIX. AWK was developed by A. V. Aho, P. J. Weinberger, and B. W. Kernighan, and the name "AWK" is an acronym composed of their initials.

AWK normally reads the input file one line at a time and parses each line into fields separated by blanks. It assigns the fields to the variables $1, $2, $3, and so on. A program consists of tests to apply to each line and actions to be performed when each test is passed. For example,

```
{ print $1, $3 }
```

is a complete AWK program that prints the first and third fields of every line. Figure 24 shows a more complete AWK program that reads a file of the form

```
USA        Georgia        23
USA        Florida        19
Canada     Ontario         5
Canada     Newfoundland    8
USA        California     52
```

and keeps totals of the numbers in the third column (one total for Canada and one for the United States). In addition, it prints out fields 2 and 3 of lines that begin with USA. If the input is the table above, the output is:

```
Program starting...
   Georgia     23
   Florida     19
California     52
USA total 94
Canada total 13
```

The program uses regular expressions to test whether each line begins with U or C. (*See* REGULAR EXPRESSION.) Then it prints results, using not only the simple `print` statement but also a `printf` statement very similar to that of C. (*See* PRINTF.)

AWK is very versatile; it provides many different ways of reading the input file, as well as standard control structures (`while`, `do`, `if`), one-dimensional arrays, and automatic interconversion of numbers and strings. All variables are automatically initialized to 0 or the empty string when the program starts. *Compare* PERL; REXX.

AWT (**A**bstract **W**indow **T**oolkit) a set of tools provided in Java for using a graphical user interface. Crucially, AWT is not tied to Windows 98, the Macintosh or any other operating system; programs that use AWT are portable.

AX.25 a standard format used in amateur radio for transmitting data in packets. It is an adaptation of the ITU-T (formerly CCITT) X.25 standard. *See* PACKET RADIO; X.25.

B

FIGURE 25. CHARLES BABBAGE (1791–1871)

Babbage, Charles (1791–1871) inventor of a number of computing machines, including the "Analytical Engine," which introduced concepts that were later used in electronic computers. Babbage was the first to envision a machine controlled by a program stored in its memory.

back browser command that returns you to the most recently viewed web page.

backbone the main communication path in a WIDE-AREA NETWORK; the set of cables or connections that carries most of the traffic. Other data paths branch off from the backbone.

back door an alternate way of entering a computer system. For example, the original programmer of the system may have programmed a secret way of logging onto the system not requiring the normal password entrance.

back end the part of a computer system not directly interacting with the user. For example, a database system running on a mainframe computer is the back end of a system, whereas the microcomputers used by those accessing the system are the front end of the system. *See* THREE-TIER ARCHITECTURE.

background the field or color against which objects are drawn or displayed on the screen.

background execution the continued execution of a program while it is not visible on the screen (or does not occupy much of the screen) and the user is free to run other programs at the same time. Background execution is possible only in multitasking operating systems. *See* MULTITASKING; WINDOWS (MICROSOFT); OS/2; UNIX.

backlit illuminated from behind (as in the liquid crystal displays on laptop computers and some calculators).

back one drawing program command that sends the selected object down one level. *See also* ARRANGE; DRAW PROGRAM; SEND TO FRONT.

backslash the character \ as opposed to the forward slash /.

backtracking a method of solving problems by trying various combinations of moves until a successful combination is found.

Backtracking works as follows: First, choose a possible move and make it. Then, proceed from there by choosing a possible move, and so on, until a solution is found. If you reach a point where you have not found a solution but no more moves are possible, back up to the most recent untried alternative. That is, undo one or more moves until you get back to an alternative you did not take. Follow that different choice to see if the solution lies in that direction. If not, keep backing up until you find what you're looking for (you may have to try all possible moves).

Backtracking is built into the programming language Prolog, which uses it extensively (*see* PROLOG). In this article we will discuss how to implement backtracking in a conventional language.

For example, consider this problem: Find three whole numbers $x[1]$, $x[2]$, and $x[3]$, each between 1 and 5, such that their sum is equal to their product. While you might try to solve this problem mathematically, it is easier just to try all the combinations. One way to get all the combinations is to set up three nested loops as follows:

```
FOR x[1]:=1 to 5 DO
 FOR x[2]:=1 to 5 DO
  FOR x[3]:=1 to 5 DO
   IF x[1]+x[2]+x[3] = x[1]*x[2]*x[3] THEN
    write (x[1],x[2],x[3],' is a solution');
```

This is possible because you know in advance that the solution will take three moves (choosing one number in each move), so you can set up three loops.

Backtracking occurs in this example because if the innermost loop doesn't find a solution, control returns to the middle loop, which increments $x[2]$ and starts the innermost loop over again. Similarly, the middle loop backtracks to the outer loop if it fails to find a solution. The loop counters keep track of untried alternatives, but it's important to understand that any method of generating alternatives one by one would work just as well.

With some problems, you don't know how many moves a solution will take. In such a case you must use recursion to nest the loops at run time. Fig. 26 shows a Pascal program that solves the problem we've just discussed but uses recursion rather than nested loops.

```
PROGRAM backtrack;

VAR { must be global }
  x: ARRAY[1..3] OF INTEGER;

PROCEDURE choose(n:INTEGER);
  { chooses a value for x[n] }
VAR
  i: INTEGER; { must be local }
  c: CHAR;
BEGIN
  IF n=4 THEN { we have chosen 3 values }
    BEGIN
      IF x[1]+x[2]+x[3] = x[1]*x[2]*x[3] THEN
        BEGIN
          writeln(x[1]:3,x[2]:3,x[3]:3,
              ' is a solution.  Continue? [y/n] ');
          readln(c);
          IF NOT (c IN ['Y','y']) THEN halt;
        END
      ELSE
        write(x[1]:3,x[2]:3,x[3]:3,
            ' is not a solution. Backtracking...')
    END
  ELSE { recurse to fill in the rest of the 3 }
    FOR i:=1 to 5 DO
      BEGIN
        x[n] := i; choose(n+1)
      END
END;

{ Main program }
BEGIN
  choose(1);
  writeln('That''s all.');
END.
```

FIGURE 26. BACKTRACKING

In Prolog, where backtracking is built in, all you have to do is specify possible values for the integers and specify the condition they must meet. You can solve our example problem by typing the query:

```
?-  member(X1,[1,2,3,4,5]),
    member(X2,[1,2,3,4,5]),
    member(X3,[1,2,3,4,5]),
    Sum is X1+X2+X3,
    Product is X1*X2*X3,
    Sum == Product,
    write([X1,X2,X3]).
```

Each clause in the query specifies a condition that the answer must meet. Whenever the computer encounters a clause whose condition cannot be satisfied, it backs up to an untried alternative in a previous clause and tries again.

backup copy a copy of working programs and related files that can be used to restore lost or damaged programs and files. You should have a full backup copy of your hard disk on zip disks, diskettes, tapes, or CD-R discs. It's a good idea to also make *daily* backups of work in progress. Store your backup copies in a secure place, preferably a fireproof box. Then, in case of any hardware or software problems, you will be able to restore your files. *See also* ARCHIVAL STORAGE; HARD DISK MANAGEMENT; GRANDFATHER TAPE; CD-R.

Backus-Naur form (BNF) a notation used to describe the syntax of languages. BNF was devised by J. Backus and Peter Naur and introduced in the first official description of ALGOL 60 (*see* ALGOL); it is sometimes referred to as Backus normal form.

Each BNF statement describes some syntactic unit by giving one or more alternative expansions of it, separated by the symbol | . For example, the following is a BNF description of the assignment statement in BASIC (we assume that <line number>, <variable name>, and <expression> have already been defined, and that <empty> stands for the absence of any written symbol):

```
<let keyword>  ::=  LET | <empty>
<assignment statement>  ::=
        <line number> <let keyword> <variable name> = <expression>
```

The first statement defines <let keyword> as standing for either the word let or no symbol, in order to indicate that the word let is optional. The second statement defines <assignment statement> as consisting of a line number, an optional let keyword, a variable name, an equals sign, and an expression.

Many languages contain syntactic rules that cannot be expressed in BNF; for instance, BNF provides no way to say that an integer cannot exceed 32,767. Still, BNF descriptions are handy because they are concise and definitive and because parsers can be generated directly from them. *See* PARSING.

Backus normal form *see* BACKUS-NAUR FORM.

balloon help a Macintosh OS help feature that identifies icons and tools as the mouse pointer is dragged over them. The speech balloon appears as close as possible to the selected object. Balloons can be very useful for novices; more advanced users can turn them off. For the PC equivalent, *see* WHAT'S THIS?

banding the appearance of strips of colors in an image due to the inherent difficulty of representing gradations of tones with a limited color palette. *See* Figure 27. Increasing the number of bands gives a smoother color transition.

FIGURE 27. BANDING

bandwidth the rate at which a communication system can transmit data; more technically, the range of frequencies that an electronic system can transmit. High bandwidth allows fast transmission or the transmission of many signals at once. On a monitor screen, high bandwidth provides a sharp image. On a computer network, the bandwidth of a connection is limited by the slowest link in the chain connecting two computers.

bang the character !, better known as an exclamation mark.

bank switching the ability to use more than one set of memory chips at different times, while giving them the same addresses. This makes it possible to equip a computer with more memory than it was originally designed for — simply store some data in one set of chips, then switch over and use the other set of chips.

Bank switching was used to give the original IBM PC more than 640K of memory (*see* EXPANDED MEMORY). Bank switching is also used on advanced color graphics cards.

banner
1. an extra page with an identifying name in large letters, printed to identify a printout.
2. a sign made by piecing together pages of computer printout.

FIGURE 28. A BAR CODE

bar code a pattern of wide and narrow bars printed on paper or a similar material. A computer reads the bar code by scanning it with a laser beam or with a wand that contains a light source and a photocell. The most familiar bar code is the Universal Product Code (Fig. 28), used with cash registers in supermarkets, but bar codes have been utilized to encode many kinds of data, including complete computer programs. Circular bar codes are sometimes used on boxes or pieces of luggage that may be scanned from many different directions.

bare metal *(slang)* the computer hardware itself. "Programming to the bare metal" means controlling the hardware directly rather than relying on operating system services. *See* API.

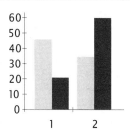

FIGURE 29. BAR GRAPH

bar graph a type of chart that displays information by representing quantities as rectangular bars of different heights. Sometimes symbols are stacked or stretched to the appropriate heights to lend some visual interest to the chart (*see* PICTOGRAPH, definition 2).

Bar graphs are usually preferred for representing and contrasting data collected over a period of time.

base

1. the middle layer of a bipolar transistor. *See* TRANSISTOR.

2. a number raised to an exponent; for example, in $y = a^x$, a is the base.

3. the number of digits used in a number system. For example, decimal numbers use base 10 and binary numbers use base 2. *See* BINARY NUMBER; DECIMAL NUMBER; HEXADECIMAL NUMBER; OCTAL.

4. the starting point for numbering the elements of an array. For example, with base 1, an array declared as X(2) will have two elements X(1) and X(2). With base 0, it would also have an element X(0).

BASIC (**B**eginner's **A**ll-purpose **S**ymbolic **I**nstruction **C**ode) a computer language designed by John Kemeny and Thomas Kurtz in 1964 and popularized by Microsoft in the 1970s.

BASIC is good for programming simple calculations quickly, and you do not have to learn much of the language in order to begin using

```
10 REM Temperature conversion program
20 PRINT "Temperature in Fahrenheit";
30 INPUT F
40 LET C=(F-32)*5/9
50 PRINT F;" F equals ";
60 PRINT C;" C"
70 END

Temperature in Fahrenheit?  98
98 F equals 36.66667 C
```

FIGURE 30. BASIC PROGRAM AND ITS OUTPUT

it. Because no declarations are required, programs can be quite short.

Fig. 30 shows a simple BASIC program and the results of running it. All lines are numbered. The keyword REM ("remark") identifies comments. Ordinary variables hold floating-point numbers. Character strings can be stored in variables whose names end in $, such as A$. Arrays are declared with the DIM statement.

The PRINT statement writes output to the screen. Items to be printed are separated by semicolons to print them adjacent to one another, or commas to align them in columns. If a PRINT statement ends with a semicolon or comma, the next PRINT statement continues writing on the same line.

The INPUT statement prints a question mark and reads data from the keyboard. Another way to obtain input is to read it from a set of DATA statements included in the program, using the READ statement. This provides a way to store large amounts of data in the program itself rather than on a separate data file.

Statements for managing flow of control include GOTO to jump to another line unconditionally, IF...THEN to jump when a condition is fulfilled, ON...GOTO to choose a destination based on the value of a variable, GOSUB to call a subroutine, and FOR...NEXT to execute a loop with a counter.

In the 1970s and 1980s, numerous software vendors, especially Microsoft, added features to BASIC to support STRUCTURED PROGRAMMING and a wide variety of DATA STRUCTURES. Today, BASIC is one of the most complex programming languages in wide use, incorporating features from Pascal, FORTRAN, and C. Line numbers are no longer necessary. However, BASIC is still easy for beginners to use, and the newest BASIC compilers still accept programs written in Kemeny and Kurtz's original language. For examples of programs in newer varieties of BASIC, *see* MANDELBROT SET; FRACTAL.

Many features of BASIC are described elsewhere in this book. For information about flow of control and program organization, *see* CONDITIONAL BRANCH; IF; FOR; LOOP; NEST; FUNCTION; SUBROU-

TINE; CALL; END. On arithmetic *see* ARRAY; ASSIGNMENT STATE-
MENT; EXPRESSION; ABS; ATN; SIN; COS; TAN; E; LOG; NUMERICAL
INTEGRATION; ROUNDING; TRUNCATION; RANDOM-NUMBER GENERA-
TOR. On string handling *see* STRING OPERATIONS. For further exam-
ples of BASIC programs *see* BUBBLE SORT; SELECTION SORT; THREE-
DIMENSIONAL GRAPHICS. On implementations of BASIC *see* INTER-
PRETER; COMPILER; BASICA; QBASIC; QUICKBASIC; VISUAL BASIC; ROM
BASIC. *See also* PEEK; POKE.

    Usage note: Since it is an acronym, *BASIC* is usually written in
all capital letters. Newer Microsoft publications, however, write *Basic*
by analogy to *Pascal.* We spell it that way when referring to newer
Microsoft products.

BASICA the command, in DOS on the original IBM PC, that called
up the built-in BASIC interpreter, most of which resided in ROM. (*See*
BASIC.) A similar interpreter for non-IBM PCs was called GW-BASIC.
Both were later replaced by QBASIC, which is still distributed with
DOS and Windows (including Windows 98).

batch processing the noninteractive use of computers. In batch processing, the user gives the computer a "batch" of information, referred
to as a *job* — for example, a program and its input data — and waits for
it to be processed as a whole. Batch processing contrasts with interactive processing, in which the user communicates with the computer by
means of a terminal while the program is running. The crucial difference is that with batch processing the user must put all of the data into
the computer before seeing any of the results, while with interactive
processing the user can decide how to handle each item on the basis of
the results obtained with earlier items.

BAT file (**batch file**) in DOS, OS/2, and Windows, a file whose name
ends in .BAT and which contains a list of DOS commands. For example,
if you store the commands

```
dir a:
dir b:
dir c:
```

on a file called THREEDIR.BAT, then you can type `threedir` and the
three `dir` commands in the file will all be executed in succession. *See
also* AUTOEXEC.BAT.

baud a unit that measures the speed with which information is transferred. The baud rate is the maximum number of state transitions per
second: for instance, a system whose shortest pulses are 1/300 second
is operating at 300 baud.

    On an RS-232 serial link, the baud rate is equal to the data rate in
bits per second (bps). With other kinds of communication, the data rate
may be considerably faster than the baud rate. For instance, a 2400-
baud modem takes 2400-baud (2400-bps) serial data and encodes it

into an audio signal whose true baud rate is 600, near the maximum rate at which a telephone line can transmit pulses. Each pulse carries more than one bit of information. At the receiving end, another modem transforms the signal back into 2400-baud serial data. Using similar techniques, newer modems go as fast as 56,600 baud.

bay a place provided for a disk or tape drive in a computer enclosure.

BBS (**B**ulletin **B**oard **S**ystem) a computer that allows users to log in from remote terminals, exchange messages, and (usually) download programs. Many BBSs are run by microcomputer hobbyists and can be accessed free of charge by dialing their telephone numbers. Other BBSs are run by computer hardware or software companies to distribute software updates and information.

    Since the mid-1980s, much of the function of BBSs has been taken over by on-line services such as CompuServe, America Online, Prodigy, and the Internet.

bcc command that invokes the Borland C Compiler. *See* C; BORLAND INTERNATIONAL; CC.

Bcc business abbreviation for "blind copies" (*compare* CC). In e-mail headers, Bcc: precedes additional addresses to which copies of the message should be sent. Unlike the Cc: header, the Bcc: header is not sent out with the message, so the copies are "blind," i.e., recipients of the message do not know that copies are being distributed.

BCD *see* BINARY-CODED DECIMAL.

BDK (**B**ean **D**evelopment **K**it) a tool for developing JavaBeans. *See* JAVA.

bean *see* JAVABEAN.

bells and whistles elaborate features added to a computer program. The phrase *bells and whistles* usually connotes that the features are unnecessary and confusing; it originally referred to sound effects devices on theater organs in the silent movie era.

benchmark a computer program used to test the performance of a computer or a piece of software. For example, the speed with which computers do arithmetic is often measured by running a prime-number-finding algorithm called the Sieve of Eratosthenes.

    Benchmark results are always somewhat untrustworthy because no single program tests all aspects of a computer's operation. A particular benchmark may exaggerate a difference between two machines that is unimportant in practice, or it may conceal an important difference. *See also* MIPS.

BeOS a microcomputer operating system developed by Be, Inc. of Menlo Park, California (www.be.com) as part of a project to develop a new type of graphics workstation.

BeOS is designed to be effective with graphics and multimedia applications and to facilitate the use of computers with multiple microprocessors. The operating system is a totally new design incorporating the best features of UNIX and Microsoft Windows but not constrained by compatibility with any older system.

Due to competition from Microsoft Windows and Linux, BeOS has recently been made available free of charge in the hopes that its market share will grow, providing a market for application products.

Bernoulli box a high-capacity removable-cartridge disk drive made by Iomega Corporation, Roy, Utah, and now largely replaced by ZIP DRIVES and JAZ DRIVES. The Bernoulli box is named after the mathematician who discovered the aerodynamic principle on which the drive head mechanism depends.

beta testing the second stage of testing a new software product that is almost ready for market. Beta testing is carried out by volunteers in a wide variety of settings like those in which the finished product will be used. *Contrast* ALPHA TESTING; GAMMA TESTING.

Bézier spline a curve that connects two points smoothly and is further defined by two more points that it does not pass through. Most draw programs represent curves as Bézier splines. For an illustration, see SPLINE.

A Bézier spline can be thought of as a gradual transition from one line to another. Call the four *control points* that define the curve P_1, P_2, P_3, and P_4. Then the curve starts out heading from P_1 toward P_2. But it curves around so that by the time it gets to P_4 it is approaching from the direction of P_3.

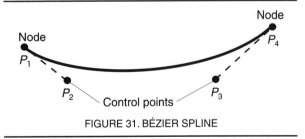

FIGURE 31. BÉZIER SPLINE

To plot a Bézier spline, let (x_1, y_1), (x_2, y_2), (x_3, y_3), and (x_4, y_4) by the coordinates of $P_1 \ldots P_4$ respectively, and let t range from 0 to 1. Then compute x and y from t as follows:

$$
\begin{array}{rcl}
a &=& -t^3 + 3t^2 - 3t + 1 \\
b &=& 3t^3 - 6t^2 + 3t \\
c &=& -3t^3 + 3t^2 \\
x &=& ax_1 + bx_2 + cx_3 + t^3x_4 \\
y &=& ay_1 + by_2 + cy_3 + t^3y_4
\end{array}
$$

Notice that as t goes from 0 to 1, a drops from 1 to 0, and t^3 rises from 0 to 1. This computation was first described by Pierre Bézier in 1970.

bid an offer to buy something for a particular price. *See* AUCTION; EBAY; RESERVE PRICE.

bidirectional

1. able to transmit data in two directions. Originally, parallel ports were used only for printers and transmitted data in only one direction, from the computer to the printer. Modern bidirectional parallel ports are often used to communicate with tape and disk drives as well as printers. *See* PARALLEL PORT.

2. able to move in two directions. Most dot-matrix printers move the print head bidirectionally for greater speed; alternating lines are printed from left to right and right to left.

big-endian a system of memory addressing in which numbers that occupy more than one byte in memory are stored "big end first," with the uppermost 8 bits at the lowest address.

For example, the 16-digit binary number 1010111010110110 occupies two 8-bit bytes in memory. On a big-endian computer such as the Macintosh, the upper byte, 10101110, is stored at the first address and the lower byte, 10110110, is stored at the next higher address. On a little-endian machine, the order is reversed. *Contrast* LITTLE-ENDIAN.

The terms "big-endian" and "little-endian" are from *Gulliver's Travels*; they originally referred to the parties in a dispute over which end of a boiled egg should be broken first.

binary addition is one of the basic arithmetic operations performed by computers, and understanding it is the key to understanding how machines do arithmetic.

If each of the numbers to be added has only one digit, addition is simple:

$$
\begin{array}{rcl}
0 + 0 &=& 00 \\
0 + 1 &=& 01 \\
1 + 0 &=& 01 \\
1 + 1 &=& 10
\end{array}
$$

A circuit that implements this function is called a *half adder* and can be made out of standard logic gates as shown in Figure 32. Notice that there are two digits of output; the higher digit is called the *carry bit* because it is carried to the next column when adding multi-digit numbers.

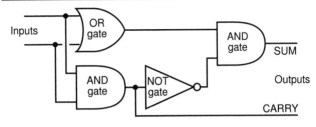

FIGURE 32. BINARY ADDITION: HALF ADDER

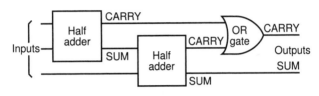

FIGURE 33. BINARY ADDITION: FULL ADDER

To add numbers with more than one digit, we proceed one digit at a time, starting at the right, just as with pencil-and-paper arithmetic. Each step of the addition can have three inputs: one digit from each of the numbers to be added, plus a digit carried from the previous column to the right. Accordingly, for each column except the rightmost, we need a circuit called a *full adder,* which takes three one-digit inputs. Its output still has only two digits because the largest value that can be obtained is $1 + 1 + 1 = 11$. A full adder can be built out of two half adders (Fig. 33).

To add two 16-bit binary numbers, a computer needs 15 full adders and one half adder, with the carry output of each adder connected to an input of the adder to its left. All of this circuitry is part of the CPU; when the CPU receives an add instruction, it sends the contents of two registers to the inputs of the set of adders, and then stores the output in a register.

binary-coded decimal (BCD) a way of representing numbers by means of codes for the decimal digits. For example, consider the number 65. In binary, 65 is 01000001, and that is how most computers represent it. But some computer programs might represent it as the code for 6 followed by the code for 5, i.e., 0110 0101.

The advantage of BCD shows up when a number has a fractional part, such as 0.1. There is no way to convert 0.1 into binary exactly; it would require an infinite number of digits, just like converting $\frac{1}{3}$ into decimal (*see* ROUNDING ERROR). But in BCD, 0.1 is represented by the code for 1 immediately after the point, and no accuracy is lost.

BCD arithmetic is considerably slower and takes more memory than binary arithmetic. It is used primarily in financial work and other situations where rounding errors are intolerable. Pocket calculators use BCD.

binary file a file containing bits or bytes that do not necessarily represent printable text. The term *binary file* usually denotes any file that is not a text file, such as executable machine language code. Crucially, special software is required to print a binary file or view it on the screen. *Contrast* TEXT FILE.

binary multiplication a basic operation in computer arithmetic. For single-digit numbers, the binary multiplication table is very simple and is the same as the Boolean AND operation (*see* AND GATE):

$$0 \times 0 = 0$$
$$0 \times 1 = 0$$
$$1 \times 0 = 0$$
$$1 \times 1 = 1$$

For numbers with more than one digit, the computer does something very similar to what we do to decimal numbers in pencil-and-paper arithmetic. To find 13×21 in decimal, we proceed like this:

$$
\begin{array}{r}
21 \\
\times\ 13 \\
\hline
63 \\
21 \\
\hline
273 \\
\end{array}
$$

First, find 3×21. Then, find 10×21, and add these two results together to get the final product. Note that the product has more digits than either of the two original numbers.

You can follow the same procedure to multiply two binary numbers:

$$
\begin{array}{r}
10101 \\
\times\ 01101 \\
\hline
10101 \\
00000 \\
10101 \\
10101 \\
00000 \\
\hline
100010001 \\
\end{array}
$$

Notice that each of the partial products is either zero or a copy of 10101 shifted leftward some number of digits. The partial products that are zero can, of course, be skipped. Accordingly, in order to multiply in binary, the computer simply starts with 0 in the accumulator, and works through the second number to be multiplied (11101 in the example), checking whether each digit of it is 1 or 0. Where it finds a 0, it does nothing; where it finds a 1, it adds to the accumulator a copy of the first number, shifted leftward the appropriate number of places.

binary number a number expressed in binary (base-2) notation, a system that uses only two digits, 0 and 1. Binary numbers are well suited for use by computers, since many electrical devices have two distinct states: on and off. Writing numbers in binary requires more digits than writing numbers in decimal, so binary numbers are cumbersome for people to use. Each digit of a binary number represents a power of 2. The rightmost digit is the 1's digit, the next digit leftward is the 2's digit, then the 4's digit, and so on:

Decimal	Binary
$2^0 = 1$	1
$2^1 = 2$	10
$2^2 = 4$	100
$2^3 = 8$	1000
$2^4 = 16$	10000

Here are examples of numbers written in binary and decimal form:

Decimal	Binary	Decimal	Binary
0	0	11	1011
1	1	12	1100
2	10	13	1101
3	11	14	1110
4	100	15	1111
5	101	16	10000
6	110	17	10001
7	111	18	10010
8	1000	19	10011
9	1001	20	10100
10	1010	21	10101

See also DECIMAL NUMBER; OCTAL; HEXADECIMAL NUMBER.

binary search a method for locating a particular item from a list of items in alphabetical or numerical order. Suppose you need to find the location of a particular word in a list of alphabetized words. To execute a binary search, look first at the word that is at the exact middle of the list. If the word you're looking for comes before the midpoint word, you know that it must be in the first half of the list (if it is in the list at all). Otherwise, it must be in the second half. Once you have determined which half of the list to search, use the same method to determine which

```
PROGRAM binsearch;
{ Binary search not using recursion.
  Searches an array of numbers for one equal to x.
  Assumes the numbers are given in ascending order. }

VAR
  n: INTEGER;
  x: INTEGER;
  a: ARRAY[1..500] OF INTEGER;

PROCEDURE readin;
  { Accepts sorted list of numbers from user }
VAR
  i: INTEGER;
BEGIN
  write('How many numbers? '); readln(n);
  FOR i:=1 TO n DO
    BEGIN
      write('a[',i,']= ');
      readln(a[i])
    END;
  write('Number to search for? '); readln(x);
END;

PROCEDURE search;
  { Finds x in a[1]...a[n] }
VAR
  lowbound, upbound, position: INTEGER;
BEGIN
  lowbound := 1;
  upbound  := n;
```

FIGURE 34. BINARY SEARCH PROGRAM

quarter, then which eighth, and so on. At most, a binary search will take about N steps if the list contains about 2^N items.

Fig. 34 shows a Pascal program that performs a binary search of a list of numbers.

binary subtraction a basic operation in computer arithmetic. The easiest way to subtract two binary numbers is to make one of the numbers negative, then add them. Circuits for doing binary addition are readily constructed with logic gates (*see* BINARY ADDITION). The negative counterpart of a binary number is called its *2-complement*.

Suppose that we have a number x, represented as a binary number with k digits. The 2-complement of x (written as $\overline{x}$) is

$$\overline{x} = 2^k - x$$

Then, to find the difference $a - x$ we can compute

$$a - x = a + \overline{x} - 2^k$$

This is easier than it looks, for two reasons. First, subtracting 2^k is trivial, because 2^k is a binary number of the form 1000, 100000, etc.,

```
    WHILE TRUE DO
      BEGIN
        writeln('It''s between position ',lowbound,
                ' and position ',upbound);
        position := (lowbound+upbound) div 2;
        IF a[position] = x THEN
          BEGIN
            writeln('Found it at position ',position);
            halt
          END
        ELSE IF upbound=lowbound+1 THEN
          { special case, search nearly over }
          lowbound := upbound
        ELSE IF position=lowbound THEN
          { the search is no longer moving }
          BEGIN
            writeln('It''s not there.');
            halt
          END
        ELSE IF a[position] > x THEN
          upbound := position
        ELSE
          lowbound := position;
      END
END;

{ Main program }
BEGIN
  readin;
  search
END.
```

FIGURE 34   (CONTINUED)

with $k + 1$ digits. So all we have to do is discard the leftmost digit to get our k-digit answer.

Second, finding the 2-complement of x is easy: just invert all the digits of x (changing 0's to 1's and 1's to 0's) and then add 1. *See* INVERTER.

Suppose we want to compute $5 - 2$ using 4-digit binary representations. That is, we want to compute:

$$0101 - 0010$$

First, change the second number to its complement, change the minus to a plus, and subtract 2^k:

$$0101 + \overline{0010} - 10000$$

To actually compute the complement, invert the digits of 0010 and add 1, so the whole computation becomes:

$$0101 + (1101 + 1) - 10000$$

Evaluate this expression by performing the two additions

$$0101 + 1101 + 1 = 10011$$

and then throwing away the leftmost digit, giving 0011 (= 3), which is the answer.

This method for handling subtraction suggests a way to represent negative numbers. Suppose we want to represent −3. Positive 3 is binary 0011 (still assuming a 4-digit system). The representation of −3 should be something similar. We can change the leftmost bit from 0 to 1 to indicate that the number is negative, thus:

$$3 = 0011 \qquad -3 = 1011$$

Now we're using the leftmost bit as a *sign bit* rather than as a digit of the number. And, conveniently, negative numbers are now the 2-complements of the corresponding positive numbers, and vice versa.

The range of numbers that can be represented is different than before. Without the sign bit, 4 binary digits can hold numbers from 0 to 15; with the sign bit, the numbers range from −8 to 7. On real computers it is typical to use 16 bits (2 bytes) to store integer values. Since one of these bits is the sign bit, this means that the largest positive integer that can be represented is $2^{15} - 1 = 32,767$, and the most negative number that can be represented is $-(2^{15}) = -32,768$. Some programming languages also provide an "unsigned integer" data type that ranges from 0 to 65,535.

binary synchronous (BiSync) a protocol for connecting IBM computer terminals together. Many terminals can share a single link, and a controller determines which terminal can transmit at a particular moment.

bind

    1. to give a variable a value; to INITIALIZE it.

    2. to start up and link together the different levels of device drivers that are necessary for network communication. For example, the driver for a protocol such as TCP/IP has to be bound to the driver for the Ethernet card.

BinHex a Macintosh utility for encoding binary files so that they can be transmitted as text through electronic mail systems and the like. (*See* BINARY FILE; TEXT FILE; ELECTRONIC MAIL.) A BinHex file is an encoded representation of a binary file, but the BinHex file consists only of printable characters arranged in lines of reasonable length. Specifically, the BinHex file consists of one hex digit (0–9, A–F) for each four bits of data in the original file. Thus the BinHex file is about twice as long as the original. *See* STUFFIT; UUENCODE; UUDECODE; BINARY FILE; TEXT FILE.

biometrics measurements of the human body. Some computer systems use biometrics, such as finger sizes, fingerprints, or scans of the human eye, to identify individuals for security purposes.

BIOS (**B**asic **I**nput **O**utput **S**ystem) a set of procedures stored on a ROM chip inside PC-compatible computers. These routines handle all input-output functions, including screen graphics, so that programs do not have to manipulate the hardware directly. This is important because if the hardware is changed (for example, by installing a newer kind of video adapter), the BIOS can be changed to match it, and there is no need to change the application programs.

The BIOS is not re-entrant and is therefore not easily usable by multitasking programs. Windows and OS/2 programs do not call the BIOS; instead, they use procedures provided by the operating system.

BIOS enumerator the BIOS routine that tells a PLUG AND PLAY system what hardware is installed.

bipolar transistor a semiconductor device formed by sandwiching a thin layer of P- or N-type semiconductor between two layers of the opposite type of semiconductor. (*See* TRANSISTOR.) The other general type of transistor is the field-effect transistor (FET).

bis Latin for "a second time," used to denote revised CCITT and ITU-T standards. *See* CCITT; ITU-T.

BIST (**b**uilt-**i**n **s**elf **t**est) a feature included in newer integrated circuits and other electronic equipment. An electronic device that has BIST can test itself thoroughly whenever it is turned on. *See* INTEGRATED CIRCUIT.

BiSync *see* BINARY SYNCHRONOUS.

bit a shorthand term for "binary digit." There are only two possible binary digits: 0 and 1. (*See* BINARY NUMBER.) Bits are represented in computers by two-state devices, such as flip-flops. A computer memory is a collection of devices that can store bits.

A *byte* is the number of bits (usually 8) that stand for one character. Memory is usually measured in units of *kilobytes* or *megabytes. See* MEMORY.

One important measure of the capability of a microprocessor is the number of bits that each internal register can contain. For example, the classic Z80 microprocessor had 8-bit registers. The Intel 8088, used in the original IBM PC, had 16-bit registers but only an 8-bit bus, leading to some confusion as to whether it should really have been called a 16-bit processor. Newer microprocessors have 32 or 64 bits per register. In general, a processor with a greater number of bits per instruction can process data more quickly (although there are other factors to consider that also determine a computer's speed). *See also* MICROPROCESSOR.

The number of colors that can be displayed is sometimes given by listing the number of bits used to represent a color. For example, a 24-bit color system uses 8 bits for red, 8 for green, and 8 for blue, so it can display $2^8 = 256$ different levels of each of the three primary colors, or $2^{24} = 16,777,216$ different mixtures of colors. *See* COLOR.

The term *bit* is also used to indicate the quality of digitized sound, as in 8 bit or 16 bit. *See* SAMPLING RATE.

bit bucket *(slang)* a place where data is lost. For example, under UNIX, the filename `/dev/null` can be used as a bit bucket; anything written to it will be ignored, but the program will think it is successfully writing to a file.

bitmap a graphical image represented as an array of brightness values. For example, if 0 represents white and 1 represents black, then

```
00000000
01111110
01000010
01000010
01111110
00000000
```

is a bitmap of a black rectangle on a white background. Each point for which there is a value is called a *pixel. See also* DIGITAL IMAGE PROCESSING.

Bitmaps can be imported into other application programs such as word processors and page layout programs, but you will not be able to edit bitmaps in those environments. You must use a PAINT PROGRAM or PHOTOPAINT PROGRAM to change bitmaps. *Contrast* VECTOR GRAPHICS. *See also* PAINT PROGRAM; DRAW PROGRAM.

bit-mapped graphics a method of displaying pictures on a computer. The picture is treated as a large array of pixels (*see* PIXEL), each of which is stored in a specific memory location. The picture is drawn by specifying the color of each pixel. *Contrast* VECTOR GRAPHICS. *See also* BITMAP; DRAW PROGRAM; PAINT PROGRAM; MEMORY-MAPPED VIDEO.

bitness the property of using a specific number of bits. For example, a single-precision integer and a double-precision integer differ in bitness.

BITNET a wide-area network linking university computer centers all over the world. It originated in the northeastern U.S. in the early 1980s and has now been combined with the Internet. Its most common use was to transmit electronic mail among scholars who are working together.

black widow a destructive computer program downloaded to the unwitting victim through the WORLD WIDE WEB as a JAVA applet. Although the Java language includes safeguards to limit the activities of downloaded programs, a malicious applet can still occupy memory and consume CPU time, slowing down the computer even if it does nothing else. *See* COMPUTER SECURITY; TROJAN HORSE; APPLET.

FIGURE 35. BLEND (DRAW PROGRAM)

blend

1. a drawing program command that computes the intermediate shapes between two selected objects. You would use the blend command to make the smooth highlights on a rendering of a three-dimensional object.

In many ways, the blend command is like the *morphing* special effects we see on television commercials. You could make the letter C turn into a cat, for example. However, blend has practical applications as well as the playful ones. You can use it to create equally spaced objects, such as lines for a business form. Align two *identical* objects, then set the intermediate blend steps to the desired number.

2. a photopaint program filter that smooths colors and removes texture over a selected area.

blind copies *see* BCC.

bloatware *(slang)* bloated software; software that requires unreasonable amounts of disk space, memory, or CPU speed. Some critics argue that much modern software is designed to sell computers larger and faster than are actually needed to do the computation efficiently.

block a group of bytes recorded on magnetic tape or similar media. Blocks are separated by blank areas called *interblock gaps.*

block move the operation of moving a section of a file from one place to another within the file. *See* EDITOR.

block protect to mark a block of text so that it will not be split across pages when printed out. This is useful to prevent a table or formula from being broken up.

Blue Screen of Death *(slang)* in Windows 95 and its successors, a serious error message displayed in white type on a blue screen, without any use of windows or graphics *(see* Fig. 36). It usually means that the entire operating system has become inoperative. The memory addresses and filenames it displays are sometimes explained on www.microsoft.com, but they are usually meaningful to only the authors of Windows.

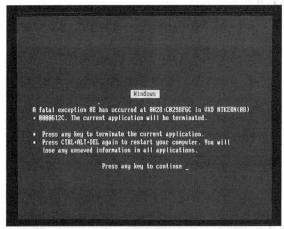

FIGURE 36. BLUE SCREEN OF DEATH

FIGURE 37. BLUR FILTER

blur a paint program filter that throws the image slightly out of focus. Blur can be repeated until the desired effect is achieved. *See also* MOTION BLUR; DIFFUSE.

BMP the filename extension for files in Microsoft Windows and OS/2 that contain bitmap representations of images. *See* BITMAP.

BNC connector a push-and-twist connector (*see* Fig. 38) used to join coaxial cables in thinwire Ethernet networks and in some types of video equipment. *See* ETHERNET; 10BASE-2; COAXIAL CABLE. *Contrast* RCA PLUG.

board

1. a printed circuit board for a computer (sometimes also called a *card*). Most computers contain *expansion slots* where you can add additional boards to enhance the capabilities of the machine.

FIGURE 38. BNC CONNECTORS

2. a bulletin board system (BBS) or similar discussion forum. *See* BBS.

boat anchor *(slang)* obsolete, useless machine.

body tag used in HTML to indicate the main part of the material for a web page, as opposed to the HEAD. For an example *see* HTML.

BOF (**B**irds **O**f a **F**eather) an informal meeting of a group of computer professionals with an interest in common, held as part of a larger convention.

bogus *(slang)* fake, incorrect, or useless. (In computer slang, this word covers a much wider range of meanings than in ordinary English; it can be applied to almost anything that is defective in any way.)

bold a type style that appears heavier and darker than normal weight type. The entry terms in this dictionary are set in **bold type**. *See* WEIGHT.

bomb to fail spectacularly (either computer programs or human performers); to CRASH. When a program bombs on a Macintosh, an alert box containing a picture of a bomb appears — the computer must be restarted and all changes made since the last "Save" will be lost. *Contrast* HANG; FREEZE.

bookmark
1. a remembered position in a file that is being edited. Some EDITORS let the user set bookmarks in order to return quickly to specific points in the file.
2. a remembered address on the WORLD WIDE WEB. Web BROWSERS normally let the user record the addresses of web pages in order to go directly to them in the future without having to type the address.
3. a placeholder that allows one to return to a specific point in a multimedia presentation.

Boolean algebra the study of operations carried out on variables that can have only two values: 1 (true) and 0 (false). Boolean algebra was developed by George Boole in the 1850s; it was useful originally in applications of the theory of logic and has become tremendously important in that area since the development of the computer.

Boolean query a query formed by joining simpler queries with *and, or,* and *not.* For example: "Find all books with author 'Downing' *and* subject 'Computers' *and not* published before 1987." *See also* SEARCH ENGINE; FULL-TEXT SEARCH.

Boolean variable a variable in ALGOL or Pascal (equivalent to a logical variable in FORTRAN) that can have one of two possible values: true or false. *See* BOOLEAN ALGEBRA.

In languages that have them, Boolean variables can be used in place of expressions such as "X is less than Y" and "Y equals Z." For example, in Pascal, the following two programs are equivalent:

```
PROGRAM one(INPUT,OUTPUT);
VAR x, y: INTEGER;
BEGIN
 read(X,Y);
 IF x=y THEN
    writeln('values are equal')
END.

PROGRAM two(INPUT,OUTPUT);
VAR x, y: INTEGER;   b: BOOLEAN;
BEGIN
  read(x,y);
  b := (X=Y);
  IF b THEN writeln('values are equal')
END.
```

Boolean variables are useful when the results of a comparison must be saved for some time after the comparison is done. Also, they can be operated on repeatedly to change their values. For example, the following Pascal program reads numbers from the input file, prints them, and reports whether a number over 100 was encountered; the Boolean variable is used somewhat as an integer would be used to keep a running total:

```
PROGRAM booleandemo (INPUT, OUTPUT);
VAR x: INTEGER; b: BOOLEAN;
BEGIN
  b := false;
  REPEAT
    read(X);
    writeln(x);
    b := b OR (X>100);
  UNTIL eof;
  IF b THEN
    writeln('There was a number over 100.')
END.
```

FIGURE 39. GEORGE BOOLE (1815–1864)

Boole, George (1815–1864) the mathematician who discovered that logical reasoning can be represented in terms of mathematical formulas (BOOLEAN ALGEBRA). Boole's work is the basis of modern digital computing.

boot to start up a computer. The term *boot* (earlier *bootstrap*) derives from the idea that the computer has to "pull itself up by the bootstraps," that is, load into memory a small program that enables it to load larger programs.

The operation of booting a computer that has been completely shut down is known as a *dead start, cold start,* or *cold boot.* A *warm start* or *warm boot* is a restarting operation in which some of the needed instructions are already in memory.

boot disk a disk or diskette that can be used to BOOT (start up) a computer.

Borland International (now renamed **Inprise Corporation**) a manufacturer of microcomputer software, founded by Philippe Kahn and headquartered in Scotts Valley, California. Its first products were Turbo Pascal, an extremely popular Pascal compiler released in 1984 (*see* TURBO PASCAL), and Sidekick, a set of IBM PC utilities that are always resident in RAM and can be called up at any time, even in the middle of another task. Later products include compilers for C and C++, the spreadsheet program Quattro, the database program Paradox, and, most recently, the Pascal-based Delphi programming tool for Windows. In 1998, Borland changed its name to Inprise Corporation, but the Borland name is still used on software products. Web address: http://www.inprise.com.

bot (*slang*) *see* ROBOT (definition 2).

bottleneck the part of a computer system that slows down its performance, such as a slow disk drive, slow modem, or overloaded network. Finding and remedying bottlenecks is much more worthwhile than simply speeding up parts of the computer that are already fast.

The *Von Neumann bottleneck* is a limit on computer speed resulting from the fact that the program and the data reside in the same memory.

Thus, at any moment the CPU can be receiving a program instruction or a piece of data to work on, but not both. Newer computers overcome the Von Neumann bottleneck by using pipelines and caches. *See* VON NEUMANN ARCHITECTURE; PIPELINE; CACHE.

bounce

    1. to return a piece of E-MAIL to its sender because of problems delivering it.

    2. to transfer a piece of incoming e-mail to another recipient without indicating who forwarded it.

FIGURE 40. BOUNDING BOX

bounding box an invisible box surrounding a graphical object and determining its size.

box

    1. *(slang)* A computer, especially a small one. For example, a Linux box is a computer that runs Linux.

    2. *(jargon)* A set of presumed limits. *See* THINKING OUTSIDE THE BOX.

Bps (with capital B, **Bps**) **b**ytes **p**er **s**econd.

bps (with lower-case b, **bps**) **b**its **p**er **s**econd. *See also* BAUD.

BR abbreviation used in HTML to indicate a line break. For an example *see* HTML.

braces the characters { and }, sometimes called *curly braces.*

brackets the characters [and], also called *square brackets.*

branch an instruction that tells the computer to jump to another part of the program, such as a GO TO statement. *See also* CONDITIONAL BRANCH.

breakpoint a place in a program where normal execution is interrupted and can be resumed after manual intervention, typically as an aid in debugging. For example, in many versions of BASIC the STOP command introduces a breakpoint in the program.

breaks, scheduling the necessary practice of allowing sufficient rest time away from the computer. Working at a computer is like playing a video game; hours can fly by, resulting in eye strain, stiff muscles, and headaches. If needed, an inexpensive timer may be used to prompt you to get up and stretch. The Macintosh operating system has a built-in timer that can be used to let you know that it's time to get a cup of coffee. (But don't drink superhuman anounts of coffee, either!)

Just remember that working harder is not the answer; you need breaks to rest your eyes, get some refreshment (mental and physical), uncramp your body, and tend to your personal needs. Ultimately, you will get more work done if you are not overworking yourself.

bridge a device that links two or more segments of a network. Unlike a hub, a bridge does not pass along all data packets that it receives. Instead, a bridge examines each packet and passes it along the path to its destination. In this way, local traffic can be prevented from flooding a larger network. *Compare* HUB; ROUTER; SWITCH (definition 2).

Briefcase the file synchronization facility in Windows 95 and its successors. *See* SYNCHRONIZATION (definition 2).

FIGURE 41. BRIGHTNESS — LIGHT, NORMAL, AND DARK

brightness
1. a photopaint filter that has the same effect as turning the brightness knob on a TV or monitor; it lightens or darkens the entire area that it's applied to. Brightness may be combined with the contrast filter since the two attributes affect each other.
2. a software control normally available with scanners, used to adjust the overall brightness of the image.

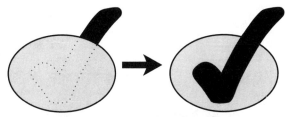

FIGURE 42. BRING TO FRONT

bring to front a graphical editing command that puts an object or window in front so that it hides other objects or windows that it overlaps. One way to hide part of an object in a draw program is to create a white object with invisible borders, then put it in front of what you want to hide. *See also* OVERLAID WINDOWS; SEND TO BACK. *Compare* BACK ONE.

brittle working correctly but easily disrupted by slight changes in conditions; the opposite of ROBUST.

broken hyperlink a link in a web page that points to a document that is no longer at that address. *See also* DEAD LINK.

broken pipe a communication failure between two programs that are running concurrently. Typically, a broken pipe occurs when a network connection is lost or one of the programs terminates while the other is still trying to communicate with it. *See* PIPE (definition 1).

brownout an extended period of insufficient power-line voltage. It can damage computer equipment. *See* POWER LINE PROTECTION.

browse
    1. to explore the contents of the World Wide Web or, more generally, the Internet. *See* BROWSER.
    2. to explore the contents of a disk drive or a computer network. *See* NETWORK NEIGHBORHOOD.

browse master in Windows 95 and its successors, the computer, on the local area network, that tells the other computers what shared resources are available. The browse master is chosen automatically from the computers that are on the network at a particular time. *See also* NETWORK NEIGHBORHOOD.

browser a computer program that enables the user to read HYPERTEXT in files or on the WORLD WIDE WEB. Popular World Wide Web browsers include Netscape and Microsoft Internet Explorer. Systems that lack graphics can use Lynx. *See* WORLD WIDE WEB; HTML; VRML.

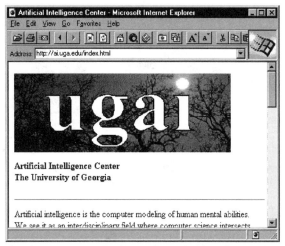

FIGURE 43. A BROWSER DISPLAYING A WEB PAGE

BSD a version of UNIX that was developed at the University of California at Berkeley (UCB). *See* UNIX; SYSTEM V. BSD UNIX introduced the vi full-screen editor and a number of other enhancements. SunOS (Solaris) and System V are combinations of BSD UNIX with the original AT&T UNIX.

B-spline a smooth curve that approximately connects two points. B-splines can be joined together to make a smooth curve passing close to any number of points. For an illustration *see* SPLINE.

Each segment of a B-spline curve is influenced by four points — the two that it lies between, plus one more in each direction. This makes computation of a B-spline much quicker than computation of a cubic spline, because every part of a cubic spline is influenced by all the points to be joined.

To plot a B-spline defined by four points (x_1, y_1), (x_2, y_2), (x_3, y_3), and (x_4, y_4), let t range from 0 to 1 and compute values of x and y for each t as follows:

$$
\begin{aligned}
a &= -t^3/6 + t^2/2 - t/2 + 1/6 \\
b &= t^3/2 - t^2 + 2/3 \\
c &= -t^3/2 + t^2/2 + t/2 + 1/6 \\
d &= t^3/6 \\
x &= ax_1 + bx_2 + cx_3 + dx_4 \\
y &= ay_1 + by_2 + cy_3 + dy_4
\end{aligned}
$$

That gives you a curve that lies approximately between (x_2, y_2) and (x_3, y_3). You can then advance by one point (letting the old x_2 become the new x_3, and so on) to plot the next segment. *See also* BÉZIER SPLINE; CUBIC SPLINE.

BTW e-mail abbreviation for "by the way."

bubble memory *see* MAGNETIC BUBBLE MEMORY.

bubble sort an algorithm for arranging items in order, as follows: First, examine the first two items in the list. If they are in order, leave them alone; if not, interchange them. Do the same with the second and third items, then with the third and fourth items, until you have reached the last two. At this point you are guaranteed that the item that should come last in the list has indeed "bubbled" up to that position.

```
10 REM BUBBLE SORT PROGRAM
15 REM Get the array elements
20 INPUT "N;";N
30 FOR I=1 TO N : INPUT A(I) : NEXT I
35 REM Sort them
40 FOR I=1 TO N
50  FOR J=1 TO N-I
60   IF A(J)>A(J+1) THEN SWAP A(J),A(J+1)
70  NEXT J
80 NEXT I
85 REM Print them out
90 FOR I=1 TO N : PRINT A(I) : NEXT I
99 END
```

FIGURE 44. BUBBLE SORT IN BASIC

Now repeat the whole process for the first $n - 1$ items in the list, then for $n - 2$, and so on.

Bubble sort is not a particularly fast sorting algorithm on conventional computers, but it works well on parallel computers that can work on different parts of the list simultaneously.

Fig. 44 shows a BASIC program that performs a bubble sort.

buffer a holding area for data. Several different things are called buffers:

1. areas in memory that hold data being sent to a printer or received from an RS-232 port. The idea here is that the printer is much slower than the computer, and it is helpful if the computer can prepare the data all at once, then dole it out slowly from the buffer as needed. Similarly, an RS-232 port needs a buffer because data may come in when the computer is not ready to receive it.

2. an area in memory that holds a file that is being edited. Some editors allow you to edit more than one file at once, and each file occupies its own buffer.

3. an area in memory that holds data being sent to, or received from, a disk. Some operating systems allow you to adjust the size or number of disk buffers to fit the speed of your disk drive.

4. an area in memory that holds signals from keys that have been pressed but have not yet been accepted by the computer. By default, the IBM PC keyboard buffer holds 16 keystrokes.

5. an electronic device whose output is the same as its input, e.g., an amplifier for driving long cables.

bug an error in a computer program. The term is somewhat misleading because it suggests that errors have a life of their own, which they do not. Bugs fall into at least three classes: *syntax errors,* where the rules of the programming langauge were not followed; *semantic errors,* where the programmer misunderstood the meaning of something in the programming language; and *logic errors,* where the programmer specified some detail of the computation incorrectly. Nowadays there is beginning to be a serious problem with a fourth class, which can be called *infrastructure errors,* where the programmer fell victim to something wrong with the operating system or a programming tool.

build

1. *(verb)* to put together a piece of software from its components by compiling, linking, and doing whatever else is necessary to make a working, deliverable version. *See* COMPILER; LINKER.

2. *(noun)* the result of building a piece of software on a particular occasion. Some software developers keep track of build numbers, which change much more rapidly than version numbers.

Case fraction   Built fraction   Piece fraction

FIGURE 45. CASE VS. BUILT VS. PIECE FRACTION

built fraction a fraction that is composed by setting the numerator and denominator as regular numerals separated by a forward slash (1/2, 1/4). *Contrast* PIECE FRACTION; CASE FRACTION.

bullet a character such as • used to mark items in a list.

bundled software software that is sold in combination with hardware. For example, software for processing speech and music is often bundled with sound cards.

burn *(slang)* to record information on a CD-R disc or an EPROM.

bus the main communication avenue in a computer. For a diagram, *see* COMPUTER ARCHITECTURE.

The bus consists of a set of parallel wires or lines to which the CPU, the memory, and all input-output devices are connected. The bus contains one line for each bit needed to give the address of a device or a location in memory, plus one line for each bit of data to be transmitted in a single step, and additional lines that indicate what operation is being performed.

Most personal computers today use a 32-bit bus, but on PC-compatibles, the bus can also work in 8-bit and 16-bit mode.

Here is how an 8-bit bus works: If the CPU wants to place the value 00011001 into memory location 10100000, it places 00011001 on the data lines, places 10100000 on the address lines, and places 1 (rather than the usual 0) on the "write memory" line. The memory unit is responsible for recognizing the "write memory" request, decoding the address, and storing the data in the right location.

The bus can transmit data in either direction between any two components of the system. If the computer did not have a bus, it would need separate wires for all possible connections between components. *See also* ISA; EISA; MICRO CHANNEL; VESA LOCAL BUS; PCI; PCMCIA; SERIAL BUS.

bus mouse a mouse that is connected to its own adapter card, which in turn connects to the bus of the computer. *See* MOUSE. *Contrast* SERIAL MOUSE. On newer PCs, the mouse connects directly to a port on the motherboard.

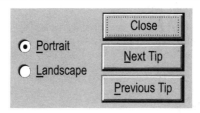

FIGURE 46. OPTION BUTTONS (LEFT)
AND COMMAND BUTTONS

button a small circle or rectangular bar within a windowed DIALOG BOX
that represents a choice to be made. One of the buttons in a group is
normally highlighted, either by having a black circle inside of it or
having a heavy black border. This represents the DEFAULT choice. You
can choose any one of the buttons by CLICKING on it with the mouse.

There are two kinds of buttons: OPTION BUTTONS (sometimes called
radio buttons) and COMMAND BUTTONS. Option buttons represent mutually exclusive settings; that is, you can choose only one. They are usually small and round, but are sometimes diamond-shaped. If you change
your mind and click on another option button, your original choice will
be grayed (dimmed). *See* HIGHLIGHT; DIMMED; DIALOG BOX.

Command buttons cause something to happen immediately when
you click on them. They are usually rectangular and larger than option
buttons. The most familiar examples are the OK and Cancel buttons
that are in almost every dialog box. If the command button brings up
another dialog box, you will see an ELLIPSIS (…) after its label.

FIGURE 47. BUTTON BAR

button bar a row of small icons usually arranged across the top of
the workspace on the screen. Each icon represents a commonly used
command; many programs allow you to customize your button bar to
suit your taste.

Byron, Augusta Ada *see* ADA.

byte the amount of memory space needed to store one character, which is
normally 8 bits. A computer with 8-bit bytes can distinguish $2^8 = 256$
different characters. See ASCII for the code that most computers use to
represent characters.

The size of a computer's memory is measured in kilobytes ($= 2^{10} =$
1024 bytes) or megabytes ($= 2^{20} = 1,048,576$ bytes).

bytecode the concise instructions produced by compiling a Java program. This bytecode is the same for all platforms; it is executed by a
Java virtual machine (*see* JAVA; JVM).

C

C a programming language developed at Bell Laboratories in the 1970s, based on the two earlier languages B (1970) and BCPL (1967). A C compiler is provided as a part of the UNIX operating system (*see* UNIX), and C was used to write most of UNIX itself. In addition, C is becoming popular as an alternative to assembly language for writing highly efficient microcomputer programs. There is a widespread (and often mistaken) belief that programs written in C are more efficient than programs written in any other language.

C is a general-purpose language like Pascal and ALGOL, but, unlike other general-purpose languages, it gives the programmer complete access to the machine's internal (bit-by-bit) representation of all types of data. This makes it convenient to perform tasks that would ordinarily require assembly language, and to perform computations in the most efficient way of which the machine is capable.

```
/* CHKSUM.C */
/* Sample program in C  -- M. Covington 1991 */
/* Based on a program by McLowery Elrod */

/* Reads a character string from the keyboard */
/* and computes a checksum for it. */

#include <stdio.h>

#define N 256

main()
{
  int i, n;
  char str[N];

  puts("Type a character string:");
  gets(str);
  printf("The checksum is %d\n",chksum(str));
}

chksum(s,n)
char* s;
int n;
{
  unsigned c;
  c = 0;
  while (n-- > 0)  c = c + *s++;
  c = c % 256;
  return(c);
}
```

FIGURE 48. C PROGRAM

In C, things that are easy for the CPU are easy for the programmer, and vice versa. For example, character string handling is somewhat clumsy because the CPU can only do it through explicit procedure calls. But integer arithmetic is very simple to program because it is simple for the CPU to execute. Most programmers who use C find themselves writing efficient programs simply because the language pushes them to do so.

Fig. 48 shows a program written in C. This language encourages structured programming; the three loop constructs are `while`, `do`, and `for`. The comment delimiters are `/* */`. A semicolon comes at the end of every statement (unlike Pascal, where semicolons only come between statements).

C allows operations to be mixed with expressions in a unique way. The expression `i++` means "retrieve the value of `i` and then add 1 to it." So if `i` equals 2, the statement `j = (i++)*3` will make `j` equal 6 (i.e., 2×3) and will make `i` equal 3 (by adding 1 to it after its value is retrieved; but notice that its *old* value was used in the multiplication).

Another noteworthy feature of C is the `#define` statement. The sample program contains the line

```
#define N 256
```

which tells the compiler that wherever N occurs as a symbol in the program, it should be understood as the number 256. *See also* ANSI C; PRINTF; C++.

C++ an object-oriented programming language developed by Bjarne Stroustrup at Bell Laboratories in the mid-1980s as a successor to C. In C and C++, the expression C++ means "add 1 to C."

Fig. 49 shows a program in C++. Comments are introduced by `//` and object types are declared as `class`. The part of an object that is accessible to the outside world is declared as `public`. For an explanation of what this program does, see OBJECT-ORIENTED PROGRAMMING, where the equivalent Turbo Pascal code is explained.

In C++, input-output devices are known as *streams*. The statement

```
cout << "The answer is " << i;
```

sends "The answer is" and the value of `i` to the standard output stream. This provides a convenient way to print any kind of data for which a print method is defined.

C++ lets the programmer *overload* operators (give additional meanings to them). For example, + normally stands for integer and floating-point addition. In C++, you can define it to do other things to other kinds of data, such as summing matrices or concatenating strings.

C++ is the basis of the Java language used for portable downloadable applications. *See* JAVA.

CA (**c**ertificate **a**uthority) an agency that issues digital certificates. *See* DIGITAL SIGNATURE.

```
// SAMPLE.CPP
// Sample C++ program -- M. Covington 1991
// Uses Turbo C++ graphics procedures

#include <graphics.h>

class pnttype {
  public:
    int x, y;
    void draw() { putpixel(x,y,WHITE); }
};

class cirtype: public pnttype {
  public:
    int radius;
    void draw() { circle(x,y,radius); }
};

main()
{
    int driver, mode;
    driver = VGA;
    mode = VGAHI;
    initgraph(&driver,&mode,"d:\tp\bgi");

    pnttype a,b;
    cirtype c;

    a.x = 100;
    a.y = 150;
    a.draw();

    c.x = 200;
    c.y = 250;
    c.radius = 40;
    c.draw();

    closegraph;
}
```

FIGURE 49. C++ PROGRAM

cable modem a MODEM that provides computer communication over television cables (either coaxial or fiber-optic) rather than telephone lines.

cache

1. a place where data can be stored to avoid having to read the data from a slower device such as a disk. For instance, a disk cache stores copies of frequently used disk sectors in RAM so that they can be read without accessing the disk.

The 486 and Pentium microprocessors have an internal instruction cache for program instructions that are being read in from RAM; an external cache is also used, consisting of RAM chips that are faster than those used in the computer's main memory. *See also* LI CACHE; L2 CACHE.

2. a set of files kept by a WEB BROWSER to avoid having to download the same material repeatedly. Most web browsers keep copies of all the web pages that you view, up to a certain limit, so that the same pages can be redisplayed quickly when you go back to them. If a web page has been changed recently, you may have to RELOAD it to see its current contents.

CAD (**C**omputer-**A**ided **D**esign) the use of a computer for design work in fields such as engineering or architecture, with the computer's graphics capabilities substituting for work that traditionally would have been done with pencil and paper. In order to do CAD, it is necessary to have a high-resolution monitor and a software package designed for the purpose.

In order to draw a building, for example, it is necessary to enter the plans by using a graphical input device, such as a mouse or graphics tablet. There are several advantages to having the plans in the computer:

1. The computer can automatically calculate dimensions. In fact, the ability to calculate dimensions is the biggest difference between CAD programs and ordinary draw programs.

2. Changes can be made easily (for example, adding a new wall).

3. Repetitive structures can be added easily.

4. The image can be enlarged to obtain a close-up view of a particular part, or it can be shrunk to make it possible to obtain an overall view. If the CAD program has three-dimensional capability, the image can be rotated to view it from many different perspectives. (*See* THREE-DIMENSIONAL GRAPHICS.) For example, the Boeing 777 airplane, first rolled out in 1994, was designed entirely on computers. Previous airplanes had been designed the traditional way with paper drawings, and then a full-scale mock-up needed to be constructed to make sure that the parts fit together in reality as they did on paper. CAD made this extra work unnecessary.

Cairo Microsoft's internal code name for a future release of Windows NT. Some people identify Cairo with Windows NT 4.0, which is already on the market, or with Windows NT 5.0. Cairo subsumes into Windows NT many of the features of Windows 95. *See* WINDOWS 95; WINDOWS 98; WINDOWS NT; CHICAGO; MEMPHIS.

calendar *see* JULIAN CALENDAR; JULIAN DATE; GREGORIAN CALENDAR; LEAP YEAR.

calibration adjustment of image values to ensure faithful rendering of colors and gray tones when output to a printer or imagesetter. The calibration loop should include your scanner, your monitor, your software, and the printer. The goal is to make sure that colors are treated identically by the scanner, the software, the screen, and the printer. *See* COLOR.

CALL a statement in FORTRAN, PL/I, some versions of BASIC, and most assembly languages, which transfers control of execution to a subprogram. When the subprogram ends, the main program resumes with the statement immediately after the CALL. Languages such as C, Pascal, and Java perform calls by simply giving the name of the routine to be called. In line-numbered BASIC, subroutines are called with the GOSUB command.

callout the line and caption marking the specific parts of a labeled illustration. For examples, see the illustration at WINDOW.

Call Waiting a service offered by many American telephone companies that makes your telephone beep if someone tries to call you while you are already using the telephone. You can then put the previous call on hold and switch to the incoming call. These beeps disrupt transmission of computer data by telephone. To make a call that will not be interrupted by beeps, dial * 7 0, wait for a dial tone, and then dial the call in the usual way. If you are using a Hayes-compatible autodial modem, give the number 555-1212 as *70W555-1212 or *70,,555-1212.

-cam abbreviation for *camera*, especially a digital or video camera whose images are made available by computer network. For instance, a camera connected to the World Wide Web is a *webcam*; a camera mounted on a tower is a *towercam*; and a camera strapped to the back of a horse might be called a *horsecam*.

CAM (**C**omputer-**A**ided **M**anufacturing) the use of computers in a manufacturing process. For example, a computer could store a three-dimensional representation of an object and then control the manufacture of the object by automated machinery. Some of the principles of CAM are the same as with computer-aided design (*see* CAD), and sometimes a system is referred to as CAD/CAM.

camera, digital *see* DIGITAL CAMERA.

camera-ready copy artwork or printed pages that are ready to be photographed and offset printed. The camera will see only black and white, not shades of gray, so the camera-ready copy must be free of smudges, dust, and stray marks. Usually, pale blue marks do not photograph, and most other colors photograph as black.

cancel
   1.   to stop the execution of a command. Most dialog boxes have a Cancel button. This clears the dialog box from the screen without taking any action.
   2.   to send a command deleting a message from a newsgroup or other public forum. (*See* NEWSGROUP.) It is important to know how to do this in case you post something that turns out to be redundant or misinformed. On Usenet, the cancellation does not take effect instantly because the cancel command has to travel to all the sites that received the original message. Normally, users can cancel only their own messages, but *see* CANCELBOT.

cancelbot (from *cancel* and *robot*; *see* BOT) a computer program that automatically cancels certain messages from a newsgroup or other public forum. Cancelbots often eliminate messages that are excessively large or are copied to excessive numbers of newsgroups (*see* SPAMMING).

Canon engine *see* ENGINE.

caps capital letters. THIS SENTENCE IS TYPED IN ALL CAPS. *Contrast with* MIXED CASE; LOWERCASE.

    Internet tip: Don't send e-mail or post to newsgroups with your message typed in all caps. Not only is it more difficult to read, but it seems as if you are shouting (all your words are emphasized).

Caps Lock a special keyboard key which acts like the Shift key for the letter keys. You do not have to hold it down; when Caps Lock is on, YOUR TYPING LOOKS LIKE THIS. A common mistake is to leave Caps Lock on when you wish to type normally. Then letters you wish to be capitalized are lowercase, but everything else is all caps lIKE tHIS. Some word processors have commands to correct capitalization errors of this sort.

capture
    1. to divert data from a serial or parallel port to a networked printer, a print spooler, or the like. For example, in Windows 95 and its successors, capturing the LPT1 parallel port address and diverting its data to a print spooler maintained by the operating system is a common practice. Thus, when DOS programs print directly to LPT1, their output is spooled by Windows rather than going directly to the port.
    2. to cause a picture or graphic to be saved as a bitmapped image. Snapshots of the screen are easy to get: for Macintosh users, hold down Command and Shift, then press 3. This places a bitmapped image of the screen in a .PICT file in your root directory. In Windows, pressing the Print Screen key puts a copy of the entire screen onto the Clipboard. Holding down Alt while pressing Print Screen saves a bitmap of the active window only.
    If you have the appropriate equipment, you can use your computer to capture images from any video source. This might be a video camera or VCR. *See* FRAME GRABBER.

carbon copy a copy of an outgoing electronic mail message kept by the sender or forwarded to someone other than the recipient. (*See* CC; BCC; FCC.) In pre-computer days, carbon copies were made in typewriters by placing a sheet of carbon-coated paper and an extra piece of plain paper behind the main document.

card
    1. *see* PUNCHED CARD.
    2. a printed-circuit board, especially one designed to be added to a microcomputer to provide additional functions (*see* Figure 50).

FIGURE 50. CARD (DEFINITION 2)

CardBus the 32-bit version of the PCMCIA (PC CARD) bus.

carpal tunnel syndrome a repetitive-use injury of the carpal tunnel (a nerve pathway in the wrist) that afflicts some typists. The main symptoms are numbness and tingling in the hand. Stretching exercises and medication help mild cases, but sometimes surgery is necessary to relieve the pain. To prevent carpal tunnel syndrome, take a break and stretch your hands frequently. Some typists find a padded wrist support to be helpful.

carriage return *See* CR.

carrier a signal that has another signal modulated onto it. For example, a modem transmits data through a telephone line by transmitting a continuous tone as a carrier. Variations in frequency and phase of the carrier encode the binary data.

cartridge a self-contained, removable part of a computer, usually small and contained in a plastic case. For example, laser printers often take *toner cartridges* (containing toner, i.e., ink) and *font cartridges* (containing memory chips on which styles of type are recorded). Game machines often accept software in plug-in cartridges. *See* FONT CARTRIDGE.

cascade to arrange multiple windows so that they look like a stack of cards, with all but the top and left edges of each window hidden by the one in front of it (see Fig. 51). When the windows on a screen are cascaded, you can see the title bar of every window. *Contrast* TILED WINDOWS; OVERLAID WINDOWS.

cascading menu a menu that leads to more menus. For an example, see START MENU.

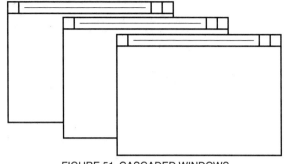

FIGURE 51. CASCADED WINDOWS

cascading style sheet a set of HTML rules governing the appearance of a set of pages at a web site on the World Wide Web. Cascading style sheets use precedence rules to decide which of two commands should take effect in case of a conflict. *See* STYLE SHEET.

CASE (**c**omputer-**a**ided **s**oftware **e**ngineering) the use of computers to help with the process of designing software.

case

    1. the property of being capitalized (uppercase, LIKE THIS) or lowercase (like this); so called because of the wooden cases in which printers' type was stored in the 1800s.

    2. a statement in Pascal that directs a program to choose one action from a list of alternatives, depending on the value of a given variable. Here is an example of a `case` statement:

```
CASE place OF
  1 : writeln('First place !!!');
  2 : writeln('Second place');
  3 : writeln('Third place')
END;
```

If the variable `place` has the value 1, then the first `writeln` statement will be executed, and so on. The `switch` statement in C and Java and the `SELECT CASE` statement in newer versions of BASIC perform similar functions.

case fraction a small fraction that is a single character in a font. *Contrast* BUILT FRACTION. *See also* EXPERT SET.

case-sensitive distinguishing between upper- and lowercase letters, such as A and a. For example, UNIX filenames are case-sensitive, so

$$\frac{3}{4} \qquad 3/4 \qquad \frac{3}{4}$$

Case	Built	Piece
fraction	fraction	fraction

FIGURE 52. CASE VS. BUILT VS. PIECE FRACTION

that `MYDATA` and `mydata` denote two different files. DOS and Windows filenames are not case-sensitive, so that `MYDATA` and `mydata` are equivalent.

Names typed in C, C++, and Java are case-sensitive; names typed in Pascal are not.

Windows 95 and Windows 98 preserve the case in which filenames were originally typed, but names that differ only in case are treated as matching.

cassette BASIC *see* ROM BASIC.

Castanet software produced by Marimba, Inc. for using push technology on the World Wide Web. A user downloads tuner software (see web address `http://www.marimba.com`), and then selects channels that will be downloaded automatically at regular intervals. Web content providers need to purchase the transmitter software.

catalog an older name for a list of the contents of a disk. *See* DIRECTORY.

catch *see* TRY.

Category 3 cable the standard 8-conductor unshielded twisted-pair cable used for 10base-T and other twisted-pair networks up to 10 Mbps; it can also be used for telephone wiring. It has been superseded by Category 5 cable. *See also* 10BASE-T; RJ-45 (wiring table).

Category 5 cable the standard 8-conductor unshielded twisted-pair cable used for 10base-T, 100base-T, and other twisted-pair networks up to 100 Mbps; it can also be used for telephone wiring. *See also* 10BASE-T; RJ-45 (wiring table); PLENUM-RATED; RISER-RATED.

CAV (constant angular velocity), in disk drives, a constant speed of rotation, regardless of whether the track being read is a long one (near the edge of the disk) or a short one (near the center). Hard disks, diskettes, and some of the newest CD-ROM drives use CAV. *Contrast* CLV.

cc the UNIX command that invokes the C compiler, now largely replaced by `gcc` (GNU C Compiler). *See* C; UNIX.

Cc business abbreviation for "copies"; the double letter C indicates the plural. In e-mail headers, `Cc:` precedes additional addresses to which copies of the message should be sent. *See also* BCC.

CCD (charge-coupled device) a semiconductor device for recording images electronically. CCDs are used in video cameras, DIGITAL CAMERAS, and SCANNERS.

CCITT (Comité Consultatif Internationale Télegraphique et Téléphonique) former name of international organization that sets standards for data communication, now known as ITU-T. *See* ITU-T; V SERIES; X.25.

CD (Compact Disc) a type of plastic optically readable disk introduced by Philips and Sony in the 1980s to store digitized music recordings. Subsequently, CDs have become popular as a way of storing computer files (*see* CD-ROM) and interactive video (CD-I). The data on CDs is encoded in microscopic grooves and is read by scanning the rotating disk with an infrared laser beam.

Unlike a diskette, a CD has its data on one long spiral track, like the groove in a phonograph record; this simplifies the design of CD players. One CD can hold 75 minutes of audio (just enough for Beethoven's *Ninth Symphony,* which was the design goal) or 680 megabytes of computer data.

Note the spellings *disc* for CDs versus *disk* for magnetic disks. *See also* RED BOOK; CD-ROM; DVD.

CD-E (Compact Disc — Erasable) an older name for CD-RW.

CDFS the CD-ROM file system under Windows 95, Windows 98, and OS/2. It corresponds to MSCDEX under Windows 3 and DOS.

CD-I (Compact Disc—Interactive) an optical disk like an audio compact disc, but storing multimedia information (images, sound, etc., but not software for a personal computer). CD-I readers are marketed as accessories for TV sets; they have not become as popular as predicted. *See also* GREEN BOOK.

CD-R (Compact Disc—Recordable) a type of CD (compact disc) that can be recorded by the user. CD-Rs have the same capacity and are readable in the same drives as ordinary CDs (except for DVD drives — *See* DVD). Instead of being manufactured by pressing, CD-Rs are recorded by bleaching ("burning") small areas of dyed plastic with a laser to create an appearance similar to the indentations in an ordinary CD.

CD-Rs are somewhat less durable than pressed CDs, though still more durable than most other computer media.

CD-ROM (Compact Disc—Read-Only Memory) an optical disk like an audio compact disc, but containing computer data. Audio and computer CDs are physically the same; in fact, a single CD can contain both computer files and music. CD-ROMs can only be read, not recorded on, by the user's computer. CD-R and CD-RW are CD-ROM-compatible media that can be recorded on by the user.

The storage capacity of a CD-ROM is about 680 megabytes (about 470 times that of a 3.5-inch diskette), and unlike diskettes, CD-ROMs are not tied to the operating system of a specific computer (although the software that is on them may be). Any computer can read the data on any CD-ROM. CD-ROM drives are rated for their speed compared with the playback speed of an audio CD. For example, a 48× drive can read a CD 48 times faster than an audio CD would be played.

CD-ROMs are a popular way to deliver digitized sound, images, and multimedia presentations that would be too bulky to put on ordinary diskettes. An entire encyclopedia or a collection of hundreds of pictures can fit on one disc. *See also* CD; CD-I; CD-R; DVD; RED BOOK; GREEN BOOK; YELLOW BOOK; ORANGE BOOK; ISO 9660; HIGH SIERRA FORMAT; MPC; MULTIMEDIA; MULTISESSION CD; MULTISPIN DRIVE; DOUBLE SPEED; PHOTO CD.

CD-ROM XA (**CD-ROM** extended **a**rchitecture) a set of extensions to the ISO 9660 format for compact disc data, allowing sound and video to be interleaved with computer data. The earlier format required sound, video, and computer files to be on separate tracks; XA removes this restriction.

CD-RW (Compact **D**isc — **R**e**W**ritable) a type of CD (compact disc) that can be recorded, erased, and reused by the user.

The surface of a CD-RW contains an alloy that can change back and forth between a bright crystalline state and a dark amorphous state; it can be switched from one state to the other by heating it to specific temperatures with a laser.

Because of the different material used in them, CD-RW discs cannot generally be read by CD-ROM or CD-R drives that are not specifically marked as CD-RW compatible.

Celeron a lower-cost version of the Intel Pentium II microprocessor, with less on-chip cache memory. Before its introduction, the Celeron was code-named *Covington,* to the delight of two of the authors of this book.

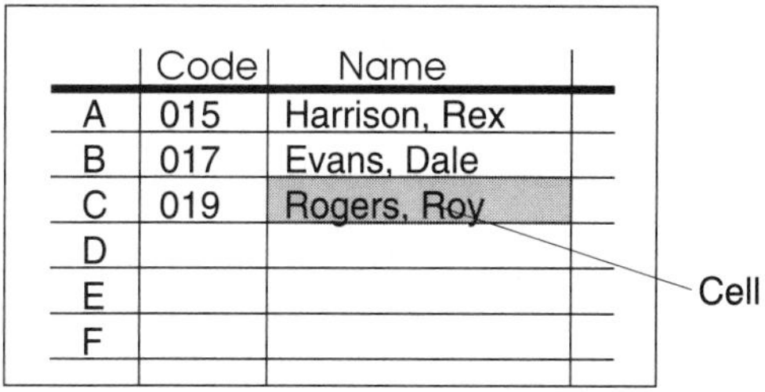

FIGURE 53. CELL IN A SPREADSHEET

cell

    1. a unit of information that forms a building block for a chart, database, or spreadsheet.

    2. one of the sections into which a city or region is divided for cellular telephone service. Each cell is served by a different antenna tower.

cellular modem a MODEM that uses a cellular telephone for wireless connection to a computer network.

cellular telephone a wireless telephone that communicates through any of a number of antenna towers, each serving a particular "cell" of the city. The user is automatically transferred from cell to cell as he or she moves around. This contrasts with earlier mobile telephones that had to be within range of a particular tower in order to work.

center to cause type or other objects to appear in the middle of the line with equal amounts of space to either side.

> This text
> is set centered.
> Centered text is
> considered
> formal.

Contrast FLUSH LEFT; FLUSH RIGHT; JUSTIFIED.

centi- metric prefix meaning $\div 100$. *Centi-* is derived from the Latin word for "hundredth." *See* METRIC PREFIXES.

central processing unit *see* CPU.

Centronics interface a standard protocol for parallel data transmission to and from microcomputer equipment, especially printers. It was originally used on Centronics printers. The PARALLEL PORT of a microcomputer is normally Centronics-compatible. *See also* IEEE 1284.

certainty factor *see* CONFIDENCE FACTOR.

CGA (**C**olor **G**raphics **A**dapter) a popular video card formerly used on IBM PCs. It supported a maximum resolution of 640×200 pixels. In the mid-1980s, the CGA was the most common video card, and many games were written for it. Software written for the CGA will usually run on the EGA, VGA, and MCGA.

CGI (**C**ommon **G**ateway **I**nterface) the standard way of interfacing computer programs with HTTP or WORLD WIDE WEB servers so that a web page can display material computed when needed, rather than just canned text and graphics. CGI programs normally output HTML text preceded by a MIME "Content-type" header. *See also* PERL.

CGM (**C**omputer **G**raphics **M**etafile) an ANSI standard file format for graphical data (both vector and bitmap). CGM files are used mainly for exchanging data between applications.

chain letter a message that is intended to be forwarded from each recipient to as many others as possible. On the Internet, chain letters are very unwelcome because they waste money; the cost of delivering e-mail is borne by the recipient's site. Many chain letters perpetrate hoaxes or pyramid schemes (*see* HOAX; PYRAMID SCHEME).

channel

1. a radio frequency or communication path (e.g., a TV channel).

2. a high-speed data communication device used to interface IBM mainframe computers with input-output devices.

3. in desktop publishing, a set of images that will compose the final image when combined. The most common use for channels is the representation of the CMYK color separations in a paint program. Each color has its own channel.

Sometimes channels can be used like layers in a DRAW PROGRAM. Selected areas can be saved to a new channel, manipulated separately from the rest of the image, and later recombined with the main channel.

4. a discussion forum in Internet Relay Chat or a similar service. *See* IRC; CHAT ROOM.

5. a web page that is constantly updated, so that viewing it is like watching a television channel. *See* CASTANET; PUSH (definition 2).

character any symbol that can be stored and processed by a computer. For example, A, 3, and & are characters. The ASCII coding system is one way of representing characters on a computer. *See* ASCII; ANSI (definition 3); EBCDIC.

character set the set of characters that can be printed or displayed on a computer. For examples *see* ASCII; ANSI; IBM PC; UNICODE; EBCDIC.

character string a series of characters, such as "JOHN SMITH" or "R2D2". *See* STRING.

charge-coupled device *see* CCD.

chat room an electronic forum in which users can communicate with each other in real time. Chat rooms are found on the Internet (*see* IRC) and on on-line services such as CompuServe and AOL.

check box a small box (in a window) that the user can turn on or off by clicking with the mouse. When on, it displays an X or check mark in a square; when off, the square is blank. Unlike option buttons, check boxes do not affect each other; any check box can be on or off independently of all the others.

FIGURE 54. CHECK BOXES

checksum a number that accompanies data transferred from one place to another and helps to ensure that the data was transferred correctly.

One way to ensure correct transmission would be to transmit all of the information twice; if there were an error, the two copies would almost certainly disagree. However, this is too time-consuming to be practical. A better approach is to divide the information into small packets, such as lines of text or disk sectors, and compute a checksum for each packet. A checksum is a number that would almost certainly be different if the information were altered.

A simple way to compute a checksum is to add up the ASCII codes for all the characters of data (*see* ASCII) and take the result modulo 256. (For a program that does this, *see* C.) Since this method gives only 256 possible checksums, it is quite possible for two different data packets to have the same checksum. However, it is very unlikely that a transmission error would change a packet of information into another packet with the same checksum. Hence errors can be detected by transmitting the checksum along with each packet, and then testing whether the checksum matches the data actually received.

Checksums are used in XMODEM and similar protocols for error-free transmission of data by telephone. *See* XMODEM.

Chicago the code name by which WINDOWS 95 was identified before its release. *Compare* CAIRO; MEMPHIS.

child an object created with the properties of another object (called the PARENT). Updating the properties of the parent object affects the children, but changing the properties of the child does not affect the parent. *See* VECTOR GRAPHICS; OBJECT-ORIENTED PROGRAMMING.

child process a process launched by and considered dependent on another process. *See* PROCESS; MULTITASKING; UNIX.

chip *see* INTEGRATED CIRCUIT.

chipset a set of integrated circuits intended to be used together. For example, many modems use a chipset made by Rockwell, and many motherboards use an Intel chipset along with a Pentium processor.

chmod UNIX command for changing file permissions. For example of its use, *see* PERMISSION.

chroma-keying the process of digitally combining video images by the use of a subtractive background. This is the method used to show a weather forecaster in front of a set of maps. The person is videotaped in front of a blue or green background. The colored background is digitally removed (hence *chroma-*, meaning color), and the desired map is placed in its stead. The weather forecaster watches a monitor off-camera so he or she can point to the correct spot.

Chroma-keying is also used for a variety of special effects in movies.

CICS (**C**ustomer **I**nformation **C**ontrol **S**ystem) an extension to the operating system of IBM mainframe computers. CICS makes it easy to write programs to enable users to enter, retrieve, and update data on their terminal screens. For example, CICS is often used in point-of-sale systems, hotel reservation systems, billing systems, and the like.

cinnamon bun *(slang)* the symbol @; *see* AT SIGN.

CIO **C**hief **I**nformation **O**fficer, an officer of a business responsible for its information management.

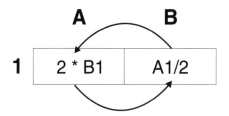

FIGURE 55. CIRCULARITY PROBLEM

circularity the problem that arises when a computer cannot finish a task until it has already finished it — an impossible situation. For example, in Lotus 1-2-3, a circularity problem arises if you enter the formula 2*B1 into cell A1 and then enter the formula A1/2 into cell B1. In order to evaluate each of the cells the computer needs the value of the other one. Thus, it cannot proceed, and it displays a warning message instead.

circumflex the symbol ^, either written by itself as an ASCII character, or written above a letter (e.g., ê).

CISC (**C**omplex **I**nstruction **S**et **C**omputer) a computer with many different machine language instructions. The IBM PC, 68000-based Macintosh, Pentium, IBM 370 mainframe, and VAX are CISC machines. *Contrast* RISC.

Cisco Systems, Inc. a company headquartered in San Jose, California that is the leading provider of high-speed networking hardware. The web address is www.cisco.com.

class an object type in object-oriented programming. *See* OBJECT-ORIENTED PROGRAMMING.

Class A *see* FCC.

Class B *see* FCC.

class library a set of classes available to programmers in an object-oriented language such as Java or C++. In addition to the base classes that come with the language itself, a programmer can use and extend other classes created from other sources.

clear
1. to set a flip-flop or memory location to zero.
2. to make the screen of a CRT go blank. In many versions of BASIC, the command CLS clears the screen.
3. in some BASIC interpreters and other interactive environments, the CLEAR command either sets all variables to zero, or frees any memory that has been allocated for specific purposes, such as arrays.

FIGURE 56. CLICK

click to press one mouse button very briefly (usually the leftmost button, if there is more than one). *Contrast* PRESS; DOUBLE-CLICK. *See also* WINDOW.

clickable image a picture on a WEB PAGE or in a HYPERTEXT document which the user can select, by clicking with the mouse, in order to call up further information. *See* IMAGE MAP.

client

    1. a computer that receives services from another computer. For example, when you browse the World Wide Web, your computer is a client of the computer that hosts the web page.

    2. an operating system component that enables a computer to access a particular kind of service. For example, computers that use Netware networks must have a Netware-compatible client installed.

client area the part of a window in which editing or drawing actually takes place. It does not include the borders, the title, the menu bar across the top, or the scroll bars, if any.

FIGURE 57. CLIP ART EXAMPLES

clip art artwork that can be freely reproduced. Many of the pictures in newspaper advertisements come from clip art. Many clip art collections are available on diskettes or CD-ROMs for use with various drawing, painting, and desktop publishing programs.

Clipboard on the Macintosh and in Microsoft Windows and OS/2, a holding area to which information can be copied in order to transfer it from one application program to another. For instance, the Clipboard can be used to transfer text from a word processor into a drawing program.

    Be aware that the contents of the Clipboard vanish when the computer is turned off. Also, only one item at a time can be on the Clipboard; the next CUT or COPY command will replace the old item with a new one. *See also* PASTE.

clipping (Macintosh OS) a fragment of text or graphic image that can be moved from one application to another simply by dragging the item with the mouse (*see* DRAG AND DROP). The clipping can even remain on the Desktop until needed. This provides another way (other than the Clipboard) for transferring information from one program to another.

clock

    1. the circuit in a computer that generates a series of evenly spaced pulses. All the switching activity in the computer occurs while the clock is sending out a pulse. Between pulses the electronic devices in the computer are allowed to stabilize. A computer with a faster clock rate is able to perform more operations per second.

    The clock speed of a computer is often given in megahertz (MHz) or gigahertz (GHz), where 1 MHz = 1,000,000 cycles per second and 1 GHz = 1000 MHz. The fastest computers have clock speeds of 500 to 1000 MHz (0.5 to 1 GHz). Often, the clock speed is doubled or tripled inside the CPU so that high-speed signals do not have to be carried outside it. The original IBM PC had a clock speed of 4.77 MHz. *See* MICROPROCESSOR.

    2. the circuit within a computer that keeps track of the date and time, often called a *real-time clock* or *clock/calendar*. Commonly, the real-time clock is powered by a battery and runs even when the computer is turned off.

clone a computer that is an exact imitation of another (e.g., a clone of the IBM PC), or a software product that exactly imitates another. In biology, a clone is an organism that has exactly the same genetic material as another, such as a plant grown from a cutting.

FIGURE 58. CLONE TOOL

clone tool

    1. a tool available in paint and photopaint programs that allows you to duplicate areas. To use the clone tool, click on the center of the area you wish to copy. Move the cursor to where you want the new area to be. Press and hold down the mouse button (the leftmost button if there is more than one) while you paint in the image. The clone tool can be used to create a crowd out of a small group of people, cover a gap left by deleting an area, or to put a third eye on someone's forehead. It is not necessary to define the outline of an area or object when using the clone tool; it works from the center out as far as needed. *See also* RUBBER STAMP.

2. (drawing program) a tool that copies the properties of an object to a secondary object.

close

1. (Windows) to exit a program and clear it from the computer's memory. This is different from MINIMIZE in that a program reduced to an icon is still running and waiting for input from you, but a closed program has been put away. Most importantly, a minimized program is still being held in the computer's memory. If you close a minimized program, you will regain the memory it is taking up.

2. (Macintosh) to reduce a window to an icon *without* quitting the application software. The Close button is at the far left of the title bar. Click once to close the open window. This sense of *close* is analogous to MINIMIZE in Windows. To clear the program from memory, choose Quit from the File menu.

This illustrates one of the most basic areas of confusion between Macintosh and Windows terminology. Be careful when talking to your cross-platform friends or you'll both end up confused!

3. (programming) to release a file when a program is finished using it.

4. (electronics) to put a switch into the position that allows current to flow.

cluster a group of disk sectors that are treated as a unit for purposes of allocating space; an ALLOCATION UNIT. *See also* LOST CLUSTER.

CLV (**c**onstant **l**inear **v**elocity), in disk drives, a speed of rotation that varies depending on whether the drive is reading a long track near the edge of the disk or a short track near the center. Thus the disk itself passes beneath the head at a constant speed. Most CD-ROM drives use CLV. *Contrast* CAV.

CMOS (**c**omplementary **m**etal-**o**xide **s**emiconductor) a type of integrated circuit noted for its extremely low power consumption and its vulnerability to damage from static electricity. CMOS devices are used in digital watches, pocket calculators, microprocessors, and computer memories. *See* FIELD-EFFECT TRANSISTOR.

CMOS RAM a special kind of low-power memory that stores information about the configuration of a computer. It is operated by a battery so that it does not go blank when the machine is turned off.

CMS (**C**onversational **M**onitor **S**ystem) the interactive part of IBM's VM/SP (VM/ESA) operating system for mainframe computers.

The key idea behind VM and CMS is that each user has a whole simulated mainframe computer all to himself. The simulated computer has a *virtual disk,* i.e., one large real disk file that simulates the function of a disk drive on which many small files can be stored. VM/CMS filenames are of the form XXXXXXXX YYYYYYYY Z, where XXXXXXXX is an identifying name, YYYYYYYY indicates the type of file, and Z indicates which of several virtual disks the file is on (A for the user's own disk, or a letter such as S for a system disk accessible to all users). In addition, there is a *virtual printer* for sending files to the system printer, and a *virtual card punch* and *virtual card reader*, used to send files to, and receive them from, other users. The help command calls up full documentation about operating system commands. *See also* VIRTUAL MACHINE; VM/ESA.

CMYK the four standard printing inks: **c**yan, **m**agenta, **y**ellow, and blac**k**. When combined, these four colors can reproduce a full-color image. If you ask your computer to make color separations for a PROCESS COLOR job, four COLOR SEPARATIONS will be generated, one for each of the standard inks. *See also* SPOT COLOR.

(You may be wondering why K is used to stand for black instead of B. It's to avoid confusion with *cyan,* which is a vivid shade of blue, and which could also lay claim to B.)

coaster *(slang)* a compact disc (CD) given away free as advertising material; if you don't need the software, you can at least put the disc under your coffee cup.

coaxial cable a cable that consists of a single conductor surrounded by insulation and a conductive shield. The shield prevents the cable from picking up or emitting electrical noise. (*Contrast* TWISTED PAIR.) Coaxial cables are rated for their *impedance*, given in ohms, which indicates how the inductance and capacitance of the cable interact. For instance, RG-58 cable is rated at 52 ohms. This impedance cannot be measured with an ohmmeter.

COBOL (**Co**mmon **B**usiness-**O**riented **L**anguage) a programming language for business data processing, developed in the early 1960s by several computer manufacturers and the U.S. Department of Defense. As the sample program in Fig. 59 shows, COBOL statements resemble English sentences, and the structure of the program requires that some documentation be included. COBOL programs are long and wordy, but easy to read, making it easy for programmers other than the author to make corrections or changes.

code
1. a way of encrypting information (making it unreadable). *See* ENCRYPTION.
2. a way of representing information on a machine or in some physical form. For example, the bit patterns in memory can be used as a code to stand for letters and digits.
3. computer programs, whether written in machine language (OBJECT CODE) or a programming language (SOURCE CODE).

codec (**co**der-**dec**oder) an electronic circuit for converting audio or video signals into and out of digital form; the essential part of a SOUND CARD or a card for processing images from a video camera.

```
IDENTIFICATION DIVISION.

PROGRAM-ID.   COBOL-DEMO.
AUTHOR.       M. A. COVINGTON.

ENVIRONMENT DIVISION.

CONFIGURATION SECTION.
SOURCE-COMPUTER. IBM-PC.
OBJECT-COMPUTER. IBM-PC.

DATA DIVISION.

WORKING-STORAGE SECTION.
77   SUM   PICTURE IS S999999, USAGE IS COMPUTATIONAL.
77   X     PICTURE IS S999999, USAGE IS COMPUTATIONAL.

PROCEDURE DIVISION.

START-UP.
    MOVE O TO SUM.
GET-A-NUMBER.
    DISPLAY "TYPE A NUMBER:" UPON CONSOLE.
    ACCEPT X FROM CONSOLE.
    IF X IS EQUAL TO O GO TO FINISH.
    ADD X TO SUM.
    GO TO GET-A-NUMBER.
FINISH.
    DISPLAY SUM UPON CONSOLE.
    STOP RUN.
```

FIGURE 59. COBOL PROGRAM

code page the table of information, inside DOS, that tells it how to display characters and interpret keystrokes. Code pages other than the usual (default) one are normally used outside the United States to accommodate the characters needed for foreign languages.

code signing attaching a DIGITAL SIGNATURE to a piece of code so a person who downloads it will know its origin. If the code comes from a trusted person or organization, the user will be more likely to grant it permission to take a wider range of actions, such as writing to the local disk drive.

coding the process of writing an algorithm or other problem-solving procedure in a computer programming language.

cold boot, cold start *see* BOOT.

cold link *see* DDE.

collate to place printed pages in order before they are bound into a book. Some photocopiers have the ability to collate multipage documents automatically.

When printing multiple copies of a document, choose "collate" if you want the pages printed in the correct order and you don't mind taking some extra time; the whole document will be sent to the printer more than once. If you do not choose "collate," you will get all the copies of page 1, followed by all those of page 2, and so on; printing will be faster because the printer will receive each page only once, followed by a command to print it repeatedly.

collating sequence the alphabetical order of all characters representable on a computer (including digits, punctuation marks, and other special characters). The collating sequence is important because it is often necessary to sort (alphabetize) data that includes characters other than letters. The collating sequence of a computer is the same as the order of the numeric codes for the characters. *See* ASCII; EBCDIC.

collector one of the three layers of a bipolar transistor. *See* TRANSISTOR.

collision the situation in which two computers are trying to transmit on the same Ethernet network segment at the same time. Each of them will try again after a random length of time (not the same length of time, or they would collide again, ad infinitum). Some collisions are normal on any busy network. Constant collisions indicate that the network is overloaded. *See* ETHERNET.

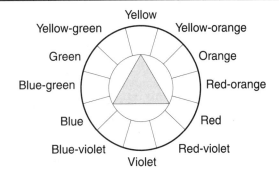

FIGURE 60. COLOR WHEEL

color the visible difference between different wavelengths of light. Fortunately, the human eye can be fooled — the color of any wavelength can be simulated by mixing light of other wavelengths. Colors on the screen are produced by mixing red, green, and blue light from tiny phosphor dots (*see* DOT PITCH). Colors on paper are produced by mixing or alternating inks in various ways.

Screen colors are specified as RGB (red, green, and blue) values in either of two ways. One way is to define a PALETTE (a working set of colors) and assign numbers to the colors on it. For example, a bitmap image with 4 bits per pixel can distinguish up to 16 colors. The other way is to give values of red, green, and blue for each pixel. For example, *24-bit color* uses 8 bits each for red, green, and blue, requiring a total of 24 bits per pixel.

Since 8 bits are used for each color, there are $2^8 = 256$ different levels for that color. Each color value is often represented as two HEXADECIMAL digits, where 00 is the minimum value and FF is the maximum value. Here are some specific examples:

Hexadecimal code	Color
FF0000	red (maximum intensity)
00FF00	green (maximum intensity)
0000FF	blue (maximum intensity)
FFFF00	yellow (mixed red and green)
FF00FF	violet (mixed red and blue)
FFC800	orange
000000	black
FFFFFF	white

In general, if the red, green, and blue values are equal, the result will be a shade of gray.

Colors on paper are usually specified as CMYK (cyan, magenta, yellow, and black) or HSB (hue, saturation, and brightness). Because the pigments being mixed are completely different from the phosphor dots on the screen, printed colors do not always match screen displays, even after extensive CALIBRATION.

color channel a representation of color information in a color bitmap image. An RGB image has three channels: **r**ed, **g**reen, and **b**lue. Each channel can be manipulated separately from the others.

color/gray map a photopaint filter that allows adjustment of a picture's color balance. In grayscale mode, it can be used to adjust the exposure of an imperfect black-and-white photo.

color replacer a tool available in paint and photopaint programs that replaces the primary color with the secondary color as you drag the tool across the image. The size and shape of the color replacer can be adjusted like any of the brush tools.

color separations camera-ready artwork that has been broken down into individual printouts, one for each color of ink that is to be printed. All the elements that should print in black will be on one sheet, and all the elements that should print in red will be on another, and so forth. Each printout will have registration marks so that the colors can be aligned properly or registered (*see* REGISTRATION, definition 2).

column move the operation of moving material to the left or right within a file (e.g., moving the material in columns 10–20 into columns 5–15 on several consecutive lines in one step). *See* EDITOR.

com

1. suffix indicating that an E-MAIL address or WEB SITE is at a commercial site in the United States, such as www.earthlink.com. *See* URL; DOMAIN.

2. the filename extension used for small, nonrelocatable machine language programs in DOS. To execute the program, type the name of the file without the final ".COM"; for example, to execute AAA.COM, type aaa. *Contrast* EXE.

In VAX/VMS, a COM file contains a list of commands to be executed, like a BAT file in DOS (*see* BAT FILE).

COM1, COM2 the filenames assigned to the first two serial ports on a PC-compatible computer under DOS.

combine a drawing program command that merges two separate objects into one so that the whole thing can become one object. This is similar to grouping objects, but there is an important distinction. A group of objects can be treated as a single object, but the individual elements retain their separate attributes. A combined object *is* a single object; it has only *one* outline (or path) and only *one* fill. Interestingly, a combined object can have holes in it that you can see through. *See* MASK; GROUP (definition 1); PATH (definition 3).

COMDEX (**Com**puter **De**alers' **Ex**position) a major computer show sponsored by The Interface Group, Inc., and held annually in several locations. New microcomputer products are often introduced at COMDEX.

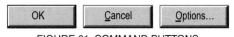

FIGURE 61. COMMAND BUTTONS

command button a small box, within a window, that can be actuated by pointing to it with the mouse and pressing a mouse button. Doing this causes the computer to perform a specific action.

Command key the key marked with a cloverleaf-like symbol (⌘) on the Macintosh. It is used like a shift key to change the meanings of other keys or to perform special functions. For example, you can print a picture of the current screen by holding down Command and Shift and pressing 4. If you press 3 instead, a picture of the current screen will be saved as a MacPaint document.

An extremely useful keyboard shortcut is ⌘. (Command-period). This will cancel any action or dialog box, including the infamous "Please insert the disk…" message.

FIGURE 62. COMMAND LINE (WINDOWS 98)

command line a place where the user can type commands to the operating system (*see* Figure 62). MS-DOS and UNIX (in its original form) rely entirely on the command line. *Contrast* GRAPHICAL USER INTERFACE.

comment information in a computer program that is ignored by the computer and is included only for the benefit of human readers. Various computer languages identify comments with markers such as C, ; , REM, or /* */.

Comments reflect the fact that programs are written to be read by human beings, not computers. If we could write in the language that best suited the computer, we would not need compilers to translate BASIC, Pascal, C, and other programming languages into machine code.

Comments can also be used to remove material from a program temporarily without deleting it. When you modify a program, it is a good idea to preserve the original form of the material you changed, in a comment, so that you can restore it or study it if the need arises.

Opinions vary as to how comments are best used. Some software engineers hold that a clearly written program needs few comments. This is certainly true in itself, but it is often impossible to write a program so clearly that another programmer — or even the author, months or years later — can tell at a glance how it works. Here are some general rules for using comments effectively, with the first four examples in Pascal:

1. Begin each program, procedure, or function with a comment stating exactly what it is supposed to do. For example:

```
PROCEDURE swap(VAR x, y: INTEGER);
  {Interchange values of x and y.}
VAR t : INTEGER;
```

```
BEGIN
  t:=x; x:=y; y:=t
END;
```

A comment of this type may run many lines or even pages.

2. Use comments to answer questions that the reader may have in mind. For example:

```
q := sin(x/57.29578);
   {x is in degrees,
    sine function expects radians.}
```

Here the comment explains the mysterious number 57.29578.

3. Do not state the obvious. This is an example of bad comment usage:

```
x := x + 1; {Add 1 to x.}
```

Here the comment adds no information.

4. Avoid misleading comments: in debugging a program, resist the temptation to believe that the statements do what the comments say they do. Here is an example of a misleading comment:

```
{ Interchange values of x and y. }
t:=x; x:=y; y:=x;
```

In spite of the comments, x and y do not come out interchanged; both end up with the value that y had at the beginning.

5. In assembly language, explain step by step what the program is doing. Assembly language is never easy to read, and the reader needs all the help you can give. Again, however, don't state the obvious. The following example is in 8086 assembly language:

```
   MOV CX,5    ; initialize loop counter
I: INT 10H     ; perform video interrupt
   LOOP I      ; decrement CX, repeat if >0
```

Here the reader of the program may not remember that INT 10H requests video services on the IBM PC, or that the LOOP instruction uses the CX register for its counter. But to explain MOV CX,5 as "put 5 in CX" would be pointless.

common logarithm a logarithm to the base 10. *See* LOGARITHM.

Common User Access *see* CUA.

Communicator product released by Netscape in 1997 containing an updated version of the Navigator web browser along with electronic mail and groupware features.

Compaq a major manufacturer of IBM PC-compatible computers. Compaq's first product, released in 1983, was the first PC *clone,* i.e., the first PC-compatible computer not made by IBM. In 1988 Compaq led a group of other computer companies in the development of a 32-bit PC bus (*see* EISA). In 1998, Compaq acquired Digital Equipment Corporation, manufacturers of the Alpha microprocessor (*see* DIGITAL EQUIPMENT CORPORATION; ALPHA). Compaq Computer Corporation is headquartered in Houston, Texas. Web address: http://www.compaq.com.

compatible

1. able to work together. For example, a particular brand of printer is compatible with a particular computer to which it can be connected.

2. able to run the same software. *See* PC COMPATIBILITY.

compiler a computer program that translates C, BASIC, Pascal, or a similar high-level programming language into machine language. The high-level language program fed into the compiler is called the *source program;* the generated machine language program is the *object program.*

Compilers contrast with *interpreters,* which store the source code and execute it statement by statement without ever producing an object program. The big advantage of a compiler is that the object program can run on any suitable computer, whether or not the compiler is installed. Further, compiled code runs 10 to 1000 times faster than interpreted code.

However, interpreters make it easier to examine and modify the program while it is running; further, many interpreters can store the source code in a compact form that takes much less space than an object program would. Traditionally, C, Pascal, and FORTRAN are always compiled; Prolog and Lisp are often interpreted because of the need to make modifications at run time; and BASIC can be handled either way. Early microcomputers almost always came with BASIC interpreters. *See* BASIC.

Some criteria often used in evaluating the performance of compilers are the following:

1. *Reliability.* Is the compiler free of errors? Does it conform to the official standards for the language that it implements?

2. *Efficiency of compilation.* How much memory and time are needed to compile a given program? This is less of an issue than it used to be, since almost all modern compilers are very fast.

3. *Efficiency of object code.* How much memory and time are needed to run the object program? This varies widely from compiler to compiler, even when the same program is compiled on the same computer. Memory requirements are especially variable because some compilers include large subroutine packages in all object programs, whether they are needed or not, while others are more selective.

4. *Optimization.* Can the compiler detect unnecessary repetitions and other inefficiencies in the source program and rearrange the instructions to make computation more efficient? This feature is normally provided only on the most sophisticated compilers.

5. *Development environment.* Does the compiler include an editor, a debugger (for testing the program statement by statement), on-line help, and other tools for the programmer? Some compilers, such as Microsoft Visual Basic, even let the programmer design the user interface graphically.

6. *Bulk.* The disk requirements of compilers range in size from about 64K bytes for a simple Pascal compiler, to 90 megabytes for a comprehensive C and C++ compiler with on-line help, extensive development and testing tools, and a library of programming examples. Some compilers are too big to fit on some computers because of the disk space they require.

compile-time error an error in a computer program that is caught in the process of compiling the program. For example, a compile-time error occurs if the syntax of the language has been violated. *Contrast* RUN-TIME ERROR. *See also* BUG.

complement either of two ways of representing negative numbers in binary:

1. The *1-complement* of a binary number is obtained by simply changing every 0 to 1 and every 1 to 0. For example, the 1-complement of 0001 is 1110. In this system, 0000 and its complement 1111 both represent zero (you can think of them as $+0$ and -0 respectively).

2. The *2-complement* of a binary number is found by reversing all the digits and then adding 1. For example, the 2-complement of 0001 is $1110 + 1 = 1111$. This is the system normally used on most computers, and it has only one representation of zero (0000). *See* BINARY SUBTRACTION.

complexity theory the mathematical study of the time (number of steps) and amount of memory needed to perform a computation.

Suppose a computer is going to process n items of input. The time complexity of the calculation may be any of the following:

- *Constant* or $O(1)$ if the computation takes the same number of steps regardless of how many items are to be processed. An example is copying a disk with the DOS `diskcopy` command, which duplicates the entire disk regardless of how much of it is actually in use.

- *Linear* or $O(n)$ if the number of steps is proportional to n. An example would be copying a set of n names and addresses from one file to another, or finding the sum of n numbers, or any program that contains only one loop.

- *Polynomial* or $O(n^k)$ if the number of steps is proportional to n raised to some constant power. For example, if the computation involves comparing each item of input with all of the other items, it will take n^2 steps. Many sorting algorithms are $O(n^2)$.

A program that contains k nested loops, each with a number of steps proportional to n, will take time proportional to n^k.

- *Exponential* or $O(k^n)$ if the number of steps is proportional to some constant k raised to the nth power. This is what happens if the computer has to try arranging n elements in all possible sequences. Exponential-time computations are generally not practical.

There are some other possibilities; for example, Quicksort takes time proportional to $n \log n$, which is less than n^2.

In calculating complexity, we ignore factors that become insignificant as n becomes large. Suppose a computation requires $n^2 + 3n + 5$ steps. For sufficiently large n, this gets closer and closer to n^2, so we say that the complexity is $O(n^2)$.

Besides the time complexity, a computation may require constant, linear, polynomial, or exponential amounts of memory. *See also* COMPUTER SCIENCE; QUICKSORT; LIMITS OF COMPUTER POWER.

complex number a number consisting of two parts, called *real* and *imaginary*. Complex numbers are written in the form $a + bi$, where a is the real part, b is the size of the imaginary part, and i is the square root of -1. (If $b = 0$, the complex number is of course equal to a real number.)

Unlike real numbers, complex numbers can produce negative numbers when squared; because of this fact, all polynomials have complex roots even though some of them lack real roots. Another use of complex numbers is to represent vectors in two-dimensional space; the imaginary number line is thought of as running perpendicular to the real number line.

Arithmetic on complex numbers obeys the ordinary laws of algebra, as follows:

$$(a + bi) + (c + di) = (a + c) + (b + d)i$$

$$(a + bi) - (c + di) = (a - c) + (b - d)i$$

$$(a + bi) \times (c + di) = ac + adi + bci + bdi^2 = (ac - bd) + (ad + bc)i$$

Complex numbers are provided as a data type in FORTRAN and C++, and in mathematical packages such as Maple, but not in most other programming languages. *See also* MANDELBROT SET.

component a section of software code that can be merged with other code to create an application. The programmer's job is easier if there are standard reusable components available to perform useful functions, but this works only if the components follow a clear standard for how they interact. For examples of systems for creating component software, *see* ACTIVEX; JAVABEAN. For a description of standards for how components can interact with each other, *see* CORBA.

composite video the kind of video signal used in a TV set. The whole signal is transmitted on one wire. By contrast, an RGB signal has separate wires for red, green, and blue. *See* MONITOR.

compositing the combining of bitmapped images from different sources or different objects in a single image. The opacity, or ALPHA, of each object determines how it combines with objects behind it. *See also* CHROMA-KEYING.

compression *see* DATA COMPRESSION.

CompuServe an on-line information service based in Columbus, Ohio, and accessible by modem from anywhere in the United States. (*See* MODEM.) CompuServe offers information on a wide range of subjects, including weather forecasts, airline schedules, the stock market, and a medical question-and-answer service. In addition, CompuServe subscribers can participate in hundreds of discussion forums (SIGs, "special-interest groups") and access the Internet. Since 1998, CompuServe has been a subsidiary of AOL. For further information, see `http://www.compuserve.com`.

computational linguistics the use of computers in the study of human language, and the study of how to make computers understand information expressed in human languages. *See* NATURAL LANGUAGE PROCESSING; PARSING.

computer a machine capable of executing instructions on data. The distinguishing feature of a computer is its ability to store its own instructions. This ability makes it possible for a computer to perform many operations without the need for a person to type in new instructions each time.

computer architecture the design and internal structure of computers.

Fundamentally, a computer is a machine that can store instructions and execute them. Thus, it consists of two major parts, MEMORY and the central processing unit (CPU), which communicate through a set of parallel electrical connections called the BUS (Fig. 64). The bus also connects to input-output devices such as a screen, a keyboard, and disk drives.

The CPU spends its time retrieving instructions from memory and doing whatever those instructions say. Each instruction is a pattern of bits (binary ones and zeroes, represented by electrical on and off signals). When the instruction reaches the CPU, the CPU must *decode* (recognize) it and activate the appropriate *functional unit* within the CPU in order to carry out the instruction. Functional units include adders, multipliers, circuits to compare bit patterns, etc., all of which are built from logic gates (for an example, *see* BINARY ADDITION).

The CPU contains REGISTERS to hold data that is being worked on. For example, in order to add two numbers, the CPU will typically

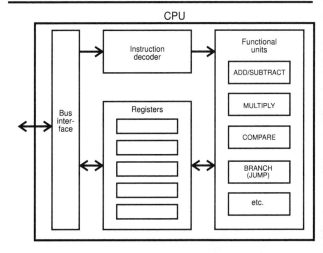

FIGURE 63. INTERNAL STRUCTURE OF A CPU
(CENTRAL PROCESSING UNIT)

retrieve the two numbers from memory into registers, perform the addition, place the result in another register, and finally store it back into memory. Fig. 63 illustrates the parts of the CPU. In most present-day computers, the CPU is a single integrated circuit (IC) called a MICRO-PROCESSOR.

Every location in memory has an ADDRESS, i.e., a bit pattern (binary number) that identifies the location. To retrieve the contents of memory location 011000011, the CPU places the bit pattern 011000011 on the address portion of the bus, activates the "read memory" line, and waits a specified length of time. The memory places the contents of that location onto the data portion of the bus so that the CPU can read it. To put data into memory, the CPU puts both the address and the data onto the bus and activates the "write memory" line. Some computers also include "read port" and "write port" lines, which are like the lines used for accessing memory except that addresses are understood as applying to input and output devices (printer ports, etc.) rather than memory.

Most computers use a VON NEUMANN ARCHITECTURE, which means that programs and data are stored in the same kind of memory. Some microcontrollers use a HARVARD ARCHITECTURE, with separate memories for program and data (mainly because programs are kept permanently recorded in ROM, but data must be changeable).

Programmers normally do not write CPU instructions. Instead, they write programs in a high-level language such as BASIC, C, or Pascal,

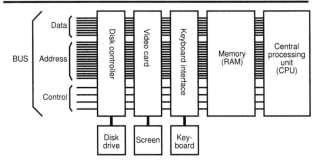

FIGURE 64. BUS CONNECTS CPU TO MEMORY
AND OTHER DEVICES

and use a COMPILER to translate the programs into machine language. It is also possible to write programs in ASSEMBLY LANGUAGE, which translates into machine language more directly. *See also* XOR GATE.

computer ethics the responsible use of computers and computer networks. Malicious misuse of computers is rare, but serious misjudgments by well-meaning people are unfortunately common. Some important points to remember are the following:

1. *People have the same legal and ethical responsibilities when using a computer as at any other time.*
   Slander, deception, harassment, etc., are just as wrong when done via computer as when done any other way, and they incur the same legal penalties.
   Using a computer without the owner's permission is prosecutable as theft of services (just like using any other machine without the owner's permission). Damaging property or data by releasing a computer virus is also prosecutable as a crime.

2. *Computers will not necessarily prevent all improper acts; users are responsible for what they do.*
   For example, if a computer is set up incorrectly so that it lets unauthorized people use it without a password, that does not justify the unauthorized usage, just as a defective door lock does not justify burglary.

3. *Some of the information stored in computers is private and confidential and should not be abused.*
   This applies particularly to credit records, educational records, and the like. Such information may also be incomplete or inaccurate because people did not correct errors that they considered inconsequential. If the information is later used for a completely different purpose, the errors can be damaging.

4. *Electronic communications are not guaranteed to be private.*
   You do not know what path your electronic mail follows or who may see it en route. Do not send credit card numbers or other confidential information through e-mail unless you have confirmed that it is traveling by a secure path.

   Also, be aware that e-mail can be faked; there is no guarantee that a piece of mail actually came from the person or site shown on the header.

5. *Users must respect software copyrights and licenses.*
   The price of a piece of software is more than just the cost of the disk and manual; it's also your share of the cost of developing the product. If people don't pay for software, there will be no software.

6. *Manufacturers, programmers, and independent consultants have responsibilities to their customers.*
   It's wrong to claim to be more of an expert than you really are; it's also wrong to sell a shoddy product while concealing defects in it. Admittedly, no one can ensure that any complex piece of software is 100% reliable, but common decency requires programmers and vendors to act in good faith — when there's a problem, do your best to correct it or at least warn the user about it.

   In the past, many manufacturers have tried to disclaim all responsibility for the performance of their products, but there are encouraging signs that the user community will no longer tolerate this dubious practice.

7. *On the Internet, you are everyone else's guest.*
   The cost of running the Internet is paid by the sites that receive messages, not just the sites that send them. Accordingly, you must be careful what you send out, and to whom.

For more about ethical aspects of computer communications see INTERNET; USENET; SPAMMING; SPOOFING; NETIQUETTE; MAIL BOMBING; DOMAIN NAME POACHING.

computer science the mathematical and scientific study of the possible uses of computers. Computer science is a wide-ranging field including pure mathematics (*see* COMPLEXITY THEORY, HALTING PROBLEM), engineering (*see* COMPUTER ARCHITECTURE), management (*see* SOFTWARE ENGINEERING), and even the study of the human mind (*see* ARTIFICIAL INTELLIGENCE). Indeed, computer scientists often work on problems in almost any field to which computers can be applied. Computer science is more than just training in the use of today's computers and software; it includes preparation to understand the technology of the future and its theoretical underpinnings.

computer security the protection of computers from tampering, physical danger, and unwanted disclosure of data. The advent of personal computers has made it easy for important business records or confidential data to be lost, sabotaged, or misused. Computers need protection from the following kinds of hazards:

1. *Machine failure.* Make backups of important files frequently. Every disk drive in the world will one day fail, losing all data.

2. *Physical hazards.* Protect the computer from fire, flood, and similar hazards, and store backups at a remote location. Remember, too, that the machine can be stolen. An increasing number of computer thieves are after data, not just equipment.
   When traveling with a laptop computer, *never let it out of your possession.* Many thefts occur at airport check-in counters: while you are preoccupied making your arrangements, someone can quietly steal the laptop computer you placed on the floor. Keep the computer in your hand. Stay close to the computer as it goes through the airport security check. Always bring your laptop on board as carry-on luggage. Checked baggage is treated far too roughly.

3. *Operator error.* It is easy to delete information accidentally. This hazard can be minimized with software that retains original files while altered copies are being made.

4. *Computer tampering.* Can someone come in and alter your records without your knowing it? Bear in mind that large numbers of people know how to use popular business software packages. If possible, use software that keeps records of changes — recording who made them and when — and requires validation (such as a password) to make unusual changes.

5. *Malicious programming.* Some computer crimes have been perpetrated by programmers who did such things as collect all the money that was lost by rounding interest payments to the nearest penny. A clever bookkeeping system run by a dishonest programmer can easily conceal abuse.
   More recently, some people have gotten their kicks by distributing destructive computer programs over the Internet. *See* TROJAN HORSE; BLACK WIDOW. Even more have gotten their kicks by circulating false warnings (*see* HOAX).

6. *Break-ins by modem or network.* Make sure you know all the possibilities for connecting to your computer from elsewhere, and that you've blocked all access that you don't want to allow. The UNIX operating system, designed originally for use in laboratories where no security was needed, is generally thought to be particularly vulnerable.

7. *Easily guessed passwords.* A computer password must never be a person's initials, nickname, child's name, birthdate, etc., nor should it be a correctly spelled word in any language. A common way to crack accounts is to try all the words in a large dictionary, as well as all names and abbreviations that are associated with a person.

Also, if a user signs onto a computer and then leaves the terminal unattended, others can tamper with it without typing the password.

8. *Insufficient protection from executable code included in web pages.* Since this code is executed when the browser connects to that page, the user may not have any warning that a potentially destructive action is occurring. Normally, web browsers impose heavy security restrictions so that code of this type cannot, for example, erase a user's hard disk or find and transmit the user's private files. These restrictions are stricter for Java applets than for ActiveX controls; also, some browsers fail to implement them properly, creating a security hazard that can be exploited by malicious web page implementors.

9. *Excessive security measures.* Excessive attempts to build security into a computer can easily make the computer so hard to use that productivity is crippled. In the final analysis, all computer security depends on human trustworthiness. Concentrate on securing the people, not the machine. That is, ensure that employees are trustworthy and that strangers have no access to the machine, then give authorized users all the access they need to do their jobs effectively.

See also FINE-GRAINED SECURITY; ENCRYPTION; MAIL BOMBING; DENIAL-OF-SERVICE ATTACK; PING FLOODING.

computers, history of Mechanical computation aids date back many centuries. The abacus, on which information is stored by moving beads along rods, was one of the earliest calculating devices. Blaise Pascal developed an adding machine in 1642 that used toothed wheels to handle carries from one digit to the next. Charles Babbage developed the concept of a stored program computer when he designed the "Analytical Engine" in 1833. Unfortunately, the mechanical devices of his day could not be made to work reliably, so the "Analytical Engine" was never completed.

An important data processing device, the punched card, was developed by Herman Hollerith to help the U.S. Census Bureau tabulate the census of 1890. (*See* PUNCHED CARD.) The first electronic digital computer was the ENIAC (Electronic Numerical Integrator and Calculator), which was built for the U.S. Army in 1946, largely because of the need to calculate ballistics tables. The ENIAC was programmed by plugging in cables to connect different units. In 1945 John von Neumann introduced the modern concept of a stored-program computer, in which the computer memory could store both programs and data.

Once the concept was established, major improvements were made by developing smaller and more reliable electronic components. The ENIAC was a huge machine made with vacuum tubes. The invention of the transistor in the late 1940s made it possible to build much smaller computers that needed less cooling. Continued improvements in integrated circuits, which were first developed in the late 1950s, made it possible to continue the miniaturization of computers.

An important advance occurred in the mid-1970s when the first microcomputers were built. Previously, all computers had been large and expensive. Microcomputers are small enough and cheap enough that they can be purchased by small businesses and individuals. A microcomputer is built around a microprocessor chip, such as the 486 or Pentium, that contains the entire central processing unit on a single crystal of silicon. The advent of powerful, low-cost microcomputers has made the computer a common household appliance.

computer virus *see* VIRUS.

computer vision *see* VISION, COMPUTER.

concatenation the operation of joining two or more character strings together, end to end. For example, `"ABC"` concatenated with `"DEF"` equals `"ABCDEF"`. *See* STRING OPERATIONS.

concurrent processing the apparently simultaneous execution of two programs, where a single CPU is actually switching its attention back and forth between them very rapidly. *See also* TIMESHARING; MULTITASKING; PARALLEL PROCESSING.

conditional branch an instruction that causes the computer to jump to another location in the program only if a specified condition is true. An example of a conditional branch in BASIC is:

```
60 IF N > 25 THEN GOTO 120
```

First, the computer checks to see whether the condition N>25 is true. If it is, then the computer will jump to statement number 120 and start executing there.

conferencing the use of computer networks to enable workers to communicate in real time (without delay) while working together. *See* IRC; MUD.

confidence factor (certainty factor) a truth value between 0 and 1, used to describe the reliability of a piece of information whose truth is unclear or uncertain. There are several systems of reasoning that use confidence factors; for one example, see FUZZY LOGIC. *Contrast* DEFAULT LOGIC, which deals with exceptions without using confidence factors.

CONFIG.SYS a file (in DOS, OS/2, and similar operating systems) that contains information about the machine configuration, including device drivers, the type of keyboard (if not the standard U.S. model), and the amount of memory to be set aside for disk buffers. CONFIG.SYS is read only when the machine boots up. *See also* AUTOEXEC.BAT.

configure to set up a computer or program to be used in a particular way. Many commercial software packages have to be configured, or installed; this involves setting them up for a particular machine (including video card and printer) and for a particular user's preferences.

console
    1. the main keyboard and screen of a multi-user computer.
    2. a keyboard and (non-graphical) screen, or a window serving the purpose of such a screen.

console mode a way of running programs without windowing under Windows 95, Windows 98, OS/2, and Windows NT. A console-mode program is started from the command line, just like a DOS program, but has access to the full facilities of the operating system, including large amounts of memory.

constant a value that remains unchanged during the execution of a program. Literal expressions, such as 3.5 and "DOLLY MADISON", are constants because they always stand for the same value. In Pascal and some other languages it is possible to define names to represent constants.

constrain (in drawing programs) to restrict or limit the available movements or shapes. For example, when drawing a circle with a circle tool, you must hold down the control key to constrain the rounded shape to a circle. If you let go of the constraining key too soon, you may get a fat oval rather than a perfect circle.
    The constrain command is also used with the rectangle drawing tool (constrains to a square) and the line drawing tool (constrains to preset angles).

contention *see* DEVICE CONTENTION.

content provider a company or organization that provides information (*content*) on line. For example, www.cnn.com (Cable News Network) is a content provider for world news and related information. *Contrast* ASP (definition 2); INTERNET SERVICE PROVIDER.

context-sensitive help information provided by a computer program when you ask for help. The help option is context-sensitive if its behavior depends on what you are doing at the time you press it. For example, a context-sensitive help key will give you information about how to edit if you press it while editing, or how to print if you press it while preparing to print.

contiguous adjacent, next to each other. For instance, the states of North Dakota and South Dakota are contiguous, but Texas and Maine are not.
    Most computers can store a disk file in either contiguous or noncontiguous sectors. (*See* DISK.) Access is slowed if the sectors are not contiguous, since to get from one part of the file to another, the read/write head must jump from one part of the disk to another. *See* FRAGMENTATION.

continuous speech speech that is spoken without pauses between words. *See* SPEECH RECOGNITION. *Contrast* DISCRETE SPEECH.

FIGURE 65. CONTRAST: LOW, NORMAL, AND HIGH

contrast the range of light and dark values in a grayscale (continuous tone) image. A *high-contrast* image is mostly white and black with very few intermediate gray shades. A *low-contrast* image has little difference between the darkest darks and lightest lights.

Contrast is best adjusted at the time of scanning the image. If that is not possible, contrast can be adjusted in a PHOTOPAINT PROGRAM. *See* SCANNER; HISTOGRAM.

control a reuseable software component in Visual Basic, ActiveX, or a similar system. Many of the first controls were user interface components—check boxes, sliding bars, and the like—hence the name.

control box (Windows, OS/2) a small box at the left of the title bar of a window. Clicking the control box pops up a menu for controlling the size of the window. Double-clicking on the control box closes the window and the application running in it.

Control key (**Ctrl** or **Cntl** key) a special key on many computer keyboards. When it is pressed in conjunction with another key, it gives the other key a new meaning that depends on the program in use. *See* ASCII to see how the Control key can be used to type nonprintable control characters.

control menu (Windows, OS/2) a menu that appears when the user clicks on the CONTROL BOX (the box at the left of the title bar). The control menu for each window allows you to maximize, minimize, restore, resize, or close the window. *See* Figure 66 for illustration. *See also* WINDOW.

In OS/2, the control menu also offers access to configuration dialog boxes and information about the application.

FIGURE 66. CONTROL MENU

Control Panel a program that gives you the ability to adjust certain features of your computer environment like the desktop color, mouse tracking, and the rate of cursor blinking. These features are easily customized and give a rather high degree of personalization to your working environment. Look for the Control Panel under the Apple menu on the Mac or under Start—Settings in Windows 95 and Windows 98.

control point *see* NODE.

CONUS abbreviation for **con**tinental **U**nited **S**tates, usually meaning the 48 contiguous states. (Alaska is part of the North American continent but is commonly overlooked.)

conversion program a program that is capable of changing a file from one format to another. For example, to use a .TIFF (Tagged Image File Format) file in a web page design, the image must be converted to .JPG or .GIF. This can be done with a separate conversion program or by using the "Save as …" command in the appropriate image-editing program. (*See* IMPORT; EXPORT; FILE FORMAT.)

Note that simply changing the file *name* from myfile.tif to myfile.jpg does *not* convert the file *type*. The data contained in the file has to be reorganized by the conversion program.

convolution an image processing computation described by a matrix. Suppose for example that you want to bring out fine detail in an image. One way to do this is to increase the difference between each pixel and its neighbors. Treating the pixels as numbers representing their brightnesses, you can use the following convolution matrix:

$$\begin{bmatrix} -1 & -1 & -1 \\ -1 & 9 & -1 \\ -1 & -1 & -1 \end{bmatrix}$$

That means: Work through the whole image, one pixel at a time. Whenever you get to a pixel, multiply it by 9, multiply each of the surrounding pixels by -1, and add them together. Then replace the original pixel with that value.

If all of the pixels are the same brightness, nothing changes, but if a pixel is brighter or fainter than its neighbors, the difference is exaggerated by a factor of 9. Other convolutions can perform other special effects, such as smoothing, elimination of details smaller or larger than a certain size, and even elimination of streaks in a particular direction.

When performing a convolution, the input is always from the original, unprocessed image. That is, the next pixel will not be affected by any changes made by the processing of the previous pixel.

convolve to perform a convolution. *See* CONVOLUTION.

cookie information stored on a user's computer by a WEB BROWSER at the request of software at a web site. Web sites use cookies to recognize users who have previously visited them. The next time the user accesses that site, the information in the cookie is sent back to the site so the information displayed can vary depending on the user's preferences.

The term *cookie* comes from a 1980s prank computer program called Cookie Monster that would interrupt users and demand that they type the word "cookie" before continuing.

coprocessor a separate circuit inside a computer that adds additional functions to the CPU (central processing unit) or handles extra work while the CPU is doing something else. Some computers have graphics coprocessors to do some of the computation necessary for displaying images on the screen. As a result, complex pictures can be displayed and changed more quickly than would be possible if the CPU had to do all the computation.

IBM-PC-compatible computers often use a math coprocessor, the Intel 8087, 80287, 80387, or 80487, to perform floating-point arithmetic. The coprocessor has no effect when the computer is running an ordinary program. However, programs that contain instructions for the math coprocessor can perform arithmetic much more quickly than programs that use the CPU alone. (An equivalent coprocessor is built into the 486DX and Pentium CPUs.)

In general, software that is designed to use the math coprocessor will not run at all if the coprocessor is not installed in the machine. However, some programs will sense whether the coprocessor is present and will use the CPU alone if the coprocessor is not there. Similar floating-point coprocessors exist for a variety of other computers.

copy

    1. to duplicate information in another place, leaving the original unchanged. In many spreadsheets, editors, and drawing programs, *copy* means either of two things:

    (a) to copy material from one place to another;

    (b) to copy material from the document being edited into a holding area, from which you can then "paste" it elsewhere. *See* CUT; PASTE; CLIPBOARD.

    2. a command, under DOS, OS/2, and Windows, that makes a copy of a disk file. For example, the command

```
COPY PGM.SRC PGMC2.SRC
```

takes the old file (PGM.SRC) and makes a copy of it under the name PGMC2.SRC. Two other examples are as follows:

```
COPY A:*.BAS C:
```

copies all files on drive A whose names end in .BAS onto drive C;

```
COPY A:*.* C:
```

copies all files from drive A onto drive C. The asterisk acts as a wild card, matching any filename (*see* WILD CARD).

copyleft *(humorous)* a copyright whose owner gives permission for the product to be distributed free subject to certain conditions. *See* GNU.

copy protection a variety of techniques that were used in the 1970s and 1980s to keep users from making unauthorized copies of program diskettes. Copy protection is usually achieved by changing the size of some of the sectors on the disk so that the software normally used to copy diskettes will not make a usable copy of the original.

Copy protection has several disadvantages and has become uncommon. Because copy-protected disks use the disk drives in ways other than the way the manufacturer intended, they are often unreadable on later model machines. Further, if there is no way to make a backup disk, the software becomes unusable when the original disk wears out.

Several commercial programs enable you to duplicate copy-protected disks or to defeat the copy protection. U.S. copyright law explicitly permits the making of backup disks, whether or not the original disks are copy protected.

copyright (the *right* to *copy*) a legal restriction on the copying of books, magazines, recordings, computer programs, and other materials, in order to protect the original author's right to ownership of, and compensations for reproduction of, an original work. Most computer programs are protected not only by copyright but also by a software license (*see* SOFTWARE LICENSE; FREE SOFTWARE). In the U.S., a program is protected by copyright if it contains a notice of the form

Copyright 1996 John Doe

or

© 1996 John Doe

in one or more prominent places. Unlike books and magazines, computer programs need not be registered with the Copyright Office or deposited in the Library of Congress.

U.S. copyright law allows limited copying of books and magazines for private study or classroom use. However, this does not apply to computer programs, which can only be copied with the permission of the copyright owner, or in order to make backup copies that will not be used as long as the original copy is intact.

Do not reproduce copyrighted material on the INTERNET or in WEB PAGES without the owner's permission. Placing something in a web page constitutes republication just as if you were making printed copies. Remember that copyrights apply to sounds and pictures as well as texts. Distributing a sound bite from a movie or a picture of a cartoon character can be a copyright violation.

Copyright protects expressions of ideas, not the ideas themselves. Copyrights do not cover algorithms, mathematical methods, techniques, or the design of machines (which, however, can be patented).

It not entirely clear to what extent copyrights protect the "look and feel" of a program, i.e., its overall visual appearance and USER INTERFACE. Fortunately, this is becoming a moot point, as most software now derives its visual appearance and user interface from the operating system (Windows 95, Windows 98, OS/2, Macintosh, etc.) more than from the programmer's independent creativity.

CORBA (**C**ommon **O**bject **R**equest **B**roker **A**rchitecture) a standard set of definitions for objects to interact with each other. CORBA was created by the Object Management Group (see OMG). CORBA defines a standard for a layer of middleware called the ORB (Object Request Broker). The way that components interact with other components is specified by IDL (Interface Definition Language). This allows client-server computing where the clients don't need to have any knowledge of the specific operation of the component they are interacting with. For example, the client doesn't need to know the language in which the component was written; it only needs to know the IDL specification of how the component interacts. For an alternative standard, *see* DCOM.

core an old term for the main memory of a computer. The term comes from the doughnut-shaped magnetic cores used as memory devices during the late 1950s and early 1960s.

Corel a corporation headquartered in Ottawa, Ontario that introduced one of the first successful DRAW PROGRAMS, CorelDraw, in 1989. In 1996, Corel acquired the WordPerfect family of business applications. Other Corel products include a suite of SCSI device drivers and a distribution of Linux. Their web address is `www.corel.com`.

correspondence points points in two objects (or images) that are associated with each other for blending or morphing. *See* BLEND; DRAW PROGRAM; MORPH.

COS the cosine function in BASIC, FORTRAN, and other programming languages. If A is an angle in a right triangle, then the cosine of A (written as $\cos A$) is defined as:

$$\cos A = \frac{\text{length of adjacent side}}{\text{length of hypotenuse}}$$

The function COS(A) in BASIC and many other languages calculates the value of cos A. Many computers require that the value for *A* be expressed in radians. For an illustration, see TRIGONOMETRIC FUNCTIONS.

cosine *see* TRIGONOMETRIC FUNCTIONS.

coulomb a unit of electric charge equivalent to the charge of 6.25×10^{18} electrons. *See* AMPERE.

Courier

```
a b c d e f g h i j k l m
n o p q r s t u v w x y z
A B C D E F G H I J K L M
N O P Q R S T U V W X Y Z
1 2 3 4 5 6 7 8 9 0 ! @ #
```
FIGURE 67. COURIER, A FIXED-PITCH FONT

Courier a typewriter-like typeface often used on laser printers. Unlike other typefaces, Courier has fixed pitch; that is, all characters are the same width. It was designed for IBM typewriters in the 1960s, but on modern laser printers, it is often unpleasantly light (thin).

CP/M (**C**ontrol **P**rogram for **M**icrocomputers) an operating system developed by Digital Research, Inc., and used on microcomputers in the 1980s. (*See* OPERATING SYSTEM.) The original CP/M (now called CP/M-80) was widely employed on computers that used the 8-bit Z80 processor. Other versions, CP/M-86 and CP/M-68, were developed for the Intel 8086 and Motorola 68000, respectively, but never became very popular. CP/M greatly influenced the early development of DOS. *See* MS-DOS.

CPU (**C**entral **P**rocessing **U**nit) the part of a computer where arithmetic and logical operations are performed and instructions are decoded and executed. The CPU controls the operation of the computer. A microprocessor is an integrated circuit that contains a complete CPU on a single chip.

CR (**c**arriage **r**eturn) the character code that tells a printer or terminal to return to the beginning of the line; ASCII code 13. On the Macintosh, CR indicates the end of a line in a text file; UNIX uses LF, and DOS and Windows use CRLF. *See* LF, CRLF.

cracker a person who "breaks into" computers via the Internet and uses them without authorization, either with malicious intent or simply to show that it can be done. *Compare* HACKER.

crash the sudden, complete failure of a computer because of a hardware failure or program error. A well-designed operating system contains protection against inappropriate instructions so that a user's program will not be able to cause a system crash.

Cray Research, Inc. a company founded by Seymour Cray, a manufacturer of supercomputers (*see* SUPERCOMPUTER). Cray's first major product was the Cray-1, introduced in 1977, a vector processor designed for repetitious numeric calculations. *See* VECTOR PROCESSOR. Web address: http://www.cray.com.

CRC (**c**yclical **r**edundancy **c**heck) an error-detecting code similar to a CHECKSUM, but computed with a more elaborate algorithm. Data stored on a disk is normally accompanied by a CRC.

creeping featurism (*slang*) the practice of trying to improve software by adding features in an unsystematic way, ultimately making it less reliable and harder to use. *Compare* BELLS AND WHISTLES.

crippleware (*slang*) software that is distributed free as an incomplete or time-limited version in the hope that the user will purchase the fully functional version.

CRLF (**c**arriage **r**eturn, **l**ine **f**eed) a pair of ASCII codes, 13 and 10, that tell a terminal or printer to return to the beginning of the line and advance to the next line. Under Windows and DOS, CRLF indicates the end of a line in a text file; the Macintosh uses CR alone and UNIX uses LF alone. *See* CR, LF.

crossover cable a cable with RJ-45 connectors that swap the input and output lines. A crossover cable can sometimes (but not always) be used to connect two computers with 10base-T networking without a hub. Crossover cables do for networking what null modems do for serial communication. *See* RJ-45 (wiring table). *Compare* NULL MODEM.

cross-platform applicable to more than one kind of computer (e.g., PC and Macintosh).

cross-post to place a single copy of a message into two or more newsgroups at once. This is less expensive than posting separate copies of it in different newsgroups. It also ensures that all replies made in any of the newgroups will be cross-posted to all of them. *See* NEWSGROUP.

CRT (**C**athode **R**ay **T**ube) a glass tube with a screen that glows when struck by electrons. An image is formed by constantly scanning the screen with an electron beam. Examples of CRTs include television screens and computer monitors. *See also* EYEGLASSES FOR COMPUTER USERS.

crunch mode *(slang)* a work situation in which a deadline is near and everyone is working hard, keeping extended hours. Crunch mode is usually the result of a mistaken estimate made by management, not a genuine emergency. *See* SOFTWARE ENGINEERING.

cryptography the technology of encoding information so that it cannot be read by an unauthorized person. *See* ENCRYPTION and its cross-references.

C/SC text typeset in capitals and small capitals (LIKE THIS). Sometimes written "C + SC." *See also* CAPS; SMALL CAPS; U/LC; *contrast* EVEN SMALLS.

CSMA/CD *see* ETHERNET.

CSS extension for a style sheet file to be used in an HTML document. *See* CASCADING STYLE SHEET.

Ctrl *see* CONTROL KEY.

Ctrl-Alt-Del the key combination that reboots a PC-compatible computer under DOS. That is, the computer reboots if you hold down Ctrl and Alt and press Del. Under OS/2, Ctrl-Alt-Del empties the file buffers (like the UNIX `sync` command) and reboots as quickly as possible.

   Under Windows 3.1, Ctrl-Alt-Del kills the currently executing program rather than rebooting the whole computer. Under Windows 95 and its successors, Ctrl-Alt-Del brings up a menu of processes; the user can then choose which ones, if any, to terminate. Under Windows NT, users must press Ctrl-Alt-Del before logging in.

CUA (**C**ommon **U**ser **A**ccess) a set of guidelines promoted by IBM for standardizing the way computer programs communicate with the people using them. CUA includes standards for the design of menus and the use of keystrokes. All software manufacturers are encouraged to follow CUA guidelines. However, it now appears that Microsoft's guidelines for the Windows user interface are more influential than IBM's CUA. The two are fairly similar. *See also* SAA; USER INTERFACE.

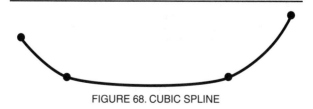

FIGURE 68. CUBIC SPLINE

cubic spline a curve that connects a set of points smoothly by solving a system of cubic equations. Unlike a Bézier spline, a cubic spline is defined only by the points that the curve must pass through; it has no control points that are not on the curve.

Cubic splines are the natural shapes of bent objects that are secured at particular points and are free to bend in between. The spline goes through each point smoothly, without sharp bends.

Each segment of the spline (from one point to the next) is modeled by a third-degree (cubic) polynomial of the form $y = ax^3 + bx^2 + cx + d$, where a, b, c, and d depend on the endpoints of the segment and the slope that the segment should have at each end.

If (x_1, y_1) and (x_2, y_2) are the endpoints and y'_1 and y'_2 are the slopes, then a, b, c, and d can be found by solving the four-equation system:

$$
\begin{aligned}
y_1 &= ax_1^3 + bx_1^2 + cx_1 + d \\
y_2 &= ax_2^3 + bx_2^2 + cx_2 + d \\
y'_1 &= 3ax_1^2 + 2bx_1 + c \\
y'_2 &= 3ax_2^2 + 2bx_2 + c
\end{aligned}
$$

More commonly, the slopes are not known, but the slope at the end of each segment is set equal to the slope at the beginning of the next segment. The slopes and coefficients are then found by solving a system of simultaneous linear equations (linear because x, x^2, and x^3 are known and can be treated as constants).

cue (animation and presentation programs) an embedded code that specifies when an action is to occur.

current the flow of electrical charge. Current is measured in amperes; 1 ampere = 6.25×10^{18} electrons per second = 1 coulomb per second.

current loop a predecessor of RS-232 serial communication; it is occasionally still seen on older equipment. (*See* RS-232.) Do not connect current loop equipment directly to RS-232 equipment; the current loop system uses voltages as high as 100 volts and can cause damage.

cursor the symbol on a computer terminal that shows you where on the screen the next character you type will appear. Cursors often appear as blinking dashes or rectangles. Many computers have cursor movement (arrow) keys that allow you to move the cursor vertically or horizontally around the screen. This ability is essential for text-editing purposes such as word processing. You can use the mouse to move the cursor quickly around the screen. *Compare* MOUSE POINTER; INSERTION POINT.

cusp node a type of NODE that marks a sudden change in the direction of the line. *See* Figure 69. *Contrast* SMOOTH NODE.

cut to remove material from the document you are editing and place it into a holding area. *See* COPY; PASTE; CLIPBOARD.

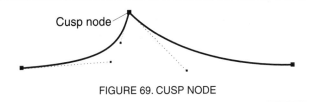

FIGURE 69. CUSP NODE

cyan a vivid greenish-blue color that is one of the standard printing ink colors. *See* CMYK.

cyber- *(prefix) see* CYBERNETICS.

cybernetics the study of the processing of information by machinery, especially computers and control systems; derived from Greek *kybernētēs* meaning "helmsman"; first conceived in the 1940s. Cybernetics has evolved into computer science, operations research, and a number of other fields. The prefix *cyber-* on numerous computer terms is derived from this word.

cyberpunk an antisocial person who uses computers as a means of self-expression, often performing destructive acts; also a genre of science fiction dating from William Gibson's 1982 novel *Neuromancer.*

cyberspace the part of human society and culture that exists in networked computer systems rather than in any particular physical location. For example, cyberspace is where most bank accounts and electronic messages reside.

cyburbia (**cyber** s**uburbia**) the community of computer users that exists in cyberspace. *See* CYBERSPACE; NETIZEN.

cycle one oscillation of a computer's CPU CLOCK; the shortest step into which computer actions can be divided. When two or more programs are running at once, they are said to be competing for cycles.

cyclical redundancy check *see* CRC.

cylinder *see* DISK.

Cyrillic the Russian alphabet. Contrast LATIN.

Cyrix a manufacturer of microprocessors, including the 5x86 and 6x86, which are compatible substitutes for Intel's 486 and Pentium. (*See* MICROPROCESSOR.) Cyrix is now part of VIA Technologies. Their web address is www.viatech.com.

D

DAC, D/A converter *see* DIGITAL-TO-ANALOG CONVERTER.

daemon (under UNIX) a program that runs continuously in the background, or is activated by a particular event. The word *daemon* is Greek for "spirit" or "soul."

dagger the character †, sometimes used to mark footnotes. *See also* FOOTNOTE. Also called an OBELISK or LONG CROSS.

daisy-chain to connect devices together in sequence with cables. For example, if four devices A, B, C, and D are daisy-chained, there will be a cable from A to B, a cable from B to C, and a cable from C to D.

daisywheel printer a printer that uses a rotating plastic wheel as a type element. Daisywheel printers were often used with microcomputers in the early 1980s. They printed high-quality text, but they were relatively slow and could not print graphics.

dash (—) a punctuation mark similar to a hyphen, but longer. On a typewriter, a dash is typed as two hyphens. (In WordPerfect, it should be typed as two required hyphens, so that a line break will not be placed between them; *see* REQUIRED HYPHEN.)

Proportional-pitch type often includes one or more kinds of dashes, such as an em dash (—), which is as wide as the height of the font, and an en dash (–), which is two-thirds as wide as the em dash. Normally, the em dash joins sentences and the en dash joins numbers (as in "1995–98").

data information. The word was originally the plural of *datum,* which means "a single fact," but is now used as a collective singular. Data processing is the act of using data for making calculations or decisions.

database a collection of data stored on a computer storage medium, such as a disk, that can be used for more than one purpose. For example, a firm that maintains a database containing information on its employees will be able to use the same data for payroll, personnel, and other purposes. *See* DATABASE MANAGEMENT.

database management the task of storing data in a database and retrieving information from that data. There are three aspects of database management: entering data, modifying or updating data, and presenting output reports. Many mainframe computers are used by businesses for database management purposes. Several software packages are available for database management on microcomputers, such as dBASE and Microsoft Access, and some data management capabilities are provided with spreadsheets such as Lotus 1-2-3 and Excel. Some examples of database applications include maintaining employee

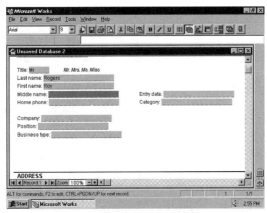

FIGURE 70. DATABASE

lists and preparing payrolls; maintaining parts order lists and keeping track of inventories; maintaining customer lists, and preparing bills for credit customers; and keeping track of the students at a school.

Information in a database system is generally stored in several different files. For example, a business will often have a file of regular customers and a file of employees. Each file consists of a series of records, each representing one person or one transaction. Each record consists of several fields, with each field containing an individual data item. For example, in an employee file there would be one record for each employee, and there would be a field containing the person's name, a field for the address, a field for the Social Security number, and so on. A database management system must make provisions for adding new records (e.g., when an employee is hired); for deleting unneeded records (e.g., when an employee retires); and for modifying existing records. Some fields (such as the Social Security number) will not change; other fields (such as year-to-date pay) must be changed frequently.

The main purpose of a database management system is to make it possible to obtain meaningful information from the data contained in the database. A database program can respond to brief queries on the screen, or it can present detailed printed reports in a format chosen by the user. Here are some general functions that a database management system should be able to fulfill:

1. Sort the records according to the order indicated by one specific field (e.g., sort in alphabetical order by name, or in numerical order by zip code). You should be able to designate a secondary field along which sorting will occur when there are ties in the

primary field. For example, if you are sorting the records by the number of months the customers are overdue in their payments, you probably would like the names of all people 1 month overdue in alphabetical order, then the names of all people 2 months overdue in alphabetical order and so on.

2. Set up selection criteria that allow you to examine only the records that meet a specific condition. For example, you may wish to look only at customers who live in your city, or you may wish to look at all employees whose job title is either "delivery driver" or "warehouse worker."

3. Count the number of records that meet a specific condition. For example, you may wish to count the number of employees who have been with the company for more than 10 years.

4. Perform calculations, such as computing the total amount owed on overdue accounts, or the year-to-date pay for each employee.

5. Connect information from more than one file. For example, a database system might contain an employee file that lists the job classification for each employee. A separate file for each job classification would contain information on wages, fringe benefits, and work schedules that apply to all workers in that classification.

(*See also* RELATIONAL DATABASE; SQL.)

data bits a parameter of RS-232 serial communication. Either 7 or 8 bits are used for each character, preceded by a *start bit* and followed by a *parity bit* (optional) and a *stop bit. See also* RS-232; XMODEM; KERMIT.

data communication the transfer of information from one computer to another. In order for communication to take place, several aspects of the communication process must be standardized. The international OSI (Open Systems Interconnection) standard (ISO Standard 7498) defines seven layers at which decisions have to be made:

1. *Physical layer.* What kind of electrical signals are sent from machine to machine? For examples of standards on this level, *see* 10BASE-T; RS-232; MODEM.

2. *Link layer.* How do the two machines coordinate the physical sending and receiving of signals? For examples, *see* HANDSHAKING; PACKET.

3. *Network layer.* How does one machine establish a connection with the other? This covers such things as telephone dialing and the routing of packets. For examples, *see* HAYES COMPATIBILITY (command chart); PACKET; COLLISION; X.25.

4. *Transport layer.* How do the computers identify each other and coordinate the sending of messages back and forth? This is the level at which most network protocols operate. For examples, *see* TCP/IP; NETBEUI; IPX/SPX.

5. *Session layer.* How do users establish connections, log on, and identify themselves?

6. *Presentation layer.* What does the information look like when received on the user's machine? The presentation layer includes file format and filename conversions and the like.

7. *Application layer.* How do software use the network—that is, how do application programs exchange data? The application layer does not consist of the programs themselves but, rather, the communication facilities that they use.

The OSI standard does not specify what any of these layers should look like; it merely defines a framework in terms of which future standards can be expressed. In a simple system, some of the layers are handled manually or are trivially simple.

data compression the storage of data in a way that makes it occupy less space than if it were stored in its original form. For example, long sequences of repeated characters can be replaced with short codes that mean "The following character is repeated 35 times," or the like. A more thorough form of data compression involves using codes of different lengths for different character sequences so that the most common sequences take up less space.

Most text files can be compressed to about half their normal size. Digitized images can often be compressed to 10 percent of their original size (or even more if some loss of fine detail can be tolerated), but machine-language programs sometimes cannot be compressed at all because they contain no recurrent patterns. *See also* ZIP FILE; STUFFIT; PCX; JPEG; MPEG.

datagram a PACKET of information transmitted by NETWORK.

data rate *see* BAUD.

data set

1. (in older telephone company nomenclature) a MODEM.

2. (in OS/360 and related IBM operating systems) a file, referred to under the name by which it is known to the operating system. (The file is known to any particular program by another name, the "filename," specified by the JCL DD statement, TSO `allocate` command, or CMS `filedef` command.)

data structures ways of arranging information in the memory of a computer. In computer programming, it is often necessary to store large numbers of items in such a manner as to reflect a relationship between them. The three basic ways of doing this are the following:

1. An *array* consists of many items of the same type, identified by number. The examination scores of a college class might be represented as an array of numbers. A picture can be represented as a large array of brightness readings, one for each of the thousands of cells into which the picture is divided.

2. A *record* consists of items of different types, stored together. For example, the teacher's record of an individual student might consist of a name (character data), number of absences (an integer), and a grade average (a floating-point number). Records and arrays can be combined. The teacher's records of the entire class form an array of individual records; each record might contain, among other things, an array of test scores.

3. A *linked list* is like an array except that the physical memory locations in which the items are stored are not necessarily consecutive; instead, the location of the next item is stored alongside each item. This makes it possible to insert items in the middle of the list without moving other items to make room. More complex linked structures, such as *trees,* can be constructed by storing more than one address with each item.

   See ARRAY; RECORD; LINKED LIST.

data types ranges of possible values that a data item might have. Some possible data types include integers, real numbers, Boolean values, and character strings. Some languages, such as Pascal and Java, are very strict about requiring that the type of each variable be declared before it can be used, and an error message occurs if a program attempts to assign an inappropriate value to a variable. Other languages make default assumptions about the types for variables if they are not declared (*see* FORTRAN.)

The advantage of requiring data types to be declared is that it forces programmers to be more disciplined with their use of variables, and the computer can detect certain types of errors. There also can be disadvantages with a language requiring strict declaration of data types. For example, some operations (such as swapping the values of two variables) are essentially the same for any data type, so it should not be necessary to include separate subroutines for each type.

Individual data items can be arranged into various types of structures. *See* DATA STRUCTURES.

daughterboard, daughtercard a small circuit board that plugs into a larger one. *Contrast* MOTHERBOARD.

day trading the practice of buying stocks or other securities and reselling them within a day (or less) to profit from short-term fluctuations. Before the Internet, day trading was possible only by spending all your time at a stockbroker's office; otherwise you would not see market results quickly enough to act upon them. Nowadays, day trading can be carried out on line. *See* ON-LINE TRADING.

dB abbreviation for DECIBEL.

dBm power level in decibels relative to a level of one milliwatt; used to measure signal strength on telephone lines. *See* DECIBEL.

DCE (**D**ata **C**ommunications **E**quipment) equipment that uses RS-232 serial communications, with conductor 2 for input and conductor 3 for output. Equipment that uses conductor 3 for input and 2 for output is called DTE (Data Terminal Equipment). A standard RS-232 cable can link two pieces of equipment only if one of them is DTE and the other is DCE; otherwise, both will try to transmit and receive on the same conductors, and a special cable that interchanges conductors 2 and 3 must be used. Most PC serial ports are configured as DTE; most modems as DCE.

DCOM (**D**istributed **C**ommon **O**bject **M**odel) a Microsoft-developed standard for allowing software components to interact with each other over a network. For an alternative standard, *see* CORBA.

DDE (**D**ynamic **D**ata **E**xchange) in Microsoft Windows and OS/2, a mechanism by which some programs can exchange data with each other while they are running. For example, through DDE, a cell in a spreadsheet can be connected to data that is being continuously updated by some other program. In this case the spreadsheet is the DDE client (the information requester) and the other program is the DDE server. A DDE connection between programs is called a *hot link* if the shared data can be updated continuously by the server, or a *cold link* if the data is updated only when the client requests it. In Windows 3.1, DDE was largely supplanted by OLE (Object Linking and Embedding), a more sophisticated technique for achieving the same results. *See* OLE.

dead link an HTML address that is no longer valid. When a dead link is selected, the browser returns an error message.

Dead links are the result of the target web page having moved to a new location, an HTML programming error (usually a mistyped filename), or the server being overloaded. Try the link again later when the Internet is not as busy. If you still get an error message, you may want to e-mail the appropriate WEBMASTER about the dead link.

deadlock a situation in which each of two processes is waiting for the other to do something; thus, neither one can proceed. *See* MULTITASKING.

dead start *see* BOOT.

deblurring the use of digital image processing to correct a blurred image. In order for this to be possible, the exact nature of the blur must be known; sometimes it can be inferred from the appearance of a small, bright object in the picture. *See* IMAGE PROCESSING; SHARPEN.

debug to remove errors from a program. With a complicated program, it often takes longer to correct errors than it did to write the program in the first place.

In DOS, the DEBUG command allows you to manipulate the contents of memory and modify disk sectors. Considerable knowledge of machine language programming is needed in order to use DEBUG

effectively. Symbolic debuggers, which show you the source program
as well as the machine code, are generally easier to use. *See* SYMBOLIC
DEBUGGER.

DEC *see* DIGITAL EQUIPMENT CORPORATION.

deca- metric prefix meaning ×10 (= 10^1). *Deca-* is derived from the
Greek word for "ten." *See* METRIC PREFIXES.

deci- metric prefix meaning ÷10. *Deci-* is derived from the Latin word
for "ten." *See* METRIC PREFIXES.

decibel (dB) a unit of relative loudness or power; one tenth of a *bel* (a
unit named for Alexander Graham Bell and now rarely used). Decibels
are used in three ways:

  1. to express the ratio of two power levels:

$$dB = 10 \log_{10} \frac{\text{first power level}}{\text{second power level}}$$

For example, multiplying power by 2 is equivalent to adding about
3 decibels; multiplying power by 10 is equivalent to adding 10
decibels; and multiplying by 100 is equivalent to adding 20 decibels.

  2. to express the ratio of two voltage levels:

$$dB = 20 \log_{10} \frac{\text{first voltage level}}{\text{second voltage level}}$$

Because power is proportional to the square of voltage, this is
equivalent to the previous formula if both voltages are driving the
same load impedance.

  3. to describe the loudness of a sound, expressed in decibels relative
to the threshold of human hearing. Clearly audible sounds range
from about 20 to 100 dB; those much above 100 dB are painful
to the ears.

decimal number a number expressed in ordinary base-10 notation,
using the digits 0, 1, 2, 3, 4, 5, 6, 7, 8, 9, whether or not there are any
digits to the right of the point. For example, 3.14 is a decimal number,
and so is 314.

deck a stack of PUNCHED CARDS (now obsolete).

declare to state the attributes of a variable. In some programming languages, such as Pascal, C, and Java, all variables must be declared. This
protects the programmer from accidentally creating another variable
by misspelling a variable name. In BASIC and FORTRAN, declaring
variables is optional, and declarations are used mainly to create arrays
or other variables of special types.

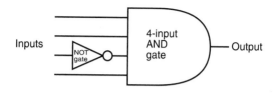

FIGURE 71. DECODER FOR THE BIT PATTERN 1101

decoder a circuit that recognizes a particular pattern of bits. Decoders are used in computers in order to recognize instructions and addresses. Figure 71 shows a decoder that recognizes the bit pattern 1101.

decryption decoding — that is, translating information from an unreadable or secret format into a form in which it can be used. *Contrast* ENCRYPTION.

dedicated assigned to only one function. For instance, a dedicated phone line is one that is always connected to the same equipment.

de facto standard a standard that is not official but is established by widespread usage.

default an assumption that a computer makes unless it is given specific instructions to the contrary. For example, a word processing program may start out assuming a particular default combination of margins, page length, and so on, which the user can change by issuing specific commands.

default directory (**current directory**) the directory on each disk in which the operating system looks for files if no directory is specified. In DOS, OS/2, Windows 95, 98, and NT, and UNIX, the user chooses the directory with the command cd or chdir. *See* DIRECTORY.

default drive (**current drive, logged drive**) the disk drive that the computer uses when not told to use another one. Under DOS, OS/2, and similar operating systems, typing a drive designator as a command (for example, c:) changes the default drive.

default logic (**defeasible logic**) a formal system of reasoning in which some facts or rules have priority over others. For example, statements about ostriches might have priority over statements about birds because an ostrich is a specific kind of bird. It is then possible to say without contradiction that birds fly, but ostriches don't fly. In classical logic, "birds fly" and "ostriches are birds" together with "ostriches don't fly" is a contradiction.

   Default logic is often used in expert systems. *See* EXPERT SYSTEM; *contrast* FUZZY LOGIC; CONFIDENCE FACTOR. *See also* BOOLEAN ALGEBRA.

defeasible logic *see* DEFAULT LOGIC.

deform (3D program) to digitally manipulate an on-screen object so that it is twisted or stretched. Some programs allow you to deform objects interactively; other transformations are done with FILTERS that can distort or break up the object during an animation.

degauss to demagnetize. Color monitors need to be degaussed when they show areas of weak or incorrect color. Some monitors degauss themselves every time they are turned on. If you wish to repeat the degauss cycle on such a monitor, wait 5 seconds each time you turn it on or off before flipping the switch again; otherwise, the power supply may be damaged.

degree measure a way of measuring the size of angles in which a complete rotation has a measure of 360 degrees (written as 360°). A right angle is 90°. *Contrast* RADIAN MEASURE.

Deja.com (more precisely, www.deja.com, formerly known as Deja-News) an Internet site that provides a search engine for newsgroups, as well as the ability to read newsgroups and post messages. Some users get the mistaken impression that Deja.com owns or runs the entire newsgroup system. In 2000 Deja.com shifted its main focus to product selection and commercial site search, although the newsgroup search engine remains available. *See* NEWSGROUP; SEARCH ENGINE.

Deja News *see* DEJA.COM.

Del the DELETE key on a computer keyboard.

delete to remove an unwanted item (character, word, art, file). *See* RECOVERING ERASED FILES for help on restoring deleted files.

delimiters symbols that mark the beginning or end of a special part of a program. For instance, { and } are the delimiters for comments in Pascal (*see* PASCAL).

Delphi a Pascal-based programming language that can be used to create Windows programs. Delphi is a product of Borland International. *See* PASCAL.

demibold in between ordinary type and boldface. Sometimes just called *demi*. *See* WEIGHT.

demon *see* DAEMON.

denial-of-service attack a malicious attack on a computer whose purpose is to interfere with the computer's normal functioning, rather than to gain services for oneself or steal confidential data. Denial-of-service attacks are often launched by people who are frustrated at not being able to break into a computer, or who are angry at the target computer's users or administrators. Often the attackers do not realize they are disrupting service for everyone, not just for a single intended victim. For examples, *see* MAIL BOMBING; PING FLOODING. *See also* COMPUTER SECURITY.

DES (**D**igital **E**ncryption **S**tandard) an encryption system using 56-bit keys in a complicated 16-round substitution process. It has been a federal standard since 1976.

j   p   q   y

FIGURE 72. DESCENDERS

descender the part of a character that extends below the baseline. For instance, the letter *p* has a descender; the letter *o* does not. *See* ASCENDER; TYPEFACE.

deselect to tell the computer you do not want to work with a particular object. There are minor differences in how different software does this, but clicking on the background or another object will usually deselect the current object. If you want to select multiple objects, you can hold down Ctrl while clicking on the desired objects. This allows you to select as many items as you want. To deselect just one item of a group, click on it again while continuing to hold Ctrl. If you are choosing between mutually exclusive options in a dialog box, choosing one button will clear the others (*see* RADIO BUTTONS; OPTION BUTTONS).

Hint: If you wish to select all but one or two objects in a drawing, the fastest way is to "Select All" (either by using the edit menu option or by MARQUEE SELECT), and then deselect the unwanted objects.

desk accessory a small, useful program that is meant to be always at hand while you are working at your computer. Examples include the clock, calculator, Character Map (KeyCaps for Mac users) and the Control Panel. All Macintosh programs provide access to the Desk Accessories under the Apple menu. Windows desk accessories are found in the Accessories program group.

deskew to straighten; to undo the effects of a SKEW command.

desktop the whole computer screen, representing your workspace. You manipulate objects (ICONS) with the mouse in much the same way that you work with papers and other objects on your physical desktop.

On the Macintosh and in OS/2, the desktop is also a special file containing information about the arrangement of icons, the programs you are using, and the like. This information is saved whenever you

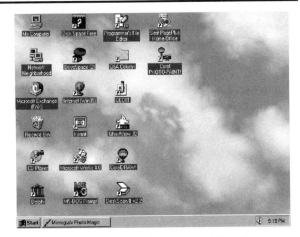

FIGURE 73. DESKTOP (WINDOWS 95)

shut the computer down and retrieved when you turn it on again. On the Macintosh, obsolete information accumulates in the desktop file and eventually the desktop needs to be rebuilt (reconstructed). *See* REBUILD DESKTOP.

In Windows 95 and 98, the desktop is a special directory called \windows\desktop. It normally contains many SHORTCUTS to program files in other locations. The shortcuts are represented by files with the extension .lnk.

The desktop is not identical with the ROOT DIRECTORY of a disk; it is more like a directory containing everything on the computer, including the disk drives. In Windows 95 and Windows 98, the disk drives are accessed through a desktop icon called "My Computer."

Desktop, Active *see* ACTIVE DESKTOP.

desktop publishing the use of personal computers to design and print professional-quality typeset documents. (*See* TYPEFACE.) A desktop publishing program such as PageMaker or QuarkXpress is much more versatile than a word processing program; in addition to typing documents, the user can specify the layout in great detail, use multiple input files, have comprehensive typographic control, insert pictures, and preview the appearance of the printed document on the screen.

Since 1990, the distinction between word processing and desktop publishing has become blurred. Most word processing programs can produce elegantly typeset documents. The difference is that desktop publishing programs put more emphasis on graphic design and facilities for handling more complex works.

A new facet of desktop publishing is ELECTRONIC PUBLISHING; producing documents that are meant to be viewed on screen, not printed out. These electronic documents are distributed by computer networks (*see* WORLD WIDE WEB) or CD-ROMs. An electronic document may have sound, music, illustrations, animations, video clips, or HYPERTEXT links (special buttons or keywords that jump the reader to a new text or picture). So, soon it will not be enough to be a master of typography, grammar, illustration, graphic design, and computer technology, but we will all need a course in film editing and musical scoring.

/dev in UNIX, the directory that contains links to specific devices such as disk drives and serial and parallel ports.

device contention the situation in which several computer programs, running concurrently, are trying to use the same device (such as a modem or printer) at the same time. Multitasking operating systems handle contention in a number of different ways, such as SPOOLING output for printers, making a program wait until the requested device is available, or simply denying access to a device that is already in use.

device driver a program that extends the operating system in order to support a specific device, such as a disk or tape drive, video card, or printer.

Device drivers are a very important part of Microsoft Windows. They insulate application programs from the hardware so that, for example, the manufacturer of a word processing program does not have to know what kind of printer you are going to be using, and if a new printer is invented in the future, you can use it even if it wasn't anticipated when the program was written. Installation of device drivers usually happens automatically when hardware or software is installed; you can also add and remove device drivers from the Control Panel (*see* CONTROL PANEL; PLUG AND PLAY).

One controversial feature of Windows 95 is that, even though it is a 32-bit operating system, it can still use 16-bit device drivers from Windows 3 and even DOS. This interferes to some extent with the multitasking capability of Windows 95 and makes it vulnerable to crashes, but it also means that old and idiosyncratic hardware can continue to be used without waiting for new device drivers that may never be written.

In DOS and OS/2, device drivers are usually installed by referring to them in the CONFIG.SYS file (*see* CONFIG.SYS). The term *device driver* also refers to programs or configuration files that enable a word processor or other applications program to use a particular device, such as a printer driver in WordPerfect.

device ID a unique name given to a hardware device for use by PLUG AND PLAY and the Windows 95–98 REGISTRY.

device node a directory entry, similar to the directory entry for a file but identifying a piece of hardware. Under UNIX, device nodes are found in the directory /dev.

/dev/null in UNIX, a "device" that is actually a place for discarding data. Anything written to /dev/null is discarded, and any software that attempts to read from /dev/null is told that no data is available. You can specify /dev/null in places where a filename is required but no data will actually be read or written. *Compare* BIT BUCKET.

dewarp to straighten; to undo the effects of a WARP manipulation.

Dhrystone *see* MIPS.

DHTML *see* DYNAMIC HTML.

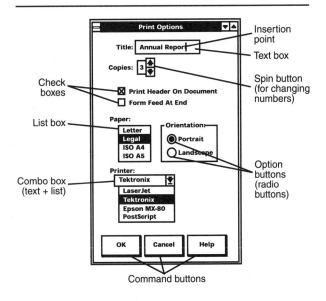

FIGURE 74. DIALOG BOX

dialog box a window that appears in order to collect information from the user. When the user has filled in the necessary information or clicked on the appropriate buttons, the dialog box disappears. Fig. 74 shows a dialog box containing several different kinds of elements. There is almost always an OK button for the user to click after filling in the information. *See also* COMMAND BUTTON; OPTION BUTTONS; LIST BOX; TEXT BOX; CHECK BOX.

dial-up connection a connection between computers established by dialing a telephone number through a MODEM.

dial-up networking computer networking that relies on communication through ordinary telephone lines via MODEM.

FIGURE 75. DIFFUSE FILTER

diffuse a photopaint filter that randomly scatters colors. The effect is rather impressionistic if you set the degree of diffusion relatively high or repeat the filter process. You might want to experiment case by case to see if the diffuse or BLUR filter gives the desired effect.

digital representing information as electrical "on" and "off" signals that correspond to binary digits and can be stored in computer memory. Digital electronics contrasts with analog electronics, which represents information with signals that vary within a predefined range. Digital signals have two advantages: they can be copied exactly, without even the slightest loss of quality, and they can be further processed by computer. *See also* DIGITAL COMPUTER.

digital audio sound represented in digital form. *See* WAVE FILE; MP3; DIGITIZED MUSIC.

digital camera a camera that takes pictures with a CCD (charge-coupled device) and transmits them directly to a computer or records them on disk without using film.

The most important specification of a digital camera is the number of PIXELS in the image. To show as much detail as a good 35-mm slide, a digital image requires about 2000×3000 pixels. Only the best digital cameras achieve this. A much lower resolution, 480 × 640 pixels, is sufficient for snapshots. The image on a TV screen is equivalent to about 400×600 pixels.

digital computer a computer that represents information in discrete form, as opposed to an analog computer, which allows representation to vary along a continuum. For example, the temperature of a room might be any value between 0° and 100°F. An analog computer could represent this as a continuously varying voltage between 0.00 and 1.00 volts. In contrast, a digital computer would have to represent it as a decimal or binary number with a specific number of digits (e.g., 68.80 or 68.81).

All modern, general-purpose computers are digital. Analog computer circuits are, however, frequently used in industrial control equipment.

A digital computer is more accurate than an analog computer because it only needs to sense the difference between clearly distinguishable states. For example, a slight voltage fluctuation would affect the result in an analog computer, but a slight voltage fluctuation would not affect a digital computer because the computer could still easily distinguish the 0 state from the 1 state of any circuit element. For the same reason, digital music reproduction (e.g., a compact disc) is more accurate than analog reproductions (e.g., a traditional record).

Digital Equipment Corporation (DEC) a large manufacturer of computer equipment headquartered in Maynard, Massachusetts. Important DEC products have included the PDP-8, PDP-11, and VAX minicomputers, the VT-100 terminal, and the Alpha microprocessor. In 1998, Digital Equipment Corporation was aquired by Compaq.

digital film the memory cards or other storage devices used in digital cameras. Unlike real photographic film, the brand of digital film does not affect the quality of the picture or the amount of light required to make it. The digital memory device simply records whatever the camera gets.

digital image processing *see* IMAGE PROCESSING.

digital press a printing press that can print directly from a computer file, bypassing the stages of CAMERA-READY COPY and PREPRESS production.

digital signal processing (DSP) the use of computers to process signals such as sound or video. Applications of DSP include decoding modulated signals (e.g., in modems), removing noise, and converting video to different formats.

digital signature a way of authenticating that an electronic message really came from the person it claims to have come from. A digital signature can be encrypted with your PRIVATE KEY. The recipient can decrypt the message with your PUBLIC KEY to verify that it is really you. Nobody who does not know your private key could create a signature that would correctly decrypt with your public key. However, the digital signature cannot be sent by itself, because then someone could simply copy the encrypted version. Instead, the signature needs to be sent as part of an abstract (or manifest or digest) of a particular message. The recipient can check to make sure that the hash function given in the manifest matches the hash function calculated from the message. If someone tampered with the original message (so they could attach their own message to your digital signature) the mismatch would be detected.

digital-to-analog converter an electronic circuit that converts digital information (binary numbers) into voltages at specific levels. DACs are used to generate sound and video signals. *Contrast* ANALOG-TO-DIGITAL CONVERTER.

digitize to convert input into a form that can be processed by a computer. *See* FRAME GRABBER; SCANNER.

digitized music music represented as computer data, either by recording the sound waves themselves (*see* WAVE FILE; SAMPLING RATE; MP3) or by storing a musical score in digital form (*see* MIDI).

dimensions (of an array) the different directions in which elements can be counted. Each dimension corresponds to one subscript. A list of objects is a one-dimensional array, while a table is a two-dimensional array. *See* ARRAY.

DIMM (**d**ual **i**nline **m**emory **m**odule) a memory module similar to a SIMM but with different signals on the two sides of the tiny circuit board. DIMMs usually have 168 pins; compared to SIMMs, they allow more memory to be installed in fewer sockets. *See* SIMM.

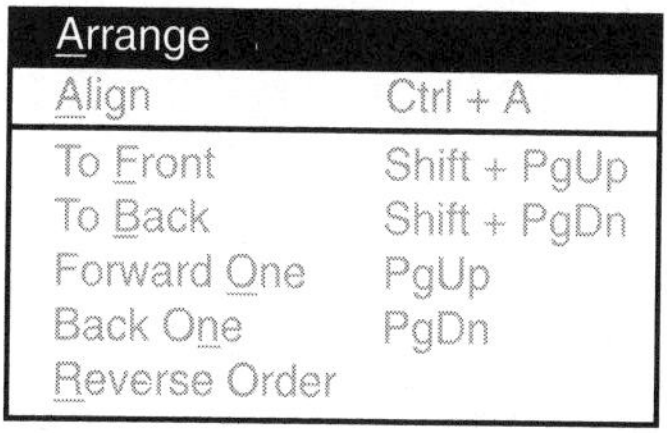

FIGURE 76. DIMMED TYPE INDICATES UNAVAILABLE ITEMS

dimmed not available for selection. If a menu option appears in light gray rather than black type, it cannot be chosen. For example, if you wish to align two objects, the align command will be dimmed until you have two or more objects selected. If you click on a dimmed command, nothing happens. *See* Figure 76.

dingbats special characters that are neither letters nor mathematical symbols, such as ‡ ♠ ♡ ◇ ♣ ↔. *See also* FLEURON.

DIN paper sizes *see* PAPER SIZES (ISO).

diode a semiconductor device that allows electric current to pass in one direction, but not in the other. Diodes are formed by joining two types of doped semiconductors: P type, with a deficiency of free electrons (and an excess of holes), and N type, with a surplus of free electrons. (*See* SEMICONDUCTOR.) The place where the two regions are joined is called the junction.

Electrons can flow from N-type to P-type material, but not the other way. The diode is said to be *forward-biased* when the voltage across it is in the right direction to make it conduct, and *reverse-biased* when the voltage is applied in the opposite direction. The diode is forward biased when a negative voltage is applied to the N region and a positive voltage to the P region; then free electrons in the N region are driven to the junction where they combine with holes from the P region. If a positive voltage is applied to the N region, electrons are pulled away from the junction and no current can flow (the diode is reverse biased).

See also TRANSISTOR; LED; ELECTRONIC CIRCUIT DIAGRAM SYMBOLS.

DIP switch a miniature switch or set of switches often used in computer equipment. DIP, or *dual inline package,* means that the switch is the same size and shape as an integrated circuit.

dir the command, under DOS, OS/2, and other operating systems, that makes the computer display all the files in a particular directory. For example,

```
dir
```

by itself lists the files in the current directory of the current disk. Here are some other examples:

```
dir a:              Current directory of drive A
dir a:\mystuff      Directory MYSTUFF of drive A
dir \mystuff        Directory MYSTUFF of the current disk
dir mystuff         Subdirectory MYSTUFF under the current
                    directory of the current disk
```

To see a directory of all of the files on the current drive that have names ending in .bas, type

```
dir *.bas
```

The asterisk acts as a "wild card," matching all filenames.

directory an area on a disk where the names and locations of files are stored. A disk can, and usually does, contain more than one directory; directories can contain other directories.

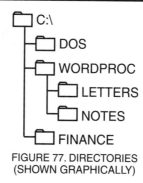

FIGURE 77. DIRECTORIES
(SHOWN GRAPHICALLY)

On the Macintosh and in Windows 95 and later, directories are called *folders.* Under Windows, OS/2, and various UNIX windowing systems, directories are pictured as tree structures or boxes within boxes (Fig. 77).

Directories are a way of classifying files; they do not divide the disk itself into sections. Any file can use as much space as needed, anywhere on the disk, regardless of what directory it is in.

disassembler a program that converts machine instructions into assembly language so that a human being can read them. DOS includes a disassembler in its debug utility; Fig. 78 shows an example of its use.

```
C:\PROG\C>debug info.exe
-u
13C9:0000 BAB319      MOV    DX,19B3
13C9:0003 2E          CS:
13C9:0004 89163502    MOV    [0235],DX
13C9:0008 B430        MOV    AH,30
13C9:000A CD21        INT    21
13C9:000C 8B2E0200    MOV    BP,[0002]
13C9:0010 8B1E2C00    MOV    BX,[002C]
13C9:0014 8EDA        MOV    DS,DX
13C9:0016 A39000      MOV    [0090],AX
13C9:0019 8C068E00    MOV    [008E],ES
13C9:001D 891E8A00    MOV    [008A],BX
-
```

FIGURE 78. DISASSEMBLING
A MACHINE-LANGUAGE PROGRAM

TABLE 3
TYPES OF DISKETTES USED ON
PC-COMPATIBLE COMPUTERS

Size	Density	Sides	Capacity	
$5\frac{1}{4}''$	DD	Single	180K	(obsolete)
$5\frac{1}{4}''$	DD	Double	360K	(obsolete)
$5\frac{1}{4}''$	HD	Double	1.2M	(occasionally used)
$3\frac{1}{2}''$	DD	Double	720K	(obsolete)
$3\frac{1}{2}''$	HD	Double	1.44M	(popular)
$3\frac{1}{2}''$	ED	Double	2.88M	(rare)

disc a compact disc (CD) or digital video disc (DVD). *See* DISK and usage note there.

disclaimer a statement absolving someone (or even oneself) of responsibility. The so-called "usual disclaimer" on e-mail messages is roughly, "These are not the opinions of my employer or the organization that transmits this message for me." Many people abbreviate this to "usual disclaimer applies." The disclaimer is unnecessary unless there is something about the e-mail message that would specifically cause people to misunderstand it.

discrete speech speech that is spoken with pauses between words to make it easier for a computer to recognize. *Contrast* CONTINUOUS SPEECH. *See* SPEECH RECOGNITION.

discretionary hyphen a hyphen that is used only when the word falls near the end of a line; sometimes called a SOFT HYPHEN. By specifying where you want the word to be broken, you override the word processor's automatic hyphenation. *Contrast* REQUIRED HYPHEN; HARD HYPHEN.

disk a round, flat device for storing computer data. There are three main kinds: DISKETTES, HARD DISKS, and OPTICAL DISKS (of which CD-ROMs are the most common kind).

Diskettes are made of flexible plastic coated with iron oxide. Information is recorded on them by magnetizing the iron oxide coating in specific places. The diskette will be erased if it comes near a magnet or a source of a magnetic field, such as an electric motor.

The iron oxide on the disk consists of microscopically small needles, each of which acts like a tiny bar magnet. Information is stored by magnetizing these needles. The read-write head, which skims the surface of the disk, can either generate a magnetic field to magnetize the needles, or detect the magnetic field of needles that are already magnetized. The binary digits 0 and 1 are represented by changes in the direction of magnetization.

Data on disks is stored in many concentric circles, each of which is called a *track*. Each track is divided into *sectors,* which are the smallest units that the computer can read into memory in a single step. On a double-sided or multilayer disk pack, the set of tracks in corresponding positions on different layers is known as a *cylinder.*

The *directory* of a disk is a special area in which the computer records the names and locations of all the files on the disk. In most operating systems, including DOS, Windows, OS/2, and UNIX, the user can create many directories on a single disk.

A disk has to be *formatted* before it can be used. Formatting is the process of marking out the tracks and sectors magnetically and creating the main directory. Diskettes for PC-compatible computers are usually sold pre-formatted.

Table 3 lists the kinds of diskettes usually used by PC-compatible computers. The $3\frac{1}{2}$-inch diskettes used by the Macintosh are physically the same as these but are formatted differently by the computer.

Hard disks are like diskettes except that the iron oxide is coated on stiff aluminum disks. There are several layers in a single disk pack, and the whole device is normally mounted permanently in the computer. Most hard disks have capacities ranging from 100 to 5,000 megabytes (equal to hundreds of diskettes).

Optical disks store information by etching a transparent plastic medium with a laser beam. *See* CD-ROM; CD-R; CD-RW.

Usage note: This word is often spelled *disc* when referring to compact discs (CDs), DVDs, and laser discs, but is always spelled *disk* when referring to magnetic disks and diskettes. The difference in spelling probably reflects the European origin of the CD.

disk drive a device that enables a computer to read (and, in most cases, write) data on disks. Microcomputers typically contain one hard disk drive, one CD-ROM drive, and one or more diskette drives. *See* DISK.

diskette a removable flexible magnetic disk on which computer programs and data can be stored (Table 3). The $5\frac{1}{4}$-inch diskettes are often called *floppy disks* because the entire diskette, including cover, is flexible. *See also* DISK.

disk farm *(slang)* a room full of disks; a large set of disk drives used by a single computer or network.

diskless workstation a computer that has no disk drive of its own, downloading the operating system and all software and data files through a network. *See* NC.

display panel a small panel that displays information on a piece of equipment that does not have a screen. For example, the HP LaserJet 4M printer has a display panel that can display the status of print jobs.

distribute a drawing program command that places objects evenly over a defined area.

distributed spread over more than one computer. For example, the WORLD WIDE WEB is a distributed library of information.

distro *(slang)* a distribution (a prepared, ready-to-install or ready-to-use copy) of a piece of free software such as Linux or TeX. Some free software packages are so complex that different people have prepared different ready-to-use distributions of the same software. *See* LINUX; TEX; FREE SOFTWARE.

FIGURE 79. DITHERING PATTERNS

dithering the representation of an intermediate color by mixing dots of two other colors. Hardware limitations make it impossible to print or display all possible colors. Dithering is used to represent shades of gray or colors on a printer or screen that cannot produce them directly.

DLL (**D**ynamic **L**ink **L**ibrary) a file containing a library of machine-language procedures that can be linked to programs as needed at run time. *See* LINK, definition 3.

DLLs are used in Microsoft Windows and OS/2. Their practical benefit is that programs don't need to include code to perform common functions because that code is available in the DLL. The program is smaller, and changes can be made once to the DLL routine instead of separately to each program.

A common source of problems with Windows 95 and its successors is that several versions of the same DLL, with the same name, can exist in different directories on the disk drive. Only one copy of each DLL is loaded into memory, and it remains there until the memory space is needed for something else. Thus, you cannot predict which version of a DLL will be in memory at a particular time. Often, newer programs crash when they encounter and use an obsolete version of a DLL.

DMA (**D**irect **M**emory **A**ddressing) the ability of a peripheral device, such as a disk controller, to access the memory of a computer directly, without going through the CPU. DMA makes it possible to transfer information to or from external devices much more quickly than would be possible if the CPU had to handle every byte of information during the transfer.

DNA

1. (**D**eoxyribo**n**ucleic **A**cid) the molecule that carries inherited information in all living things. The operation of DNA is somewhat like that of a computer. It consists of nucleotides that can be strung together in any sequence to encode a blueprint for other molecules. In this manner, a set of DNA molecules contains the entire plans for building a plant, animal, or human being. Like computer programs, DNA contains "go to" instructions that skip over some of the material.

2. (Windows **D**istributed **I**nternet **A**rchitecture) Microsoft's model for developing distributed computing applications with Windows.

DNS

1. (**D**omain **N**ame **S**erver) a computer that determines IP addresses from domain names. If your browser reports a DNS problem, it means that it could not find the computer you asked it to find. *See* NAME SERVER.

2. (**D**o **N**ot **S**et) a copyediting abbreviation used to mark marginal notations or special typesetting instructions on a manuscript.

dock to anchor; to fix into position. Many applications allow the user to move toolboxes from the default position to a new location at the side, top, or bottom of the window. This action is called "docking the toolbox."

docking station an accessory that gives a laptop computer additional capabilities when it is used at a fixed location. A typical docking station will include a charger for the laptop's battery, connection to a larger monitor, and possibly additional disk drives or other peripherals.

document a file containing a text to be printed (e.g., a letter, term paper, or book chapter) or a drawing or other piece of work that a human being is editing with the aid of the computer.

documentation written descriptions of computer programs. Documentation falls into several categories:

1. *Internal documentation,* consisting of comments within the program. (*See* COMMENT.) Internal documentation is addressed mostly to future programmers who may have to make corrections or other modifications.

2. *On-line documentation,* information that is displayed as the program runs or that can be called up with a command such as `help`. The user should be able to control the amount of information displayed (more for beginners, and less as the user's experience increases). Also, help commands should be sensitive to the context in which they are invoked; for instance, typing `help` within an editor should call up information about the editor, not the whole operating system.

3. *Reference cards,* containing easily forgotten details for quick reference. A reference card assumes that the user is already familiar with the general principles of the program. Reference cards

printed on paper are becoming obsolete, but the same kind of documentation is often made available on-line.

4. *Reference manuals,* setting out complete instructions for the program in a systematic way. Related information should be grouped together, and a good index should be provided.

5. *Tutorials,* serving as introductions for new users. Unlike a reference manual, a tutorial gives the information in the order in which the user will want to learn it; items are grouped by importance rather than by function or logical category.

document mode the normal way of typing documents that are to be printed. The word processor includes codes that indicate hyphenation, page breaks, and the like, thereby producing a special word processing file rather than a text file. *See also* NONDOCUMENT MODE; TEXT FILE.

dodge/burn tool a photopaint tool that simulates the effects of traditional dodging and burning methods in the photgraphic darkroom: the burn tool gradually increases the darkness of the area you pass the tool over; likewise, the dodge tool lightens the area.

DOM (Document Object Model) a system in which a web page is viewed as a collection of objects that can be manipulated by an object-oriented scripting language such as JAVASCRIPT. *See also* DYNAMIC HTML.

domain address an Internet address in conveniently readable form, such as jones.com, as opposed to the IP ADDRESS, which consists of numbers. *See* INTERNET.

domain name hoarding the practice of registering multiple domain names, some of which will remain unused, simply to prevent a competitor from using them.

domain name poaching the practice of registering an internet domain name with the intention of reselling the domain name rights to a corporation or individual. For example, you might want to register www.ford.com for yourself in the hope that Ford Motor Company would then buy it from you. Also called *domain name hijacking.*

dongle a device that attaches to a computer, typically on a parallel port, and must be present in order to run a particular piece of software, but has no other purpose. Dongles are used to prevent unauthorized copying. *See* COPY PROTECTION.

DoS abbreviation for "**D**enial **o**f **S**ervice." *See* DENIAL-OF-SERVICE ATTACK.

DOS (Disk Operating System) the name of various operating systems produced by various computer manufacturers, including an early operating system for the IBM 360; the disk operating system for the Apple II (Apple DOS); MS-DOS, developed by Microsoft for 16-bit microcomputers; PC-DOS, a version of MS-DOS commonly sold with the IBM

PC; and Novell DOS (formerly DR-DOS), a replacement for MS-DOS sold by Novell.

Since 1983 the name DOS has almost always referred to MS-DOS or equivalent operating systems, as it does throughout this book.

After the introduction of Windows 3.0 in 1990, it became common to refer to an IBM PC program as "for DOS" if it did not require Windows.

Users of Windows 95 and 98 can still enter commands using the DOS command line by choosing the MS-DOS option off the Program Menu (which is off the Start menu).

DOS 640K limit a limit on the size of programs executing under DOS in real mode, actually imposed by the architecture of the PC rather than by DOS. Any other operating system operating in real mode would have the same limit. *See* MS-DOS; REAL MODE.

dot

1. the character . (period), often used in filenames and Internet addresses.

2. the decimal point. For example, "nineteen dot two" means 19.2 thousand bytes per second, a standard data transmission rate.

dot com an Internet address ending in .com; more generally, a business that operates on the Internet. *See* COM.

dot-matrix printer a printer that forms characters as patterns of dots made by pressing pins onto a ribbon. These printers were widely used in the 1980s, but inkjet printers give comparable or higher quality and speed without making as much noise. *See also* INKJET PRINTER; LASER PRINTER.

dot pitch the spacing of the dots of red, green, and blue phosphor on the screen of a color monitor.

These dots do not correspond to pixels; instead, the dot pitch of a screen imposes a blur on any image regardless of its electronic resolution. For example, on a 15-inch screen with 0.28-mm dot pitch, a 1024×768-pixel image is no sharper than an 800×600 image, although it may look slightly smoother.

The smaller the dot pitch, the sharper the image; 0.28 mm is generally considered satisfactory, and anything higher than 0.35 mm is too blurry for serious work. Monochrome screens do not have dots, and their dot pitch is effectively 0, making them sharper than even the best color screens.

dots per inch *see* DPI.

double buffering

1. in graphics, the practice of computing the next frame of an animation in memory while the previous frame is being displayed, then copying the new frame to the screen quickly. That way, the process of drawing each frame is visible on the screen and does not produce flicker.

2. more generally, the use of two buffers (memory areas) to hold data being sent to an output device. One buffer can continue to accept data while the other buffer is being copied from memory to the device.

FIGURE 80. DOUBLE CLICK

double-click to depress the button of a mouse twice very rapidly (if the mouse has more than one button, use the leftmost one). This is usually the shortcut to open or launch the selected file. If you find it difficult to double click quickly enough, you can adjust the mouse's double-click speed. You'll find the mouse adjustments in the Control Panel (Macintosh and Microsoft Windows).

double dagger the character ‡, which is sometimes used to mark footnotes. *See* FOOTNOTE for more information.

double density a type of diskette that puts twice as many bits into a given area as the obsolete single-density format. *See* DISK; *contrast* HIGH DENSITY.

double precision a way of representing floating-point numbers with about twice the usual number of significant digits. Double-precision data types are available in several programming languages, including C, Java, and newer versions of BASIC; computation is slower in double precision than in single precision. *See* ROUNDING ERROR.

down not available for use. A computer is said to be down when it malfunctions or when it is being tested or maintained.

download to transmit a file or program from a central computer to a smaller computer or a computer at a remote site. *See* KERMIT; XMODEM; FTP. *Contrast* UPLOAD.

downward compatibility the ability to work with older equipment and/or software than that for which a computer program or accessory was designed. *Contrast* UPWARD COMPATIBILITY.

dpi (**d**ots **p**er **i**nch) the number of pixels or printer dots per linear inch. The first generation of laser printers could print with a resolution of

300 dots per inch. 600 and 1200-dpi laser printers are now available. *See* RESOLUTION for further details.

draft quality a printout in low resolution, unsuitable for CAMERA-READY COPY, but adequate for proofing the copy and checking the placement and alignment of graphics.

FIGURE 81. DRAG

drag to move an object by using a mouse. To do this, move the mouse pointer to the object, then hold down a mouse button (usually the left-most button if there is more than one), and move the mouse. The selected object will move with the mouse pointer, as if the pointer were *dragging* the object. When you are finished, drop the object by releasing the button.

drag and drop
    1. a method of opening an application program quickly. Simply pick up a file icon and drag it to the icon of an application program that can open the file.
    2. the ability to move text or graphics by dragging it to a new location with the mouse.
    On the Macintosh (System 7.5 and up), objects can be selected and then dragged onto the desktop or into another program. *See* CLIPPING.

drain one of the three regions in a field-effect transistor.

DRAM (**D**ynamic **R**andom-**A**ccess **M**emory, pronounced "D-ram") a computer memory that requires a refresh signal to be sent to it periodically. Almost all computers use DRAM chips for memory. *See* MEMORY; RAM; FPM; EDO. *Contrast* SRAM.

draw program one type of program for drawing pictures on a personal computer. Unlike a paint program, a draw program treats the picture as a collection of objects, each of which will be printed as sharply as the printer can print. Thus, the sharpness of the picture is not limited by the resolution of the screen. Also, individual circles, lines, rectangles, and

FIGURE 82. DRAW PROGRAM

other shapes can be moved around without affecting other objects they overlap. However, individual pixels cannot be edited. Draw programs are sometimes called *vector graphics* or *object-oriented graphics* programs.

Draw programs are preferred for drawing diagrams, while paint programs are sometimes superior for pictorial artwork. Some popular draw programs include MacDraw and Adobe Illustrator (for the Macintosh), Micrografx Designer, CorelDraw, and DrawPerfect (for Microsoft Windows). *Contrast* PAINT PROGRAM.

DR-DOS a substitute for MS-DOS (PC-DOS) developed independently by Digital Research, Inc.; subsequently known as Novell DOS and Caldera DOS.

drive bay a space in a computer enclosure that can hold a disk drive.

driver *see* DEVICE DRIVER.

FIGURE 83. DROP-DOWN MENU

drop-down menu a menu that appears when a particular item in a menu bar is selected (*see* Figure 83). Also called a pop-up menu. *See also* MENU BAR; PULL-DOWN MENU.

DSA (**D**igital **S**ignature **A**lgorithm) a U.S. federal standard for digital signatures using public key encryption, developed in 1991 by the National Institute of Standards and Technology. *See* DIGITAL SIGNATURE; ENCRYPTION.

DSL (**D**igital **S**ubscriber **L**ine) a system for transmitting digital data over ordinary copper phone lines. This service is available to individual subscribers if they are close to a telephone central office with a special router that transmits the digital signals to a backbone network. DSL allows speeds up to 7 Mbps. *Contrast* ISDN; T1 LINE; CABLE MODEM; POTS.

DSP *see* DIGITAL SIGNAL PROCESSING.

DSS (**D**igital **S**ignature **S**tandard) a federal standard for digital signatures using the Digital Signature Algorithm (DSA).

DTD abbreviation for "**d**ocument **t**ype **d**efinition." *See* XML.

DTE (**d**ata **t**erminal **e**quipment) *see* DCE.

DTMF (**d**ual-**t**one **m**ulti-**f**requency) the signaling system used on push-button telephones. Each signal consists of two tones transmitted simultaneously.

dual boot capable of running more than one operating system. Typically, the user chooses the desired operating system at boot-up time.

dump to transfer data from one place to another without regard for its significance. A dump (on paper) is a printout of the contents of a computer's memory or disk file, shown byte by byte, usually in both hexadecimal and character form. Dumps are usually very hard to read and are used only when there is no other convenient way to get access to the data. Large-scale copying of files from disk to tape, or vice versa, is sometimes referred to as dumping.

dusty deck (*slang*) an ancient, poorly understood computer program that goes back to the days of punched cards; something that is obsolete but has to be kept usable because someone needs it. *Compare* LEGACY.

Dutch auction an auction in which several items, all alike, are being sold at once to the highest bidders. Dutch auctions are popular on eBay and similar on-line auction services. *See* EBAY.

DVD (**D**igital **V**ersatile **D**isc, originally **D**igital **V**ideo **D**isc) an optical disc similar to CD-ROM but with much greater capacity, up to 16 gigabytes depending on format. Most DVD drives will also read CD-ROMs, but because of the different wavelength of laser light used, they may have trouble with CD-R discs.

DVD was introduced in order to store a complete, digitized feature-length movie on a single disc. However, despite "video" in the name, DVD can store any kind of computer data. *See also* CD-ROM.

DVI file
1. (**D**igital **V**ideo **I**nterface) Intel's file format for storing video on disk.
2. **d**evice-**i**ndependent output from TEX or LATEX, which can be printed on any printer using the appropriate DVI program.

dweeb *(slang)* an unsophisticated, untidy, obnoxious person.

DX suffix denoting higher-performance versions of some Intel microprocessors. The 386DX has a 32-bit external bus; the 386SX has a 16-bit external bus, although it uses 32 bits internally. The 486DX includes a math coprocessor; the 486SX does not. *Contrast* SX.

dyadic operation an operation on two numbers (operands). For example, addition, multiplication, subtraction, and division are all dyadic operations because each of them operates on two numbers. Negation is not a dyadic operation because it operates on only one number.

dye-sublimation printer a type of color printer that gives excellent color proofs. Dye-sub printouts appear to be continuous-tone images like photographs. Actually they, too, are composed of tiny dots (like laser or thermal-wax printouts), but the dots of dye have spread together. The intense colors, glossy finish, and lack of apparent halftone dots make these printouts especially suitable for presentations to clients.

Dye-sublimation printers are expensive machines and are out of the reach of most individuals, but many service bureaus have them.

dynamic data exchange *see* DDE.

dynamic HTML enhancements to HTML that allow the display of a page to change in response to user actions, such as mouse movements, without having to reload the page from the server. A page is viewed as a set of objects (see DOM) whose appearance can be changed by scripts (see JAVASCRIPT) in response to user actions such as mouse clicks. For example, a page can contain headings that are supported by detailed text which will only be visible when the user clicks on the headings.

Unfortunately, some of the advanced features have not yet been standardized, so Microsoft and Netscape browsers will not always display the same result.

See also CASCADING STYLE SHEETS.

dynamic link library *see* DLL.

dynamic RAM *see* DRAM.

E

e (in mathematics) an important number whose value is approximately 2.71828. The reason *e* is important is that the function e^x is its own derivative. In BASIC and other programming languages, the function EXP(X) computes e^x. If $y = e^x$, then x is the natural logarithm of y.

e- prefix meaning *electronic,* especially when applied to terms in the context of the Internet or World Wide Web. *See* E-MAIL; E-ZINE; and E-COMMERCE for examples.

Usage note: Spelling of *e-* words is not yet standardized, and the new words are often spelled without hyphenation (e.g., *email, ezine*).

(A)   (B)

FIGURE 84. (A) EAR, DEFINITION 1   (B) EARS, DEFINITION 2

ear

1. the small stroke on the right side of the letter g.
2. a small box of information on either side of a headline or masthead. In newspapers, an ear is commonly used for the weather forecast.

Easter egg *(slang)* a hidden part of a computer program. Easter eggs are usually activated only by a bizarre series of actions—then the user is treated to an amusing presentation that usually includes the names of the development team. The actions necessary to see an egg are very complex and would never be performed by a casual user of the program; one has to be looking for the Easter egg. Information about program eggs is often spread on the World Wide Web.

eBay (www.ebay.com) an on-line auction house established in 1995 and headquartered in San Jose, California. By acting as an auctioneer, eBay enables individuals to buy and sell almost anything through the World Wide Web.

An on-line auction has several advantages over a conventional one. Bids on an item can be collected for several days, typically a week, rather than having to be delivered all at once. Perhaps more importantly, the actual bidding can be done by computer. Would-be buyers specify their maximum bids, but the computer places actual bids that are just high enough to outbid the other bidders. Finally, the computer can search quickly through thousands of item descriptions. *See also* BID; RESERVE PRICE; DUTCH AUCTION.

EBCDIC (**E**xtended **B**inary **C**oded **D**ecimal **I**nformation **C**ode) the numeric representation of characters on IBM mainframe computers. (Contrast ASCII, which is used on most other computers.) The decimal and hexadecimal numbers corresponding to the most commonly used EBCDIC characters are shown in Table 4. Note that the numbering of the letters of the alphabet is discontinuous. Some EBCDIC devices support a variety of additional characters.

An advantage of EBCDIC is that digits (0, 1, etc.) can be converted into numbers (0, 1, ...) by masking off the upper four bits of their EBCDIC codes, without doing any table lookup or arithmetic. For example, the EBCDIC code for 3 is hexadecimal F3, binary 11110011, and the binary number 3 is 00000011.

e-book a book distributed electronically (on line or on CD-ROM or similar media) rather than on paper.

EC abbreviation for ELECTRONIC COMMERCE (or European Community).

echo to send information back to where it came from. With computers, this refers to two things:

1. When communicating by modem, a computer echoes typed characters if it sends them to its own screen as well as to the other computer. If you can't see what you're typing, turn echoing on; if what you type appears twice, turn echoing off.

2. In DOS, Windows, OS/2, and UNIX, the echo command sends a message to the screen; for example,

   ```
   echo Hello there!
   ```

   writes "Hello there!" on the screen. In a DOS .BAT file or OS/2 .CMD file, the command echo off tells DOS not to print commands on the screen as they are executed. In DOS 3.3 and higher, OS/2, Windows 95 and its successors, you can prevent the echo off command itself from being displayed by prefixing it with @, like this:

   ```
   @echo off
   ```

   In fact the @ prevents display of any command, not just echo.

e-commerce *see* ELECTRONIC COMMERCE.

ECP (**E**xtended **C**apabilities **P**ort) an advanced type of parallel port for personal computers, incorporating fast bidirectional communication.

TABLE 4
EBCDIC (IBM MAINFRAME) CHARACTER CODES

Each code is shown in decimal, hexadecimal, and character form.

129	81	a	193	C1	A	240	F0	0
130	82	b	194	C2	B	241	F1	1
131	83	c	195	C3	C	242	F2	2
132	84	d	196	C4	D	243	F3	3
133	85	e	197	C5	E	244	F4	4
134	86	f	198	C6	F	245	F5	5
135	87	g	199	C7	G	246	F6	6
136	88	h	200	C8	H	247	F7	7
137	89	i	201	C9	I	248	F8	8
						249	F9	9
145	91	j	209	D1	J			
146	92	k	210	D2	K	64	40	blank
147	93	l	211	D3	L	76	4C	<
148	94	m	212	D4	M	77	4D	(
149	95	n	213	D5	N	78	4E	+
150	96	o	214	D6	O	79	45	|
151	97	p	215	D7	P	80	50	&
152	98	q	216	D8	Q	90	5A	!
153	99	r	217	D9	R	91	5B	$
						92	5C	*
162	A2	s	226	E2	S	93	5D	)
163	A3	t	227	E3	T	94	5E	;
164	A4	u	228	E4	U	96	60	–
165	A5	v	229	E5	V	97	61	/
166	A6	w	230	E6	W	107	6B	,
167	A7	x	231	E7	X	108	6C	%
168	A8	y	232	E8	Y	109	6D	_
169	A9	z	233	E9	Z	110	6E	>
						111	6F	?
122	7A	:	125	7D	'			
123	7B	#	126	7E	=			
124	7C	@	127	7F	"			

ECP is similar to EPP but includes protocols for speed negotiation and addressing of multiple devices. The ECP standard was introduced by Hewlett-Packard and Microsoft in 1992. *See also* ECP, IEEE 1284.

edge detect a photopaint filter or image processing technique that outlines the edges of objects. See Fig. 85.

EDI *see* ELECTRONIC DATA INTERCHANGE.

edit to examine a file and make changes in it, usually with the aid of an editor. (*See* EDITOR.)

editor a computer program that enables the user to create, view, and modify text files. Early interactive computers used *line editors* that identified the lines by number and accepted commands only at the bottom of the screen. Almost all computers today offer *full-screen editing*,

FIGURE 85. EDGE DETECT

enabling the user to put the cursor anywhere on the screen and scroll upward, downward, and even horizontally through the text.

EDLIN a line editor provided with earlier versions of DOS. It has been superseded by a full-screen editor called EDIT. *See* EDITOR.

EDO (**e**xtended **d**ata **o**ut) a type of dynamic random-access memory (DRAM) that holds its output on the BUS until the beginning of the next bus cycle. This enables the computer to retrieve data from memory in one bus cycle instead of two. (To further gain speed, memory is attached to a fast bus that connects directly to the CPU, rather than the slower bus that connects to expansion cards.) EDO DRAM is often used with Pentium processors. *Contrast* FPM; SDRAM.

edu suffix indicating that an E-MAIL address or WEB SITE is at an educational site in the United States, such as www.uga.edu. *See* URL; DOMAIN ADDRESS.

EEPROM (**E**lectrically **E**rasable **P**rogrammable **R**ead-**O**nly **M**emory) a type of memory chip whose contents can be both recorded and erased by electrical signals, but do not go blank when power is removed. (It is called "read-only" because the recording process is too slow to be used more than occasionally.) EEPROM contrasts with permanently recorded ROM chips and with EPROMs that can be programmed electrically but cannot be erased electrically. *See* EPROM; ROM.

effector key a key that changes the meaning of the other keys. The most often used effector key is the shift key. Other effector keys are CTRL and ALT. Also called a MODIFIER KEY.

efficiency the conservation of scarce resources. In order to measure efficiency, you have to decide which resource you want to conserve. For example, one program might be more "efficient" than another if it uses less memory, and another program might be more "efficient" in terms of speed; the question is whether you would rather conserve memory or time.

With computers, some of the most important resources are:

1. computer execution time;
2. computer memory capacity;
3. auxiliary storage capacity (i.e., disk space);
4. programmer's time.

The general rule is: it is more important to work to conserve a resource if it is more scarce. With early computers, which were very slow and had limited memory (compared to computers available now), it was more important to write programs that would not require much memory and would not require as many steps for the computer to execute. Now that computers are faster and have more memory, it is often the case that the programmer's labor is the most scarce resource. This means that it is more efficient to write software in a way that simplifies the programmer's job, even if it uses more computer time and memory. An added benefit is that if the programmer's job is simplified, errors (bugs) are less likely.

E format *see* EXPONENTIAL NOTATION.

EGA (**E**nhanced **G**raphics **A**dapter) the second major type of graphics card for the IBM PC, successor to the Color Graphics Adapter (CGA). The EGA provided a resolution of 640×350 pixels. All of its functions are included in the VGA.

EIA (**E**lectronics **I**ndustries **A**ssociation) an American organization that promotes industrial standards. On older computer equipment, "EIA" often marks an RS-232 or EIA-232D serial port.

EIA-232D the new official designation for the RS-232 standard for data communication. *See* RS-232.

EIDE (**E**xtended **I**ntegrated **D**evice **E**lectronics) a newer type of IDE disk drive and controller that allows a larger number of sectors per track and thereby overcome the original limit of 528 megabytes per drive. Some operating systems, such as OS/2, provide EIDE support in software even when used with a conventional IDE controller.

EISA (**E**nhanced **I**ndustry-**S**tandard **A**rchitecture) a standard 32-bit bus for IBM PC-compatible computers using the 386, 486, or Pentium microprocessor. EISA was developed by a group of competitors as an alternative to IBM's Micro Channel, retaining more compatibility with the original (ISA) bus.

In general, EISA computers can use ISA as well as EISA cards. The extra contacts on the EISA card edge connector are in a second row above the contacts that correspond to those on ISA cards.

See ISA; MICRO CHANNEL; BUS.

electronic circuit diagram symbols graphical symbols used in schematic diagrams of electronic circuits. Examples are shown in

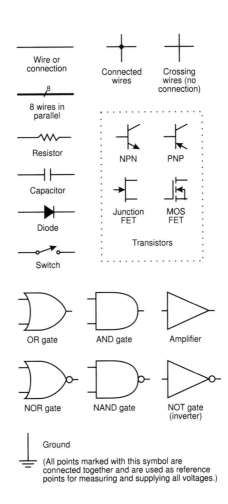

Wire or connection

8 wires in parallel

Resistor

Capacitor

Diode

Switch

Connected wires

Crossing wires (no connection)

NPN

PNP

Junction FET

MOS FET

Transistors

OR gate

AND gate

Amplifier

NOR gate

NAND gate

NOT gate (inverter)

Ground

(All points marked with this symbol are connected together and are used as reference points for measuring and supplying all voltages.)

FIGURE 86. ELECTRONIC CIRCUIT DIAGRAM SYMBOLS

Figure 86. *See also* NOT GATE; OR GATE; AND GATE; NAND GATE; LOGIC CIRCUITS; TRANSISTOR.

electronic commerce (**EC**) the carrying out of business transactions by computers. For example, computers at a store can monitor inventory levels and automatically order more merchandise when it is needed. Electronic commerce also includes transactions where there is a human participant, but the process is highly computerized, such as making purchases over the Internet. *See also* ELECTRONIC DATA INTERCHANGE; E-TAIL.

electronic data interchange (**EDI**) the transfer of information between organizations in machine-readable form in order to carry out business transactions. Electronic data interchange is becoming popular because it minimizes the errors that can occur if the same information has to be typed into computers several times.

For example, consider a department ordering an item from a supplier. In a paper-based system, the department will typically fill out a requisition that needs to be approved by the purchasing department, which fills out a purchase order, which is sent to the supplier. The supplier will need to generate its own paperwork to direct the billing and shipment of the item. When the item is received, the receiving department will need to fill out more paperwork for verification. More paperwork will be required for the accounts payable department to receive authorization to pay the bill, and then a paper check must be sent. All that paperwork is required even if the process operates correctly; if an error is made or another inquiry is necessary, still more paperwork will be generated. At each stage of the process, a person can make mistakes typing the relevant information, such as the name of the supplier and the part number of the item being ordered.

In an electronic data interchange system, the basic flow of information is the same, except that electronic messages take the place of paper. These messages are similar to electronic mail, except that there is a standard format for each type of message so that software can read it and automatically generate the next message in the process. The part number, quantity, and supplier get typed only once, at the beginning, and then are automatically transferred from computer to computer. At the end, even the payment may take place by electronic funds transfer rather than by writing a check.

Electronic data interchange systems can work only if all of the companies involved have agreed on the same standards. Extra care must be taken to protect against fraud, and the legal system needs to adjust to the fact that in the absence of paper documents, it is not possible to use signatures as evidence of approval. Nevertheless, the advantages of electronic data interchange are such that this type of system will become more common in the future. *See also* ELECTRONIC MAIL.

electronic document a document intended to be read as it is displayed on a monitor. An electronic document can use HYPERTEXT to create an interactive environment for the reader. It can also use special effects such as animation, sounds, and music. Unlike with traditional printed documents, there is no extra cost for full color. WEB PAGES are a type of electronic document; so are catalogs, documentation, and MULTIMEDIA presentations distributed on CD-ROM. *See also* AUTHORING SOFTWARE.

electronic mail (**e-mail**) the transmission of messages by computer from one person to another. Messages are saved until the recipient chooses to read them. E-mail is much more convenient than ordinary mail or telephone calls because it arrives immediately but does not require the recipient to be present, nor does it interrupt anything else the recipient may be doing. Messages are easily printed out, saved on disk, or forwarded to other people.

In e-mail messages, the symbols :) or -) (smiling face or tongue in cheek) denote remarks that are not to be taken seriously; this is important because the recipient cannot hear the sender's tone of voice. (*See* EMOTICON.) Ill-considered angry messages are fairly common and are called *flames.*

All users of e-mail should be aware that backup copies of the messages can be saved on disk or tape and that perfect privacy cannot be guaranteed.

For abbreviations commonly used in electronic mail, *see* AFAIK; AFAIR; BTW; FWIW; IANAL; IMHO; IRL; RYFM; TIA; YMMV.

See also ELECTRONIC DATA INTERCHANGE; LOCAL-AREA NETWORK; WIDE-AREA NETWORK.

electronic publishing

1. the creation, manufacturing, and distribution of paperless documents. Examples of electronic documents are CD-ROM encyclopedias and the HOME PAGES on the WORLD WIDE WEB. Each of these new formats brings new challenges and technical problems, but all need the skill of someone who knows how to work with type and how to produce a pleasing combination of graphics and text.

2. the use of specialized computer-controlled equipment in the publishing and printing industries. Desktop publishing may be considered part of this trend, but electronic publishing encompasses the use of equipment not readily available to the mass market (powerful workstation class computers and DIGITAL PRESSES, for example). Electronic publishing is superseding traditional methods of PREPRESS production.

electrostatic printer a printer that operates by using an electric charge to deposit toner on paper. Laser printers are electrostatic printers.

element one of the items in an array or list.

elephant's ear *(slang)* the symbol @; *see* AT SIGN.

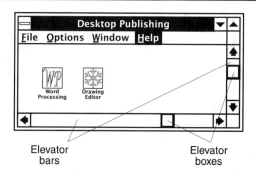

Elevator
bars

Elevator
boxes

FIGURE 87. ELEVATOR BARS

elevator bar a scroll bar; a part of a window frame that provides a
convenient way of moving vertically or horizontally through a document or drawing that is too big to display all at once. The position of the
elevator box (THUMB) gives you a graphical representation of where
you are in the document. If the elevator box is near the top of the bar,
you are near the top of the document, and likewise for bottom, left, and
right. You can DRAG the thumb with the mouse for fast scrolling or you
can CLICK on the arrows at the ends of the bar to scroll line by line.
Unlike real elevators, elevator bars can be either vertical or horizontal.

elite a typewriter typeface that prints 12 characters per inch. See PITCH;
PICA. The nearest computer equivalent to elite typewriter type is 10-
point (12-pitch) Courier.

ELIZA a computer program developed by Joseph Weizenbaum of
M.I.T. in 1966 to demonstrate that it is easy to make computers *seem*
intelligent. ELIZA carries on a conversation with the user in the style
of a psychotherapist, but it actually responds only to certain patterns of
words in the input, ignoring the rest. For example, if the user mentions
"mother," ELIZA might reply, "Tell me more about your mother."
    ELIZA passes the TURING TEST in a crude way, thereby demonstrat-
ing that human-like intelligence is easily faked. *See also* ARTIFICIAL
INTELLIGENCE.

ellipsis typographic convention of using three dots (...) to indicate the
trailing off of a thought. In Windows 3.1 and up, the ellipsis is typed
by holding down Alt while keying 133 on the numeric keypad. Mac-

intosh users can type an ellipsis by holding down Option and typing :
(colon). Note that the three dots are actually one character. The spacing
is different than simply typing three consecutive periods. (Ellipsis …;
Three periods ...)

The ellipsis also has an important function in the menu system
of Microsoft Windows (3.1 and up). The appearance of '...' after a
menu item means that a dialog box will appear when that command is
selected.

e-mail *(noun)* electronic mail; *(verb)* to send a message or file by electronic mail. *See* ELECTRONIC MAIL.
 Usage note: The spelling *e-mail,* with the hyphen, is now widely
 preferred. The older spelling is *email.* Either way, the noun and verb
 are spelled alike.

embedded font a FONT that is included within a file to ensure faithful
reproduction of the formatted document.

embedded object an object included in your file that was created in
another software package and that still maintains a LINK to the other
software. If the object is changed in the original software, it will be
updated in the second file. *See* OLE for more details.

embedded system a computer that forms part of a larger machine
of some other kind. The microprocessor that controls an automobile
engine is an example. Embedded systems must usually be extremely
reliable. They must also respond to events in real time (that is, as
they happen) without undue delay. *See* MICROCONTROLLER; REAL-TIME
PROGRAMMING.

em dash a long dash (—). *See* DASH.

emitter one of the three layers of a bipolar transistor. *See* TRANSISTOR.

emoticon a typewritten symbol for a facial expression, often used in
electronic mail. For example, :) denotes a grin (look at it sideways),
and -) means "tongue in cheek."

EMS *see* EXPANDED MEMORY.

emulation the process of achieving the same results as if you had a
different machine than the one you're actually using. For example,
VT-100 emulation means making a computer act exactly like a VT-
100 terminal. Emulation is different from *simulation,* which involves
imitating the internal processes, not just the results, of the thing being
simulated.

emulsion the coated surface of photographic film. Normally, a photographic negative looks right (not flipped) if the emulsion of the negative faces away from the person viewing it. Some graphics software
offers output choices of "emulsion up" and "emulsion down" to produce flipped images for systems in which a photographic negative is
going to be used backward.

Encapsulated PostScript (EPS) a file format that is widely supported by different computers, printers, and software. Most desktop publishing software supports the importation of Encapsulated PostScript files, thus providing a common denominator for exchanging files. *See also* POSTSCRIPT.

encryption the act of converting information into a code or cipher so that people will be unable to read it. A secret key or password is required to decrypt (decode) the information. More and more confidential data is being sent along computer networks, so it is becoming increasingly important to develop ways to send information over computer networks securely.

For example, suppose we wish to send this message:

> HELLOGOODBYE

One way to encrypt it is to replace each letter with the letter that comes 10 places later in the alphabet, so that letter 1 (A) becomes letter 11 (K), letter 2 (B) becomes letter 12 (L), and so forth, starting over at A when we go past Z, like this:

> *Plain:* ABCDEFGHIJKLMNOPQRSTUVWXYZ
> *Encrypted:* KLMNOPQRSTUVWXYZABCDEFGHIJ

Mathematically speaking, we change letter n to $(n + 10)$ mod 26. Here *mod* stands for *modulo* and refers to the remainder after division by 26. For example, letter 20 (T) is shifted to 30, which becomes 30 mod 26 = 4, which is the letter D. Using this method, our message becomes:

> ROVVYQYYNLIO

The recipients can easily decrypt the message as long as they know the algorithm (each letter is shifted by a certain number of places) and the key (in this case, 10).

Unfortunately, this algorithm is so simple that it would be easy for a spy to crack the code. There are only 25 possible keys (a key of 26 would have no effect, and a key of 27 or higher would have the same effect as a lower one). It is easy to check all 25 possibilities:

Trying key: 1	Message decodes as: QNUUXPXXMKHN
Trying key: 2	Message decodes as: PMTTWOWWLJGM
Trying key: 3	Message decodes as: OLSSVNVVKIFL
Trying key: 4	Message decodes as: NKRRUMUUJHEK
Trying key: 5	Message decodes as: MJQQTLTTIGDJ
Trying key: 6	Message decodes as: LIPPSKSSHFCI
Trying key: 7	Message decodes as: KHOORJRRGEBH
Trying key: 8	Message decodes as: JGNNQIQQFDAG
Trying key: 9	Message decodes as: IFMMPHPPECZF
Trying key: 10	Message decodes as: HELLOGOODBYE

In this case the spy can stop after the tenth try.

To make the code harder to crack, we can use a longer key. For example, say that the first letter of the message will be shifted 10, the second will be shifted 8 letters, the third will be shifted 17, and so on. If you use a key with 8 numbers, then you can repeat the pattern after every 8 letters (that is, the ninth letter will be shifted the same as the first letter, the tenth letter will be shifted the same as the second letter, and so on). The longer the key is, the harder it will be for the spy to try all possibilities. If you can design it so that the time required to check all possibilities exceeds the lifetime of the universe, you're probably safe from this kind of attack. Even if you can design it so that the expense of cracking the code is greater than the benefit the spy would receive by cracking your code, you're probably safe.

However, there are other means of attack. Not all letters of the alphabet are used with equal frequency. A spy can program a computer to make a guess for the length of the key; collect all letters encrypted with a particular part of the key; and then check the frequency of encrypted letters, guessing that the most frequently appearing letter represents E, and so on. That guess may not be right, but guessing with this system will likely proceed much faster than guessing all the possibilities. This kind of attack is easier if the message is longer, but it won't work for numerical data where the digits are equally likely to appear.

Another likely means of attack would be to attack the key itself. If the spy gets hold of the key, it will be easy to decrypt all the messages. If a lot of people are sending messages to lots of other people, it is hard for them to deliver the keys to the recipients of the messages without letting them fall into the wrong hands.

One way to solve this problem is with public key encryption. In this approach, each person has both a *public key* (which everyone knows) and a *private key* (which is kept secret). If Alice is sending a message to Bob, then the message will be encrypted using an algorithm that is based on Bob's public key. Anyone can use this key to encrypt a message to Bob, but it can only be decrypted using Bob's private key.

Here is one example of how this can work, using the algorithm developed by Whitfield Diffie and Martin Hellman in 1976. Alice and Bob agree on two numbers: $n = 37$ and $g = 7$. (In reality, n and g would be much larger than this.) Each of them has a private key, which we'll call a and b respectively. Alice and Bob generate their public keys A and B using the formula:

$$\text{Public key} = g^{(\text{private key})} \bmod n$$

Thus:

$$
\begin{aligned}
\text{Alice's private key } a &= 8 \\
\text{Alice's public key } A &= 7^8 \bmod 37 \\
&= 5{,}764{,}801 \bmod 37
\end{aligned}
$$

$$= \quad 16$$

$$\text{Bob's private key } b \quad = \quad 6$$

$$\text{Bob's public key } B \quad = \quad 7^6 \text{ mod } 37$$

$$= \quad 117,649 \text{ mod } 37$$

$$= \quad 26$$

Alice now generates another key K to use for the actual message using this formula:

$$K \quad = \quad B^a \text{ mod } n$$

$$= \quad 26^8 \text{ mod } 37$$

$$= \quad 208,827,064,576 \text{ mod } 37$$

$$= \quad 10$$

This key is known as the *session key*. Now she can encrypt the message. For example, if she is sending the message HELLOGOODBYE, it will be encrypted as shown at the beginning of this entry.

When Bob receives the message, he will calculate the session key using a very similar formula:

$$K \quad = \quad A^b \text{ mod } n$$

$$= \quad 16^6 \text{ mod } 37$$

$$= \quad 16,777,216 \text{ mod } 37$$

$$= \quad 10$$

Notice that this is the same value even though it is calculated from different numbers using a different formula. This works because of the following mathematical identities:

$$(a \times b) \text{ mod } n = [(a \text{ mod } n) \times (b \text{ mod } n)] \text{ mod } n$$

$$a^c \text{ mod } n = (a \text{ mod } n)^c \text{ mod } n$$

$$a^{bc} = (a^b)^c = (a^c)^b$$

$$a^{bc} \text{ mod } n \quad = \quad (a \text{ mod } n)^{bc} \text{ mod } n$$

$$= \quad [(a \text{ mod } n)^b]^c \text{ mod } n$$

$$= \quad [(a \text{ mod } n)^c]^b \text{ mod } n$$

$$a^{bc} \text{ mod } n = (a \text{ mod } n)^{bc} \text{ mod } n = (a^c \text{ mod } n)^b \text{ mod } n$$

$$a^{bc} \text{ mod } n = (a \text{ mod } n)^{bc} \text{ mod } n = (a^b \text{ mod } n)^c \text{ mod } n$$

To calculate the private key (equivalent to c), given the public key and the session key, you need to solve an equation of this general form:

$$k = j^x \text{ mod } n$$

If n happens to be a large prime number, it is very difficult to discover the value of x even if you know the values of k, j, and n. Thus, large prime numbers play a crucial role in public-key encryption.

In practice, when computers are used for encryption, the calculations are usually carried out directly on the binary digits of the data, using a key given as a binary number. A longer key provides greater security, but the calculation process becomes more complicated.

All this presumes that you can get people's public keys reliably so that you can be sure you're really using Bob's public key when you send messages to Bob. Since public keys are not secret, all you need is a trustworthy database in which you can look up people's public keys.

Another issue is that the U.S. Government presently regulates the export of strong encryption software in the same way that it regulates the export of weapons. This regulation dates from the 1940s, before general-purpose digital computers existed; encryption machines at that time were considered to be munitions, and they still are. Almost everyone in the computer industry wants this outdated regulation to be repealed.

See also DIGITAL SIGNATURE; DES; PGP; RSA ENCRYPTION; SSL; ONE-WAY FUNCTION; HASH FUNCTION.

end

1. keyword that marks the end of a particular program structure in several programming languages. In BASIC, the END keyword tells the computer to stop executing the program. In Pascal, END marks the end of blocks of statements that start with BEGIN.

2. the key on your keyboard that takes your cursor to the end of the current line. Some word processors use Ctrl-End as a keyboard shortcut to take you to the end of the document.

en dash a short dash (–). *See* DASH.

end-of-file mark a symbol that indicates the end of a file. For example, in CP/M, all text files ended with ASCII character 26 (Ctrl-Z) because the computer did not otherwise keep track of the exact length of the file, only the number of disk sectors. In DOS, Windows, and OS/2, Ctrl-Z is often used the same way even though the computer knows exactly where the file ends whether or not an end-of-file mark is present. The UNIX end-of-file mark is Ctrl-D.

end user the person ultimately intended to use a product, as opposed to people involved in developing or marketing it.

Energy Star a set of guidelines proposed by the U.S. Environmental Protection Agency in 1992 to reduce the amount of electricity consumed by personal computers. An Energy Star-compliant computer consumes less than 30 watts of power when idling (i.e., when turned on but not in use) and switches automatically into low-power mode if several minutes elapse without any keyboard activity. *See* GREEN PC.

engine

1. the part of a computer program that implements a special technique; *see* INFERENCE ENGINE, MONTE CARLO ENGINE, SEARCH ENGINE.

2. the printing mechanism of a laser printer, not including the computer control circuitry. Many laser printers use an engine made by Canon in Japan.

ENIAC (**E**lectronic **N**umerical **I**ntegrator **A**nd **C**alculator) the first electronic computer, built at the University of Pennsylvania in the mid-1940s. It contained about 18,000 vacuum tubes. Initially, the ENIAC was programmed by plugging cables into circuit boards. Today, one of the Internet nodes at the University of Pennsylvania is named `eniac` but is, of course, not the same machine.

Enter key the key on a computer keyboard that you press at the end of each line in order to send the contents of that line into the computer. On most keyboards, the Enter key is the same as the Return key. However, IBM 3270-series terminals make a distinction: the Return key starts a new line, but the Enter key sends the contents of the whole screen to the computer.

Under windowed operating systems, pressing the Enter key is usually equivalent to clicking on the currently selected icon or other highlighted item.

enumerator a device driver or operating system component that identifies all hardware devices of a particular type. *See* BIOS ENUMERATOR.

FIGURE 88. ENVELOPE MANIPULATION

envelope

1. (in a draw program) the imaginary outline enclosing an object. You can edit the envelope, turning it from a rectangle into a curved shape, and thereby distorting everything inside it.

2. (in engineering) the limits imposed by physical or technical constraints (called an "envelope" because they can be envisioned as surrounding an area on a graph). "Pushing the envelope" means working close to, or at, the limits.

environment

1. the display and human interface provided by software. On a computer, an environment defines what you can do with the computer. For instance, the operating system, a word processor, and a spreadsheet provide (at least) 3 different environments that respond to different commands. For example, if you type a word processing command while you are in the operating system environment, or vice versa, the command will not be understood.

2. (in DOS, Windows, OS/2, and UNIX) a data area in which you can store information for use by programs. To put information there, use the `set` command; for example, under DOS, Windows, or OS/2,

```
set prompt=$p$g
```

tells the computer to display the current disk and directory (such as `C:\MYDIR>`) when it is ready for a command. To see the contents of the environment area, type `set` by itself.

EPP (**E**nhanced **P**arallel **P**ort) an advanced type of parallel port for personal computers, incorporating fast bidirectional communication. The EPP standard was introduced by Xircom, Zenith, and Intel in 1992. *See also* ECP; IEEE 1284.

EPROM (**E**rasable **P**rogrammable **R**ead-**O**nly **M**emory) a type of memory chip that can be programmed electrically and erased by exposure to ultraviolet light. *See also* ROM; PROM; EEPROM.

EPS *see* ENCAPSULATED POSTSCRIPT.

Epson a prominent Japanese manufacturer of printers and other computer peripherals, distributed in the United States by Epson America, Inc., of Torrance, California. More information about Epson can be found at `http://www.epson.com`.

The Epson MX-80 dot-matrix printer received wide acceptance during the early 1980s and set many standards to which other manufacturers subsequently adhered. Epson dot-matrix printers are capable of many special effects, including dot-by-dot graphics. Today, Epson makes high-quality color inkjet printers and other computer peripherals.

equalize a photopaint filter that adjusts the brightness range of a picture so that all levels of brightness become equally common. If some brightnesses are not used (because the picture is too bright or too dark, or because of a contrast problem), the equalized picture will often look much better. Equalizing can dramatically improve the appearance of objects that are nearly the same brightness as their background.

erase the command that erases a file or set of files from disk in DOS, OS/2, and other operating systems. *See also* RECOVERING ERASED FILES.

FIGURE 89. ERASER

eraser a paint and photopaint program tool that does to a bitmap what its real-life counterpart does to marks on paper. The eraser is used by holding down the mouse button (the leftmost if there is more than one) and dragging the eraser tool. You can adjust the size and shape of your eraser to suit your needs. Some programs will even adjust how well the eraser works; it can erase thoroughly or just lighten the color. *See* NATURAL MEDIA.

ergonomics the science of designing machines and working environments to suit human needs (from the Greek words meaning "the study of work"). An ergonomically designed machine is one whose design is based on the scientific study of human requirements such as vision, posture, and health risks. After all, let's not forget that the most important part of a desktop publishing system is the human being who is operating the computer.

Ergonomics goes beyond considering your comfort. Smart workers know that they need to work efficiently. When you work efficiently, you can get more done. Here are some things you can do:

- *Desk.* Your computer desk should be deep enough to comfortably accommodate all of your equipment. If the system unit keeps threatening to dump the keyboard in your lap, you may not have enough room. Investigate putting the system unit on the floor or to the side of the monitor. There are special stands that can turn the box on end.

  Check the height of your desk. Is it too tall for you to type comfortably? You may want to attach a keyboard drawer. This lowers the keyboard to a more comfortable level and gives you a storage place for the keyboard.

- *Chair.* Your chair is most vital to the health and well-being of your back. You should choose a chair that has adjustments for height and good lumbar support. Try to find a chair that lets you adjust the tilt of the seat. Take frequent stretching breaks. It also helps to periodically make minor changes to the seat tilt or angle of the chair back during a long work session. You might also consider a *kneeling chair*.

- *Monitor.* The monitor is one of the big-ticket items when you purchase your computer system. Ergonomically speaking, you do not want to skimp here. A cheap monitor with lots of flicker can literally give you a headache. (See MONITOR for a more thorough discussion of how to choose a monitor.) Make sure you are comfortable with the height and tilt of the screen. You may need a swivel monitor stand, especially if you are taller than most people. You may need a special pair of glasses for working at the computer. (*See* EYEGLASSES FOR COMPUTER USERS.)

  If you work where there's more than one computer system running, make sure that you are *not* positioned directly to the side or back of a fellow worker's monitor. The research on the dangers of electromagnetic emissions shows that the greatest risk is to the *side* and *back* of the monitor, extending 3 to 4 feet away. Most researchers feel that you are safe enough in front of the monitor.

- *Mouse and keyboard.* The big risk is CARPAL TUNNEL SYNDROME, a condition that creates a buzzing feeling or numbness in your hands. Prevention is the key. You should keep your wrists straight when typing; don't allow them to bend. Some people enjoy a cushioned wrist rest for their keyboard. If using the mouse gives you any discomfort, try using another pointing device such as a TRACKBALL.

- *Lighting.* To prevent glare on the screen, do not place your computer opposite a window. Overhead lighting should be soft (not as bright as it would be for reading). There are add-on anti-glare screens for monitors.

- *Posture.* Good posture *is* important. Try to imagine that an invisible string is pulling your head up and back in line with your spine. Be relaxed rather than stiff. Sit with your feet in front of you; if they don't reach the floor, your chair is too high or you need a footrest. Take frequent stretching breaks.

error a malfunction; a situation in which a computer cannot follow its instructions, or in which recorded data cannot be retrieved correctly. In computing, *error* does not necessarily denote a mistake made by a human being. *See* ERROR MESSAGE; HARD ERROR; SOFT ERROR.

error message a message that indicates that a computer cannot do what is requested or that some part of the software or hardware is defective. Error messages range from "You can't divide by zero" to "The disk drive isn't working." They do not necessarily mean that the user of the computer has made a mistake. *See also* ERROR.

error trapping *see* TRAPPING.

escape code a code that indicates that the following character is to be handled specially (e.g., as a printer control code), or a code that stands for a character that cannot otherwise be typed. For example, in HTML, the characters < > mark the beginning and end of a command, so if you want them to appear on the screen, you have to type them as the escape codes < and > respectively.

Escape key a key on a computer keyboard that has a special meaning depending on what software is being used. In many programs and under Microsoft Windows, the Escape key means "get out of where you are now and get back to where you were before" (e.g., back out of a menu without making any of the choices on it). The Escape key transmits ASCII character code 27, which is a character used to send special messages to devices. *See* ESCAPE SEQUENCE.

escape sequence a special sequence of character codes that cause a screen or printer to perform some action (such as changing type style) rather than displaying the characters. For examples, see ANSI SCREEN CONTROL and ESCAPE CODE.

ESDI (Enhanced Small Device Interface) a standard introduced by Maxtor in 1983 as an alternative to the ST-506 standard interface for hard disks. Compared to ST-506, ESDI allows somewhat faster data transfer. It has now largely been superseded by IDE and SCSI. *See* ST-506; ESDI; SCSI; IDE.

e-tail retail sales conducted on the Internet. For an example, *see* AMAZON.COM.

/etc in UNIX, a directory that contains system configuration information; often pronounced "et-see."

Ethernet a type of local area network originally developed by Xerox Corporation. Communication takes place by means of radio frequency signals carried by a coaxial cable. The name "Ethernet" apparently comes from "aether," the 19th-century name for the medium through which light waves were thought to travel. *See* LOCAL-AREA NETWORK; DATA COMMUNICATION.

On the physical level, there are four types of Ethernet connections. Thin-wire Ethernet uses RG-58 coaxial cable. Twisted-pair Ethernet is similar but uses a pair of unshielded wires. Conventional baseband Ethernet uses a thicker coaxial cable about $\frac{3}{8}$ inch in diameter, and broadband Ethernet modulates the whole Ethernet signal on a higher-frequency carrier so that several signals can be carried simultaneously on a single cable, just like cable TV channels. *See* 10BASE-2; 10BASE-T; 100BASE-T.

The control strategy of Ethernet is called CSMA/CD (Carrier Sense, Multiple Access, Collision Detection). Each computer listens to see if another computer is transmitting. If so, it waits its turn to transmit. If two computers inadvertently transmit at the same time, the collision is detected and they retransmit one at a time.

Different Ethernet systems use different software protocols, including TCP/IP and Novell Netware. *See* TCP/IP.

FIGURE 90. EURO CURRENCY SYMBOL

Euro the common European currency introduced in 1999 and intended to replace national currencies in Austria, Belgium, Finland, France, Germany, Ireland, Italy, Luxembourg, the Netherlands, Portugal, and Spain. More information about the European currency is available from the European Union at www.europa.eu.int and the European Central Bank, which manages the currency, at www.ecb.int. As of early 2000, one Euro is almost exactly equal to one U.S. dollar, but this can change.

The Euro symbol is shown in Figure 90. In Windows, this can be typed by holding down Alt and typing 0128 on the numeric keypad. However, to display and print this symbol, users of versions prior to Windows 2000 may need to download updated fonts from www.microsoft.com.

European paper sizes *see* PAPER SIZES (ISO).

even smalls type that is set in all small capital letters, with no capital letters, LIKE THIS. The cross-references in this book are set in even smalls. *Contrast* C/SC.

event-driven programming programming in which the computer spends its time responding to events rather than stepping through a prearranged series of actions. Computers that control machinery are almost always event-driven. So are computer programs that run under graphical user interfaces such as the Macintosh operating system or Microsoft Windows. Such programs respond to events such as the user choosing an item on a menu or clicking the mouse on an icon. *See* OBJECT-ORIENTED PROGRAMMING; VISUAL BASIC; GRAPHICAL USER INTERFACE; WINDOW.

exa- metric prefix meaning $\times 1,000,000,000,000,000,000$ (10^{18}). *Exa-* is derived from the Greek word for "beyond" or "outside." *See* METRIC PREFIXES.

Excel a popular SPREADSHEET program, originally released in 1985 by Microsoft for the Macintosh, and later adapted for Microsoft Windows.

exception an event that cannot be handled by a normal process. Examples include division by zero, numeric overflow, or attempting to read data from a file that isn't there. In Java, if the exception occurs during a block of code enclosed by TRY, then it can be handled by a subsequent block of code enclosed by CATCH.

exclusive-OR gate *see* XOR GATE.

execute to do what an instruction says to do. A computer alternates between a fetch cycle, when it locates the next instruction, and an execute cycle, when it carries the instruction out. *See* COMPUTER ARCHITECTURE.

executive size a size of paper sometimes used for stationery in the United States, $7\frac{1}{4} \times 10\frac{1}{2}$ inches.

EXE file a file that contains an executable machine-language program in DOS, Windows, OS/2, and VAX/VMS. To execute the program from the command line, type the name of the file without the final `.exe`; for example, to execute AAAA.EXE, type `aaaa`. In VAX/VMS, however, an .EXE file is executed by the RUN command (e.g., `run aaaa.exe`). To execute an .EXE file from its icon, just double-click on it.

   Most application programs are distributed as .EXE files. Most compilers translate source code into .EXE files. *See* COMPILER. *Contrast* BAT FILE; COM (definition 2).

exit to clear an application program from memory; to QUIT. Most software prompts you to save changes to disk before exiting. Read all message boxes carefully. *Compare* CLOSE.

EXP the function, in many programming languages, that calculates the value of e^x. *See* E.

expanded memory a method of accessing more than 640K of memory on a computer that is emulating an early-model IBM PC.

   Ordinarily, the 8088 processor in the PC could address only one megabyte (1024K) of memory. The upper 384K of this is reserved for special purposes, leaving only 640K available for ordinary use. Expanded memory used bank switching to swap many different sets of memory chips into a single block of addresses within this 640K region. Special memory cards and special software were required.

By contrast, *extended* memory (on the 80286 and higher processors) is directly accessible at addresses higher than one megabyte. Microsoft Windows, OS/2, and UNIX use extended memory automatically. Under DOS, a device driver can be used to make extended memory accessible to software that expects expanded memory.

1234567890

abd123₁₂₃ ff fi fl ffi ffl ¢ Ł ¿

¼ ½ ¾ ⅛ ⅜ ⅝ ⅞ ⅓ ⅔

ABCDEFGHIJKLMNOPQRSTUVWXYZ

FIGURE 91. EXPERT SET
(MINION TYPEFACE, PARTIAL FONT)

---

expert set a font that includes a full set of accented vowels, ligatures, small caps, and other special characters (such as an extended group of CASE FRACTIONS). It is assumed that someone using such a font will have the know-how and the software to be able to set the special characters. Not every typeface has a matching expert set; you may have to take this into consideration when selecting a typeface for a particular job or when purchasing fonts.

expert system a computer program that uses stored information to draw conclusions about a particular case. It differs from a database, which merely calls up stored information and presents it to the user unchanged. Expert systems are widely used to troubleshoot defects in machines; they have also been used successfully to diagnose diseases or recommend manufactured products.

Every expert system consists of three parts: (1) a user interface, which is a way of communicating with the user through such devices as menus, commands, or short-answer questions (*see* USER INTERFACE); (2) a knowledge base containing stored expertise; and (3) an inference engine, which draws conclusions by performing simple logical operations on the knowledge base and the information supplied by the user. *See also* PROLOG; ARTIFICIAL INTELLIGENCE; DEFAULT LOGIC; FUZZY LOGIC.

Explorer the part of Windows 95 and its successors that is used for exploring directories, files, and desktop menus. To access it, right-click on the START BUTTON and choose "Explore." Explorer roughly corresponds to File Manager in earlier versions of Windows. For Windows 98, the Explorer user interface is closer to the Internet Explorer browser.

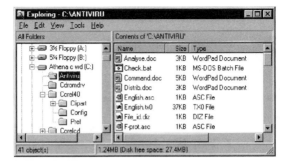

FIGURE 92. EXPLORER (WINDOWS 95)

exponent a number or letter that indicates repeated multiplication. Thus the exponent n in the expression a^n means to multiply n number of a's together. For example:

$$3^2 = 3 \times 3 = 9$$
$$4^5 = 4 \times 4 \times 4 \times 4 \times 4 = 1{,}024$$
$$10^6 = 10 \times 10 \times 10 \times 10 \times 10 \times 10 = 1{,}000{,}000$$

Also, $a^2 = a \times a$ is called a to the second power, or a *squared.* The number that when multiplied by itself gives a is called the *square root* of a (written as $\sqrt{a}$). That means $\sqrt{a} \times \sqrt{a} = a$. For example, $\sqrt{9} = 3$, since $3 \times 3 = 9$.

exponential function a function of the form $y = a^x$, where a can be any positive number except 1 and is called the *base* of the function. The most commonly used exponential function is e^x. *See* E.

exponential notation (scientific notation, E format) a way of writing very large or very small numbers conveniently. For example, 2,500,000 can be written as 2.5×10^6 or (in E format) 2.5E6 or 2.5E+6. For very small numbers, the exponent is negative; thus $0.003 = 3.0 \times 10^{-3}$ = 3.0E-3.

export to save a file in a format other than the application program's native format. Many word processing and graphics programs have the ability to export to several different formats. Look under the "Save As…" dialog box for the available file formats.

Because the export process is a type of file conversion (instead of a simple copy operation) there is the possibility of a loss of image quality or text formatting.

expression a series of symbols that can be evaluated to have a particular value. For example, $2 + 3$ is an expression that evaluates to 5.

Here are some more examples, in BASIC, of numeric expressions (i.e., expressions that evaluate to give numbers):

```
3.5
(4/3)*PI*R^3
SQR(A^2 + B^2)
```

Some programming languages have expressions whose values are character strings or Boolean (true-false) values. For example,

```
"WALLA" + "WALLA"
```

is a character string expression, and

```
(P OR Q) AND R
```

is a Boolean expression.

Extended Industry Standard Architecture *see* EISA.

extended memory memory at addresses higher than 1 megabyte on 80286 and higher PC-compatible processors, including the Pentium. It contrasts with *expanded memory*, which is bank-switched. Windows, OS/2, and UNIX use extended memory. *See* EXPANDED MEMORY; BANK SWITCHING.

extends a Java keyword indicating that a class inherits all of the functionality of that class, and then adds additional data or methods. For example, all programmer-defined applet classes include a declaration similar to this:

```
class myapplet extends Applet
```

This allows the class you write (myapplet) to include all of the features defined in the standard class Applet.

extension

1. (Macintosh) a program that adds to the power and ability of the operating system or application program. Operating system extensions are loaded at boot-up time. Examples of common extensions are AppleShare and QuickTime. Other extensions customize the operating system for a particular printer.

2. the part of a filename following the period, in DOS and similar operating systems. For example, the file PROG1.BAS has .BAS as its extension.

The purpose of extensions is to indicate the type of file, but it is important to realize that the extension does not actually cause the file to be of a particular type; you can rename any file to have any extension, but when you do, your software may no longer recognize it for what it is.

TABLE 5
FILENAME EXTENSIONS IN DOS, WINDOWS, AND OS/2

`.ai`	Adobe Illustrator subset of .EPS
`.asc`	ASCII text file
`.bak`, `.bk`	Backup copy of a file that has been edited
`.bas`	BASIC program file
`.bat`	Batch job (file of commands, in DOS)
`.bmp`	Bitmap (Windows or OS/2 graphics)
`.c`	C program file
`.cdr`	Vector graphics (CorelDraw)
`.class`	Java bytecode file
`.cmd`	File of commands (in OS/2)
`.com`	Command file (smaller version of `.exe`)
`.cpp`	C++ program file
`.doc`	Document file (ASCII or Microsoft Word)
`.dll`	Dynamic link library
`.eps`	Vector graphics, encapsulated PostScript format
`.exe`	Executable file (machine-language program)
`.gif`	Bitmap graphics file (often used in Web pages)
`.hlp`	Help file
`.htm`, `.html`	Hypertext Markup Language
`.ico`	Icon (Windows or OS/2)
`.ini`	Initialization file (configuration settings)
`.java`	Java program source file
`.jpeg`	Bitmap graphics; popular on the Web
`.log`	Log of installation or usage (various software)
`.mak`	Makefile (Visual Basic and other environments)
`.mid`	MIDI digitized music file
`.pas`	Pascal program file
`.pcx`	Bitmap graphics file (Zsoft format)
`.pif`	Program information file (Windows)
`.prj`	Project file (various compilers)
`.pl`	Perl or Prolog program
`.ps`	PostScript printable file
`.sys`	Component of the operating system
`.tif`, `.tiff`	Bitmap graphics file (TIFF format)
`.ttf`	TrueType font
`.tmp`	Temporary file
`.txt`	ASCII text file
`.wav`	Sound wave file
`.wks`, `.wk2`, `wk3`	Lotus 1-2-3 worksheet file or Microsoft Works file
`.wp`, `.wp5`, `.wp6`	WordPerfect document
`.wri`	Document file (Windows Write)
`.xls`	Excel worksheet file
`.zip`	File compressed with PKZIP or equivalent

Some file extensions have standard meanings; see Table 5. See the individual entries in this book for more information on some of the more important types.

A practical problem arises when the same extension is used by different software packages for different purposes. For example, .tex denotes both a TEX word processing document and a Corel Draw texture. When this happens, an extension may end up associated with the wrong piece of software. See ASSOCIATE for information on how to change the software that is associated with a particular extension.

Prior to Windows 95, all extensions could be no more than 3 characters. Newer file extensions can be longer.

external viewer *see* VIEWER.

FIGURE 93. EXTRUDED TYPE

extrude a special effect provided by drawing programs that creates a three-dimensional shadow. It looks as if the type (actually any object) has been extruded from a cookie gun.

FIGURE 94. EYEDROPPER TOOL

eyedropper a tool available in PAINT and PHOTOPAINT PROGRAMS that allows you to match a color in the existing picture, and cause it to become the active color. All you have to do is click the eyedropper on the area of color you desire and *that* becomes the selected color. You can sample for your primary, secondary, and background colors.

If at first this tool seems senseless, consider what would happen if you were working on a digitized 24-bit color photograph. There are literally millions of colors available in this format — how are you going to find the right one to extend that background shade over that telephone line? Or how are you going to remember which of those colors you were using yesterday? The eyedropper will let you pick up the right color to use. *See* 24-BIT; COLOR.

eyeglasses, computer eyeglasses for viewing a computer screen. Most eyeglasses are designed for vision at a great distance or for reading at about 18 inches. Neither of these is suitable for looking at a computer screen two or three feet away. In addition, the slight fuzziness of screen images causes some people's eyes to strain as they try to focus. As a result, many eyeglass wearers think the computer has harmed their vision, although in fact there is no evidence that computer work (or any other kind of close work) harms the eyes.

Computer screens emit tiny amounts of ultraviolet (UV) light, and special glasses are available that block this. However, there is much more UV in ordinary sunlight than in the image on a computer screen, so UV-blocking glasses are probably more beneficial outdoors than in the office.

EZ drive a line of removable-cartridge disk drives made by Syquest Technology, Inc., of Fremont, California, starting with a 135-megabyte cartridge introduced in 1996. *See also* ZIP DRIVE; JAZ DRIVE.

e-zine *(slang)* electronically published magazine, i.e., a magazine published on a web page or the like. *See* WORLD WIDE WEB.

F

facsimile *see* FAX.

factorial the product of all the integers from 1 up to a specified number. The factorial of a number n is symbolized by an exclamation point: $n!$. For example:

2!	=	2×1	=	2
3!	=	$3 \times 2 \times 1$	=	6
4!	=	$4 \times 3 \times 2 \times 1$	=	24
5!	=	$5 \times 4 \times 3 \times 2 \times 1$	=	120

fair use in copyright law, a limited kind of use of copyrighted material that does not require the copyright holder's permission. For example, quoting a few sentences from a book and acknowledging the source is fair use.

The essential characteristic of fair use is that it does not decrease the market for the original; it may in fact increase it. Fair use does not permit reproduction of a complete essay, poem, or other copyrighted work, nor does it extend to music, artwork, or software. *See* COPYRIGHT.

FAQ (**f**requently **a**sked **q**uestions) a file maintained by volunteers in connection with a Usenet NEWSGROUP. FAQ files for newsgroups are available by FTP from rtfm.mit.edu.

FAT (**F**ile **A**llocation **T**able) the part of the disk that contains information about the sizes and locations of the files. In OS/2 and Windows NT, a FAT file system is a file system that is compatible with DOS, as opposed to an OS/2 high-performance file system (HPFS) or a Windows NT native file system (NTFS). *See also* FAT32.

FAT16 the original form of the FAT file system used by DOS and by Windows 95 and its predecessors. *Contrast* FAT32.

FAT32 (**F**ile **A**llocation **T**able, 32 bits) a modified form of the FAT file system that was introduced in Windows 98 and some late releases of Windows 95. FAT32 allows each disk to be divided into a larger number of clusters (allocation units); thus, space can be allocated in smaller units and used more efficiently. More importantly, FAT32 supports disk drives larger than 2 gigabytes.

favorites recorded addresses on the WORLD WIDE WEB. Web browsers normally let the user record the addresses of frequently visited web pages in order to go directly to them in the future without having to type the full web address or use a search engine. Also called *bookmarks*.

fax (originally an abbreviation for *facsimile*) a method of transmitting copies of paper documents over telephone lines by converting the appearance of the document into an electronic signal. The output looks much like a photocopy. Computers can send and receive fax signals by using suitable software and a fax modem. A fax document consists of a BITMAP image, not a file of characters.

fax modem a MODEM that can transmit FAX messages as well as computer-to-computer connections.

FCC

1. (**F**ederal **C**ommunications **C**ommission) the agency of the U.S. Government that regulates all equipment that produces radio-frequency signals, including computers. The FCC issues two levels of approval for computers: Class A (suitable for use in industrial or business areas) and Class B (suitable for use in the home). *See* RFI PROTECTION.

2. business abbreviation for **f**ile **c**arbon **c**opy, a copy of an electronic mail message that is kept by the sender. *Compare* CC, BCC.

FCS (**F**inal **C**ustomer **S**hipment) the stage at which a product has completed the beta-testing phase and is available to be shipped to customers.

FDD (**f**loppy **d**isk **d**rive) a diskette drive.

feedback a phenomenon that occurs when a control device uses information about the current state of the system to determine the next control action. For example, when a thermostat controls the temperature in a house, it needs to know the current temperature in the house before it decides whether to turn on the furnace. Thus, information about the temperature "feeds back" into the device that controls the temperature.

femto- metric prefix meaning $\div 1,000,000,000,000,000$. *Femto-* is derived from the Danish word for "fifteen" (because it signifies 10^{-15}). *See* METRIC PREFIXES.

fencepost error an OFF-BY-ONE ERROR; a programming error caused by doing something one less, or one more, time than necessary. So called because a person who is asked how many fenceposts, one foot apart, are needed to build a 10-foot fence, is likely to answer "ten" rather than the correct "eleven."

FET *see* FIELD-EFFECT TRANSISTOR.

fiber optics cables that carry light rather than electrical energy. Fiber-optic cables are made of thin fibers of glass. Large amounts of data can be carried by a single fiber-optic cable. Unlike wire cables, fiber-optic cables are not subject to crosstalk or electromagnetic noise, and they cannot be tapped into (e.g., by an eavesdropper) without producing a noticeable drop in signal level.

field

1. a portion of a record in a database, containing one piece of information. For instance, in an address list, the zip code might be stored in a 10-character field. *See also* RECORD; DATABASE.

2. a place where information can be typed on the screen, such as one of the cells in a spreadsheet. *See* SPREADSHEET.

field-effect transistor (FET) a transistor in which the flow of current from source to drain is controlled by a charge applied to the gate. This charge attracts electrons into the area between source and drain or repels them away from it, thus changing its semiconductor properties. No current actually flows into the gate (in practice, there is a tiny current, on the order of 10^{-12} ampere). Thus, field-effect transistors consume little power and can be packed very densely on integrated circuit chips.

MOSFETs (metal-oxide-semiconductor FETs) have an insulating layer of metal oxide between the gate and the rest of the transistor. They consume the least power of all kinds of transistors. *See* TRANSISTOR; CMOS; INTEGRATED CIRCUIT.

FIFO (first-in-first-out) a QUEUE (definition 1); a data structure or memory device from which items are retrieved in the order in which they were stored. *Contrast* LIFO.

fifth-generation computers computers built with advanced large-scale integrated circuits that break out of the traditional Von Neumann architecture by making extensive use of pipelining and/or vector processing. *See also* COMPUTER ARCHITECTURE; PIPELINE; VECTOR PROCESSOR.

Fifth Generation Project a project begun by the Japanese government in 1981 to develop a new generation of computers that manipulate data in sophisticated ways and understand human languages. During the first decade it yielded considerable progress in development of parallel computers and logic programming. *See* PARALLEL PROCESSING; PROLOG.

file a block of information stored on disk, tape, or similar media. A file may contain a program, a document, or a collection of data (such as a mailing list). A file need not occupy a contiguous block of disk space. *See* TEXT FILE; BINARY FILE; DATABASE MANAGEMENT; RECORD; DISK.

file compression *see* DATA COMPRESSION.

file format a way of arranging information in a file. Almost every computer program has one or more file formats of its own; for example, WordPerfect documents are not in the same format as Microsoft Word documents, and similar programs from different manufacturers cannot necessarily process each other's files. There are three reasons why file formats are diverse:

1. Different programs handle different kinds of data (text vs. pictures vs. spreadsheets, for example).

2. Different programmers simply pick different ways of doing the same thing. Sometimes, inventing a new format is a point of pride,

or is necessary to avoid infringing someone else's copyright or patent.

3. Even when the end result is the same, the way different programs achieve it may be very different. For example, a Windows Paint-brush picture is a *bitmap* (a large grid of dots), but a CorelDraw picture consists of *vector graphics* (instructions to draw lines or shapes in particular positions). The two kinds of pictures are very different from the computer's point of view.

Many programs have the ability to *import* (bring in) files that are not in their own format. But the format of the imported file may not be very well suited to the way the program works, resulting in a loss of quality or partial loss of information (disappearance of italics or footnotes, loss of graphics resolution, inability to edit the imported material, or the like). It is also possible to *export* files to a format other than the usual one, but again, loss of information may occur. *See* SAVE AS. *See also* CONVERSION PROGRAM; EXTENSION.

filename the name of a file. *See also* FILE; 8.3 FILENAME; LONG FILE-NAME; EXTENSION.

Usage note: Many publishers prefer to write *file name* as two words.

file permissions *see* PERMISSION.

file server a computer that provides file access for other computers through a local-area network. This saves disk space because each computer no longer needs its own copy of all the software that it uses. Also, it enables separate computers to share and update a single set of files. *See* LOCAL AREA NETWORK; NFS; NOVELL NETWARE.

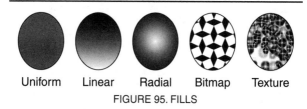

Uniform   Linear   Radial   Bitmap   Texture

FIGURE 95. FILLS

fill (graphics programs) the color of an object. Fills may be of a uniform tone, or they may contain shades that gradually change from one color to another. A fill may even be a pattern. *See also* UNIFORM FILL; LINEAR FILL.

film, digital *see* DIGITAL FILM.

film recorder a device for recording computer-generated images on film in a camera. The most common application is making 35-mm slides for use in presentations or as an output device for photographs that have been electronically retouched.

filter

1. a program that reads a file, byte by byte, and creates another file from it in some way. For example, the DOS sort command can be used as a filter. If you type

```
dir | sort | more
```

you are sending the output of the dir command through the sort command, which acts as a filter to put the lines in alphabetical order; then the result is sent to the more command to be displayed on the screen. This technique originated in UNIX. *See* UNIX.

2. a program that translates files from one format to another when called by the import or export command in a word processor or graphics program. *See* IMPORT; EXPORT; CONVERSION PROGRAM.

3. in paint and photopaint programs, a tool for modifying the image. See IMAGE PROCESSING and its cross-references.

4. in electronics, a device that blocks certain signals or frequencies. *See* ANTIALIASING; RFI PROTECTION.

5. a device that blocks light of certain wavelengths or polarizations. Filters are used in front of computer screens to reduce glare.

6. a material that removes dust particles from air, sometimes used in front of a computer's cooling fan.

7. in Windows programming, a set of patterns that match desired filenames. For example, `*.c;*.h` is a filter that picks out files whose names end in `.c` and `.h`.

find

1. a UNIX command that searches directories to find files with particular attributes. For example, this command starts in the current directory and searches all subdirectories to find files whose name starts with *pas*:

```
find . -name "pas*" -ls
```

In Windows 95 and its successors, a similar function is available from the Start button at the lower left-hand corner of the screen.

2. a DOS command that finds all lines in a text file that contain a particular character string; a less powerful version of the UNIX grep command. For example, this command will display all the lines in myfile.txt that contain the word *birthday*:

```
find "birthday" <myfile.txt
```

To find the lines that do *not* contain *birthday*, add the option /V immediately after find.

find and change (find and replace) SEARCH AND REPLACE.

Finder part of the operating system of the Apple Macintosh. It allows users to copy and manipulate files and execute programs by moving icons on the screen.

fine-grained security a security model allowing the user to control the specific level of access that a particular program has to the computer. For example, a fine grain security system would allow downloaded programs from certain providers to have read/write access to specified directories; read only access to other directories; and no access to other directories. This is generally better than an all-or-nothing approach to security, which forces the user to choose between crippling the functionality of a downloaded program by preventing it from having any access to the local machine, or else risking a breach of security by giving the downloaded program complete access. *See also* SANDBOX.

finger a UNIX command that provides you with information about users of your own or other machines. For example, if you type

```
finger smith@gizmo1.ai.uga.edu
```

your computer will connect with GIZMO1 (the host computer's name) at the University of Georgia and look for a user named Smith; if one exists, you will get that person's full name and e-mail address, along with some other information depending on the exact version of the operating system.

Because the finger command has been abused (to collect addresses for junk e-mailing or even to deliberately overload a machine with requests), many larger UNIX systems no longer answer finger queries. *See* COMPUTER SECURITY.

firewall a link in a network that relays only data packets clearly intended and authorized to reach the other side. Firewalls are helpful in keeping computers safe from intentional hacker attacks and from hardware failures occurring elsewhere.

firewire a serial bus standard more formally known as IEEE 1394. *See* IEEE 1394; SERIAL BUS. *Contrast* USB.

firmware software (i.e., computer programs) that is stored in some fixed form, such as a read-only memory (ROM). *Contrast* SOFTWARE; HARDWARE.

first-generation computers the computers that were built in the late 1940s and early 1950s, using vacuum tubes as switching elements.

fit text to path a draw program command that warps the baseline of a line of text so that it follows the shape of a specified line (PATH). *See* Figure 96 for an example.

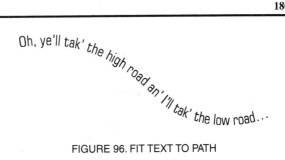

FIGURE 96. FIT TEXT TO PATH

fix a solution to a software defect; typically a new version of a program issued in order to correct a problem. *Compare* PATCH.

fixed disk a disk drive that cannot be removed from the computer in normal use. *See* HARD DISK.

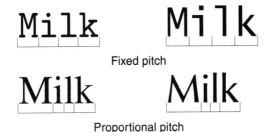

Fixed pitch

Proportional pitch

FIGURE 97. FIXED PITCH VS. PROPORTIONAL PITCH

fixed-pitch type type in which all letters are the same width (e.g., I is the same width as M). Most typewriters and older printers and computer screens use fixed-pitch type. *Contrast* PROPORTIONAL PITCH.

fixed-point number a number in which the position of the decimal point is fixed. For example, amounts of money in U.S. currency can always be represented as numbers with exactly two digits to the right of the point (1.00, 123.45, 0.76, etc.). Contrast FLOATING-POINT NUMBER.

F keys *see* FUNCTION KEYS.

flame *(slang)* an angry, ill-considered e-mail message or newsgroup posting. *See* ELECTRONIC MAIL; NEWSGROUP.

flame war *(slang)* an angry, uninformative quarrel in a NEWSGROUP or other electronic discussion forum.

flash memory a type of EEPROM (electrically erasable programmable read-only memory) that can only be erased all at once; unlike ordinary EEPROM, it cannot be altered one byte at a time.

flatbed scanner a scanner in which the object to be scanned is held flat against a piece of glass. *See* SCANNER.

flat-file database a database like a relational database except that it has only one table. *See* RELATIONAL DATABASE.

flavor
   1. *(slang)* a variety or type of something. For example, CD-ROM, CD-R, and CD-RW might be described as three "flavors" of compact disc.
   2. (in early object-oriented programming experiments at MIT) an inheritable object class.

FIGURE 98. FLEURONS

fleuron a decorative typographic ornament. See Fig. 98 for examples. Fleurons may be used for purely decorative purposes or to mark the beginnings of paragraphs.

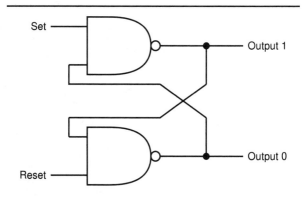

FIGURE 99. FLIP-FLOP CONSTRUCTED FROM NAND GATES

flip-flop an electronic circuit that can switch back and forth between two states (called 0 and 1) and will remain in either state until changed. Flip-flops are the basic component of which CPU registers are composed.

Figure 99 shows how to construct a flip-flop from two NAND gates. It has two possible states: state 1 (in which output 1 = 1) and state 0 (in which output 1 = 0). (Output 0 is always the opposite of output 1.)

If both inputs are 1 when the flip-flip is first powered up, it will settle into one state or the other, at random. Bringing the "set" input momentarily to 0 will put the flip-flop into state 1, and bringing the "reset" input to 0 will put the flip-flop into state 0. Whenever both inputs are 1, the flip-flop stays in whatever state it was already in. Thus, a flip-flop is a 1-bit memory.

More elaborate flip-flops include control circuitry so that the data to be stored in them can be delivered through a single input. A 16-bit CPU register consists of 16 flip-flops side by side.

flip horizontal a command that creates a mirror image of the original object. The image still appears right-side-up, but left and right are reversed.

FIGURE 100. FLIP HORIZONTAL; FLIP VERTICAL

flip vertical a command that turns an image upside down, but maintains the image's left-right orientation, just like a reflection in still water. This is *not* equivalent to rotating the object or defined area 180 degrees. (Try it and see.)

floating illustrations illustrations that should appear near, but not necessarily at, specified positions in a text. For instance, many of the tables in this book are floating illustrations; they appear near the articles that refer to them, but not between particular words. The page-layout software places the illustrations wherever it is convenient to put them.

floating-point number a number in which the decimal point can be in any position. For instance, a memory location set aside for a floating-point number can store 0.735, 62.3, or 1200. By contrast, a fixed-point memory location can only accommodate a specific number of decimal places, usually 2 (for currency) or none (for integers). Floating-point numbers are often written in scientific notation, such as 4.65E4, which means $4.65 \times 10^4 = 46,500$. *See* REAL NUMBER; ROUNDING ERROR; DOUBLE PRECISION. *Contrast* FIXED-POINT NUMBER.

floppy disk *see* DISKETTE.

floppy disk drive a disk drive for diskettes (floppy disks).

floppy tape drive *(slang)* a tape drive connected to a diskette drive controller (floppy disk drive controller). (There is no such thing as "floppy tape.")

flowchart a chart consisting of symbols and words that completely describe an algorithm (i.e., how to solve a problem). Each step in the flowchart is followed by an arrow that indicates which step to do next.

The flowchart in Figure 101 shows how to calculate the cube root of a number a using Newton's method, where x is the guess for the cube root of a, and δ indicates how accurate the result must be. The procedure will follow around the loop until $|x^3 - a| < \delta$.

"Start" and "stop" statements are written with ovals, action statements are written with squares, and decision statements are written in diamonds. A decision statement asks a yes-or-no question. If the answer is yes, the path labeled "yes" is followed; otherwise the other path is followed.

Writing a flowchart often helps to solve a complex programming problem, although flowcharts are seldom used now that structured programming has become popular. A flowchart is often much bulkier than the program it describes. *See* STRUCTURED PROGRAMMING.

flush

> **1.** flat against a margin, as in FLUSH RIGHT and FLUSH LEFT.
> **2.** to finish an output operation by emptying the buffer in which the information is stored while waiting to be output.

flush left an arrangement of text with each line starting at the same horizontal position, making a neat left edge. *Flush left, ragged right* means that the length of the lines are allowed to vary. The right edge looks like a torn piece of paper — in other words, *ragged*.

This is
an example of some
flush-left type.

Flush left is how type is ordinarily arranged on a typewriter. *Contrast* JUSTIFICATION; FLUSH RIGHT; CENTER.

flush right an arrangement of text with each line of type ending at the same horizontal position. The beginnings of the lines are irregular, but the right margin is smooth.

> This is
> an example of
> flush-right type.

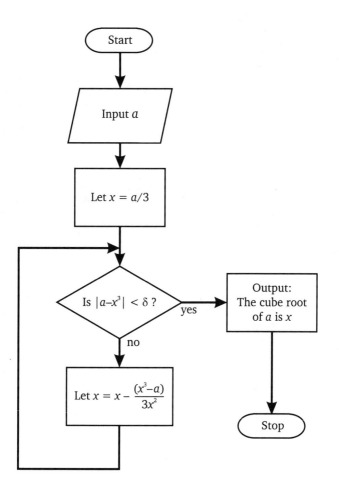

FIGURE 101. FLOWCHART

Flush-right alignment is seldom used except in charts or tables. *Contrast* FLUSH LEFT; JUSTIFICATION; CENTER.

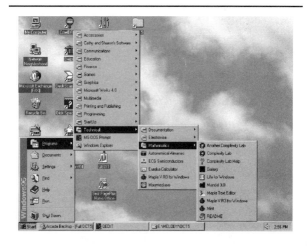

FIGURE 102. FLY-OUT MENUS IN WINDOWS 95

fly-out menu a secondary menu that appears to the side when you select an item on the primary menu.

FM synthesis (**f**requency **m**odulation **s**ynthesis) a technique of synthesizing musical sounds by using one waveform to modulate (vary) the frequency of another waveform. FM synthesis is an older technique for generating electronic music. It produces a wide variety of sounds, but does not imitate conventional musical instruments as closely as WAVETABLE SYNTHESIS does. *Contrast* WAVETABLE SYNTHESIS.

FOAF (**f**riend **o**f **a** **f**riend) an unidentified source of a piece of information. *See* HOAX.

focus the part of a DIALOG BOX that is ready to receive input from the keyboard. The focus is generally indicated by highlighting with a special color or with an extra dotted line around a BUTTON.

folder a subdirectory (Macintosh, Windows 95 and its successors) or a group of program icons (OS/2). *See* DIRECTORY.

font a complete collection of characters (including upper- and lowercase letters, numerals, punctuation, ligatures, reference marks, etc.) in a consistent style and size. Desktop publishing programs and word processors let you use more than one font in a single document. When

ABCDEFGHIJKLMNOPQRSTUVWXYZ
abcdefghijklmnopqrstuvwxyz
!"#$%&'()*+,-./0123456789:;<=>?
@[\]^_`~,ƒ„…†‡ˆ‰Š‹Œ''""•——˜™š›œŸ¡¢
£¤¥¦§¨ª«¬-®¯°±²³´µ¶·¸¹º»¼½¾¿
ÀÁÂÃÄÅÆÇÈÉÊËÌÍÎÏÐÑ
ÒÓÔÕÖ×ØÙÚÛÜÝÞß
àáâãäåæçèéêëìíîïðñòóôõö÷øùúûüýþÿ

FIGURE 103. A FONT (TIMES NEW ROMAN)

you switch to italics or to bold or to a larger size, you are changing the *font* even though you may still be in the same TYPEFACE.

Some fonts are specifically designed to be printed at a particular size. For instance, if you have 8-point Dutch Roman and 12-point Dutch Roman on your laser printer font cartridge, you cannot use intermediate sizes such as 9-point. If the largest font you have is 72 points, then you will not be able to set 96-point type. Current systems use SCALABLE FONTS that can be used at any size. *See also* MULTIPLE MASTER FONT; TYPE I FONT; TRUETYPE.

font cartridge a plug-in device for a laser printer or certain other printers that contains additional fonts (kinds of type) recorded on ROM chips. *Contrast* INTERNAL FONT; SOFT FONT.

foolscap a traditional British paper size, 8 × 13 inches, now being superseded by ISO A4. *See* PAPER SIZES (ISO).

foot the bottom of the page. *Contrast* HEAD.

footer text that is placed at the bottom of each page of a printed document. *Contrast* HEADER.

footnote a short comment placed at the bottom (FOOT) of a page that provides a citation or insightful comment to the text.[*] Some word processors cannot handle footnotes properly, placing them at the end of the chapter or article rather than at the foot of the page where they belong.

Footnotes should be numbered consecutively throughout an entire book, or beginning again for each chapter or page. Sometimes footnotes are not numbered, but are referenced by a traditional set of symbols.

---

[*]This is a footnote. Notice that the asterisk in the footnote matches the asterisk in the text. The typeface used for the footnote is smaller than the font used for the body copy. A horizontal rule or extra vertical space should be used to separate the footnote from the text.

They should be used in this order: ASTERISK (*), DAGGER (†), DOUBLE DAGGER (‡), SECTION SIGN (§), and PILCROW (¶).

footprint the amount of space on a desk that a device takes up. For example, a laptop computer has a smaller footprint than a full-size PC. A smaller footprint is desirable because it leaves more space for other items on your desk. *See also* REAL ESTATE.

for a keyword that identifies one type of loop in BASIC, Pascal, C, Java, and Algol. (It corresponds to DO in PL/I and FORTRAN.)

A FOR loop causes a certain variable, known as the loop variable, to take on several values in sequence. For example, these groups of statements, in BASIC and Pascal, respectively, print out the whole numbers from 1 to 10:

```
05 REM This is BASIC:
10 FOR I= 1 TO 10
20    PRINT I
30 NEXT I
```

```
{ This is Pascal: }
FOR i:= 1 TO 10 DO writeln(i);
```

A FOR loop can be used either to obtain repetition or to make the values of the variable available for some purpose. For example, here is how to calculate the sum of the whole numbers from 1 to 100:

```
05 REM In BASIC:
10 LET T = 0
20 FOR I = 1 TO 100
30    LET T = T + I
40 NEXT I
50 PRINT T
```

```
{ In Pascal: }
PROGRAM addup (output);
VAR i,t: INTEGER;
BEGIN
   t := 0;
   FOR i:= 1 TO 100 DO t := t + i;
writeln(t)
END.
```

Although the statements within the loop can examine the value of the loop variable, they should not attempt to change it, since the result of doing so is unpredictable.

In Pascal, the way to include more than one statement in the loop is to bracket the statements between BEGIN and END, like this:

```
FOR i:=1 TO 5 DO
```

```
BEGIN
  writeln(i);
  j := j+i
END
```

In C and Java, the for statement is more general; it takes the form

for (*init*; *test*; *step*) { *statements* }

where *init* is a statement that is executed once, before beginning the loop; *test* is a condition that must be true at the beginning of every pass through the loop; *step* is a statement executed at the end of each pass; and *statements* are the statements within the loop, if any. For example, here is how to print the integers from 1 to 10 in C:

for (i=1; i<11; i++) { printf("%d\n", i); }

In Java, this is written:

for (i=1; i<11; i++) { System.out.println(i); }

Unlike its BASIC and Pascal counterparts, the C and Java for statement need not step a number through a series of values; it can be used for many other kinds of repeated actions, because *init, test,* and *step* can be statements and tests of any kind.

force quit (Macintosh) to escape from a frozen or hung program by pressing the Option, Command (⌘), and Escape keys simultaneously. It is highly recommended to restart your Mac after a force quit—the operating system may be unstable.

The iMac does not respond to Option-Command (⌘)-Escape. However, a recessed reset button can be pressed with a straightened paper clip.

See FREEZE; HANG; CRASH.

form a screen display in which the user is expected to type in information and then press Enter or click OK. Forms enable readers of WEB PAGES to send information to the host site.

formal parameter a name used within a function or subroutine for a value that will be passed to it from the calling program. *Contrast* ACTUAL PARAMETER.

format any method of arranging information that is to be stored or displayed. The word *format* can therefore refer to many different things relating to computers. Four of its most common uses are as follows:

1. The format of a file (or of any storage medium) refers to the way the information is stored in it. *See* FILE FORMAT.

2. To format a disk or tape is to make the computer record a pattern of reference marks on it. A brand-new disk or tape must always be formatted before it can be used, unless it was formatted at the factory. Formatting a disk or tape erases any information previously recorded on it.

3. In FORTRAN, the FORMAT statement specifies the form in which data items, especially numbers, are to be read or written. *See* FORTRAN.

4. In a spreadsheet, the format of a cell determines the appearance of the output (how many digits are displayed, whether there is a dollar sign, etc.).

formatting the special codes in a document that indicate italics, underlining, boldface, and the like. Formatting information is lost when a file is saved as ASCII text.

form factor the size and shape of a piece of equipment or material. Diskette drive form factors include HALF-HEIGHT and FULL-HEIGHT. Motherboard form factors include AT (like the original PC AT), "Baby AT" (a smaller board that mounts in the same case), and ATX (a newer type of motherboard introduced by Intel and others in 1996).

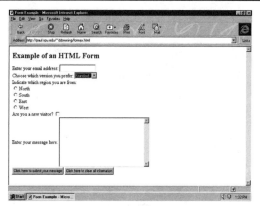

FIGURE 104. HTML FORM (AS DISPLAYED ON SCREEN)

form, HTML a web page that allows users to enter data, which can then be sent back to the server. Here is an example of the HTML code for a form where users can enter an e-mail address into a text field, use a list box to select either the deluxe, special, or standard version; use radio buttons to indicate which region they are from; use a check box to indicate whether they are a first-time visitor or not; and enter a brief message into a text area.

The ACTION command of this form will simply e-mail the result of the form to the specified address. It is also possible to specify a

```
<HTML><HEAD><TITLE>Form Example</TITLE></HEAD>
<BODY>
<H2>Example of an HTML Form</H2>
<FORM METHOD=POST ACTION="MAILTO:yourcompany@xyz.com">
Enter your e-mail address:
<INPUT TYPE="TEXT" NAME="EMAIL" WIDTH=25><BR>
Choose which version you prefer:
<SELECT NAME="VERSION">
<OPTION SELECTED> Standard
<OPTION> Special
<OPTION> Deluxe</SELECT><BR>
Indicate which region you are from:<BR>
<INPUT NAME="REGION" TYPE="RADIO"
     VALUE="North"> North<BR>
<INPUT NAME="REGION" TYPE="RADIO"
     VALUE="South"> South<BR>
<INPUT NAME="REGION" TYPE="RADIO"
     VALUE="East"> East <BR>
<INPUT NAME="REGION" TYPE="RADIO"
     VALUE="West"> West <BR>
Are you a new visitor?
<INPUT TYPE="CHECKBOX" NAME="NEWVISITOR"
     VALUE="yes"><BR>
Enter your message here:
<TEXTAREA COLS=60 ROWS=10 NAME="MESSAGETEXT"><BR>
<INPUT TYPE="SUBMIT"
     VALUE="Click here to submit your message">
<INPUT TYPE="RESET"
     VALUE="Click here to clear all information">
</FORM>
</BODY>
</HTML>
```

FIGURE 105. HTML FORM (SOURCE CODE)

CGI script as the ACTION. This script needs to be specially written to process the results of the form once they are sent back to the server. The text that is not enclosed by < > are labels; see Figure 104, which shows how this form appears on the screen. Each element of the form needs to have a name by which it is identified to the server; in this example, the names are EMAIL, VERSION, NEWVISITOR, REGION, and MESSAGETEXT. Finally, the form has a submit button for the user to click when ready to send the information, and a reset button to clear information if desired.

For another example of an HTML form, see JAVASCRIPT.

FORTH a programming language invented by Charles Moore around 1970. FORTH is noted for requiring few machine resources and giving very rapid execution.

In FORTH, programmers define their own statements in terms of

```
C FORTRAN IV program to
C find sum of integers 1-100
      INTEGER I, SUM
      SUM=0
      DO 1 I=1, 100
    1 SUM = SUM + I
      WRITE (6,2) SUM
    2 FORMAT(1X,I5)
      STOP
      END
```

FIGURE 106. FORTRAN IV PROGRAM

simpler statements. FORTH is a *threaded interpretive language,* meaning that a program is represented in the computer as a list of addresses of subroutines, each of which is composed of addresses of other subroutines, and so on until the primitive operations of the language are reached. Because it has little to do except read addresses and jump to them, a FORTH interpreter can run very fast; in fact, there is little difference between an interpreter and a compiler for FORTH.

FORTRAN (**For**mula **Tran**slation) a programming language developed by IBM in the late 1950s, the first major programming language that allowed programmers to describe calculations by means of mathematical formulas. Instead of writing assembly language instructions such as

```
LOAD A
ADD B
MULTIPLY C
STORE D
```

the FORTRAN programmer writes

```
D = (A+B)*C
```

where * is the symbol for multiplication. Almost all subsequent programming languages have adopted this useful feature.

FORTRAN has existed in several versions, of which the most important are FORTRAN IV (USASI Standard FORTRAN, 1966) and FORTRAN 77 (ANSI FORTRAN, 1977). Fig. 106 shows a sample FORTRAN IV program.

Comments begin with C in column 1; all other statements begin in column 7, though they may have numbers in columns 2–5. Any line with column 6 nonblank is treated as a continuation of the previous statement.

The FORMAT statement in the example specifies that the output should consist of a single blank, followed by an integer occupying 5 character positions. The blank is not actually printed; it serves as *carriage control* and tells the printer to print a new line in the normal manner. This is a relic of early IBM printers that used the first character of each line as a control code for various printer functions. The number 6 in the WRITE statement refers to the printer — another relic of early IBM computer architecture.

FORTRAN variable names contain up to six letters or digits; the first character must be a letter. Variables can be declared as INTEGER, REAL (floating-point), DOUBLE PRECISION (like real, but with more significant digits), COMPLEX (*see* COMPLEX NUMBER), LOGICAL (Boolean), or (in FORTRAN 77) CHARACTER. If a variable is not declared, it is assumed to be integer if its name begins with I, J, K, L, M, or N, or real otherwise.

Compared to FORTRAN IV, FORTRAN 77 includes more sophisticated input-output statements, especially for file handling; the ability to process character-string data; and block-structured IF-ELSE-ENDIF statements to facilitate structured programming (see STRUCTURED PROGRAMMING).

forward one a graphics program command that moves the selected object up one in the stacking order. *See also* BACK ONE; SEND TO BACK; SEND TO FRONT; DRAW PROGRAM; VECTOR GRAPHICS.

FIGURE 107. FOUNTAIN FILLS

fountain fill a fill that is composed of two or more colors. In between the colors is a smooth blending. You are able to rotate the angle of the fill (linear) or have the blend radiate from a central point (radial). Figure 107 shows a sampling of different fountain fills. *See also* UNIFORM FILL; GRADIENT PAINT ROLLER. Also called a GRADIENT FILL.

fourth-generation computers computers built around integrated circuits with large-scale integration. Some people view these computers as being advanced third-generation computers.

FPM (**f**ast **p**age **m**ode) the conventional type of dynamic random-access memory (DRAM) used in the early 1990s. Memory access normally takes two bus cycles. (These cycles are cycles of a fast bus that connects directly to the CPU, rather than the slower bus that connects to expansion cards.) FPM memory is being superseded by EDO memory. *See also* EDO; SDRAM.

FPS (**F**rames **P**er **S**econd) the rate at which a moving video image is displayed. For example, American TV images are displayed at 30 fps, with each frame divided into two interlaced scans to reduce flicker.

FPX file extension for a graphical file in FlashPix format.

FIGURE 108. A FRACTAL BUILT FROM A TRIANGLE
(THE KOCH SNOWFLAKE)

fractal a shape that contains an infinite amount of fine detail. That is, no matter how much a fractal is enlarged, there is still more detail to be revealed by enlarging it further. Fractals are common in nature; they are the shapes of clouds, coastlines, broken rocks, the edges of torn pieces of paper, and the like. Fractals are important in generating realistic images of everyday objects on the computer.

Figure 108 shows how to construct a fractal called a Koch snowflake. Start with a triangle and repeatedly replace every straight line with a bent line of the form:

The picture shows the result of doing this 0, 1, 2, and 3 times. If this were done an infinite number of times, the result would be a fractal.

Fig. 109 shows a QBASIC program that can generate this pattern. Note that it uses recursion, since each part of the pattern can be generated by using even smaller repetitions of the same pattern. *See* RECURSION. *See also* MANDELBROT SET.

fragmentation a situation in which many files on a hard disk are broken into little chunks and stored in physically different areas of the disk platter. This can dramatically slow down access time and create long waits while files are being read or written.

A disk becomes fragmented when many files are created and erased on it over a long period of time. Files are recorded continuously on an empty disk, but as files of various sizes get erased, empty spots develop that gradually become filled in with parts of newly recorded files. Eventually, when the user creates a large file, the file will be given space in many disconnected places all over the disk (*see* Figure 110 for an illustration).

```
' QBASIC program to draw Koch snowflake
' D. Downing and M. Covington 1991, 1995

INPUT "How many levels of recursion"; levels%
SCREEN 11
snowflake 280.0,  10.0, 164.5, 210.0, levels%
snowflake 164.5, 210.0, 395.5, 210.0, levels%
snowflake 395.5, 210.0, 280.0,  10.0, levels%
END

SUB snowflake (x1, y1, x2, y2, levels%)
  IF levels% = 0 THEN
    ' just draw a line
    LINE (x1, y1)-(x2, y2)
  ELSE
    ' compute 3 more points
    x4 = x1*2/3 + x2*1/3
    y4 = y1*2/3 + y2*1/3
    x5 = x1*1/3 + x2*2/3
    y5 = y1*1/3 + y2*2/3
    x6 = (x4+x5)/2 + (y4-y5)*SQR(3)/2
    y6 = (y4+y5)/2 + (x5-x4)*SQR(3)/2
    ' call snowflake recursively
    snowflake x1, y1, x4, y4, levels%-1
    snowflake x4, y4, x6, y6, levels%-1
    snowflake x6, y6, x5, y5, levels%-1
    snowflake x5, y5, x2, y2, levels%-1
  END IF
END SUB
```

FIGURE 109. FRACTAL-DRAWING ALGORITHM

A disk can be defragmented by copying all the files to another disk. Programs exist for some machines that will defragment a disk "in place" by carefully rearranging the files without copying to another disk.

frame

1. one in a succession of pictures in a video or animation. When displayed rapidly one after the other, successive frames give the impression of movement. *See* ANIMATION.

2. a boxed area in a web page. *See* FRAME, HTML.

3. a boxed area that is to contain text or a graphic (WORD PROCESSING, PAGE LAYOUT SOFTWARE).

Fragmented disk   Defragmented disk
FIGURE 110. FRAGMENTATION
DARK AREAS SHOW SECTORS OCCUPIED BY ONE FILE

frame grabber an accessory device that takes an image from a video camera, VCR, or other video input and digitizes it, creating a bitmap image. A video image consists of *frames* (successive pictures) transmitted at the rate of 30 per second, and the frame grabber must *grab* and digitize one of them.

frame, HTML an area in a web page that scrolls independently of the rest of the web page. A web page can be divided into multiple frames. For example, one frame can include a navigation bar that always stays on the screen as the user moves around the text of the page that appears in the other frame.

Here is an HTML file that divides the browser window into two frames. The two files mentioned in it, `navbar.html` and `main.html`, are the source files for the separate frames.

```
<HTML>
<frameset rows="100%, *"  cols="35%,100%">
<frame src="navbar.html" name="NavigationBar"
    scrolling=auto>
<frame src="main.html" name="main"
    scrolling=auto>
</frameset>
</HTML>
```

Here is file `navbar.html`, which produces the navigation bar in the left-hand frame:

```
<HTML><BODY>
<P><A TARGET="main" HREF="main.html#sec1">
        Section 1</A>
```

FIGURE 111. HTML FRAMES

```
<P><A TARGET="main" HREF="main.html#sec2">
        Section 2</A>
<P><A TARGET="main" HREF="main.html#sec3">
        Section 3</A>
</BODY></HTML>
```

The following file, main.html, produces the main frame:

```
<HTML><BODY>
<H1><A NAME="sec1"> Section 1</A></H1>
The rest of the text for section 1 would go here
<H1><A NAME="sec2"> Section 2</A> </H1>
The rest of the text for section 2 would go here
<H1><A NAME="sec3"> Section 3</A></H1>
The rest of the text for section 3 would go here
</HTML></BODY>
```

Figure 111 shows the appearance of this page when displayed by the browser. If the right hand frame did contain a large amount of text, the user could scroll through it while the links on the left hand side always stayed in the same place, making it easier to jump to other sections of the document.

framing error an error that occurs when an asynchronously transmitted character appears to contain the wrong number of bits. *See* ASYNCHRONOUS; RS-232. Framing errors usually result from transmitting or receiving at the wrong speed.

free software several kinds of computer software that can legally be copied and given free of charge to other users:

1. *Public-domain software.* This is software that is not covered by any kind of copyright. Few substantial public-domain programs exist, but the term public-domain is often used incorrectly to refer to other kinds of free software.

2. *Software that is copyrighted but is distributed free with permission of the copyright owner.* Two famous examples are the Kermit communication program and the TeX typesetting program (*see* KERMIT; TEX). Many UNIX utilities are also in this category.

3. *Shareware.* This is copyrighted software that can be distributed free to anyone, but which requests or requires a payment from satisfied users directly to the author. Shareware is often misleadingly described as "free."

Free Software Foundation *See* GNU.

freeware *see* FREE SOFTWARE.

freeze to stop responding to input; to HANG. A frozen computer shows no activity on screen or on the front panel of the computer system and will not respond to the keyboard. Many times, the mouse cursor disappears. In Windows 95 and its successors, control can often be regained by pressing Ctrl-Alt-Del simultaneously and letting the operating system close the offending software. Macintosh users can often escape from a frozen program by pressing ⟨Option⟩⟨Command⟩⟨Esc⟩ and then selecting the FORCE QUIT button.

freeze date a date after which the specifications for a software project cannot be changed. *See* SOFTWARE ENGINEERING.

friendly name the most familiar or meaningful of several names denoting the same thing. For example, a networked printer might be known as \\gizmo1\ttya-lj4 and as Office Printer. The latter is its friendly name.

front end a computer or a program that helps you communicate with another computer or program. For example, supercomputers usually do not communicate with their users directly; instead users submit programs through another computer called the front end.

FS e-mail abbreviation for "**f**or **s**ale."

FTP (**F**ile **T**ransfer **P**rotocol) a standard way of transferring files from one computer to another on the Internet and on other TCP/IP networks. (*See* TCP/IP.) FTP is also the name of any of various computer programs that implement the file transfer protocol.

When you connect to a remote computer, the FTP program asks you for your user name and password. If you do not have an account on the computer that you have connected to, you can use *anonymous FTP* to retrieve files that are available to the general public. In that case the procedure is to give *anonymous* as your user name and then type your e-mail address in place of the password. Also remember to use

```
C:\> ftp
ftp> open ai.uga.edu
Connected to ai.uga.edu FTP server.
ftp> user
User name: anonymous
Password: yourname@your.site.address
User 'anonymous' logged in.
ftp> cd /pub/pc.utilities
ftp> binary
ftp> dir
pkzip.exe
ahed.zip
pred.zip
ftp> get pred.zip
pred.zip transferred, 17895 bytes in 2.5 seconds
ftp> quit
```

FIGURE 112. FTP SESSION
(USER'S COMMANDS ARE IN ITALICS)

the command `binary` if the file you are transferring is anything other than plain ASCII text. Figure 112 shows an example of an anonymous FTP session.

You can also retrieve files by FTP using a web browser. For example, to retrieve the file whose name is `filename` in directory `pub/directoryname` on host `ftp.cdrom.com`, give the URL as:

`ftp://ftp.cdrom.com/pub/directoryname/filename`

If you need to specify an account name and password, do this:

`ftp://userid:password@zzzzz.com/directoryname/filename`

Most browsers will prompt you for the password if you leave it out.

One of the most popular FTP sites, offering large amounts of free software, is `ftp.cdrom.com`. *See also* WORLD WIDE WEB; INTERNET.

FTP site a computer that makes files available for downloading by FTP.

FUD (**F**ear, **U**ncertainty, and **D**oubt) the tactic of trying to make customers afraid of adopting a rival product by creating doubts about its future.

full adder a logic circuit that accepts three one-digit binary numbers (two addends and one digit carried from the previous column) and produces two outputs, a sum output and a carry output. *See* BINARY ADDITION.

full duplex the transmission of data in two directions simultaneously. *Contrast* HALF DUPLEX; *see* MODEM.

full-height drive a $5\frac{1}{4}$-inch disk drive that is approximately $3\frac{1}{4}$ inches high, twice the height of a half-height drive. Full-height drives are now obsolete; the standard sizes are half-height (about 1.6 inches) and one-inch.

full-text search the act of searching through every word in a set of documents to retrieve information you are interested in. This is a slow but thorough way to use a computer to search through web pages, court records, scholarly journals, or other material to retrieve items that you are interested in. *See also* BOOLEAN QUERY; SEARCH ENGINE.

function

1. (in mathematics) a value that depends on one or more *arguments* in such a way that, for any particular set of arguments, the function has only one value. For example, the positive real square root of a number is a function of that number. The sum of two numbers is a function of the two numbers. A function need not exist for all possible arguments; for example, negative numbers have no (real) square roots.

2. (in computer programming) a subprogram that acts like a mathematical function: given a particular set of argument values, the function returns a unique result. In traditional BASIC, functions are defined using the DEF command. For example:

```
10   DEF FNR(X) = (INT(100*X + .5))/100
```

This statement defines a function called FNR that rounds any number off to the nearest hundredth. X represents the argument of the function. To use the function in a program, type the function name followed, in parentheses, by the number you want rounded. For example, FNR(3.457) will have the value 3.46, and FNR(104.011) will have the value 104.01.

In FORTRAN, Pascal, and newer versions of BASIC, a function is a subprogram of any length. Here is an example of a simple Pascal function that doubles a number:

```
FUNCTION double(b: REAL): REAL;
BEGIN
   double := 2*b
END;
```

For example, double(23.4) will have the value 46.8. Here is an example of a more complicated Pascal function that calculates the factorial of a number (*see* FACTORIAL):

```
FUNCTION fact(n:INTEGER): REAL ;
VAR z:REAL; i:INTEGER;
BEGIN
   z := 1;
   IF n>1 THEN
     FOR i:=1 TO n DO
```

```
      z := z*i;
   fact := z
END;
```

The top line tells the computer that the name of the function is `fact`, the argument is of type integer, and the result is of type real. For example, `fact(6)` has the value 720.

In C and LISP, all procedures are called functions, and the value returned is often ignored. *See* PROCEDURE.

function keys (F keys) keys labeled F1 to F12 on the IBM PC and PS/2 keyboards (F1 to F10 on earlier models), and similar keys on other kinds of computers. Their function depends on the software being run. *See also* PROGRAMMABLE FUNCTION KEY.

fuzzy logic a formal system of reasoning developed by Lotfi Zadeh in which the values "true" and "false" are replaced by numbers on a scale from 0 to 1. The operators *and*, *or*, and the like are replaced by procedures for combining these numbers. *See* BOOLEAN ALGEBRA.

Fuzzy logic captures the fact that some questions do not have a simple yes-or-no answer. For example, in ordinary English a 6-foot-high man might or might not be described as tall. In fuzzy logic, a 6-foot man might be tall with a truth value of 0.7, and a 7-foot man might be tall with a truth value of 1.0. A problem with fuzzy logic is that there is often no clear way to come up with the numbers that are used as truth values. For an alternative, *see* DEFAULT LOGIC.

Fuzzy logic is often used in expert systems; it nicely bridges the gap between logical inference and mathematical modeling. *See* EXPERT SYSTEM; CONFIDENCE FACTOR.

FWIW e-mail abbreviation for "for what it's worth."

G

gain the amount of amplification in an audio amplifier or similar circuit. Adjusting the gain is one way to control the loudness of the sound from a sound card.

gamma (γ)
　　1.　in computer graphics, a measure of the nonlinear response of a video screen. The brightness of a pixel on the screen is not proportional to the brightness value sent to it from software. Instead, the actual brightness B is

$$B = aV^\gamma$$

where a is a constant, V is the brightness value, and the exponent γ is usually about 2 to 2.5. If gamma is known, it can be corrected so that all parts of the image are displayed with the specified brightness.
　　2.　in photography, a measure of contrast. Normally, the gamma of film is about 0.7 and the gamma of photographic paper is about 1.4. When multiplied together, the two give a gamma of 1 so that the picture has the same contrast as the original subject.

gamma testing a third stage of software testing sometimes peformed after beta testing but before commercial release. In gamma testing, the software is believed to be complete and free of errors, but the manuals and packaging may not yet be in final form. *See also* ALPHA TESTING and BETA TESTING.

gamut
　　1.　in music, the range of notes in the scale.
　　2.　in color graphics, the range of colors that a screen or output device can display. No output device can produce all the colors that the eye can see. Color video screens are particularly limited. Their primary red is actually pinkish orange, and they cannot display strong ruby reds and purples. Printing inks are subject to different limits. Some graphics software packages provide gamut warnings to indicate colors that are out of the gamut of the intended output device. *See also* RGB MONITOR; HSB; and CMYK.

Gantt chart a diagram that shows the schedule for a series of tasks. *See example at* PROJECT MANAGEMENT.

garbage collection clearing out objects that are taking up space in memory but are no longer in use by a program. In Lisp, Prolog, and Java, garbage collection happens automatically. In C++, there is no garbage collection; the programmer must specifically release the memory taken up by an object when it is no longer needed.

gas plasma display a computer display that works on the same principle as a neon light; the display is usually orange on black. Gas plasma screens were used on early laptop computers. They are bright and easy to read, but they consume considerably more electricity than LCD displays. A plasma is a glowing, ionized gas.

gate
  1. one of the three parts of a field-effect transistor. *See* FIELD-EFFECT TRANSISTOR.
  2. any of several logic circuits. *See* AND GATE; OR GATE; NOT GATE; NOR GATE; NAND GATE; LOGIC CIRCUITS.

gateway a link between different computer networks.

GB *see* GIGABYTE.

GC *see* GARBAGE COLLECTION.

gcc *See* CC.

general failure in DOS and similar operating systems, the inability to complete an operation for an unknown reason, apparently a hardware failure. If a disk drive is defective or incorrectly installed, you will get "general failure" error messages when you try to use it. *See also* ABORT, RETRY, FAIL.

germanium a chemical element used to make semiconductor devices. (*See* SEMICONDUCTOR.) Germanium semiconductors have now been almost completely replaced by silicon.

FIGURE 113. GHOSTING

ghosting superimposing an image or object onto another image by making the upper object translucent. A popular use of ghosting is to lighten or darken part of a photograph so that overprinted type will be legible. *See* Figure 113 for example.

GIF (**G**raphics **I**nterchange **F**ormat) a file format developed by CompuServe for storing bitmap images on disk. (*See* BITMAP; COMPUSERVE.) GIF images can have up to $65,536 \times 65,536$ pixels and 256 colors. GIF is a common format for images on the World Wide Web. *Compare* TIFF; PCX.

giga- metric prefix meaning $\times 1,000,000,000$ (10^9) or, in rating computer memories and disks, $\times 1,073,741,824$ $(= 1024^3)$. *Giga-* is derived from the Greek word for "giant." *See* METRIC PREFIXES.

gigabyte (GB) approximately one billion bytes. With computer memories, one gigabyte is always $2^{30} = 1,073,741,824$ bytes = 1024 megabytes. With disk drives, a gigabyte is sometimes understood as 1000 megabytes. *See also* MEGABYTE.

gigahertz (GHz) one billion cycles per second, a unit of frequency equal to 1000 megahertz; a measure of the frequency of a radio signal or an electrical oscillation. *See* HERTZ; MEGAHERTZ; CLOCK; MICROPROCESSOR; WIRELESS COMMUNICATION; RF.

glitch erroneous response that occurs inside a computer because signals that are supposed to be simultaneous actually arrive at slightly different times. Software errors are occasionally called glitches. *See* BUG.

Global Positioning System *see* GPS.

global variable a variable that can be recognized anywhere in a program. *Contrast* LOCAL VARIABLE.

glue logic additional, relatively simple logic circuits needed to connect one major part of a computer to another. For example, many microprocessors require some glue logic between the CPU and the memory. *See* LOGIC CIRCUITS.

glyph any printable character; the printed appearance of a character.

Gnu a project led by Richard Stallman of the Free Software Foundation. *Gnu* stands for "**G**nu is **n**ot UNIX"; the Gnu project's original goal was to develop a freely distributed substitute for UNIX, but Linux and other projects, starting later, have already reached that goal. The most important Gnu products are the Emacs editor and the Gnu C Compiler.

Gnu software is copyrighted and is distributed free subject to certain conditions (typically, you must distribute it complete and intact, with source code). This set of conditions is sometimes called "copyleft" (i.e., a copyright with the opposite of its usual function) and also applies to some other free software, such as Linux. *See also* FREE SOFTWARE.

gooey pronunciation of *GUI*. *See* GRAPHICAL USER INTERFACE.

Gopher a computer program, and an accompanying data transfer protocol, for reading information that has been made available to the public on the Internet. Gopher is supported by the University of Minnesota and uses a menu-driven user interface. It has mostly been superseded by HTTP (Hypertext Transfer Protocol) and browsers such as Netscape (which can read Gopher information as well as HTTP information). The name "gopher" is a pun on "go for" (i.e., go and get things). *See* WORLD WIDE WEB.

gotcha *(slang)* a pitfall; a feature that leads to mistakes. *Compare* MISFEATURE.

GO TO or **GOTO**; a statement in Fortran, BASIC, and other programming languages that transfers execution to another place in the program. For example, here is a BASIC program that prints "Hello" 1000 times:

```
10     LET X=0
20     PRINT "HELLO"
30     LET X=X+1
40     IF X<1000 THEN GO TO 20
```

Use of the GO TO statement has been strongly discouraged since the 1970s, when E. W. Dijkstra and others discovered that it was very error-prone. If a program contains GO TO statements, it's hard to tell, by looking at it, exactly how it will work, because execution can jump from any point to any other point. Instead, statements such as FOR, WHILE, and REPEAT are much easier for the programmer to get correct. *See* STRUCTURED PROGRAMMING.

gov suffix indicating that an E-MAIL address or WEB SITE is at a government site in the United States, such as www.whitehouse.gov. *See* URL; DOMAIN.

GPF (**G**eneral **P**rotection **F**ault) an error that arises in Microsoft Windows when a program tries to access a location in memory that is not allocated to it. GPFs are usually caused by programming errors such as uninitialized pointers. Software that produces GPFs is defective or improperly configured. *See also* ILLEGAL OPERATION.

GPS (**G**lobal **P**ositioning **S**ystem) a network of 24 satellites allowing users with portable GPS devices to determine precise locations on the surface of the Earth. The portable GPS device measures the exact time taken for signals to reach it from at least four different satellites; from this, the instrument can compute its location.

GPS was developed by the U.S. Department of Defense for military purposes, but it has plenty of civilian applications. Hikers and campers can use it to plot their position on maps. GPS-equipped automobiles can call up computerized maps showing their exact position. Police cars can transmit their exact position to the dispatcher automatically. Boats and ships can use GPS for practically effortless navigation.

To keep GPS from being accurate enough for enemy military use, the Department of Defense originally introduced constantly varying errors that limited GPS's accuracy to about 300 feet (100 m). This system of intentional errors was called *Selective Availability.* When Selective Availability was turned off in May 2000, the accuracy became approximately 100 feet (30 m).

gradient fill a fill that is composed of two or more colors. In between the colors is a smooth blending. You are able to rotate the angle of the fill (linear) or have the blend radiate from a central point (radial). *See also* UNIFORM FILL; GRADIENT PAINT ROLLER. *See also* FOUNTAIN FILL.

FIGURE 114. GRADIENT PAINT ROLLER

gradient paint roller a tool available in some paint and photopaint programs that fills an area with a gradual transition from one color to another. This is analogous to a FOUNTAIN FILL in a DRAW PROGRAM.

grandfather tape a tape that is two generations older than the current data; for example, a backup tape from two days ago if backups are done daily. *See also* HARD DISK MANAGEMENT.

graph a graphical display of information, designed to make it easier for the reader to interpret and understand numerical data. *See* BAR GRAPH and PIE CHART for examples.

graphical user interface (GUI) a way of communicating with the computer by manipulating icons (pictures) and windows with a mouse. Before GUIs became widespread, it was common for computers to operate in a mode where only text (no graphics) could be displayed on the screen.

Xerox developed a machine with a graphical user interface in the 1970s, but the first widely used GUI machine was the Apple Macintosh in 1984. The release of Microsoft Windows 3.0 in 1990 led to widespread use of a graphical user interface on IBM PC-compatible computers. For examples, *see* WINDOWS; MACINTOSH.

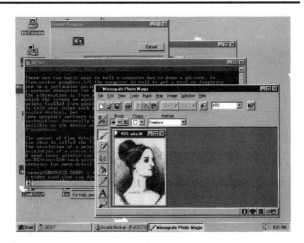

FIGURE 115. GRAPHICAL USER INTERFACE (WINDOWS 95)

graphics the use of computer output devices, such as screens, printers, and plotters, to produce pictures. The applications of computer graphics include publishing, education, entertainment, and the visualization of computed data (such as graphs of mathematical functions).

There are two basic ways to tell a computer how to draw a picture. In *vector graphics,* the computer is told to put a real or imaginary pen in a particular position and then draw a line a certain distance in a certain direction (or draw a line to another specific point). The alternative is *raster graphics* or *bitmap graphics,* in which the screen or plotting area is divided into a rectangular array of points (called *pixels,* from "picture cells"), and the computer is told what color each point should be. Computer screens and printers are raster devices, but some graphics software uses vector-style instructions internally so that all lines will appear as sharp as possible on the device actually used to display them.

The amount of fine detail that a particular graphics device can show is called the *resolution.* The resolution of a printer is usually given in dots per inch; the resolution of a screen is given as the size of the whole image. A good laser printer can print 600 dots (pixels) per inch, so that an 8×10-inch picture is a 4800×6000 array of pixels and contains far more detail than the screen can display.

graphics card a video card that can display graphics as well as text. All modern video cards are graphics cards. *See* VGA; SUPER VGA.

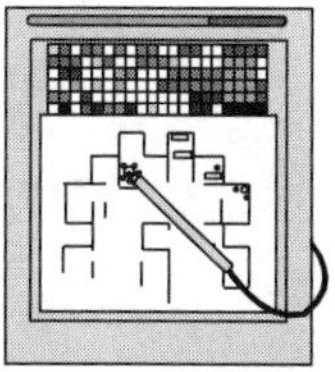

FIGURE 116. GRAPHICS TABLET

graphics tablet an alternative pointing device. A graphics tablet consists of a pressure-sensitive pad on which you draw with a special pen called a STYLUS. This is much more natural than attempting to draw with a mouse. *See* DRAW PROGRAM; PAINT PROGRAM.

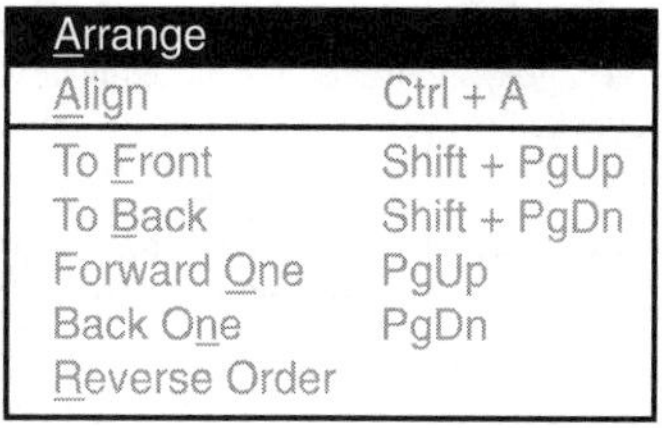

Arrange	
Align	Ctrl + A
To Front	Shift + PgUp
To Back	Shift + PgDn
Forward One	PgUp
Back One	PgDn
Reverse Order	

FIGURE 117. GRAYED MENU SELECTIONS

grayed displayed in gray type and not available for selection. If a menu option appears in light gray rather than black type, it cannot be chosen. Menu selections are grayed whenever it is impossible to do the thing they call for (e.g., "Save" may be grayed if there is no data to be saved).

grayscale

1. a series of boxes filled with a range of black tints from pure white to 100 percent black. A grayscale is used to test a printer, monitor, scanner, or printing press.

2. (scanner terminology) the range of grays in an image as measured by the scanner.

3. a description of any image that contains shades of gray as well as black and white.

FIGURE 118. GREEKING

Greek the alphabet used in ancient and modern Greece, $ABΓΔ...Ω$ and $αβγδ...ω$. Greek letters are often used as mathematical symbols. For the complete Greek alphabet see p. 554. *Contrast* LATIN; CYRILLIC.

greeking the use of random letters or marks to show the overall appearance of a printed page without showing the actual text. With computers, greeking is used when the page is displayed too small for the text to be readable on the screen.

Green Book the Philips/Sony standard for multimedia interactive compact discs (not including personal computer software). *See* CD-I.

Green PC a personal computer that draws little electrical power when idle, even though still turned on. A Green PC typically stops spinning its hard disk and shuts down power to the monitor if several minutes elapse with no keyboard activity. *See also* ENERGY STAR.

Gregorian calendar the calendar system presently in use, introduced by Pope Gregory in 1582 and adopted in England in 1752 and in Russia in 1918. It is exactly like the Julian calendar except that years divisible by 100 are not leap years unless they are also divisible by 400. The Gregorian calendar thus follows the earth's revolution around the sun more accurately than the Julian calendar did. *See* LEAP YEAR.

grep the UNIX command that reads a text file and outputs all the lines that contain a particular series of characters. For example, the command

```
grep abc myfile
```

reads the file *myfile* and outputs every line that contains "abc."

Instead of specifying the exact characters to be searched for, you can give a regular expression that defines them. For example:

```
grep [bB]ill myfile
```

outputs all the lines that contain either "bill" or "Bill." *See* REGULAR EXPRESSION.

The origin of the word *grep* is disputed, but it may be an abbreviated editing command, g/*re*/p, where *re* stands for "regular expression," g means "global search," and p means "print" (i.e., display all lines that match the search criteria). Grep programs have been written for other operating systems, such as DOS.

grid a feature of various draw programs and paint programs that allows lines to be drawn only in certain positions, as if they were drawn on the lines of graph paper. The grid makes it much easier to draw parallel and perpendicular lines, lay out diagrams, and avoid irregular breaks. However, when the grid is turned on, there are positions in which you cannot draw. *See also* DRAW PROGRAM; PAINT PROGRAM.

grid system a way of standardizing the layout of many related pages, such as the pages of a multipage document. The designer first draws a grid that will define the possible positions of columns, horizontal divisions, and pictures. Not all the possibilities of the grid are used on any single page, but the grid ensures that column positions do not vary haphazardly, and thereby makes the pages look related.

grounding the establishment of a uniform reference voltage level across several pieces of electrical equipment that are connected together.

In any electrical device, "ground level" is the voltage level to which all other voltages are compared. In most computers, the ground level is connected to the ground pin (the third, rounded pin) of the power plug, and the power line then connects it to the earth itself, thereby assuring that the ground level for all machines is the same. This helps prevent cables from picking up noise or emitting radio frequency interference. It also reduces the danger of damage from lightning. *See* POWER LINE PROTECTION; RFI PROTECTION; ELECTRONIC CIRCUIT DIAGRAM SYMBOLS.

group
   1. (in a draw program) to cause the computer to treat a number of objects as a single object. The individual objects of a group retain their own attributes (*contrast* COMBINE). Most importantly, a group can be sized, stretched, and moved as if it were one object. If you have a complex element of a drawing, it is a good idea to group the objects to allow them to retain their relative position. It is surprisingly easy to make a mistake with the mouse and dislocate something. The grouped object can be ungrouped if needed.
   2. (in Windows 3.1 Program Manager) a set of application programs whose icons are in a single small window that can be collapsed into an icon. Placing programs into groups is entirely up to the user; any program can be placed into any group. It is helpful to arrange related icons into groups that will help you find them. By default, every commercial software package puts its icons into a different group, so unless

you move the icons around, software that you use together will not be together on the screen.

In Windows 95 and its successors, groups are replaced by CAS-CADING MENUS starting from the START MENU — effectively, groups within groups, nested to any depth. This makes it easier to group related material together.

groupware software that makes it easy for a group of people to work on the same data through a network, by facilitating file sharing and other forms of communication. Lotus Notes is an example of widely used groupware.

GUI *see* GRAPHICAL USER INTERFACE.

guideline a nonprinting line that aids in aligning text and other objects in a draw program or page layout program. Some programs allow you to turn on a *snap-to-guidelines* feature that causes the guidelines and objects to have a magnetic attraction for each other. *See also* SNAP-TO-GRID.

gutter the blank space between columns of type or between pages of a book.

GW-BASIC Microsoft's interpreter for the dialect of BASIC that was implemented in ROM on the IBM PC. GW-BASIC runs on machines that need not contain the IBM ROM chip. It has now been replaced by Microsoft QBASIC and Microsoft QuickBASIC. *See* BASICA.

H

hack attack *(slang)* a sudden inspiration or compulsion to work on a computer program. Despite what it sounds like, a "hack attack" has nothing to do with computer security violations.

hacker

    1.   an exceptionally skilled computer programmer.

    2.   a person who programs computers for recreation or as a hobby.

    3.   a person who "breaks into" computers without authorization, either for malicious reasons or just to prove it can be done; a CRACKER. *See* COMPUTER SECURITY.

hairline	————————
½ point	————————
1 point	————————
2 points	————————
4 points	■■■■■■■■■

FIGURE 119. LINE WIDTHS

hairline a very thin line, usually about .003 inch wide.

half adder a logic circuit that adds two one-digit binary numbers, producing two digits of output. *See* BINARY ADDITION.

half duplex the transmission of data in only one direction at a time. *Contrast* FULL DUPLEX; *see* MODEM.

half-height drive is a disk drive approximately 1.6 inches high, half the height of older full-height drives.

FIGURE 120. HALFTONE SCREEN (ENLARGED)

halftone the reproduction of a *continuous-tone* image (containing shades of gray or colors) by converting it into a pattern of very small dots of various sizes. (For an example, look closely at a picture in a newspaper or magazine.) Laser printers and printing presses can print shades of gray only as halftones.

halting problem the problem of determining whether a particular computer program will terminate or will continue forever in an endless loop; a famous theoretical result in computer science.

Consider a computer program A that analyzes other programs; call the analyzed program B. Suppose A can always determine, with complete certainty, whether B will ever terminate. You could arrange for A to repeat endlessly if it finds that B terminates, and terminate if it finds that B repeats endlessly.

You could then feed A a copy of itself (that is, let $B = A$), and you'd have a program that terminates if and only if it does not terminate. This is a contradiction, proving that A, as described, cannot exist.

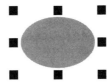

FIGURE 121. HANDLES ON SELECTED OBJECT

handles (in graphics programs) the little black boxes at the corners and midpoints of an object that has been selected for editing. As the name suggests, handles give you a place to "grab" onto an object with the mouse and manipulate it. Dragging a corner handle (any one of the four) will change the size of the object. Dragging a midpoint handle will stretch or shrink the object in one dimension.

handshaking the exchange of signals between two computers to indicate that data transmission is proceeding successfully. For examples, *see* X-OFF, X-ON, and XMODEM.

hand tool a tool available in some graphical environments that looks like a human hand and allows you to move the picture around the screen. If there is a hand tool provided, there will usually not be a SCROLL BAR at the side and bottom of the viewing window.

hang
1. to make a computer stop in its tracks because of a software bug or hardware failure.
2. (modem) to disconnect from the telephone line (hang up).

hanging indent (**hanging tab**) a new paragraph indicated by letting the first word extend to the left past the normal margin into the gutter. Also called OUTDENT. Each entry in this dictionary begins with a hanging indent.

Happy Mac the icon of a smiling Macintosh that greets you when you turn on your Macintosh and everything is well. *Contrast* SAD MAC.

hard copy a printout on paper of computer output. *Contrast* SOFT COPY, which is a copy that is only viewable on the screen.

hard disk a data storage medium using rigid aluminum disks coated with iron oxide. Hard disks have much greater storage capacity than diskettes. In the early 1980s, 10 megabytes was a common size for hard disks. More recently, 1 and 2-gigabyte hard disks have become common, and even larger sizes are available.

The read-write head travels across the disk on a thin cushion of air without ever actually touching the disk. However, hard disks have the disadvantage that they are usually built into the machine and cannot be removed, as can diskettes. Hard disks are also called *Winchester disks. See* DISK; DISKETTE; HARD DISK MANAGEMENT. For information on the interface between the hard disk and the computer, see ST-506; IDE; ESDI; SCSI.

hard disk management a task faced by almost all computer users. Here are some tips for using a hard disk effectively.

1. Learn how to back up your hard disk, and do it frequently. Every hard disk in use today *will* break down within just a few years! Individual files can be backed up on diskettes, but backing up large amounts of data is much easier if you have a tape backup system, a Zip drive, or a Jaz drive. You can simplify the process by backing up only the files you have created, not the installed software, which you could reinstall from its own original disks if necessary.

2. Divide the disk into subdirectories (FOLDERS) and put related files in each subdirectory (e.g., all word processing files in one directory and all spreadsheet files in another). Use a further level of subdirectories where appropriate, e.g., to separate letters from reports within the word processing directory. (*See also* DIRECTORY.)
   An alternative is to group files according to the projects that they pertain to, so that all files pertaining to a particular piece of work will be in the same directory, even if some of them are texts and others are spreadsheets or drawings.

3. Use the DOS PATH command or its equivalent so that commonly used commands will work no matter what directory you are in. Put the PATH command in your AUTOEXEC.BAT file.

4. In DOS, use the command
   ```
   prompt $p$g
   ```

so that the command prompt will tell you what directory you are in (e.g., C:\MYDIR> rather than just C>). Again, this command can be in your AUTOEXEC.BAT file. In fact, it's probably already there.

5. Delete files that you no longer need. Make a directory called JUNK or TEMP in which to put files that will not be needed for very long, so that they will not clutter up other directories.

6. Periodically run chkdsk, scandisk, or its equivalent to check for lost clusters. (*See* CLUSTER.)

7. Run a defragmentation program every few months, or eliminate fragmentation by backing up the whole disk, erasing all files, and restoring all files from the backup. *See* FRAGMENTATION.

8. (Macintosh) Periodically rebuild the desktop by holding down Command and Option at bootup. This should speed up system performance.

hard edge an edge that is smooth and sharp, with no blending or blurring of the boundary. *Contrast* SOFT EDGE.

hard error a persistent, reproducible error (defect) on a data storage device. *Contrast* SOFT ERROR.

hard hyphen *see* REQUIRED HYPHEN.

hard page a forced page break; a place where the word processor must begin a new page whether or not the previous page was full. In WordPerfect and Windows Write, the way to type a hard page is to hold down the Ctrl key while pressing Enter.

hardware the physical elements of a computer system; the computer equipment as opposed to the programs or information stored in the machine. *Contrast* SOFTWARE.

hardware interrupt a CPU interrupt triggered by a hardware event, such as pressing a key. *See* INTERRUPT.

Harvard architecture a type of computer design in which the program and the data are stored in separate memories. *Contrast* VON NEUMANN ARCHITECTURE. *See* COMPUTER ARCHITECTURE.

hash function a function that converts a string of characters to a number or a shorter string. During data transmission, the value of an agreed-upon hash function can be transmitted along with the data so it can be verified if the data has been transmitted correctly. For example, *see* CHECKSUM. A one-way hash function is a hash function that is also a one-way function. *See* ONE-WAY FUNCTION; ENCRYPTION.

hashing a storage mechanism where data items are stored at locations that are determined by a mathematical function of the data. For example, suppose you need to store a list of 100 numbers in memory locations whose addresses run from 1 to 100. One example of a hashing function

TABLE 6
HAYES MODEM DIALING COMMANDS

ATDT9W555-1212	Dial 9, wait for another dial tone, and dial 555-1212 (using tone dialing).
ATDP9W555-1212	Same, but use pulse dialing.
ATH0	Hang up.
ATA	Answer an incoming call (right now).
ATO	Resume communicating (use this after you have typed +++ to issue commands in the middle of a session). Note that this command uses the letter O, not the digit 0.
ATS0=1	Answer when the phone rings.

is to divide each number by 100 and use the remainder as the storage address. For example, the number 538 would be stored at memory location 38, and 1124 would be stored at location 24.

The use of hashing makes it possible to store and retrieve the data items quickly, since it is not necessary to search through the list in order to find the item. However, there is one complication: A hashing function will sometimes assign more than one data item to the same address. For example, using the rule given above, the number 638 would also be stored in location 38. To avoid that problem, a hashing system needs to be able to resolve collisions by storing the new data item in a separate place.

hat a name for the character ^. *See also* CIRCUMFLEX.

Hayes compatibility the ability of a modem to respond to the same set of autodialing commands as the Hayes Smartmodem (made by Hayes Microcomputer Products, Inc., Norcross, Georgia). Almost all modems nowadays are Hayes compatible.

Two modems need not be Hayes compatible in order to communicate with each other. Hayes compatibility refers only to the commands used by the computer to control the modem. A sampling of such commands is given in Table 6.

The modem accepts commands whenever it is not connected via phone lines to another modem. To set the modem baud rate, simply start sending commands at the baud rate you desire. To send a command to the modem while communicating to another computer, stop typing for 1 second, type +++, and again stop typing for about a second. The modem will respond "OK," and you are free to give a command.

Table 7 gives Hayes commands that change the configuration of the modem. *See also* MODEM; RS- 232.

HD (**h**igh **d**ensity) *see* DISKETTE.

HDD **h**ard **d**isk **d**rive.

TABLE 7
HAYES MODEM CONFIGURATION COMMANDS

AT&F	Reset modem to factory default configuration (useful to fix a modem in an unknown state).
AT&W	Store current configuration in nonvolatile RAM.
ATZ	Reset modem to stored configuration (also done when modem is turned on).
ATB0	At 1200 baud, use V.22 protocol (Europe).
ATB1	At 1200 baud. use Bell 212A protocol (U.S.A.).
ATE0	Do not echo (display) commands typed to modem.
ATE1	Echo commands.
ATL1	Speaker volume low.
ATL3	Speaker volume high (also ATL2 in between).
ATM0	Speaker always off.
ATM1	Speaker on during dialing, until connected.
ATM2	Speaker always on.
AT&C0	CD (carrier detect signal) always on (necessary to allow some communication programs to send commands to the modem).
AT&C1	CD on only when connection is present.
AT&D1	Modem ignores DTR signal from computer.
AT&D2	Modem hangs up when DTR signal turns off (e.g.. upon exiting from communication program).
AT&D3	Modem hangs up and resets when DTR turns off.

head

1. the part of a disk drive that reads and writes information magnetically. A double-sided disk drive or multilayered hard disk has a head for each side of each layer. (*See* DISK.)

2. tag used in HTML to indicate the beginning of the heading material of a web page, which includes material such as the title. *Contrast* BODY. For an example, *see* HTML.

3. the top of a page or printed piece (such as a newsletter).

4. short for headline.

heap a block of memory that belongs to a program but has not yet been given a specific use. For example, when a BASIC program creates character strings, it typically places them in space obtained from its heap.

hecta- metric prefix meaning $\times 100$ (10^2). *Hecta-* is derived from the Greek word for "hundred." *See* METRIC PREFIXES.

hello-world program a program that simply writes "Hello, world" on the most convenient output device, and terminates. Hello-world programs are the traditional way to verify that programming languages and output devices are working, at least to a minimal degree.

help information provided by a computer program to assist the user. Many computer programs contain an on-screen help facility that a user can turn to when questions arise. For example, if you have forgotten how a particular command works, you can consult a help facility (if one is available) to refresh your memory.

In Windows programs, one of the menu choices is usually *Help*. Windows 95 and its successors have an elaborate help system accessible from the Start button. *See also* DOCUMENTATION; CONTEXT-SENSITIVE HELP.

Helvetica

abcdefghijklm
nopqrstuvwxyz
ABCDEFGHIJKLM
NOPQRSTUVWXYZ
1234567890!@#

FIGURE 122. HELVETICA (NORMAL WEIGHT)

Helvetica a popular sans-serif typeface designed around 1957 by M. Miedinger.

Hercules graphics card an early third-party substitute for the IBM Monochrome Display Adapter (MDA), adding high-resolution graphics capability to the original IBM PC and PC XT. It became largely obsolete with the advent of the EGA and VGA.

hertz the number of times something is repeated per second; a unit of frequency, abbreviated Hz and named for Heinrich Hertz, discoverer of radio waves. *See also* MEGAHERTZ; GIGAHERTZ.

heuristic a method of solving problems that involves intelligent trial and error. By contrast, an algorithmic solution method is a clearly specified procedure that is guaranteed to give the correct answer. (*See* ALGORITHM.) For example, there is no known algorithm that tells how to play a perfect game of chess, so computer chess-playing programs must use a heuristic method of solution, using methods that are likely but not certain to give good results in any particular case.

Hewlett-Packard a leading manufacturer of computers, laser printers, inkjet printers, and electronic test equipment. Hewlett-Packard is headquartered in Palo Alto, California, and can be reached on the web at: http://www.hp.com. *See also* LASERJET.

TABLE 8
HEXADECIMAL EQUIVALENTS OF BINARY NUMBERS

Binary	Hex	Binary	Hex
0000	0	1000	8
0001	1	1001	9
0010	2	1010	A
0011	3	1011	B
0100	4	1100	C
0101	5	1101	D
0110	6	1110	E
0111	7	1111	F

hexadecimal number a number written in base 16. Hexadecimal numbers use 16 possible digits, written 0, 1, 2, 3, 4, 5, 6, 7, 8, 9, A (= 10), B (=11), C (=12), D (= 13), E (= 14), and F (= 15). For an example, the number A4C2 in hexadecimal means:

$$10 \times 16^3 + 4 \times 16^2 + 12 \times 16^1 + 2 \times 16^0 = 42,178$$

Hexadecimal numbers provide a good shorthand way of representing binary numbers, since binary numbers can be converted to hexadecimal numbers by looking at only four digits at a time. For example, binary 1111 equals hexadecimal F, binary 0100 equals hexadecimal 4, and binary 11110100 equals hexadecimal F4:

$$\underbrace{1111}_{F}\underbrace{0100}_{4}$$

When converting a binary number to hexadecimal by this method, start by adding zeros at the left in order to make the number of digits a multiple of 4.

Table 8 shows the hexadecimal equivalents of the four-digit binary numbers, and Table 9 shows the decimal equivalents of the hexadecimal numbers from 00 to FF.

hidden files files, in DOS and similar operating systems, that are not listed by the `dir` command and are invisible to some programs. In DOS 5.0 and higher, you can see hidden files by using the command `dir /ah`.

Any DOS boot disk has two hidden files on it, named either IBM-BIO.SYS and IBMDOS.SYS, or IO.SYS and MSDOS.SYS. These files are hidden so that they will not be copied or moved; DOS relies on their being in a specific position on the disk when the machine boots up. Other programs occasionally use hidden files to implement copy protection. The `copy` and `xcopy` commands do not copy hidden files, but the `diskcopy` command duplicates an entire disk, hidden files and all.

TABLE 9
DECIMAL EQUIVALENTS OF HEXADECIMAL NUMBERS
(PART 1)

00	=	0	20	=	32	40	=	64	60	=	96
01	=	1	21	=	33	41	=	65	61	=	97
02	=	2	22	=	34	42	=	66	62	=	98
03	=	3	23	=	35	43	=	67	63	=	99
04	=	4	24	=	36	44	=	68	64	=	100
05	=	5	25	=	37	45	=	69	65	=	101
06	=	6	26	=	38	46	=	70	66	=	102
07	=	7	27	=	39	47	=	71	67	=	103
08	=	8	28	=	40	48	=	72	68	=	104
09	=	9	29	=	41	49	=	73	69	=	105
0A	=	10	2A	=	42	4A	=	74	6A	=	106
0B	=	11	2B	=	43	4B	=	75	6B	=	107
0C	=	12	2C	=	44	4C	=	76	6C	=	108
0D	=	13	2D	=	45	4D	=	77	6D	=	109
0E	=	14	2E	=	46	4E	=	78	6E	=	110
0F	=	15	2F	=	47	4F	=	79	6F	=	111
10	=	16	30	=	48	50	=	80	70	=	112
11	=	17	31	=	49	51	=	81	71	=	113
12	=	18	32	=	50	52	=	82	72	=	114
13	=	19	33	=	51	53	=	83	73	=	115
14	=	20	34	=	52	54	=	84	74	=	116
15	=	21	35	=	53	55	=	85	75	=	117
16	=	22	36	=	54	56	=	86	76	=	118
17	=	23	37	=	55	57	=	87	77	=	119
18	=	24	38	=	56	58	=	88	78	=	120
19	=	25	39	=	57	59	=	89	79	=	121
1A	=	26	3A	=	58	5A	=	90	7A	=	122
1B	=	27	3B	=	59	5B	=	91	7B	=	123
1C	=	28	3C	=	60	5C	=	92	7C	=	124
1D	=	29	3D	=	61	5D	=	93	7D	=	125
1E	=	30	3E	=	62	5E	=	94	7E	=	126
1F	=	31	3F	=	63	5F	=	95	7F	=	127

Under UNIX, files whose names begin with a dot, such as `.newsrc`, are considered "hidden" because the regular `ls` command does not display them, but `ls -al` does display them.

hierarchical arranged in such a way that some items are above or below others in a tree-like structure. Examples of hierarchies include the organizational chart of a corporation, the arrangement of directories on a disk, and the arrangement of windows on a screen (because some of the windows are within others).

The *root* of the hierarchy is the main item that is above all of the others, such as the CEO of a corporation, the root directory of a disk, or the window that comprises the whole screen.

Many menu systems are arranged hierarchically, as menus within menus. For other examples of hierarchical data structures, *see* DIRECTORY; OUTLINE; TREE.

TABLE 9
DECIMAL EQUIVALENTS OF HEXADECIMAL NUMBERS
(PART 2)

80	=	128	A0	=	160	C0	=	192	E0	=	224
81	=	129	A1	=	161	C1	=	193	E1	=	225
82	=	130	A2	=	162	C2	=	194	E2	=	226
83	=	131	A3	=	163	C3	=	195	E3	=	227
84	=	132	A4	=	164	C4	=	196	E4	=	228
85	=	133	A5	=	165	C5	=	197	E5	=	229
86	=	134	A6	=	166	C6	=	198	E6	=	230
87	=	135	A7	=	167	C7	=	199	E7	=	231
88	=	136	A8	=	168	C8	=	200	E8	=	232
89	=	137	A9	=	169	C9	=	201	E9	=	233
8A	=	138	AA	=	170	CA	=	202	EA	=	234
8B	=	139	AB	=	171	CB	=	203	EB	=	235
8C	=	140	AC	=	172	CC	=	204	EC	=	236
8D	=	141	AD	=	173	CD	=	205	ED	=	237
8E	=	142	AE	=	174	CE	=	206	EE	=	238
8F	=	143	AF	=	175	CF	=	207	EF	=	239
90	=	144	B0	=	176	D0	=	208	F0	=	240
91	=	145	B1	=	177	D1	=	209	F1	=	241
92	=	146	B2	=	178	D2	=	210	F2	=	242
93	=	147	B3	=	179	D3	=	211	F3	=	243
94	=	148	B4	=	180	D4	=	212	F4	=	244
95	=	149	B5	=	181	D5	=	213	F5	=	245
96	=	150	B6	=	182	D6	=	214	F6	=	246
97	=	151	B7	=	183	D7	=	215	F7	=	247
98	=	152	B8	=	184	D8	=	216	F8	=	248
99	=	153	B9	=	185	D9	=	217	F9	=	249
9A	=	154	BA	=	186	DA	=	218	FA	=	250
9B	=	155	BB	=	187	DB	=	219	FB	=	251
9C	=	156	BC	=	188	DC	=	220	FC	=	252
9D	=	157	BD	=	189	DD	=	221	FD	=	253
9E	=	158	BE	=	190	DE	=	222	FE	=	254
9F	=	159	BF	=	191	DF	=	223	FF	=	255

hierarchical file system a file system that allows subdirectories or folders to belong to a higher-level subdirectory or folder (Fig. 123). *See* DIRECTORY.

hierarchical menu a menu with other menus under it; a CASCADING MENU. For an example, see START BUTTON.

high density a diskette that records considerably more data per inch than the earlier double-density (DD) format. High-density diskettes can only be used in high-density diskette drives. *See* DISKETTE.

high-level language a computer programming language designed to allow people to write programs without having to understand the inner workings of the computer. BASIC, C, Pascal, and Java are examples of high level languages. By contrast, a *machine language* is at the lowest level, since machine language programming requires detailed

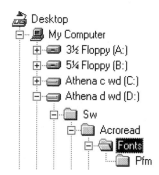

FIGURE 123. HIERARCHICAL FILE SYSTEM

knowledge of the computer's inner workings. An *assembly language* is at a slightly higher level than a machine language, since it uses a notation more convenient for the programmer.

highlight
    1. to make a menu item prominent (either lighter or darker than the others) to show that it is selected. In most graphical user interfaces, you can choose the highlighted item by pressing Enter.
    2. the lightest part of an image. In artwork, highlights show texture, shape, and the direction of the source of light.

High Sierra format a standard format for recording files and directories on CD-ROMs, now superseded by ISO 9660. The two formats are closely compatible, but some of the earliest CD-ROM software could read only High Sierra format disks.

hinting additional information encoded into a digital font to help the computer software correctly display and print the letters at different sizes and resolutions.

hiragana *see* KANA.

histogram a bar graph in which the bars represent how many times something occurs. Histograms are often used in photopaint programs and scanner software to allow direct manipulation of the image characteristics. Each bar represents the total number of pixels of a particular shade of gray. By sliding the endpoints closer together, you decrease the image contrast; sliding the endpoints apart increases contrast. *See also* BRIGHTNESS; CONTRAST.

history folder a folder that contains a list of the locations you have visited on the Internet.

FIGURE 124. HISTOGRAM

hit

1. something found by a searching. For instance, if you search the Web for instances of the word "aardvark" and find 250 of them, you've found 250 hits.

2. on the World Wide Web, an instance of someone elsewhere calling up the web page and viewing it. The popularity of a web site is measured in hits per day.

hoax a piece of misinformation circulated as a deliberate prank; common on the Internet. (*Compare* MEME VIRUS.) Hoaxes usually arrive in e-mail messages that say "mail this to all your friends" — that is, the hoaxer does not want you to post the message in a public forum where knowledgeable people might debunk it. The most common Internet hoaxes are the following:

1. "A dying child (or maybe a charity) wants a gigantic number of postcards or a gigantic amount of e-mail."
   One young cancer victim, Craig Shergold, did appeal for post-cards in 1989; his story is told in the *Guinness Book of World Records,* and his family is begging for the flood of postcards to stop. Unfortunately, his story is still circulating, often with altered names and addresses.
   Nobody wants a gigantic amount of e-mail; e-mail costs money to receive.

2. "Some branch of government, such as the FCC, is about to do something outlandish."
   Sometimes these warnings come from well-meaning activists; more often they are pranks. In the 1970s a disgruntled license applicant started a rumor that the FCC was about to ban all religious broadcasting; the story is still circulating and the FCC can't afford to answer the flood of correspondence that it has generated. Newer hoaxes include a "modem tax" or bans on various uses of the Internet.

3. "If you get e-mail titled 'Good times' (or 'Happy birthday' or 'Deeyenda' or something else), it will erase your hard disk (or do other great harm)."

Any file attached to e-mail could easily contain a virus or destructive program; do not open such files unless you are sure of their origin. However, the viruses described in these particular hoaxes apparently do not exist.

Any piece of e-mail that is designed to spur you to immediate action is likely to be a hoax; before passing it on, you should check it out with your system administrator, your local computer security team, or another knowledgeable person. Better yet, post it in a newsgroup where better-informed people can respond. *See also* FOAF; PYRAMID SCHEME.

hole a place where an electron is missing from the crystal structure of a P-type semiconductor. A hole acts as a moving positive charge. *See* SEMICONDUCTOR.

/home in UNIX, a directory that contains individual users' home directories.

home directory the main directory belonging to a particular user of a UNIX system or of a file server shared by multiple users.

home page
    1.   the main WEB PAGE for a person or organization; the page that users are expected to read first in order to access other pages.
    2.   the WEB PAGE that a person sees first, immediately after starting up the BROWSER. Most browsers let you choose what web page this will be.
    See also WORLD WIDE WEB; HTML.

hook a provision, in a computer program, for interaction with other programs that have yet to be written. For example, Adobe Photoshop and Netscape Navigator provide hooks for plug-ins that add additional features. *See* PLUG-IN.

Hopper, Grace (1906–1992), mathematician and U.S. naval officer (later admiral) who worked on the first electronic computers. She developed the first compiler and contributed to the development of COBOL. For many years, she was the highest-ranking woman in the U.S. Navy.

horizontal side to side; across.

host computer a computer that provides services to others that are linked to it by a network; generally, the more remote of two or more computers that a person is using at once. For example, when a user in Florida accesses a computer in New York, the New York computer is considered the host.

HotJava a web browser developed by Sun Microsystems, notable for being the first browser to run Java applets.

hot link a DDE connection in which the shared program information is updated continuously. *See* DDE.

hot list a list of bookmarks or favorites; a stored list of web addresses, filenames, or other data of immediate interest to the user. *See* BOOK-MARK; FAVORITES.

hot-pluggable able to be plugged in and unplugged while a computer is powered on and running.

hot spot
   1. the exact spot of a pointer (or any mouse cursor) that must touch an object in order to select it. The very tip of the arrow is the hot spot for the pointer.
   2. a place in a hypertext document where a user can click to call up further information. Hot spots are generally highlighted words or small pictures. Some large graphics can have multiple hot spots. *See* ANCHOR; HYPERLINK; IMAGE MAP.

hot-swappable able to be replaced (swapped out) while a computer is powered on and running.

hot zone the area at the end of a line of type that triggers the computer to hyphenate words. If a word extends into the hot zone, it will be hyphenated to make it fit on the line. *See* HYPHENATION.

FIGURE 125. HOURGLASS ICON

hourglass icon (in Microsoft Windows) the shape of the mouse pointer while the computer is too busy to accept any input from the keyboard or mouse. The pointer returns to its usual shape when the wait is over. *See also* WATCH ICON.

HR keyword used in HTML to indicate a horizontal rule. For an example, *see* HTML.

HSB (**H**ue, **S**aturation, **B**rightness) a standard method of describing color. Hue is what artists call color (red vs. green vs. purple, etc.). Saturation refers to how *pure* the hue is (e.g., red vs. pale red vs. pink). If you add a contrasting color (let's say we add some red to a pure green) you *decrease* its saturation. Brightness refers to how light or dark the hue is (whether we add white or black). HSB is the preferred method of describing colors for someone who paints; the process is very similar to mixing pigments. Be aware that this is an internal description, just between you and your software. *See* RGB; COLOR.

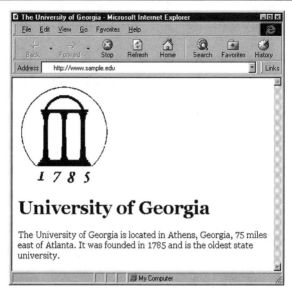

FIGURE 126. HTML EXAMPLE AS DISPLAYED BY BROWSER

HTML (**H**ypertext **M**arkup **L**anguage) a set of codes that can be inserted into text files to indicate special typefaces, inserted images, and links to other hypertext documents.

The main use of HTML is to publish information on the Internet (*see* WORLD WIDE WEB). Here is a simple example of an HTML document.

```
<HTML>
<HEAD>
<TITLE>The University of Georgia</TITLE>
</HEAD>
<BODY>
<P>
<IMG SRC="ugaseal.gif">
<H1>University of Georgia</H1>
<P>
The University of Georgia is located in
Athens, Georgia, 75 miles east of Atlanta.
It was founded in 1785 and is the oldest
state university.
</BODY>
</HTML>
```

Figure 126 shows how this looks when displayed by a web browser. HTML features are indicated by special codes, called *tags*. If there were an HTML tag called XXX, then the characters <XXX> would mark the beginning of this feature, and </XXX> would mark the end. For example, the keywords <TITLE> and </TITLE> mark the beginning and end of the title. <P> marks a paragraph break, and <IMG SRC=*filename*> embeds an image in the document; many image formats are supported but GIF is the most popular. Codes for special typefaces include the following:

<H1> ...</H1>	Heading, size 1 (largest)
<H6> ...</H6>	Heading, size 6 (smallest)
<B> ...</B>	Boldface
<I> ...</I>	Italics
<U> ...</U>	Underline
<T> ...</T>	Typewriter type (like this)

The tag <BR> inserts a line break; note that the line breaks on the displayed web page will not necessarily match the line breaks on the original HTML text. The tag <HR> inserts a horizontal rule.

An unnumbered list of items can be inserted as follows:

```
<UL>
<LI> put first item in list here </LI>
<LI> put second item here </LI>
<LI> put third item here </LI>
</UL>
```

An ordered (numbered) list is created in the same manner, except with <OL> used in place of <UL>.

A link to another document looks like this:

```
<A HREF="XXXX.HTML"> Click here.</A>
```

That means "Jump to file XXXX.HTML (another HTML document) if the user clicks on the words 'Click here.'" A URL can appear in place of the filename. A link to another place in the same document looks like this:

```
<A HREF="#XXXX">
This is the text that will display the link</A>
```

When the user clicks on this link, the browser will jump to the location in the current document marked with

```
<A NAME="XXXX"> This is the target of the link</A>
```

Comments (to be ignored by the HTML system) look like this:

```
<! This is a comment>
```

Even with no special codes in it, a text file is still a valid HTML document.

Although you can use almost any word processor or page layout program to produce HTML, it is much easier to use a program specially designed for the job (Adobe PageMill, Corel Xara, Microsoft FrontPage, and other "web publishers"). Many of the newer programs provide a WYSIWYG environment for designing web pages, then automatically produce the correct HTML codes.

For other examples of HTML, *see* FORM, TABLE, FRAME, JAVASCRIPT, JAVA, and DYNAMIC HTML.

HTTP (**H**ypertext **T**ransfer **P**rotocol) a standard method of publishing information as hypertext in HTML format on the Internet. URLs (addresses) for web sites usually begin with `http:`. *See* URL; HYPERTEXT; HTML; INTERNET; WORLD WIDE WEB.

HTTPS a variation of HTTP that uses SSL encryption for security.

hub on a network with star topology, the device that links several computers together. A hub is typically a small box with five or more RJ-45 connectors that accept cables from the individual computers (nodes). One of the connectors may be labeled uplink, which means that it has the transmit and receive signals swapped in order to connect to another hub rather than to a computer. *See* TOPOLOGY; 10BASE-T; 100BASE-T. *Contrast* ROUTER; BRIDGE; SWITCH (definition 2).

hue color (red vs. green vs. orange, etc.). *See* HSB.

hunt and peck *(slang)* to type by gazing at the keyboard, hunting for the letters, and pressing them one by one with one finger, rather like a trained chicken.

hyperdocument *see* HYPERTEXT.

hyperlink an item on a WEB PAGE which, when selected, transfers the user directly to another location in a hypertext document or to some other web page, perhaps on a different machine. Also simply called a LINK. For an example, *see* HTML.

hypertext (**hyperdocuments**) electronic documents that present information that can be read by following many different connections, instead of just sequentially like reading a book. The World Wide Web is an example of hypertext, as are Microsoft Windows help files and CD-ROM encyclopedias.

A hypertext document typically starts with a computer screen full of information (text, graphics, and/or sound). The user then will have different options as to what related screen to go to next; typically, options are selected with a mouse.

Encyclopedia information is especially suitable for hypertext presentation. Each entry can be a screen of information, and each cross-reference can be a button that the user can click on in order to jump to that entry. Software help files are also a good application for hypertext because the user generally needs to find a particular piece of information as quickly as possible rather than reading through the whole document.

There is a danger that the user might become lost in the middle of a hyperdocument. A good hyperdocument should include some form of navigational aid that allows the user to see an overview of the document. Also, it is helpful if the computer maintains a record of the path that has been followed, both so the user can go backwards and so it is possible to retrace the same path at a future date if so desired. Often a hyperdocument follows a particular sequence automatically if the user does not want to make all of the choices individually.

A large hyperdocument (an encyclopedia, for example) requires large amounts of storage such as provided by a CD-ROM. The World Wide Web is a way of publishing hypertext on the Internet, using many different computers as servers for different parts of the information. *See* WORLD WIDE WEB; HTML; BROWSER.

hyphenation the practice of breaking words between syllables at the end of a line, so that the lines will be more nearly the same length.

Most desktop publishing software can automatically hyphenate text. The computer tries to put as many words as possible on one line. When it enters the last half inch of the line (the HOT ZONE), it calculates whether the next word will fit; if not, the word is looked up in the hyphenation dictionary, or hyphenated according to phonetic rules. The basic idea is that both parts of the word should be pronounceable. There is often more than one acceptable way to hyphenate a word, and dictionaries sometimes disagree with each other. The most basic rule is, "Make both pieces pronounceable."

Fully justified type will always look better when hyphenated; otherwise loose lines (lines with big gaps between the words) become a problem. If you are setting type flush left, ragged right, be aware that the size of the hot zone will affect how ragged the right margin is.

Proofread carefully for unfortunate line breaks. The traditional example is the word "therapist" — don't let the computer hyphenate it as "the-rapist." Learn how to mark required hyphens so that hyphenated names and phone numbers won't be broken across lines.

See also REQUIRED HYPHEN, DISCRETIONARY HYPHEN.

Hz *see* HERTZ.

I

I2 *see* INTERNET 2.

IANA (Internet Assigned Numbers Authority) an organization based at the University of Southern California with the responsibility to make sure all IP addresses are unique. Their web address is `www.iana.org`. *See* IP ADDRESS.

IANAL e-mail abbreviation for "**I** **a**m **n**ot **a** **l**awyer," often used as a disclaimer when discussing matters of law or ethics.

I-bar the shape of the mouse pointer in a text editing environment. The height of the I-bar indicates the size of type currently selected. Sometimes called an *I-beam*.

IBM (International Business Machines) the industry's largest computer manufacturer. IBM makes other office equipment as well as computers, which it started manufacturing in the 1950s. By the late 1960s, IBM controlled about 80 percent of the computer market with models such as the IBM System/360 mainframe computer, and the name IBM was practically synonymous with computing. Today, the company continues to make 360-compatible mainframe computers, such as the 390 series.

In 1981 IBM introduced the IBM Personal Computer (PC), which quickly became one of the most popular microcomputers. Users felt that with IBM behind it, the personal computer had come of age as a practical business machine, not just an experimental machine for laboratories or hobbyists. The IBM PC was designed in some haste, and very little of its design was patented; as a result, other companies (beginning with Compaq in 1983) were able to produce *clones* (compatible imitations) of it. Nowadays IBM controls a relatively small part of the PC market.

Other important IBM products include the PS/2 line of microcomputers (PC-compatible, but with a redesigned bus, introduced in 1987 and discontinued in 1995); RS/6000 RISC workstations; and AS/400 business minicomputers. IBM is headquartered in Armonk, New York.

IBM 3270 a type of terminal commonly used with IBM mainframe computers. IBM 3270 terminals use the EBCDIC character set. An unusual aspect of 3270 series terminals is that most of the user's interaction is with a terminal cluster controller rather than with the computer itself. The cluster controller maintains the contents of the screen, and when the user presses Enter, the whole screen is sent to the computer. *See also* IBM 7171.

IBM 7171 a communications controller that allows ASCII terminals such as the VT-100 (or personal computers emulating ASCII terminals) to take the place of IBM 3270 EBCDIC terminals. The 7171 performs ASCII-to-EBCDIC translation and takes the place of the 3270 cluster controller.

IBM PC and PS/2 popular lines of microcomputers manufactured by IBM. There are many variations of each; this article will mention only the most historically important.

The IBM Personal Computer (PC), introduced in 1981, was the first of a family of very popular microcomputers, including not only IBM products but also "clones" (imitations) made by other companies. The original IBM PC used very little proprietary technology. Thus, it was easy for competitors to build compatible machines without violating patents. *See* CLONE; PC COMPATIBILITY.

IBM has maintained a high level of upward compatibility within the PC and PS/2 line. This means that later-model machines will run virtually all software written for earlier models. Nowadays, most PC-compatible computers are made by other companies; IBM continues to market PC-compatibles that are very similar to competitors' products.

FIGURE 127. IBM PC (1981) AND PC AT (1984)

IBM's two original machines, the PC and PC XT, are virtually identical, featuring 4.77-MHz 8088 microprocessors with an 8-bit bus. The only difference was that the XT had a 10-megabyte hard disk and had eight expansion slots instead of five. The PC AT, introduced in 1984, was the first PC to use the 80286 microprocessor, enabling programs to run much faster. The PC AT had what is now known as the ISA (Industry Standard Architecture) bus; it accepted both 8-bit (XT-style) and 16-bit plug-in cards.

The PS/2 machines were introduced in 1987 and discontinued in 1995. They were more compact than comparably configured PCs or ATs, and all but the lowest models used the Micro Channel bus, which made it possible in some situations to use more than one CPU in a single machine. Unlike the PC, XT, and AT, the PS/2 machines had built-in video adapters.

In 1990, IBM introduced the PS/1 as a low-priced, self-contained, ready-to-run home computer, sold complete with software. IBM has

á 160	é 130	í 161	ó 162	ú 163
à 133	è 138	ì 141	ò 149	ù 151
â 131	ê 136	î 140	ô 147	û 150
ä 132	ë 137	ï 139	ö 148	ü 129
å 134	É 144		ö 153	Ü 154
Ä 142		æ 145		
Å 143		Æ 146		ÿ 152

ç 135	¢ 155	α 224	Ω 234	∫ 244
Ç 128	£ 156	ß 225	δ 235	∫ 245
ñ 164	¥ 157	Γ 226	∞ 236	÷ 246
Ñ 165	₧ 158	π 227	ø 237	≈ 247
	ƒ 159	Σ 228	ε 238	° 248
¿ 168		σ 229	∩ 239	• 249
¡ 173	ª 166	µ 230	≡ 240	· 250
« 174	° 167	τ 231	± 241	√ 251
» 175	┌ 169	Φ 232	≥ 242	ⁿ 252
	¬ 170	Θ 233	≤ 243	² 253

218 □ 191	201 ▢ 187	213 ▢ 184	
192 217	200 188	212 190	

214 ▯ 183	220 ▄ 220	■ 219	▒ 177
211 189	221 ▐ 222		
	223 223	▓ 178	░ 176

| 179	┤ 180	‖ 186	╣ 185 ╫ 215
– 196	├ 195	= 205	╠ 204
+ 197	┴ 194	╬ 206	╦ 203 ╪ 216
	┬ 193		╩ 202

(Note the arrangement: these are not in numerical order. 218 is the upper left corner box-drawing character; 192 is the lower left corner, and so on.)

FIGURE 128. IBM PC SPECIAL CHARACTERS

also marketed PC-compatible computers under the names PS/Value-point and, more recently, Aptiva.

All the computers in the PC and PS/2 line can run appropriate versions of DOS (PC-DOS, also known as MS-DOS). Those with 386, 486, or Pentium microprocessors can also run current versions of Microsoft Windows and OS/2. *See* MS-DOS; MICROPROCESSOR; WIN-DOWS (MICROSOFT); OS/2.

These computers use the ASCII character set (*see* ASCII). In addition, they define printed representations for all character codes from 0 to 255, even those that are not defined by the ASCII standard. Some of these characters can never be printed because they are equivalent to codes such as Return or Line Feed, but they can be displayed on the screen by placing the appropriate code directly into video memory.

Figure 128 shows the printable part of the special character set. Under DOS, these characters are typed by holding down the Alt key and typing the appropriate number on the numeric keypad at the right side of the keyboard. For example, to type a shaded block, hold down Alt, type 178, and then release Alt. (*See also* ASCII; ANSI)

An unusual characteristic of all IBM PCs, ATs, and PS/2s, but not of clones, is that if the machine is unable to load an operating system from disk, it calls up a BASIC interpreter that is stored on a ROM chip. This BASIC interpreter ("Cassette BASIC") was originally implemented so that low-budget computer hobbyists could use IBM PCs without disk drives, storing their programs on cassette tape. The same ROM code was included in later machines because it is used by the BASIC interpreter that runs under DOS. (*See* BASICA; GW-BASIC.)

IBM RS/6000 *see* WORKSTATION.

IC *see* INTEGRATED CIRCUIT.

ICANN (Internet Corporation of Assigned Names and Numbers) a non-profit corporation established in 1998 to oversee the assignment of Internet domain names and addresses. *See also* NETWORK SOLUTIONS, INC.

Letter Writer MarkVision Printer Utility Memory Check Notepad

Paint Phone Dialer QEDIT Superpad

FIGURE 129. ICONS REPRESENTING PROGRAMS

icon a small picture on a computer screen that represents a particular object, operation, or group of files. Icons are used extensively in graphical user interfaces such as Microsoft Windows, the Macintosh, and the OS/2 Desktop.

On the Macintosh, the trash can icon stands for "delete." Use the mouse to move a file to the trash can, and it will be deleted. In Windows 95 and its successors, the Recycle Bin serves the same function. *See* GRAPHICAL USER INTERFACE; MOUSE; WINDOW; WINDOWS (MICROSOFT).

iconify to turn a window into an icon (same as MINIMIZE).

IDE (Integrated Device Electronics) a type of hard disk that has most of the controller circuitry built into it, to save space. IDE controllers are functionally similar to the older ST-506 standard. *See* ST-506; ESDI; SCSI.

identifiers symbolic names used in a program and defined by the programmer. Most identifiers stand for variables (*see* VARIABLE); however, some languages allow the use of identifiers to represent constants, so that the value of a particular constant, wherever it occurs in the program, can be changed by changing the statement that defines the identifier. *See* CONSTANT.

identity in Outlook Express or similar mail-reading programs, a setting that determines which of several individuals is using the computer. This enables several people to share a computer and keep their e-mail separate even though the operating system is not set up for multiple users.

identity theft *(jargon)* the crime of impersonation, i.e., pretending to be someone else, using forged documents of various kinds. Crucially, identity theft goes beyond the theft of a single credit card number or the forgery of a single document. It is an attempt to assume a person's entire identity, including name and credit rating, in order to create new accounts under the victim's name.

   Identity theft often involves electronic communications media by taking advantage of the fact that on-line and mail-order merchants are often not very thorough in checking credit card users. However, despite wide publicity in the late 1990s, identity theft remains a relatively uncommon crime. *See also* COMPUTER ETHICS.

ideogram, ideograph a written symbol that represents an idea rather than the pronunciation of a word. Symbols such as &, $, numerals, and computer icons are ideograms.

IDL (Interface Definition Language) *see* CORBA.

IE (Internet Explorer) a web browser developed by Microsoft.

IEC power connector the type of connector commonly used to attach a PC's power cord to the computer, using three prongs oriented in the same direction.

IEEE (Institute of Electrical and Electronics Engineers) the leading professional society for electrical and computer engineers in the United States. It publishes journals, holds conferences, and publishes many standards applicable to computer equipment. The IEEE is headquartered in Piscataway, New Jersey, and can be reached on the Web at http://www.ieee.org.

IEEE 1284 an IEEE standard for PC parallel ports, compatible with the designs used previously, but including provision for high-performance bidirectional communication with tape drives, disk drives, and other devices, not just printers. It is fully compatible with earlier EPP and ECP standards.

The IEEE 1284 standard defines three connectors: the traditional 25-pin socket on the PC (IEEE 1284A), the 36-pin Centronics connector on the printer (IEEE 1284B), and a new miniature connector (IEEE 1284C).

Parallel ports are IEEE 1284 *compliant* if they implement the whole IEEE 1284 standard; they are IEEE 1284 *compatible* if they implement one or more of the older standards of which IEEE 1284 is a superset.

See PARALLEL PORT; CENTRONICS INTERFACE; EPP; ECP.

IEEE 1394 an IEEE standard for a serial bus more commonly known as "Firewire." It provides a data transfer rate of at least 200 million bits per second, fast enough for uncompressed video. Its main rival is Universal Serial Bus (USB). *See* SERIAL BUS; USB.

IETF (Internet Engineering Task Force) an international group of network professionals who work on advances in Internet architecture and work to ensure smooth operation of the Internet. The IETF is organized into several working groups on specific topics. Their web address is www.ietf.org.

IF a keyword in many programming languages that specifies that different actions are to be performed depending on the result of some test. Here is an example of an IF statement in BASIC:

```
100 PRINT "INPUT PRICE"
110 INPUT P
120 IF P<0 THEN PRINT "PRICE CAN'T BE < 0!":GOTO 100
```

If the condition P<0 is true, then the two commands:

```
PRINT "PRICE CAN'T BE <0!"
GOTO 100
```

will be executed. Here is an example of an IF statement in Pascal:

```
IF hours <= 40 THEN
  BEGIN
    pay := hours * wage;
    writeln('No overtime hours')
  END
ELSE
  BEGIN
    pay :=  wage*40 + 1.5*wage*(hours-40);
    writeln('Overtime wages paid')
  END;
```

If the condition hours < = 40 is true, then the two statements between the first BEGIN/END pair will be executed. If the condition is false, the computer will instead execute the statements enclosed in the second BEGIN/END pair. Here is an example in Java:

```
if (hours<=40) {
  pay = hours * wage;
  System.out.println("no overtime hours");
}
else {
  pay = wage*40+1.5*wage*(hours-40);
  System.out.println("overtime wages paid");
}
```

IIOP (Internet Inter-ORB Protocol) a protocol that extends TCP/IP by adding CORBA defined messages for objects to connect to each other over the network. *See* CORBA.

IIRC e-mail abbreviation for "if I remember correctly."

IIS abbreviation for Internet Information Server, web server software developed by Microsoft.

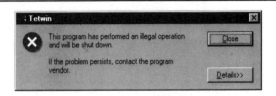

FIGURE 130. ILLEGAL OPERATION MESSAGE (WINDOWS 95)

illegal operation an operation that a program is not permitted to perform, such as writing on a read-only disk or using memory allocated to some other program. Illegal operations are almost invariably the result of errors in programming. *See also* GPF.

iMac Apple Computer's G3-based Macintosh built within an unconventional, brightly colored, one-piece enclosure. Sales of the iMac have been brisk, partly because of its innovative case design (*see* Figure 131).

One of the more controversial points of the iMac's design is its lack of an internal diskette drive, although easy access to peripheral devices (e.g., a Zip drive) through USB ports should make this a moot point. *See also* MACINTOSH; APPLE.

image map a web page graphic to which multiple LINKS have been assigned. It is possible to click on different parts of the picture and activate different links. For example, you might create a map of your community that appears on the web page; if the user clicks on the part of the map representing one neighborhood, then the browser will jump

FIGURE 131. IMAC (COURTESY OF APPLE COMPUTER, INC.)

to a link providing information about that neighborhood. This gives the links a visual meaning that would not be there in a list of text-only links. Image maps can be created with some web-creation software programs, or they can be defined directly by hand-coding the proper HTML.

image processing the use of a computer to modify pictures (usually bitmap images). Applications of image processing include retouching or enhancement of photographs, computer vision, and creation of works of art. Many image processing functions are built into paint and photopaint programs as FILTERS (definition 2). For examples, see ADD NOISE; BLEND; BLUR; BRIGHTNESS; COLOR/GRAY MAP; EDGE DETECT; EQUALIZE; MOTION BLUR; PIXELATE, PIXELIZE; REMOVE SPOTS; SHARPEN; UNSHARP MASKING. *See also* VISION (COMPUTER); DEBLURRING; CONVOLUTION.

imagesetter a high-quality output device. Imagesetters can deliver up to 2400 DPI (dots per inch) instead of the 300 or 600 DPI of ordinary laser printers.

IMG tag used in HTML to indicate an image file. For example, *see* HTML.

IMHO e-mail abbreviation for "**i**n **m**y **h**umble **o**pinion."

IMO e-mail abbreviation for "**i**n **m**y **o**pinion."

impedance a measure of how easily an alternating current can pass through an electrical circuit. The impedance of a resistor is the same as its resistance. Capacitors and inductors also affect impedance, depending on the frequency of the current. The impedance of a capacitor decreases as the frequency increases; the impedance of an inductor increases as the frequencey increases. The characteristic impedance of coaxial cable results from the interaction of its inductance and capacitance. It is not a resistance and cannot be measured with an ohmmeter. *See* COAXIAL CABLE.

import to load a file from a format other than the application program's native format. Many word processing and graphics programs have the ability to import text and graphics from several different file formats. Because importing is a type of file conversion, formatting and image detail may be lost in the process. *See* CONVERSION PROGRAM.

incremental backup a backup operation that only copies files that have changed since the last backup. *See* BACKUP COPY.

incremental compiler a compiler that compiles the lines of a program as they are typed into the computer, rather than compiling the whole program at once. The purpose is to keep the programmer from having to wait a long time for the complete program to be compiled when it is finished. *See* COMPILER.

indent to leave a space at the beginning of the first line of a paragraph. Indented margins are also used to set off long quotations. *See also* HANGING INDENT.

index
    1. an alphabetical listing of important words and concepts found in a book and the pages on which these terms may be found. Many page layout and word processing programs have the ability to automatically generate indexes from properly tagged terms (*see* DESKTOP PUBLISHING; TAGS). Note that the process is not wholly automatic; the human still has to specify which words should be indexed.
    2. a pictograph of a pointing hand. Sometimes called a *fist*.

FIGURE 132. INDEX (DEFINITION 2)

    3. the number that picks out an element of an array. For example, in A[2], 2 is the index. *See* ARRAY.

indexed file a file in which the order of the items is recorded in a separate file called the index. For example, if the computer is looking for John Smith's billing records, it first looks up "Smith, John" in the index, and then the index tells it where to look in the billing record file.

Indexed files have two advantages. First, the index can be sorted (alphabetized) without moving the contents of the main file. This saves time because the index is much smaller. Second, it is possible to maintain multiple indexes to the same file — for example, to index by name and also by account number, zip code, or date.

Industry Standard Architecture *see* ISA.

inference engine the part of an EXPERT SYSTEM that draws conclusions by reasoning logically from information. *See also* PROLOG; ARTIFICIAL INTELLIGENCE.

inferior character a subscript; small letters and numbers set on or below the baseline like this. Used mainly in mathematical typesetting (*see* SUBSCRIPT; *contrast* SUPERSCRIPT, SUPERIOR).

INF file a type of file, with extension .inf, that tells the Windows Setup program how to install a particular piece of hardware or software.

Infobahn German for INFORMATION SUPERHIGHWAY.

informatics the study of information and computation; a European name for computer science. *See* COMPUTER SCIENCE.

information hiding *see* STRUCTURED PROGRAMMING.

Information Superhighway a network of electronic and digital communication equipment that is quietly revolutionizing businesses and our private lives (*see* INTERNET).

Not only is information being disseminated faster than ever, but worldwide electronic communication is creating a unique community — one that does not have a physical location, but rather exists in what is called CYBERSPACE. Some portions of cyberspace are rather lawless right now; an ill-considered message may bring down an avalanche of angry messages (called FLAMES) upon your e-mail account. However, some standards of ethics and personal behavior are being worked out.

The term *information superhighway* is also used to refer to a system of fiber-optic cables that may one day link every home to the Internet, replacing the current television and telephone cables.

infrared a kind of radiation similar to light but at a slightly longer wavelength, used to transmit data through the air in TV remote controls, wireless mice, wireless keyboards, and the like, and occasionally for short-distance computer-to-computer links. Like light, infrared signals require a clear line of sight and cannot go through walls.

Infrared radiation is abundant in ordinary sunlight and, at the levels used for communication, is not hazardous.

inheritance the process by which one object is defined to be just like another except for some specified differences. The second type of object

then "inherits" the properties of the first. *See* OBJECT-ORIENTED PRO-
GRAMMING.

INI file a file (with the extension `.ini`) that stores initialization information for Microsoft Windows, OS/2, or a specific piece of software.
Windows INI files consist of editable text; OS/2 INI files are generated
by the operating system.

initialize
    1. to store a value in a variable for the first time. If a program tries
to use a variable that has not been initialized, it will get a random value
and the results will be unpredictable.

    2. to prepare a tape for use, erasing any data that may already be
on it.

inkjet printer a printer that forms characters by shooting tiny droplets
of ink at the paper. Advantages include speed, high resolution, and
quiet operation. An ink jet printer is often an economical alternative
to a laser printer; in black and white, the image quality is comparable,
but printing is slower. Some color inkjet printers can print near-photo-
quality pictures on special plastic-coated paper; with ordinary paper,
the picture quality is lower.

inlining the conversion of a FUNCTION or PROCEDURE into machine
instructions that perform the computation directly, without calling the
function or procedure. In effect, the statement that calls the procedure is
replaced by a copy of the procedure itself. This speeds up execution but
requires slightly more memory. *See* FUNCTION; PROCEDURE; COMPILER.

Inprise Corporation ("Integrating the Enterprise") a software
company headquartered in Scotts Valley, California, and formerly
known as Borland International. Inprise can be reached on the web at
`http://www.inprise.com`. For history and products *see* BORLAND
INTERNATIONAL.

input information that is given to a computer; the act of giving information to a computer. (Note that the terms *input* and *output* are always used
from the computer's point of view.) The input data may be either numbers or character strings (e.g., a list of names). The computer receives
input through an input device, such as a keyboard, or from a storage
device, such as a disk drive.

insertion point the place, in a full-screen editor or drawing program,
where characters will appear if you start typing. The insertion point is
usually indicated with a cursor or a thin vertical bar. The insertion point,
which is different from the mouse pointer, looks like an arrowhead or,
in some contexts, a tall, thin letter "I".

insertion sort an algorithm for placing the elements of an array in
ascending or descending order. This method is efficient if the list is
already close to being in order.

To perform an insertion sort, examine every item in the list except the first. Whenever you find an item that should come before the item that immediately precedes it, pick up the current item, shift its neighbor on the left one space to the right, and see whether you can put the current item in the space thus vacated. If not, shift that item to the right and try again.

Consider for example the following list:

2404   8653   1354   5781

The steps of the insertion sort are the following:

1. 2404 and 8653 are in the right order, so proceed to the next pair.
2. 8653 and 1354 are in the wrong order, so pick up 1354:

2404   8653   5781

Shift 8653 one space to the right:

2404   8653   5781

Can 1354 be put into the empty space? No; its neighbor on the left would be 2404, a larger number. So shift 2404 one space to the right:

....   2404   8653   5781

Now you can put 1354 into the empty space:

1354   2404   8653   5781

3. Now examine 8653 and 5781. They are in the wrong order, so pick up 8653 and shift it one space to the right, then put 5781 into the empty space:

1354   2404   8653   ....
1354   2404   8653
1354   2404   5781   9653

Now all the elements are in order, and the process is complete.

Fig. 133 shows a Pascal program that performs an insertion sort. *See also* SHELL SORT.

instance variables the variables (*fields*) that contain data unique to each object in OBJECT-ORIENTED PROGRAMMING.

instantiated created or initialized. Once a new instance of a particular object type is created, it is said to be instantiated. In Prolog, a variable is said to be instantiated when it is given a value. *See* INSTANCE VARIABLES; OBJECT-ORIENTED PROGRAMMING; PROLOG.

INT 13 the interrupt service routine that provides disk access through the BIOS under DOS. Advanced operating systems such as Windows 98 normally bypass INT 13, but they can be told to use it if necessary for compatibility with unusual hardware or device drivers.

integers whole numbers and negated whole numbers, such as 1, 2, 3, 0 , −10, −26, 157, 567, and −2,397. An integer does not contain a fractional part. Thus, 3.4 and $2\frac{2}{3}$ are not integers.

```
PROGRAM insertionsort;
VAR
  a: ARRAY [1..10] OF INTEGER;
  i, value, position: INTEGER;
BEGIN
  { Read in the data }
    FOR i := 1 TO 10 DO
      BEGIN
        write('Enter item ',i:2,':');
        readln(a[i])
      END;
  { Perform the insertion sort }
    FOR i := 2 TO 10 DO
      BEGIN
        value := a[i];
        position := i;
        WHILE (position > 1) AND
              (a[position-1] > value) DO
          BEGIN
            a[position] := a[position-1];
            position := position-1
          END;
        a[position] := value
      END;
  { Print the results }
    FOR i := 1 TO 10 DO write(a[i]:5);
    writeln
END.
```

FIGURE 133. INSERTION SORT IN PASCAL

integrated circuit (**IC**) an electronic device consisting of many miniature transistors and other circuit elements on a single silicon chip. The
first integrated circuits were developed in the late 1950s, and since then
there has been continued improvement. The number of components that
can be placed on a single chip has been steadily rising.

The advantages of integrated circuits over discrete components
include the facts that they are very small (most are less than $\frac{1}{4}$ inch
square), their internal connections are more reliable, they consume
much less power, they generate much less heat, and they cost less than
similar circuits made with separate components.

Integrated circuits are classified by their level of complexity. *Small-
scale integration* describes circuits containing fewer than 10 logic
gates; *medium-scale integration,* circuits containing 10 to 100 gates;
and *large-scale integration,* circuits with more than 100 gates.

An integrated circuit is made by adding impurities to a silicon crystal in specific places to create P-type and N-type regions, and adding
metal conductive paths to serve as wires. (*See* SEMICONDUCTOR.) The
whole process uses light-sensitive chemicals whose action is controlled
by a tiny image projected through a device that is like a microscope
working backward; thus, tiny regions on the IC can be created from a
much larger picture of the desired layout.

Integrated circuits are mass produced by making many identical circuits at the same time from a single wafer of silicon. Each circuit must be individually tested, because a single defect in the crystal can completely ruin the circuit.

The ultimate integrated circuit is the microprocessor, which is a single chip that contains the complete arithmetic and logic unit of a computer, and sometimes other parts of the computer as well. *See* MICROPROCESSOR.

Integrion a company formed by IBM and leading banks to develop electronic home banking, available on the World Wide Web at `http://www.integrion.net`.

Intel the manufacturer of the microprocessors used in PC-compatible computers, although other companies also make compatible equivalents. Intel products include the 8088, 80286, 386, 486, Pentium, Pentium Pro, and Pentium II. *See* MICROPROCESSOR. Earlier, Intel developed the first microprocessors (4004, 8008) and the microprocessor for which CP/M was developed (the 8080, soon superseded by Zilog's Z80). Intel Corporation is headquartered in Santa Clara, California. Its web address is `http://www.intel.com`.

interactive system a computer system in which the user communicates with the computer through a keyboard and screen. The computer presents the results almost immediately after an instruction has been entered, and the user can type in new instructions after seeing the results of the previous ones. Nowadays, almost all computing is interactive. *Contrast* BATCH PROCESSING.

interblock gap a blank space on a magnetic tape between two adjacent blocks. The presence of the gap makes it easier to keep track of the locations of the blocks when the tape is started and stopped.

intercap a capitalized letter in the middle of a word. The word *PostScript* contains an example. The companies that have coined such trademarks contend that the unusual capitalization is part of the correct spelling of the trademark.

Not everybody accepts these unusual spellings. At one time there was a company that claimed the only correct spelling of its name was "en●vōs." Almost everyone printed it as Envos. The moral of the story is that names need not reproduce trademarks and logos. In fact, a company can be at a real disadvantage if it makes its name too hard to print — journalists may simply ignore it.

intercharacter spacing the spacing in between characters within words. Also called LETTERSPACING. *See* KERNING; TRACKING.

interface the connection between two systems through which information is exchanged. For example, in computer hardware, an interface is an electrical connection of the proper type. In software, it is a standard format for exchanging data. The USER INTERFACE of a piece of software is the way it interacts with the human being who is using it. *See also* DATA COMMUNICATION; USER INTERFACE.

interlaced GIF a BITMAP file that has been optimized for downloading to a remote site. An interlaced GIF displays faster because it can be displayed in rough form before all the information has been received. The picture initially appears in coarse blocks, which refine themselves into finer detail as the complete file is downloaded. *See* GIF.

interlacing a way of arranging a video display so that the CRT scans all the odd-numbered rows first, then all the even numbered rows, or vice versa. This is supposed to reduce flicker because the whole screen is scanned twice as often as it would be if the rows were scanned in order.

In practice, interlacing reduces flicker only if adjacent rows are similar so that they can blend together. Thus interlacing works well with an ordinary TV picture but not so well on a computer screen, where a horizontal line, for example, might occupy only one row. With computer graphics, best results are obtained with a noninterlaced display that scans the whole screen at least 50 times per second. *See* MONITOR; CRT.

internal font a description of a kind of type to be printed on a printer. Unlike soft fonts and font cartridges, internal fonts are permanently built into the printer, where they reside on ROM chips. *Contrast* FONT CARTRIDGE; SOFT FONT.

International Business Machines *see* IBM.

Internet a cooperative message-forwarding system linking computer networks all over the world. Users of the Internet can exchange electronic mail, participate in electronic discussion forums (newsgroups), send files from any computer to any other via FTP, retrieve information via Gopher or HTTP, and even use each other's computers directly via Telnet or rlogin if they have appropriate passwords. *See* ELECTRONIC MAIL; FTP, TELNET; RLOGIN; FINGER; GOPHER; HTTP; WORLD WIDE WEB; IRC; INFORMATION SUPERHIGHWAY.

Every user of every machine on the Internet has an address. For example, the address

```
covington@beetle.ai.uga.edu
```

means:

covington	individual user (Covington)
beetle	machine ("beetle")
ai	subnetwork (Artificial Intelligence Lab)
uga	site (University of Georgia)
edu	type of site (U.S. educational)

Here `beetle.ai.uga.edu` is a domain address that gets translated into a numeric IP address, in this case 128.192.12.9, by the network itself.

U.S. commercial, government, and military sites have addresses that end in `com`, `gov`, and `mil` respectively. Other countries have distinctive suffixes, such as `ca` for Canada and `uk` for Great Britain.

The cost of running the Internet is paid largely by the sites that receive messages, and the sites that pass them along, not by the sites that send messages out. This has important legal and ethical implications. *Unsolicited advertising via e-mail or in newsgroups is almost always unwelcome*, as is any self-serving misuse of electronic communications, because the sender of the material is not paying the cost of distributing it. For further ethical guidelines *see* USENET; COMPUTER ETHICS.

The Internet grew out of the ARPAnet (a U.S. Defense Department experimental network) as well as BITNET, Usenet, and other wide area networks. *See* WIDE-AREA NETWORK; USENET. *Contrast* INTRANET.

Usage note: Many people confuse the Internet with the World Wide Web, which is only one of several forms of communication that take place on the Internet. *See also* E-MAIL; NEWSGROUP; FTP.

Internet 2 a group of colleges working on advanced Internet features. For further information, *see* `http://www.internet2.edu`.

Internet radio the transmission of sound from a radio station, or similar real-time audio programs, to computer users over the Internet. This makes hearing distant and specialized radio stations possible. However, it can clog up networks because a separate copy of each data packet has to be sent to each computer. (Real radios all pick up the same signal at the same time.) The BBC World Service can be heard by Internet radio at `www.bbc.co.uk`.

Internet service provider (**access provider**) a company that provides its customers with access to the INTERNET, typically through DIAL-UP NETWORKING. Major service providers in the United States include Microsoft, Netcom, and Earthlink. America Online, CompuServe, and Prodigy provide Internet access among their other services.

Typically, the customer pays a monthly fee, and the Internet service provider supplies software that enables the customer to connect to the Internet by modem. Some ISPs also provide file space for pages on the WORLD WIDE WEB and FTP file storage.

interoperability the ability of machines or programs to work together. Two computers are interoperable if they can be used together in some useful way, working on the same files or sharing data through a network.

interpolation

1. in mathematics, the process of estimating an unknown value of a function in between two known values. For example, if it takes 18

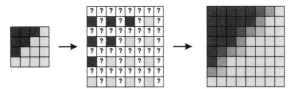

FIGURE 134. INTERPOLATION FILLS IN MISSING PIXELS
WHEN AN IMAGE IS ENLARGED

minutes to cook a 1-inch-thick steak and 40 minutes to cook a 2-inch steak, you can interpolate and find that it should take about 30 minutes to cook a $1\frac{1}{2}$-inch steak.

2. in computer graphics, the process of smoothing the pixels in an image that has been enlarged by filling in intermediate colors or shades of gray, thus reducing the stairstep appearance that would otherwise result from enlarging a small bitmap; also known as resampling. *See* RESAMPLE.

interpreter a program that executes a source program by reading it one line at a time and doing the specified operations immediately. Most early BASIC systems were interpreters. *Contrast* COMPILER.

interrupt an instruction that tells a microprocessor to put aside what it is doing and call a specified routine. The processor resumes its original work when the interrupt service routine finishes. Interrupts are used for two main purposes:

1. to deal with hardware events such as a key being pressed or a character arriving through a serial port. These events cannot be ignored; the incoming data must be either processed immediately or stored in a buffer.

2. to call subroutines that are provided by the hardware or operating system. On the IBM PC, most DOS and BIOS services are called through interrupts rather than through the ordinary instruction for calling a subroutine. OS/2 and Windows services, however, are called as ordinary subroutines.

These correspond to the two main ways of causing an interrupt: by receiving a signal from outside the microprocessor (a hardware interrupt) or by executing a machine instruction (a software interrupt).

interrupt service routine *see* INTERRUPT.

intersection the set of elements that are in both of two other sets. For example, the intersection of $\{a, b, c\}$ with $\{c, b, r\}$ is $\{b, c\}$.

interword spacing The spacing between words. Sometimes called WORDSPACING.

intranet the opposite of INTERNET; a network confined to a single organization (but not necessarily a single site). Intranets are often set up as web pages, so a web browser can be used to view the content. This makes the intranet appear just the same as part of the World Wide Web; the only difference is that it is not accessible to those outside the organization. Keeping it separate from the outside world is essential if it carries confidential data, such as internal business records.

Intuit leading producer of personal financial software (the program Quicken). Web address: `http://www.intuit.com`.

intuitive obvious without conscious thought. The operation of a piece of software is said to be *intuitive* if the operation fits the task so well that the user can guess how to perform common operations without consulting manuals or pausing to figure things out. *Compare* USER-FRIENDLY.

invalid media disks or tapes that cannot be used because of physical defects or because they have been partly erased by a magnetic field. In the latter case the media can be formatted (erased) and used again. *See also* ABORT, RETRY, FAIL.

FIGURE 135. INVERTED PHOTOGRAPH

invert
   1. to turn an image into a photographic negative of itself, substituting black for white and white for black, and changing colors to their complements.
   2. (less commonly) to turn an image upside down.
   For other senses, *see* INVERTER.

inverter
   1. a NOT gate. (*See* NOT GATE.)
   2. a device that converts direct current to alternating current for power supply purposes (e.g., to power a computer from a car battery).

invisible watermark a code secretly hidden in a picture to carry copyright information or other secret messages. An invisible watermark consists of a very slight change of contrast over large areas of the picture, invisible to the human eye, even fainter than the watermark on a piece of paper. Suitable software can recover the invisible watermark even if the image has been printed out, photographed, and scanned in again.

Iomega manufacturer of Zip and Jaz drives. Their corporate web site is at `http://www.iomega.com`.

IOW e-mail abbreviation for "in other words."

IP
    1. **I**nternet **P**rotocol. *See* TCP/IP.
    2. **i**ntellectual **p**roperty. i.e., patents, copyrights, and trademarks, especially patented or copyrighted designs for components of equipment or software.

IP address (**I**nternet **P**rotocol address) the numeric address of a machine, in the format used on the Internet. For example, the IP address of one of the University of Georgia's computers is 128.192.12.9.
    Three blocks of IP addresses are reserved for private networks and will never be officially assigned. Therefore, if you must make up an unofficial IP address, you should choose it from one of these blocks. They are 10.0.0.0–10.255.255.255, 172.16.0.0–172.16.255.255, and 192.168.0.0–192.168.255.255. The address 127.0.0.1 on any machine connects it back to itself. *Contrast* DOMAIN ADDRESS. *See* INTERNET.

IPO (**I**nitial **P**ublic **O**ffering) the first sale of a corporation's stock to the public. Innovative computer companies have often begun as privately held corporations, motivating employees by offering stock options that become valuable after the IPO if the market price rises. Outside investors who buy stock soon after the IPO will profit from further increases in the stock price. However, this type of investment is very risky because there is no guarantee the stock price will rise.

IP spoofing *see* SPOOFING.

IPX/SPX (**I**nternetwork **P**acket **E**xchange/**S**equenced **P**acket **E**xchange) a data transmission protocol developed by Novell and widely used in local-area networking. *See* PROTOCOL. *Contrast* TCP/IP; NETBEUI; ATM.

IRC (**I**nternet **R**elay **C**hat) a multi-user conversation conducted over the Internet in real time. Fig. 136 shows what a chat session looks like. Numerous CHANNELS (conversation forums) exist. Participants normally identify themselves by nicknames.
    In addition to typing remarks for transmission to the other participants, the IRC user can type commands such as `/list` to see what channels are available, `/join #frogs` to join a channel called `frogs` or create it if it doesn't exist, and `/bye` to sign off. *See also* CHAT ROOM.

```
<JohnBoy> Does anybody know where I can
get some information about SCSI?
<Gweep> Hello, John Boy!
<JohnBoy> Hello, Gweep!
<Hermes> There's a newsgroup called
comp.periphs.scsi.  Look there.
<JohnBoy> Thanks, Hermes.
<Gweep> What's a newsgroup?
```

FIGURE 136. AN IRC SESSION

IRL e-mail abbreviation for "**i**n **r**eal **l**ife," meaning the mundane, real, physical world as opposed to the glamorous exciting life in CYBERSPACE.

TABLE 10
IRQ NUMBERS (FOR PC COMPATIBLES)

IRQ	Function
0	Hardware timer
1	Keyboard
2	Cascade from IRQ9
3	COM2, COM4
4	COM1, COM3
5	LPT2
6	Diskette controller
7	LPT1
8	Real-time clock
9	Video
10	Unassigned (often used by network cards)
11	Unassigned (often used by SCSI adapters)
12	Unused
13	Math coprocessor
14	Hard disk controller
15	Unassigned (often used by sound cards)

IRQ (**I**nterrupt **Req**uest) a type of bus signal used on PC-compatible computers to allow input-output devices to interrupt the CPU.

When installing a network card or other new peripheral in a PC, you will often have to choose an unused IRQ number and assign it to the new device. To find out what IRQ numbers are already in use, use the command msd to run Microsoft Diagnostics, a program supplied with Windows, or use Device Manager under Windows 95 and its successors. Table 10 shows how IRQ numbers are normally assigned. Some devices can share IRQ numbers with other devices.

ISA (**I**ndustry-**S**tandard **A**rchitecture) a term often used to describe the conventional IBM PC AT (16-bit) bus and the associated card edge connector, as opposed to EISA or Micro Channel. *See* EISA; MICRO CHANNEL; BUS.

ISA slot a slot in a computer where ISA accessories can be added.

ISDN (**I**ntegrated **S**ervices **D**igital **N**etwork) a type of all-digital telephone service. ISDN lines can transmit digital data as well as voice, without a modem. ISDN service began in the U.S.A. in 1988 and may eventually replace conventional telephone service. The capacity of an ISDN line is 128 kbps, much slower than a T1 or T3 line. *See* T1 LINE; T3 LINE; MODEM.

ISO

    1. International Organization for Standardization (abbreviated ISO in all languages), an organization that sets standards for many industries. For example, there are ISO standards for the Pascal and Prolog programming languages and for sizes of printer paper. *See also* ANSI; PAPER SIZES (ISO).

    2. e-mail abbreviation for "**i**n **s**earch **o**f."

    3. a system for rating the sensitivity (speed) of photographic film or CCDs, based on an ISO standard, equivalent to the older ASA system. An ISO 100 film or CCD will make a correctly exposed picture of a sunlit landscape when exposed for 1/100 second at $f/16$.

ISO 9000 an ISO standard specifying various ways of ensuring the quality of manufactured products. It does not denote any specific computer technology.

ISO 9660 the basic standard format for recording computer data on compact discs (CD-ROMs). Unlike most disk formats, CD-ROMs are not tied to the operating system of a particular computer; any computer can read the data files from any standard CD-ROM. (Software recorded on the CD-ROM may of course require a specific computer in order to run.) ISO 9660 format supersedes the earlier High Sierra format, with which it is closely compatible. *See* JOLIET FILE SYSTEM.

ISOC (**I**nternet **Soc**iety) a global organization that discusses issues related to the Internet. Their web address is www.isoc.org.

ISO paper sizes *see* PAPER SIZES (ISO).

ISP (**I**nternet **s**ervice **p**rovider) a company that provides accounts allowing customers to access the Internet. *See* INTERNET SERVICE PROVIDER or ACCESS PROVIDER.

ISTR e-mail abbreviation for "**I** **s**eem **t**o **r**ecall …"

ISV (**I**ndependent **s**oftware **v**endor) a company that writes software independently of the company selling the hardware.

IT (**i**nformation **t**echnology) computers and electronic communication.

italics letters slanted to the right and designed with a more calligraphic feel than their roman counterparts. *This sentence is set in italics.* Italics are used for emphasis, for setting the titles of books and articles, and for foreign words. Italic type corresponds to underlining on a typewriter.

iteration the process of repeating a particular action. A *definite iteration* occurs when the specified action will be repeated a fixed number of times. For example, you can find the sum of all the integers from 1 to 100 with the following BASIC program, which uses iteration:

```
10   T = 0
20   FOR I = 1 TO 100
30      T = T + I
40   NEXT I
```

See LOOP.

An *indefinite iteration* occurs if the repetitions stop when a particular condition is met, but you don't know in advance how many repetitions will take place before that happens. An example of an indefinite iteration is a binary search routine. (*See* BINARY SEARCH.) In that case the iteration will continue until the item you're looking for has been found, or you establish that it is not in the list.

I-triple-E *See* IEEE.

ITU (**I**nternational **T**elecommunication **U**nion) an organization head-quartered in Geneva, Switzerland, that sets standards for electronic communication technology. For more information see the Web page `http://www.itu.int`.

ITU-T the telecommunication section of the ITU, formerly known as the CCITT.

iway (or **i-way**) abbreviation for INFORMATION SUPERHIGHWAY.

J

jack a connector into which a plug can be inserted.

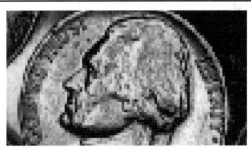

FIGURE 137. JAGGIES (STAIRSTEPS)
IN AN IMPROPERLY-SIZED BITMAP

jaggies the property of an improperly sized bitmap that shows the image broken into blocky squares. *See* BITMAP; ANTIALIASING; RESOLUTION.

Japanese writing *see* KANA.

JAR file (Java Archive) a file containing a collection of Java class files that can be downloaded more efficiently than would be possible if each file were downloaded separately.

Java a programming language developed at Sun Microsystems in the mid-1990s to enable networked computers to transmit computations to each other, not just data. For example, an Internet user can connect to a Java APPLET (program) on the World Wide Web, download it, and run it, all at the click of a mouse, using a Java-compatible WEB BROWSER. Applets can include features such as animation. Fig. 138 shows an example of a Java program.

Java is designed for OBJECT-ORIENTED PROGRAMMING. The language is extensible: classes are defined in terms of other more general classes, and they inherit their properties. It is closely based on C++ but is fundamentally different in a number of ways that make it easier to use. Its special features include:

- architecture neutrality (a Java program can, in principle, run under any windowed operating system);

```
/* File showball.java */

/* Displays red or blue circles when user clicks mouse */

import java.awt.*;
import java.applet.*;

public class showball extends Applet {
   Graphics g;   int rc,gc,bc;   ball ballobject;

  public void init() {
     setLayout(null);
     Button bluebutton = new Button("Blue");
     add(bluebutton);
     bluebutton.reshape(0,0,100,20);
     Button redbutton = new Button("Red");
     add(redbutton);
     redbutton.reshape(110,0,100,20);
     ballobject = new ball();
  }

  public boolean action(Event e, Object o) {
        if ("Red".equals(o))
             {rc=255;  gc=0; bc=0;}
     else if ("Blue".equals(o))
             {rc=0;    gc=0; bc=255;}
       return false;
  }

  public boolean mouseDown(Event e, int x, int y) {
     ballobject.xc = x;   ballobject.yc = y;
     ballobject.redcode = rc; ballobject.greencode = gc;
     ballobject.bluecode = bc;
     repaint();         return false;
  }

  public void paint(Graphics g) {
     ballobject.drawball(g);
  }
}
```

```
/* File ball.java */

import java.awt.*;
import java.applet.*;

public class ball {
     int xc,yc,redcode,greencode,bluecode;

  public void drawball(Graphics g2) {
        Color rgbcolor = new Color(redcode,greencode,bluecode);
        g2.setColor(rgbcolor);
        g2.fillArc(xc,yc,25,25,0,360);
        /* fillArc is included with the class applet*/
  }
}
```

FIGURE 138. JAVA PROGRAM (COMPRISING 2 FILES)

- garbage collection (memory is cleared automatically when objects no longer need it, eliminating one of the major headaches of C++ programming);

- security (Java applets downloaded from the web are restricted in their access to the machine's files and operating system; this is an essential feature of programs loaded through the Internet from a possibly untrustworthy source);

- uniform support for windowing environments (programs produce similar screen displays no matter where they are run);

- support for multiple threads of program action (concurrency).

Java programs are compiled, not into machine code, which would not be portable, but into a concise code (known as Java bytecode) for downloading to the recipient's Java interpreter. A compiled Java program resides on a file of type .class that can be incorporated into a web page through HTML commands such as:

```
<applet code="showball.class"
    width=200 height=200> </applet>
```

Java is important not only because it allows computations to be downloaded through web pages, but also because it is the first portable programming language for windowed operating systems. It does for windowing what BASIC did for the keyboard and screen, making it possible to write programs that run the same way regardless of the kind of machine. *See also* HTML; WORLD WIDE WEB; BLACK WIDOW.

JavaBean a software component written in Java. The goal of JavaBeans is to facilitate software development by letting programmers assemble programs from previously written and tested components that will work on many different platforms. This only works when there are consistent specifications for the ways for the components to work with other components. A JavaBean consists of data and methods, similar to an ordinary Java class. The data can only be accessed through accessor methods, whose names begin with *get* (to receive values from the bean) or *set* (to send values to the bean). This standardization allows an application builder tool to examine the bean and determine its properties, and how those properties can be changed.

A JavaBean may have a visual representation (for example, it may appear as a button or a dialog box, allowing users with a visual development system to drop it onto the screen at the desired location). Beans are typically included in a JAR (Java Archive) file, which may also include other elements such as a graphical image that the bean uses. For an alternative example of component technology for Windows, *see* ACTIVEX.

Java chip an integrated circuit using the Java bytecode as its machine language.

JavaScript a language that allows a web page to include commands to be executed by the web browser. For example, you may wish your web page to have dialog boxes that appear when the user clicks on certain places. Or, if your web page will send information back to the server, you can use JavaScript to catch some common data entry errors before it is sent. This will save work for the server.

The name comes from the fact that JavaScript shares some syntax and object-oriented features with Java, but they are actually quite different languages. JavaScript commands are interpreted by the web browser (*see* INTERPRETER), rather than being compiled into bytecode as Java programs are. JavaScript is easier to learn than Java, particularly if you already know HTML, but, unlike Java, it does not have the features of a complete programming language.

Here is an example of how JavaScript can be used together with an HTML form to receive information from a customer. In this example, the user enters the item number, price, and quantity for two different items into the form. Two different JavaScript functions are defined. The function *addup* is called by the event handler onChange that is located in the HTML code for the form. Whenever one of these fields is changed, JavaScript checks for negative values and then multiplies the price times the quantity and adds up the total dollar amount.

```
<HTML>
<HEAD><TITLE> JavaScript Example</TITLE>
<SCRIPT LANGUAGE="JavaScript">

function multiply(a,b) {
  if ((a>=0)&(b>=0)) {return a*b;}
  else {window.alert("Value can't be negative");
    return "invalid";}
      }

function addup() {
  var totalamount=0;  var amount=0;
    for (i=1; i<=2; i++) {
      amount=
        multiply
          (document.orderform.elements[i*4-2].value,
          document.orderform.elements[i*4-1].value);
      document.orderform.elements[i*4].value=amount;
      totalamount+=amount;
                   }
  document.orderform.total.value=totalamount;
       }
</SCRIPT>
</HEAD>

<BODY>
```

FIGURE 139. JAVASCRIPT IN ACTION

```
<H1> Order Form Example </H1>

<FORM NAME="orderform">
<ACTION "mailto:youraddress@xyz.com">
Your Name: <INPUT TYPE= "text" NAME="customername"
  SIZE=20><br>

Item Number:<INPUT TYPE="text" NAME="item1" SIZE=5>
Price:<INPUT TYPE="text" NAME="price1"
  SIZE=5 onChange="addup();">
Quantity:<INPUT TYPE="text" NAME="quant1"
  SIZE=5 onChange="addup();">
Value: $<INPUT TYPE="text" NAME="value1"
  SIZE=8 onChange="addup();"><BR>

Item Number:<INPUT TYPE="text" NAME="item2" SIZE=5>
Price:<INPUT TYPE="text" NAME="price2"
  SIZE=5 onChange="addup();">
Quantity:<INPUT TYPE="text" NAME="quant2"
  SIZE=5 onChange="addup();">
Value: $<INPUT TYPE="text" NAME="value2"
  SIZE=8 onChange="addup();"><BR>

Total Value: $<INPUT TYPE="text" NAME="total"
  SIZE=8 onChange="addup();"><BR>

<INPUT TYPE="SUBMIT" NAME="submit"
  VALUE="E-Mail your order" SIZE=40>
</FORM>
</BODY>
</HTML>
```

Figure 139 shows the appearance of the screen when this web page is loaded.

For another example of programming in JavaScript, *see* ROLLOVER.

Jaz drive a 1-gigabyte removable-cartridge disk drive made by Iomega Corporation of Roy, Utah. *See also* ZIP DRIVE; BERNOULLI BOX.

JCL (Job Control Language) the command language used in batch jobs to tell a computer what to do. (*See* BATCH PROCESSING.) The acronym JCL usually refers to the job control language used on large IBM computers, but sometimes designates very different languages used for the same purpose on other computers.

The following is an example of JCL for an IBM 360; the language is the same for all IBM mainframe computers running operating systems derived from OS/360, such as OS/VS2 and MVS:

```
//JONES JOB 123456,TIME=5
// EXEC PLIXCG
//PLI.SYSIN DD DSN=JONES.SAMPL.PLI,DISP=SHR
//GO.SYSIN DD *
1 2 3 4
/*
//
```

The first statement is the JOB card, which gives the job a name, specifies the user's account number, and establishes a CPU time limit of 5 minutes for the whole job. The EXEC PLIXCG statement calls up the procedure to compile and execute a PL/1 program; its operation happens to consist of two steps, PLI (compile) and GO (execute).

The DD (data definition) statements define files. SYSIN (standard system input) for the PLI step is defined as a cataloged disk data set named JONES.SAMPL.PLI; SYSIN for the GO step is given in the job itself, beginning after DD * and ending with /*. The // card marks the end of the job.

In IBM JCL, each statement has up to four fields per this example:

```
//GO.SYSIN DD * INPUT FILE
```

Here GO.SYSIN is the name field, DD is the operation field, * is the operand field, and INPUT FILE is the comment field. The rules for coding the fields are as follows:

1. The fields are separated by at least one blank. Only the first 71 characters of every line (not 72, as you might expect) are significant.

2. The name field is immediately adjacent to the two slashes at the beginning of the line. Often the EXEC statement has no name field; when this is the case, be sure to type

   // EXEC

   and not

   //EXEC

   The name field cannot contain any blanks.

3. The next field after the name field is the operation field, usually JOB, EXEC, or DD. The operation field also cannot contain any blanks.

4. The next field after the operation field is the operand field; this too cannot contain any blanks unless they are in quotation marks. If the operand field will not fit on one line, it can be continued to a second line, as in this example:

```
//GO.SYSIN DD DSN=JONES.OLD.DATA,
//            DISP=SHR,
//            DCB=(LRECL=80,BLKSIZE=3120)
```

Here every line except the last ends with a comma. Every line except the first begins with two slashes followed by from 1 to 13 blanks. (A common error is to include too many blanks.)

5. Anything after the operand field is considered to be a comment and is ignored by the computer.

JCL also includes a null statement (consisting of // by itself), which marks the end of a job, and a comment statement, which begins with //*. Comment statements are ignored by the operating system itself but are often used to convey information to utilities that have been added onto the operating system for various purposes (e.g., automatic allocation of tape drives).

The details of JCL vary considerably from installation to installation; consult local manuals for more information. 𝄍

JDK (**J**ava **D**evelopment **K**it) a system provided free by Sun Microsystems that can be used to write Java programs. It comes with a Java compiler, standard class library, and an applet viewer.

jewel case a rigid clear-plastic case that protects compact discs (CDs).

JIT compiler (just-in-time compiler) a Java VM that converts Java bytecode into native machine language the first time it is encountered; this allows subsequent execution of that code to occur faster.

job *see* BATCH PROCESSING.

Job Control Language *see* JCL.

join *see* RELATIONAL DATABASE.

Joliet file system an extension to the ISO 9660 format for recording CD-ROMs, created by Microsoft in order to support long filenames and long directory names. It is the usual format for CD-ROMs to be used under Windows 95 and later.

joule a unit for measuring amounts of energy. 1 joule equals 1 kilogram-meter^2/second^2. One watt is equivalent to one joule per second. *See* WATT; WATT-HOUR; VOLT.

joystick a computer input device especially helpful when playing computer games. The joystick consists of a handle that can be pointed in different directions. Because the computer can sense in which direction the joystick is pointed, the joystick can be used to control the movements of objects displayed on the computer screen.

JPEG (**J**oint **P**hotographic **E**xperts **G**roup) a file format for storing bitmap images, including lossy compression (that is, a file can be compressed to a very small size if some blurring of detail is tolerable). JPEG file format is often used for high-quality photographic images.

JScript a version of JAVASCRIPT developed by Microsoft.

jukebox a device for automatically selecting disks (usually CD-ROMs) from a library and inserting the desired one into the disk drive.

Julian calendar the calendar introduced in 46 B.C. by Julius Caesar, with a leap year every four years. *See* LEAP YEAR; GREGORIAN CALENDAR.

Julian date

1. the number of days elapsed since January 1, 4713 B.C., counting that date as day 1. The Julian date is now used primarily by astronomers. It is unrelated to the Julian calendar. The Julian date was introduced in 1582 A.D. by J. J. Scaliger, who named it for his father Julius. Its original purpose was to convert dates between various ancient calendars without using negative numbers. The Julian date of January 1, 2000 is 2,451,544.

2. more loosely, any date expressed as a day count rather than as year, month, and day.

jumper a removable electrical connector that joins two pins on a circuit board. Many of the internal settings in computers are made by moving or removing jumpers.

jump list a WEB PAGE consisting mostly of links to other web pages. *See* HTML; INTERNET; WORLD WIDE WEB; LINK (definition 3).

junction the part of a diode or transistor where two opposite types of semiconductor material meet. *See* DIODE; TRANSISTOR.

junk e-mail unsolicited electronic mail, usually containing advertisements; presently legal but very unwelcome because it imposes an expense on the recipient. Many of the businesses that advertise through junk e-mail are obviously untrustworthy. As this is written, legislation is before Congress to ban or heavily restrict junk e-mail. *See also* JUNK FAX; COMPUTER ETHICS; SPAMMING.

junk fax unsolicited advertisements transmitted by fax. Junk faxing is illegal in the United States because it imposes an expense on the recipient (who has to pay for the paper) and ties up machines that are needed for more important messages.

justification the insertion of extra space between words in lines of type so that the left and right margins are even and smooth. Most of the type in this book is justified.

Most word processors and desktop publishing programs can automatically do the computations necessary to justify type. Problems generally arise only when the column width is too narrow, or too large a HOT ZONE has been specified. Then you will get RIVERS of white space running down the column (not too attractive). To cure this, make sure hyphenation is enabled, shrink the hot zone, go to a smaller type size, or increase the column width.

JVM (Java Virtual Machine) software that executes Java bytecode. A program written in Java is first compiled into class files, written in bytecode. To execute these files, the computer needs to use the JVM to interpret the code. The JVM is built into web browsers that are capable of executing Java applets. The bytecode is the same for all platforms, but the JVM will be different on different platforms because it needs to execute using the native code of the machine it is running on.

K

k, K abbreviation for KILOBYTE (or, less commonly, *kilohm* or other metric units). By convention, a capital K stands for a factor of 1,024, and a lowercase k stands for a factor of 1000, as in the metric system (kilograms, kilometers, etc.). *See also* MEMORY; BYTE; MEGABYTE.

K6 chip microprocessor introduced by AMD in 1997 as a competitor to the Intel Pentium. *See* MICROPROCESSOR.

K56flex a standard formerly used by Rockwell and other modem manufacturers for transmitting data on telephone lines at speeds up to 56,600 bits per second, now superseded by v.90.

kana the Japanese phonetic writing system. There are two styles, *hiragana* and *katakana*. Kana contrasts with *kanji,* the Chinese-derived symbols for whole words. Written Japanese uses a mixture of kana and kanji.

kanji *see* KANA.

katakana *see* KANA.

kBps kiloBytes per second. *See also* KILOBYTE; BAUD.

kbps kilobits per second. *See* BIT.

Kerberos an authentication protocol that allows users and computers to identify each other without risk of impersonation and to communicate securely by encrypting their data. A Kerberos system uses a central authentication server to issue *tickets,* which are temporary authorizations to communicate. Each ticket is valid only for a specific user and for a limited length of time. Thus, an intercepted or stolen ticket is of little use. Because of the encryption used, forged tickets are virtually impossible to produce.

Kerberos was developed at the Massachusetts Institute of Technology, which distributes an implementation of it free of charge (web.mit.edu/kerberos/www/). Kerberos has many commercial implementations. In Greek mythology, Kerberos (in Latin, Cerberus) is the dog that guards the gate of Hades.

Kermit a protocol for transferring files from one computer to another. Kermit is also the name of a program (distributed free by Columbia University) that implements this protocol. (Other communications programs also implement part or all of the Kermit protocol.)

Like XMODEM, Kermit makes an exact copy of the original file even when transmitting over a noisy line. All data packets are error-checked, and erroneous packets are retransmitted. Kermit is slightly slower than XMODEM but is more versatile and has been ported to a wider variety of computers.

kernel the central part of an OPERATING SYSTEM. In many operating systems, only the kernel can access hardware directly.

Usage note: For obscure reasons this term is often spelled *kernal*. This may be nothing more than a typing error that appeared in an influential manual and caught on.

To   Without kerning

To   With exaggerated kerning

FIGURE 140. KERNING

---

kerning adjustment of the amount of space between certain combinations of letters in proportional-pitch type. If the combination "To" is typeset with the same letter spacing as "Th," the letters seem to be too widely spaced. "To" looks better if the top of the "T" is allowed to overhang the "o" slightly. *See* Figure 140.

key

    1. a button on a computer keyboard.

    2. the item by which a data file is sorted or searched. For instance, if a file of names and addresses is sorted by zip codes, then the zip code is the key.

    3. The password or other secret information needed to decode an encrypted message. *See* ENCRYPTION.

keyboard the primary computer input device for alphanumeric data. There are many different types of keyboard layouts; for the most part the alphabet and numbers are consistently placed, but there is considerable variation in the placement of the auxiliary characters, editing keys, and function keys. Most keyboards have a numeric keypad (for typing digits) at the right; if you use a mouse a lot, but don't type many numbers, you may prefer a narrower keyboard that omits the keypad and lets you put your mouse closer to where you sit. Some keyboards have a mouse-like pointing device built in; these are generally fine for menu selection but not precise enough for drawing.

    When buying a new computer, be sure to evaluate the keyboard carefully. A keyboard that feels "dead" can be tiring to use. Practice typing on several different models to find one that feels good to you. Some of the newest keyboards are bent in the middle so that your hands can stay in a more comfortable position. Spending a few extra dollars for a good keyboard can be a wise investment; after all, it is the part of your computer that you are in contact with constantly.

keyboarding entering data through the keyboard; typing.

keyboard shortcut *see* SHORTCUT.

key disk a non-copyable diskette that must be inserted into a computer in order to run a particular program. The key disk does not contain the whole program, only an essential part of it. Key disks are sometimes used so that a single licensed program can be installed on multiple machines but only used on one of them at a time.

key frame (animation software) an artist-supplied image representing a single moment in an animation. The computer creates intermediate frames between the key frames.

keying
1. typing; inputting information into the computer by means of the keyboard.
2. the process of digitally combining video images by using a subtractive background. *See* CHROMA-KEYING.

keywords words that have special meaning in a particular programming language. For example, GOSUB is a keyword in BASIC, and BEGIN is a keyword in Pascal.

killer app *(slang)* a software application that becomes so desirable that it is the reason people purchase a computer, computer peripheral, or operating system. For example, Visicalc was a killer app for the Apple II, and Lotus 1-2-3 was a killer app for the original IBM PC. Some operating systems, such as OS/2, have failed to become popular because of the lack of a killer app.

kilo- metric prefix meaning $\times 1000$ (10^3) or, in rating computer memories and disks, $\times 1024$. *Kilo-* is derived from the Greek word for "thousand." *See* METRIC PREFIXES.

kilobyte a unit of computer memory capacity equal to 1024 characters. The number 1024 is significant because $2^{10} = 1024$.
By convention, a capital K stands for a factor of 1024, and a lower-case k stands for a factor of 1000, as in the metric system (kilograms, kilometers, etc.). *See also* MEMORY; BYTE; MEGABYTE.

kilowatt-hour a unit of electrical energy consumption equal to 1000 watt-hours. *See* WATT-HOUR.

kiosk a small stand containing a computer that people can walk up to and use to retrieve information. Kiosks often display current information about local events. They are used in museums, airports, and other public places.

kluge (pronounced "klooge") an improvised, jury-rigged, and poorly-thought-out solution to a problem, usually intended only for temporary use. The word *kluge* may be derived from German *klug,* which means "clever." In Britain it is sometimes spelled *kludge* and pronounced to rhyme with "sludge."

knife (drawing program) a tool that cuts an object into pieces, defining a new outline along the cut edge and thus preserving the fill attributes of the original object.

knockout an area where an underlying color has been cut out so that the overprinting color can remain pure. Some DESKTOP PUBLISHING software automatically creates knockouts and TRAPS when preparing files for duplication on a printing press (*see* PREPRESS).

knowledge base a collection of knowledge that is used as the basis for solving problems or making recommendations. *See* EXPERT SYSTEM.

Koch snowflake *see* FRACTAL.

L

L1 cache (level-1 cache) the memory cache that is closest to the CPU or included within it.

L2 cache (level-2 cache) a memory cache outside the CPU. *Contrast* L1 CACHE.

l8r, l8tr humorous e-mail abbreviation for "later."

label

    1. an identifying name or number attached to a particular statement in a computer program.

    2. a block of information recorded on a tape to identify it.

    3. an identifying name recorded on a disk and displayed by the `dir` command in DOS, OS/2, and similar operating systems.

LAN *see* LOCAL-AREA NETWORK.

 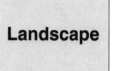

FIGURE 141. LANDSCAPE VS. PORTRAIT ORIENTATION

landscape a way of orienting paper so that it is wider than it is high, like a landscape painting. That is, the paper is positioned sideways compared to the way it would otherwise be used ("portrait orientation"). Laser printers typically offer a choice of portrait or landscape orientation.

LAP-B (**L**ink **A**ccess **P**rocedure-**B**alanced) a method for detecting and correcting errors in data transmission. (For a description of another method in detail, *see* XMODEM.) LAP-B error correction is built into some high-speed modems so that erroneous data is never sent to the computer.

TABLE 11
SOME LASERJET PCL COMMAND CODES

ASCII code numbers	Action
27 38 108 ## 80	Set page length to ## lines per page
27 38 108 ## 69	Set top margin to ## lines
27 38 97 ## 76	Set left margin to column ##
27 38 97 ## 77	Set right margin to column ##
27 38 108 54 68	Set vertical spacing to 6 lines per inch
27 61	Halfline feed
27 38 97 ## 82	Position cursor at row ##
27 38 97 ## 67	Position cursor at column ##
27 38 108 48 79	Switch orientation to portrait
27 38 108 49 79	Switch orientation to landscape
27 40 56 85	Switch font to internal Roman-8
27 40 115 ## 72	Set primary pitch to ## characters per inch
27 40 115 ## 86	Set primary point size to ##
27 40 115 48 83	Set primary style to upright
27 40 115 49 83	Set primary style to italics
27 40 ## 88	Set primary font to number ##

laptop a small, lightweight computer (under 8 pounds) with a flip-up screen. Such a computer is powered by rechargeable batteries and is easily portable. Laptops are especially valuable for people who travel frequently and need to be able to work on a computer while on the road. *See also* PCMCIA; DOCKING STATION. Because of their portability, laptops need special precautions against theft. *See* COMPUTER SECURITY.

large-scale integration the construction of integrated circuits that contain more than 100 logic gates. (*See* INTEGRATED CIRCUIT.)

laser (**l**ight **a**mplification by **s**timulated **e**mission of **r**adiation) an electronic device that produces rays of light that are exactly matched in wavelength and phase. Laser beams can be used to detect microscopically tiny detail (such as the pattern on a CD-ROM) and to concentrate energy in a small, precisely located space (as in a laser printer).

LaserJet a popular line of laser printers produced by Hewlett-Packard. Each successive model has incorporated improvements in the command language and a larger number of built-in fonts. Additional fonts can be added by plugging in font cartridges and by downloading fonts from the computer. Models with the suffix P, such as the IIIP and 4MP, are "personal" printers designed for low-volume use.

Table 11 shows a number of control codes in HP PCL (Hewlett-Packard Printer Control Language, the command language of the LaserJet series). Each control code begins with ASCII code 27 (Escape), and ## denotes ASCII codes that are treated as numbers. Note that LaserJet-compatible software will send these codes to the printer automatically as needed. Some LaserJet models, such as the LaserJet 4M, support PostScript as an alternative command language.

laser printer a computer printer that generates an image by scanning a photoconductive drum with a laser beam, then transfers the image to paper by means of electrostatic toner. Laser printers provide high-quality output of text and graphics; they are quiet and run fast. *Contrast* DOT-MATRIX PRINTER; INKJET PRINTER.

Laserwriter trademark for laser printers marketed by Apple for use with the Macintosh computer. Most models of Laserwriter use the PostScript command language. *See* MACINTOSH; POSTSCRIPT.

FIGURE 142. LASSO TOOL

lasso a selection tool commonly found in PAINT PROGRAMS; it looks like a rope lariat, and you use it to define an area that you wish to work with. Crucially, the area need not be rectangular; it can be any shape. After selecting the lasso icon, you drag the mouse *freehand* around the desired area. Once the area is defined, you can scale, move, rotate, change color, apply filters, or perform any operation that is available.

Because the lasso is a freehand tool, it is dependent upon your skill as a mouse operator. Knowing how difficult it is to draw accurately with a mouse, you may want to see if your paint program has other selection tools (such as a MAGIC WAND) that would suit your needs better. *See* SELECT.

LaTeX (pronounced "la-tekh" or "lay-tekh"; often written LƎTƎX) a type-setting system designed by Leslie Lamport and implemented as a set of macros for Donald Knuth's TeX (*see* TEX). There are two versions in wide use, LaTeX 2.09 and LaTeX 2_ϵ; LaTeX 3 is under development.

The key idea of LaTeX is to separate the job of the author from that of the publication designer. The author uses commands such as \chapter{...} and \section{...} to mark chapter and section titles, figures, quotations, and the like. (Fig. 143 shows an example.) Separately, a file called a *style sheet* specifies how these things should be printed and keeps them consistent. So, while other word processing

```
\documentstyle{article}

\title{An Example}
\author{Michael A. Covington}
\date{June 27, 1998}

\begin{document}
\maketitle

\section{Overview}
This is a sample of a short paper typed with \LaTeX.
Notice the commands I use to get \emph{italics} and
\textbf{boldface}. I can also typeset mathematical
formulas such as $\sum_{x=1}^{5} A_x$.

Notice that I skip lines between paragraphs in the
input. This is the second paragraph.

\section{Another section}
This is the second section.  It is very short.

\end{document}
```

An Example

Michael A. Covington

June 27, 1998

1. Overview

This is a sample of a short paper typed with LaTeX. Notice the commands I use to get *italics* and **boldface**. I can also typeset mathematical formulas such as $\sum_{x=1}^{5} A_x$.

Notice that I skip lines between paragraphs in the input. This is the second paragraph.

2. Another section

This is the second section. It is very short.

FIGURE 143. LATEX INPUT AND OUTPUT

programs work like a computerized typewriter, LaTeX does the job of an expert typist and layout artist.

LaTeX is especially popular for typesetting scientific and mathematical books because the full power of the TeX mathematical typesetting system is available. Many scholarly journals are typeset with LaTeX, as are most of the books published by several major publishers. LaTeX is also popular with graduate students writing theses and dissertations because it is easy to conform to standard formats—just use your university's official style sheet.

Implementations of LaTeX are available for a wide range of computers. This book was typeset with LaTeX 2_ε on a Pentium III under Windows 98, using a highly customized style sheet.

Latin the language of the ancient Romans; the Roman alphabet (including j, v, and w, which were added to it in modern times), as opposed to the Greek or Russian alphabet.

launch

1. to advertise and release a new product. Windows 95 was launched on August 24, 1995.

2. to start a computer program, especially in a multitasking operating system.

LCD (**L**iquid **C**rystal **D**isplay) the type of display used on most digital watches, calculators, and laptop computers, and in overhead-projector computer displays.

LCDs consume much less power than any other kind of display, but they are sometimes hard to read because of a lack of contrast ("black" is not much darker than "white"). "Supertwist" LCDs have more contrast than earlier types.

LCDs use liquid crystals, which are chemicals whose response to polarized light can be controlled by an electric field. A polarizing filter is built into the LCD; through this filter, the liquid crystal compound looks light or dark depending on its electrical state.

LCD panel *see* PROJECTION PANEL.

leader a line of dots that connects one side of the page with another, often used in tables of contents, like . . . . this.

leading (pronounced "ledding") the insertion of extra space between lines of type. On old printing presses, this was originally done by inserting strips of lead between rows of type cast in lead. *See* TYPEFACE.

> These lines
>
> are typeset with
>
> extra leading.

In some cases, it is actually beneficial to use *negative leading*—for instance, when setting type in all caps, it is not necessary to allow space for descenders. Such headlines usually look best with negative leading.

**THESE LINES ARE TYPESET
WITH NEGATIVE LEADING.**

leak an error in a program that makes it fail to release memory or other system resources when it terminates. Thus, the available memory, disk space, or other resources are gradually eaten up until the computer is rebooted. Memory leaks are a common error in Windows programs.

Java programs avoid this problem because of the garbage collection process, which automatically releases memory locations that are no longer being referenced by the program.

leap year a year in which an extra day, February 29, is added to keep the calendar year in step with the earth's revolution around the sun. If there were no leap years, the calendar would get out of step with the earth's motion, so that after several centuries, January 1 would occur in the summer instead of the winter.

The rule for identifying leap years is as follows:

- Years divisible by 400 are always leap years. Thus, 2000 and 2400 are leap years.

- Years divisible by 100, but not by 400, are not leap years. Thus, 1900 and 2100 are not leap years.

- Otherwise, years divisible by 4 are leap years. Thus, 2004, 2008, etc., are leap years.

Leap years were introduced by Julius Caesar. *See* JULIAN CALENDAR; GREGORIAN CALENDAR.

learning curve a graph representing mastery of a skill plotted against the time spent on learning it. If something is hard to learn to use, it is sometimes described as having a steep learning curve (although, logically, a steep curve should indicate rapid learning). The term originated in behaviorist psychology but is now used very imprecisely.

LED (**l**ight-**e**mitting **d**iode) a semiconductor device that emits light when an electric current passes through it. The bright red display on some digital clocks is made of LEDs. Other available LED wavelengths are infrared, orange, yellow, green, and blue.

left-click to CLICK with the left-hand mouse button (or the right-hand button if the mouse is set up for a left-handed person).

legacy anything left over from a previous version of the hardware or software. For example, *legacy applications* are applications from earlier versions of DOS or Windows; *legacy hardware* is hardware that does not support PLUG AND PLAY.

legacy-free not burdened by the need for compatibility with substantially older equipment or software. Microsoft is promoting legacy-free PC design as a way to make PCs more reliable and easier to upgrade.

Since 1984, the IBM PC AT architecture has reserved a number of port addresses, interrupt request (IRQ) numbers, and memory addresses for various purposes. These were assigned long before sound cards, video capture devices, and other modern computer peripherals were invented. Because of this, the person installing a sound card into a modern PC often has to choose memory addresses and IRQ numbers for it—a job that should be left to the designer of the machine. *Legacy-free PCs* break free of these requirements by allowing the operating system to control the hardware directly. *Legacy-reduced PCs* are intermediates between legacy-free and conventional PCs. *See also* IRQ; PC 2001; PLUG AND PLAY.

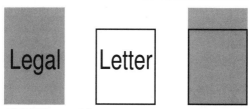

FIGURE 144. LEGAL- AND LETTER-SIZED PAPER

legal size the size of paper used for legal documents in the United States, $8\frac{1}{2} \times 14$ inches. *Contrast* LETTER SIZE, EXECUTIVE SIZE. *See also* PAPER SIZES.

letter quality a quality of printing equal to the best typewriters, or better. All laser printers and daisywheel printers are letter quality; so are most inkjet printers.

letter size the size of paper used for business letters in the United States, $8\frac{1}{2} \times 11$ inches. Elsewhere, ISO size A4 is the nearest equivalent. *Contrast* LEGAL SIZE, EXECUTIVE SIZE. *See also* PAPER SIZES.

letterspacing the space between letters (characters). *See* Figure 145. Look for the letterspacing controls with other FRAME attribute commands (letterspacing is sometimes called TRACKING).

LF (line feed) the character code that tells a printer or terminal to advance to the next line; ASCII code 10. UNIX uses LF to indicate the end of a line in a text file. The Macintosh uses CR; DOS and Windows use CRLF. *See* CR; CRLF.

library
1. a collection of files, computer programs, or subroutines. A loader library is a file containing subroutines that can be linked into a machine language program.

verylo o s e
l o o s e
normal
tight
touching

FIGURE 145. LETTERSPACING

2. a collection of reference materials and software tools, such as clip art, prerecorded sounds, and predefined objects.

license permission to use patented or copyrighted material. *See* SOFTWARE LICENSE; SHRINKWRAP LICENSE.

LIFO (last-in-first-out) a STACK (definition 1); a data structure or memory device from which items are retrieved in the opposite of the order in which they were stored. *Contrast* FIFO.

ff fi fl ffi ffl
FIGURE 146. LIGATURES

ligature a printed character representing a combination of two or three letters (Fig. 146). Some of the most sophisticated word processing programs, such as TeX, change pairs of letters into ligatures automatically.

light
1. visible electromagnetic radiation.
2. type that is designed and drawn with very fine strokes; the opposite of BOLD.

light-emitting diode *see* LED.

light pen a pen-like light-sensitive device that can be used like a mouse to communicate with a computer. The operator holds the pen up to the screen, and the computer can sense what point on the screen the pen is touching. Light pens were popular in the 1970s but have largely been replaced by mice.

lights (3D, animation software) virtual devices that mimic the effect of real lights upon the computer-generated scene. Computer lights can be adjusted in many of the same ways as their real-life counterparts: intensity, position, direction, and color. *See also* AMBIENT LIGHTING.

LIM-EMS *see* EXPANDED MEMORY.

limitcheck PostScript error that occurs when a drawing is too complex to be printed.

limits of computer power a subject of continuing theoretical study.

Computers can perform only tasks that can be reduced to mechanical procedures (algorithms). They are therefore inapplicable to tasks that cannot or should not be reduced to mechanical form, such as judging the greatness of a work of art or administering psychotherapy. Rather surprisingly, however, there are some tasks that are mathematically precise but that present-day computers cannot perform. These fall into two major types: (1) problems with no known algorithmic solution, and (2) problems whose best known algorithmic solutions require unreasonable amounts of time.

An example of a problem of the first type (one with no presently known algorithmic solution) is how to get a computer to recognize the structures of sentences in a human language such as English. Obviously, this is something computers will have to be able to do if we are ever to be able to communicate with them in English, and there is no reason to think it impossible. The difficulty is simply that English (and all other human languages) are so complicated that complete algorithms for processing them have not yet been discovered.

A good example of the second type of problem, one that takes an unreasonable amount of time to solve, is the so-called traveling salesman problem. The task is to find the shortest route by which a salesman can visit a particular set of cities (in any order). The only known way to solve this problem is to try all possible routes. A few shortcuts are possible — for instance, the testing of each route can be abandoned as soon as its length exceeds the shortest length already found, without pursuing it to the end — but the number of steps is never substantially fewer than N factorial, where N is the number of cities (*see* FACTORIAL). Suppose the fastest imaginable computer could perform one step in this algorithm by moving an electric charge a distance of 1 millimeter at the speed of light. This would mean that it could perform 3×10^{11} steps per second. Then the times required to solve the traveling salesman problem (in $N!$ steps) would work out as follows:

Number of Cities	Number of Steps	Time Required
5	120	0.36 picosecond
10	3,628,800	12 microseconds
15	1.3×10^{12}	4.4 seconds
20	2.4×10^{18}	94 days
25	1.6×10^{25}	1.6 million years
30	2.7×10^{32}	2.8×10^{13} years

And this is with a computer millions of times faster than any that presently exist. Obviously, it will never be feasible to solve the traveling salesman problem for more than a few cities unless a much better algorithm is found.

Another interesting class of computational problems, known as *NP-complete* problems, has been proved to be equivalent to the traveling salesman problem; if a better algorithm is found for any NP-complete problem, it will be applicable to all of them.

line

1. in geometry, the shortest path connecting two points. A geometric line is always perfectly straight and has no width.

2. in graphics, a visible representation of a geometric line. A line in this sense has a definite color and width (normally at least 0.5-point for good visibility on paper; *see* HAIRLINE) and may be continuous, dashed, or dotted.

3. a printed line of type. Punched cards and non-graphical computer screens usually accommodate 80 characters per line, but text is most readable with a line length of about 65 characters. *See also* WORD WRAP; LINESPACING.

4. an electronic communication path, such as a telephone line. *See* T1 LINE; T3 LINE.

linear fill a way of filling an object with color so that it makes a smooth transition from one color at one side of the object to another color at the other side. You can specify the angle of the linear fill. *Contrast* RADIAL FILL.

line cap the end of a drawn line. In most DRAW PROGRAMS, you can choose square or rounded ends, or even arrowheads.

line drawing an illustration that can be represented as a series of hard-edged black lines and black areas on a white background. Line drawings are easily converted to vector images by tracing them.

line feed *see* LF.

line spacing the spacing in between lines of type. Also called LEADING.

link

1. any kind of communication path between two computers.

2. an entry in one directory or menu that points directly to something in some other directory or menu; a SHORTCUT. Links can be used to make the same file accessible from more than one directory or to put the same program on more than one menu.

3. an item on a WEB PAGE which, when selected, transfers the user directly to some other web page, perhaps on a different machine. Also called a HYPERLINK. For example *see* HTML.

4. in Windows, a DDE or OLE communication path between programs. *See* DDE; OLE.

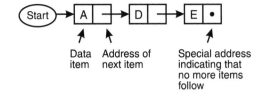

Data   Address of   Special address
item   next item   indicating that
                     no more items
                     follow

FIGURE 147. A LINKED LIST

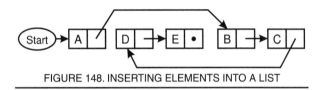

FIGURE 148. INSERTING ELEMENTS INTO A LIST

5. to combine the machine instructions for a program with the machine instructions for any predefined procedures that it uses. For example, a program that does trigonometric calculation might use predefined procedures to find sines, cosines, and tangents. Some compilers perform linking automatically; others require you to execute a linker as a separate command.

6. a pointer in a linked list or tree. *See* LINKED LIST; TREE.

link, dead *see* DEAD LINK.

linked list a way of organizing data items in a computer so that they are retrievable in a particular order that is not necessarily the same order as the physical locations in which they are stored. Each data item consists of two parts: the data itself, and a number giving the location of the next item. Figure 147 shows how this is usually diagrammed. To read the items in order, you need only know which item is in the beginning (the head) of the list; having located it, you can go next to the item whose address was stored with it; and so on.

Linked lists allow items to be added or removed without requiring that other items be moved to make room. For instance, the list A–D–E of Figure 147 can be changed into A–B–C–D–E by adding two items. As Figure 148 shows, the newly added items B and C can be placed in the unused area after the E, and *inserted* into the list by changing the address associated with item A.

Figure 149 shows that an item can be *deleted* by changing the addresses so that there is no longer a path to that item. In either case, using linked lists can eliminate the need to move hundreds or thousands of data items whenever an insertion or deletion takes place.

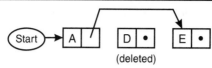

(deleted)

FIGURE 149. DELETING AN ELEMENT

Item No.	Data item	Address of next item
1	A	4
2	D	3
3	E	0
4	B	5
5	C	2

FIGURE 150. A LINKED LIST STORED IN AN ARRAY

Figure 150 shows a way to construct a linked list in an ordinary two-dimensional array; this can be done in practically any programming language. Each row of the array contains a data item and an integer indicating which row the next item is on (or zero, to indicate that there are more items). In the example, it is assumed that the first item in the list will always be in row 1; if you wish to be able to delete the first item, you can use a separate integer, outside the array, to keep track of where the list starts. *See also* DATA STRUCTURES.

linker a program that puts separately compiled routines together to make a complete, working program. *See* LINK (definition 5).

Linux (usually understood as "**Lin**us' **UNIX**") a freely distributed UNIX-compatible operating system for PCs and a number of other processors.

Linux was developed by Linus Torvalds and others and is distributed under terms similar to those of Gnu's "copyleft" (*see* GNU). Copies can be given away free provided they are complete and intact, but most users prefer to purchase commercially produced CD-ROMs containing Linux together with application software.

Linux is quite reliable and highly compatible with UNIX; as a result, it is very popular with universities, Internet service providers, and small businesses that need multi-user computing at minimum cost. More information can be found on the World Wide Web at http://www.linux.org.

Linux box *(slang)* a small computer running Linux.

liquid crystal display *see* LCD.

Lisp (**List** **P**rocessor) a programming language developed in the late 1950s at MIT under the direction of John McCarthy. Because of the ease with which it can handle complex data structures, Lisp is used for artificial intelligence research and for writing programs whose complexity would render them unmanageable in other languages.

A Lisp program is easy to recognize because of the accumulation of closing parentheses at the end of the program. All Lisp statements and most Lisp data structures are linked lists, written as lists of elements in parentheses (*see* LINKED LIST). Programmers build a complete program by defining their own statements (actually functions) in terms of those previously defined. For example, a function that computes the factorial of *X* is:

```
(DEFUN FACTORIAL (X)
  (IF (= X 0)
      1
      (* FACTORIAL(-X 1))))
```

Translating into English: "This is the definition of a function called FACTORIAL whose parameter is *X*. If *X* is zero, its factorial is 1; otherwise, its factorial is equal to *X* times the factorial of *X* − 1." The IF keyword works like a Pascal if-then-else statement. This function calls itself recursively; recursion is the normal way of expressing repetition in LISP.

list
    1. a set of data items that are to be accessed in a particular order; for instance, a list of the students in a class might be accessed in alphabetical order. Lists are stored in arrays or linked lists. *See* ARRAY; LINKED LIST.
    2. to display a program line by line (especially in BASIC).
    3. a MAILING LIST distributed by e-mail.

list administrator the person responsible for maintaining a MAILING LIST.

list box an area in a dialog box where the user can choose among a list of items, such as files, directories, printers, or the like. For an illustration, *see* DIALOG BOX.

list processing
    1. the manipulation of linked lists. *See* LINKED LIST; LISP.
    2. the processing of mailing lists and similar data is sometimes called list processing. *See* DATABASE MANAGEMENT.

listserv a program often used to maintain mailing lists. *See* MAILING LIST. *Compare* MAJORDOMO.

literals symbols in a computer program that stand for particular values and are not programmer-defined (i.e., cannot possibly stand for any other value). For example, in the following BASIC program:

```
10    LET A = 2.4
20    LET B$ = "THE ANSWER IS"
30    PRINT B$, A
```

the literals are "THE ANSWER IS" and 2.4.

little-endian a system of memory addressing in which numbers that occupy more than one byte in memory are stored "little-end-first," with the lowest 8 bits at the lowest address.

For example, the 16-digit binary number 1010111010110110 occupies two 8-bit bytes in memory. On a little-endian computer such as the IBM PC, the lower byte, 10110110, is stored at the first address and the upper byte, 10101110, is stored at the next higher address. On a big-endian machine, the order is reversed. *Contrast* BIG-ENDIAN.

The terms "big-endian" and "little-endian" are from *Gulliver's Travels*; they originally referred to the parties in a dispute over which end of a boiled egg should be broken first.

ln the function, in Pascal and some other languages, that calculates the natural (base *e*) logarithm of its argument. For example, `ln(X)` finds the natural logarithm of X. *See* LOGARITHM; E.

LNIB (**L**ike **N**ew **I**n **B**ox) describes merchandise offered for sale in almost-new condition. *Compare* NOS (definition 2).

load to transfer information from a disk or other outside device into the memory of a computer. *Contrast* SAVE. *See also* LOADER.

loader a computer program whose function is to load another program into memory and transfer control to it. All operating systems include loaders. For example, if you have a program named `myfile.exe` and you type the DOS command

```
C:\> myfile
```

you are telling the DOS loader to find `myfile.exe` and load it.

local located at the user's computer or site. *Contrast* REMOTE.

local-area network a network that connects several computers that are located nearby (in the same room or building), allowing them to share files and devices such as printers. For examples, see ETHERNET; TOKEN RING. *Contrast* WIDE-AREA NETWORK.

A local-area network can be very valuable if several people must constantly enter data into a single database. Some database programs, such as Paradox, have network versions designed specifically for this purpose. For example, several workers might work on the same inventory-control system, one of them logging new merchandise as it comes in, the other logging sales as they take place.

For an example of a popular local-area network system, *see* NOVELL NETWARE.

local bus a separate bus in a computer, designed to provide extra-fast access to the CPU for specific devices, such as video cards. It contrasts with the main bus, which connects to most other parts of the computer. For examples *see* VESA LOCAL BUS, PCI.

localization the process of adapting software to run in a particular part of the world. Localization might involve translating screen displays into French or German, adapting to a foreign-language keyboard, printing the date differently (e.g., 1999 Dec 31 in Japan vs. 31 Dec 1999 in Britain and Dec. 31, 1999 in the United States), setting the clock for daylight saving time on different dates, or even writing numbers differently (3,000.95 vs. 3 000.95 or even 3.000,95).

local variable a variable that has meaning only within a particular function or subroutine. The name of a local variable can be used in another subroutine elsewhere in the program, where it will refer to an entirely different variable. Local variables contrast with *global variables,* which are recognized throughout the program.

The advantage of using local variables is not obvious in short programs. However, it is a good idea when writing a long program to make as many variables as possible local, because then there will be no problem if you wish to use the same name to mean something else elsewhere in the program. This rule is even more important if several different people are writing subroutines that will be combined into one main program. *See also* SIDE EFFECT.

lock
   1. (Macintosh) to mark a file or disk as "Do not change" by clicking on the "Locked" box in the "Get Info" window.
   2. (various operating systems) to mark a file as in use so that other programs running concurrently will not change it. Under DOS, the share command implements file locking.
   3. to prevent a diskette from being written on. A $3\frac{1}{2}$-inch diskette can be physically locked by sliding the small plastic tab (on the back of the diskette) toward the edge. This uncovers a square hole that tells the disk drive that the diskette is "READ-ONLY." This is called *write protection.* (*See* WRITE-PROTECT.)
   Any disk sent to a service bureau should be locked so that VIRUSES cannot be written on it.

LOG the function, in many versions of BASIC and other languages, that calculates the natural (base-e) logarithm of its argument. However, in some languages and spreadsheets, LOG(X) is the common (base-10) logarithm and LN(X) is the natural logarithm. *See* LOGARITHM.

logarithm the power to which a number must be raised in order to give another number.

If $y = a^x$, then x is the logarithm of y to the base a (written as $x = \log_a y$). The most commonly used bases for logarithm functions are 10 and e (approximately 2.718). Base-10 logarithms are called *common logarithms;* base-*e* logarithms, *natural logarithms* (because integrals and derivatives are simpler with base *e* than with any other base). For example, the common logarithm of 10,000 is 4 ($\log_{10} 10,000 = 4$) because $10^4 = 10,000$.

If no base is specified in the expression log *a*, then usually base 10 is meant; the natural logarithm of *a* is written $\log_e a$ or ln *a*.

logical

1. possessing or pertaining to logic (in any of various senses).

2. described from the viewpoint of software. For example, if a single disk drive is divided into two partitions which the computer handles separately, it can be said to comprise two logical disk drives.

logical design

1. the design of an electronic circuit using logic gates. *See* GATE and cross-references there.

2. the design of the logic of a computer program (as opposed to its user interface or data files).

3. the practice of designing a document by using tags to indicate the function rather than the appearance of each element. For example, chapters are labeled as such rather than just being indicated by words typed in a particular arrangement on the page.

Logical design is the approach followed by LATEX, SGML, and XML; it is not followed by WYSIWYG word processors. Logical design is generally superior for complicated documents because decisions about the appearance of elements of the document can be made independently of the text. If you want to change the appearance of chapter headings, for instance, you need to make the change in only one place because all chapter headings are recognized as instances of the same unit. In a WYSIWYG system, you would need to change each heading individually because the computer does not know that they are alike. Documents with tags specifying the logical design are also easier to handle effectively in computer databases.

logical drive one of several divisions of a single partition on a hard disk. Logical drives are treated as separate disk drives.

logic circuits electronic circuits that accept binary digits (bits) as inputs and produce an output bit according to a specified rule. For examples *see* AND GATE; OR GATE; NAND GATE; NOR GATE; NOT GATE; FLIP-FLOP. For information on how logic circuits are used, *see* BINARY ADDITION; COMPUTER ARCHITECTURE; DECODER; XOR GATE.

A typical computer represents 1 (logic "true") as +5 volts and 0 as 0 volts. More precisely, 1 is represented by a connection to the +5-volt power supply (directly or through a resistance), and 0 is represented by a connection to ground. Note that 0 is not merely the absence of a voltage; logic circuits differ as to how they handle an unconnected input.

Basically, logic circuits are switching circuits. Figure 151(A) shows

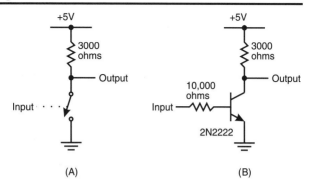

FIGURE 151. NOT GATE BUILT WITH
A SWITCH (A) AND A TRANSISTOR (B)

a NOT gate implemented as a switch. The output is +5 volts (binary 1, logic "true") whenever the switch is *not* closed. (When the switch is closed, the resistor dissipates the voltage and the output is connected to ground.) That is, the output is the negation of the state of the switch.

For this to be usable in a computer, the switching has to be controlled by an electrical signal. Figure 151(B) shows what happens when the switch is replaced by a switching transistor. The transistor conducts when its base is at least 0.6 volts above ground, i.e., when its input is binary 1. When the transistor is conducting, the effect is the same as the closed switch, and the output is 0. Thus, the output is the negation of the input, and the NOT gate works correctly.

Figure 152 shows how to build a NAND gate out of two diodes, two resistors, and a transistor. This circuit is very similar to what is used inside TTL integrated circuits. The output is 0 ("false") if and only if both of the inputs are binary 1 (+5 volts). In that situation, the diodes do not conduct, the base of the transistor receives current through the resistor, and the transistor conducts. But if even one of the inputs is binary 0 (connected to ground), the base of the transistor is held low and the transistor does not conduct, so the output is binary 1. To understand this circuit, it is very important to remember that binary 0 is represented by a connection to ground, not merely the absence of a voltage. Like real TTL ICs, this circuit happens to treat disconnected inputs as binary 1.

NAND gates are important because all the other gates can be built from them (Fig. 153). A NOT gate is simply a NAND gate with only one input, or with all its inputs tied together; an AND gate is a NAND gate followed by a NOT gate; and so on. In a similar way, all the types

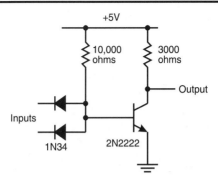

FIGURE 152. NAND GATE BUILT WITH
TRANSISTORS AND DIODES

of gates can be built from NOR gates.

Instead of TTL circuits, newer ICs use CMOS (complementary metal-oxide semiconductor) switching transistors, which come in pairs that respond to opposite polarities, so that one switches off whenever the other switches on. This makes it easy to connect the output either to +5 volts or to ground depending on the input. However, the circuits inside practical CMOS gates are too complicated to diagram here.

logic diagram an electronic circuit diagram that shows gates and other components that affect logic signals, but does not show the power supply or other non-digital electronic subsystems. *See* ELECTRONIC CIRCUIT DIAGRAM SYMBOLS.

logic programming a method of writing computer programs based on the mathematical study of logical reasoning. Logic programming is used in the computer modeling of human thinking. For examples, *see* PROLOG.

log in *see* LOG ON.

logo a trademark or printed emblem; short for *logotype*.

LOGO a programming language developed by Seymour Papert of MIT for use in teaching programming to children. Papert's fundamental insight was that computer-aided instruction is of little use unless the pupil can control the computer, rather than the other way around. To experiment with this idea, he designed a language that is markedly easier to use than BASIC and does not share BASIC's preoccupation with numerical calculation.

Although LOGO offers a full range of computer functions, most elementary LOGO exercises revolve around the "turtle," originally a

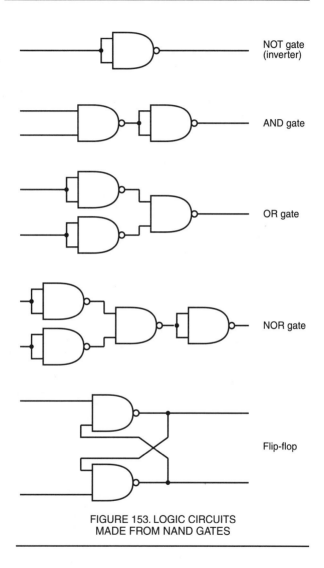

NOT gate
(inverter)

AND gate

OR gate

NOR gate

Flip-flop

FIGURE 153. LOGIC CIRCUITS
MADE FROM NAND GATES

robot that rolled around on a sheet of paper making marks with a pen. (The present-day turtle is a triangle that moves around the screen, drawing a line if told to do so.) Drawing shapes with the turtle appeals to children who would not be attracted to mathematical calculation or verbal input-output; at the same time, it serves as a good medium for teaching geometry and logical problem solving.

LOGO is an extensible language; that is, programs are constructed by defining statements in terms of previously defined statements. For example, the following procedure draws a square:

```
TO SQUARE
  CLEARSCREEN
  FORWARD 50
  RIGHT 90
  FORWARD 50
  RIGHT 90
  FORWARD 50
  RIGHT 90
  FORWARD 50
END
```

That is: "Clear the screen (and put the turtle in the center), go forward (up) 50 units, do a 90-degree right turn, go forward 50 units, do a 90-degree right turn," and so forth. Since LOGO procedures can call themselves recursively, complicated snowflake-like patterns are relatively easy to generate. *See also* KOCH SNOWFLAKE.

log on (**log in**) to identify yourself as an authorized user of a computer or a network at the beginning of a work session.

long a variable of type long is an integer with more bits stored than the normal-length integer. For example, in Java, a variable of type int fills 32 bits; a variable of type long fills 64 bits (allowing 2^{64} different values, ranging from -2^{63} to $2^{63} - 1$ (approximately $\pm 9 \times 10^{18}$).

long cross the character †, a symbol used to mark footnotes. *See also* FOOTNOTE. Also called a DAGGER or OBELISK.

long filename a filename longer than the 11-character DOS limit. Long filenames are supported by OS/2 HPFS, Windows 95 and its successors, Macintosh OS, and most versions of UNIX. Under Windows 95 and later, a filename can be up to 255 characters long and can contain blanks and some special characters. Uppercase and lowercase letters are distinguished. Long filenames that contain blanks must be surrounded by quotation marks when used in commands, like this:

```
C:\> dir "My Program Files"
```

Long filenames are automatically translated into short filenames such as MY~PRO~1 for compatibility with DOS and Windows 3 software running under Windows 95 and its successors. *Contrast* 8.3 FILENAME.

look and feel the overall visual appearance and USER INTERFACE of a computer program. *See* COPYRIGHT.

loop a series of statements in a computer program that are to be executed repeatedly. For example, the BASIC program

```
10 FOR I = 1 TO 5
20   PRINT I, I^2
30 NEXT I
```

contains a loop. Statement 20 will be executed five times, first with I equal to 1, then with I equal to 2, and so on. The output from the program will look like this:

```
1    1
2    4
3    9
4    16
5    25
```

This program contains a loop that will always be executed the same number of times. It is also possible to establish a loop that will be executed until a particular condition occurs. *See* REPEAT; WHILE; ITERATION.

loose letterspacing that has been adjusted to increase the space between the letters. *Contrast* TIGHT. *See* LETTERSPACING for an illustration.

lost cluster a group of disk sectors that are not marked as free but are not allocated to a file. Lost clusters result when the operation of creating a file is interrupted. They waste space and should be cleaned up periodically; under DOS and Windows, this is done with the CHKDSK or SCANDISK command.

Lotus (Lotus Development Corporation) a corporation headquartered in Cambridge, Massachusetts, which produces the widely-used spreadsheet Lotus 1-2-3 and the program Lotus Notes, as well as other products. In 1995, Lotus was acquired by IBM. You can find Lotus on the web at http://www.lotus.com.

Lotus 1-2-3 a popular SPREADSHEET program, widely used on IBM PCs since its introduction in 1983. The original Lotus 1-2-3 contained significant advances in graphing and data handling ability. Later versions include release 2.4, with additional features for formatting data; release 3, which allowed three-dimensional spreadsheets; and Lotus 1-2-3 for Windows.

lowercase the "small" letters a, b, c, d, etc., as opposed to uppercase or capital letters, A, B, C, D, etc. The term *lowercase* goes back to the early days of letterpress printing. The metal type was kept in divided drawers called cases; the capital letters were traditionally kept in the upper case, and the small letters in the lower.

LPI (lines per inch) a measure of the resolution of a halftone screen (*see* HALFTONE). Most newspaper screens are 85 LPI; good quality magazines use 150 LPI. 300-DPI screened output is roughly equivalent to a 50-LPI screen (draft quality). 600 DPI on a plain paper typesetter should be acceptable for most work; it can produce the equivalent of a 100-LPI halftone. When higher resolutions are needed, the file should be output to a 2400-DPI imagesetter.

LPT1 the filename by which DOS and related operating systems refer to the first parallel printer port. Additional parallel ports are known as LPT2 and LPT3. The DOS command

```
mode lpt1:=com1:
```

redefines LPT1 as equal to COM1 (the first serial port).

luminosity brightness; the property of glowing with light. Some 3D programs can render objects that seem to be emitting light by setting a high luminosity level.

lurk (*slang*) to read a NEWSGROUP regularly without contributing any messages of your own. It's advisable to lurk in a newsgroup for a while before posting any messages in order to make sure you understand the purpose and nature of the discussion. Most newsgroups have more lurkers than the participants realize.

Lycos a company headquartered in Waltham, Massachusetts that runs a portal web site, a web search engine, a guide to the Internet, and other services. Their web address is www.lycos.com. The name is apparently derived from the Greek word *lykos*, which means *wolf.*

Lynx a text-based WEB BROWSER that is unable to display images, but is popular on systems that only offer non-graphical access. Lynx was written by Lou Montulli of the University of Kansas. It runs on UNIX systems and is distributed free. The name is a pun on "links." *See* WORLD WIDE WEB.

M

Mac nickname for MACINTOSH.

MacApp a programming tool for developing application programs on the Macintosh. It was introduced in 1986 and was one of the first APPLICATION FRAMEWORK programs. MacApp is essentially an "empty" program: it knows how to use the graphical user interface but does not do any actual work. To create a real application, the programmer adds menus and supplies procedures to do whatever the application program is supposed to do.

MacApp uses object-oriented Pascal. It is similar to object-oriented Turbo Pascal and to Visual Basic, both of which came later. *See* OBJECT-ORIENTED PROGRAMMING; VISUAL BASIC.

machine-dependent program a program that works on only one particular type of computer.

machine-independent program a program that can be used on many different types of computers. The usual way to make a program machine-independent is to write it in a widely used programming language, such as FORTRAN or C, and compile it separately for each machine. A Java program is machine-independent because it is compiled to a standard bytecode, which can be run using the Java virtual machine (JVM) available for each specific machine.

machine language instructions that a computer can execute directly. Machine language statements are written in a binary code, and each statement corresponds to one machine action.

The difference between machine language and assembly language is that each assembly-language statement corresponds to one machine language statement, but the statements themselves are written in a symbolic code that is easier for people to read. (*See* ASSEMBLY LANGUAGE.) A single statement in a high-level language such as BASIC may contain many machine instructions.

machine-readable data data in any form that can be fed into a computer through an input device. Examples of machine-readable data include magnetic disks and tapes, optical disks, punched cards, and bar codes.

Macintosh a family of personal computers introduced by Apple in 1984; the first widely used computers with a graphical user interface, windowing, and a mouse. Users copy files and activate software by pointing to symbols (icons) on the screen rather than by typing commands. The screen is always in graphics mode: it is divided into windows and can display all the typefaces that the printer can print. The Macintosh user interface was derived from that of Xerox workstations;

it has been imitated by a number of other operating systems, including Microsoft Windows and OS/2 Presentation Manager.

Most importantly, the mechanisms for using windows, icons, and mouse menus are provided by the operating system, which means they look virtually the same in all programs. Thus, anyone who knows how to use any Macintosh software package will also know how to perform similar operations in any other software package.

The original Macintosh used a 7.80-MHz Motorola 68000 microprocessor with 128K of RAM (see MICROPROCESSOR). This was not enough for the software to perform well, and later models used 68020 and 68030 processors with several megabytes of RAM. The latest Macintoshes use PowerPC CPUs, which can software-emulate the Motorola 68000 to run older software.

Macintoshes have always been on the forefront of practical computer graphics and related technology. QuickTime video and TrueType scalable fonts originated on the Macintosh. Macintosh hardware, although expensive, is simple to set up because of Apple's early commitment to widely recognized standards such as PostScript and SCSI. Things work easily or not at all; little experimenting is required (or possible).

A disadvantage of the Macintosh is that programming has always been somewhat difficult due to the complex operating system. Users do not normally write their own programs, and the selection of software available, though adequate, is smaller than with PCs. Most recent models can read and write PC diskettes, and some can run PC software (in emulation mode, not using the full power of the Macintosh CPU).

See also MICROPROCESSOR; POWERPC; IMAC; QUICKTIME; TRUE-TYPE FONT; SCSI; POSTSCRIPT. For Macintosh serial port pinouts, *see* RS-232.

Mac OS the operating system for Macintosh computers; the latest version is version 9. System X, the next scheduled upgrade, is already available for Macintosh servers.

Mac OS 9 continued in the tradition of its preceding versions by presenting an uncluttered and consistent user interface. Since the advent of the Macintosh in 1984, the goal has been to let the user do what he or she wants to (within and sometimes beyond reason) and to let the computer deal with the housekeeping details. The elegantly simple idea of *choosing* an object and then telling the computer what to do with it has been carried through all versions of the Mac operating system, desktop accessories, and third-party applications. The idea was even adopted by the PC world (*see* WINDOWS). Today, a person familiar with one operating environment can pretty much sit down at any computer and, within minutes, be doing productive work.

Mac OS 9 includes many Desk Accessories (DAs) that aid productivity: SimpleText, a simple text editor; Stickies, electronic sticky notes; and Sherlock 2, a highly customizable search engine that works on the Internet as well as on an individual computer.

Key improvements included subtantial performance upgrades and support for a new hard disk format to increase storage space. The ability to work with PC files and media has been greatly inhanced. Java support has been improved to speed Internet and World Wide Web access.

macro an instruction that stands for a sequence of simpler instructions:

1. a user-defined abbreviation for one or more lines of assembly-language code. In C, a macro instruction is a user-defined abbreviation for an expression or a sequence of statements.

2. a series of keystrokes that have been combined so that they can be easily accessed. Many software packages make it possible to define macros for commonly used keystroke combinations. For example, in Lotus 1-2-3, a macro is defined by entering characters into a cell (or range of cells) and then giving that cell a name.

Suppose you frequently have to format a group of cells to have currency format with two decimal places. The commands to do this are / Range Format Currency 2. To spare yourself from typing these characters each time, enter the expression '/RFC2˜ into a convenient cell. The quotation mark at the beginning indicates that this is a label; the 2 indicates that two decimal places are to be taken, and the ˜ symbol represents the return key. Use the /Range Name Create command to give this cell a name that consists of a backslash followed by a letter. We could give the macro the name \F, since F stands for format. The macro has now been defined.

In order to execute the macro, press the ALT key and the letter that names the macro (in this case F). The result will be the same as if you had pressed each of the keys / R F C 2 (return) individually.

Macros in Lotus 1-2-3 can be much more complicated. For example, it is possible to create a macro that pauses at some point to obtain input from the user.

macro assembler any program that translates assembly language programs into machine code (*see* ASSEMBLY LANGUAGE) and allows the programmer to define macro instructions (*see* MACRO).

Macromedia San Francisco-based company that makes products to enhance the audiovisual content of web pages, including Shockwave Player. Their web address is www.macromedia.com/.

macro virus a virus written using the macro language of a particular application. For example, if a Microsoft Word document contains a macro virus that is designed to execute when the file is opened, an unsuspecting user who downloads the file and then opens it with Word will suffer the consequences of whatever the virus is programmed to do. Macro viruses are particularly dangerous because they can hide in word processing documents. Formerly, viruses could only be placed in executable code. *Contrast* VIRUS; TROJAN HORSE.

magenta a purplish-red color that is one of the standard printing ink colors. *See* CMYK.

magic number *(slang)* an important number (such as an interest rate or a file size limit) buried deep within a computer program where those revising the program are likely to overlook it.

FIGURE 154. MAGIC WAND SELECTION TOOL

magic wand an editing tool that selects an entire area of a particular color, regardless of its shape; magic wands are found in many photo editing programs (Adobe Photoshop, Aldus Photostyler, Corel Photo-Paint). You use the magic wand to select an area for editing. Its power lies in its ability to do a lot of tedious work for you. When you click on a pixel, the magic wand selects an area of that particular color, no matter how jagged the edges. You can then copy, delete, move, rotate, flip, shrink, stretch, or apply filters to this area as if it were a single object. *See also* SELECT, SELECTION TOOLS, BITMAP, PAINT PROGRAM.

magnetic bubble memory a form of nonvolatile storage for computers; that is, it does not go blank when power is turned off. Magnetic bubble memories are used in some very lightweight, portable computers when a disk drive would be too bulky or too fragile and battery-backed-up RAM would be too risky.

mail *see* ELECTRONIC MAIL.

mail bombing the practice of trying to flood an obnoxious person with gigantic amounts of e-mail. This is a very bad idea for several reasons. It clogs up facilities needed by other people, not just the intended recipient. More importantly, people who act obnoxious on the Internet generally falsify their addresses, thereby bringing down floods of wrath upon innocent victims. *See* DENIAL-OF-SERVICE ATTACK.

mailing list an online discussion conducted by relaying copies of all messages to all the participants by ELECTRONIC MAIL. Mailing lists are preferable to NEWSGROUPS when the group of interested people is relatively small or the discussion would be heckled if it were open to the general public. *See also* NETIQUETTE.

```
# Each entry consists of:
#    A filename
#    A list of other files that file depends on
#    A command to generate it from them
#
myprog:    myprog1.o  myprog2.o
           cc myprog1.o myprog2.o -o myprog
#
myprog1.o:  myprog1.c
            cc -c myprog1.c
#
myprog2.o:  myprog2.c
            cc -c myprog2.c
```

FIGURE 155. A MAKEFILE

mail merge *see* MERGE.

mainframe computer a large computer occupying a specially air-conditioned room and supporting typically 100 to 500 users at one time. The IBM 370 and IBM 3090 are examples of mainframe computers. *Contrast* MINICOMPUTER; PERSONAL COMPUTER.

Majordomo a program often used to maintain mailing lists on UNIX systems. (The major-domo is the head servant in an aristocratic household.) *See* MAILING LIST. *Contrast* LISTSERV.

make a command, in UNIX and similar operating systems, that manages the steps of creating a machine-language program or some other complex product of computation.

Typically, a large machine-language program is made by compiling several different source files, producing a group of object files, and then linking the object files together. (*See* SOURCE CODE; OBJECT CODE.) The make command manages this process. It looks at a makefile (Fig. 155) that tells it how to create each of the files needed to generate the complete program. Then it looks at the date on which each file was last modified. If any file is newer than the other files made from it, make will do whatever is needed to update those files (typically compiling or linking). By using make, the programmer avoids recompiling anything that has not been changed.

The make command can actually manage any process in which files are made from other files. All it needs is a makefile containing the appropriate commands.

makefile a file that controls the operation of the MAKE command. Under UNIX, by default, it is named makefile or Makefile and resides in the current directory.

FIGURE 156. MANDELBROT SET

management information systems (MIS) a field of study that deals with effective systems for the development and use of information in an organization. The complete information system includes not just the computers but also the people. Any effective information system must determine:

1. what the goals of the organization are;
2. what information is needed to accomplish those goals;
3. how that information is originated;
4. how the information needs to be stored and transferred to accomplish those goals.

Mandelbrot set a famous fractal, i.e., a shape containing an infinite amount of fine detail. It was discovered by Benoit Mandelbrot. The Mandelbrot set is the set of values of c for which the series $z_{n+1} = (z_n)^2 + c$ converges, where z and c are complex numbers and z is initially (0,0). *See* COMPLEX NUMBER.

   The detail in the Mandelbrot set fascinates mathematicians. In Figure 156, the x and y axes are the real and imaginary parts of c. The Mandelbrot set is the black bulbous object in the middle; elsewhere, the stripes indicate the number of iterations needed to make $|z|$ exceed 2.

   Fig. 157 is an IBM PC BASIC program to plot the Mandelbrot set. A complete plot can take several hours to generate.

manifest a list of the contents of a shipment; a list of files transmitted as a group.

```
100 ' Choose area to be plotted
110 XMIN = -2
120 XMAX = 2
130 YMIN = -1.5
140 YMAX = 1.5
150 ' Select 320x200 4-color graphics
160 SCREEN 1
170 KEY OFF
180 ' Plot the Mandelbrot set
190 FOR IX = 0 TO 319
200    FOR IY = 0 TO 199
210       ' Locate this point
220       X = (IX/319)*(XMAX-XMIN) + XMIN
230       Y = (IY/199)*(YMAX-YMIN) + YMIN
240       ' Does the function converge?
250       COUNT = 0
260       QX = X
270       QY = Y
280       WHILE COUNT < 128 AND (QX*QX + QY*QY) < 4
290          COUNT = COUNT + 1
300          TEMP = 2*QX*QY + Y
310          QX = QX*QX - QY*QY + X
320          QY = TEMP
330       WEND
340       ' Plot point in color depending on count
350       PSET (IX, IY), (COUNT MOD 4)
360    NEXT IY
370 NEXT IX
380 END
```

FIGURE 157. MANDELBROT SET PROGRAM
(IBM PC BASIC)

man pages (**man**ual **pages**) the on-line documentation built into UNIX and accessed by the command

man *command*

where *command* is the command or system function you want to know about. A selling point of UNIX since the earliest days has been that its manuals are on-line. *See* UNIX.

Map Network Drive the operation, in Windows 95 and higher, that makes a directory on another computer act as if it were a local disk drive. To map a network drive, right-click on the My Computer icon and select the Map Network Drive menu item. You will need to specify the server name, directory to map, and the drive letter to use. *See also* NETWORK NEIGHBORHOOD; UNC.

mapping software software that contains data making it possible to create various types of maps for different applications. The map data is stored in digital form, consisting of the coordinates describing where to draw lines and labels. (*See* VECTOR GRAPHICS.) The map can be viewed at different scales, and other information can be displayed, e.g., by using different colors to illustrate sales figures for each district.

Map data typically require a large amount of memory and disk space. If maps consisted of straight lines, it would be necessary to store only the end points of the lines, but a realistic description of a curvy coast can require thousands of bytes. Detailed mapping programs typically are released on CD-ROM. For example, you can obtain a CD-ROM containing all of the streets in the entire United States. Also, maps are often provided as clip art with draw programs.

marching ants *(slang)* the moving dashed lines that indicate the borders of a selected object in a paint or draw program (*see* MARQUEE SELECT). Some programs allow you to hide the ants if they distract you.

markup language any language that provides ways to indicate underlining, italics, paragraph breaks, section headings, etc., in text. For examples, *see* SGML; HTML; TEX.

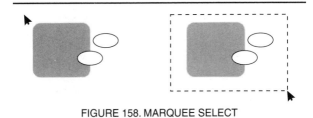

FIGURE 158. MARQUEE SELECT

marquee select a method of selecting more than one object at a time in a graphical user interface (GUI). It gets its name from the animated effect of the dashed line of the bounding box — it resembles a theater marquee.

To marquee-select items, sight along the top and the left edge of the group of items you wish to select. Position the mouse cursor there. While holding down the mouse button, pull diagonally down and to the right. When the marquee encloses all the items, release the mouse button. *See also* MOUSE; GUI; SELECT.

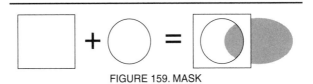

FIGURE 159. MASK

mask

1. (draw program) to create an object with a hole in it, so that the view of an underlying object is controlled.

2. (paint program) to mark an area of the drawing as protected from the drawing tools. The mask can be removed as the drawing progresses. This is analogous to the masking used in watercolor painting.

3. (programming) to isolate part of a binary number by ANDing it with another binary number. For example, the first four bits of any byte can be isolated by ANDing the byte with 11110000. *See* AND GATE.

master

1. the controlling unit in a pair of linked machines. *Contrast* SLAVE (definition 1).

2. one of a pair of IDE hard disks or other devices connected to the same IDE cable. Generally, jumpers have to be set on IDE devices to identify them as master and slave. *Contrast* SLAVE (definition 2).

master page a design template that defines the overall appearance of every page of a printed document. *See also* GRID SYSTEM.

math coprocessor an auxiliary CPU that provides additional mathematical operations. A descendant of the Intel 387 math coprocessor is built into the Pentium. *See* COPROCESSOR.

MathML (**M**athematics **M**arkup **L**anguage) an extension of HTML designed to facilitate the display of mathematical expressions. (See the W3C web site at http://www.w3.org.)

matrix *see* ARRAY.

matrix printer a printer that forms letters and other symbols by patterns of dots. *See* DOT-MATRIX PRINTER.

maximize to make a window take over the whole screen or become as large as possible. To do this, click the mouse on the maximize button (*see picture at* WINDOW). *See also* MINIMIZE; RESTORE. Maximize is also an option under the CONTROL MENU.

On a Macintosh, use the ZOOM box (at the far right side of the window's title bar) to enlarge a window.

MB abbreviation for MEGABYTE.

MBps **m**ega**b**ytes **p**er **s**econd. *See also* MEGABYTE; BAUD.

Mbps **m**ega**b**its **p**er **s**econd. *See* BIT.

MCGA (**M**onochrome/**C**olor **G**raphics **A**dapter) a video system built into two early IBM PS/2 models (25 and 30). Its features are a subset of those of the VGA. *See* VGA.

MDA (**M**onochrome **D**isplay **A**dapter) the very first video system used in early-model IBM PCs. It provided very sharp, readable text, but no graphics, on a monochrome screen.

MDI (**m**ultiple **d**ocument **i**nterface) the ability to edit more than one file or drawing with a single copy of a Windows program.

media plural of MEDIUM.

media error a defect in the surface of a disk or tape, sometimes curable by formatting the disk or tape again.

media, invalid *see* INVALID MEDIA.

medium (plural **media**)

    1. material used for storage of information. Magnetic disks, tapes, and optical disks are examples of storage media.

    2. a way of presenting information to the computer user. Vision is one medium; sound is another. Multimedia computing uses visible displays of several types together with sound.

    3. a means of mass communication, such as television.

medium-scale integration the construction of integrated circuits that contain from 10 to 100 logic gates. *See* INTEGRATED CIRCUIT.

meg short for MEGABYTE.

mega- metric prefix meaning $\times 1{,}000{,}000$ or, in rating computer memories and disks, $\times 1{,}048{,}576$ ($= 1024 \times 1024$). *Mega-* is derived from the Greek word for "big." *See* MEGABYTE; METRIC PREFIXES.

megabyte (**MB**) an amount of computer memory equal to $2^{20} = 1{,}048{,}576$ bytes $= 1{,}024$ kilobytes. One megabyte can store more than one million characters. The internal memory (RAM) of a microcomputer is often measured in megabytes; 32 to 64 MB is now a typical size, up from 32 to 64 KB (1024 times smaller) in the early 1980s. *See* MEMORY.

    Hard disk capacity is also measured in megabytes; 500 to 5000 megabytes are typical sizes. In measuring disk capacity, *megabyte* sometimes means the same as when measuring memory. Sometimes, however, *megabyte* is used to mean 1 million bytes, or even 1,024,000 bytes (1024×1000). These different systems of measurement result in different numbers being used to describe the capacity of the same disk.

megahertz (**MHz**) million hertz or million cycles per second, a measure of the clock speed of a computer or the frequency of a radio signal. *See* CLOCK; MICROPROCESSOR.

megapixel an image containing about one million pixels or more. For example, a 1024×1024-pixel image is often referred to as a megapixel image. *See* BITMAP.

meme virus (*slang,* from *mimetic*) an idea or belief that spreads quickly from person to person, like an infection, whether or not it is true; meme viruses do to the human mind what computer viruses do to software.

End-of-the-world predictions, fads, and hoaxes are examples of meme viruses. Some people deliberately spread meme viruses on the Internet. *See* HOAX.

memory (formerly called *core*) the space within a computer where information is stored while being actively worked on. Most microcomputers have a small amount of read-only memory (ROM), containing the built-in programs that start the operation of the computer when it is turned on, and a large amount of random-access memory (RAM) for user's programs and data. Except for ROM, memory goes blank when the computer is turned off; any data in it must be copied to disk or tape to be saved.

The memory requirements of a computer are dictated by the software that is to be run on it. In the early 1980s, 64K was a common size for a microcomputer memory. The memory requirements of newer software continued to increase, however, so by the end of the decade 640K became the minimum amount of memory necessary for a business microcomputer. Memory sizes of four to eight megabytes became common in the 1990s. Computers running Windows perform best if at least 32 megabytes are available.

See also EXPANDED MEMORY; EXTENDED MEMORY; MS-DOS; SIMM; DRAM; EDO; FPM.

memory leak *see* LEAK.

memory-mapped video a type of computer video display where the contents of the screen are controlled by storing appropriate values in a block of memory that is directly accessible to the CPU. (*See* VIDEO MEMORY.) For example, the IBM PC has memory-mapped video; many UNIX systems do not.

memory-resident program a computer program that remains in memory after being run so that it can be called up later. Before Windows 3.0, a memory-resident program was a special class of program; now, Windows makes switching between programs possible at any time.

Memphis Microsoft's internal code name for the Windows 98 development project. *See* WINDOWS 98. *Compare* CHICAGO, CAIRO.

menu a list of choices that appears on the screen in response to your actions. Most windows have a MENU BAR just under the title bar. When you click on an item in the menu bar, its corresponding menu will appear. You select the command you want by moving the mouse pointer to it. Commands with ellipsis dots (…) after them will pop up a dialog box for you to give the computer further instructions before executing the command. If there are keyboard shortcuts for any command, they will often be listed to the right of the command.

Menus make a program user-friendly. It's very easy to learn and use software with a menu-driven command system. You don't need to

FIGURE 160. MENU

memorize all the commands. By looking at the menus, you can see all the options.

The problem with menus is that it often takes a substantial amount of time and mouse movement to work through them. Experienced users use the keyboard shortcuts to speed up their work. Also, if you are not careful, it is possible to get lost in a series of nested menus. Many manuals provide a tree-shaped diagram of the menus; when learning a new program it's a good idea to have that chart at hand.

menu bar a horizontal menu across the top of the screen or window. Depending on the software, the items in the menu bar are chosen by clicking on them with a mouse, or by typing the first letter of each item, or possibly by typing the first letter while holding down Alt. Usually each item is a further menu. For an illustration, *see* MENU.

merge to insert data (e.g., names and addresses) from one file into a document that resides in another file (e.g., the text of a form letter).

merge sort an algorithm for sorting data (*see* SORT). Merge sort takes advantage of the fact that it is easy to combine two lists that are already sorted; just keep looking at the first element of each list and taking whichever element comes first. For example, to combine the lists

Adams	Bush
Buchanan	Clinton
Lincoln	Kennedy

do the following: Compare Adams to Bush; take Adams. Then compare Buchanan to Bush and take Buchanan. Then compare Lincoln to Bush and take Bush, and so on. This will give you a list of all six names in alphabetical order.

To perform a complete merge sort, first divide your data into several small sorted lists. These can be sorted with some other sorting algorithm; or they can be two-element lists which are sorted by swapping the two elements where needed; or they can even be one-element lists, which do not need sorting. Then combine these lists, two at a time, until they all have been put together into a single sorted list.

A big advantage of merge sort is that you never need to see more than the first element of any list. Thus, merge sort can take its data from tapes or from linked lists, which cannot easily be sorted by any other algorithm. *See* SEQUENTIAL-ACCESS DEVICE; LINKED LIST.

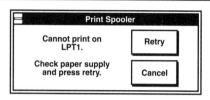

FIGURE 161. MESSAGE BOX

message box a small window that appears to present information to the user. When the user acknowledges reading the message by pressing a mouse button, the message box disappears. See Figure 161 for an example of a message box. *See also* ALERT BOX.

message sending one way of describing object-oriented programming: objects receive "messages," which are calls to procedures associated with them. *See* OBJECT-ORIENTED PROGRAMMING.

metacrawler a program that submits search queries to the major Internet indexes (such as Yahoo or Lycos) and creates a summary of the results, thus giving the searcher the benefit of using all the SEARCH ENGINES (*crawlers*) simultaneously.

metafile a file format that provides a common ground between two or more proprietary formats, and thus a translation path from one piece of software to another. For example, a Windows Metafile (.wmf) is a vector-based drawing format that is recognized by most drawing, page-layout, and word-processing programs. *See also* CGM.

metal *see* BARE METAL.

metalanguage any language used to describe another language. For example, Backus-Naur Form can be used as a metalanguage to describe the syntax of programming languages. Lisp and Prolog have the interesting property that the programs can read and modify themselves, so these programming languages can be put to practical use as metalanguages for themselves. *See* BACKUS-NAUR FORM; PROLOG; LISP.

TABLE 12
METRIC PREFIXES

Prefix	Abbreviation	Meaning
yotta-		×1,000,000,000,000,000,000,000,000
zetta-		×1,000,000,000,000,000,000,000
exa-		×1,000,000,000,000,000,000
peta-		×1,000,000,000,000,000
tera-	T	×1,000,000,000,000 (or 1,099,511,627,776)
giga-	G	×1,000,000,000 (or 1,073,741,824)
mega-	M (not m)	×1,000,000 (or 1,048,576)
kilo-	k	×1000 (or 1024)
hecta-		×100
deca-		×10
deci-	d	÷10
centi-	c	÷100
milli-	m (not M)	÷1000
micro-	μ	÷1,000,000 (unofficially abbreviated u)
nano-	n	÷1,000,000,000
pico-	p	÷1,000,000,000,000
femto-	f	÷1,000,000,000,000,000
atto-	a	÷1,000,000,000,000,000,000

method (in object-oriented programming) a procedure associated with an object type. *See* OBJECT-ORIENTED PROGRAMMING.

metric prefixes the prefixes used in the metric system to denote multiplication of units, such as *kilo-* meaning "thousand." The complete set is shown in Table 12.

When measuring computer memory or disk capacity, *kilo-*, *mega-*, *giga-*, and *tera-* often stand for powers of 1024 (= 2^{10}) rather than powers of 1000; those are the alternative values shown in the table. Even more confusingly, *mega-* occasionally means $1000 \times 1024 = 1,024,000$.

In Greek, *kilo-*, *mega-*, *giga-*, and *tera-* mean, respectively, "thousand," "big," "giant," and "monster."

mezzanine bus a special bus that connects the CPU to some of the faster peripherals, such as memory modules, and is separate from the slower bus used for slower peripherals. *See* BUS.

MFM (**M**odified **F**requency **M**odulation) the original way of recording data magnetically on disks. *See* ST-506. *Contrast* RLL.

MHz *see* MEGAHERTZ.

micro- metric prefix meaning ÷1,000,000 (one millionth). For example, a microsecond is one millionth of a second (0.000001 second), and a microfarad is one millionth of a farad. *Micro-* is derived from the Greek word for "small." *See* METRIC PREFIXES.

Micro Channel the bus design used in the IBM PS/2 computers, model 50 and higher (*see* BUS). It contrasts with the bus design of the IBM PC, XT, and AT, which was also used in the lowest PS/2 models. Plug-in cards designed for one bus cannot be used with the other.

     Unlike the original bus, the Micro Channel is designed to allow use of more than one CPU in a single computer. IBM discontinued Micro Channel products in 1995 on the ground that the PCI bus provides equal or better performance. Historically, Micro Channel was an important predecessor of EISA, PCI, and Plug and Play. *See also* EISA; PCI; PLUG AND PLAY.

microcomputer a computer whose CPU consists of a single integrated circuit known as a microprocessor. Commonly, a microcomputer is used by only one person at a time. All home computers are microcomputers. *See* INTEGRATED CIRCUIT; MICROPROCESSOR.

microcontroller a microprocessor designed specifically for controlling equipment. Microcontrollers usually contain some memory and input-output circuitry on the same chip with the microprocessor. This enables the microcontroller to work as a self-contained unit. Microcontrollers are used in consumer products such as telephones, automobiles, and microwave ovens, as well as in industrial equipment. *See also* EMBEDDED SYSTEM.

microprocessor an integrated circuit containing the entire CPU of a computer, all on one silicon chip, so that only the memory and input-output devices need to be added. The first popular microprocessor, the Intel 8080, came out in 1973 and cost approximately $400; its successor, the Zilog Z80, now sells for about $1.

     Microprocessors are commonly described as 8-bit, 16-bit, or the like. The number can refer either to the number of bits in each internal data register, or to the number of bits on the data bus (*see* BUS); these two numbers are usually, but not always, the same. Other things being equal, larger registers and a larger bus enable the processor to do its work faster.

     Clock speed is also important. The clock is the oscillator that causes the microprocessor to proceed from one step to the next in executing instructions. (Each machine instruction takes several clock cycles.) Clock speed is measured in megahertz (MHz): 1 MHz is 1 million cycles per second. Higher clock speeds result in faster computation — but only if exactly the same machine instructions are being executed; this is why it is misleading to compare the clock speeds of processors of different types. It is even possible for two microprocessors with the same instruction set and clock speed to perform computations at different rates because of differences in internal design. A 100-MHz Pentium II, for example, is faster than a 100-MHz Pentium.

     Table 13 describes a number of important microprocessors. The processors in each group (e.g., the 68020 and 68030) use the same machine language and run the same programs.

TABLE 13
SOME IMPORTANT MICROPROCESSORS

Mfr./ Type	Register size (bits)	Bus size (bits)	Clock speed (MHz)	Where used/ Comments
Zilog				
Z80	8	8	2	Kaypro (1982)
MOS Technology				
6502	8	8	1	Apple II (1977)
Intel				
8088	16	8	4.77	IBM PC (1981)
8086	16	16	8	Like 8088, wider bus
80286	16	16	8	IBM PC AT (1984)
386	32	32	33	Begins current generation of PCs
486	32	32	100	Faster 386, built-in coprocessor
486SX	32	32	33	Cheaper 486, no coprocessor
486DX2	32	32	33 (66)	Clock internally doubled
486DX4	32	32	33 (100)	Clock internally tripled
Pentium	64	64	200	Successor to 486
Pentium Pro	64	64	166–200	Faster Pentium
Pentium II	32	64	450	Faster, upgraded Pentium
Celeron	32	64	533	Cheaper Pentium II, smaller cache
Pentium III	32	64	800	Faster yet, more instructions
AMD				
Am5x86 (586)	32	32	133	Replacement for 486
K5	32	64	166	Replacement for Pentium
K6, K6-2, K6-III	32	64	450	Replacement for Pentium II, III
Athlon	32	64	1000	Pentium-compatible, 200-MHz bus
Cyrix				
5x86	64	32	120	Replacement for 486
6x86	64	64	233	Replacement for Pentium
M II	32	64	433	Replacement for Pentium II
Motorola				
68000	32	16	8	Original Macintosh
68030	32	32	40	Macintosh IIfx
68040	32	32	40	68030 with coprocessor
PowerPC (IBM/Motorola/Apple)				
MPC601 (G1)	32	64	80	Original PowerPC (1991)
MPC750 (G3)	32	64	300	Used in Macintosh PowerBook
MPC7400 (G4)	32	64	1000	Superscalar, 3 instructions at once
Sun Microsystems				
UltraSPARC-III	64	64	600	RISC for UNIX workstations
Compaq (formerly Digital)				
Alpha	64	64	1000	Fastest microprocessor (as of 2000)

Clock speeds shown are highest available for each processor as of early 2000.

Microsoft the world's leading software-producing company, headquartered in Redmond, Washington, and founded by William Gates and Paul Allen in 1975 when they wrote a version of BASIC for an early hobbyist microcomputer, the Altair. In the late 1970s the company grew as it sold versions of BASIC to other computer makers, but it was still fairly small when it was approached by IBM to design the operating system for the IBM PC (released in 1981). This operating system (known as PC-DOS, MS-DOS, or simply DOS) became a huge seller, since almost all PC and PC clones used it. After 1993, IBM and Microsoft developed new versions of DOS separately, and PC-DOS and MS-DOS became separate, though virtually identical, products.

In the late 1980s Microsoft worked with IBM on the development of a new multitasking operating system, OS/2. However, in the 1990s Microsoft and IBM split over operating system strategy, with IBM pushing OS/2 and Microsoft focusing on Windows. The collaboration has ended, and OS/2 is now solely an IBM product.

In 1990 Microsoft introduced version 3.0 of Windows, a much improved version of an earlier product that provides a graphical user interface for computers in the IBM PC line. Windows 3.0 rapidly became a best seller, and many other software makers wrote programs to operate within the Windows environment. Windows 3.1 added minor improvements and greater reliability and became the standard operating system for PC-compatible machines. It was superseded by Windows 95, a true 32-bit operating system, in 1995. *See* WINDOWS (MICROSOFT).

Microsoft is also a big seller of applications software for both PCs and Macintoshes. The suite Microsoft Office includes the word processing program Microsoft Word, the spreadsheet Excel, the database program Access, and the presentation program Powerpoint. Microsoft also produces compilers or interpreters for several different programming languages. Microsoft BASIC is one of the most widely used programming language implementations the world has ever seen (*see* BASICA; GW-BASIC; QBASIC; QUICKBASIC.) In 1991 Microsoft introduced Visual Basic, an advanced version of BASIC that allows the programmer to take advantage of the graphical environment of Windows. It now provides development environments for other languages in the Visual Studio series. Other products include the Microsoft Network Online service and the web browser Internet Explorer.

For further information about Microsoft and its products, *see* http://www.microsoft.com.

Microsoft antitrust charges

Microsoft has been accused of violating U.S. antitrust laws (laws that prohibit businesses from monopolizing a market or conspiring to stifle competition).

In 1994, while under investigation by the U.S. Department of Justice, Microsoft accepted a consent decree in which it promised to change some of its licensing practices. For example, prior to 1994, Microsoft gave computer manufacturers a discount on Windows if the manufacturers paid Microsoft a fee for every computer made, regardless of the operating system installed on it. In effect, this amounted to requiring them to license a Microsoft operating system for every computer.

In 1997, a new antitrust case was filed against Microsoft, charging that it violated antitrust laws by including its Internet Explorer browser free with Windows, because this killed off the market for other browsers (e.g., Netscape) that were available commercially. An appeals court threw out this case. However, in 1998, the U.S. Department of Justice filed a broader antitrust case against Microsoft. In 2000, Judge Thomas Penfield Jackson ruled that Microsoft had violated the Sherman Antitrust Act. The final resolution of the case had not been decided when this book went to press. The case has raised concerns because the main antitrust statute (Section 2 of the Sherman Antitrust Act) is so vague that it does not specify exactly which behavior is illegal. Some feel that Microsoft is being punished for technological innovation and financial success.

Microsoft Internet Explorer web browser produced by Microsoft. *See* BROWSER; WORLD WIDE WEB.

Microsoft Windows *see* WINDOWS.

microspacing the insertion of extra space in a printed document in units smaller than the size of one character. *See* JUSTIFICATION.

middleware in a three-tier system, the system that is between the user interface and the database access software. *See* THREE-TIER ARCHITECTURE.

MIDI (**M**usical **I**nstrument **D**igital **I**nterface) a standard way for communicating information about music between different electronic devices, such as computers and sound synthesizers.

MIDI comprises two things: an electrical connection between musical instruments and computers, and a file format for representing musical sounds. MIDI files are more like musical scores than digitized audio; they represent notes and instrumentation, not sound waves, and the computer must "play" them like a musician. Thus, MIDI files are much more compact than WAVE FILES.

mil suffix indicating that an E-MAIL address or WEB SITE is at a military location.

millennium bug a software defect reflecting the Year 2000 Problem. Despite dire predictions that electric power, water systems, aircraft, and even coffee makers would fail on January 1, 2000, only minor problems occurred in some business software that had not been properly updated. *See* YEAR 2000 PROBLEM.

milli- metric prefix meaning ÷1000 (one thousandth). For example, one millisecond is one thousandth of a second (0.001 second), and a millimeter is one thousandth of a meter. *Milli-* is derived from the Latin word for "thousandth." *See* METRIC PREFIXES.

MIME (Multipurpose Internet Mail Extensions) a standard proposed by N. Borenstein and N. Freed for including material other than ASCII text in e-mail messages. MIME messages can be recognized by the "Content-Type" declaration in the header, and the range of content types is potentially unlimited. Most e-mail software now supports at least partial use of MIME encoding. *See also* CGI.

mind virus *see* MEME VIRUS.

minicomputer a computer intermediate in size between a mainframe computer and a microcomputer; two examples are the Digital Equipment Corporation VAX and the IBM AS/400. A minicomputer typically occupies a large area within a room and supports 10 to 100 users at a time. Minicomputers are typically used by medium-sized businesses and academic institutions. They are rapidly being replaced by networks of microcomputers. *Contrast* MAINFRAME COMPUTER; PERSONAL COMPUTER.

minimize to make a window as small as possible; usually this means it becomes an icon rather than a window. In Windows 95 and its successors, minimized icons go to the taskbar at the bottom of the screen.

To minimize a window, click on the minimize button (*see* WINDOW). This is a handy way to get one piece of software out of the way temporarily while you turn your attention to something else. You can then RESTORE the window when you want to resume working with it.

Caution: the minimized program is still taking up memory and you'll find that graphics intensive programs (such as paint programs) need all the memory you can give them. You should CLOSE all minimized programs before launching a program that needs lots of memory. Some utilities can run minimized in the background (print spoolers, for example). *See also* MAXIMIZE; RESTORE; LAUNCH.

MIPS (Million Instructions Per Second) a measurement of the speed with which computer programs are run. Because different instructions take different amounts of time, speed measured in MIPS depends on the exact program that the computer is running. For this reason, speed tests are usually done with standard programs such as Whetstone and Dhrystone.

Another problem is that equivalent programs take different numbers of instructions on different CPUs. To compare different computers meaningfully, it is common practice to calculate MIPS using the number of instructions that a program would require on a VAX rather than on the computer actually being tested. This way, equivalent programs are always viewed as having the same number of instructions and the speed of the computer under test is the only variable.

FIGURE 162. MIRROR, DEFINITION 1

mirror

    1.   to flip an image so that the resulting image is a mirror image of the original.

    2.   to reproduce the entire contents of an FTP or WEB SITE so that the same files are available from more than one location.

MIS *see* MANAGEMENT INFORMATION SYSTEMS.

misfeature *(slang)* an ill-conceived feature; a feature with unforeseen and unfortunate effects. For example, the choice of / as the option character in DOS 1.0 was a misfeature because it made it impossible to use / as the directory separator when DOS 2.0 introduced directories. As a result, DOS and Windows use \ where UNIX has /, to the annoyance of programmers everywhere.

FIGURE 163. MITERED VS. UNMITERED JOINT

miter to cut at an angle. A way of specifying how lines should intersect; *mitered* joints come to neat points. If intersecting lines are not properly mitered, there are ugly gaps at the intersection, or the square endpoints of the lines overlap.

    Most drawing programs let you set the *miter limit*; the threshold at which the computer bevels a sharp angle when two lines have a narrow angle of intersection. This prevents the pointed joint from extending way past the end of the line.

mixed case type set with normal capitalization, neither all caps nor all lowercase.

mixed-signal handling both ANALOG and DIGITAL signals. For example, a sound card is a mixed-signal device.

mixer a software control that determines the relative loudness of various kinds of sound produced by a SOUND CARD, such as MIDI music, wave file playback, and synthesized speech.

MMX (**m**ulti**m**edia e**x**tensions) a set of additional instructions added to the later models of the Pentium microprocessor and its successors to support high-speed processing of animation and sound. The MMX instructions support a limited form of vector processing. *See* VECTOR PROCESSOR.

mnemonic a symbol or expression that helps you remember something. For example, the expression "Spring forward, fall back" helps you remember which way to adjust your clocks in the spring and fall for daylight saving time.

A mnemonic variable name is a variable name that helps the programmer remember what the variable means. For example, in a payroll program the variable to represent the hours worked could be named X312W17HK, but it would be much better to give it a mnemonic name such as HOURS.

MNP (**M**icrocom **N**etworking **P**rotocol) a set of methods for detecting and correcting errors in data transmission. MNP error correction is built into some high-speed modems so that erroneous data is never sent to the computer. MNP level 5 and above also includes data compression.

MO (**m**ega-**o**ctet) French abbreviation for MEGABYTE.

mobo *(slang)* **mo**ther**bo**ard.

MOD abbreviation for *modulo,* used to refer to the remainder in integer division. For example, in Pascal, the expression 24 mod 7 has the value 3, since 3 is the remainder when 24 is divided by 7. In C, C++, and Java, this operation is symbolized by %.

modal dialog box a dialog box that requires an immediate response from the user; other windows cannot be used until the modal dialog box has been dealt with. Modal dialog boxes generally warn of problems such as running out of printer paper or losing a network connection. *See* DIALOG BOX.

mode the state that a piece of hardware or software is in, defining the way it can be used. For example, the 386 microprocessor can be used in real mode (to run DOS) or in protected mode (to run Windows 95 and its successors).

modem (**mo**dulator-**dem**odulator) a device that encodes data for transmission over a particular medium, such as telephone lines, coaxial cables, fiber optics, or microwaves.

An *internal* modem is housed inside the computer's case; an *external* modem is a separate box connected to a serial port. Either way, modern computers use device drivers to access the modem, so that the details of the modem's operation are of no concern to the user. Virtually

```
MODULE Demo;
FROM InOut IMPORT WriteInt;
VAR k : INTEGER;
BEGIN
   k := 1;
   REPEAT
     WriteInt(k,4);
     k := k*2
   UNTIL k>1000
END.
```

FIGURE 164. MODULA-2 PROGRAM

all modems accept a set of commands originally designed for Hayes modems (*see* HAYES COMPATIBILITY).

The *baud rate* of a modem determines how fast it can communicate. In the 1980s, 300, 1200, and then 2400 baud were standard speeds. Nowadays, modems automatically negotiate the highest speed permitted by the quality of the telephone connection, and this can be as high as 56,600 baud (*see* V.90). Most modern modems can communicate with fax machines as well as computers.

Normally, a modem performs the entire job of translating serial data into telephone-line signals and vice versa. However, on computers running Microsoft Windows, a *soft modem* or WINMODEM gives part of that task to the CPU, lowering the cost of the modem. Soft modems give reduced performance and are generally not compatible with operating systems other than Windows.

Telephone-line modems are gradually being replaced by digital network cables that go directly to subscribers' houses. *See* CABLE MODEM.

modem eliminator an RS-232 cable that interchanges conductors 2 and 3; it is known as a *modem eliminator* or *null modem* because it allows two computers to be connected together without modems. *See* DCE; for a diagram, *see* RS-232.

modem, null *see* MODEM ELIMINATOR.

modifier key a key that changes or extends the meaning of a keyboard key. Examples of modifier keys are SHIFT, CTRL, and ALT.

Modula-2 a programming language developed by Niklaus Wirth in the late 1970s as a replacement for Pascal, which Wirth had developed some 10 years earlier. Modula-2 replaces an earlier version, called simply Modula. As its name suggests, Modula-2 is designed to encourage modularity (*see* STRUCTURED PROGRAMMING). Modula-2 is very similar to Pascal, especially the extended versions of Pascal that most compilers now implement. The main differences are:

1. In Modula-2, routines can be compiled separately and linked at load time. Compiled units are called *modules*.

2. The IMPORT and EXPORT declarations control recognition of names. IMPORT means "Recognize names here that are declared in another module"; EXPORT means "Allow other modules to IMPORT names that are declared here."

3. Modula-2 allows the programmer to divide the program into concurrent tasks that run simultaneously. *See* TIMESHARING.

4. The BEGIN and END statements are used only to mark the beginning and end of the program. Within the program, each IF, WHILE, or FOR construct is terminated with an END. (As in Pascal, REPEAT is terminated with UNTIL.)

5. Each standard input-output statement handles only one item of a specific type. For instance, the Pascal statement

   ```
   WRITELN ('The answer is ',A)
   ```

   is replaced by the sequence:

   ```
   WriteString('The answer is');
   WrlteReal(A);
   WriteLn;
   ```

   This feature makes it easier for users to write their own replacements for input-output routines, but it also makes programs longer and clumsier.

6. As in PL/I, procedures can determine, at run time, the size of arrays passed to them as parameters. This makes it practicable to handle variable-length character strings.

7. The CASE statement has an ELSE clause (as it already has in most implementations of Pascal).

8. Upper and lowercase are distinguished throughout the program; reserved words must be entirely in uppercase, and names differing only in case (e.g., WRITELN vs. WriteLn) are not equivalent. An entire name is significant, not just its first eight characters.

Fig. 164 shows a sample program in Modula-2.

module a part of a larger system. A module in a computer program is a part of the program that is written and tested separately and then is combined with other modules to form the complete program. *See* TOP-DOWN PROGRAMMING.

moiré an unintended and distracting pattern that occurs when two or more halftone screens are overprinted at the wrong angle. *See* Fig. 165.

monadic operation an operation on one piece of data. For example, negation (finding the negative of a number) is an operation that requires only one operand and is therefore monadic. Addition is not monadic because it requires two numbers to be added. *Contrast* DYADIC OPERATION.

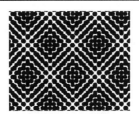

FIGURE 165. MOIRÉ

monitor

1. a computer program that supervises the activity of other programs.

2. a device similar to a television set that accepts video signals from a computer and displays information on its screen. The monitor itself does no computing at all.

Each advance in computer video requires a new kind of monitor. For example, super VGA cards require monitors that can handle higher scan rates than ordinary VGA cards, which in turn require a completely different kind of monitor than was used with earlier PCs.

Types of monitors that have been used with computers include blurry, TV-like COMPOSITE VIDEO monitors; TTL monochrome monitors, which give a very sharp image and accept the same signal voltages as TTL integrated circuits; RGB color monitors, which accept digital signals for red, green, and blue on separate wires; analog color monitors, in which the intensities of red, green, and blue range along a continuum, making a larger number of colors possible; and multiscan (multisync) monitors, which can scan the screen at different rates when in different video modes. *See also* VGA; SUPER VGA; DOT PITCH; EYEGLASSES, COMPUTER.

monochrome monitor a computer screen that can display only one color. Monochrome monitors are becoming uncommon, but they generally produce a sharper, brighter image than color monitors and are worth trying if eyestrain is a problem. *See* DOT PITCH.

monospace a typeface design that gives each letterform the same width, `like this`. *See* TYPEFACE; FIXED-PITCH TYPE; COURIER.

Monte Carlo engine a computer or program used for MONTE CARLO SIMULATION.

Monte Carlo simulation a simulation method that uses random numbers to estimate complex probabilities.

Suppose that you know the probability that a particular event will happen, but it is too difficult to calculate the probability that a complicated combination of events will occur. In the Monte Carlo method

Monospace

Proportional pitch

FIGURE 166. MONOSPACE VS. VARIABLE-PITCH TYPE

you use a random number generator to calculate a random number between 0 and 1, and then compare that number with the probability of the event. For example, if the probability of the event is .62, and the random number generated is .58, then the program will simulate that the event has occurred. You can simulate thousands of such events and look at how the combinations of them add up. The name Monte Carlo comes from the fact that this method is a bit like a game of chance.

MOO (MUD, Object Oriented) a type of MUD (Internet game or interaction environment). *See* MUD.

Moore's Law the prediction that the number of transistors that can be placed in an INTEGRATED CIRCUIT of any given size will double every two years. That is why microprocessors and other integrated circuits become cheaper and more efficient year by year.

Moore's Law was first expressed in 1967 by Gordon Moore, co-founder of Intel, and has proved accurate so far, although there is speculation that true physical limits will be reached within a few more years.

FIGURE 167. MORPH

morph to transform one image gradually into another. A *moving morph* is an animation of the morphing process; a *still morph* is a single image of the transition in progress. *See also* COMPOSITING; ANIMATION.

Mosaic a pioneering computer program for reading publicly available information on the Internet using HTTP and other protocols. Mosaic includes the ability to display graphics in a variety of formats. It is distributed free by the National Center for Supercomputing Applications (NCSA), and versions exist for X Windows (under UNIX), Microsoft Windows, and the Macintosh. Mosaic has been largely superseded by NETSCAPE NAVIGATOR and MICROSOFT INTERNET EXPLORER. *See* WORLD WIDE WEB.

motherboard the main circuit board of a computer, containing the CPU and memory. Some computers have other devices, such as printer ports, also built into the motherboard.

FIGURE 168. MOTION BLUR

motion blur (PHOTOPAINT, 3-D PROGRAMS) a filter that blurs the image along a specified axis to give the effect of motion.

Motorola a major manufacturer of electronic equipment and parts, headquartered in Schaumburg, Illinois. Motorola makes a number of microprocessors, including the 68000 series used in the Apple Macintosh, the PowerPC, and the 6800, used in some early microcomputers in the 1970s. Web address: `http://www.mot.com`.

Motorola 68000 *see* MICROPROCESSOR.

mount to put a disk or tape into a computer and make it known to the operating system. Under UNIX, a list of all currently mounted file systems can be displayed by typing the command `mount`.

mount point in UNIX and Windows 2000, a directory that is actually a separate disk drive. For example, if a UNIX system has two disks, one of them will likely be mounted as / (the root directory) and the other as /home. Then the second disk drive will function as if it were a subdirectory of the first one.

mouse a computer input device that is used by moving it around on your desk and pressing one or more buttons. Moving the mouse moves a pointer on the screen (*see* MOUSE POINTER). Graphical user interfaces such as Microsoft Windows and the Apple Macintosh operating system are built around the mouse. So are paint and draw programs. *See* WINDOWS (MICROSOFT); MACINTOSH; GRAPHICAL USER INTERFACE; PAINT PROGRAM; DRAW PROGRAM; TRACKBALL.

In OS/2 and in Windows 95 and its successors, clicking on the *right* mouse button will bring up a menu of properties or operations pertaining to the object you click on.

There are two basic ways to add a mouse to a PC-compatible computer that was not originally wired for one: to connect a bus mouse to the bus via a special adapter card, or to connect a serial mouse to a serial port.

mouse pointer a small symbol on the screen (usually an arrow) that indicates what the mouse is pointing to, and moves whenever the mouse is moved. Also called *mouse cursor.*

mouse potato *(slang)* a computer-user addicted to web-surfing and other computer-related activities. Obviously adapted from *couch potato*, a person who incessantly views television.

MOV

1. (**m**etal **o**xide **v**aristor) an electronic component used to protect electronic equipment from momentary voltage spikes. *See* SURGE PROTECTOR; POWER LINE PROTECTION.

2. abbreviation for "move" in most ASSEMBLY LANGUAGES. The direction of the arguments depends on the language. On Intel processors, MOV 7,8 means move the value 8 into location 7; on Motorola processors it means move the value 7 into location 8.

Mozilla an open-source web browser established by Netscape; also the name of a lizard used as Mozilla's mascot. Their website is www.mozilla.org.

MP3 a file compression format for music that allows users to download music over the web. MP3 is short for MPEG, layer 3 (layer 1 and layer 2 refer to previous, less-advanced compression formats) and is promoted by the Motion Picture Experts Group (*see* MPEG).

Sound waves can be represented as numbers indicating the amplitude of the wave at each moment in time. High-fidelity sound requires storing a 16-bit number 44,100 times per second (a sampling rate of 44.1 kilohertz). This means that one minute of stereo music requires over 10 megabytes of disk space. This is generally too large to be practical, but MP3 compression reduces the file size to about 1 megabyte per minute. The compression method was developed after carefully studying human auditory perception and then designing the compression algorithm so that the information lost is imperceptible.

To listen to MP3 files, users need to download a software player from a company such as RealNetworks and then download music from various web pages. (Portable hardware devices are also available that can play music stored in MP3 format.) MP3 format now allows many artists to make samples of their work available to the general public over the web, but the ease of copying music in MP3 format raises concerns about piracy. *See also* WAVE FILE; SOUND CARD; COPYRIGHT.

MPC (**m**ultimedia **p**ersonal **c**omputer) a personal computer that meets requirements specified by the MPC Marketing Council for compact disc, sound, and graphics capabilities. These requirements are revised frequently.

MPEG (**M**otion **P**icture **E**xperts **G**roup) an ISO working group that sets standards for digital sound and video and the associated data compression requirements. Web address: `http://www.mpeg.org`.

MRU **m**ost **r**ecently **u**sed.

MRU list a list of most-recently-used files or web addresses. Many word processors, web browsers, etc., maintain MRU lists so the user can quickly return to a document that was used recently. Windows 95 and its successors maintain MRU lists on the Start button, under "Documents."

ms (**m**illisecond) one thousandth of a second. *See* ACCESS TIME.

MS a common abbreviation for Microsoft. *See* MICROSOFT; MS-DOS.

MSCDEX the component of DOS that gives access to files stored on CD-ROM. MSCDEX is distributed free by Microsoft and has been updated more often than DOS itself. It is not needed under Windows 95 and its successors.

MSD (Microsoft Diagnostics) a program provided with Windows for examining the configuration of the computer. For an example of its use, see IRQ.

MS-DOS Microsoft Disk Operating System, the original operating system for IBM PC-compatible computers. Early versions were also marketed by IBM as PC-DOS; today MS-DOS and PC-DOS are separate products derived from the same original code. A version of MS-DOS is also included with Windows 95. Users of Windows 95/98 can still enter commands using the MS-DOS command line by choosing the MS-DOS option from the Program Menu (which is off the Start Menu).

Caldera DOS (formerly Novell DOS and DR-DOS) is an independently developed CLONE (imitation) of MS-DOS.

MS-DOS originated as a CP/M-like operating system for 8086 and 8088 microprocessors. Since version 2.0, however, DOS has included UNIX-like tree-structured directories and pipes. DOS file and directory names have the form XXXXXXXX.XXX (up to 8 letters and/or digits, a period, and up to 3 more letters or digits). The part after the period is called the EXTENSION.

At any time, any DOS system has a particular *default disk* (*current disk*) and a particular *default directory* on each disk. These are where a file is assumed to be if there is no indication to the contrary. Here are some examples of filenames with and without directory information:

XXXX.XXX	File XXXX.XXX in current directory on current disk
A:XXXX.XXX	File XXXX.XXX in current directory of disk A
A:\XXXX.XXX	File XXXX.XXX in main (root) directory of disk A
A:ZZZ\XXXX.XXX	File XXXX.XXX in directory ZZZ, which is in the current directory of disk A
A:\ZZZ\XXXX.XXX	File XXXX.XXX in directory ZZZ, which is in the main (root) directory of disk A

Crucially, if the directory information (the path) starts with a backslash, it is understood as beginning in the root directory; otherwise it begins in the current directory of the appropriate disk.

Here are some common DOS commands:

`a:`	Make disk A the default disk
`cd c:\progs`	Make \PROGS the default directory on disk C
`dir b:`	List the files on disk B
`copy a:zzz b:`	Copy file ZZZ from disk A to disk B

To understand how DOS processes commands, imagine you've just typed `qwerty` at the command prompt. The following things happen:

1. DOS looks for a built-in command named QWERTY. A few commands, such as DIR, are built in. Of course QWERTY isn't.
2. DOS looks for a file that may be named QWERTY.BAT, QWERTY.COM, or QWERTY.EXE in the current directory of the current disk.
3. DOS looks for files with those names in the search path (a list of directories stored in memory with the `path` or `set path` command). If DOS doesn't find QWERTY in any of these places, you get the message "Bad command or file name."

The output of most commands can be redirected to a file or to the input of another command. For example,

```
dir c: > b:directry
```

writes the output of `dir c:` onto file B:DIRECTRY, and

```
dir c: | sort | more
```

sends the output of `dir c:` through the sort program to put lines in alphabetical order, and then through the command MORE, which displays it one screenful at a time.

DOS runs with the CPU in real mode, so that memory space is limited to 1024K, of which addresses above 640K are reserved for video memory. This is the famous "DOS 640K limit" that is actually an artifact, not of DOS, but of the IBM PC video architecture. Versions 5.0 and higher can use the CPU in protected mode to access higher memory addresses for some purposes.

See also PATH; EXTENSION; REAL MODE; BAT FILE; COM; EXE; OS/2; WINDOWS.

MSN (**M**icrosoft **N**etwork) an on-line network established by Microsoft which provides content as well as a connection to the Internet.

MSRP **m**anufacturer's **s**uggested **r**etail **p**rice.

MTBF (**m**ean **t**ime **b**etween **f**ailures) a measure of the reliability of equipment. For example, equipment with an MTBF of 25,000 hours can be expected to run, on the average, 25,000 hours without failing. Some disk drives have an MTBF as high as 800,000 hours (90 years). However, the MTBF is only an average; there is always a risk that any particular piece of equipment will fail sooner.

MUD (**m**ulti-**u**ser **d**omain or **m**ulti-**u**ser **d**imension, formerly **m**ulti-**u**ser **d**ungeon) a type of real-time Internet conference in which users not only talk to each other, but also move around and manipulate objects in an imaginary world.

Originally conceived as multi-user ADVENTURE GAMES, MUDs have developed into a promising format for collaboration and education through the Internet. To access a MUD, the user must, in general, TELNET to the computer that hosts it. *Compare* IRC.

multimedia the combination of sound and visual information presented either to inform or to entertain.

A multimedia PC (MPC) has a high-resolution color monitor, a sound card, and a CD-ROM drive. The combination of sound and related visuals has great promise for the educational software market, as well as for providing a new type of interactive reference work — a HYPERTEXT encyclopedia. Business presentations can now include music, sound effects, and animations along with the usual graphs and charts.

Because of the tremendous demands of displaying complex graphics and animations, a multimedia PC requires state-of-the-art hardware. The CD-ROM is necessary to store the large amounts of data for multimedia presentations.

See also MPC; CD-ROM; MMX; HYPERTEXT.

Multimedia PC *see* MPC.

multimedia speaker an amplified speaker for use on a multimedia computer. The name is a bit misleading because, of course, speakers use only one medium (sound), not multiple media. *See* MULTIMEDIA; AMPLIFIED SPEAKER.

multiple inheritance a technique in object-oriented programming whereby an object type is defined to be a combination of two or more pre-existing types. Some programming languages, such as C++, permit this, and others, such as Java, do not. *See* OBJECT-ORIENTED PROGRAMMING.

Width

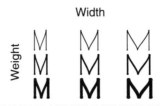

FIGURE 169. MULTIPLE-MASTER FONT

---

multiple-master font a font with two or more master designs, with the intermediate variations generated by the computer.

With multiple-master technology, the type designer specifies two extremes (e.g., the lightest and heaviest weights of the typeface). These are called the *design axes*. The desired combination of characteristics can be generated by the computer as needed. See Figure 169.

multiple virtual mode the mode in which a 386, 486, or Pentium CPU can emulate multiple 8088s (original IBM PCs). *See* VIRTUAL 8086 MODE.

multiprocessing the use of more than one CPU in a single computer system.

multiprogramming the apparently simultaneous execution of more than one program on a single computer through timesharing. *See* MULTITASKING; TIMESHARING.

multiscan, Multisync a monitor that can scan the screen at more than one speed, needed in order to support multiple video modes or work with different kinds of hardware. *Multisync* is a trademark of NEC and *multiscan* is the generic term. *See* MONITOR.

multisession CD a compact disc (CD-ROM) that was not recorded all at once; rather, some files were recorded on it at one time and more files were added later. The directory of a multisession CD occupies more than one block of disc space, and earlier CD-ROM software cannot necessarily read multisession CDs. *See* CD-ROM *and references there.*

multispin drive a CD-ROM drive that runs at more than the original standard speed.

multitasking the execution of more than one program apparently at the same time on the same computer. In reality, the CPU rapidly switches

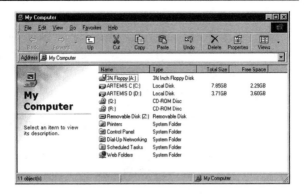

FIGURE 170. "MY COMPUTER" (WINDOWS 98)

its attention among the various programs (*see* TIMESHARING). Multitasking makes it possible to print one document while editing another, or to perform lengthy computations "in the background" while working on something else on the screen. *See* OS/2; WINDOWS; UNIX.

The programs that run concurrently are called *processes* or *tasks*. An important concern is to keep tasks from interfering with each other. For example, two tasks cannot use the same area of memory or the same input-output device, such as a printer, at the same time. *See* PROTECTED MODE.

If tasks communicate with each other, it is important to prevent *deadlocks*, in which two tasks are each waiting for the other to do something, so that neither one can make any progress.

Multitasking can be either *preemptive* or *cooperative.* In preemptive multitasking (as under UNIX or OS/2), the operating system forces the CPU to switch regularly from each process to the next. In cooperative multitasking (as in Windows 3.0 and 3.1), each process has to voluntarily give up the CPU periodically so that other processes can run.

A more primitive form of multitasking allows you to switch from one program to another, but only one program at a time actually runs; the others are frozen until you return to them. This kind of multitasking was implemented in versions of Microsoft Windows before 3.0 and in early versions of the Macintosh operating system.

MVS (**M**ultiple **V**irtual **S**torage) an operating system for IBM mainframe computers; from the user's point of view, it is almost completely compatible with OS/360. *See* OS/360; JCL; TSO.

My Computer a FOLDER on the DESKTOP of Windows 95 and its successors that contains all the disk drives, the control panel, and other information about the system.

Ordinarily, folders are directories. The root directory of a disk drive is also a folder. My Computer is a special folder that gives you access to the entire machine.

My Documents a FOLDER on the DESKTOP of Windows 95 and its successors in which the user is invited to store his or her files in the absence of a more elaborate file system. The My Documents folder was created to discourage beginners from storing files in the same folder as the software that created them.

My Network Places the FOLDER on the Windows 2000 DESKTOP that takes the place of Windows 95's Network Neighborhood. It enables the user to BROWSE (examine) the computer resources available through the network, if any. *See* NETWORK NEIGHBORHOOD.

N

NACK *see* NAK.

nagware shareware that always opens with a message begging for remuneration. Some nagware is exceptionally persistent and interrupts your work sessions with messages reminding you to register (and pay!). *See* SHAREWARE; FREE SOFTWARE.

NAK an abbreviation for ASCII code 21, which stands for "not acknowledged" in older teletype systems and in XMODEM and some other protocols. NAK is sent when a data packet is received incorrectly or is not received when expected. *Contrast* ACK.

nameserver a computer whose job is to translate names into IP ADDRESSES for other computers.

Most computers on the Internet do not contain their own directories of the whole network. Instead, they rely on nameservers to interpret names for them.

namespace the set of names available for naming things such as files, variables in a program, or computers in a network. If two parts of a program have different namespaces, the same name can be used in both places for different purposes without conflict. *See also* LOCAL VARIABLE.

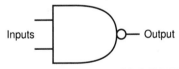

FIGURE 171. NAND GATE (LOGIC SYMBOL)

NAND gate (Figure 171) a logic gate whose output is 0 if both of the inputs are 1, and is 1 otherwise, thus:

Inputs		Output
0	0	1
0	1	1
1	0	1
1	1	0

A NAND gate is equivalent to an AND gate followed by a NOT gate. NAND gates are important because all the other types of logic circuits can be built out of them. *See* LOGIC CIRCUITS.

nano- metric prefix meaning ÷1,000,000,000. For example, 1 nanosecond is one billionth of a second. *Nano-* is derived from the Latin word for "dwarf." *See* METRIC PREFIXES.

nanosecond a unit of time equal to 10^{-9} second, that is to say, $1/1,000,000,000$ second. During one nanosecond, a light wave, electrical field, or radio wave travels about one foot. The access time of many computer memories is about 60 to 70 nanoseconds.

national characters the characters on a computer are those whose appearance varies from country to country. For example, on IBM mainframes, the characters $, #, and @ are called national characters because they may be replaced by other characters such as £ or ¥ for use outside the United States.

native

    1. designed for a specific hardware or software environment (rather than for compatibility with something else).

    2. consisting of CPU machine instructions rather than instruction codes to be interpreted by a program.

native file format the file format proprietary to an application program; the format in which it normally saves documents or drawings. Most programs can, with the IMPORT command, convert similar file types to their own format. If you want to convert a native file to a more generic file type, use the SAVE AS or EXPORT commands. *Contrast* METAFILE.

native method a computer program compiled in the machine language of the specific computer on which it is being run. For example, a Java program is normally compiled to Java bytecode, but in some cases it might link to a native method that was written in a language such as C++ and compiled into machine language.

natural language processing the use of computers to process information expressed in human (natural) languages.

    At present, almost all human communication with computers is done in artificial languages such as BASIC and Pascal. Computers would be much more useful if they could understand instructions in ordinary human languages (natural languages) such as English and French. In the early days of computers, it was assumed that successful natural language processing programs would be easy to construct, given sufficient computing power. However, progress has been slow. There are three main problem areas:

    1. *Syntax.* No one has yet produced a complete, mathematically precise description of the possible sentence structures of any human language. There are a number of promising approaches (all derived directly or indirectly from the work of Noam Chomsky in the 1950s), but all of them run into difficulties with some types of sentences.

The correct interpretation of pronouns such as *himself* and *each other* is especially problematic; human beings seem to know intuitively how to use such words in a sentence as soon as they learn what they mean, but no one has ever captured this knowledge in a completely satisfactory set of explicit rules. Facts such as this have led Chomsky and his followers to suspect that the human brain is genetically "preprogrammed" in quite specific ways for certain features of human languages.

2. *Semantics.* If the computer is to understand sentences, it must have some kind of internal representation of their meanings. The most straightforward way to represent meanings in a computer is to decompose them into a finite set of primitive elements; for example, *grandfather* can be represented as *male parent of parent of self,* where *male, parent, of,* and *self* are part of a small built-in vocabulary.

There are, however, many words whose meanings defy representation in this form. For example, as Geoffrey Sampson has pointed out, the word *picturesque* cannot be broken up into simpler elements; but one would hardly want to say that the human brain acquired a new "built-in" primitive concept, PICTURESQUE, just a couple of centuries ago when the word first came into use. Many meanings seem to consist of mental images or sets of associated ideas that admit of considerable vagueness.

3. *Phonetics.* Although computers can now produce reasonably intelligible synthetic speech, it is difficult to get them to recognize human speech. The problem is that, although speech seems to consist of strings of distinct sounds (*m, a,* and *n* for *man*), in reality the sounds are merged together, even in the clearest radio-announcer speech. (The *a* and *n* in *man,* for instance, are almost completely simultaneous.) In addition, variations between speakers often lead to ambiguity; for instance, many New Yorkers pronounce *man* almost exactly the way Southerners pronounce *men.* There are even substantial differences between the sound waves produced when the same person pronounces the same word twice.

The best speech-recognition systems available today recognize only a few hundred words and usually have to be "trained" for the speech of a particular person.

There are many approaches to natural language processing. Some programs attempt to model processes in the human brain, while others use any available procedure to obtain practical results, even if it is something human speakers could not possibly do (e.g., processing the words of each sentence in reverse order). There is some controversy over whether it is better to try to determine the sentence structure first, and then the meaning, or whether the computer should construct a representation of the meaning of a sentence in one step; the latter approach results in programs that are less neatly organized but can use information about meaning to help make decisions about sentence structure.

The best currently available natural language processors often perform impressively (e.g., Yale University has developed one that reads incoming news stories from a teletype line and prepares summaries of them), but none of them is highly reliable; each program misinterprets certain types of sentences, often producing ludicrously incorrect results. Natural conversations between human beings and computers are still several years away. (*See also* PARSING; ELIZA.)

natural logarithm logarithm to the base *e* (about 2.718). *See* LOGARITHM.

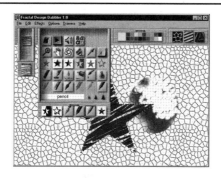

FIGURE 172. NATURAL MEDIA PAINT PROGRAM

natural media actual artists' materials (paint, canvas, etc.) realistically simulated by a computer program. In a natural-media paint program, you can specify the kind of paper or canvas you are working on. The tools available behave very much as their real world counterparts would act — the chalk smears, the watercolors spread, and markers bleed. The main difference is the ability to combine unlikely media (try to paint watercolors over chalk in real life), and you don't have to wait for anything to dry.

Natural-media programs are very demanding of your hardware; they create huge files and require lots of RAM, fast video boards, and fast CPUs.

navigation finding your way around a complex system of menus, help files, or the WORLD WIDE WEB. This can be a real challenge, but there are a few tricks to help you.

- *Menu navigation.* Learning how to navigate menus requires an adventurous spirit. Make yourself a map (if there's not one already in the manual), as any good explorer would do. Sometimes the logic of grouping certain commands together will not be apparent to you and you'll have to learn some rather arbitrary distinctions. The best defense is to be familiar with your software. If you know that there *is* a command to do whirligigs, but can't remember whether it's under File or Arrange, it's only a matter of a fraction of a second to look under both categories.

  Menus can nest like wooden Russian dolls. One will lead to another in a rather infuriating way. Just remember to take one thing at a time. After making your decisions at each level, click OK. If you've gotten lost in the menus, you can back out at any time by choosing Cancel. Note: if you cancel out, the changes you made will not take place. Be aware that menus can interconnect at lower levels. This means that there *can* be more than one way into the same DIALOG BOX.

- *Help and hypertext files.* Programs for viewing HYPERTEXT FILES usually have a command called Back that allows you to backtrack to the previous screens. This is similar to Tom Sawyer using a rope to find his way around caves. A frequent frustration is to have a vague memory of a subject you read about yesterday, but can't remember how to get there. Some programs have bookmarks to mark important sections; use them. Also, familiarize yourself with the search capabilities of the hypertext system; it can save you a lot of time. As always, a good index is worth its weight in gold. If the index is too general to be useful, write a complaint to the software vendor. (If enough users complain, something might be done.) In the meantime, you may want to make a few notes on an index card and slip it into the manual.

- *World Wide Web.* The links that make up the World Wide Web can lead you literally in thousands of different directions from any starting point. When searching for information on a particular topic, use one of the standard web search engines such as Yahoo!, Lycos, or Excite (try `http://www.search.com` to access the major indexes). *See* SEARCH ENGINE to get specific search tips.

  When browsing the WWW for pleasure, you may want to explore a JUMP LIST; most service providers have one. Usually, a web site will contain a page of new links to follow. (This will take care of all the rest of your free time.)

  When you find a web page you think you'll want to return to, bookmark it, or add it to your Favorites folder. During the same web-surfing session, you can also use the Back and Forward buttons on your browser. Back returns you to the previous web page; after backing up, you can use Forward to retrace your steps.

Your browser maintains a list of where you've been (the HISTORY FOLDER). The most recently visited sites are a mouse-click away under the Go menu.

Navigator web browser developed by Netscape (and often simply called Netscape). *See* NETSCAPE NAVIGATOR.

NC (**n**etwork **c**omputer) a computer that downloads all software and data from a network, having little or no disk storage of its own; a DISKLESS WORKSTATION. Network computers have some advantages because the system managers do not have to keep updating software and files on each individual worker's computer. Network computers are not yet in wide use. NC software, as envisioned, may consist of Java applets.

near letter quality (NLQ) a type of printer whose output resembles the print of a cloth-ribbon typewriter (which often looks gray, broken, or smudged). Near-letter-quality printing is not considered satisfactory for dissertations or correspondence on corporate letterheads. Nine-pin dot-matrix printers and thermal printers are considered near-letter-quality printers. Most current printers are letter-quality, but some offer a *draft mode* which saves toner or ink by printing lighter. (*See* LETTER QUALITY)

FIGURE 173. A NEGATIVE IMAGE

negative a photographically reversed image; black becomes white, white becomes black, and colors become their complements.

In desktop publishing, white letters on a black background are usually called a REVERSE. A *negative* is the physical film that is the intermediate step between camera-ready copy and a printing plate. *See* INVERT.

nest to put a structure inside another structure of the same kind. For example, in BASIC, three nested FOR loops look like this:

```
FOR I=1 TO 100
  FOR J=1 TO 100
    FOR K=1 TO 100
```

```
    ...statements to be repeated go here...
      NEXT K
   NEXT J
NEXT I
```

Note that indenting is used so that human readers can see how the loops are nested.

net suffix indicating that an E-MAIL address or WEB SITE is located at a network with a particular name. Names ending in `.net` generally designate sites that provide Internet connectivity to other networks.

Net, the a colloquial name for the INTERNET.

NetBEUI (**NetB**IOS **E**xtended **U**ser **I**nterface) a data transmission protocol developed by IBM and Microsoft and widely used in local-area networking. It is usually the preferred protocol for networking Windows systems but does not support routing. *See* PROTOCOL; ROUTER. *Contrast* TCP/IP; IPX/SPX; ATM.

NetBIOS (**Net**work **B**asic **I**nput-**O**utput **S**ystem) an operating system extension designed by IBM to allow software to access a network. NetBIOS includes a network protocol that was later extended to form NetBEUI. *See* NETBEUI.

netiquette (network etiquette) the conventional practices that make the INTERNET usable. More than just politeness, netiquette involves fundamental respect for the rights of other users who are helping pay the cost of running the network.

For example, it is unacceptable to post off-topic material in NEWS-GROUPS, be rude during chats, ask people to do your homework for you, or bother them with commercial solicitations. *See also* NEWSGROUPS; COMPUTER ETHICS; ACCEPTABLE-USE POLICY.

netizen (Internet citizen) a person who is part of the Internet community in CYBERSPACE.

NetPC an initiative announced in 1997 by Microsoft and Intel to create a computer that will be easier to administer because it will be in a sealed box, so the user will not have to install any software or insert disks. Instead, software will come from a server. *See* NC.

Netscape Navigator a popular WEB BROWSER for several types of computers, produced by Netscape Comunications Corporation (see their web site at `http://www.netscape.com`). In 1998 Netscape was acquired by AOL. Netscape Navigator includes VIEWERS for many different graphics formats, and the newest versions support Java (*see* Figure 174). *See also* WORLD WIDE WEB; HTML; JAVA.

net surfing *see* SURFING.

NetWare *see* NOVELL NETWARE.

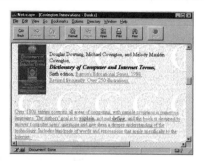

FIGURE 174. NETSCAPE NAVIGATOR

network a set of computers connected together. *See* LOCAL-AREA NETWORK; WIDE-AREA NETWORK; INTRANET; INTERNET.

network computer *see* NC.

FIGURE 175. NETWORK NEIGHBORHOOD

Network Neighborhood in Windows 95 and later, the desktop icon that identifies computers and printers accessible on the local-area network (*see* Figure 175). The information in Network Neighborhood is not always up-to-date; it comes from the browse master and can be as much as 15 minutes old. *See* BROWSE MASTER.

In Windows 2000, Network Neighborhood is called My Network Places.

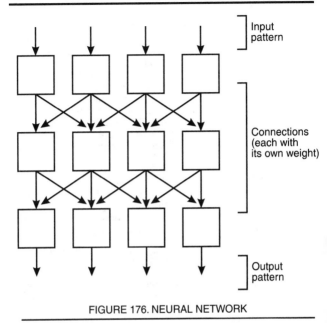

Input pattern

Connections (each with its own weight)

Output pattern

FIGURE 176. NEURAL NETWORK

Network Solutions, Inc. the organization that, until 1998, had sole responsibility for maintaining the registry of top-level domain names (TLDs) ending in .com, .net and .org, under a contract with the United States Government. Its web address is www.networksolutions.com.

Since 1998, Network Solutions is one of several competing domain name registrars. This process is supervised by ICANN. *See also* DOMAIN NAME HOARDING; DOMAIN NAME POACHING.

neural networks computer programs that model the way nerve cells (neurons) are connected together in the human brain. Neural networks enable a computer to train itself to recognize patterns in a strikingly human-like way. Like the human brain, neural networks give only approximate results, but they can do things that no other kind of computer program can efficiently.

Figure 176 shows how a neural network is set up. Each neuron has several inputs but only one output. Some of the inputs excite (activate) the neuron while others inhibit it, each with a particular strength. The idea is that each output neuron will be activated when one particular kind of pattern is present at the input. In the computer, the neurons and connections are simulated by arrays of numbers.

Training a neural network is like training an animal. Patterns are applied to the input, and a simple algorithm adjusts the weights of the connections to try to get the desired output. After many training runs in which many different patterns are utilized, the neural network "learns" to recognize patterns of a certain kind. Even the programmer need not know exactly what these patterns have in common, because the patterns are analyzed by the neural network itself.

Neural networks are good at recognizing inputs that are vague, ill-defined, or likely to contain scattered variation. For example, a neural network can recognize images of human faces, or patterns of weather data, or trends in stock market behavior. However, a neural network is never 100 percent reliable, and even simple calculations can be quite slow.

newbie *(slang)* newcomer (to the Internet, a newsgroup, etc.).

new media the means of communication that are displacing newspapers and television at the beginning of the 21st Century. Chief among them is the World Wide Web or, more generally, the Internet. Some differences between the Web and earlier media include the following:

- *Lack of central control.* Almost anyone can publish almost anything without an editor's or publisher's approval.

- *Very low cost of production.* You do not have to own a TV station or newspaper company to express yourself; everyone has a voice. In the 1500s, the printing press had a similar impact. It allowed any educated and reasonably prosperous person to print handbills and give them out. Later, newspapers and magazines arose as means of mass communication through printing.

- *Computer-assisted access.* Computers can help you find material you are interested in and filter out things you do not want to see. (*See* SEARCH ENGINE.)

- *Multimedia.* New media can combine the effects of print, painting, photography, music, motion pictures, and animation while adding new capabilities of their own, such as hypertext. *See* HYPERTEXT.

- *Volatility.* The contents of a web page can be changed at any time; it is possible to rewrite history and deny what you published a few weeks earlier. Libraries need to address this by archiving the World Wide Web for the public good.

One thing everyone agrees on is that the new media are in their infancy and their most common uses fifty years hence will probably involve techniques that have not yet been invented or foreseen.

newsgroup a public forum or discussion area on a computer network. All users of the network can post messages, and every user can read all the messages that have been posted. The most famous newsgroups are those distributed worldwide by the Usenet system, covering thousands of topics. *See* USENET.

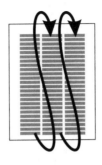

FIGURE 177. NEWSPAPER COLUMNS

newspaper columns a word processor mode that specifies a newspaper-like format with text flowing from one column into the next.

newsreader a piece of software that enables the user to read Usenet newsgroups. *See* NEWSGROUP.

Newton a PDA (personal digital assistant) introduced by Apple in 1993. *See* PDA.

NFS (Network File System) an extension to UNIX that enables computers on a network to share disk drives. NFS was developed by Sun Microsystems but is available on computers from a wide variety of manufacturers. *See* LOCAL-AREA NETWORK; FILE SERVER.

nibble a group of 4 bits, or half of 1 byte.

NIC (Network Interface Card) the circuit board inside a computer that connects it to a local-area network. Usually, the first step in networking a computer is to install a NIC.

nicad (**ni**ckel-**cad**mium) a type of rechargeable battery often used in laptop computers. Nickel-cadmium batteries are toxic and should not be discarded in ordinary trash.

NiMH (**Ni**ckel-**M**etal **H**ydride) a type of rechargeable battery electrically similar to nickel-cadmium (NICAD) but having greater capacity.

node

1. an individual computer (or occasionally another type of machine) in a network.

2. a connection point in a data structure such as a linked list or tree.

3. (draw programs) a point on a curve or line that helps define the shape of the line. *See* SPLINE; SMOOTH NODE; CUSP NODE.

nom suffix indicating that an E-MAIL address or WEB SITE is a personal site.

nondocument mode a type of word processing that produces plaintext (ASCII) files with no special codes for hyphenation, page breaks, fonts, or the like. The most common way of saving a file in nondocument mode is to use the "Save as" menu and choose "text file" or "text only." *See* TEXT FILE.

noninterlaced a type of monitor that scans the entire screen in one pass, minimizing flicker. *See* INTERLACING.

nonvolatile not erased when turned off. Disks are a nonvolatile storage medium; memory (RAM) is volatile.

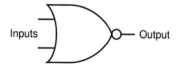

FIGURE 178. NOR GATE (LOGIC SYMBOL)

NOR gate (Figure 178) a logic gate whose output is 0 when either or both of the two inputs is 1, thus:

Inputs		Output
0	0	1
0	1	0
1	0	0
1	1	0

A NOR gate is equivalent to an OR gate followed by a NOT gate. NOR gates are important because all the other types of logic circuits can be built from them. *See* LOGIC CIRCUITS.

Norton Utilities a set of programs written by Peter Norton for IBM PC-compatible computers (a Macintosh version is also available). Their most important function is to recover erased files and correct other problems with disks. *See* RECOVERING ERASED FILES.

NOS

    1. (**N**etwork **O**perating **S**ystem) any special operating system or operating system extension that supports networking. For an example, *see* NOVELL NETWARE.

    2. (**N**ew **O**ld **S**tock) old but unused and still in original packaging; this describes parts for obsolete equipment or the like. *Compare* LNIB.

notebook a computer about the same size as a looseleaf notebook, weighing less than six pounds. Notebooks are slightly smaller than laptop computers, which can weigh up to eight pounds.

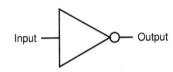

FIGURE 179. NOT GATE (INVERTER)

NOT gate (Figure 179) a logic gate whose output is 1 if the input is 0, and vice versa, thus:

Inputs	Output
0	1
1	0

    A NOT gate is also called an *inverter* because it reverses the value of its input. *See* LOGIC CIRCUITS.

Novell NetWare a popular software package for networking PC-compatible computers. It is produced by Novell, Inc. of Provo, Utah (web address: http://www.novell.com). NetWare runs with many kinds of network hardware and communication protocols (including Ethernet, Arcnet, and IBM token ring) and enables computers to share files and printers.

NP-complete problem *see* LIMITS OF COMPUTER POWER.

NPN one of the two types of bipolar TRANSISTORS (*contrast* PNP).

NSFnet a network, subsidized by the National Science Foundation, that formerly served as the BACKBONE of the Internet for academic users in the United States.

NSI *see* NETWORK SOLUTIONS, INC.

NT short for Windows NT. *See* WINDOWS (MICROSOFT).

NTFS the file system used by WINDOWS NT. *Contrast* FAT; CDFS.

NTSC (National Television System Committee) the type of color TV signal used in the United States. It was designed to be compatible with a pre-existing black-and-white system. The screen consists of 525 lines, interlaced, and a complete scan takes 1/30 second. Color information is modulated on a 3.58-MHz subcarrier. *Contrast* PAL; SECAM.

nudge to move a selected object in small increments by using the arrow keys instead of the mouse.

null modem (or **modem eliminator**) a cable for connecting two computers together without a modem. *See* MODEM ELIMINATOR. For a diagram, see RS-232.

null-terminated string a CHARACTER STRING that ends with ASCII code 0. Null-terminated strings are used in the C programming language and in many of the system routines of UNIX and Windows.

number crunching *(slang)* arithmetical calculation, especially for scientific or engineering purposes.

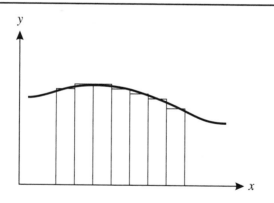

FIGURE 180. NUMERICAL INTEGRATION

numerical integration the process of finding the area under a particular curve by dividing the area into many tiny rectangles, adding up the heights of individual rectangles, and then multiplying the sum by their common width. *See* Figure 180. Numerical integration is a good

```
1       REM THIS PROGRAM FINDS THE AREA UNDER
2       REM THE STANDARD NORMAL PROBABILITY
3       REM CURVE FROM X=0 TO X=B
10      INPUT B
20      A = 0
30      P = SQR(2 * 3.14159265)
40      FOR I = 1 TO INT(100*B)
50        X = I/100 - .005
60        Y = EXP(-X^2/2)
70        A = A + Y
80      NEXT I
90      PRINT A/(100*P)
100     END
```

FIGURE 181. NUMERICAL INTEGRATION IN BASIC.

example of a calculation that is practical to do on a computer but not by hand.

For example, in probability theory it is important to find the area under the bell curve defined by:

$$y = \frac{1}{\sqrt{2\pi}} e^{-x^2/2}$$

This area can be found with the BASIC program in Fig. 181, which uses a loop to perform a numerical integration. As you might imagine, it would take a long time to perform this calculation with a calculator, and it would be entirely impractical to do it by hand.

numeric keypad a separate set of keys at the end of the keyboard, contains the digits 0 to 9 and a decimal point key. The digits are arranged in the same way as they are on an adding machine. If you have to type large quantities of numeric data, a numeric keypad is quicker to use than the number keys on the regular keypad. Some people prefer a keyboard without a numeric keypad because it lets them place the mouse closer to where they sit. *See also* KEYBOARD.

Num Lock a key on PC-compatible computers that switches the NUMERIC KEYPAD between two functions: typing numbers or moving the cursor with arrow keys.

O

Ob- *(slang)* "obligatory"; used in newsgroup postings to signify a belated return to the intended topic. *See* TOPIC DRIFT.

obelisk the character †, a symbol used to mark footnotes. *See also* FOOTNOTE. Also called a DAGGER or LONG CROSS.

object

1. a data item that has procedures associated with it. *See* OBJECT-ORIENTED PROGRAMMING.

2. one of the parts of a graphical image. *See* DRAW PROGRAM.

object code the output of a compiler; a program written in machine instructions recognizable to the CPU, rather than a programming language used by humans. *Contrast* SOURCE CODE.

object linking and embedding (OLE) (in Microsoft Windows 3.1 and later versions) a method of combining information that is processed by different application programs, such as inserting a drawing or a portion of a spreadsheet into a word processing document. The main document is called the *client* and the document or application that supplies the embedded material is the *server*. OLE supersedes an older feature of Windows called *dynamic data exchange* (DDE).

OLE can be done in either of two ways. An *embedded* object becomes part of the document that it is inserted into. For example, if you embed a drawing into a word processing document, the whole thing becomes one file, and to edit it, you use the word processor, which will call up the drawing program when you double-click on the drawing to edit it. A *linked* object has a life of its own; it remains a separate file and can be edited separately. When you edit it, the information that is linked from it into other documents is automatically updated. Thus, you can use a word processor to create a report that has links to a spreadsheet, and when you update the information in the spreadsheet, the corresponding information in the report will be updated automatically. Embedding and linking correspond to "cold links" and "hot links" in Windows 3.0 DDE. *See also* ACTIVEX.

object-oriented graphics graphical images that are represented as instructions to draw particular objects, rather than as light or dark spots on a grid. *See* DRAW PROGRAM.

object-oriented programming a programming methodology in which the programmer can define not only data types, but also procedures that are automatically associated with them.

Many programming languages let the programmer define new data types such as records, arrays, and linked lists (*see* DATA STRUCTURES). In object-oriented programming, the programmer can associate a set of procedures (methods) with each type. Types with procedures associated with them are called *classes*. Crucially, the same name can be given to different procedures that do corresponding things to different types; this is called *polymorphism*. For example, there could be a "draw" procedure for circles and another for rectangles.

Some uses for object-oriented programming include the following:

1. *Graphical objects.* A program that manipulates lines, circles, rectangles, and the like can have a separate "draw" and "move" procedure for each of these types.

2. *Mathematical objects.* In order to work with vectors, matrices, or other special mathematical objects, the programmer has to define not only data structures for these objects, but also operations such as addition, inversion, or finding a determinant.

3. *Input-output devices.* The procedure to draw a line might be quite different on a printer or plotter than on the screen. Object-oriented programming provides a simple way to ensure that the right procedure is used on each device.

4. *Simulation.* In a program that simulates traffic flow, for example, cars, trucks, and buses might be types of objects, each with its own procedures for responding to red lights, obstructions in the road, and so forth. This, in fact, is what object-oriented programming was invented for. The first object-oriented programming language was Simula, introduced in 1967.

5. *Reusable software components.* Object-oriented programming provides a powerful way to build and use components out of which programs can be built. For example, a programmer might use a predefined object class such as "sorted list" (a list that automatically keeps itself in order) rather than having to write procedures to create and sort a list.

Here is an example of object-oriented programming in Turbo Pascal. Imagine a program that manipulates points, lines, and circles. A point consists of a location plus a procedure to display it (just draw a dot). So the programmer defines a type called *pointtype* as follows:

```
TYPE pointtype = OBJECT
   x, y: INTEGER;
   PROCEDURE draw
END;
```

This is just like a record declaration except that it refers to procedure draw, defined like this:

```
PROCEDURE pointtype.draw;
BEGIN
  PutPixel(x,y,white)
END;
```

Now variables of type `pointtype` can be declared, for example:

```
VAR  a, b: pointtype;
```

Here the objects `a` and `b` are like records, each containing an `x` and a `y` field; `x` and `y` are called *instance variables*. In addition, `a` and `b` are associated with the `point.draw` procedure. Here's an example of how to use them:

```
a.x := 100;
a.y := 150:
a.draw;
```

This sets the `x` and `y` fields of `a` to 100 and 150, respectively, and then calls the `draw` procedure that is associated with `a` (namely `pointtype.draw`).

Now let's handle circles. A circle is like a point except that in addition to `x` and `y`, it has a radius. Also, its `draw` method is different. We can define `circletype` as another type that inherits from `pointtype` (i.e., contains everything that `pointtype` contains) except that it adds an instance variable called `radius` and substitutes a different draw method. Here's how it's done:

```
TYPE circletype = OBJECT(pointtype)
                    radius: INTEGER;
                    PROCEDURE draw;
                END;

PROCEDURE circletype.draw;
BEGIN
   Circle(x,y,radius)
END;

VAR c: circletype;
...
c.x := 200;
c.y := 250;
c.radius := 49;
c.draw;
```

It is important to remember that instance variables belong to individual objects such as `a`, `b`, and `c`, but methods (procedures) belong to object types. The advantage of object-oriented programming is that it automatically associates the right procedures with each object: `c.draw` uses the circle draw procedure because object `c` is a circle, but `a.draw` uses the point draw procedure because object `a` is a point.

The act of calling one of an object's methods is sometimes described as "sending a message" to the object (e.g., `c.draw` "sends a message" to `c` saying "draw yourself"). All object-oriented programming systems allow one class to inherit from another (like `circletype` and `pointtype` above); some also allow *multiple inheritance*, in which a class can be defined as the combination of two or more preexisting classes. *See also* C++; SMALLTALK; JAVA.

object program a program that has been translated into machine language and is ready to be run. *See* COMPILER; *contrast* SOURCE PROGRAM.

OBO abbreviation for "**o**r **b**est **o**ffer," often used when advertising things for sale on the Internet.

OCR *see* OPTICAL CHARACTER RECOGNITION.

octal a way of writing numbers in base-8 notation. Octal numbers use only the digits 0, 1, 2, 3, 4, 5, 6, and 7, and the next column represents multiples of 8. For example, the octal number 23 means 2 eights and 3 ones, or 19. Here are some further examples:

Binary	Octal	Decimal
001 000	10	$1 \times 8^1 = 8$
001 001	11	$1 \times 8^1 + 1 = 9$
001 010	12	$1 \times 8^1 + 2 = 10$
010 001	21	$2 \times 8^1 + 1 = 17$
011 001	31	$3 \times 8^1 + 1 = 25$
100 001	41	$4 \times 8^1 + 1 = 33$
101 010 100	524	$5 \times 8^2 + 2 \times 8^1 + 4 = 340$

Note that each octal digit corresponds to three binary digits.

octet a group of exactly eight bits, regardless of whether eight bits represent a character on any particular computer. *Contrast* BYTE.

octothorpe the character #; originally a map-maker's representation of a village with eight fields (thorpes) around a central square. Also called a POUND SIGN.

OEM (**O**riginal **E**quipment **M**anufacturer) a company that assembles complete pieces of equipment from parts. In some Microsoft documentation, "OEM" is used as a euphemism for "IBM" in order to avoid naming the competitor directly; but it also refers to other manufacturers.

OEM character set the native character set of the IBM PC. For a chart, *see* IBM PC.

off-by-one error a programming error caused by doing something the wrong number of times (one time too many or one time too few); also called a FENCEPOST ERROR.

Office, Microsoft suite of applications including Word, Excel, Access, and PowerPoint. This product became the leading business application software used on microcomputers in the 1990s.

offset the distance, in a computer memory, between one location and another. The offset of a data item is its address relative to the address of something else (0 if they are in the same position, 5 if they are 5 bytes apart, and so forth).

On a microprocessor such as the 8088, each memory address is given as two numbers, a *segment* and an *offset*. To find the actual address, the segment is shifted one hexadecimal digit to the left and the offset is added to it. For instance, the address F123:1114 (segment F123, offset 1114) means:

$$
\begin{array}{r}
\text{F1230} \\
+ \quad \text{1114} \\
\hline
\text{F2344}
\end{array}
$$

where F2344 is the absolute address. Note that F000:2344 refers to exactly the same address: so does F200:0344, and so on. *See also* SEGMENT.

offset printing a way of printing on paper by means of ink transferred by a rubber roller from another surface. Offset printing is a cheap way for a print shop to produce hundreds of copies of a laser-printed original.

ohm the unit of measure of electrical resistance. If an object has a resistance of 1 ohm, then an applied voltage of 1 volt will cause a current of 1 ampere to flow. *See* OHM'S LAW.

Impedance is also measured in ohms. Impedance is similar to resistance but is defined in terms of alternating current rather than direct current. *See* IMPEDANCE.

Ohm's law a basic law describing the behavior of electricity. It states that the current that flows through a circuit element is equal to the voltage applied across that element divided by the resistance of that element:

$$
I = V/R
$$

where I = current, in amperes; V = voltage, in volts; and R = resistance, in ohms. In effect, voltage is the force that drives a current through a resistance.

OLE *see* OBJECT LINKING AND EMBEDDING.

OMG (Object Management Group) a consortium of hundreds of computer companies that develop standards for software components to interact with each other. See web address: `http://www.omg.org`. *See also* CORBA.

on-board included within a piece of equipment. For example, it is common for a sound card to have an on-board amplifier that can drive speakers, so that an external amplifier is not needed.

one-way function a function whose inverse is very hard to calculate. A function f is a one-way function if, given x, it is relatively easy to calculate $y = f(x)$, but it is hard to calculate the inverse function (that is, calculate the value of x if you are given the value of y). One-way functions are used in public key encryption schemes; *see* ENCRYPTION.

onionskin (animation software) a translucent drawing layer placed on top of a reference image for purposes of tracing.

on line connected to a computer or available through a computer. For example, on-line help is information that can be called up immediately on a computer screen rather than having to be looked up in a book.

    Usage note: *On-line* takes a hyphen when used before a noun, as in *on-line processing* (but not *the computer is on line*). Influenced by the trade name *America Online,* some publishers prefer to write *online* as a single word in both situations.

    In New York City, but not elsewhere, *on line* means "in a queue," as in *We are standing on line* – the rest of the country says *standing in line*.

on-line trading the buying and selling of stocks or other securities through the Internet. Instead of paying a broker to type transactions into a computer, you type them in yourself. Brokerage fees are much lower, and transactions are completed more promptly. Unfortunately, the broker's wise counsel is absent, and fortunes have been lost through speculative day trading. *See* DAY TRADING.

OOC abbreviation for "**o**ut **o**f **c**haracter" in e-mail and on-line games. To act out of character is to pretend to be something you are not (whether in a game or in real life).

OOP *see* OBJECT-ORIENTED PROGRAMMING.

open

    1.   to call a file, document, or drawing up from disk in order to work with it.

    2.   (programming) to prepare a file to have data transferred into or out of it.

    3.   (electronics) to put a switch into the position that does not allow current to flow.

open architecture a computer architecture whose details are fully made public so that other manufacturers can make clones and compatible accessories. The architecture of the original IBM PC is open; that of the original Macintosh is not.

open source software software whose source code is published so that a variety of people can add contributions. This is different from proprietary software such as Microsoft Windows, where the source code is a trade secret and only employees of that corporation work on the software's development. Significant examples of open source software include the Linux operating system, the Apache web server, and various Gnu products. *See* SOURCE CODE; GNU; LINUX; APACHE.

open systems interconnection *see* DATA COMMUNICATION.

OpenType a proposed type format that will take the place of both TrueType and Type 1 fonts.

operands the items on which a mathematical operation is performed. For example, in the expression $2 + 3$, the operands are 2 and 3, and the operation is addition.

operating system a program that controls a computer and makes it possible for users to enter and run their own programs.

A completely unprogrammed computer is incapable of recognizing keystrokes on its keyboard or displaying messages on its screen. Most computers are therefore set up so that, when first turned on, they automatically begin running a small program supplied in read-only memory (ROM), or occasionally in another form (*see* BOOT). This program in turn enables the computer to load its operating system from disk, though some small microcomputers have complete operating systems in ROM.

Under the control of the operating system, the computer recognizes and obeys commands typed by the user. In addition, the operating system provides built-in routines that allow the user's program to perform input-output operations without specifying the exact hardware configuration of the computer. A computer running under one operating system cannot run programs designed to be run under another operating system, even on the same computer. For articles on specific operating systems, *see* CP/M; MS-DOS; UNIX; MVS; OS/2; VM/SP; WINDOWS (MICROSOFT); LINUX; MAC OS; BEOS.

operations research the mathematical modeling of repetitive human activities, such as those involved in traffic flow, assembly lines, and military campaigns. Operations research makes extensive use of computer simulation.

optical character recognition (OCR) the recognition of printed or handwritten characters in an image of a piece of paper. OCR software is commonly used with scanners so that information received on paper will not have to be retyped into the computer. A difficulty is that the computer usually cannot recognize letters and digits with complete certainty, so it has to make intelligent guesses based on the spellings of known words. For example, if you type "chack" an OCR device is likely to read it as "check." Obviously, OCR has difficulty distinguishing l from 1 or O from 0; so do humans if they don't know the context. Information obtained through OCR should be carefully checked for accuracy. *See also* SCANNER.

optical disk a high-density storage device that stores information by etching tiny grooves in plastic with a laser. *See* CD-ROM and references there; WORM.

option buttons small circles in a dialog box, only one of which can be

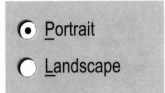

FIGURE 182. OPTION BUTTONS

chosen at a time. The chosen button is black and the others are white. Choosing any button with the mouse causes all the other buttons in the set to be cleared. Because option buttons work like the buttons on older car radios, they are sometimes called *radio buttons*.

Option key a key on the Macintosh keyboard that acts as another kind of Shift key, allowing special characters to be typed quickly. *See also* COMMAND KEY; MODIFIER KEY.

Oracle a leading producer of database software. Oracle Corporation is headquartered in Redwood Shores, California. Web address: http://www.oracle.com.

Orange Book
   1. the official standard for compact discs that can be recorded by the user. *See* CD-ROM.
   2. the U.S. Government's *Trusted Computer System Evaluation Criteria,* published in 1985 and defining standards for computer security.

ORB (**O**bject **R**equest **B**roker) a system that allows objects to connect to other objects over a network. See CORBA for a description of one set of standards that define how ORBs connect different components.

order of magnitude a factor-of-10 difference in size. If one number is 10 times larger than another, they differ by one order of magnitude. Personal computers have sped up by two orders of magnitude — that is, a factor of 100 — since the early days of the IBM PC.
   More formally, the order of magnitude is the exponent in exponential notation. *See* EXPONENTIAL NOTATION.

org suffix indicating that an E-MAIL address or WEB SITE is at a nonprofit organization.

OR gate (Figure 183) a logic gate whose output is 1 when either or both of the inputs is 1, as shown in the table:

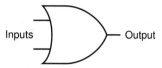

FIGURE 183. OR GATE (LOGIC SYMBOL)

Inputs		Output
0	0	0
0	1	1
1	0	1
1	1	1

See also LOGIC CIRCUITS; COMPUTER ARCHITECTURE.

orphan

1. the last line of a paragraph if it appears by itself as the first line of a page. Some word processors automatically adjust page breaks to avoid creating orphans. *See also* WIDOW.

2. a computer product that is no longer supported by its manufacturer, or whose manufacturer is out of business. For example, the Amiga is now an orphan computer.

OS/2 a multitasking, virtual memory operating system for 386 and higher PC-compatible computers. OS/2 was an important predecessor of Windows 95 (another descendant of the same IBM-Microsoft joint development project) but is now declining in popularity.

Like Windows 95, OS/2 provides multitasking, extended memory, a graphical user interface, and the ability to multitask DOS programs as well as programs written for OS/2. Versions 2.1 and up also provide some integration of Windows 3.1 applications into OS/2.

OS/2 was originally developed by Microsoft in cooperation with IBM. Since version 2 it has been solely an IBM product, competing against newer versions of Windows. *See also* MULTITASKING; VIRTUAL MEMORY; SWAP SPACE; WINDOWS; WARP; WORKPLACE SHELL; INI FILE.

OS/360 the operating system released with the IBM 360 in the early 1960s, and which formed the basis of many subsequent operating systems (OS/VS2, MVT, MVS, etc.). *See also* TSO; JCL; MVS.

oscilloscope an instrument for viewing sound waves or electrical waveforms.

OSI *see* DATA COMMUNICATION.

OSR (OEM Service Release) any of several updates to Windows 95 that were issued to original equipment manufacturers (OEMs, companies that bundle Windows 95 with their computers). The last OSR, number 2.5, was issued in February 1998.

outdent to mark the first line of a paragraph by letting it extend into the left margin; HANGING INDENT; the opposite of INDENT. The entry terms in this dictionary are outdented.

FIGURE 184. OUTLINE (DEFINITION 1)

outline
   1.   a graphical image showing only the edges of an object.

```
I. Animal classification
   A. mammals
          1. dogs and wolves
                 a. pets
                 b. wild animals
          2. cats
                 a. domestic
                 b. large cats
          3. primates
   B. marsupials
```

FIGURE 185. OUTLINE (DEFINITION 2)

   2.   a way of representing the main points of a text without giving all the details. People have been making outlines on paper for centuries, but a computer can simplify the process in two ways. First, with a word processor, it is easy to create a document by first typing an outline of it, and then going back and filling in the sections one by one. Second, software has been developed to let you display just the desired parts of an outline while concealing the rest. While you are working on one section, the details of other sections, even if they have already been written, can be removed from the screen.

Outlook Express the e-mail-reading software provided with Microsoft Windows and also made available by Microsoft for other operating systems. A more elaborate commercial version is called Outlook.

output the information that a computer generates as a result of its calculations. Computer output may be either printed on paper, displayed on a monitor screen, or stored on magnetic tapes or disks.

output device a device that shows, prints, or presents the results of a computer's work. Examples of output devices include MONITORS, PRINTERS, and IMAGESETTERS.

overflow the error condition that arises when the result of a calculation is a number too big to be represented in the available space. For example, adding $65,535 + 1$ will cause an overflow on a computer that uses 16-bit unsigned integers, because $2^{16} - 1 = 65,535$ is the largest integer representable in that format. (Or, worse, if the computer does not detect overflows, it may simply compute $65,535 + 1 = 0$ without letting you know anything is wrong.)

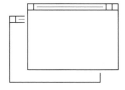

FIGURE 186. OVERLAID WINDOWS

overlaid windows windows that can overlap; when they do, one window hides the parts of others that are behind it (Fig. 186). To bring another window to the front, move the mouse pointer into it and click the button. *Contrast* TILED WINDOWS; CASCADE.

overwrite to write over information that is already on a disk. For example, if you copy a file called ABC.TXT onto a disk that already has a file with the same name, some operating systems will ask you whether you want to overwrite the old file. If you say no, the new file will not be copied.

P

packet a group of consecutive characters sent from one computer to another over a network. For an example, *see* XMODEM. On many local-area networks, all communications are in the form of packets that begin with labels indicating the machine to which they are addressed. *See* X.25.

packet radio the transmission of data (in packets) by radio. It is a fast-growing hobby among radio amateurs ("hams") and also has commercial applications as a way of linking computers without wires.

A typical amateur packet system consists of a computer linked by a terminal-node controller (TNC) to a VHF radio transmitter and receiver. The TNC constructs and recognizes packets. The packet radio protocol effectively prevents two systems from transmitting at the same time, and all data are error-checked. Packet systems are often used to run bulletin boards (*see* BBS). Unlike telephone-line BBSs, packet BBSs are inherently multiuser systems because each packet contains a label indicating its sender and receiver. Thus, the computer can keep track of many users concurrently.

Commercial packet systems often involve portable computer terminals carried by delivery or service personnel. The terminals are linked by radio to a main computer many miles away. *See also* AX.25.

packet switching a technique that enables many computers to share a single communication channel, such as a cable, by transmitting all data in packets which specify the machine to which they are addressed. *See* PACKET.

page
    1. a section of memory that is accessible at one time. *See* VIRTUAL MEMORY.
    2. information available on the World Wide Web; see WEB PAGE; HOME PAGE.

page fault the situation that arises when the computer needs to access an area of memory that has been swapped out to disk. *See* VIRTUAL MEMORY.

page frame an indication of the edges of the paper displayed by your computer's software. The area around the page frame is called the *pasteboard*.

page layout software software specially designed for creating CAMERA-READY COPY. Page layout programs, such as PageMaker, QuarkXPress, and Corel Ventura Publisher, allow the desktop publisher to combine many separate files of different types into a specified design. These special designs, called TEMPLATES or STYLESHEETS, pro-

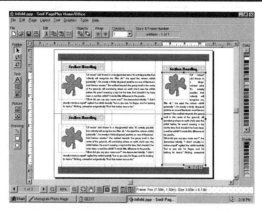

FIGURE 187. PAGE LAYOUT SOFTWARE

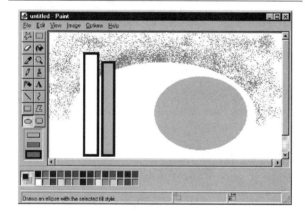

FIGURE 188. PAINT PROGRAM

vide a framework to put the individual elements into. Most programs come with a library of predefined stylesheets.

Page layout software also allows more control over typography than most word processors. *See* DESKTOP PUBLISHING; FRAME.

paint program one type of program for drawing pictures on a personal computer. The user draws with the mouse pointer (or a graphics tablet), and commands are provided for drawing circles, lines, rectangles, and other shapes, as well as for drawing freehand and choosing colors.

Paint programs treat the picture as a grid of pixels (*see* PIXEL; BITMAP). Shadings are easy to produce by manipulating the color of each individual pixel. It is hard to move an element of the picture if it is not where you want it. *Contrast* DRAW PROGRAM.

More sophisticated paint programs are called *photopaint programs* because of their ability to retouch photographs and produce realistic images. *See* PHOTOPAINT PROGRAM.

PAL (**P**hase-**A**lternate-**L**ine) the type of color TV signal used in Great Britain and many other countries. The screen consists of 625 lines, interlaced, and a complete scan takes 1/25 second. Color information is modulated on a 4.43-MHz subcarrier. *Contrast* NTSC; SECAM.

palette a set of colors chosen from a much larger set. For instance, the original IBM VGA can display more than 250,000 different colors, but the programmer or user must choose a palette of no more than 256 to use at a time. The whole set of displayable colors is also sometimes called a palette.

Palm Pilot a popular handheld computer made by Palm Computing, Inc. of Santa Clara, California (`www.palm.com`); the first in a series that now includes the Palm III, Palm V, and Palm VII. All models include software for personal information management and can transfer data to and from personal computers. The newest version includes wireless Internet access.

pan (animation and 3-D software) to move the viewing area left or right to see additional sections of the scene.

Pantone Matching System (PMS) a color matching and calibration system designed by the Pantone company. (Web address: `http://www.pantone.com`.) There are a wide variety of products all keyed to the same numbering system. If you want a certain color, you can specify it by its Pantone number and be assured of consistent reproduction. Some software also utilizes the Pantone system. A competing system is TRUMATCH. *See* COLOR.

paper sizes *see* A4; FOOLSCAP; LEGAL SIZE; LETTER SIZE; PAPER SIZES (ISO); QUARTO.

paper sizes (ISO) a set of standard sizes of paper used everywhere except the United States, of which A4 is the best known (*see* A4). The sizes are shown in Table 14. Each size is made by cutting the next larger size in half, and all sizes have the same height-to-width ratio (1.414:1). A0 paper has an area of 1 square meter, and B0 paper is 1 meter wide.

Note that A4 paper is usually mailed in C6 or DL envelopes.

These standards are administered by the International Standards Organization (ISO). They were formerly a German industrial standard (**D**eutsche **I**ndustrie-**N**orm) and were known as DIN paper sizes.

TABLE 14
ISO PAPER SIZES

Each size is made by cutting the next larger size in half.

	mm (exact)	inches (approximate)
A0	841 × 1189	33.1 × 46.8
A1	594 × 841	23.4 × 33.1
A2	420 × 594	16.5 × 23.4
A3	297 × 420	11.7 × 16.5
A4	210 × 297	8.3 × 11.7
A5	148 × 210	5.8 × 8.3
A6	105 × 148	4.1 × 5.8
B0	1000 × 1414	39.4 × 55.7
B1	707 × 1000	27.8 × 39.4
B2	500 × 707	19.7 × 27.8
B3	353 × 500	13.9 × 19.7
B4	250 × 353	9.8 × 13.9
B5	176 × 250	6.9 × 9.8

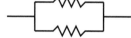

FIGURE 189. PARALLEL CIRCUIT (TWO RESISTORS)

parallel flowing through more than one path at once:

1. two electronic circuit elements are connected in parallel if the electric current will reach the same destination by flowing through either element. Figure 189 shows two resistors connected in parallel. *Contrast* SERIES.

2. parallel data transmission is the transmission of several bits at the same time over separate wires; it is usually faster than serial transmission (*see* SERIAL). In connecting a printer to a microcomputer, it is important to know whether the printer requires a parallel or a serial (RS-232) connection.

3. a parallel computer has more than one CPU and can therefore execute more than one instruction at the same time.

parallel columns adjacent columns of printed text in which the second column is not a continuation of the first; instead, the second column may give notes, comments, or a translation into another language. Many Canadian documents are printed in parallel columns of English and French. *Contrast* NEWSPAPER COLUMNS.

parallel port an output device that lets a computer transmit data to another device using parallel transmission — that is, several bits sent simultaneously over separate wires. It is common for a microcomputer to have a parallel port that is connected to a printer. *See* IEEE 1284.

parallel printer a printer that connects to a computer's parallel port (rather than, for example, to a serial port or a network cable).

parallel processing computation carried out at the same time on different CPUs, or on a CPU that can execute more than one instruction at the exact same time.

By contrast, most multitasking is accomplished by making a single CPU switch its attention among several tasks. This is called concurrent processing or timesharing.

parameter a symbol that will be replaced in a procedure by supplied values when the procedure is called. *See* ACTUAL PARAMETER; FORMAL PARAMETER.

Here is a Pascal program containing a procedure called swap. The procedure uses two parameters: x and y. The first time the procedure is called, the variables a and b are substituted for the parameters. The next time b and c are used.

```pascal
PROGRAM swapnum (INPUT, OUTPUT);
VAR a, b, c : INTEGER;

  PROCEDURE swap(VAR x, y : INTEGER);
  VAR temp : INTEGER;
  BEGIN
     temp := x;
     x := y;
     y := temp
  END;

BEGIN { Main program }
  readln(a,b,c);
  writeln('a=',a,' b=',b,' c=',c);
  swap(a,b);
  writeln('a=',a,' b=',b,' c=',c);
  swap(b,c)
  writeln('a=',a,' b=',b,' c=',c)
END.
```

Here is a sample run of this program with the numbers 239, 535, and 66 as input:

```
a=239 b=535 c=66
a=535 b=239 c=66
a=535 b=66  c=239
```

The names that are used for the parameters in the procedure declaration (x and y in this case) are known as the *formal parameters*. The names used when the procedure is called (a, b, and c in this case) are known as actual parameters.

parent an object that gives its properties to a newly created object (the CHILD). Updating the properties of the parent object affect the children, but changing the properties of the child do not affect the parent. *See* DRAW PROGRAM; OBJECT-ORIENTED PROGRAMMING.

parity the property of whether a number is odd or even. Often, when groups of bits (1's and 0's) are being transmitted or stored, an extra bit is added so that the total number of 1's is always odd (or, alternatively, always even). This is called the parity of the data.

One incorrectly transmitted bit will change the parity, making it possible to detect the error; the parity would be unchanged only if there were two (or an even number of) incorrect bits. Thus, if errors are frequent, some of them will be detected and the recipient of the information will have some warning that errors are present.

If you are setting up a computer terminal for an older system and do not know how to set the parity and related parameters, try the following, which is the most popular combination:

Baud rate	9600
Parity	None
Data bits	8
Stop bits	1
Duplex	Full

This is often described briefly as "9600,N,8,1." A popular alternative is to use even parity with 7 data bits. A terminal set to the wrong parity can often be recognized because about half of the characters are incorrect, while the rest are received normally.

The memory of many PC-compatible computers is parity-checked to detect erroneously recorded bits. The message PARITY ERROR is displayed if a memory chip fails the test.

park to disengage the head of a hard disk so that the disk will be protected from possible damage when the computer is moved or shaken. Most hard disks nowadays park themselves when powered off.

parsing the analysis, by computer, of the structure of statements in a human or artificial language. For instance, DOS has to parse the command

```
dir b: /p
```

to determine that dir is the name of the command, b: specifies the files to be shown, and p is another parameter (in this case, it means "pause when the screen is full"). Compilers and interpreters have to parse

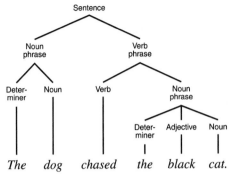

FIGURE 190. PARSED STRUCTURE OF A SENTENCE

(1)	Sentence	→	Noun Phrase + Verb Phrase
(2)	Noun Phrase	→	Determiner + Noun
(3)	Noun Phrase	→	Determiner + Adjective + Noun
(4)	Verb Phrase	→	Verb + Noun Phrase
(5)	Determiner	→	*the*
(6)	Noun	→	*dog*
(7)	Noun	→	*cat*
(8)	Adjective	→	*black*
(9)	Verb	→	*chased*

FIGURE 191. GRAMMAR RULES USED FOR PARSING

statements in programming languages. (*See* COMPILER, INTERPRETER.) Programs that accept natural-language input have to parse sentences in human languages.

Parsing is done by comparing the string to be parsed to a *grammar*, which defines possible structures. For example, Figure 190 shows the structure of the sentence "The dog chased the black cat." Figure 191 shows a small part of the grammar of English.

Parsing can be done either *top-down* or *bottom-up*. In top-down parsing, the computer starts by looking for a particular constituent. It consults the grammar to determine what this constituent consists of, and then looks for those constituents instead, thus:

```
Look for Sentence
Rule 1 : Sentence consists of Noun Phrase + Verb Phrase
  Look for Noun Phrase
  Rule 2: Noun Phrase consists of Determiner + Noun
    Look for Determiner
      Accept Determiner the from input string
    Look for Noun
      Accept Noun dog from input string
  Look for Verb Phrase (etc.)
```

The process is complete when the input string is empty and all of the elements of a sentence have been found.

In bottom-up parsing, the computer accepts elements from the input string and tries to put them together, thus:

Accept *the*, which is a Determiner
Accept *dog*, which is a Noun
Determiner + Noun make a Noun Phrase
Accept *chased*, which is a Verb
Accept *the*, which is a Determiner
Accept *black*, which is an Adjective
Accept *cat*, which is a Noun
Determiner + Adjective + Noun make a Noun Phrase
Verb + Noun Phrase make a Verb Phrase
Noun Phrase + Verb Phrase make a Sentence

Parsing algorithms must be able to *backtrack* (back up and try alternatives) because the grammar provides alternatives. For example, a noun phrase may or may not contain an adjective, and a word like *leaves* can be a verb or a noun. Further, parsing algorithms usually use *recursion* to handle the recursive structure of human languages. For example, a noun phrase can contain a noun phrase, which can contain another noun phrase, as in *the discoverer of the solution to the problem. See* RECURSION; BACKTRACKING; NATURAL LANGUAGE PROCESSING.

Part 15 device a radio transmitter that is allowed to operate without a license under the terms of Part 15 of the Federal Communications Commission's regulations (known to lawyers as 47 CFR 15). Examples include cordless telephones, wireless intercoms, and some kinds of wireless computer communication devices (wireless LANs). Because individual Part 15 transmitters are not licensed, there is no way to guarantee that they will not interfere with each other, but spread-spectrum technology makes interference unlikely. By contrast, licensed transmitters can be given exclusive use of a particular frequency in a particular area. *See also* SPREAD-SPECTRUM.

partition a part of a HARD DISK that is treated by the computer as if it were a separate disk drive. Naturally, most hard disks consist of only one partition. Multiple partitions are sometimes used with very large drives, especially if the drive is larger than those the operating system was designed for.

Under DOS, Windows, and OS/2, the FDISK command sets the partition structure of a hard disk. Any change in the partition structure makes the previous contents of the disk completely unreadable, so don't run FDISK unless you have backed up all your data first.

Pascal a programming language developed by Niklaus Wirth in the early 1970s. Pascal is essentially a modernized version of ALGOL, and it has greatly influenced the design of other languages, as well as becoming popular in its own right. *See* TURBO PASCAL for information on a popular version.

```
PROGRAM primecheck;
  { This is Turbo Pascal. }
VAR n,i,max: INTEGER;
    continue: BOOLEAN;
    status: STRING[13];
BEGIN
 REPEAT
  write('Enter a whole number (type 0 to quit): ');
  readln(n);
  status := ' is prime';
  IF n>2 THEN continue := TRUE
         ELSE continue := FALSE;
  i := 1;
  max := TRUNC(SQRT(n));
     { max is the largest divisor that must be
       checked to see if n is prime}
  WHILE continue DO
    BEGIN
      i := i + 1;
      IF (n MOD i)=0 THEN
        BEGIN
          status := ' is not prime';
          continue := FALSE
        END;
      continue := (i < max);
    END; {end of WHILE loop}
  write(n);
  writeln(status);
 UNTIL n=0
END.
```

FIGURE 192. A PASCAL PROGRAM

Fig. 192 shows a sample program in Pascal. A Pascal program
consists of:

- A PROGRAM statement to give the program a name (and, in older
  versions, to declare input and output files);

- Declarations of global variables;

- Declarations of procedures and functions;

- The keyword BEGIN, the action part of the main program, the
  keyword END, and finally a period to mark the end.

Procedures and functions, in turn, can contain their own declarations,
including more procedures and functions (a kind of nesting that is not
permitted in C).

Pascal is not case-sensitive (e.g., X and x are equivalent). In this
book, uppercase letters are used for *reserved words* (keywords that

cannot be redefined, such as IF, THEN, and ELSE), and lowercase letters for everything else.

Semicolons are used as separators *between* statements. Thus a statement ends with a semicolon only when what follows is the beginning of another statement. This contrasts with C and PL/I, which end every statement with a semicolon regardless of the context.

Comments in Pascal are enclosed in braces, { }, or the symbols (* *). A statement does not have to fit on one line; lines can be broken anywhere that blank space is permitted.

Pascal provides four standard data types: real, integer, Boolean, and character. Integer variables can take on only values that are whole numbers or the negatives of whole numbers. Real variables can take on numerical values that include fractional parts, such as 23.432. Boolean variables are logic variables that can have only two possible values: true or false. Char variables can take on single character values. Here is an example of how to declare variables:

```
VAR count, total: INTEGER;
    average: REAL;
    initial: CHAR;
```

A character string is simply an array of char items. Most modern versions of Pascal, however, have added variable-length strings.

An assignment statement in Pascal looks like this:

```
x := 3;
```

This statement gives the value 3 to the variable x. Note that the symbol for assignment is :=, not =. The arithmetic operators are + for addition, − for subtraction, * for multiplication, / for floating-point division, div for integer division, and mod for modulo (remainder from division). Some implementations have added ** for exponentiation.

The two input commands are read and readln, each of which can take any number of arguments. The difference is that readln consumes an entire line of input (ignoring anything after the data that it is told to read), while read consumes only the data that you ask for. Thus, you can read two numbers from the same line of input by using two read statements in succession, or by using a readln with two arguments.

The two output commands are write and writeln, which likewise take any number of arguments. The difference between them is that writeln starts a new line after writing its output. You can specify the number of spaces to be used to write a number; thus write(i:6) means to write the value of i right-justified in 6 character positions, and write(x:6:3) means that x should occupy 6 character positions of which 3 are to the right of the decimal point.

For file input and output, read, readln, write, and writeln take an optional first argument indicating the file. Details of how this is done are somewhat implementation-dependent.

The IF-THEN-ELSE statement can be used to control the actions of a program. For example:

```pascal
IF x > 0 THEN
   writeln('x is positive')
ELSE
   writeln('x is negative');
```

Note the general structure:

IF *condition* THEN *statement* ELSE *statement*

To put a series of statements where the language permits only one, use the keywords BEGIN and END to group the statements into blocks, like this:

```pascal
IF x > 0 THEN
  BEGIN
    writeln('The value of x is positive.');
    writeln('The square root of x is:',SQRT(x):6:3)
  END
ELSE
  BEGIN
    writeln('The value of x is negative.');
    writeln('It has no real square root.')
  END
```

Pascal has three kinds of loops, REPEAT, WHILE, and FOR. Each of the following program segments prints the whole numbers from 1 to 10:

```pascal
number := 0;
REPEAT
   number := number + 1;
   writeln(number);
UNTIL number >= 10;

number := 1;
WHILE number <= 10 DO
  BEGIN
    writeln(number);
    number := number + 1
  END;

FOR number := 1 TO 10 DO
  writeln(number);
```

Arrays are declared by listing the highest and lowest allowable values for their subscripts. For example, the declaration

```
VAR officenum: ARRAY[1..20] OF INTEGER;
```

defines officenum as a 20-element one-dimensional array of integers, and the declaration

```
VAR table: ARRAY[0..10,0..15] OF REAL;
```

defines table as being a two-dimensional array of real numbers with 11 rows (labeled 0 to 10) and 16 columns (labeled 0 to 15).

One of the most valuable features of Pascal is the way it encourages the programmer to divide a program cleanly into procedures and functions rather than writing just one long list of instructions. A *procedure* is a miniature Pascal program defined in the declaration section of the main program. The procedure can be executed from the main program simply by giving its name and any parameters that are to be passed to it. Any variables that are declared within the procedure are local to that procedure; like-named variables in different procedures do not conflict. *Functions* are like procedures except that a function returns a value to the calling program. For examples, see PROCEDURE; FUNCTION.

Pascal lets the programmer define new data types that can be used in addition to the four standard types. Pascal also allows the programmer to define sets, and then perform a set operation such as union or intersection. By using a structured data type called a record, it is possible to organize related data of different types. *See* RECORD. Fig. 192 is a sample program written in Pascal.

See also MODULA-2.

FIGURE 193. BLAISE PASCAL (1623–1662)

Pascal, Blaise (1623–1662) a French mathematician who, in 1642, built a mechanical adding machine that was one of the early forerunners of calculators and computers.

passive matrix an older type of liquid crystal display that produces lower contrast than newer ACTIVE MATRIX displays.

password a secret sequence of typed characters that is required to use a computer system, thus preventing unauthorized persons from gaining access to the computer.

If you are using a password to protect your computer:

- Protect your password. Keep it a secret and don't share it.

- Don't choose an obvious password. Use some imagination and forethought. What would be hard to guess? Your password is not your mantra and should *not* express your personality or indicate in any way who you are.

- Don't use a word in any language; some people crack computers by automatically trying every word in a dictionary.

- Change your password regularly.

paste to transfer material from a holding area into the document you are editing. In Windows 95 and its successors, the keyboard shortcut for *paste* is Ctrl-V. *See* CUT; COPY; CLIPBOARD.

patch to correct a defective piece of software by modifying one or more of the files on which it resides, rather than by installing a complete, corrected copy.

patent legal protection for the design of a machine or mechanical process, preventing others from using the same idea without the inventor's permission. Unlike a copyright, a patent protects an idea itself, not just an expression of the idea. In the United States, a patent remains in force for 17 years.

Computer programs have not traditionally been considered patentable, but some software patents have been issued in recent years and present law and practice are unclear. Integrated circuits are often protected by both patents (for the circuit design) and copyrights (for the artwork from which the tiny etch pattern is made, or for data recorded on the chip). *See also* COPYRIGHT.

path

1. a designation that specifies how to find a file on a disk that has more than one directory. In DOS and related operating systems, paths have either of two forms. For example:

`\AAA\BBB\CCC`

means, "In the root directory there is a directory called AAA. In AAA there is a directory called BBB. In BBB there is a directory or file called CCC."

If the initial backslash is left out, the path starts at the directory currently in use rather than at the root directory. For example, the path

`AAA\BBB\CCC`

means, "In the current directory there is a directory called AAA. In AAA there is a directory called BBB. In BBB there is a directory or file called CCC." Paths in UNIX are written the same way but with forward slashes (/ rather than \).

2. (DOS, OS/2, and Windows) a command that specifies directories in which to search for command files (BAT, COM, and EXE files) if they are not found in the current directory. The PATH command is often included as part of the AUTOEXEC.BAT file so it will always be executed when the machine starts up. For example, if AUTOEXEC.BAT contains the command

```
PATH C:\PROGS
```

then the computer will automatically look on drive C in the directory PROGS, as well as in the current directory. More commonly, the PATH command specifies more than one directory where command files are kept, like this:

```
PATH C:\PROGS;C:\DOS
```

Equivalently, you can set the path as an environment variable, like this:

```
SET PATH=C:\PROGS;C:\DOS
```

In UNIX, PATH is an environment variable, not a command. Paths work much the same way as in DOS, but command files are assumed to be in a directory that is on the path; UNIX does not look for them in the current directory unless the path contains "." (which means "current directory"). *See* DIRECTORY; AUTOEXEC.BAT; HARD DISK MANAGEMENT.

3. a contour or outline. Objects in a draw program are defined by paths. *See* VECTOR GRAPHICS; DRAW PROGRAM; POSTSCRIPT.

4. a line that defines the movement of an object in an animation.

PC 97 a standard promoted by Microsoft in 1997 for personal computers to run Windows 95 or 98. PC 97 computers use the PCI bus and may also include ISA bus slots.

PC 98 a standard promoted by Microsoft in 1998 for personal computers to run Windows 98; successor to the PC 97 standard. PC 98 computers use the PCI bus, and, unlike PC 97 computers, need not contain any ISA slots.

PC 99 a standard promoted by Microsoft and Intel in 1999 for personal computers to run Windows 98 and 2000, the successor to PC 98 and PC 97. PC 99 systems are expected to have a 300-MHz Pentium with 32 MB RAM (slower processors are acceptable in laptops). The main new requirement is ACPI (Advanced Configuration and Power Interface) with features to enable the computer to power on and off quickly without rebooting.

PC 2001 a specification issued by Intel and Microsoft for the design of LEGACY-FREE personal computers, i.e., computers that run the latest PC operating systems but are not burdened by the need for full compatibility with the original PC hardware. *See* LEGACY-FREE. *Compare* PC 97 (predecessor of PC 2001).

PC Card a newer name for PCMCIA expansion cards. *See* PCMCIA.

PC compatibility the ability of a computer to run the same programs and use the same hardware accessories as the original IBM Personal Computer (PC) or newer computers of the same general type. In order to be fully PC-compatible, a computer needs an 8088-family processor (which nowadays means a 386, 486, Pentium, or equivalent). Some other computers can software-emulate a 386 and thereby run PC software on a completely different CPU, such as a Sun RISC CPU or a PowerPC chip.

If a computer merely needs to exchange data with an IBM PC, it need not be IBM-compatible at all; all it needs is a suitable communications medium, such as phone lines or a local-area network, with suitable software.

PCI (**P**eripheral **C**omponent **I**nterface) an improved bus for PC-compatible computers, introduced by Intel in 1992. PCI is faster than EISA and has been expanded to 64 bits to meet the needs of the Pentium processor. PCI-bus computers can use a bus interface unit on the motherboard to connect to EISA or ISA cards, so that the same motherboard has both PCI and ISA slots. *See* BUS.

PCMCIA (**P**ersonal **C**omputer **M**emory **C**ard **I**nternational **A**ssociation) an organization that defines standards for connecting peripherals to miniaturized computers such as notebooks and laptops. The standard ISA, EISA, PCI, and VLB buses are too bulky for laptop computers; the PCMCIA bus (now known as PC Card and CardBus) is a widely accepted standard. *See* BUS; CARDBUS.

PCX a standard format for graphic image files developed by ZSoft, manufacturer of a popular paint program called PC Paintbrush. PCX files use RUN-LENGTH ENCODING to store bitmaps compactly. (*See* BITMAP, DATA COMPRESSION.)

As the name suggests, PCX files are closely tied to the format of IBM PC video memory; this enables them to be displayed on the PC screen very quickly. The PCX format has been revised several times to support newer video hardware.

In addition to ZSoft products, many other programs also recognize PCX format. Filenames usually end in .PCX. *Compare* TIFF; GIF.

PDA (**p**ersonal **d**igital **a**ssistant) a pocket-sized, special-purpose personal computer that lacks a conventional keyboard. PDAs do such things as send and receive fax messages, maintain an electronic address book and telephone directory, and serve as notepads on which files can be created for subsequent processing on a larger computer.

PDD *see* Portable Digital Document.

PDF (**P**ortable **D**ocument **F**ile) a document that maintains its formatting and displays correctly on any output device. PDF files are viewable with Adobe Acrobat software. Large documents, such as reference books, are often distributed on CD-ROM in PDF format. Unlike HTML, PDF is designed to represent images of printed pages. *See* ADOBE SYSTEMS, INC.

peak a way of measuring the voltage of alternating current from zero volts up to the most positive point. The peak voltage of any symmetrical waveform is exactly half of the peak-to-peak voltage. *See also* PEAK-TO-PEAK; RMS.

peak-to-peak a way of measuring the voltage of alternating current from the most positive to the most negative point. For example, the audio output of a microphone is about 0.002 volt peak-to-peak; the "line out" from a piece of audio equipment is about 1 volt peak-to-peak. Peak-to-peak measurement is used mostly with low-level signals that are viewed on oscilloscopes; ordinary voltmeters usually read rms voltage. The peak-to-peak voltage of a sine wave is $2.828 \times$ the rms voltage. *Contrast* RMS; PEAK.

PEBKAC *(humorous)* (**P**roblem **E**xists **B**etween **K**eyboard **A**nd **C**hair) an uncomplimentary way to indicate that a computer problem is the fault of the user. A legendary, and apparently recurrent, PEBKAC consists of the user mistaking the CD-ROM disk tray for a coffee cup holder and eventually breaking it.

PEEK a function in BASIC that allows the programmer to read the contents of a particular memory location, identified by its address. PEEK was used extensively on small microcomputers in the early 1980s. Its uses depended on the details of the hardware and software. *See also* POKE; BASIC.

FIGURE 194. PELS

pel (picture **el**ement) PIXEL; one of the small dots of which a bitmap image is composed.

FIGURE 195. BITMAP PEN TOOL

pen (in draw or paint programs) a tool used to create lines. Sometimes a similar tool is shown as a pencil. Most programs allow control of the width of the stroke the pen makes, the shape of the nib of the pen, the miter limit, and the shape of the endcaps. These settings are usually under an *Attributes* or sometimes *Preferences* menu item. See your program's manual for details.

Pentium a high-performance microprocessor introduced by Intel in 1993, software-compatible with the 8088 used in the original IBM PC.

The name "Pentium" is from the Greek word *pente* meaning "five." If the original numbering scheme had continued, the Pentium would have been known as the 586. *See* MICROPROCESSOR.

Pentium II a high-performance microprocessor introduced by Intel in 1997 as a successor to the Pentium and Pentium Pro. The CPU and its L1 and L2 caches are packaged in a single module that plugs into the motherboard via an edge connector. For specifications *see* MICROPROCESSOR.

If the original numbering system had continued, the Pentium II would have been known as the 786.

Pentium Pro a high-performance 64-bit microprocessor introduced by Intel in 1996 to replace the Pentium; it runs the same software faster by making additional use of superscalar techniques (*see* SUPER-SCALAR PROCESSOR). That is, different CPU instructions can execute simultaneously rather than one after another. For specifications *see* MICROPROCESSOR.

If the original numbering scheme had continued, the Pentium Pro would have been known as the 686.

peripheral a device connected to a computer. Examples of peripherals include terminals, tape drives, disk drives, and printers.

Perl (**P**ractical **E**xtraction and **R**eport **L**anguage) a programming language developed by Larry Wall for writing utilities that perform large amounts of string handling, text file processing, and interaction with the operating system. Like AWK and REXX, which it resembles, Perl

```
#!/usr/local/bin/perl

@path = split(/:/,$ENV{'PATH'});
$n = 1 + $#path;

print "You have $n directories on your path.\n";
print "They are:\n";
foreach $i (0..$#path) { print "$path[$i] \n"; }
```

FIGURE 196. PERL PROGRAMMING EXAMPLE

is normally interpreted, not compiled. It is designed to minimize the programming effort needed for computations that are relatively simple and quick.

Fig. 196 shows a simple Perl program. The overall syntax resembles C. Numbers and strings are interconvertible and are not distinguished; as far as Perl is concerned, 4 = '4'.

Every variable name begins with a character indicating its type: $ for scalars (numbers and strings), @ for ordinary arrays, and % for associative arrays (arrays whose elements are retrieved by keyword rather than by position). Array elements are numbered from 0; the operator $# retrieves the index of the highest element, which is one less than the total number of elements. Lines that begin with # are comments.

Under UNIX, Perl programs are often called *scripts* and begin with the line

```
#!/usr/local/bin/perl
```

so that if the program is passed to UNIX as a SHELL SCRIPT, it will be given to the Perl interpreter for execution.

On the WORLD WIDE WEB, Perl is often used to implement web pages that perform computations. Instead of writing a web page in HTML, the programmer writes a Perl program that generates the HTML from other sources of information, such as database files, calculations, and even the user's menu choices. *See also* AWK; REXX; HTML; CGI.

permission an attribute of a file that indicates who is allowed to read or modify it. For example, the UNIX command

```
chmod ugo+r-wx myfile.txt
```

sets permissions for the *u*ser, *g*roup, and *o*ther users of file `myfile.txt` by adding read permission (+r) and removing write and execute permission (-wx).

personal computer a computer designed to be used by only one person, either at home or in a business setting. One of the first personal computers was the Digital Equipment Corporation PDP-8, a minicomputer often used in scientific laboratories in the early 1970s. *See also* IBM PC, PS/1, PS/2; MACINTOSH.

personal digital assistant *see* PDA.

PERT (**P**rogram **E**valuation and **R**eview **T**echnique) a method for project planning by analyzing the time required for each step. *See* PROJECT MANAGEMENT.

peta- metric prefix meaning ×1,000,000,000,000,000 (10^{15}). *Peta-* is apparently derived from the Greek word for "to fly" or "to soar." *See* METRIC PREFIXES.

PGA
   1. **p**in **g**rid **a**rray, the arrangement of pins on a Pentium or similar microprocessor, making it possible to plug the processor into a socket.
   2. **P**rofessional **G**raphics **A**dapter, an early high-performance graphics system for the IBM PC, marketed in the mid-1980s.

PGP (**P**retty **G**ood **P**rivacy) a public-key encryption system developed by Philip Zimmerman. More information about PGP can be found at http://www.nai.com.

phono plug *See* RCA PLUG.

Photo CD Kodak's proprietary format for storing digitized photographs on CD-ROM in a format similar to that of CD-I, viewable with a computer that has suitable software or with a "Photo CD player" that attaches to a TV set. Each photograph is stored in several different sizes ranging up to 4 megabytes per image (16 megabytes in the case of professional-grade Photo CDs).
   Photo CDs use a data compression algorithm that has not been made public; all software that reads them must be based on code licensed from Kodak. Further, Photo CDs are not ISO 9660 compliant; that is, they do not consist of files that the computer's operating system can recognize. Special software is needed to read the disc even if the files are not to be decoded.

photograph a continuous-tone image created with a camera. Because photographs closely reproduce what we are able to see with our eyes, we credit them with being more "real" than drawings. Photographs make any document more interesting and convey much more information to the readers than words alone.
   You can choose to use photographs from collections of stock photographs or have some of your own pictures scanned in. If the original photograph is deficient in some way, it can be altered digitally with a PHOTOPAINT PROGRAM. It's best to scan the photo at the finished size and at the resolution of the output device (usually your laser printer). The contrast and brightness of the image can be adjusted while scanning it. You'll notice that photographs (especially color ones) create large files. A $3\frac{1}{2}$×5-inch color snapshot, scanned at 100%, 300 DPI, 24 bit (millions of colors), creates a 3.3-megabyte file. Transporting and managing files of this size can be quite a headache! Files of black-and-white photos are smaller; they don't have to include as much information.

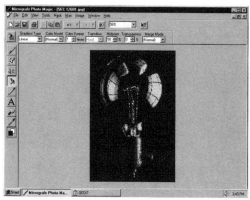

FIGURE 197. PHOTOPAINT PROGRAM

Once the photograph is digitized, you can use a photopaint program to alter it. Spots and flaws can be removed, distracting elements erased, backgrounds changed, or the overall color balance adjusted. (*See* RETOUCHING). Then import the digital photo into your page layout or word processing program, or publish it on the World Wide Web. *See also* DIGITAL CAMERA.

photography, digital the use of digital cameras to take pictures. *See* DIGITAL CAMERA.

photopaint program a type of bitmap editing program with special tools and filters for manipulating photographs. You can also create illustrations from scratch with the drawing tools provided. *Compare* PAINT PROGRAM. *Contrast* DRAW PROGRAM.

In many ways, photopaint programs are the professional versions of the limited paint programs that come with operating systems. They are proportionately difficult to learn and master. Be prepared to spend enough time reading the manual and experimenting. *See also* ADD NOISE; AIRBRUSH; BLUR; BRIGHTNESS; CONTRAST; CLONE; EDGE DETECT; FILTER; MAGIC WAND; MOTION BLUR; PIXELATE.

phreak (or **phone phreak**) a person who makes a game of defrauding telephone companies by means of fake control signals, stolen credit card numbers, and the like.

pi the Greek letter π, which stands for a special number that is approximately equal to 3.14159. If the radius of a circle is r, then the circumference is $2\pi r$ and the area is πr^2.

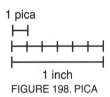

FIGURE 198. PICA

pica

    1.   a pica typewriter prints 10 characters per inch; so do most fixed-pitch computer printers.

    2.   in typesetting, a pica is $\frac{1}{6}$ inch, or 12 points.

pick tool a mouse cursor shaped like an arrow that is used to pick up or pick out (select) objects in an image.

pico- metric prefix meaning $\div 1{,}000{,}000{,}000{,}000$. *Pico-* is derived from a Spanish word that means, among other things, "small quantity." *See* METRIC PREFIXES.

pictograph

    1.   a picture that represents an idea. Computer icons are a type of pictograph.

    2.   a bar graph that uses stacked or stretched symbols instead of plain vertical bars. Although this lends some visual interest to the graph, it can also be confusing if not handled correctly.

| Case fraction | Built fraction | Piece fraction |

FIGURE 199. CASE VS. BUILT VS. PIECE FRACTION

piece fraction a fraction constructed of three characters: small numerals for the numerator and denominator separated by a forward slash or a horizontal bar ($^1/_2$, or $\frac{1}{2}$). *Contrast* BUILT FRACTION; CASE FRACTION.

pie chart a type of chart that resembles a pie and graphically shows the relative size of different subcategories of a whole.

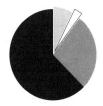

FIGURE 200. PIE CHART

PIF (**P**rogram **I**nformation **F**ile) in Microsoft Windows, a file that contains information about how to run a DOS program — how much memory it requires, whether it can run in a window, whether it can multitask, and the like. PIF files have names ending in `.pif`.

pilcrow the symbol ¶, which is used to mark the beginning of a new paragraph when the text is set with continuous paragraphs. The pilcrow can also be used as a footnote symbol. *See* FOOTNOTE.

pin
    1. a movable stiff wire that presses on the ribbon of a dot-matrix printer under computer control in order to make dots on the paper. A 9-pin printer produces readable but inelegant type. Some 9-pin printers have a near-letter-quality mode in which they simulate 18 pins by making two passes across each line; the result resembles the type from a cloth-ribbon typewriter. Printers with 24 pins produce sharp letter-quality text.
    2. a stiff prong in an electronic connector. For example, a VGA video connector has 15 pins; a serial port connector has 9 or 25 pins.

PIN (**P**ersonal **I**dentification **N**umber) a number used as a password by a computer user.

ping the command, on a TCP/IP network, that sends a test data packet to another site and waits for a response.

ping flooding the practice of maliciously disrupting a computer by *pinging* it continuously, i.e., flooding it with test data packets to which it must respond. Also known as SMURFING. *See* DENIAL-OF-SERVICE ATTACK.

pipe
    1. in UNIX, DOS, Windows, OS/2, and other operating systems, a way of stringing two programs together so that the output of one of them is fed to the other as input. For example, the DOS command

```
C:\> dir | sort | more
```

invokes `dir` (which lists the names of the files on a disk), feeds its output to `sort` (which puts the items in alphabetical order), and feeds that output to `more` (which displays it one screenful at a time).

Under DOS, the three programs execute in succession, each writing its output on a file that is read by the next. Under UNIX, however, they run concurrently and communicate without writing the piped data to disk. *See also* BROKEN PIPE.

2. the character | (the pipe symbol).

pipeline a device within a CPU that enables it to fetch (read) instructions in advance of executing them, so that whenever an instruction is completed, the next instruction is ready to execute. This is a way of partly overcoming the Von Neumann bottleneck. *See also* COMPUTER ARCHITECTURE.

piracy the unauthorized copying of software, which is forbidden by law. *See* SOFTWARE LICENSE; COPYRIGHT.

It is in your own best interests not to use pirated software. You cannot get (nor should you expect) user support from the software vendor if you are running an illegal copy. You won't have a copy of the manual. You are at greater risk of VIRUSES because, commonly, you don't know exactly where your copy came from. And if the software company isn't getting the revenues from sales of their program, they will not be able to maintain the program (i.e., fix the bugs) or to keep adding new features. Why should other people pay them when you don't?

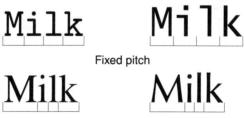

Fixed pitch

Proportional pitch

FIGURE 201. PITCH, FIXED VS. PROPORTIONAL

pitch the number of characters per inch in a particular size and style of type. Fixed-pitch type has every character the same width; proportional-pitch type has some characters wider than others (e.g., *M* wider than *I*), and the pitch can be measured only approximately as the average of many different letters.

pitch (monitor) *see* DOT PITCH.

pivot table a multi-dimensional data table that can be rearranged to allow different views of the data. For example, suppose you need to keep track of a budget with two divisions and three spending categories for three months. Here is the original data:

```
DIVISION        MONTH      CATEGORY     AMOUNT
   NORTH      January     EMPLOYEES        564
   NORTH      January      SUPPLIES        320
   NORTH      January          RENT         40
   NORTH     February     EMPLOYEES        602
   NORTH     February      SUPPLIES        348
   NORTH     February          RENT         40
   NORTH        March     EMPLOYEES        620
   NORTH        March      SUPPLIES        352
   NORTH        March          RENT         40
   SOUTH      January     EMPLOYEES        212
   SOUTH      January      SUPPLIES        180
   SOUTH      January          RENT         20
   SOUTH     February     EMPLOYEES        240
   SOUTH     February      SUPPLIES        200
   SOUTH     February          RENT         20
   SOUTH        March     EMPLOYEES        265
   SOUTH        March      SUPPLIES        160
   SOUTH        March          RENT         20
```

It would be easier to understand the data if it were arranged in a pivot table, like this:

```
NORTH
             EMPLOYEES   SUPPLIES      RENT     TOTAL
   January         564        320        40       924
  February         602        348        40       990
     March         620        352        40      1012
     TOTAL        1786       1020       120      2926

SOUTH
             EMPLOYEES   SUPPLIES      RENT     TOTAL
   January         212        180        20       412
  February         240        200        20       460
     March         265        160        20       445
     TOTAL         717        540        60      1317
```

Sometimes it helps to rearrange the data. Here are two different ways of doing this:

```
January
             EMPLOYEES   SUPPLIES      RENT     TOTAL
     NORTH         564        320        40       924
     SOUTH         212        180        20       412
     TOTAL         776        500        60      1336

February
             EMPLOYEES   SUPPLIES      RENT     TOTAL
     NORTH         602        348        40       990
     SOUTH         240        200        20       460
     TOTAL         842        548        60      1450
```

```
March
                EMPLOYEES   SUPPLIES      RENT       TOTAL
        NORTH       620        352        40         1012
        SOUTH       265        160        20          445
        TOTAL       885        512        60         1457

****************************************************
EMPLOYEES
                NORTH       SOUTH       TOT
    January       564         212        776
   February       602         240        842
      March       620         265        885
       TOT:      1786         717       2503

SUPPLIES
                NORTH       SOUTH       TOT
    January       320         180        500
   February       348         200        548
      March       352         160        512
       TOT:      1020         540       1560

RENT
                NORTH       SOUTH       TOT
    January        40          20         60
   February        40          20         60
      March        40          20         60
       TOT:       120          60        180
```

Or, you might wish to consolidate all of the spending categories and create a view like this:

```
ALL CATEGORIES

            January   February     March      TOTAL
    NORTH       924        990      1012        2926
    SOUTH       412        460       445        1317
    TOTAL      1336       1450      1457        4243
```

Recent versions of Excel contain a wizard that automatically creates pivot tables.

pixel one of the individual dots that make up a graphical image. For example, a VGA color screen in high-resolution mode consists of a 640×480 pixel array. A program can draw pictures on the screen by controlling the color of each pixel. *See* GRAPHICS.

pixelate, pixelize a photopaint filter that transforms the bitmap into rectangular blocks of uniform color, as if the pixels were much larger than before.

PKCS (**P**ublic-**K**ey **C**ryptography **S**tandards) a set of standards developed by RSA laboratories and others. Information on the web is available at http://www.rsa.com/rsalabs/pubs/PKCS.

FIGURE 202. PIXELATE

```
PRMCHK: PROCEDURE OPTIONS (MAIN);
   /* Reads a list of numbers and
      identifies which ones are prime */

          DECLARE (N, I) FLOAT;
          ON ENDFILE GO TO STOP;

   START: GET LIST(N);

   LOOP: DO I = 2 TO (TRUNC(SQRT(N))+1);
            IF N/I = TRUNC(N/I) THEN
               GO TO NPRIME;
         END LOOP;
         PUT SKIP(2) LIST (N, 'IS PRIME');
         GO TO START;

 NPRIME: PUT SKIP(2) LIST(N,'IS NOT PRIME');
         PUT SKIP LIST ('IT IS DIVISIBLE BY',I);
         GO TO START;

   STOP: END PRMCHK;
```

FIGURE 203. PL/1 PROGRAM TO TEST
WHETHER A NUMBER IS PRIME

PL/1 (PL/I) a powerful programming language developed by IBM
in the early 1960s to accompany its System/360 computer. The name
stands for Programming Language One.

PL/1 can be described as a combination of ALGOL 60 block structure, FORTRAN arithmetic, and COBOL data structuring. PL/1 is the
language of choice for writing complex programs on IBM mainframe
computers, but it has received little use on other types of machines.

Fig. 203 shows an example of a PL/1 program. Note that the main
program is declared as a procedure with the option MAIN. This program
is written in a FORTRAN-like style with GO TO statements, but a pure
structured PL/1 style (like Pascal, without GO TO) is equally practical.

planar

    1. *(adjective)* flat. For example, planar transistors are made of flat pieces of silicon.

    2. *(adjective)* situated on the motherboard of a computer (e.g., *planar RAM*).

    3. *(noun)* motherboard. *See* MOTHERBOARD; *contrast* DAUGHTER-BOARD; RISER.

plane

    1. in geometry, all the points on a flat surface. Thus a plane is a two-dimensional space on which things have length and width but no thickness.

    2. in computer graphics, one of several images that are superimposed to produce the final image. For example, many video cards have separate planes (internal bitmaps) for red, green, and blue. The complete image is a combination of the images stored on the three planes. *See* CHANNEL.

plasma glowing ionized gas. *See* GAS PLASMA DISPLAY.

platen the roller in a typewriter or printer that holds the paper as the keys or pins strike it.

platform a piece of equipment or software used as a base on which to build something else. For example, a mainframe computer can serve as a platform for a large accounting system. Microsoft Windows serves as a platform for application software.

plenum-rated describes cable suitable for use in places where air circulates, such as above suspended ceilings. (A *plenum* is a place full of air, the opposite of a vacuum.) Plenum-rated cable is fire resistant and does not give off noxious fumes when overheated. *Contrast* RISER-RATED.

plotter a device that draws pictures on paper by moving pens according to directions from a computer. *See* GRAPHICS.

Plug and Play a standard way of configuring PC-compatible computer hardware automatically, developed by Microsoft and a number of other companies in the mid-1990s. Plug and Play hardware is compatible with conventional hardware (ISA, PCI, PCMCIA, Micro Channel, etc.) but has additional capabilities. Each card or accessory inserted into a computer contains identifying information that can be read by the BIOS and the operating system. Thus, the computer can see all the installed accessories and can configure itself to use them appropriately.

plug-in an accessory program that provides additional functions for a main application program. Plug-ins have to be loaded at the same time as the main program; they then show up as an option in an appropriate menu. Plug-ins are also added to a web browser to allow it to view additional file formats, such as multimedia shows.

PMJI e-mail abbreviation for "**p**ardon **m**e for **j**umping **i**n."

PMS *see* PANTONE MATCHING SYSTEM.

PNP one of the two types of bipolar TRANSISTORS (*contrast* NPN).

PnP abbreviation for PLUG AND PLAY.

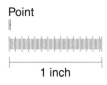

FIGURE 204. POINT

point a unit of typographical measurement equal to $\frac{1}{72}$ inch. The height of type is usually expressed in points. However, this is not a measurement of the size of the letters, but rather of the wooden blocks on which the metal type was mounted for printing presses. This usually included some space at the top of the tallest capital letters and below the descenders. Therefore, different typefaces of the same point size may actually differ in size. To this day, even digitized typefaces show some of the same idiosyncrasies. A desire to be faithful to the original designs has prevented the type's apparent size from being regularized.

FIGURE 205. 24-POINT TYPE SAMPLES

In a typical book-sized line of type, about 25 picas wide, readability is greatest with 10-point type with 2 points of leading. This works out to 6 lines to the inch. Greater width calls for larger type, and lesser width (as a newspaper column) calls for smaller type. *See* LEADING; TYPEFACE; TYPESETTING MISTAKES.

pointer

1. an arrow-like symbol that moves around a computer screen under the control of the user. For example, to execute a command in a windowed operating system, use the mouse to move the pointer to

the icon representing that command, and then quickly press the mouse button twice.

2. a data item consisting of an address that tells where to find a desired item. For examples, *see* LINKED LIST; TREE. Pascal and C++ provide a specific data type called a pointer variable that can be used to keep track of data structures that vary in size as the program is executed.

pointing device a computer peripheral that allows you to control your computer in a graphical user interface (GUI). The most familiar pointing device is a MOUSE, but some people prefer a TRACKBALL or a GRAPHICS TABLET.

point-of-sale system a computer used in place of a cash register where merchandise is sold. Besides keeping track of cash, the computer can keep track of inventory and print informative invoices and receipts, and perhaps automatically deduct funds from the customer's account.

point release a minor upgrade of a piece of software, such as the upgrade from version 2.0 to 2.1.

point-to-point protocol *see* PPP.

POKE a BASIC instruction that allows you to put a specific value in a specific memory location. POKE was used extensively on small microcomputers in the early 1980s. Its effect depends on the details of the hardware and software environment. *See also* PEEK; BASIC.

Polish notation a way of writing algebraic expressions that does not require parentheses to state which operations are done first. It is named in honor of its inventor, Jan Lukasiewicz (1878–1956), whose name most English-speaking mathematicians cannot pronounce. The ordinary algebraic expression

$$4 + (5 - 3) + 2$$

translates into Polish notation as

$$4\ 5\ 3\ -\ +\ 2\ +$$

To evaluate the expression, work through it from left to right until you encounter an operation (a plus or minus), then perform that operation on the numbers immediately to the left of the operator, replace the numbers and the operator with the result of the operation, and keep going in the same manner. Thus $4\ 5\ 3\ -\ +2+$ simplifies to $4\ 2\ +\ 2+$, then $6\ 2+$, and finally 8.

This is technically known as reverse Polish notation (RPN); the expression can also be written in the other direction and worked through from right to left. Many calculators and programming language interpreters translate expressions into Polish notation in order to evaluate them. Also, Hewlett-Packard calculators use Polish notation rather than parentheses on the ground that Polish notation is easier to work with once the user becomes accustomed to it.

FIGURE 206. POLYGONS

polygon a closed geometric figure with any number of straight sides. Triangles, squares, pentagons (five-sided), hexagons (six-sided), heptagons (seven-sided), and octagons (eight-sided) are all examples of polygons.

polymorphism the use of different procedures, each with the same name, which are associated with different object types. For example, procedures named `draw` could be associated with the types `point`, `circle`, and `square`. Calling `draw` for any particular object then activates the right drawing procedure for that type. *See* OBJECT-ORIENTED PROGRAMMING.

Ponzi scheme *see* PYRAMID SCHEME.

pop to remove the topmost item from a stack. *See* STACK.

POP
    1. **P**ost **O**ffice **P**rotocol, a standard protocol for delivering e-mail to personal computers.
    2. **p**oint **o**f **p**urchase (point of sale). For example, a POP computer is a computer used as a cash register. *See* POINT-OF-SALE SYSTEM.
    3. **p**oint **o**f **p**resence, a place where an INTERNET SERVICE PROVIDER can be accessed, such as a local telephone number.

pop-up menu *see* PULL-DOWN MENU.

pop-up utility *see* MEMORY-RESIDENT PROGRAM.

port
    1. to adapt a program from one kind of computer to another. For example, some IBM PC programs have been ported to the Macintosh.
    2. a connection where a computer can be connected to an external device, such as a modem, printer, or tape drive. *See* SERIAL; PARALLEL; SCSI.
    3. a unique number used by a microprocessor to identify an input-output device. For example, the hexadecimal number 3F8 is the port address for part of the circuitry that controls the first serial port (COM1) on the IBM PC.
    4. a number identifying the type of connection requested by a remote computer on the Internet. *See* URL.

portable

    1. able to be carried around. A portable computer is larger than a laptop computer, but still easily movable.

    2. (said of programs) able to run on more than one type of computer.

Portable Digital Document a file format supported by Macintosh computers with QuickDraw GX. A document saved in this format can be viewed on any other Mac with QuickDraw GX, even if the two computers do not have the same application software or fonts. *See* QUICKDRAW GX; ELECTRONIC PUBLISHING.

Portable Document File *see* PDF.

portal a web site designed for people to visit when they are looking for links to other sites. Examples include `www.lycos.com` and `www.yahoo.com` as well as the home pages of various Internet service providers.

 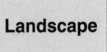

FIGURE 207. PORTRAIT VS. LANDSCAPE ORIENTATION

portrait the position in which a sheet of paper is higher than it is wide, like a portrait painting. Most printers print with the paper in portrait orientation. If the printed image can be turned sideways, the result is called *landscape orientation*. Laser printers typically offer a choice of portrait or landscape (horizontal) orientation.

POS

    1. **p**oint **o**f **s**ale. *See* POINT-OF-SALE SYSTEM.

    2. **p**rogrammable **o**ption **s**elect, the system for recording the configuration of a computer into CMOS RAM so that the computer can boot successfully. *See* CMOS RAM.

POSIX (usually understood as "**p**ortable **o**perating **s**ystem **i**nterface based on UNIX" though this is not its official definition) an IEEE

```
%!PS-Adobe-2.0 EPSF-2.0
%%BoundingBox: 1 800 1 800
% PostScript program to print a gray square
% and the words 'PostScript Example'
/Helvetica-Bold findfont 12 scalefont setfont
newpath
72 720 moveto              % start drawing rectangle
142 720 lineto
142 648 lineto
72 648 lineto
closepath
.75 setgray                % choose 75% gray
fill
0 setgray                  % restore color to black
162 700 moveto
(PostScript) show          % print text
162 600 moveto
(Example) show
```

FIGURE 208. POSTSCRIPT PROGRAM

---

standard set of operating system functions available to software. The POSIX standard makes it possible to write programs that will run under any POSIX-compliant operating system by simply recompiling them. Windows 95 and its successors are partially POSIX-compliant; Windows NT and 2000 are more so. POSIX is a trademark of the IEEE. *See* IEEE.

post to place a message in a NEWSGROUP, BBS, or other public discussion forum.

posting a message placed in a NEWSGROUP, BBS, or other public discussion forum.

PostScript a programming language for controlling laser printers and other graphical output devices, developed by Adobe Systems of Palo Alto, California. A PostScript printer accepts not only characters to be printed but also commands to change the size of type fonts or to draw lines or circles in specific positions. An application designed to work with PostScript will automatically send Postscript codes to the printer. The user can also write programs in the Postscript language. Fig. 208 shows an example. The text following the percent signs is treated as comments, but some of the comments (such as BoundingBox) are used by some types of software. This program is suitable for encapsulation into larger programs; to print it by itself, add the command showpage after the last line.

PostScript works with a coordinate system with the origin at the lower left-hand corner of the page, with units $\frac{1}{72}$ of an inch long. The program demonstrates the use of the moveto command, the lineto command (which draws a line from the previous point to the indicated point), and the fill command (which fills an area with a desired

PostScript Example

FIGURE 209. OUTPUT FROM THE SAMPLE
POSTSCRIPT PROGRAM

shade of gray). Text is printed by enclosing it in parentheses and then using the command show. Before printing, the appropriate font must be selected; fonts can be scaled to different point sizes. PostScript also lets the programmer use variables and define abbreviations and procedures. Figure 209 shows the output of Figure 208.

Many printers expect a Ctrl-D (UNIX end-of-file mark) at the end of every PostScript job. Some software also generates a Ctrl-D at the beginning of the job, to clear out anything that may have previously been sent to the printer.

PostScript was introduced in 1985; Level 2 PostScript, an extended version of the language, was introduced in 1991 and is now standard. *Encapsulated PostScript* (EPS) is a file format for using the PostScript language to exchange graphics between programs. EPS files must contain a BoundingBox comment, must follow certain other restrictions, and can contain bitmap previews of the image. Notoriously, software that imports some EPS files does not necessarily understand the entire PostScript language; many programs confine themselves to the Adobe Illustrator (AI) subset of EPS.

POTS (**P**lain **O**ld **T**elephone **S**ervice) humorous name for conventional analog telephone lines compatible with all telephones made since the 1920s. Designing modems for POTS lines has been a challenging engineering problem. At present, the highest possible data rate is thought to be about 56 kbps, but other, much lower, rates were thought to be the highest possible rate in past years. *Contrast* ISDN; T1 LINE; CABLE MODEM; DSL.

pound key the key on a telephone marked with the symbol #. It is often used to signal the end of an international telephone number.

pound sign the character #. Also called an OCTOTHORPE.

power cycle to switch off electric power to a device, then switch it on again. This is one way to REBOOT a computer. However, it should be done only in emergencies because many operating systems (including UNIX and also Windows 95 and it successors) will lose data if not shut down properly. After turning power off, always wait a few seconds for capacitors to discharge and disks to spin down before turning the power on again.

power line protection measures taken to protect a computer from problems caused by the AC power supplied by the wall outlet. Several things can go wrong:

1. Brief bursts ("spikes") of excessive voltage can damage the computer. These spikes come from lightning or from large electric motors switching off. They are easily absorbed by a surge protector (*see* SURGE PROTECTOR).

2. Power failures cause the computer to shut down or restart suddenly, losing the data that you were working on. A surge protector cannot prevent this. If the problem is frequent, you may want to invest in an uninterruptible power supply (UPS).

3. The computer can emit radio or TV interference through the power line. *See* RFI PROTECTION.

PowerPC a family of high-performance 32- and 64-bit microprocessors developed jointly by IBM, Motorola, and Apple, to compete with the Intel microprocessors and Microsoft software that presently dominate the personal computer market. For specifications *see* MICROPROCESSOR (Table 13).

Introduced in 1994, PowerPC processors are specially designed to emulate other kinds of CPUs efficiently. Thus a PowerPC-based computer can run DOS and/or conventional Macintosh software by running a special program on the PowerPC that recognizes and executes the machine instructions of the 386 or 68030 CPU respectively.

The first PowerPCs to reach the market were Macintoshes. *See also* MACINTOSH; OS/2; RISC; MICROPROCESSOR.

Powerpoint presentation software sold with Microsoft's Office suite. The user can create an outline version of a talk and then display it one page at a time or one line at a time, and graphics can be included as well. Speaker notes or handouts can also be printed.

power supply the part of a computer or other electronic equipment that supplies power to the other parts. The power supply generally includes stepdown transformers and voltage regulators. *See also* SWITCHING POWER SUPPLY.

The watt and ampere ratings of a power supply represent the maximum that it can deliver; the actual power consumed will depend on the devices attached to it. Correct practice is to use a power supply with the *correct* voltages and *correct or higher* watt and ampere ratings.

p-p (**p**eak-to-**p**eak) a way of measuring AC voltage. *See* PEAK-TO-PEAK.

PPM (**p**ages **p**er **m**inute) a measure of the speed of a printer.

PPP (**P**oint-to-**P**oint **P**rotocol) a communications protocol often used in DIAL-UP NETWORKING. *Compare* SLIP.

PRE tag used in HTML to indicate that the material is pre-formatted; that is, the exact pattern of spacing and line breaks in the source is to be preserved when displayed on a web browser. This formatting begins with the <PRE> tag and ends with the </PRE> tag.

precedence the property of arithmetic operations in a programming language that determines which operations are done first in a complex expression.

For example, in BASIC, as in many other languages, exponentiations are done first, then multiplications and divisions, and finally additions and subtractions. For example, the BASIC expression

```
2 + 3 * 4 ^ 2
```

means $2 + 3 * 16 = 2 + 48 = 50$. You can use parentheses to change the order of the operations when you need to, since any operation in parentheses will be done first.

precision the exactness with which a quantity is specified. For numbers, the precision is the number of significant digits that the computer keeps track of when it carries out arithmetic operations. *See* ROUNDING ERROR. For examples in Java, *see* LONG; DOUBLE PRECISION.

Precision is entirely separate from accuracy. If I weigh 175 pounds and you say that I weigh 150.03535 pounds, your assertion is precise but not accurate.

preferences settings for a computer program to allow for individual differences. The preferences menu is sometimes a rather obscure catchall for adjustments to mouse tracking, the double-click rate, the NUDGE rate, and the brush style. Take the time to become familiar with the "Preferences" settings in your software; sometimes a problem can be quickly solved by making a small adjustment.

preflight the step just before printing an image or document. During preflight checking, software can detect missing fonts, images too large for the paper, and the like. The name apparently alludes to the preflight checks performed on aircraft just before taking off.

prepend to append at the beginning; to put in front. For example, if you prepend // to a line in a C++ program, that line becomes a comment.

prepress the preparation of material to be printed in quantity on a printing press. Many prepress functions are highly automated and well suited to being performed with computers. For example, there are software packages that take a PostScript file and slightly increase the outline of color areas to create TRAP. The graphic arts industry is moving toward a totally digital production system where the printing plates will be prepared directly from computer files.

presentation graphics the use of software to create business or educational presentations that integrate drawings, charts, and texts. Examples of software include Persuasion (from Aldus), Hollywood (IBM), Freelance Graphics (Lotus), and PowerPoint (Microsoft). Typically, these programs include drawing tools and the ability to make charts out of data taken from a spreadsheet program. Users can create a complete show by arranging the images in the desired order and standardizing the color scheme for all of the images. By viewing miniature images of the presentation all on the same screen, the user can obtain an overview of the finished product. Of course you will ultimately need a way to show the presentation to the audience, using a video projector or LCD projection panel or outputting the presentation onto overhead projector transparencies or 35-mm slides.

More sophisticated programs can also incorporate music, sound effects, and animation into the presentation. *See also* MULTIMEDIA.

Presentation Manager the windowed user interface of OS/2. It enables the user to control files and software graphically by using a mouse. *See* OS/2.

FIGURE 210. PRESS

press to depress a mouse button and hold it down until the mouse action is completed. *Contrast* CLICK.

pretzel *(slang)* nickname for ⌘, the Macintosh command key.

preview a viewing mode that displays the appearance of the finished document or drawing. In order to let you work quickly, many drawing programs show you only an outline of the objects on screen. (This is called WIREFRAME mode.) When you want to see what the final printed piece would look like, you have to use the "Preview" command. Then all of the objects appear with their fills so that you can check whether they are layered correctly.

Most drawing programs will allow you to work in preview mode, but the time spent redrawing the screen after each action can be quite irritating. It is best to work with the wireframe and preview to check your work. Another method is to open two windows containing the same file, one in wireframe and the second in preview.

Some word processors will also allow you to preview your document.

primary mouse button the button used to select objects on a mouse with more than one button. For a right-handed user, this is usually the left mouse button. The SECONDARY MOUSE BUTTON is the button used to call up the action menu.

Left-handed users have the option of reversing the default order for mouse buttons; they can use the right mouse button as the primary button and the left button as the secondary.

primitive a basic element or concept in terms of which larger elements or concepts are formed. For example, in programming languages such as FORTH and LISP, it is common for the programmer to create his own statements by defining them in terms of primitives provided by the language.

printer a device for putting computer output on paper. *See* DAISY-WHEEL PRINTER; DOT-MATRIX PRINTER; INKJET PRINTER; ELECTRO-STATIC PRINTER; LASER PRINTER; THERMAL PRINTER.

printf the statement in C and C++ that performs formatted output. For example, the statement

```
printf("The answer is %d\n",i):
```

prints "The answer is," then the value of i as a decimal integer, then starts a new line. The scanf statement is very similar, but performs formatted input instead. For example,

```
scanf("%d",&i);
```

reads the value of i as a decimal integer from standard input. Its argument is &i (the address of i), rather than i itself, so that it can store a new value in this location. Otherwise it would not be able to change i.

The first argument of printf or scanf is a string with format codes in it. Table 15 gives examples of format codes. There are many others; consult your manual.

Print Manager the PRINT SPOOLER built into Microsoft Windows 3.1.

print server a computer that handles printing for other computers via a NETWORK. A print server is often mounted on a card inside the printer itself.

print spooler a program that stores computer output in memory so that the user's program can finish creating the output without waiting for

TABLE 15
PRINTF/SCANF FORMAT CODES

Code	Meaning
%d	Decimal integer
%7d	Decimal integer with 7 digits
%u	Unsigned decimal integer
%x	Hexadecimal integer
%f	Floating-point decimal number
%6.3f	Floating-point decimal, occupying a total of 6 characters, with 3 digits to the right of the decimal point
%e	Floating-point number in E format
%c	One character
%s	A character string (`printf` prints the entire string; `scanf` reads until a nonblank character is found)
%\n	Start a new line (`printf` only)

the printer to print it. The spooler then sends the stored output to the printer at the proper speed. The print spooler in Microsoft Windows is called Print Manager. *See also* SPOOLING; BUFFER.

private key the key (password, code word) that the recipient of a message uses to decrypt a message that was encrypted with the recipient's PUBLIC KEY. Only the recipient of a message knows his or her own private key. *See* ENCRYPTION.

procedure a smaller program that is part of a main program. The procedure is executed when the main program calls it. Fig. 211 shows an example of a Turbo Pascal program with a procedure.

There are two main advantages to using procedures when writing programs:

1. Procedures eliminate the need to program the same thing more than once. In the example program, the procedure `readint` is called twice, but the programmer only has to write it once, and only one copy of it occupies space in the computer's memory.

2. A large program is easier to understand if it consists of procedures. Each procedure should have a well-understood purpose. (*See* TOP-DOWN PROGRAMMING.)

For another example of a Pascal procedure, see PARAMETER. For an example of the equivalent concept in BASIC, *see* SUBROUTINE.

process a series of instructions that a computer is executing in a multitasking operating system. Many processes execute concurrently. From the user's viewpoint, processes may be programs or parts of programs (such as the editing routine and the printing routine in a word processor

```
PROGRAM divide(INPUT,OUTPUT);
   { Reads 2 integers, performs the division,
     and reports both the quotient and the remainder }

VAR a, b: INTEGER;

  PROCEDURE readint(VAR z:INTEGER);
    { This procedure reads in an integer from
      the keyboard.  In case of invalid input,
      it will ask the user to reenter the data. }
  VAR x: STRING; code, z2: INTEGER;
  BEGIN
    write('Enter integer value:');
    readln(x);
    val(x,z2,code);
    WHILE code<>0 DO
      BEGIN
        write('|',X,'|' is invalid; enter integer;');
        readln(x);
        val(x,z2,code)
      END;
    z := z2
  END;

BEGIN {main program}
  readint(a);   {The procedure is called in each}
  readint(b);   {of these two lines}
  writeln('Quotient: ',(a DIV b));
  writeln('Remainder:',(a MOD b))
END.
```

FIGURE 211. PROCEDURE IN A PASCAL PROGRAM

that can print while editing). In a multiuser operating system such as UNIX, each user has one or more processes. *See* MULTITASKING, UNIX.

process color four-color printing, usually used for producing full-color pictures. *See* CMYK. *Contrast* SPOT COLOR.

processor *see* MICROPROCESSOR; COPROCESSOR; CPU.

Prodigy an Internet service provider (www.prodigy.com). Before the Internet was made available to nonacademic users, Prodigy was a popular on-line service available by subscription.

profile a file of saved information that indicates how the user normally wants something done.

ProgMan short for PROGRAM MANAGER (part of Windows 3.1).

program a set of instructions for a computer to execute. A program can be written in a programming language, such as BASIC or Pascal, or in an assembly language. *See* APPLICATION PROGRAM; UTILITY.

program group in Microsoft Windows, a set of application programs whose icons appear in a single window or on a single menu. In many ways, a program group is similar to a SUBDIRECTORY or a Macintosh

FOLDER. An application program can appear in more than one program group.

When Windows 95 is installed on a system that previously used Windows 3.1, the program groups are preserved in the START MENU.

programmable function key a key on a computer keyboard whose function depends on the software being run. In many cases, programmable function (PF) keys can be defined as equivalent to combinations or sequences of other keys.

programmable option select *see* POS (definition 2).

Program Manager a program supplied with Microsoft Windows 3.1 that allows you to organize and run application programs. Program Manager by default takes over most of the screen and lets you control all the other applications from within it.

programmer a person who prepares instructions for computers.

programming the process of composing instructions for a computer to carry out. A programmer needs to develop a well-defined concept of how to solve a problem. (*See* ALGORITHM.) Then this concept must be translated into a computer language. (*See* PROGRAMMING LANGUAGE.) Finally, the program needs to be typed into the computer, tested, and debugged before being placed into service.

programming language a language used to give instructions to computers. During the 1960s and 1970s, a huge variety of programming languages were developed, most of which are no longer in wide use. Moreover, a substantial amount of programming is now done with special program development tools (e.g., Visual Basic), or in programming languages that pertain to specific pieces of software (e.g., Maple) rather than by simply writing instructions in a general-purpose language.

The following is a rough classification of programming languages. Most of these languages are treated in separate articles in this book.

1. General-purpose languages for large, complex programs: PL/I, C, C++, Pascal, Modula-2, Ada, Java.
2. General-purpose languages for smaller programs: BASIC, Visual Basic, Pascal.
3. Mathematical calculation, science, and engineering: FORTRAN, APL, Maple, and the general-purpose languages named above.
4. Business data processing: COBOL, RPG. Where microcomputers are involved, BASIC, C, and languages associated with specific database products are also widely used.
5. Artificial intelligence and programs of extreme logical complexity: LISP and Prolog.

Another useful classification is based on the way the program is organized.

1. Sequential languages treat the program as a series of steps, with an occasional GOTO statement as a way of breaking out of the sequence. In this category are FORTRAN, BASIC, and COBOL (though COBOL also allows programs to be written in a style more like a block-structured language).

2. Block-structured languages encourage structured programming by allowing the programmer to group statements into functional units. (*See* STRUCTURED PROGRAMMING.) This category originated with Algol and now includes Pascal, Modula-2, C, PL/I, and Ada.

3. Object-oriented languages allow the programmer to define new data types and associate procedures with them. Languages of this type include C++, Java, object-oriented extensions of Pascal, and Smalltalk.

4. Symbolic languages allow the program to examine and modify itself, treating instructions as data. Lisp and Prolog fall into this category.

Usage note: Although names of some programming languages are normally written in all capital letters, names of most languages are not, even if they are acronyms. Usage varies from language to language. With some, usage has shifted over the years. *See also* BASIC (Usage note).

project the set of all files needed to produce the ready-to-use version of a program. Typically, the compiler accepts procedures from several different files and combines them into one executable (EXE) file. *See* LINK; MAKE.

projection panel a semitransparent panel that connects to a computer and is placed on an overhead projector in order to project an image of the computer screen. Also called an LCD PANEL.

project management the scheduling of a complex project involving many different tasks. A typical task requires some resources and a certain amount of time; it also requires that certain other tasks have already been finished. You may sometimes schedule two tasks to be performed simultaneously if they don't overtax the supply of available resources, but when the tasks are sequential, you must schedule them in the proper order. For example, the engines on the wings of an airplane cannot be installed until the wings have been built. A project manager program takes the information the user enters for each task and then determines how to schedule the tasks. The results are often presented in the form of a diagram called a Gantt chart (see Figure 212).

Prolog a programming language developed in the early 1970s by Alain Colmerauer at the University of Marseilles and standardized by the ISO in 1995. Prolog is used for writing computer programs that model human thinking. It exemplifies *logic programming,* a kind of programming developed by Robert Kowalski of the University of London.

Task	Weeks						
	1	*2*	*3*	*4*	*5*	*6*	*7*
visit houses	▓	▓					
make decision		▓					
loan application			▓	▓	▓		
shop for furniture		▓					
send notices of address change					▓		
sign closing papers						▓	
order phone						▓	
move							▓

FIGURE 212. PROJECT MANAGEMENT: GANTT CHART
FOR MOVING TO A NEW HOME

In ordinary programming, a program describes the steps that a computer is to work through in order to solve a problem. In logic programming, the program gives the computer facts about the problem, plus rules by means of which other facts can be inferred. The computer then applies a fixed procedure to solve the problem automatically.

Suppose, for example, we want to know whether Atlanta is in North America. We have the following information to work from:

1. X is in North America if X is in the United States.
2. X is in North America if X is in Canada.
3. X is in the United States if X is in Georgia.
4. X is in the United States if X is in Florida.
5. Atlanta is in Georgia.

As Kowalski has pointed out, this can be described equally well in terms of reasoning procedures as follows:

1. To show that X is in North America, show that X is in the United States.
2. To show that X is in North America, show that X is in Canada.
3. To show that X is in the United States, show that X is in Georgia.
4. To show that X is in the United States, show that X is in Florida.
5. To show that Atlanta is in Georgia, do nothing.

It is then obvious that our problem can be solved by chaining statements 1, 3, and 5 together. We express the available information in Prolog as follows:

```
/* Rule 1 */ north_america(X)  :- united_states(X).
/* Rule 2 */ north_america(X)  :- canada(X).
/* Rule 3 */ united_states(X)  :- georgia(X).
/* Rule 4 */ united_states(X)  :- florida(X).
/* Rule 5 */ georgia(atlanta).
```

The symbol /* indicates the beginning of a comment, and */ indicates the end of the comment. All of these statements are rules. X is a variable that can be matched with any constant, and :- means "if." Rule 1 means "If X is in the United States, then X is in North America." Rule 5 is a special kind of rule called a *fact* because it does not contain an "if."

   To find out whether Atlanta is in North America, we then give Prolog the following query:

```
?- north_america(atlanta).
```

To solve the query, Prolog looks for a rule the first part of which will match the query. Rule 1 will work, provided that variable X is given the value atlanta. Then the second part of the rule becomes the new query

```
?- united_states(atlanta).
```

Again, we look for a rule that will match the query. Rule 3 will work, and the new query becomes

```
?- georgia(atlanta).
```

When we look for a rule that matches this query, we find that rule 5 matches it exactly and does not contain an "if"—hence it does not introduce a new query, the process is complete, and the question can be answered "yes." If the process had ended with a query that no rule would match, the question would be answered "no."

   One of the most important properties of Prolog is its ability to backtrack, that is, to back up and try alternative solutions. This is necessary whenever the search starts pursuing a chain of rules that do not lead to a solution. For example, rules 2 and 4 do not lead to a solution in our example; if the computer tried either of them, it would need to back up and try alternatives.

   Prolog is not confined to the simple kind of logic described here. It can implement all types of algorithms, including sorting, numerical computation, and parsing. Prolog is coming into favor as a programming language for managing windows because the idea of backing out of an operation is built into it. *See also* ANONYMOUS VARIABLE; SINGLETON VARIABLE.

PROM (**P**rogrammable **R**ead-**O**nly **M**emory) a type of computer memory that can be programmed once but not reprogrammed. *See also* EPROM.

promiscuous mode a mode in which a computer reads all the data packets on the network, not just those addressed to it. *See* SNIFFER.

prompt a symbol that appears on a computer terminal screen to signal to the user that the computer is ready to receive input. Different programs use different prompts. For example, under most versions of DOS, the prompt is C> if C is the default disk drive.

In DOS, the PROMPT command can be used to change the appearance of the prompt. For an example, see HARD-DISK MANAGEMENT.

prop an object placed within the scene of an animation.

properties the attributes of any object. Under OS/2 and Windows, menus titled "Properties" are the usual way of changing settings. In Windows 95 and 98, right-click on an object to change its properties. For example, the properties of an icon specify what it looks like and what should happen when the user clicks on it.

proportional pitch the use of characters with different widths in a single typeface. For example, in proportional-pitch type, *M* is wider than *I*. Compared to a fixed-pitch typewriter or printer, this improves the appearance of the type and makes it more readable. Most books and newspapers are set in proportional type. *See* TYPE; TYPEFACE. For an illustration, *see* PITCH.

Because the letters are of different widths, it is not possible to count letter spaces in proportional-pitch type the way one does on a typewriter. *See* TYPESETTING MISTAKES.

proprietary owned by a specific company or individual. A feature of a computer is proprietary if one company has exclusive rights to it.

protected mode the mode in which an 80286, 386, 486, or Pentium microprocessor can access the largest possible amount of memory. In this mode, these processors can only run programs designed for protected mode, not programs designed for earlier processors such as the 8088. In Microsoft Windows and OS/2, the user can switch between protected mode (for running Windows or OS/2 programs) and real mode or multiple virtual 8086 mode (for running DOS programs).

In protected mode, different parts of memory are allocated to different programs, and memory is "protected" in the sense that a program can only write to the memory allocated to it. *Contrast* REAL MODE; MULTIPLE VIRTUAL MODE.

protocol a standard way of carrying out data transmission between computers. *See* HANDSHAKING; X-OFF; X-ON; XMODEM; KERMIT; HTTP; FTP; TCP/IP; NETBEUI; IPX/SPX; ATM.

proxy an item that represents something else. *See also* PROXY SERVER.

proxy server a computer that saves information acquired from elsewhere on the INTERNET and makes it available to other computers in its immediate area. For example, if several users connect to the same WEB SITE through a proxy server, each page of information will be downloaded from that site only once and then provided to all the users.

A disadvantage of proxy servers is that they make it impossible to count HITS accurately.

PS/1, PS/2 *see* IBM PC AND PS/2.

PS 2 an advanced version (Level 2) of the POSTSCRIPT graphics language.

PS/2 mouse a mouse with a small round connector of the type originally used on the IBM PS/2 but now widely used on other PC-compatible computers.

pseudocode an outline of a computer program, written in a mixture of a programming language and English. Writing pseudocode is one of the best ways to plan a computer program. For example, here is a pseudocode outline of a Pascal program to find the largest of a set of 10 numbers:

```
begin
  repeat
    read a number;
    test whether it is the largest found so far
  until 10 numbers have been read;
  print the largest
end.
```

Here is the program that results from translating all of the pseudocode into genuine Pascal:

```
PROGRAM findthelargest (INPUT, OUTPUT);
VAR num, largest, count : INTEGER;
BEGIN
  count := 0;
  largest := 0;
  REPEAT
    count := count + 1;
    read(num);
    IF num > largest THEN largest := num;
  UNTIL count = 10;
  writeln('The largest number was ',largest)
END.
```

(This program assumes that the largest number will be greater than zero.)

The advantage of pseudocode is that it allows the programmer to concentrate on how the program works while ignoring the details of the language. By reducing the number of things the programmer must think about at once, this technique effectively amplifies the programmer's intelligence.

pub the usual name for the DIRECTORY on an FTP SITE that contains files downloadable by the public. *See also* ANONYMOUS FTP.

public_html typical name for a user's directory containing HTML files that are available for anyone on the World Wide Web to read.

publication (desktop publishing) the collection of files that describe all the elements of a given project—namely, the text, the graphics, the layout elements, and any other supporting files generated by the DTP software. Each publication should have its own subdirectory.

public domain the status of literature, art, music, or software that is not copyrighted.

A computer program is in the public domain if it is not covered by any kind of copyright. Few substantial public-domain programs exist, but the term "public domain" is often used incorrectly to describe other kinds of freely copyable software (*see* FREE SOFTWARE). *See also* COPYRIGHT.

public key The sender of a message uses the public key of the recipient to encrypt the message. The recipient then uses his or her own secret PRIVATE KEY to decrypt the message. See ENCRYPTION.

pull the process whereby the user retrieves information from a network at the user's request, as in traditional web browsing; *contrast* PUSH (definition 2).

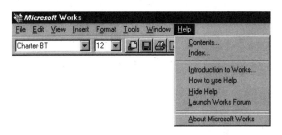

FIGURE 213. PULL-DOWN MENU

pull-down menu a menu that appears when a particular item in a menu bar is selected. *See also* MENU BAR.

punched card a stiff paper card on which holes can be punched according to a particular pattern that can be read by a computer. In the

1960s, punched cards were the dominant way of feeding programs into computers, but they have now been replaced by interactive terminals. Standard punched cards were $7\frac{3}{8}$ inches long and $3\frac{1}{4}$ inches high, with 80 columns and 12 rows. The pattern of holes in each column represented one character.

The use of punched cards for data processing actually preceded the invention of the computer by more than 50 years. Herman Hollerith realized that it took several years to process data from the 1880 census. He figured that, unless a faster method was found, the U.S. Census Bureau would still be working on the results from the 1890 census when it came time to start the 1900 census. Hollerith developed a system in which census data were punched on cards, and machines were used to sort and tabulate the cards. Even earlier, in 1801, a system of punched cards was used to direct the weaving pattern on the automatic Jacquard loom in France.

push

1. to place an item on a stack. *See* STACK.

2. the process whereby the network delivers information to a client machine without waiting for the user to request it. Push technology makes the World Wide Web work rather like TV; the user selects a "channel" and views whatever is being sent out at the moment. This contrasts with the way web browsers traditionally work, where the user manually selects information to retrieve from the Web. (*Contrast* PULL.) Push technology is useful for delivering information that has to be updated minute by minute, such as stock market quotes or news bulletins. However, the user demand for push technology is not what had once been expected. Users do not want to give up control of the Internet in order to watch it passively like television. *See* CASTANET.

pushdown stack (**pushdown store**) a data structure from which items can only be removed in the opposite of the order in which they were stored. *See* STACK.

pushing the envelope working close to, or at, physical or technological limits. *See* ENVELOPE.

push technology *See* PUSH (definition 2).

pyramid scheme (**Ponzi scheme**) a get-rich-quick scheme in which you receive a message containing a list of names. You're expected to send money to the first person on the list, cross the first name off, add your name at the bottom, and distribute copies of the message.

Pyramid schemes are presently common on the Internet, but they are illegal in all 50 states and in most other parts of the world. They can't work because there is no way for everyone to receive more money than they send out; money doesn't come out of thin air. Pyramid schemers often claim the scheme is legal, but that doesn't make it so.

Q

QBASIC the version of Microsoft's QuickBASIC compiler that is provided with later versions of MS-DOS. *See* QUICKBASIC.

QIC **q**uarter-**i**nch **c**artridge, an abbreviation used in the designation of several types of computer tapes.

quarto a traditional British paper size, 8×10 inches, now being superseded by ISO A4. *See* PAPER SIZES (ISO).

query language a language used to express queries to be answered by a database system. For an example, *see* SQL.

queue
    1. a data structure from which items are removed in the same order in which they were entered. *Contrast* STACK.
    2. a list, maintained by the operating system, of jobs waiting to be printed or processed in some other way. *See* PRINT SPOOLER.

QuickBASIC Microsoft's fast compiler for BASIC under DOS. It accepts programs written for BASICA or GW-BASIC, but it also adds many new kinds of statements and allows the programmer to leave out line numbers. A similar compiler, which does not generate standalone executables, is provided with MS-DOS under the name QBASIC.

    Beginning with version 4.0, QuickBASIC has two unusual technical features. First, it is an incremental compiler, meaning that lines are compiled as soon as they are typed in. Second, it compiles into threaded code, a special kind of machine language that corresponds line-by-line to the original program. Thus, compilation is very fast and can be undone to reconstruct the BASIC program that was compiled.

QuickDraw GX a new version of the Macintosh's graphics control language. Improvements include support for GX FONTS, transparent graphics, improved rotation and skewing, and allowing documents to be saved in a Portable Digital Document format (PDD). This means that any other Mac with QuickDraw GX can view the file, even if the other computer does not have the same application program or fonts.
    See ELECTRONIC PUBLISHING; GX FONTS.

quicksort a sorting algorithm invented by C. A. R. Hoare and first published in 1962. Quicksort is faster than any other sorting algorithm available unless the items are already in nearly the correct order, in which case it is relatively inefficient (*compare* MERGE SORT).

    Quicksort is a recursive procedure (*see* RECURSION). In each iteration, it rearranges the list of items so that one item (the "pivot") is in its final position, all the items that should come before it are before it, and all the items that should come after it are after it. Then the lists

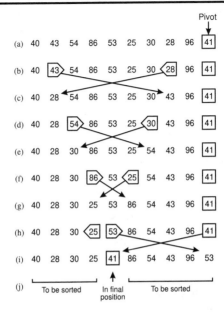

FIGURE 214. QUICKSORT IN ACTION

of items preceding and following the pivot are treated as sublists and sorted in the same way. Figure 214 shows how this works:

(a) Choose the last item in the list, 41, as the pivot. It is excluded from the searching and swapping that follow.

(b), (c) Identify the leftmost item greater than 41 and the rightmost item less than 41. Swap them.

(d), (e), (f), (g) Repeat steps (b) and (c) until the leftmost and rightmost markers meet in the middle.

(h), (i) Now that the markers have met and crossed, swap the pivot with the item pointed to by the leftmost marker.

(j) Now that the pivot is in its final position, sort each of the two sublists to the left and in right of it. Quicksort is difficult to express in languages, such as BASIC, that do not allow recursion. The amount of memory required by Quicksort increases exponentially with the depth of the recursion. One way to limit memory requirements is to switch to another type of sort, such as selection sort, after a certain depth is reached. (*See* SELECTION SORT.) Fig. 215 shows the Quicksort algorithm expressed in Pascal.

```
{ Quicksort in Pascal - M. Covington 1991 }
{ To sort a[1..n], an array of integers. }

PROCEDURE swap(VAR x,y: INTEGER);
VAR
  t: INTEGER;
BEGIN
  t:=x; x:=y; y:=t
END;

PROCEDURE partition(first,last:INTEGER; VAR p:INTEGER);
  {Partitions a[first]...a[last] into 2 sub-arrays}
  {using a[first] as pivot.  p is position where}
  {pivot ends up.}
VAR
  i, j: INTEGER;
  pivot: INTEGER;
BEGIN
  pivot := a[first];
  i:=first;
  j:=last+1;
  REPEAT
    REPEAT i:=i+1 UNTIL a[i]>=pivot;
    REPEAT j:=j-1 UNTIL a[j]<=pivot;
    IF i<j THEN swap(a[i],a[j])
  UNTIL j<=i;
  swap(a[j],a[first]);
  p := j
END;

PROCEDURE quicksort(first,last:INTEGER);
  {Sorts the sub-array from a[first] to a[last].}
  {To sort the whole array, call quicksort(1,n).}
VAR p: INTEGER;
BEGIN
  IF first < last THEN
    BEGIN
      partition(first,last,p);
      quicksort(first,p-1);
      quicksort(p+1,last)
    END
END;
```

FIGURE 215. QUICKSORT IN PASCAL

QuickTime the standard way of storing digitized sound and video on
the Macintosh. Using QuickTime files and associated software, the
Macintosh user can create and edit movies and play them back on the
screen. QuickTime includes RUN-LENGTH ENCODING and JPEG data
compression. *Compare* AVI FILE.

quit to clear an application program from memory; to EXIT. Most software prompts you to save changes to disk before quitting. Read all
message boxes carefully.

R

FIGURE 216. RADIAL FILL

radial fill a way of filling a graphical object with two colors such that one color is at the center, and there is a smooth transition to another color at the edges. *See* FOUNTAIN FILL. *Contrast* LINEAR FILL.

radian measure a way of measuring the size of angles in which a complete rotation measures 2π radians. The trigonometric functions in most computer languages expect their arguments to be expressed in radians. To convert degrees to radians, multiply by $\pi/180$ (approximately 1/57.296).

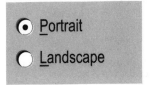

FIGURE 217. RADIO BUTTONS

radio button small circles in a dialog box, only one of which can be chosen at a time. The chosen button is black and the others are white. Choosing any button with the mouse causes all the other buttons in the set to be cleared. Radio buttons acquired their name because they work like the buttons on older car radios. *Also called* OPTION BUTTONS.

Radio Shack a division of Tandy Corporation, of Fort Worth, Texas, maker of Tandy computers. Radio Shack operates one of the most widespread chains of retail computer stores. For further information, see http://www.tandy.com.

Their TRS-80 Model I, introduced in 1977, was one of the first home computers. Subsequent Radio Shack computers of many different types have shared the name TRS-80.

radix the base of a number system. Binary numbers have a radix of 2, and decimal numbers have a radix of 10.

radix sort an algorithm that puts data in order by classifying each item immediately rather than comparing it to other items. For example, you might sort cards with names on them by putting all the A's in one bin, all the B's in another bin, and so on. You could then sort the contents of each bin the same way using the second letter of each name, and so on. The radix sort method can be used effectively with binary numbers, since there are only two possible bins for the items to be placed. For other sorting methods, *see* SORT and references there.

ragged margin a margin that has not been evened out by justification and at which the ends of words do not line up.

This is
an example of
flush-left, ragged-right type.

See also FLUSH LEFT; FLUSH RIGHT.

RAID (**R**edundant **A**rray of **I**nexpensive **D**isks) a highly reliable way of storing data using a set of disk drives rather than just one.

One type of RAID system divides up each byte of data into bits and stores each bit on a different disk. If the data consists of 8-bit bytes, there will be 10 disks, one for each of the 8 bits, and two more for an error-correcting code. The error-correcting code makes it possible to reconstruct any single missing bit in any byte. Thus, if one of the disk drives fails completely, only one bit will be missing from each byte, and the contents of the failed disk can be reconstructed completely from the error-correcting code.

RAID also includes other ways of combining disk drives, including a simple scheme in which one drive stores a copy of the information on the other.

RAM (**R**andom-**A**ccess **M**emory) a memory device whereby any location in memory can be found, on average, as quickly as any other location. A computer's RAM is its main working memory. The size of the RAM (measured in megabytes) is an important indicator of the capacity of the computer. *See* MEMORY; DRAM; FPM; EDO.

RAM disk (**virtual disk**) an area of RAM (random-access memory) that is used to simulate an additional disk drive (*see* DISK). Data can be written and read much more quickly on a RAM disk than on a real disk. Like memory, a RAM disk goes blank whenever the computer is turned off; its contents must be copied onto it from a real disk whenever the computer is turned on. RAM disks are ordinarily employed to store frequently used programs or temporary working files.

RAM disks are especially popular under the DOS operating system (*see* MS-DOS). A RAM disk is created by modifying the operating system so that an area of RAM is treated in a special way; no modification to the machine is required.

Because it uses RAM to replace disk space, a RAM disk is the exact opposite of VIRTUAL MEMORY, which is the use of disk space to replace RAM. Thus, RAM disks are not used under Windows, VMS, or OS/2.

random-access device any memory device in which it is possible to find any particular record as quickly, on average, as any other record. The computer's internal RAM and disk storage devices are examples of random-access devices. *Contrast* SEQUENTIAL-ACCESS DEVICE.

random-access memory *see* RAM.

random-number generator a computer program that calculates numbers that seem to have been chosen randomly. In reality, a computer cannot generate numbers that are truly random, since it always generates the numbers according to a deterministic rule. However, certain generating rules produce numbers whose behavior is unpredictable enough that they can be treated as random numbers for practical purposes. The RND function in BASIC is an example of a random-number generator contained in a computer programming language. Random-number generators are useful in writing programs involving games of chance, and they are also used in an important simulation technique called MONTE CARLO SIMULATION.

raster a scan pattern that fills the screen of a CRT. Like television sets, present-day computers scan the entire screen continuously with an electron beam. Earlier graphics terminals worked more like oscilloscopes — they directed the electron beam only at places where lines were to be drawn. *See* BIT-MAPPED GRAPHICS; VECTOR GRAPHICS.

raster graphics graphics in which an image is generated by scanning an entire screen or page and marking every point as black, white, or another color, as opposed to VECTOR GRAPHICS.

A video screen and a laser printer are raster graphics devices; a pen plotter is a vector graphics device because it marks only at specified points on the page.

raster image processor (**RIP**) a device that handles computer output as a grid of dots. Dot-matrix, inkjet, and laser printers are all raster image processors.

rasterize to convert an image into a bitmap of the right size and shape to match a raster graphics output device. *See* BITMAP; RASTER GRAPHICS; VECTOR GRAPHICS.

ray tracing the computation of the paths of rays of light reflected and/or bent by various substances.

Ray-tracing effects define lighting, shadows, reflections, and transparency. Such computations often are very lengthy and may require several hours of computer time to produce a RENDERING (realistic drawing of three-dimensional objects by computer).

FIGURE 218. RCA PLUG

RCA plug (also called PHONO PLUG) an inexpensive shielded plug sometimes used for audio and composite video signals (*see* Figure 218); it plugs straight in without twisting or locking. *Contrast* BNC CONNECTOR.

read to transfer information from an external medium, such as a diskette, into a computer.

readme (from *read me*) the name given to files that the user of a piece of software is supposed to read before using it. The readme file contains the latest information from the manufacturer; it often contains major corrections to the instruction manual.

read-only pre-recorded and unable to be changed. *See* LOCK; CD-ROM; WRITE-PROTECT; ATTRIBUTES.

read-only memory computer memory that is permanently recorded and cannot be changed. *See* ROM.

RealAudio a communication protocol developed by Real Networks (http://www.realaudio.com) that allows audio signals to be broadcast over the Internet. The user hears the signal in real time, rather than waiting for an audio file to be downloaded and then played. RealAudio is sometimes used to distribute special-interest radio broadcasts and the like.

real estate *(slang)* the space occupied by a computer on a desktop or an electronic component on a circuit board (*compare* FOOTPRINT).

real mode the operating mode in which an 80286, 386, 486, or Pentium microprocessor acts like an 8086 or 8088, with a maximum of one megabyte of memory of which only 640K is available to user programs.

DOS runs in real mode; Windows and OS/2 run in protected mode and multiple virtual mode.

In real mode, the segment and offset registers contain the true addresses of memory locations, while in protected mode, segment registers point to entries in a lookup table. *See* PROTECTED MODE; MULTIPLE VIRTUAL MODE.

real-mode driver a DEVICE DRIVER that runs in REAL MODE under a protected-mode operating system such as Windows 95 and its successors. Real-mode drivers are slower than their protected-mode counterparts.

real number any number that can be represented either as an integer or a decimal fraction with any finite or infinite number of digits. Real numbers correspond to points on a number line.

Examples are $0, 2.5, 345, -2134, 0.00003, \frac{1}{3}, \sqrt{2}$, and π. However, $\sqrt{-1}$ is not a real number (it does not exist anywhere among the positive or negative numbers). *Contrast* COMPLEX NUMBER.

On computers, real numbers are represented with a finite number of digits, thus limiting their accuracy. (*See* ROUNDING ERROR.)

In many programming languages, "real number" means "floating-point number." *See* FLOATING-POINT NUMBER.

real soon now *(slang)* at an indefinite time in the future, probably much later than promised. *See* VAPORWARE.

real-time programming programming in which the proper functioning of the program depends on the amount of time consumed. For instance, computers that control automatic machinery must often both detect and introduce time delays of accurately determined lengths.

ream a package of 500 sheets of paper.

reboot to restart a computer, that is, turn it off and then on again. Many operating systems, including UNIX and also Windows 95 and its successors, have to be shut down properly before power to the computer is turned off; otherwise, data will be lost. *See* BOOT.

rebuild Desktop a housecleaning operation that needs to be performed monthly on the Macintosh.

The Desktop system file is an invisible file that stores information about icons, comments from the "Get Info" box, and links to application files for all the document files. As this file grows larger, the computer's response will begin to slow to unacceptable levels. At regular intervals, the Desktop should be rebuilt. This will improve system performance.

To rebuild the desktop, hold down the Command and Option keys during bootup.

record a collection of related data items. For example, a company may store information about each employee in a single record. Each record consists of several fields — a field for the name, a field for a Social Security number, and so on.

Here is an illustration of the Pascal record data type. Suppose information for each customer at a store will be kept in a record with three fields: name, address, and account balance. Create the record type "customer" as follows:

```
TYPE
  customer = RECORD
              name    : STRING;
              address : STRING;
              class   : INTEGER:
              balance : REAL
             END;
```

Then we can create the array `clist`, which will be an array of items of type `customer`:

```
VAR clist: ARRAY[1..number] OF customer;
```

Now the expression

```
clist[7].name
```

will refer to the name for customer 7,

```
clist[8].balance
```

will refer to the balance for customer 8, and so on.

In object-oriented languages, the same concept is used in a more general fashion: an OBJECT can include methods as well as data items.

recovering erased files retrieval of deleted files whose space has not yet been overwritten by other data.

When you erase a file on a computer disk, the space that the file occupied is marked as free, but it is not actually overwritten until the space is needed for something else. If you erase a file accidentally, you can often get it back by using programs such as Norton Utilities or analogous programs on other machines. As soon as you realize you want to recover a file, do everything you can to stop other programs from writing on the same disk so that nothing else will be written in the space that the file occupied.

On the Macintosh and in Windows 95 and its successors, deleted files usually go into a trash can or recycling bin from which they can be retrieved. The disk space is not actually freed until the user empties the trash. Until then, the files can be restored to their original locations.

```
PROGRAM factorial(INPUT,OUTPUT);
VAR x:INTEGER;

   FUNCTION fact(x: INTEGER) : INTEGER;
     VAR t:INTEGER;
     BEGIN
       writeln('Now looking for factorial of',x);
       IF x > 0 THEN z := x * fact(x-1) ELSE z := 1;
       { Here is the recursion^^^^^^^^^^}
       writeln('The factorial of ',x,'is',z);
       fact :=z
   END; {end of procedure fact}

BEGIN  { main program begins here }
   readln(x);
   writeln(fact(x))
END.
```

FIGURE 219. RECURSION IN PASCAL

recursion the calling of a procedure by itself, creating a new copy of the procedure.

To allow recursion, a programming language must allow for local variables (thus, recursion is not easy to accomplish in most versions of BASIC). Each time the procedure is called, it needs to keep track of values for the variables that may be different from the values they had the last time the procedure was called. Therefore, a recursive procedure that calls itself many times can consume a lot of memory.

Recursion is the natural way to solve problems that contain smaller problems of the same kind. Examples include drawing some kinds of fractals (*see* FRACTAL); parsing structures that can have similar structures inside them (*see* PARSING); sorting (*see* QUICKSORT); and calculating the determinant of a matrix by breaking it up into smaller matrices.

A recursive procedure can be used to calculate the factorial of an integer. (*See* FACTORIAL.) Fig. 219 shows a Pascal program that does so.

The recursion occurs when the function fact calls itself. Note that the ELSE clause is crucial. That clause gives a nonrecursive definition for the factorial of zero. If it were not there, the program would end up in an endless loop as the function fact kept calling itself until the computer ran out of memory. Any time recursion is used, it is necessary to make sure that there is some condition that will cause the recursion to halt.

Following is an example of the output from this program when the number 4 is given as the input. In practice, you would want to remove the two writeln statements from the function, but they are included here to make it possible to see the order of execution.

```
Now looking for factorial of 4
Now looking for factorial of 3
Now looking for factorial of 2
Now looking for factorial of 1
Now looking for factorial of 0
The factorial of 0 is 1
The factorial of 1 is 1
The factorial of 2 is 2
The factorial of 3 is 6
The factorial of 4 is 24
24
```

Any iterative (repetitive) program can be expressed recursively, and recursion is the normal way of expressing repetition in Prolog and Lisp.

FIGURE 220. RECYCLE BIN

Recycle Bin in Windows 95 and its successors, the place where deleted files are stored, corresponding to the TRASH on the Macintosh. You can put a file in the Recycle Bin by dragging it there or by choosing "delete" in Explorer and similar applications. However, software can also delete files directly and irretrievably.

Red Book the Philips/Sony standard format for audio compact discs. *See* CD.

redline to mark a portion of a printed document that has been changed. Redlining is usually a line (originally red) in the margin or a gray shading applied to the marked area. It is used with manuals, laws, regulations, etc., where changes need to be marked.

redo to reverse the effect of the most recent UNDO command.

redundancy

   1. unnecessary repetition; lack of conciseness. Data files can be compressed by removing redundancy and expressing the same data more concisely. *See* DATA COMPRESSION.

   2. the provision of extra information or extra hardware to increase reliability. For example, a simple way to protect a message from errors in transmission is to transmit it twice. It is very unlikely that both copies will be corrupted in exactly the same way.

Redundant hardware is extra hardware, such as one disk drive serving as a backup for another. *See also* RAID.

reentrant procedure a procedure that has been implemented in such a way that more than one process can execute it at the same time without conflict. *See* MULTITASKING.

reflow (**rewrap**) to rearrange a written text so that the ends of lines come out more even. For example, reflowing will change this text:

```
Four score and seven years ago our
forefathers
brought forth upon this continent a
new
nation, conceived in liberty...
```

into this:

```
Four score and seven years ago our
forefathers brought forth upon this
continent a new nation, conceived in
liberty...
```

Reflowing changes the total number of lines and thus the positions of the page breaks. *See* WORD WRAP.

refresh

1. to update the contents of a window to show information that has changed; to REPAINT the screen.

2. to RELOAD the contents of a WEB PAGE from the machine on which it resides.

3. to regenerate the display on a video screen by scanning the screen with an electron beam. Though it seems to, the screen does not glow continuously; instead, it is refreshed 30 to 60 times per second, rather like a movie screen.

4. to freshen the contents of a memory chip. Dynamic RAM chips have to be refreshed many times per second; on each refresh cycle, they read their own contents and then store the same information back into the same memory location.

refresh rate the rate at which a video screen is repeatedly scanned to keep the image constantly visible; typically 30 to 75 hertz (cycles per second).

regional settings the settings in an operating system that pertain to the user's location, such as language, currency, and time zone.

register a row of flip-flops used to store a group of binary digits while the computer is processing them. (*See* FLIP-FLOP.) A flip-flop can be in either of two states, so one flip-flop can store 1 bit. A register consisting of 16 flip-flops can store words that are 16 bits long.

registration

1. the act of informing the manufacturer of a product that you have purchased and installed it. Registering software is a good idea because it makes you eligible for customer support and upgrades from the manufacturer.

2. the alignment of color plates in a multi-color printing job on a printing press. If the colors are not perfectly aligned, there may be MOIRÉS, or there may be unitentional gaps between colors. *See* TRAPPING.

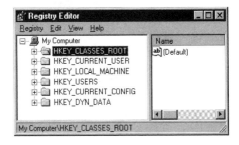

FIGURE 221. WINDOWS 95 REGISTRY EDITOR

Registration Editor *see* REGISTRY.

Registry the part of Windows 95, 98, 2000, and NT that stores setup information for the hardware, software, and operating system. It takes over most of the function performed by INI files and the Registration Editor in earlier versions of Windows.

The information in the Registry is supplied by the Control Panel and the setup routines for particular applications. You can also view the contents of the Registry directly by choosing Run from the START MENU and typing regedit. This is rarely necessary unless unusual problems arise.

regular expression a way of defining a possible series of characters. Table 16 gives some examples. In UNIX, the grep command searches a file for character strings that match a regular expression; regular expressions are also used in the programming language AWK and in some editors. *See* GREP; AWK.

Regular expressions are efficient to process because the computer can always tell whether a string matches a regular expression by working through the string and the expression from left to right, one item at a time. This is simpler than the methods used to parse Backus-Naur

TABLE 16
REGULAR EXPRESSIONS

Expression	Matches
abc	The string abc
a.c	Like abc but with any character in place of b
a*bc	Zero or more a's, followed by bc
a*b+c	Zero or more a's, one or more b's, and c
*	An asterisk
\\	A backslash
[BbCx]	The character B, b, C, or x
[A-E2-4]	The character A, B, C, D, E, 2, 3, or 4
[^A-E2-4]	Any character except A, B, C, D, E, 2, 3, or 4
[Ff]ill	Fill or fill
^abc	abc at beginning of line
abc$	abc at end of line

form or other kinds of syntactic description. *See* PARSING; BACKUS-NAUR FORM.

relational database a database that consists of tables made up of rows and columns. For example:

Name	City	State
Downing, D.	Seattle	Washington
Covington, M.	Athens	Georgia

The table defines a relation between the things in each row: It says that Seattle is the city for Downing, Athens is the city for Covington, and so on.

One important operation in a relational database is to *join* two tables, i.e., cross-reference information between them. For example, the names in this table could be cross-referenced to another table containing names and salaries; the result would be a table relating name, city, state, and salary.

A database with only one table is called a *flat-file database.* Every relational database has a *query language* for expressing commands to retrieve data. *See* QUERY LANGUAGE; SQL.

relative address

1. in computer memory, a memory address measured relative to another location. To convert a relative address into an absolute (true) address it is necessary to add the address of the point it is measured from. *Compare* OFFSET.

2. in a spreadsheet program, a cell address that indicates the position of a cell relative to another cell. If this formula is copied to another location, the address will be changed so that it refers to the cell in the same position relative to the new cell. In Lotus 1-2-3 and Microsoft

Excel, a cell address is treated as a relative address unless it contains dollar signs. (*See* ABSOLUTE ADDRESS.) For example, if the formula 2*D7 is entered into the cell E9, the D7 in the formula really means, "the cell that is one column to the left and two rows above." If this formula is now copied to cell H15, the formula will now become 2*G13, since G13 is the cell that is one column to the left and two rows above the cell H15.

relative URL a URL for a document in the same directory as the current document. For example, if a web page contains the link <a href="http://doc1.html"> it will look for the document doc1.html in the same directory as the page containing the link. If you copy both of these files to a different directory or different machine, the link will still work. *Contrast* ABSOLUTE URL.

release
    1. the edition or version number of a software product. Most commonly, whole-number increments in the release number (e.g, from 1.0 to 2.0) signify a major upgrade to the program. Fractional increases are for minor upgrades and bug fixes.
    2. to let go of the mouse button. *Contrast* CLICK; PRESS.

reload to obtain a fresh copy of information that is already in a computer; an example is reloading a WEB PAGE that may have changed recently, rather than viewing a copy stored in a CACHE on your own computer.

relocatable program a machine-language program that can execute correctly regardless of the location where it is loaded into the computer's memory. The loader changes the addresses referred to within the program to reflect the program's actual position. In DOS, relocatable programs reside on EXE files.

remote located on a computer far away from the user. *Contrast* LOCAL.

remove spots a photopaint filter that erases spots from digitized photographs and pictures. Technically, it removes all pixel groups below a certain size; image detail may be lost.

render (3-D program) to apply a color, texture, and lighting to a WIREFRAME model.

rendering the technology of drawing three-dimensional objects realistically on a computer. It involves computations of texture and light reflections. Rendering is performed automatically by VRML viewers. *See also* VRML; RAY TRACING.

repaginate to allow a word processor or page layout program to reposition page breaks by working forward from the current cursor position. *See also* REFLOW; WRAP

repaint to regenerate the display on all or part of a computer screen.

repeat keyword used to define one kind of loop in Pascal. The word

REPEAT marks the beginning of the loop, and the word UNTIL marks the end. Here is an example:

```
REPEAT
  writeln(x);
  x := 2*x;
  writeln('Type S if you want to stop.');
  readln(c); {c is of type CHAR}
UNTIL c = 'S';
```

The computer always executes the loop at least once because it does not check to see whether the stopping condition is true until after it has executed the loop. *Contrast* WHILE.

repeater a device that receives signals by network cable or by radio and retransmits them, thereby overcoming limits of cable length or radio range. A repeater can also conserve BANDWIDTH by retransmitting only the data packets that are addressed to sites in its area.

required hyphen a hyphen that does not indicate a place where a word can be broken apart. For instance, if the hyphenated word "flip-flop" falls at the end of the line, then "flip-" can appear on one line, with "flop" at the beginning of the next. But if you type "flip-flop" with a required hyphen, it will not be split up. In WordPerfect, a required hyphen is typed by hitting the Home key and then the hyphen key.

required space a space that does not denote a place where words can be split apart at the end of a line. For instance, you might not want a person's initials (as in "T. S. Eliot") to be split at the end of a line. You should therefore use required spaces between them rather than ordinary spaces. In WordPerfect, a required space is typed by hitting the Home key and then the space bar. In TEX, a required space is typed as ~ (TILDE).

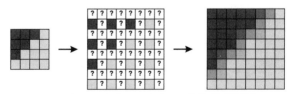

FIGURE 222. RESAMPLING (INTERPOLATION)
FILLS IN MISSING PIXELS WHEN AN IMAGE IS ENLARGED

resample to change the size of a bitmap image or the sampling rate of a digital audio file, using interpolation to fill in the intermediate samples (Fig. 222). *See also* INTERPOLATION (definition 2).

reseat to remove an integrated circuit (IC) or a printed circuit board from its socket and reinsert it. This often yields a better electrical connection.

ResEdit (**Res**ource **Edit**or) a program distributed by Apple Computer for configuring the operating system of the Macintosh and for editing resources of all types. *See* RESOURCE.

reserved word a word that has a special meaning in a particular programming language and cannot be used as a variable name. For example, in BASIC and Pascal, IF is a reserved word. COBOL has dozens of reserved words. FORTRAN and PL/I have none, since in these languages it is always possible to tell from the context whether or not a word is a variable name.

reserve price a secret minimum bid in an auction. Ordinarily, the minimum bid (the lowest price that the seller will take) is announced to would-be buyers. However, auction services such as eBay allow the seller to specify a secret minimum bid, called a reserve price. The amount of the reserve price is not disclosed, but bids below it are rejected. *See* AUCTION; EBAY.

resistance the measure of how difficult it is for electric current to flow through a circuit or component. Resistance is measured in a unit called the ohm. *See* OHM'S LAW.

resize to change the size or dimensions of; to SCALE.

To resize an object interactively with the mouse in most environments, select the object, then drag one of the HANDLES in the desired direction. Dragging a corner handle will keep the vertical and horizontal aspects of the object in the same proportion to each other (like reducing or enlarging something on a photocopier). Dragging one of the handles at the midpoint of the BOUNDING BOX will affect only one dimension of the object. This way, you can stretch or shrink the object to the desired shape.

resolution a measure of the amount of detail that can be shown in the images produced by a printer or screen. For instance, many laser printers have a resolution of 300 dots per inch (dpi), meaning that they print characters using a grid of black or white squares each 1/300 of an inch across. This means that their resolution is 150 lines per inch printing line art, or 50 lines per inch printing halftone shadings (e.g., photographs), which use pixels in groups of six.

The human eye normally resolves about 150 lines per inch at normal reading distance, but a person examining a page critically can distinguish two or three times this much detail.

The resolution of a screen is given as the total number of pixels in each direction (e.g., 640×480 pixels across the whole screen). The equivalent number of dots per inch depends on the size of the screen. Present-day video screens resolve about 80 dots per inch; they are not nearly as sharp as ink on paper.

A big advantage of draw programs, as opposed to paint programs, is that they can use the full resolution of the printer; they are not limited to printing what they display on the screen. However, some paint programs can handle very detailed images by displaying only part of the image at a time. *See* DRAW PROGRAM; PAINT PROGRAM; VECTOR GRAPHICS.

resource

   1.   anything of value that is available for use. *Resources* can refer to computers on a network, preallocated memory blocks in an operating system, or money in a budget.

   2.   a modifiable part of a program on the Macintosh or under Microsoft Windows or OS/2, separate from the program instructions themselves. Resources include menus, icons, and fonts.

resource leak *see* LEAK.

FIGURE 223. RESTORE BUTTON

restore to make a window go back to its previous size after being minimized or maximized. In Windows 95 and later, the restore button is to the right of the minimize button on the title bar and alternates with the maximize (full-screen) button. Or, right-click the application's icon on the taskbar; the top choice of the pop-up menu is "Restore."

   See also WINDOW; MINIMIZE; MAXIMIZE.

retouching altering a photograph or illustration to eliminate flaws and unnecessary elements. The preferred software for this job is a PHO-TOPAINT PROGRAM, which has the appropriate tools and FILTERS to seamlessly correct digitized photographs.

retrocomputing the hobby of preserving old computer technology, either by maintaining the machines themselves or by emulating them on newer equipment.

Return key the key on a computer keyboard that tells the computer that the end of a line has been reached. On most keyboards the Return key is marked Enter. On IBM 3270 terminals, the Return and Enter keys are separate.

reusable components pieces of software that can be used in other programs. For example, Java classes are reusable; they can be used by programs other than the one for which they were originally created.

FIGURE 224. EXAMPLES OF REVERSED TYPE

reverse to replace white with black and black with white. A reversed block of type can be a dramatic design element—however, legibility can become a factor. A large block of reverse text is difficult to read. Typefaces with hairline strokes do not reverse well. The COUNTERS of the letters may spread and fill in if the font size is too small. Always evaluate a proof of reverse type carefully.

Type can also be reversed out of a color or a tint. Check that there is enough contrast between the type and the background for the text to be read.

revert to reload from disk a previously saved version of a file, losing all intermediate changes. Revert is therefore a super-undo command. Save your file before attempting a potentially dangerous command (search and replace or applying a filter), and you will have the option of reverting to the older file in case something goes wrong.

rewrap *See* REFLOW.

REXX a programming language used to write procedures that contain operating system commands. REXX is used in OS/2 .CMD files, IBM PC-DOS 7.0 .BAT files, and some IBM mainframe operating systems. REXX is also a convenient language for testing algorithms and writing sample utility programs when execution speed is not important.

Fig. 225 shows a simple REXX program. Communication with the user and with the operating system is particularly easy: *arg* retrieves command-line arguments, PULL breaks up a line of input into arguments separated by spaces, and any string or string expression, when used by itself as a statement, is passed to the operating system as a command.

Depending on the operating system, REXX programs are required to begin with / or with a line containing REXX so they can be distin-

```
/* REXX program to display space available on a disk */
/* under OS/2 */

'@echo off'
ARG diskdrive
if diskdrive='' then diskdrive='c:'

/*Execute dir command, extract the line that contains*/
/*"bytes free", and write it on tempfile.tmp*/

'dir ' diskdrive '/w | find "bytes free" >tempfile.tmp'

/* Read that line into 2 variables, b and junk */

parse value linein('tempfile.tmp') with b junk

/* Report results and delete temporary file */

say b/1048576 ' megabytes are free on drive ' diskdrive

junk = stream('tempfile.tmp','c','close')
erase tempfile.tmp
```

FIGURE 225. REXX PROGRAM

guished from command procedures written in other languages. *Compare* AWK, PERL.

RF (**r**adio **f**requency) a frequency in the range that is typical of radio waves, approximately 0.5 to 2000 megahertz. *Contrast* AF.

RFC

    1. (**R**adio-**F**requency **C**hoke) an inductor (coil) designed to keep high-frequency signals from flowing into power supply lines and other interconnections. *See* RFI PROTECTION.

    2. (**R**equest **F**or **C**omment) one of numerous documents defining the standard for the Internet. All are supposedly unofficial, although most are followed universally. For example, RFC 822 specifies the format for E-MAIL messages in transit. RFCs are available on line at http://www.cis.ohio-state.edu/hypertext/information/rfc.html and other sites.

RFI protection protection of electronic equipment from radio-frequency interference.

    Computers use the same kind of high-frequency electrical energy as radio transmitters. This often causes RFI (radio-frequency interference), also called EMI (electromagnetic interference). All computers interfere with nearby radio and TV reception to some extent, and sometimes the problem is severe. On rare occasions, the opposite happens — a strong signal from a nearby radio transmitter disrupts the computer, or two computers interfere with each other.

    Here are some suggestions for reducing RFI:

1. If possible, move the radio or TV receiver away from the computer, and plug it into an outlet on a different circuit.

2. Supply power to the computer through a surge protector that includes an RFI filter (*see* SURGE PROTECTOR).

3. Ground the computer properly (*see* SURGE PROTECTOR).

4. Use high-quality shielded cables to connect the parts of the computer system together. Make sure all cable shields and ground wires are connected properly. This is especially important for the monitor cable and the printer cable. If possible, wind the cable into a coil to increase its inductance.

5. Check that the computer has the appropriate approval from the FCC (Federal Communications Commission). Some computers are not approved for use in residential areas. *See* FCC; CLASS A; CLASS B.

RFP (**R**equest **F**or **P**roposal) an invitation to submit a price quotation, sales pitch, or grant proposal.

RGB monitor a color monitor that uses separate signals for the three additive primary colors (red, green, and blue). *Contrast* COMPOSITE VIDEO. *See also* ANALOG MONITOR.

ribbon bar a row of small icons arranged just below the menu bar of a window. Each icon gives the user acces to a frequently used command.

rich text text that contains codes identifying italics, boldface, and other special effects. WORD PROCESSING programs deal with rich text rather than plain ASCII text. *Contrast* TEXT FILE, NONDOCUMENT MODE.

right-click to CLICK with the right-hand (or SECONDARY) mouse button. In Windows 95 and its successors, right-clicking the mouse will pop-up an action menu that includes access to the "Properties" dialog for the selected object.

RISC (**R**educed **I**nstruction **S**et **C**omputer) a CPU design with a small number of machine language instructions, each of which can be executed very quickly. The Sun Sparcstation and the PowerPC are examples of RISC computers. The opposite of RISC is CISC.

RISC architecture was developed for speed. A RISC computer can execute each instruction faster because there are fewer instructions to choose between, and thus less time is taken up identifying each instruction.

RISC and CISC computers can run the same kinds of software; the only difference is in what the software looks like in machine code. CISC is faster than RISC if memory access is relatively slow; the RISC machine has to fetch more instructions from memory than the CISC machine to do the same work. RISC is faster than CISC if memory access is very fast. *See also* CISC; COMPUTER ARCHITECTURE; POWERPC.

riser a small circuit board inserted perpendicularly into the motherboard, containing slots for cards. *Compare* DAUGHTERBOARD. *See also* MOTHERBOARD; CARD (definition 2).

riser-rated (describing cable) suitable for use inside walls and in open areas but not in places where air circulates, such as above suspended ceilings. Riser-rated cable is fire-resistant but can give off noxious fumes when overheated. *Contrast* PLENUM-RATED.

river a series of white spaces between words that appear to flow from line to line in a printed document, like the white patch in the example below. Rivers result from trying to justify type when the columns are too narrow or the available software or printer is not versatile enough. *See* JUSTIFICATION.

> Quo usque tandem
> abutere,   Catilina,
> patientia   nostra?
> quamdiu etiam furor
> iste tuus nos eludet?

FIGURE 226. RJ-45 CONNECTOR (*LEFT*) AND
RJ-11 CONNECTOR (*RIGHT*)

RJ-11 the 4-pin modular connector used to connect telephones and modems to the telephone line (*see* Figure 226, *right*). One RJ-11 connector can support two telephone lines, one on the inner pair of pins and one on the outer pair.

RJ-11 connector the flat-cable connector ("modular connector") commonly used on telephone wires.

RJ-45 the 8-pin modular connector used on the ends of 10base-T and 100base-T cables (*see* Figure 226, *left*); it resembles a 4-pin telephone connector but is wider. The color code for wiring RJ-45 connectors is shown in Table 17. *See also* CATEGORY 3 CABLE; CATEGORY 5 CABLE.

RL abbreviation for "real life" in e-mail and on-line games.

TABLE 17
WIRING OF RJ-45 CONNECTORS FOR
10BASE-T AND 100BASE-T NETWORKS

	T568A		T568B
1	white-orange	1	white-green
2	orange	2	green
3	white-green	3	white-orange
4	blue	4	blue
5	white-blue	5	white-blue
6	green	6	orange
7	white-brown	7	white-brown
8	brown	8	brown

Pins are numbered from left to right as seen with the plug
pointing away from you, contacts up.

Note that one twisted pair (on pins 3 and 6) goes to
nonadjacent pins.

Normal cables are T568A or T568B at both ends. A crossover
cable is T568A at one end and T568B at the other.

RLL (**r**un-**l**ength **l**imited) a type of hard-disk controller that was used in
the late 1980s to get about 50 percent more data on the same disk as a
conventional hard disk controller by using data compression technology. Thus, the Shugart ST-225 hard disk has 20 megabytes of capacity
with a conventional MFM controller, or 30 megabytes with an RLL
controller. *Contrast* MFM. For newer technologies *see* IDE; ESDI; SCSI.

rlogin (**r**emote **login**) the UNIX command that allows you to use your
computer as a terminal on another computer. Unlike telnet, rlogin
does more than just establish a communication path: it also tells the
other computer what kind of terminal you are using and sends it your
user name.

RMI (**R**emote **M**ethod **I**nvocation) technique for calling a method in a
Java class located on a machine (such as a web server) different from the
machine (such as the browser client) on which the current application
is running.

rms (**r**oot-**m**ean-**s**quare) the most common method of measuring the
voltage of an alternating current; the square root of the mean of the
square of the instantaneous voltage. This method of measurement is
used because power (wattage) depends on the voltage squared; thus,
120 volts AC rms will light a light bulb to the same brightness as 120
volts DC. With a sine wave, the rms voltage is $0.707 \times$ the peak voltage
or $0.353 \times$ the peak-to-peak voltage. *Contrast* PEAK; PEAK-TO-PEAK.

robot

    1. a computer that moves itself or other objects in three-dimensional space under automatic control. Robots are now widely used in manufacturing. *See also* ARTIFICIAL INTELLIGENCE.

    2. *(slang;* also *bot)* a computer program that performs a human-like communication function such as replying to E-MAIL or responding to messages in a NEWSGROUP. *See also* DAEMON.

robust reliable even under varying or unforeseen conditions. *Contrast* BRITTLE.

ROFL e-mail abbreviation for "rolling on the floor laughing."

rollerball *see* TRACKBALL.

rollover

    1. an important change in the date or another gradually increasing number, such as the date rollover from 1999 to 2000.

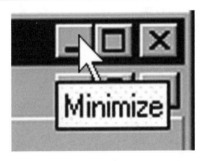

FIGURE 227. ROLLOVER, DEFINITION 2

    2. an explanatory note that appears as the mouse cursor is placed onto (*rolls over*) a key word, icon, or graphic even though the mouse has not been clicked. Rollovers are used by operating systems and application programs, but are especially common on web pages.

    JavaScript can be used to provide rollover effects on a web page. The following example uses the status line at the bottom of the browser window to include a description of a link when the mouse passes over it:

```
<html><head><title>Mouse Rollover example</title>

<script language='javascript'>  <!-- hide
```

```
function rollOn(choicedescription) {
  window.status=choicedescription;
}

function rollOut() {
  window.status=" ";
}
-->
</script></head>
<body>
<h1>Example of a Mouse Rollover, using the status line</h1>
<ul>
<li><a href="#choice1"
      onMouseOver="rollOn('Here is text that describes
            choice 1'); return true;"
      onMouseOut="rollOut(); return true;">
      Choice 1 </a>
<li><a href="#choice2"
      onMouseOver="rollOn('Here is text that describes
            choice 2'); return true"
      onMouseOut="rollOut(); return true;">
      Choice 2 </a>
</ul>
<a name="choice1"><h2>Here is choice 1</h2></a>
Here is some text for choice 1.<br>
<a name="choice2"><h2>Here is choice 2</h2></a>
Here is some text for choice 2.<br>
</body></html>
```

The next example changes the display of the image when the mouse
rolls over the links:

```
<html><head><title>Mouse Rollover example</title>

<script language='javascript'>  <!-- hide

function rollOn(choicenum) {
if (choicenum==1)
      { document.image1.src="image_for_choice_1.jpg"; }
else {document.image1.src="image_for_choice_2.jpg"; }
}

function rollOut() {
   document.image1.src="default_image.jpg";
}
--></script></head>

<body>
<h1>Example of a Mouse Rollover with a changing image</h1>
<ul>
<li><a href="#choice1"
      onMouseOver="rollOn(1); return true;"
      onMouseOut="rollOut(); return true;">
      Choice 1 </a>
<li><a href="#choice2"
      onMouseOver="rollOn(2); return true;"
      onMouseOut="rollOut(); return true;">
      Choice 2 </a>
</ul>
```

```
<img name="image1" height="200" width="300"
     src="default_image.jpg">

<a name="choice1"><h2>Here is choice 1</h2></a>
Here is some text for choice 1.<br>
<a name="choice2"><h2>Here is choice 2</h2></a>
Here is some text for choice 2.<br>
</body></html>
```

See also WHAT'S THIS?; HTML; JAVA; JAVASCRIPT; RIGHT-CLICK.

FIGURE 228. ROLL-UP MENU

roll-up menu a dialog box that stays open on screen while you choose among the settings it offers. The roll-up can be positioned anywhere you like and when you are finished with it, it can be "rolled up" to just the size of its title bar. It is very similar in concept to a TOOLBOX.

ROM (**R**ead-**O**nly **M**emory) a computer memory that contains instructions that do not need to be changed, such as permanent parts of the operating system. The computer can read instructions out of ROM but cannot store new data in it. *See also* CD-ROM; PROM; EPROM.

roman the kind of type that books are normally typeset in, as opposed to italics or boldface. The type you are reading now is roman type. *See* TYPEFACE.

ROM BASIC a version of Microsoft BASIC that was built into a ROM chip on early IBM Personal Computers, making it possible to use BASIC on a machine with no disk drives. (Programs could be stored on cassette tape.)

Some older PCs display a message such as "No ROM BASIC; system halted" if turned on with no disk drives attached.

ROM BIOS *see* BIOS.

root the account name used by the system administrator under UNIX. (From ROOT DIRECTORY.)

root directory the main directory of a disk, containing files and/or subdirectories. *See* DIRECTORY.

root-mean-square *see* RMS.

rot13 (rotate 13) a type of ENCRYPTION commonly used on the Internet to conceal answers to puzzles and the like. To encode a message, the first 13 letters of the alphabet are swapped with the last 13. Performing the same swap again decodes the message. This is not a secure code, of course, but it provides a way to make things temporarily unreadable.

Qba'g lbh jbaqre jung guvf fnlf?

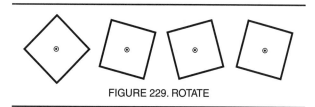

FIGURE 229. ROTATE

rotate in draw programs, to turn an object around a specific center. By default, the center of rotation is at the center of the object itself. You can drag this center to wherever you want it to be and then rotate the object around it. Rotation can be done interactively with the mouse, or if you require more precision, you can use the DIALOG BOX to set the angle of rotation in degrees.

ROTFL e-mail abbreviation for "rolling on the floor laughing."

rounding the act of replacing a number with the nearest number that has a smaller number of significant digits. For example, 2.76 rounded to one decimal place is 2.8. The rule is that if the first digit to be discarded is 5 or greater, the last digit that is kept should be increased. Thus 2.74 → 2.7, but 2.76 → 2.8. *Contrast* TRUNCATION.

An alternative way to do rounding — easier on the computer — is to add 0.5 (or 0.05, or 0.005, etc.) to the number before discarding digits. For example:

$$2.74 + 0.05 = 2.79 \rightarrow 2.7$$

$$2.76 + 0.05 = 2.81 \rightarrow 2.8$$

The addition changes 7 to 8 in the desired cases; then the subsequent digits can simply be discarded.

In BASIC, you can round X to the nearest integer by evaluating INT(X+0.5). You can round X to 2 decimal places by evaluating

INT(100*X+0.5)/100 (unless the result is thrown off by *rounding error*; see next entry).

rounding error an error that occurs because the computer cannot store the true value of most real numbers; instead, it can store only an approximation of a finite number of digits.

If you wish to write $\frac{1}{3}$ as a decimal fraction, you can approximate it as 0.333333333, but it would require an infinite number of digits to express it exactly. The computer faces the same problem except that internally it stores the numbers in binary, and it can lose accuracy in converting between binary and decimal. For example, 0.1 has no exact representation on a computer; if you add the computer's representation of 0.1 to 0 ten times, you will not get exactly 1. To avoid rounding error, some computer programs represent numbers as decimal digits. *See* BINARY-CODED DECIMAL.

Route 128 a highway that skirts the west side of Boston, Massachusetts, passing through the cities of Needham and Waltham. Route 128 is the home of a number of computer companies, including Digital Equipment Corporation and Lotus. *See* DIGITAL EQUIPMENT CORPORATION; SILICON VALLEY; SILICON CREEK.

router a network component that joins several networks together intelligently. A router is more powerful than a bridge because instead of just choosing network segments based on previous traffic, a router can look up the best route to a distant site. The Internet relies heavily on routers. *Compare* HUB; BRIDGE; SWITCH (definition 2). *See also* DNS (definition 1).

RPG (**R**eport **P**rogram **G**enerator) a programming language developed by IBM in the 1960s in an attempt to simplify programming for business applications. RPG is based on the principle that most business computer programs have the same structure: a large file is read one record at a time, some actions are performed for each record (e.g., adding numbers to a running total, or perhaps writing an altered form of the record onto another file), and other actions are performed only at the end (e.g., printing out the totals). The RPG programmer specifies only the details of these actions, not the overall structure of the program.

Because RPG programming can be reduced to a fixed procedure for filling out forms, RPG was often the first programming language taught to trainees. However, RPG programs are markedly less readable than programs in other languages, and complex algorithms are difficult to express in RPG.

RPM (**r**evolutions **p**er **m**inute) a measure of speed of rotation. For example, many newer hard disks rotate at 7200 RPM.

RPN *see* POLISH NOTATION.

RS-232 an Electronics Industries Association (EIA) recommended standard for transmitting serial data by wire. This standard is now officially

TABLE 18
RS-232 PIN CONNECTIONS (25-PIN)

(Pin numbers are embossed on the connector.)

Pin	Signal	Direction	Explanation
1	GND	Both	Frame ground — ties together chassis of terminal and modem; often omitted
2	TxD	To modem	Transmitted data
3	RxD	To terminal	Received data
4	RTS	To modem	Request to send — high when terminal is on and able to communicate
5	CTS	To terminal	Clear to send — high when computer on other end is able to receive
6	DSR	To terminal	Data set ready — high when modem is on and functioning
7	SG	Both	Signal ground — reference point for all signal voltages
8	CD	To terminal	Carrier detect — high when a connection to another computer has been established
20	DTR	To modem	Data terminal ready — high when terminal is on and functioning. Most modems hang up phone when DTR goes low.
22	RI	To terminal	Ring indicator — high when telephone is ringing.

known as EIA-232D. Almost all modems, asynchronous computer terminals, and serial printers follow, at least to some degree, the RS-232 standard.

The connection includes lines for sending and receiving data, ground connections, and, usually, one or more control lines such as Carrier Detect or Data Terminal Ready (see Table 18). The data are sent as a stream of bits at a constant speed. Each character is preceded by a *start bit* and followed by one or two *stop bits*.

The signal voltages are +5 to +15 volts (binary 0 on the data lines, "high" or "true" on the control lines) and −5 to −15 volts (binary 1 on the data lines, "low" or "false" on the control lines). A disconnnected wire can be recognized because it is neither positive nor negative, but few RS-232 ports do this.

RS-232 ports usually have 25-pin connectors, but the connector is not part of the standard and its usage varies somewhat. Table 18 shows the usual pin assignments. Table 19 describes the 9-pin connector used on the IBM PC AT. (The Macintosh follows the RS-422 standard; *see* RS-422.) Figure 230 shows the solution to some common cabling problems. *See also* SERIAL; PARALLEL; BAUD; RS-422; RS-423.

RS-422, RS-423A two standards, recommended by the Electronics Industries Association (EIA), which define a format for transmitting serial data by wire, intended to replace the older RS-232 format. The

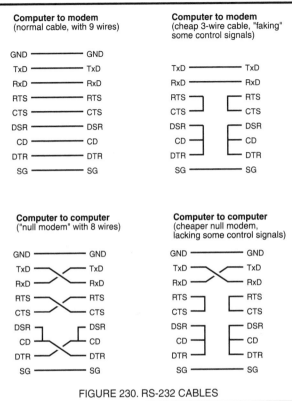

FIGURE 230. RS-232 CABLES

new format offers faster data rates and greater immunity to electrical noise.

The format exists in two versions. RS-422 uses balanced (differential) signaling with two wires for each signal. The computer responds only to the difference between the two wires and ignores any noise that is picked up by both. RS-423A is a simpler format using only one wire per signal; at suitable data rates, it is compatible with older RS-232 equipment. The Apple Macintosh has an RS-422/RS-423A port; Table 20 shows the pin connections. For RS-232 compatibility, use only the line marked "−" in each pair.

RS/6000 *see* WORKSTATION.

TABLE 19
RS-232 PIN CONNECTIONS (9-PIN PC SERIAL PORT)

Pin	Signal
1	Carrier detect
2	Receive data
3	Transmit data
4	Data terminal ready
5	Signal ground
6	Data set ready
7	Request to send
8	Clear to send
9	Ring indicator

TABLE 20
RS-422 PIN CONNECTIONS (MACINTOSH)

(Pin numbers are embossed on the connector.)
Original Macintosh (9-pin D-connector):

Pin	Signal
1	Frame ground
2	+5V power to external device
3	Signal ground
4	Transmit +
5	Transmit −
6	+12V power to external device
7	Clear to send
8	Receive +
9	Receive −

Macintosh SE, Macintosh II (8-pin mini-DIN connector):

Pin	Signal
1	Data terminal ready
2	Clear to send
3	Transmit −
4	Signal ground
5	Receive −
6	Transmit +
7	Carrier detect or clock input (Not used on Macintosh Plus)
8	Receive +

RSA encryption a public key encryption algorithm named after the initials of its developers (Ron Rivest, Adi Shamir, and Leonard Adleman). The security of the system relies on the difficulty of factoring very large numbers. More information about RSA encryption can be found at http://www.rsa.com. *See also* ENCRYPTION.

RSN *see* REAL SOON NOW.

RTFM (**r**ead **t**he **f**riendly **m**anual) an exhortation to computer users who are unwilling to look things up for themselves. *Compare* RYFM.

FIGURE 231. RUBBER STAMP

rubber stamp a paint program tool that duplicates a selected area of a drawing. Similar to the CLONE TOOL.

FIGURE 232. RULER

ruler a strip at the top (and sometimes the side) of the on-screen work area, marked in units of measurement. Like its physical counterparts, an on-screen ruler is used to help you measure things. Rulers can be found in word processors, drawing programs, and page layout programs. You have the option to display the ruler, or to hide it and give yourself some more working room. You can also have the ruler show units of measurement other than inches (PICAS might be more useful for many applications). A ruler is especially useful when using a high degree of zoom because it helps you keep your orientation.

In a word processor, the ruler is used to set the TABS and MARGINS.

run to make the computer execute a program. A distinction is often made between *compile time* (the time when the program is compiled; *see* COMPILER) and *run time* (the time when the program is run).

Run... a menu choice under Windows 3's PROGRAM MANAGER and Windows 95 and its successors' START BUTTON that allows you to run a program by typing its filename. For instance, to run `myprog.exe` from drive A, choose "Run..." and type `a:\myprog.exe` or simply `myprog` (it isn't necessary to type the extension). This is the usual way to run setup programs when installing new software.

run-length encoding a way of storing data in less than the usual amount of space by using special codes to indicate repeated bytes. *See* DATA COMPRESSION.

running head a small headline that appears at the top or bottom of each page. Running heads are usually there to remind the reader which chapter (or section) he or she is reading. In a dictionary like this one, the running heads tell you the first and last entries on the page spread.

run-time error an error that occurs when a program is being executed. For example, a run-time error might occur if division by 0 is attempted or if the subscript for an array is outside the allowable bounds for that array. A run-time error may cause the program to stop execution, or it may be handled by an error-trapping routine (*see* TRAPPING). *Contrast* COMPILE-TIME ERROR.

run-time player a software module that allows a presentation to run without the application software being present on a computer. Thus, the presentation becomes smaller, and is able to be played on any computer system.

RYFM (read your friendly manual, pronounced "riff-um") a computer user who pesters his colleagues with questions rather than look things up for himself. *Compare* RTFM.

S

SAA (Systems Application Architecture) a set of guidelines promoted by IBM for standardizing the design of large pieces of software. It includes a set of user interface guidelines called Common User Access (CUA), as well as guidelines for data communication, programming languages, and procedure libraries. *See also* CUA; USER INTERFACE.

Sad Mac the icon of a frowning Macintosh computer that announces the Mac has found a hardware problem and cannot finish booting. Jot down the number displayed below the icon, turn off the computer, and make sure all the cables are secure. Try to boot the computer again. If the Sad Mac appears again, it's time to look up the number of the repair station.

safe mode a way of running Windows 95, 98, and 2000 (not NT 4.0 or earlier) with many special hardware drivers disabled, to work around problems with improperly installed hardware or software. Safe mode is used only for testing.

sampling rate the number of times per second that sound waves are sampled and digitized. The highest frequency that can be reproduced is half the sampling rate. High-fidelity audio is usually sampled at 44.1 kHz (44,100 samples per second) in order to reproduce frequencies up to 22.05 kHz, just above the limit of human hearing. Speech can be stored more compactly by sampling at a lower rate, 22.05 or 11.025 kHz.

Another parameter is the number of bits of data stored in each sample. High-fidelity audio requires 16 bits per sample; speech can be reproduced adequately with 8 bits. One minute of sound, sampled at 44.1 kHz with 16 bits per sample, requires about 5 megabytes of disk space.

sandbox a safe environment to play in; a protective mechanism that prevents a program from accessing or changing memory or disk space outside of its own permitted area. This is a security feature preventing programs from damaging the system they run on. For example, a Java applet loaded from the World Wide Web runs in a sandbox where it is prohibited access to the hard disk on the browser's computer.

sans-serif a typeface that does not have serifs, such as this one. Serifs are small perpendicular marks at the ends of the strokes (*sans* is French for "without"). *See* Figure 233. *Contrast* SERIF; *see also* TYPEFACE.

saturation the intensity of a color. A highly saturated color is recognized as a vivid, brilliant color; to dull a color (decrease its saturation), you add small amounts of its *complement*, making it closer to gray. *See* HSB; COLOR.

FIGURE 233. SANS-SERIF TYPE

save to transfer information from the computer's memory to a storage device such as a disk drive. Saving data is vital because the contents of the computer's memory are lost when power is turned off. The opposite process is known as loading or retrieving.

Save As…

1. to save a document or drawing under a different name. The first time you save an untitled work, you will use "Save As …" instead of "Save."

2. to save a file in a different format (e.g., to save a CorelDraw file as a Windows Metafile). *See also* EXPORT.

SBC *see* SINGLE-BOARD COMPUTER.

scalable able to be used on a large or small scale without major changes. For example, much of the appeal of the UNIX operating system is its scalability; it can be used on small or large computers with little change in the way it works.

scalable font a font that can be used to print characters of any size. Many newer laser printers include scalable fonts; also, the TrueType fonts used by windowed operating systems are scalable. The shapes of the characters in a scalable font are stored in the form of vector graphics rather than bitmaps. *See* FONT; VECTOR GRAPHICS.

scalar a quantity represented by a single number, as opposed to an ARRAY or LIST.

scalar processor a computer that operates on only one piece of data at a time. Most computers are scalar processors. *Contrast* VECTOR PROCESSOR. *See also* SUPERSCALAR PROCESSOR.

scale to change the size of a graphical object without changing its shape. In most draw programs, you can scale any object by selecting it and then dragging one of the dots (called HANDLES) that appear at its corners.

scan converter a device that accepts video signals from a computer and converts them into standard television format (NTSC, PAL, SECAM) so that the computer screen display can be used in videotapes and television broadcasts. Conversion is necessary because computers scan the screen more rapidly, and with a greater number of horizontal lines, than do television sets. *Contrast* FRAME GRABBER. *See also* NTSC; PAL; SECAM.

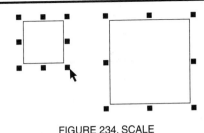

FIGURE 234. SCALE

scanf the formatted input procedure in the programming language C. For a table of format codes, *see* PRINTF.

scanner a device that enables a computer to read a printed or handwritten page. The simplest scanners give the contents of the page to the computer as a graphic image — a handy way of putting pictures into the computer (*see* DESKTOP PUBLISHING). There are four main types of scanners:

1. *Hand-held scanners* are inexpensive and adequate for inputting sketches into a draw program. But they have some difficulty scanning images wider than they are; the image has to be scanned in two or more passes and then assembled into one file.

2. *Page scanners* accept loose sheets of paper and generally include good software for graphical input and optical character recognition.

3. *Flatbed scanners* are the next step up; they can scan pages in books without requiring the page to be fed through the machine. This type of scanner is reasonably priced and generally suitable for all the desktop publisher's needs.

4. *Drum scanners* are expensive but give results superior to the other types of scanners. Some service bureaus have drum scanners and can scan artwork or photographs for you.

There are many nuances involved in scanning artwork. In some ways, it is quite similar to photography and if you are comfortable with a camera, it will make the transition to working with a scanner very smooth. Scanners can adjust the contrast and brightness of the image. Controls for setting the *highlight* and *shadow* area are usually provided. Color images can be color-corrected at the scanning stage.

With appropriate software, scanners can read the letters of typewritten text, transmitting them into the computer as if they were typed on the keyboard (OCR). This process, however, is seldom 100 percent accurate. You will find it necessary to proofread scanned copy very carefully.

Several other kinds of electronic devices are called scanners, including bar code readers (*see* BAR CODE) and devices for scanning the radio spectrum.

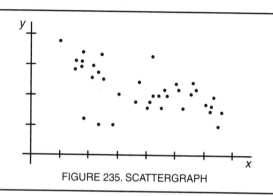

FIGURE 235. SCATTERGRAPH

scattergraph, scatter plot a graph that shows points of data plotted on an *x*-*y* coordinate system. Also called an *x*-*y* *graph*.

scientific notation *see* EXPONENTIAL NOTATION.

FIGURE 236. SCISSORS ICON

scissors

1. a tool available in paint and photopaint programs that allows you to define an area of the picture that you wish to separate from its surroundings. The resulting cutout may be resized (scaled), stretched, rotated, or moved.

The scissors tool is one of several SELECTION TOOLS available to you. Others include the LASSO, MAGIC WAND, and box selection tools. To save space, these tools may be grouped together in your toolbox and only one may be visible at a time.

2. icon for "cut the selected item to the Clipboard." *See also* COPY; PASTE.

scrapbook a special directory that contains frequntly used text or graphics. Each object can be quickly selected and then dragged into the file you are editing.

scratch disk, scratch tape a disk or tape that one can erase and reuse at any time because it does not contain anything that needs to be kept for future use.

screen
1. a computer display; a monitor.
2. a screenful of information.
3. to process a grayscale image for printing by breaking down the various shades of gray into very small dots. *See* HALFTONE.

screen saver a program that automatically blanks the screen of a computer, or displays a moving picture, when the computer has not been used for several minutes.

The original purpose of screen savers was to prevent "burn-in" (i.e., to keep the screen coating from wearing out in places where bright parts of the image were constantly displayed). Modern screens are less vulnerable to burn-in, and today, screen savers serve mainly to protect the privacy of users who are away from their desks, and to save energy when used in conjunction with monitors that turn themselves off when the screen goes blank. Screen savers also provide entertainment. *See also* GREEN PC; ENERGY STAR.

screen shot, screen snapshot (**screen capture**) an image of the current screen, saved as a bitmap.

Snapshots of the screen are easy to obtain: on the Macintosh, hold down Command and shift, then press 3. This places a bitmapped image of the screen in a PICT file in your root directory. For Windows, pressing the Print Screen key puts a copy of the entire screen onto the CLIPBOARD. Holding down Alt while pressing Print Screen saves a bitmap of the active window only.

Handgloves

Handgloves

Handgloves

FIGURE 237. SCRIPT TYPE

script

1. a style of type that resembles cursive handwriting (not italics), as shown in Fig. 237.

2. a file containing commands to be executed, such as a SHELL SCRIPT or a script of dialing commands for a communication program. *See also* JAVASCRIPT; VBSCRIPT; PERL; CGI.

3. a file or printout containing a copy of information that was displayed on the screen.

scroll

1. to move information across the screen as if the screen were a window or porthole through which you are looking. For example, all word processing programs can scroll vertically, and some can also scroll horizontally.

2. to type gibberish rapidly and repeatedly in order to disrupt a discussion in a chat room. (This makes all the real messages scroll by too fast for people to read them.) *See* CHAT ROOM.

scroll bar the bar at the right-hand side and/or bottom of a window that enables you to scroll the window, i.e., look at different areas of the data that the window is displaying, treating the window as a portion of a larger picture. To scroll, click on the arrows at the ends of the scroll bar or use the mouse to move the scroll box along the bar. For an illustration, *see* WINDOW.

FIGURE 238. SCSI CONNECTORS
(TWO OF SEVERAL COMMON TYPES)

SCSI (**S**mall **C**omputer **S**ystems **I**nterface, pronounced "scuzzy") a standard way of interfacing a computer to disk drives, tape drives, and other devices that require high-speed data transfer. Up to seven SCSI devices can be linked to a single SCSI port. Thus, a single SCSI adapter can interface a computer to one or more hard disks, a CD-ROM drive, a tape drive, and a scanner (*see* Figure 238).

SCSI is especially popular with Macintoshes and UNIX workstations but is also used on some PC-compatible computers, where it is supported by device drivers. Almost all SCSI hard disks use the same device driver, with no need for further settings to be made; that makes SCSI hard disks easier to install than any other type. Other SCSI devices such as CD-ROM drives require additional device drivers. This is often done in two layers: an ASPI (Advanced SCSI Programming Interface) device driver for the SCSI system, and various drivers that issue ASPI commands to specific devices.

The cable that comes out of a SCSI port is essentially an 8-bit bus (or 16- or 32-bit if it follows the newer SCSI-2 standard). The devices connected to it are daisy-chained with a *SCSI terminator* (a resistor pack) at the end. Each device, including the SCSI port itself, has an address between 0 and 7 inclusive; most addresses are switch-selectable to prevent conflicts.

See also BUS; DEVICE DRIVER. *Contrast* ST-506; ESDI; IDE.

scuzzy a common misspelling of SCSI.

SDK
1. **S**oftware **D**evelopment **K**it.
2. **S**ervlet **D**evelopment **K**it.

SDRAM (**s**ynchronous **d**ynamic **r**andom **a**ccess **m**emory) a type of RAM chip whose output is synchronized with the system bus, making data available to the CPU more quickly than with FPM or EDO RAM. *Contrast* EDO; FPM.

search and replace to work through a file, changing every occurrence of a particular sequence of characters into some other sequence of characters. In Macintosh software, this is usually called *Find and Change. See* EDITOR.

search engine a computer program that searches through large amounts of text or other data. For example, a search engine for the WORLD WIDE WEB can be accessed at `http://www.yahoo.com` or at `http://www.search.cnet.com`. For searching Usenet newsgroups, use the search engine at `http://www.deja.com`.

Depending on the search engine, there are generally several ways to search. If you type a phrase such as *golden isles,* the search engine will normally search for all documents that contain *golden* and/or *isles,* giving highest priority to those that contain both words. Alternatively, you can specify that you want only the documents that contain the whole phrase, and you can specify boolean ("and" and "or") relationships between words you are searching for (e.g., "Visa OR MasterCard"). There is generally a help button that explains how to perform various kinds of searches. *See also* BOOLEAN QUERY; FULL-TEXT SEARCH.

searchware software used to search through a database. For example, an encyclopedia available on CD-ROM must come with searchware to allow the user to find specific entries. *See* FULL-TEXT SEARCH; HYPER-TEXT.

seat

   1.   *(noun)* a place where a person can use a computer system or software product. The cost of software is often calculated in terms of seats. For example, a multi-user computer that supports five users has five seats; so does a group of five personal computers.

   2.   *(verb)* to insert an integrated circuit (IC) or a printed circuit board into a socket.

SECAM (**Sé**quentiel **C**ouleur **a**vec **M**émoire) the type of color TV signal used in France. The screen consists of 625 lines, interlaced, and a complete scan takes 1/25 second. Color information is modulated on two subcarriers at 4.406 and 4.250 MHz. *Contrast* NTSC; PAL.

secondary mouse button the mouse button used to call up the action menu. For a right-handed user, this is usually the right mouse button. The left mouse button (the PRIMARY MOUSE BUTTON) is used to select objects.

   Left-handed users have the option of reversing the default order for mouse buttons; they can use the right mouse button as the primary button and the left button as the secondary.

second-generation computers computers made with discrete transistors in the 1950s and 1960s.

section sign the symbol § which is used to mark sections of text for reference (usually in legal documents). The section sign can also be used for a footnote symbol. *See* FOOTNOTE.

sector part of a track on a disk. For example, the original IBM PC diskette system partitions the diskette into 40 circular tracks with each track having 8 sectors. *See* TRACK; DISK.

seed a number that is used to start a series of seemingly random numbers. If the seed remains the same, a random-number generator will produce the same "random" numbers (in sequence) every time you use it. To get an unpredictable seed, programs sometimes look at the system clock. In Microsoft BASIC, this is done by the statement RANDOMIZE TIMER. *See also* RANDOM-NUMBER GENERATOR.

seek time the average time taken by a disk drive to *seek* (move) from one track to another; usually on the order of 10 milliseconds.

segment one of two numbers that define a memory location on a microprocessor such as the 8088. For an example of its use, *see* OFFSET.

   On the 80286, 386, 486, and Pentium, in protected mode, the segment address itself is not added to the offset; rather, it serves as a pointer to a table of segment descriptors that define the locations to which offsets are added. This allows a much larger amount of memory to be addressed and gives more flexibility in the way memory is utilized.

segmentation fault an error in a program causing it to try to access a memory address that does not belong to it.

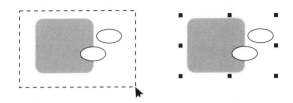

FIGURE 239. SELECTING A GROUP OF OBJECTS

select to tell the computer you are ready to work with an object. You can select one or more objects at a time. Usually, you select an object by clicking on it with the mouse. To select a group of objects, use MARQUEE SELECT or hold down the Shift key while clicking on individual objects until they are all included in the bounding box.

FIGURE 240. SELECTING AN AREA OF A BITMAP

selection area the selected part of an image (Fig. 240).

selection marqee *see* MARQUEE SELECT.

selection sort algorithm for sorting the elements of an array by first selecting the lowest-valued item, then the next lowest, and so on. In practice, the lowest-valued item is interchanged with the first item in the part of the array being searched, and the search is confined to the remainder of the array from then on.

```
1       REM Selection sort in BASIC
10      INPUT "N:";N
20      FOR I=1 TO N: INPUT X(I): NEXT I
30      FOR I = I TO N
40         M = I
50         FOR J = (I+1) TO N
60            IF X(J)>= X(M) THEN 80
70            M = J
80         NEXT J
90         Y = X(M)
100        X(M) = X(I)
110        X(I) = Y
120     NEXT I
130     END
```

FIGURE 241. SELECTION SORT IN BASIC

Selection sort is probably the easiest to remember of the many general-purpose sorting algorithms. The program in Fig. 241 implements selection sort in BASIC.

selection tools tools provided to define an area or choose an object to be worked with. Examples include the POINTER, LASSO, MAGIC WAND, and SCISSORS.

selvage detachable perforated strips on the edges of printer paper.

semiconductor a material that is neither a good conductor of electricity nor a good insulator, and whose conduction properties can therefore be manipulated easily.

Semiconductor devices, such as diodes, transistors, and integrated circuits, are the essential parts that make it possible to build small, inexpensive electronic machines.

The most widely used semiconductor material is silicon. Each atom in a silicon crystal contains four outer-level (or valence) electrons. A pure silicon crystal is not a very good conductor because these electrons normally stay bound to their atoms.

An N-type semiconductor region is formed by adding a bit of impurity to the pure silicon. This process is known as *doping*. The impurity added is a material such as phosphorus, in which each atom has five valence electrons. The result is a crystal much like the original one, except that there are now a few extra electrons floating around (one for each atom of phosphorus that was added). The whole crystal is called an N-type region because it contains movable negative charges.

If an impurity with only three valence electrons, such as boron, is added to the silicon crystal, gaps are left in the crystal structure because there are not enough electrons to fill all the spaces in the crystal. Each gap is called a *hole*. Even though a hole is nothing but the absence of an electron, it can be thought of as carrying a mobile positive charge. A semiconductor region with an excess of holes is called a P-type semiconductor region.

Electric current can flow in an N-type region in much the same way that it flows in a regular conductor. In a conductor, the current is made up of outer-level valence electrons that are not too tightly bound to their atoms. When a negative voltage is applied to one end of the N-type region and a positive voltage is applied to the other, the loose electrons will be repelled by the negative voltage and attracted by the positive voltage.

Current can flow in the P-type region, but the process is quite different. If a negative voltage is applied to one end of the P-type region, the electrons will be repelled. However, the P-type region does not contain any mobile electrons. What an electron can do is jump into one of the holes. This process creates a new hole where the original electron used to be. We can think of the hole itself as moving toward the negative voltage, carrying a positive charge with it.

A semiconductor diode is formed by joining a P-type region and an N-type region. A transistor consists of a thin layer of one type of semiconductor between two layers of the opposite type. A semiconductor integrated circuit is made by placing many P and N regions on a single chip, so as to form a complex circuit containing many miniature transistors and other circuit elements.

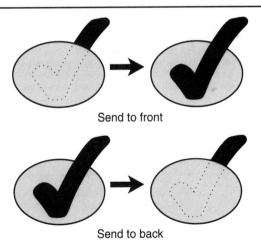

FIGURE 242. SEND TO FRONT; SEND TO BACK

send to back in some graphical editing environments, a command that puts an object or window "at the back" so that other objects or windows are allowed to overlap it (*See* Figure 242). *See also* OVERLAID WINDOWS; BRING TO FRONT. *Compare* FORWARD ONE; BACK ONE.

send to front in a graphical editing environment, a command that brings the selected object to the front of all other objects (*See* Figure 242). *Contrast* SEND TO BACK.

sequential-access device a data-storage device in which it is necessary to read through all preceding records before the computer finds the record it is looking for. Tape storage devices are examples of sequential-access devices. *Contrast* RANDOM-ACCESS DEVICE.

serial method of transmitting data one bit at a time over a single wire. Serial transmission is the normal way of linking computers to modems and is often used to link microcomputers to printers, especially relatively slow ones. *See* BAUD; RS-232. *Contrast* PARALLEL.

serial-access device *see* SEQUENTIAL-ACCESS DEVICE.

serial bus a system for rapid communication among components of a computer using a minimum number of wires. Successive bits of each byte or word travel along the same wire, rather than along separate wires as in a conventional bus. *See* BUS. For examples, *see* FIREWIRE; USB.

serial mouse a mouse that is attached to a serial port of a computer. *See* MOUSE.

serial port a connection by which a computer can transmit data to another device using serial transmission — that is, one bit at a time. It is usual for a microcomputer to have a serial port that is connected to a modem or printer. IBM PC-compatible computers typically have two serial ports labeled COM1 and COM2; UNIX systems often identify their serial ports as /dev/ttya and /dev/ttyb. Most serial ports follow the EIA-232D (RS-232) standard. *See* RS-232. *Contrast* PARALLEL PORT.

serial printer a printer that connects to a computer's serial port. *See* SERIAL PORT; PARALLEL PORT.

FIGURE 243. SERIES CIRCUIT (TWO RESISTORS)

series connection of two electronic components so that current flows through one and then the other (*see* Fig. 243). *Contrast* PARALLEL.

Serif

FIGURE 244. SERIF (ON A LETTER)

serif the short finishing strokes of the letterforms in a roman typeface, present in I F A and absent in I F A (Fig. 244). It is thought that the horizontal nature of serifs helps guide the reader's eye along the line of type. *Contrast* SANS-SERIF. *See also* TYPEFACE.

server a computer that provides services to another computer (called the *client*). On multitasking machines, a process that provides services to another process is sometimes called a server. For specific examples, *see* FILE SERVER; X SERVER; DDE; WEB SERVER.

service bureau a business that provides services to computer users, such as high-quality color printing, disk format conversions, or the like.

service provider a company that provides computer or networking services to customers. *See also* ACCESS PROVIDER; INTERNET.

servlet a Java program that runs on a web server. By contrast, an applet is a Java program running on a web browser client. Servlets provide some advantages over writing CGI scripts for the server: 1) a developer writing the applet in Java can use the same language for the server side of the process; 2) the servlet can run as a thread, not requiring a new CGI process to be restarted with each client request; and 3) the servlet runs in a SANDBOX where it is prevented from doing damage to the server system.

session
    1. a period of time during which a person is using a particular computer service, such as a connection to the Internet.
    2. an occasion upon which data is written to a recordable CD-ROM. Multisession CDs have had data written to them more than once.

set
    1. the input of a flip-flop that places it into state 1, as opposed to the *reset* input. *See* FLIP-FLOP.
    2. the command, in DOS, OS/2, Windows, and UNIX, that stores information in the operating system's environment area (*see* ENVIRONMENT). In other operating systems (e.g., VM/CMS and VAX/VMS), the SET command allows the user to customize many aspects of the operating system.
    3. in mathematics, a collection of objects of any kind. For example, $\{2, 4, -425\}$ is a set of numbers, and $\{\{2, 3\}, \{4, 5\}\}$ is a set of

sets. *See* SET DIFFERENCE, UNION, INTERSECTION.

4. a data type in Pascal that consists of a group of values of a specified type. For example, a set can be declared with the statement

```
VAR smallnums: SET OF INTEGER;
```

and can then be assigned a set of values with an assignment statement such as:

```
smallnums := [1,2,3,4];
```

Now you can use a statement such as

```
IF x IN smallnums THEN ...
```

to test whether a given integer is contained in this set. The expression x IN smallnum is true if x has the value 1, 2, 3, or 4; otherwise, it is false. Pascal also provides for standard set operations, such as union (symbolized by +), intersection (∗), and set difference (−).

set difference the set of elements that belong to one set and not to another. For example, the difference between $\{a, b, c\}$ and $\{b, c\}$ is $\{a\}$.

seven layers *see* DATA COMMUNICATION.

SGML (**S**tandard **G**eneralized **M**arkup **L**anguage) a standard set of codes for marking boldface, italics, etc., in ASCII text files, which became the basis for HTML. *See* HTML; XML.

shadow the darkest area of a photograph or drawing that is being scanned. The image contrast can be adjusted by marking the shadow and HIGHLIGHT areas for the computer.

shadow RAM random-access memory (RAM) that holds a copy of the ROM BIOS. The copy is made at boot-up for faster access because RAM is faster than ROM. *See* RAM; ROM; BOOT; BIOS.

shape tool in CorelDraw, the triangular tool that is used to edit the nodes that define the shape of an object.

shareware software that is copyrighted but can be distributed free of charge to anyone. Users are asked or required to make a payment directly to the author if they use the program regularly. Shareware is often misleadingly described as "free" (*see* FREE SOFTWARE).

Shareware has been criticized for relying on the unpaid work of users to do much of the advertising and distribution while the income goes only to the author. On the other hand, shareware products can be much less expensive than comparable commercial products.

sharpen a photopaint filter that sharpens the focus of a defined area. It can improve a slightly blurred image. (Don't expect miracles — the computer cannot compute information that is not in the original picture!) If overused, the sharpen filter can overemphasize small random specks or film grain because it works by increasing the difference between adjacent pixels. *See* PIXELATE; PIXELIZE; UNSHARP MASKING.

shell a program that accepts operating system commands and causes them to be executed. For example, when you type a DOS command such as `dir`, the command is read by the shell.

In DOS, the shell is normally the program COMMAND.COM. UNIX users have a choice of shells, such as the C shell (`csh`), the Bourne shell (`sh`), and the Korn shell (`ksh`).

The term *shell* often refers to a second shell that is loaded into unused memory on top of an application program (such as a word processor or spreadsheet). By using a shell, the application program can pass commands to DOS or allow the user to use DOS without leaving the application program, provided enough memory is available. To leave a shell, type the DOS or UNIX command `exit`.

shell script a file of commands to be executed by the SHELL (the command processor of an operating system). DOS BAT files are shell scripts. In UNIX, a shell script can begin with a line to indicate which of several shells should process it; for example, the line

```
#!/bin/csh
```

identifies a script for the C shell. The PERL and REXX programming language interpreters can be used as shells to execute scripts written in their respective languages.

Shell sort a variation of the insertion sort algorithm (*see* INSERTION SORT) invented by D. L. Shell. A Shell sort is a series of insertion sorts in which each item, instead of being compared with the items next to it, is compared with items a certain number of elements away. On each pass, this number (the *skip count*) becomes smaller until it reaches 1; thus, the last pass is an ordinary insertion sort. The earlier passes take care of large moves that would be time-consuming in a pure insertion sort.

Fig. 245 shows a Pascal program that reads 10 numbers and performs a Shell sort.

Shergold, Craig a young cancer victim who, in 1989, circulated an appeal for postcards. He no longer wants any postcards, but people won't stop circulating his appeal, which now haunts the Internet, often with altered names and addresses. For more information, see the *Guinness Book of World Records*. See also HOAX.

shift register a register in which all the bits can be moved one place to the left (or the right) when a particular control signal is pulsed. For example, the register containing 0 0 0 0 1 1 0 1 when shifted left once is 0 0 0 1 1 0 1 0, and when shifted twice is 0 0 1 1 0 1 0 0. For an application, *see* BINARY MULTIPLICATION.

```pascal
PROGRAM shellsort;
  { Based on R. Sedgewick, ALGORITHMS (1983) }

LABEL 1;
CONST n = 10;
VAR
  a: ARRAY[1..n] OF INTEGER;
  i, value, position, skip: INTEGER;

BEGIN
  { Read in the data }
    FOR i := 1 TO n DO
      BEGIN
        write('Enter item ',i:2,': ');
        readln(a[i])
      END;

  { Choose initial skip count }
    skip := 1;
    REPEAT
      skip := 3*skip + 1
    UNTIL skip > n;

  { Perform the Shell sort }
    REPEAT
      skip := skip DIV 3;
      FOR i:=skip+1 TO n DO
        BEGIN
          value := a[i];
          position := i;
          WHILE a[position-skip]>value DO
            BEGIN
              a[position] := a[position-skip];
              position := position - skip;
              IF position <= skip THEN GOTO 1
            END;
  1:        a[position] := value
        END
    UNTIL skip = 1;

  { Print the results }
    FOR i:=1 TO n DO write(a[i]:5);
    writeln
END.
```

FIGURE 245. SHELL SORT IN PASCAL

Shockwave a file format for presenting audiovisual shows on the Web, designed by Macromedia, Inc., which produces the software that interprets it. A free Shockwave player is available for users to download from www.macromedia.com.

shoeshine *(slang)* to move tape back and forth repeatedly like a shoeshine cloth, often done by tape drives that are experiencing media errors.

shortcut

    1. in Windows 95, its successors, and OS/2, an ICON that serves as a LINK to a file or icon elsewhere on the same computer. Shortcuts let you put the same program or file into the menu system in more than one place. In Windows 95 and Windows 98, shortcut icons are recognizable by an arrow displayed in the corner, and they are represented by files with the extension .lnk in the directory corresponding to the folder in which they reside.

    2. a faster way to access a command without having to pick it from a menu. Shortcuts are often indicated by underlined letters on menus; typing the letter (perhaps while holding down Alt) will take you directly to that menu selection. Some menus also indicate explicit shortcuts (such as Ctrl-S), which you can hit at any time, even when that part of the menu is not on the screen.

shrinkwrap the clear plastic coating that covers the boxes in which commercial software is sold.

shrinkwrap license a software license that the purchaser is deemed to accept by opening the package. Obviously, if the license is hidden inside the package, there will be some difficulty enforcing it in court, and many provisions of shrinkwrap licenses have never been tested. *See also* LICENSE; COMPUTER ETHICS.

shrinkwrapped product a product packaged in SHRINKWRAP; a product that is sold in retail stores, not just through mail order catalogs or through personal contact with a specialist.

side effect an effect of a program or subprogram other than simply computing its output from its input. For example, this Pascal procedure swaps two values, and also has the side effect of changing the global variable t:

```
PROCEDURE swap (VAR a,b: INTEGER);
BEGIN
  t := a;
  a := b;
  b := t;
END;
```

Side effects are usually undesirable because they disrupt variables used by other parts of the program. If t were declared local, the side effect would not occur.

sidelit illuminated from the side. Some liquid crystal displays (LCDs) on laptop computers are sidelit. *Contrast* BACKLIT.

SIG

    1. a **s**pecial **i**nterest **g**roup within various organizations and on-line services.

    2. a SIGNATURE FILE.

sigma

1. the uppercase Greek letter Σ, which stands for the sum of all possible values of an expression. For example,

$$\sum_{i=1}^{3} i + 1$$

is read "the sum of $i + 1$ from $i = 1$ to 3" and stands for $(1 + 1) + (2 + 1) + (3 + 1)$.

2. the lowercase Greek letter σ, which stands for the standard deviation in statistics.

signature an identification code sent with a message identifying the sender of the message. *See* DIGITAL SIGNATURE.

signature file a file automatically appended to outgoing e-mail and Internet postings, giving the sender's name, e-mail address, and other pertinent information. Many people use their signature file ("sig file") as a means of artistic expression, containing elaborate displays of ASCII GRAPHICS, poetry, or favorite quotes.

Users sometimes embarrass themselves by forgetting what is in their signature file. Inside jokes and funny mottoes can be quite out of place on serious correspondence such as job applications.

silicon the material most often used to make semiconductor devices. Its electrical properties can be changed by adding small amounts of impurities. *See* SEMICONDUCTOR; INTEGRATED CIRCUIT.

Silicon Creek an area in suburban Atlanta, Georgia, centered on the city of Norcross, the home of several major computer companies, including Hayes, Quadram, and American Megatrends (AMI). *See* SILICON VALLEY; ROUTE 128.

Silicon Valley the Santa Clara Valley and surrounding area between San Jose and San Francisco, California, including the cities of Cupertino, Sunnyvale, and Palo Alto. It is the home of numerous semiconductor and computer companies, including Hewlett-Packard, Intel, and Apple, as well as Stanford University. *Compare* SILICON CREEK; ROUTE 128.

SIMM (single in-line memory module) a tiny printed circuit board to which several memory chips are attached. It plugs into a slot on a larger printed circuit board and is handled as if it were a single integrated circuit. *See also* DIMM.

simulation the process of representing the actions of one system by those of another. A computer simulation is a computer program that carries out a step-by-step representation of the actions of something in the real world. For example, a computer model of population growth can simulate the behavior of a real population. A deterministic simulation occurs when the future path of the system is exactly determined by the parameters of the system. A Monte Carlo simulation occurs when probabilities are known and a selection of random numbers is used to guide the system. *See also* EMULATION.

sin the trigonometric sine function. If A is an angle in a right triangle, then the sine of A (written as sin A) is given by

$$\sin A = \frac{\text{length of opposite side}}{\text{length of hypotenuse}}$$

The function SIN(A) in many programming languages calculates the value of sin A, if A is in radians. For an illustration, *see* TRIGONOMETRIC FUNCTIONS.

sine *see* TRIGONOMETRIC FUNCTIONS.

single-board computer a complete computer that resides on a single printed circuit board, usually a small one. Single-board computers are often built into industrial equipment. *See also* EMBEDDED SYSTEM.

singleton something that is in a set by itself; the only member of a one-member set.

singleton variable in Prolog, a variable that occurs only once in a fact or rule. Since all variables are local, a singleton variable does not carry information from one place to another, and it should be replaced by an anonymous variable. *See* ANONYMOUS VARIABLE; PROLOG.

site license a software license that allows unlimited copying of a computer program for use by a single organization at a specified site. A site license is often much cheaper than the purchase of multiple copies. *See also* SOFTWARE LICENSE.

size *see* SCALE.

FIGURE 246. SKEW

skew a drawing program command that lets you alter the overall shape of an object. When you skew an object, you slide one side of its bounding box to the left or to the right. This will slant it or shift its bottom edge uphill or downhill. Skewing can be done interactively with the mouse, or, for more precision, the degree of skew can be specified in a dialog box.

SKU (**s**tock **k**eeping **u**nit) a numbered warehouse bin or package; more generally, a code to identify a product being sold. SKU numbers are often used to identify merchandise in computerized inventory and POINT-OF-SALE SYSTEMS.

skunk works *(slang)* a group of engineers and programmers who are deliberately isolated from their employer in an attempt to foster creativity and boost morale.

slash the character /, as opposed to the backslash \.

slave

    1. the dependent unit in a pair of linked machines. *Contrast* MASTER (definition 1).

    2. one of a pair of IDE hard disks or other devices connected to the same IDE cable. Generally, jumpers have to be set on IDE devices to identify them as master and slave. *Contrast* MASTER (definition 2).

slide a single image in a presentation. The slide can be textual, pictorial, or graphical. Slides can also contain animations, sounds, music, and video.

slide sorter an on-screen representation of an entire presentation. The individual slides are shown in rows, very small. It is then easy to reorder the slides, assign special effects and timings to the slides, or select the next slide to work on.

SLIP (**S**erial **L**ine **I**nternet **P**rotocol) an adaptation of TCP/IP for DIAL-UP NETWORKING. *Compare* PPP.

slot a socket in a microcomputer designed to accept a plug-in circuit board. *See* CARD.

small caps a specially designed alphabet of capital letters that are approximately two-thirds the cap height of the font, LIKE THIS. Text set in small caps has the same visual texture as normal text but gives the emphasis of setting text in all caps. The cross references in this book are set in small caps. *See* C/SC; EVEN SMALLS.

Smalltalk one of the first object-oriented programming languages. It was developed at Xerox Palo Alto Research Center (PARC) in the late 1970s and included a powerful graphical user interface that influenced the design of the Macintosh and Microsoft Windows. *See* OBJECT-ORIENTED PROGRAMMING; GRAPHICAL USER INTERFACE.

smart card a portable card containing a microprocessor and memory. Smart cards can carry identification information for the individual, and they can be used for electronic payment systems.

smear a retouching tool available in most PHOTOPAINT PROGRAMS. The smear paintbrush drags color from one area over another, as if you had run your finger over a chalk picture. The smear paintbrush works with the colors already present in the picture; contrast SMUDGE, which adds random mixed colors to the image.

smoke test *(slang)* to start up a machine or computer program for the first time and "see if smoke comes out," i.e., see if it fails catastrophically.

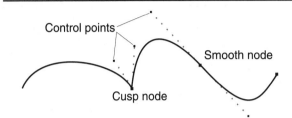

FIGURE 247. SMOOTH AND CUSP NODES

smooth node a point (NODE) that defines the shape of a curve but does not mark a sudden change of direction. (The *control points* lie on a straight line with the node; see Fig. 247.) *Contrast* CUSP NODE.

SMTP (**S**imple **M**ail **T**ransfer **P**rotocol) a protocol used to transfer electronic mail between computers on the Internet and other TCP/IP networks. *See* INTERNET; TCP/IP.

smudge a retouching tool available in most PHOTOPAINT PROGRAMS. The smudge spray can randomly mixes colors in an area. The smudge spray can adds texture to the image; with coarse settings, the effect achieved is rather impressionistic. *Contrast* SMEAR; SPRAY CAN.

smurfing the practice of maliciously disrupting a computer by *pinging* it continuously, i.e., flooding it with test data packets to which it must respond. (*Smurf* is the name of a program often used to do this.) Also known as PING FLOODING. *See* DENIAL-OF-SERVICE ATTACK.

snail mail *(slang)* ordinary postal mail, as opposed to E-MAIL.

snap point (in a draw program) a point on an object that clings to the GRID or user-defined guidelines. Most objects have multiple snap points; generally speaking, they will be at every *node* that defines the shape of the object. *See* Figure 248.

snap to grid a mode in which a drawing program lines up all objects on a (nonprinting) grid. This makes it easy to line up parts of diagrams that are drawn separately, rather like drawing with a pencil on graph paper.

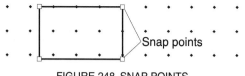

FIGURE 248. SNAP POINTS

sneakernet *(slang)* the practice of transferring files from one computer to another by carrying a diskette across the room.

sniffer a hardware device or computer program for intercepting data packets as they pass through a network either to test the network or to intercept other people's confidential data. *See* FIREWALL.

SNOBOL a language for processing character-string data, developed at Bell Telephone Laboratories in 1962. It is based on the theory of finite-state Markov processes, and surprisingly concise and powerful programs can be written in it. However, since nearly every SNOBOL statement contains at least one conditional jump, structured programming in SNOBOL is impossible and nowadays the language is little used.

snow small, flickering white spots on a computer screen. The IBM Color/Graphics Adapter (CGA), used in the mid-1980s, produced snow when the contents of video memory were changed rapidly, because random data were put on the screen momentarily during the change. *See* CGA.

snowflake *see* FRACTAL; KOCH SNOWFLAKE.

socket
    1. an electrical connector into which another connector, with pins, can be inserted.
    2. a communication path between two computer programs not necessarily running on the same machine. Sockets are managed by a socket DEVICE DRIVER that establishes network connections as needed; the programs that communicate through sockets need not know anything about how the network functions. *See also* WINSOCK.

soft brush (in paint and photopaint programs) a category of tools that includes PAINTBRUSHES, AIRBRUSHES (or SPRAY CANS), SMEAR paintbrush, and CLONE tools. All of these tools leave soft edges and have transparent strokes. These tools are sometimes grouped together in the toolbox and have similar dialog boxes for their settings.

soft copy computer output that is only viewable on the computer screen. *Contrast* HARD COPY.

soft edge in a graphical image, a boundary between two areas that is diffuse and somewhat blurred. *Contrast* HARD EDGE.

soft error an error or defect on a data storage device that is present only intermittently; an error that goes away when the same operation is tried again. *Contrast* HARD ERROR.

soft font a font that is downloaded to a laser printer by the computer.

Unlike a font cartridge or an internal font, a soft font consists of data transmitted to the printer by the computer before the text is printed. The soft font will vanish from the printer's memory when the power to the printer is turned off, so it will be necessary to reload it each time the printer is powered on. The availability of a wide variety of soft fonts provides users with great flexibility. *Contrast* FONT CARTRIDGE; INTERNAL FONT.

soft hyphen a hyphen that is used only when the word falls at the end of a line; sometimes called a DISCRETIONARY HYPHEN. *Contrast* REQUIRED HYPHEN; HARD HYPHEN.

soft modem a modem that relies on the CPU to do part of the signal processing traditionally done by the modem itself. *See* MODEM.

soft page an invisible control code that indicates where the text will break at the end of a page. Unlike a HARD PAGE, a soft page break is inserted by the program and will move if the amount of text on the page changes. *See* WRAP.

soft-sectored disk a diskette whose sectors are positioned by FORMATTING the disk in a disk drive, rather than by using physical marks or holes. Almost all diskettes nowadays are soft-sectored.

software programs that tell a computer what to do. The term contrasts with *hardware,* which refers to the actual physical machines that make up a computer system. The hardware by itself is of little value without the instructions that tell it what to do.

Software can be classified into *system software* (*see* OPERATING SYSTEM) and *application software.* For examples of common types of application software, *see* WORD PROCESSING, SPREADSHEET, DATABASE MANAGEMENT. For information on creating software, *see* PROGRAMMING and PROGRAMMING LANGUAGE.

software engineering the art and science of designing and constructing software. The computer industry has learned from bitter experience that large programs cannot be constructed as casually as small ones. Some principles of software engineering include the following:

1. Before starting a project, estimate the amount of labor it will require, based on previous experience. Err on the side of caution. Do not reduce an estimate just because a manager or customer wishes it were lower.

2. Allow adequate time for planning. Decide exactly what is needed, and if possible, write some of the documentation for the finished product before starting to write the program.

3. "Freeze" the specifications when planning is complete. Make sure clients and higher management understand that any further changes will delay completion and raise costs. The only exceptions are changes proposed by the programmers in order to simplify implementation and improve performance.

4. Set priorities. Which is more important, finishing on time or implementing the full set of features? Can the product be developed incrementally, as a minimal first version followed by upgrades?

5. Use reliable programming techniques, including structured programming and appropriate use of comments.

6. Insist that programmers remove errors as soon as they are found; do not leave debugging for later. You cannot build the upper stories if the foundation is not solid.

7. Keep programmers' morale high. Long working hours, although traditional in Silicon Valley, do not increase productivity; few people really work more than eight hours a day no matter how long they are at the office.

8. Do not add personnel to a project that is running late; the time taken to orient the new programmers will delay it further. Instead, find ways to help the current programmers work more efficiently. Shield them from unnecessary meetings, administrative chores, and even telephone calls.

9. Deadline crises are a symptom of incompetent management. A well-managed project gets finished on time without going into "crunch mode." If a manager does not know how long a project will take, that's not the employees' fault. If the time needed cannot be estimated in advance, everyone should realize it rather than relying on wishful thinking.

See also STRUCTURED PROGRAMMING; COMMENTS; CREEPING FEATURISM.

software interrupt *see* INTERRUPT.

software license an agreement between the publisher of a computer program and the person who buys a copy of it, allowing the software to be used.

Some licenses specify that when you buy a copy of a program, you do not really own the copy but have merely bought the right to use it in certain ways. Normally, the license allows you to make a working copy of the program, which would otherwise be forbidden by copyright law (*see* COPYRIGHT).

Most licenses allow a single copy of the program to be used on only one machine at a time. It can be copied for backup purposes, and it can be moved from one machine to another, but it cannot be actually in use in two places at once. Thus you are forbidden to load the same program into more than one machine through a network (*see* LOCAL-AREA NETWORK). However, it is usually permissible for several people to use the same program on a multiuser machine with a single CPU.

A *site license* allows unlimited copying of a program for use by a single organization at a specified site. A site license is often much cheaper than the purchase of multiple copies. Another alternative for schools and colleges is the use of student editions of software; these are less powerful than the commercial versions and are sold at much lower prices.

Many aspects of software licenses have not yet been tested in court. In particular, the license document is sometimes packed where the user cannot see it until after buying and opening the software package. In such cases, it can hardly be described as a valid contract. When dealing with unclear or unreasonable licenses, users should make a good-faith effort to obey copyright law and to avoid depriving the publisher of income. *See also* FREE SOFTWARE; SHRINKWRAP LICENSE.

SOHO abbreviation for "**s**mall **o**ffice, **h**ome **o**ffice." (Soho is also the name of districts in London and New York City.)

Solaris the version of UNIX sold by Sun Microsystems. *See* SUN WORK-STATIONS.

solver a computer program that solves equations that may have variables on either side of the equal sign, such as $x = 1 + 1/x$. This contrasts with ordinary calculators, spreadsheets, and programming languages, which can evaluate only expressions that consist entirely of known values.

sort to arrange items in numerical or alphabetical order.

There are many different algorithms that can be used to sort a group of items. If the number of items is small, it is probably best to use an algorithm that can be represented by a short program. If the number of data items is large, then it is more important to use a faster algorithm, even if it is complicated. Some algorithms assume that the data items have been read into the memory of the computer. However, if there is a very large number of items, it will be necessary to use an algorithm that works when the data are stored on an auxiliary storage device. Since sorting is such a common operation, many operating systems include built-in sorting algorithms. For examples of specific sorting algorithms, *see* BUBBLE SORT; INSERTION SORT; MERGE SORT; QUICKSORT; RADIX SORT; SELECTION SORT; SHELL SORT.

Sound Blaster a line of popular sound cards for PCs marketed by Creative Labs, Inc., of Milpitas, California.

sound card (**sound board**) a circuit board that can be added to a computer to enable it to record and reproduce sound. Sound cards often include other features such as a MIDI musical instrument interface, a controller for a CD-ROM drive, and an audio amplifier that can drive speakers.

source
    1. a place from which information is copied; the opposite of TAR-GET.
    2. one of the three parts of a field-effect transistor (*see* FIELD-EFFECT TRANSISTOR).

source code a programming language designed for use by human beings, as opposed to OBJECT CODE, which is used internally in the computer. A compiler translates source code into object code.

source program a program written in a programming language (such as C, Pascal, or FORTRAN) and fed into a computer. The compiler translates the program into a machine-language *object program.*

spaghetti code *(slang)* a disorganized computer program using many GO TO statements; as easy to read as a plate of spaghetti. *Contrast* STRUCTURED PROGRAMMING.

spam unsolicited and unwelcome advertisements sent to people via e-mail or posted in newsgroups. "Spammers" have discovered that they can reach a large audience at low cost on the Internet by posting the same message to all available newsgroups or e-mailing it to all possible addresses.
    Spamming is considered seriously unethical for two reasons. First, newsgroups and e-mail would be useless if they routinely contained unwanted material. Second, the cost of transporting e-mail and news-group postings is not paid by the sender; it is paid by the recipient's site and other sites along the way. Thus, it is important not to impose expenses on people by sending them unwanted material.
    In some places, spamming by e-mail is illegal, and there is a strong movement to prohibit it everywhere. More importantly, almost all Internet service providers (ISPs) flatly prohibit both e-mail and newsgroup spam. The few ISPs that allow spamming are ostracized by other sites, which refuse to accept any data from them. *See* COMPUTER ETHICS; NETIQUETTE.
    It is not clear why spam was named after a processed-meat product made by Hormel. For Hormel's response to the situation, *see* www.spam.com.

SPARC (**S**calable **P**rocessor **A**rchitecture) a microprocessor developed by Sun Microsystems and used in Sun Sparcstations as well as computers made by other manufacturers. It uses RISC architecture to achieve very high speed. *See* WORKSTATION; SUN WORKSTATIONS; RISC.

special characters characters that cannot be typed directly from the keyboard, but require entering a special code or selection through the KeyCaps applet (Macintosh) or the Character Map (Windows).

Windows software accesses these special characters by holding down the Alt key and typing a four-digit code on the numeric keypad. (See the table of standard Windows characters at ANSI.) Macintosh users can type special characters by holding down the Option button while typing (here the Option key acts like another Shift key). You'll need to consult a keyboard map to find where the desired character is.

See also ANSI; EXPERT SET; IBM PC.

specular highlight a bright point of light on a reflective or shiny surface.

speech recognition the use of computers to recognize spoken words. This is a nontrivial task because the same spoken word does not produce entirely the same sound waves when pronounced by different people or even when pronounced by the same person on more than one occasion. The computer must digitize the sound, then transform it to discard unneeded information, and finally try to match it with words stored in a dictionary.

Most speech recognition systems are *speaker-dependent*; they have to be trained to recognize a particular person's speech and can then distinguish thousands of words (but only the words they were trained on). *Speaker-independent* speech recognition is less effective. The biggest demand for speech recognition arises in situations in which typing is difficult or impossible, such as equipment for the handicapped, highly portable equipment, and computers that are to be accessed by telephone.

It is easier to recognize DISCRETE SPEECH (speech with pauses between words) than CONTINUOUS SPEECH, but discrete speech is slow and awkward. Hesitation noises ("uh," "um"), coughs, and sneezes are sometimes mistaken for words.

speech synthesis the generation of human-like speech by computer (by computing the pronunciation of each word, not by playing back recordings).

Originally handled by special hardware, speech synthesis is now usually done by means of software running on a personal computer with a sound card. The technology to generate understandable speech has existed since the 1960s, but the speech is not completely natural; the intonation and timing are not perfect, and the voice may be monotonous and robot-like.

Speech synthesis is important in making computers accessible to blind people and delivering computer data by telephone.

spell checker a program that checks the spelling of every word in a document by looking up each word in its dictionary. If the word does not appear in the dictionary, the user is alerted to a possible misspelling, and possible corrections are often suggested. Many word processing programs include spell checkers. An effective spell checker needs to store a large number of words using efficient data compression techniques, and it must be able to search the list quickly with a binary search. *See* DATA COMPRESSION; BINARY SEARCH.

A spell checker will not recognize unusual proper names or specialized terms, but it will often allow you to create your own personal dictionary of specialized words you often use. (Be sure not to put misspelled words into it!) Spell checkers are valuable aids to proofreading, but they cannot catch the substitution of one correctly spelled word for another (such as *form* for *from* or *to* for *too*). Thus they do not guarantee that a document is free of spelling errors.

Copies: 3

FIGURE 249. SPIN BUTTON

---

spin button a dialog box element that allows the user to change numbers rapidly by clicking on the up and down arrows or by typing the desired number directly into the number box.

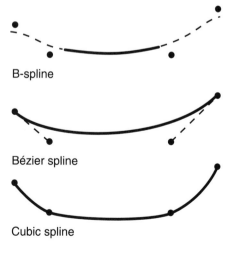

B-spline

Bézier spline

Cubic spline

FIGURE 250. THREE TYPES OF SPLINES

spline a curve that connects a set of points smoothly. Fig. 250 shows some examples. For details of computation, see B-SPLINE; BÉZIER SPLINE; CUBIC SPLINE.

spoofing the act of impersonating a user or a machine. For example, *IP spoofing* is the act of attaching a computer to the Internet using an IP ADDRESS assigned to a different computer, thereby intercepting communications intended for the other machine.

spooling the process of storing computer output before sending it to the printer. This enables the main program to run quickly, sending its output to the print spooler, which will then dole the information out to the printer at the proper speed. The print spooler normally runs concurrently with the main program.

spot color the use of a specified color of ink in a printing job. Spot color can be used for emphasis or to add interest to documents. *Contrast* PROCESS COLOR.

FIGURE 251. SPRAY CAN

spray can a tool found in various paint and photopaint programs that leaves a circular pattern of the selected color. To use it, you press and hold down the mouse button and drag the mouse. The center of the spray pattern will be solid, but the edges will feather out to the background color. If you need a dense, solid, color, move the mouse slowly; if you want a wispy trace of color, move the mouse rapidly. You can change the size of the spray can's coverage area — usually by changing the brush size.

A similar tool is the AIRBRUSH. Generally, a program will have either an airbrush or a spray can tool, but not both.

spreadsheet a table of numbers arranged in rows and columns. Paper spreadsheets were used for business data long before computers were invented. The first computer spreadsheet was VisiCalc, used on the Apple II computer in the late 1970s. Recently the most popular spreadsheets have been Lotus 1-2-3 and Excel. Here are some general features of these programs:

1. Data is arranged in rows (labeled with numbers) and columns (labeled with letters). Each location in the spreadsheet is called a cell. You can enter numbers or letters in a cell, as in this example, which records the sales of different types of products at a small store:

	A	B	C	D
1	Item	Price	Quantity	
2	cereal	3.99	10	
3	milk	2.15	25	
4	toothpaste	1.95	7	

2. The computer will do calculations automatically if you enter formulas. For example, to calculate the revenue from the sale of cereal, enter the formula +B2*C2 in cell D2. (The asterisk * represents multiplication; the initial plus sign indicates this is a formula and not a label. In Excel, an equal sign is put at the start of a formula.)

	A	B	C	D
1	Item	Price	Quantity	Revenue
2	cereal	3.99	10	39.90
3	milk	2.15	25	
4	toothpaste	1.95	7	

When a formula is entered, the spreadsheet will display the result of the formula, not the formula itself, in that cell. However, moving the cell pointer to a cell will let you see the formula for that cell at the top of the screen, and you can edit it if needed.

3. A formula in one cell can be copied to other cells. For example, the formula in cell D2 above can be copied to cells D3 and D4, which will give the total revenue for the other products:

	A	B	C	D
1	Item	Price	Quantity	Revenue
2	cereal	3.99	10	39.90
3	milk	2.15	25	53.75
4	toothpaste	1.95	7	13.65

When Lotus 1-2-3 runs under DOS, not Windows, the copy command is part of the menu that appears at the top of the screen when the / key is pressed. Commands in Windows spreadsheets are called using the standard menu structure for Windows.

The copy command automatically changes formulas when they are copied to new cells. In the example above, when you copy the formula +B2*C2 from cell D2 to cell D3, it will become the

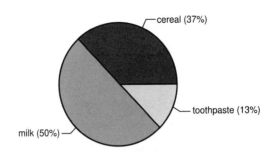

FIGURE 252. PIE CHART CREATED BY A
SPREADSHEET PROGRAM

formula +B3*C3, and in cell D4 it will become +B4*C4. This
is because B2 and C2 in the formula in the original cell (D2)
were written in the form of a RELATIVE ADDRESS. *See* ABSOLUTE
ADDRESS to learn how to prevent the cell addresses from being
changed by the copy command.

4. A formula can contain built-in functions, such as a command
   to sum all cells in a range. Entering the Lotus 1-2-3 formula
   @SUM(D2..D4) or the Excel formula =SUM(D2:D4) into cell
   D5 will automatically calculate the column total (cells D2, D3,
   and D4). Many such functions are included with spreadsheet programs.

5. Spreadsheets are especially valuable because the formulas will
   be automatically recalculated whenever one of the numbers is
   changed. For example, if later in the month you update your sales
   figures, the program will automatically recalculate the revenue for
   each item, and the total revenue. This makes spreadsheets especially useful for "what-if" analysis. You can design a spreadsheet
   with many variables, and see how the result changes when one or
   more of those variables are changed.

6. Spreadsheets can automatically create graphs of your data. For
   example, Fig. 252 shows a pie chart giving the fraction of the sales
   of each item. Graphs can also illustrate how a variable changes
   with time, or how two variables are related to each other.

7. MACROS can be used to combine a series of keystrokes into one
   command, and advanced macros are themselves computer programs that can interact with users and process data.

8. Modern spreadsheets have added many features to improve the appearance of the output. For example, some cells can be displayed in boldface type, or a cell can be emphasized with shading.

9. Originally, spreadsheets were two-dimensional, making them analogous to putting all of your work on one giant piece of paper. Later spreadsheets added three-dimensional capability, which is analogous to keeping your work on different pages in a notebook. In that case a cell address could be written as C:B1, meaning page C, column B, row 1. Also, modern spreadsheets allow different worksheets to be automatically linked together. For example, you can put your monthly sales figures in 12 different worksheets, and then have those linked to a single spreadsheet with year-end summary data.

See also LOTUS 1-2-3; EXCEL; MACRO.

spread-spectrum a technique of radio transmission in which the frequency changes many times per second in a predetermined but seemingly random sequence. The receiver knows the sequence and follows the frequency changes. Spread-spectrum transmission overcomes interference because two transmitters will never be on the same frequency for more than a moment. Spread-spectrum transmission also provides privacy because the signal is almost impossible to intercept without knowing the sequence of frequency changes. *See* WIRELESS COMMUNICATION.

sprite a moving element in a graphical display. Most video games use sprites.

SQL (Structured Query Language, formerly Sequel) a standard query language used by many programs that manipulate large databases. Here is an example of an SQL query:

```
SELECT NAME, SALARY FROM TABLE1
WHERE SALARY > 35000
```

This means "Give me the name and salary from each row in TABLE1 where the salary is more than 35,000." *See* RELATIONAL DATABASE; QUERY LANGUAGE.

SRAM (Static Random-Access Memory, pronounced "S-ram") a type of computer memory that does not require a periodic refresh signal. SRAM is more expensive than DRAM and is rarely used as the main memory of a computer system, but it is often used for caches, video memory, and microcontroller systems. *See* MEMORY; RAM. *Contrast* DRAM.

SRC HTML keyword that indicates the file that serves as the source of an image or multimedia data. For example, *see* HTML.

SSL (Secure Socket Layer) an encryption system developed by Netscape based on RSA ENCRYPTION. SSL protects the privacy of data exchanged by the web site and the individual user. It is used by web sites whose names begin with `https` instead of `http`.

ST-506 standard electrical interface between hard disk and controller used in PC-compatible computers in the 1980s. The ST-506 interface was used for both MFM and RLL data encoding. ST-506-compatible disks and controllers were made by many different companies. (*See* MFM; RLL.) ST-506 interfaces have been replaced by IDE, ESDI, and SCSI. (*See* IDE; ESDI; SCSI.)

stack

　1. a data structure from which items are removed in the reverse order from which they were inserted; also called a *pushdown stack* or *pushdown store*.

　For example, when a program calls a subroutine, information about how to return to the main program is usually placed on the stack. If the subroutine then calls another subroutine, information about how to return to the first subroutine is placed on the stack. Since this information is retrieved from the stack in the opposite order from which it was placed there, each subroutine returns control to the right place.

　Stacks are very useful for dealing with one operation nested inside another. To *push* a data item is to place it on a stack; to *pop* the stack is to remove an item from it. *Contrast* QUEUE.

　2. A set of DEVICE DRIVERS loaded in a specific order to implement a function such as TCP/IP.

stacking order the order in which objects are arranged in a drawing program. This order determines which objects overlay others. Commands to reorganize the stacking order (Send to Front, Send to Back, Forward One, Back One) are usually found under an Arrange menu.

Standard Generalized Markup Language (SGML) a standard set of codes for marking boldface, italics, etc., in ASCII text files, which became the basis for HTML. *See* HTML; XML.

star the character * (asterisk).

star dot star the WILD CARD character sequence *.*, which matches all DOS filenames.

star key the key on a telephone keypad marked with the symbol *. It is often used to give commands to software at the telephone company (e.g., to disable CALL WAITING).

start bit the bit that indicates the beginning of an asynchronous RS-232 character. *See* RS-232.

Start button a button, labeled "Start…", that is normally on the screen whenever Windows 95 or 98 is running. By clicking on the Start button, you can access application programs and other functions of the computer through the START MENU.

If the Start button is not visible, it's probably because the TASKBAR at the bottom of the screen has been reduced to minimum width. By dragging the taskbar with the mouse cursor, you can restore it to normal width and make it readable again.

You can also display the Start menu at any time by pressing Ctrl-Esc.

FIGURE 253. START BUTTON AND START MENU
WINDOWS 95 AND 98

Start menu the menu that is called up by the START BUTTON in the corner of the screen under Windows 95 and 98. It leads to all the application software that is installed on the computer. To edit or modify the Start menu, open it with the right mouse button rather than the left button.

startup disk any disk (either a hard drive or diskette) that contains enough of the computer's OPERATING SYSTEM for the disk to be used to BOOT the computer in an emergency. In DOS, a startup disk is created by formatting with the /s option. A Windows 95 or Windows 98 startup disk can be created at the time the operating system is installed, or it can be created by clicking on buttons in this sequence: Start; Settings; Control Panel; double-click on Add/Remove Programs; Startup Disk.

startup folder a FOLDER under the Windows 95 and 98 Start menu containing programs that are to be run automatically when Windows starts up. It corresponds to the PROGRAM GROUP called Startup under Windows 3.1.

statement a single instruction in a computer programming language. One statement may consist of several operations, such as LET X = Y+Z/W (a division, an addition, and an assignment). *See* PROGRAMMING LANGUAGE.

static RAM *see* SRAM.

statistics program a software package for performing statistical calculations.

A statistics program works with lists of numbers instead of single values. It should have built-in commands for calculating the average and standard deviation of the elements of a list, for testing hypotheses about the relationships between variables through methods such as multiple regression, for performing transformations (such as taking the logarithm of each of the elements in a list), and for drawing graphs of the data. Examples of statistics programs include SAS (**S**tatistical **A**nalysis **S**ystem) and SPSS (**S**tatistical **P**rogram for the **S**ocial **S**ciences).

status line a line of information on the computer screen that gives valuable data about the current settings of the software and the current cursor position. The contents of a status line will vary depending on the software used; some programs give different information during the execution of different commands. It is a good idea to get into the habit of noticing what is in the status line. If you do not understand what you see there, take a moment to review the manual.

steganography the concealment of a small message inside a larger file that appears to consist entirely of something else. For example, an encrypted message might be hidden among some some slight variations of color at selected points in a picture. Crucially, a person viewing the picture would not know that a message was concealed in it. Messages can also be hidden in inaudible low-level noise superimposed on digitized music.

Steganography goes hand-in-hand with encryption but is not the same thing. Encryption makes a message unreadable by unauthorized persons; steganography hides the very existence of the message. *See also* CRYPTOGRAPHY; ENCRYPTION.

stochastic random; constantly varying; unpredictable; scattered.

stop bit the bit that indicates the end of an asynchronous RS232 character. (*See* RS-232.) Normal practice is to use two stop bits at 110 baud and one stop bit at higher baud rates.

store
    1. to transmit a data item from the computer to a memory device.
    2. suffix indicating that an E-MAIL address or WEB SITE is at a store providing goods for sale.

stored program computer a computer that can store its own instructions as well as data. All modern computers are of this type. The concept was originated by Charles Babbage in the nineteenth century and was developed by John Von Neumann. The ability of a computer to store instructions allows it to perform many tasks without human intervention. The instructions are usually written in a programming language. (*See* COMPUTER.)

stream
1. *(noun)* in C++, Lisp, and other computer languages, a file or device that can be read or written one character at a time. For example, the screen and keyboard can be treated as streams.
2. *(verb)* to move tape past a read-write head continuously, rather than making short movements with pauses in between.

streaming
1. moving a tape continuously. *See* STREAM (definition 2).
2. delivering audio or video signals in real time, without waiting for a whole file to download before playing it. *See* REALAUDIO.

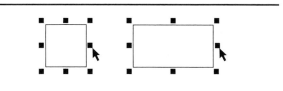

FIGURE 254. STRETCH

stretch to increase either the vertical or horizontal dimension of an object. To use the mouse to stretch a selected object interactively, drag out one of the handles at the midpoints of the BOUNDING BOX. *Contrast* SCALE, which maintains the height-to-width ratio of the object.

string (**character string**) a sequence of characters stored in a computer and treated as a single data item. *See* STRING OPERATIONS.

string operations operations that are performed on character string data. A programming language that is capable of working on string data will normally include built-in commands or operators to perform the functions listed below. Here are some examples from Microsoft BASIC, where A$ represents the string "GEORGE" and B$ represents "WASHINGTON":

1. Compare two strings to see if they are the same (often symbolized =) or if one string comes before the other in alphabetical order (often symbolized <). Alphabetical order is determined on the

basis of ASCII codes, so lowercase letters come after uppercase letters (*see* ASCII).

2. Join two strings together (concatenation). This is often symbolized by +. For example,

   `A$+" "+B$`

   is:

   `"GEORGE"+" "+"WASHINGTON"`

   which is equal to:

   `"GEORGE WASHINGTON"`

3. Calculate the length of a string. In BASIC, this is symbolized by LEN. For example, LEN(B$) is 10.

4. Select specified characters from any position in string. In BASIC, this is symbolized by MID$. For example, MID$(A$,3,2) means "select two characters from A$ beginning at position 3" and yields "OR".

   BASIC also provides LEFT$ and RIGHT$ to select a specified number of characters from the left or right end of the string, respectively.

5. Determine if one string is contained in another string, and if so, at what position it starts. In BASIC, this is accomplished by the function INSTR. For example, INSTR("OR",A$) is 3; INSTR("AND",A$) is 0.

6. Determine the ASCII code of an individual character. In BASIC, this is done by the function ASC. For example, ASC("A") is 65.

7. Determine the character associated with a given ASCII code. In BASIC, this is done by the function CHR$. For example, CHR$(65) is "A".

8. Determine the numerical value of a string that represents a number. In BASIC, this is done by the function VAL. For example, VAL("86") is the number 86. If the string does not represent a number, then the result is 0 (for example, VAL("what") is 0).

9. Convert a numeric value into a string. In BASIC, this is done by the function STR$. For example, STR(86) is the string "86", possibly with one or more blanks added.

structured programming a programming technique that emphasizes clear logic, modularity, and avoidance of GO TO statements (which are intrinsically error-prone).

One of the most important barriers to the development of better computer software is the limited ability of human beings to understand the programs that they write. Structured programming is a style of programming designed to make programs more comprehensible and programming errors less frequent. Because it is more a popular movement than a precise theory, structured programming can be defined in several ways, but it usually includes the following;

1. *Block structure.* The statements in the program must be organized into functional groups. For example, of the following two Pascal program fragments, the first is structured, while the second is not:

```
Structured:               Unstructured:
IF x<=y THEN              IF x>y THEN GOTO 2;
  BEGIN                    z := y-x;
     z := y-x;             q := SQRT(z);
     q :=SQRT(z);          GOTO 1;
  END                     2: z:= x-y;
ELSE                       q:=-SQRT(z);
  BEGIN                   1: writeln(z,q);
     z:= x-y;
     q := -SQRT(z)
  END;
WRITELN(z,q);
```

   Note that it is much easier to tell what the first example does.

2. *Avoidance of jumps* ("GO-TO-less programming"). It can be proved mathematically that, if a language has structures equivalent to the (block-structured) IF-THEN and WHILE statements in Pascal, it does not need a GO TO statement. Moreover, GO TO statements are often involved in programming errors; the programmer becomes confused as to the exact conditions under which a particular group of statements will execute.

   Advocates of structured programming allow GO TO statements only under very restricted circumstances (e.g., to deal with error conditions that completely break out of the logic of a program) or not at all.

3. *Modularity.* If a sequence of statements continues uninterrupted for more than about 50 lines, human beings have a hard time understanding it because there is too much information for them to keep track of. As an alternative, programs should be broken up into subroutines, even if some of the subroutines are called only once. Then the main program will read like an outline, and the programmer will never need to understand more than about one page of code at a time. (The programmer must know what the subroutines do, but not how they do it.) This principle is sometimes called *information hiding* — irrelevant information should be kept out of the programmer's way.

StuffIt a data compression program for the Macintosh written by Raymond Lau. Like ZIP and WinZip on the IBM PC, StuffIt allows several files to be combined into one. StuffIt can also encode and decode Bin-Hex files. *See* DATA COMPRESSION; ZIP FILE; BINHEX.

Normal *Italic* **Bold** ***Bold Italic*** Condensed Extended

FIGURE 255. STYLES OF TYPE

style (of type) a particular kind of type, either plain, boldface, or italic, belonging to a specified font. *See* FONT; TYPEFACE.

style sheet a file (in WordPerfect, LaTeX, HTML, and other publishing programs) that defines the overall layout and type specifications of a document or web page. *See* CASCADING STYLE SHEETS; DESKTOP PUBLISHING; GRID SYSTEM.

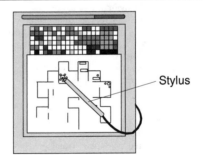

FIGURE 256. STYLUS

stylus the pen-like part of a graphics tablet.

subdirectory a disk directory that is stored in another directory. *See* DIRECTORY.

subroutine a set of instructions, given a particular name or address, that will be executed when the main program calls for it. In many programming languages, subroutines are called *procedures* (*see* PROCEDURE).

In line-numbered BASIC, a subroutine is labeled by the statement number of its first line and is executed when a GOSUB command transfers control to it. For example, suppose that X is a time of day, measured as a floating-point number of hours past midnight. Here is a program that uses a subroutine to convert X into hours, minutes, and seconds and tell whether it is A.M. or P.M.:

```
10   INPUT "NUMBER OF HOURS AFTER MIDNIGHT:";X
20   GOSUB 100
30   PRINT H;":";M;":";"S";D$
40   END               :REM END OF MAIN PROGRAM
100  REM START OF SUBROUTINE
110  H = INT(X)         :REM NUMBER OF HOURS
120  F = 60*(X - H)
130  M = INT(F)         :REM NUMBER OF MINUTES
140  S = 60*(F - M)     :REM NUMBER OF SECONDS
150  IF X>=12 THEN D$ = "P.M."
160  IF X<12 THEN D$ = "A.M."
170  IF H>12 THEN H = H - 12
180  IF H=0 THEN H=12
190  RETURN             :REM END OF SUBROUTINE
```

The command RETURN marks the end of the subroutine and tells the computer to return to the main program.

There are two main advantages to using subroutines when writing programs. If a complicated set of instructions is needed at different locations in the program, then making the instructions into a subroutine can save considerable work since it will be unnecessary to type the instructions more than once. Also, a complicated program is best written as a collection of smaller parts, each with a well-understood purpose.

See also TOP-DOWN PROGRAMMING; STRUCTURED PROGRAMMING.

subscript a number or other indicator used to identify a particular element in an array. In mathematics, subscripts are written below the main line, as in x_1 or a_k. In most computer languages, however, subscripts are enclosed by parentheses, as in X(1) or A(K), or square brackets, as in X[1] or A[K]. *See* ARRAY.

subscripted variable array variable (*see* ARRAY).

subwoofer a speaker designed to reproduce very low-pitched sounds which would not be audible through an ordinary speaker. A subwoofer generally contains its own amplifier. *See* AMPLIFIED SPEAKER.

suit *(slang)* a manager or salesman; a (male) worker in the computer industry who is neither an engineer nor a programmer and is therefore not allowed to dress casually.

suitcase *(Macintosh)* a special kind of folder that contains system resources (fonts, sounds, desk accessories). For example, you can manage your fonts by keeping them grouped logically in suitcases. Some prefer to store their fonts in typeface families — others group fonts used for specific projects in separate suitcases.

suite a set of application software from a single vendor that attempts to span the basic uses of a computer. A suite usually has a word processor, a database, and a spreadsheet. The advantage of using a suite is compatibility; you are assured that all of the programs can accept data from any of the others and incorporate them in their own files. On the downside, the individual programs of a software suite sometimes lack desirable features. If additional software is purchased, it may be difficult to get the programs to work together.

Sun Microsystems, Inc. (Mountain View, California) the company that developed SPARC microprocessors, SUN WORKSTATIONS, the SOLARIS operating system, and the JAVA programming language. Web address: http://www.sun.com.

Sun workstations high-performance desktop computers manufactured by Sun Microsystems of Mountain View, California. Most are marketed as single-user systems although each can support more than one user. All run Solaris (SunOS), a proprietary version of UNIX based on System V and incorporating some BSD features. Current Sun workstations are descendants of the Sun-4, which introduced the SPARC CPU; earlier products used Motorola 68000 and Intel 386 processors. *See* UNIX; SYSTEM V; BSD; WORKSTATION; SPARC.

superclass a class from which another class in an object-oriented programming language is descended. For example, if your applet program `myapplet` extends the class `Applet`, then `Applet` is the superclass for `myapplet`.

supercomputer a computer designed to run markedly faster than ordinary mainframe computers, generally by using parallel processing. Examples are the Cray vector processors and the Intel iPSC parallel processor.

superior character a superscript; small letters and numbers set above the baseline $^{\text{like this}}$. Used mainly in mathematical typesetting (*see* SUPERSCRIPT; *contrast* SUBSCRIPT, INFERIOR CHARACTER).

superscalar processor a computer that is in between conventional SCALAR PROCESSOR and VECTOR PROCESSOR architectures; it accepts instructions like those of a scalar processor but has some ability to double them up and do more than one thing at once at run time. The PENTIUM is an example of a superscalar processor.

superscript a small character written above the baseline, $^{\text{like this}}$. In mathematics, a superscript indicates an exponent, which denotes repeated multiplication. For example, $4^3 = 4 \times 4 \times 4$.

supertwist a newer type of liquid crystal display (LCD) that produces higher contrast than earlier types. An LCD works by twisting light waves to change their polarization. Supertwist displays produce more of a change in polarization than their predecessors.

super VGA any video card incorporating all the functions of IBM's VGA plus additional modes with higher resolution and/or more colors usable at once. Many different companies make super VGAs that work in slightly different ways. Super VGAs typically offer resolutions of 800×600 and 1024×768 pixels, with up to 64K colors (65,536 colors) available in each. Not all resolutions are available with any particular combination of card and monitor.

Some super VGAs also incorporate *Windows accelerator* functions —that is, they take care of operations such as moving a window that would ordinarily require the full attention of the CPU.

Super VGAs are practical because operating systems such as Microsoft Windows and OS/2 Presentation Manager handle all graphical output. Thus, individual programs do not have to be modified to use special video modes; the user simply installs a device driver to support the super VGA card in the desired mode, and the operating system takes care of the details. That is why the great diversity of super VGA cards has not raised software compatibility problems. However, some device drivers are unreliable, and if software performs unreliably — even if the problem does not seem to be video-related — it is worthwhile switching to a plain VGA driver to see if the problem disappears. *See also* DEVICE DRIVER; VGA.

surface mapping the act of applying a surface (complete with color, pattern, shading, and texture) to a 3D wireframe model. *See* RENDER.

surfing *(slang)* the practice of browsing through the contents of NEWS-GROUPS, the WORLD WIDE WEB, or other information services, much like a surfer riding one wave and then another.

surge protector device that absorbs brief bursts of excessive voltage coming in from the AC power line. These surges are created by lightning or by electric motors switching off.

Surge protectors do little good unless the power line is properly grounded. Always plug the computer into a properly grounded outlet. If possible, do not plug a laser printer into the same outlet strip or extension cord as the computer, because laser printers draw heavy current intermittently.

Many surge protectors also incorporate RFI protectors to help reduce radio and TV interference emitted by the computer into the power line. (*See* RFI PROTECTION.) A surge protector cannot do anything about momentary power failures; for that, you need an uninterruptible power supply.

See also POWER LINE PROTECTION; UNINTERRUPTIBLE POWER SUPPLY.

SVGA *see* SUPER VGA.

SVR4 (**S**ystem **V R**elease **4**) a widely used version of UNIX. *See* UNIX.

swap file a file used for swap space. In OS/2, the swap file is named SWAPPER.DAT and changes size as needed (provided enough disk space is free). In Windows, the swap file is hidden and does not normally appear in directory listings. It can be either permanent, and fixed in size, or temporary, and varying in size. Permanent swap files give faster execution.

Besides the swap file used by the operating system, there are also swap files used by particular applications, such as CorelDraw. *See* SWAP SPACE.

swap space disk space that an operating system or program uses as a substitute for additional memory. *See* VIRTUAL MEMORY; SWAP FILE.

FIGURE 257. SWASH CAPITAL LETTERS

swash a capital letter with a decorative flourish. Swashes are best when used sparingly.

swf (**S**hockwave **f**ile) filename extension used by Macromedia Shockwave. *See* SHOCKWAVE.

switch

1. in electronics, a device for interrupting or rerouting the flow of electric current.

2. in telecommunications and networking, a device for establishing connections between one location and another, doing the work of a telephone operator. For instance, on a computer network, a switch is a device that temporarily creates high-speed paths between different segments as they are needed. It works like a bridge, but faster. *See* BRIDGE. *Compare* HUB; ROUTER.

switched line an ordinary (POTS) telephone line on which you establish connections by dialing; the path actually taken by the signals need not be the same when you call the same number twice on different occasions. *Contrast* T1 LINE; T3 LINE; POTS.

switching power supply a power supply that regulates the voltage of direct current by switching it off and on very rapidly and then smoothing out the variations. Most computer power supplies are of this type. The advantages of a switching power supply are that it does not waste energy and does not require a heavy transformer, since the incoming AC is chopped to give a high frequency that can be handled by a smaller, lighter transformer. The disadvantage is that it produces radio-frequency interference (*see* RFI; POWER SUPPLY).

SWMBO e-mail abbreviation for "She Who Must Be Obeyed." Used facetiously to refer to one's wife in imitation of Rumpole, the eccentric and somewhat henpecked lawyer in stories by John Clifford Mortimer.

SX suffix denoting lower-end models of some Intel microprocessors.

The 386 SX is a microprocessor like the 386 except that it has a 16-bit rather than a 32-bit bus and is therefore slower. The 486 SX is like the 486 except that it lacks the 486's built-in math coprocessor. *See* MICROPROCESSOR.

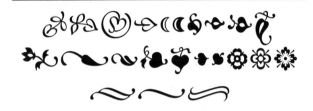

FIGURE 258. SYMBOL FONT
(MINION ORNAMENTS)

symbol font a font containing symbols or ornaments rather than a regular alphabet. Also called a PI FONT or DINGBATS.

symbolic algebra the manipulation of mathematical symbols (not just their numerical values). For example, we can calculate that $(a + b) \times (c + d) = ac + ad + bc + bd$ without knowing the values of a, b, c, or d.

Symbolic algebra on computers began with the MACSYMA project at MIT in the 1960s. Today, popular symbolic algebra programs for personal computers include MathCad, Maple, and Mathematica. They greatly simplify the formerly tedious process of deriving and manipulating mathematical formulas.

symbolic debugger program that lets you step through a compiled program, interrupting it at any point and examining or changing the values of variables.

"Symbolic" means that programmer-assigned names in the program are recognized. A symbolic debugger analyzes the source code and the object code together, so that even though the program has been compiled, you can work with it as if you were editing the source program.

symbolic programming a kind of programming in which variables can stand for pieces of the program itself (symbolic expressions), not just numbers, strings, or other values. Lisp and Prolog are examples of symbolic programming languages. *See* LISP; PROLOG; SYMBOLIC ALGEBRA.

synchronization

1. the act of making a video display scan each line at exactly the right time, so that the image is displayed correctly. The input to a monitor consists of SYNC PULSES as well as red, green, and blue video.

2. the process of keeping two or more disk drives up to date relative to each other, by copying the latest version of each file to each device. This is a practical problem if you work with more than one computer, such as a laptop and a desktop machine. The Briefcase feature of Windows 95 and 98 helps users synchronize files.

synchronous occurring in unison with a separate signal. In synchronous data transmission, there are two signals, *data* and *clock*. The clock signal indicates exactly when the *data* line should be read in order to obtain each successive bit. *Contrast* ASYNCHRONOUS.

sync pulse the part of a video signal that indicates when the electron beam should scan each line. *See* SYNCHRONIZATION.

syntax the set of rules that specify how the symbols of a language can be put together to form meaningful statements. A syntax error is a place in a program where the syntax rules of the programming language were not followed.

synthesizer

1. a device or program for generating speech sounds by computer. *See* SPEECH SYNTHESIS.

2. a device for generating musical sounds by computer, usually from MIDI data. *See* MIDI.

Syquest drive *see* EZ DRIVE.

sysadmin (**sys**tem **admin**istrator) a person who manages a multiuser computer.

sysop (**sys**tem **op**erator) person who manages a bulletin-board system. *See* BBS.

Sys Req key key on IBM mainframe terminals that enables the user to communicate with the communications system itself rather than the application program. The IBM PC AT and subsequent PCs have a Sys Req key, but little or no software makes use of it.

Systems Application Architecture *see* SAA.

systems programmer person who writes the programs needed for a computer system to function (as opposed to the programs that do particular kinds of useful computation). Some of the programs that systems programmers write include operating systems, language processors and compilers, and data file management programs. Systems programming, which is often done in an assembly language, requires considerable knowledge of the particular computer system being used. *Contrast* APPLICATIONS PROGRAMMER.

System V one of the most widely used versions of the UNIX operating system. *See* UNIX; BSD.

T

T1 line a special type of telephone line for digital communication only, with a maximum data rate of 1.544 million bits per second. Many Internet sites are connected to each other through T1 lines. *Contrast* SWITCHED LINE; ISDN; T3 LINE.

T3 line a high-speed digital telephone line with a maximum data rate of 45 million bits per second, 28 times that of a T1 line. Larger Internet sites use T3 lines to link to each other. *Contrast* SWITCHED LINE; ISDN; T1 LINE.

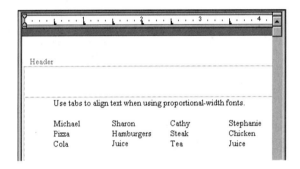

FIGURE 259. USING TABS TO ALIGN TEXT

Tab

1. the key on a computer keyboard that is marked with forward and backward arrows. The Tab key advances the cursor to a preset spot; Shift-Tab goes back to the previous tab stop. Most word processors and page layout programs let you set the TAB STOPS where you want them and otherwise provide a reasonable set of defaults, usually every half inch.

Always use the Tab key instead of the space bar to align type. When setting proportional type, it is impossible to get columns to line up by adding space characters; you *must* set the tabs.

The Tab key has ASCII code 9 and is equivalent to Ctrl-I. The backward Tab (Shift-Tab) key has no ASCII code.

When entering text into a dialog box, the Tab key often moves the cursor from one field to the next.

table 472

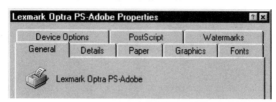

FIGURE 260. TABS IN DIALOG BOX

2. a visual indication of multiple pages in a dialog box. Click on the appropriately-labeled tab to get to the desired page.

table an arrangement of data in a database where each row defines a relationship between the items in that row. *See* RELATIONAL DATABASE.

table, HTML special HTML tags and commands for displaying tabular material. A web page can include various items arranged in a table by using the TABLE tag in HTML. Here is an example:

```
<HTML><HEAD><TITLE>Table Example</TITLE></HEAD>
<BODY>
<H2> HTML Table Example</H2>
<TABLE BORDER>
<TR><TD>President</TD><TD>Years in Office</TD>
    <TD>Home State</TD></TR>
<TR><TD>George Washington</TD><TD>1789-1797</TD>
    <TD>Virginia</TD></TR>
<TR><TD>John Adams</TD><TD>1797-1801</TD>
    <TD>Massachusetts</TD></TR>
<TR><TD>Thomas Jefferson</TD><TD>1801-1809</TD>
    <TD>Virginia</TD></TR>
</TABLE>
</BODY></HTML>
```

The BORDER attribute automatically sets up a border for the table; the border can be set wider by specifying its width in pixels (BORDER=3). If no border is desired, simply delete the BORDER attribute.

Each row of the table is enclosed between the <TR> and </TR> tags, and each data item in the table is enclosed between <TD> and </TD> tags. The web browser will automatically line up the items correctly; it doesn't matter where the line breaks in the HTML code occur. Figure 261 shows how this table is displayed.

FIGURE 261. TABLE (IN HTML)

The table elements do not have to be text; they can also include graphic images and links.

tab stops adjustable markers that indicate the next horizontal position of the cursor when the Tab key is pressed.

tag a code inserted into a FILE or data structure indicating how something is to be interpreted. Many pieces of software use tags of various kinds for various purposes. HTML commands are often called tags. *See* HTML; DATA STRUCTURES.

talent (digital video) hired human actor, as opposed to computer-generated characters. *Contrast* ACTOR.

tall paper orientation that is taller than it is wide; also called PORTRAIT or VERTICAL orientation.

tan the trigonometric tangent function.

If A is an angle in a right triangle, then the tangent of A (written as $\tan A$) is defined to be

$$\tan A = \frac{\text{length of opposite side}}{\text{length of adjacent side}}$$

The function TAN(A) in many programming languages calculates the value of $\tan A$. Many computers require that the value of A be expressed in radians. *See* TRIGONOMETRIC FUNCTIONS for an illustration.

tangent

1. a line that just touches a circle or other curve.

2. the trigonometric tangent function. *See* TRIGONOMETRIC FUNCTIONS.

tape a thin, flexible material on which data can be stored magnetically. Tapes are an excellent way to make backup copies of your files and to transport large files (greater than the capacity of a high-density disk) to a service bureau. You should verify that the service bureau has the equipment to read a tape from your particular tape drive; there are a large variety of formats and sizes available.

Be aware that recording a tape takes time — as much as several hours to back up 1 gigabyte. Also, each tape may need to be formatted before it is used; formatting a tape can take a couple of hours. Thus, tapes are not a practical substitute for disk drives.

Large mainframe computers use reel-to-reel tapes of a type that originated in the 1950s. Microcomputers use tape cartridges of various sizes.

tape drive a device that enables a computer to read and write magnetic tape.

tar file in UNIX, a collection of files made into one file with the `tar` (**tape ar**chive) program. (Nowadays, tar files are almost always stored on disk, not tape.) To extract the contents of a tar file, use the command:

```
% tar -xvf filename.tar
```

Unlike ZIP, `tar` does not compress files; thus, tar files are often compressed with another utility (such as `compress`, which adds `.Z` at the end of the filename). *See* ZIP FILE.

target

1. the place to which information is copied (e.g., the "target disk" when copying disks); the opposite of *source.*

2. something that is being searched for (as when searching for a word in a document).

task a PROCESS; one of several computer programs that are executing concurrently.

FIGURE 262. WINDOWS TASKBAR

taskbar the area at the bottom of the screen in Windows 95 and its successors, containing the START BUTTON and a button for every program that is currently running. It also contains tiny icons for the speaker (volume control), clock, printer (if printing), fax modem (if active), and other specialized programs.

The taskbar is normally wide enough for one row of buttons, but you can widen it, shrink it, or move it to a different edge of the screen by dragging it with the mouse. If you can't see the taskbar, look closely to see whether it has been reduced to minimum width or moved to an unusual location.

Task List (Windows, OS/2) a menu of open (running) and minimized software, some of which may be hidden by overlaid windows. In Windows 3.1, the task list is accessed by pressing Ctrl-Esc. In Windows

95 and its successors, the taskbar at the bottom of the screen shows a button for each of the open or minimized windows.

A similar feature for Macintosh users is the APPLICATION MENU, which is located at the far right end of a window's menu bar.

TCL/TK (**T**ool **C**ommand **L**anguage and [graphical] **T**ool **K**it) a programming language developed by John Ousterhout in the tradition of Perl and Awk. As its name suggests, TCL/TK is for building customized tools. It links together pre-existing software and system facilities, including network communication, along with new code to generate easy-to-use programs with a graphical user interface. It is one of the easiest ways to do GUI programming under UNIX, and implementations for Microsoft Windows also exist. TCL/TK is an open-source project, and most implementations of it are distributed free of charge. For more information *see* `www.scriptics.com`.

TCP/IP (**T**ransmission **C**ontrol **P**rotocol/**I**nternet **P**rotocol) a standard format for transmitting data in packets from one computer to another. It is used on the Internet and various other networks. The two parts of TCP/IP are TCP, which deals with construction of data packets, and IP, which routes them from machine to machine. *See* INTERNET; WIDE-AREA NETWORK.

telecommute to work at a job from a home office with the aid of a computer, modem, telephone, fax, and other specialized equipment.

telecompute to use the computer facilities at another location by using a WIDE-AREA NETWORK or a modem link.

telnet a command that lets you use your computer as a terminal on another computer through a network; widely used on the Internet. Some versions are known as `tn` rather than `telnet`.

Normally, the telnet program provides a direct path so that the remote computer communicates directly with the terminal you are actually using. But if you are connecting to an IBM mainframe, you should use `tn3270`, which emulates an IBM 3270 full-screen terminal even though your real terminal is something else. *See* TCP/IP; INTERNET; RLOGIN.

template a pattern for arranging or matching things.

    1. a plastic card with flowchart symbols cut out of it. A programmer using a template card can easily trace out the symbols that are needed in drawing a flowchart.

    2. a particular pattern for a spreadsheet program, a database program, or page layout program that is frequently used. Therefore, storing the template will save you from having to retype the specifications each time.

    3. a regular expression (or other pattern to be matched) is sometimes called a template. *See* REGULAR EXPRESSION.

ter Latin for "a third time," used to denote revised CCITT and ITU-T standards. *See* CCITT; ITU-T.

tera- metric prefix meaning $\times 1{,}000{,}000{,}000{,}000$ (10^{12}) or, in rating computer memories and disks, $\times 1{,}099{,}511{,}627{,}776$ ($= 1024^4$). *Tera-* is derived from the Greek word for "monster" or "freak." *See* METRIC PREFIXES.

terminal an input-output device consisting of a screen and keyboard for communicating with a computer.

The earliest terminals were teletype machines. Today, personal computers are often used as terminals on larger computers. *See* DATA COMMUNICATION; MODEM; UPLOAD; DOWNLOAD.

terminal-node controller *see* PACKET RADIO.

terminate-and-stay-resident *see* MEMORY-RESIDENT PROGRAM.

TEX (pronounced "tekh"; also written TeX) a computer typesetting program used by the American Mathematical Society and many book publishers and educational institutions. TEX was designed and first implemented by D. E. Knuth of Stanford University. It was used to typeset this book.

Unlike most desktop publishing systems, TEX does not attempt to show you the appearance of the finished document on the screen as you edit it (though screen previews can be generated). Instead, you type a document with codes in it that indicate boldface, italics, special characters (e.g., \int for an integral sign), and the like (Table 21).

The rationale is that correct typesetting relies on distinctions that are too subtle to see on a computer screen. A user who wants an em dash rather than an en dash should say so with explicit codes rather than trying to make a mark that appears the right length on the screen. Likewise, large-scale aspects of design should be automated; you should be able just to give the title of a chapter, and let the computer take care of numbering the chapter and putting the title in the right place on the page.

Most TEX users access TEX through LATEX, a package of ready-to-use document designs and command shortcuts that make the system easier to use. *See* LATEX.

TEX is generally considered the most sophisticated computer typesetting system, as well as (for an experienced user) one of the easiest to use. It sets a standard that other desktop publishing systems try to emulate.

Usage note: The logo TEX is easily produced from within TEX or LATEX. Otherwise, it is usually typed "TeX."

Texas Instruments (TI) a manufacturer of semiconductors and computers, headquartered in Dallas, Texas. Jack S. Kilby developed the first working integrated circuit ("silicon chip") at TI in 1958, making it possible to miniaturize electronic equipment to a degree far beyond earlier

TABLE 21
T_EX NOTATIONS USED IN MATHEMATICAL FORMULAS

∞	`\infty`
$\pm$	`\pm`
$\times$	`\times`
$\div$	`\div`
$'$	`^\prime`
$\circ$	`^\circ`
$\leq$	`\leq`
$\geq$	`\geq`
$\in$	`\in`
$\subset$	`\subset`
$\subseteq$	`\subseteq`
$\rightarrow$	`\rightarrow`
$\Rightarrow$	`\Rightarrow`
α, β	`\alpha, \beta` (etc.)
Γ, Δ	`\Gamma, Delta` (etc.)
a^{bcd}	`a^{bcd}`
a_{bcd}	`a_{bcd}`
$\frac{xyz}{abc}$	`{xyz}\over{abc}`
$\sqrt{xyz}$	`\sqrt{xyz}`
$\sum_{abc}^{def} ghi$	`\sum_{abc}^{def} ghi`
$\int_{abc}^{def} ghi\,dx$	`\int_{abc}^{def} ghi~dx`

expectations. Currently, TI produces parts for practically all makes of computers, as well as computers and printers of its own. Web address: `http://www.ti.com`.

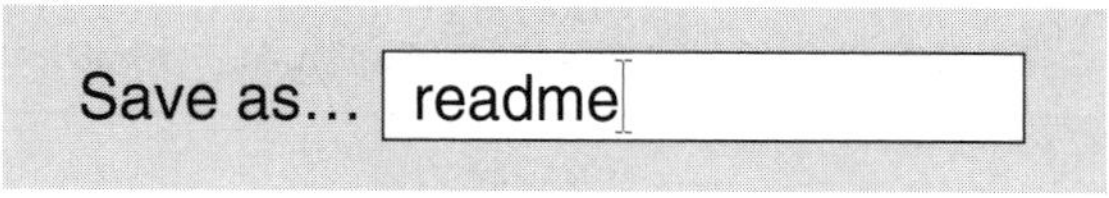

FIGURE 263. TEXT BOX

text box an area within a window where the user can type or edit characters.

text editor an editor designed primarily or exclusively for handling textual material (letters, manuscripts, etc.) rather than programs. *See* EDITOR.

text file a file that contains lines of written information that can be sent directly to the screen or printer by using ordinary operating system commands.

The files produced by word processors are usually not text files. Although they contain text, they also contain special codes (for margins, underlining, etc.) whose meaning is known only to the word processing software. Many word processors can, however, produce text files. Windows programs often provide an option under the save command allowing a file to be saved as text only.

On machines that use the ASCII character set, text files are often called ASCII files.

texture mapping the act of applying a texture to the surface of a 3D wireframe model.

text wrap *see* WORD WRAP; REFLOW.

thermal printer a printer that prints by heating spots on the paper with an array of tiny, fast-acting heating elements. Thermal printers are among the least expensive printers and are often used in calculators and low-priced fax machines. They require special paper that may discolor with age.

thickwire the thicker type of Ethernet coaxial cable. *See* 10BASE-5.

thinking outside the box *(jargon)* thinking outside presumed limits; thinking creatively. For example, you might think that the dots in Figure 264 cannot be connected with just two straight lines. But they can.

Notice that the dots do not form a perfect square. Draw a line through the top two dots; draw another line through the bottom two dots. Extend both lines. They are not parallel; they meet several inches to the right of the picture. With just two lines, you've joined all four dots.

FIGURE 264. THINKING OUTSIDE THE BOX. CAN YOU
CONNECT ALL 4 DOTS WITH JUST TWO STRAIGHT LINES?

No one told you that your two lines needed to meet within the picture, but you probably assumed it. A similar puzzle involving nine dots is a popular training example.

thinnet thinwire Ethernet. *See* ETHERNET; 10BASE-2.

thinwire the thinner type of Ethernet coaxial cable. *See* 10BASE-2.

third-generation computers computers made with integrated circuits. Current computers built with circuits that have large-scale integration are often called fourth-generation computers.

third party someone other than the maker of a machine and the END USER. For example, third-party software is software that does not come from the manufacturer, nor is it developed by the user. Most software today is third-party software.

thread
   1. a series of messages in a discussion forum, each responding to the previous one. *See* NEWSGROUP.
   2. a task or process in a computer program that uses MULTITASKING. For example, a word processor might have one thread to accept keystrokes from the keyboard, and another thread, running concurrently, to keep the screen updated. The Java programming language is designed to facilitate the creation of programs with more than one thread.

threaded interpretive language a programming language in which programs are stored almost exclusively as lists of addresses of subroutines. *See* FORTH.

three-dimensional graphics the process of representing three-dimensional images on a two-dimensional computer screen. This ability is especially important in CAD and in games. For example, imagine that you are designing a house, and your computer program lets you simulate walking through the different rooms. The computer needs to keep track of three-dimensional coordinates of the points of the house, and it needs to know which points are connected with lines, which planes should be filled in (as in a wall) or left open (as in a door). To allow the user to view the image from different points, the computer needs to be able to translate or rotate the points as directed. Particularly in a game setting, the computer needs to redraw the entire screen very quickly to maintain the illusion of rapid motion.

A simple kind of image is a wireframe view, which shows only the basic structure of an object, not the details of surfaces. This type of image is particularly helpful when designing pieces that need to fit together. Fig. 265 demonstrates how to draw a wireframe image of a cube, which can then be rotated using trigonometry.

Three-dimensional images can be transmitted to other computers using the VRML language. *See* VRML.

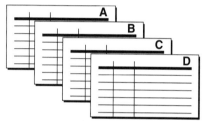

FIGURE 267. THREE-DIMENSIONAL SPREADSHEET

three-dimensional spreadsheet a spreadsheet in which each cell is identified by three coordinates — page, column, and row — which makes it possible to organize work into separate pages. This makes it much easier to manage large spreadsheets.

Suppose you were organizing a large paper spreadsheet with several hundred rows and columns arranged on one giant two-dimensional page. That would be very awkward; it is easier to organize paper in the form of pages in a book. In the early 1990s, most spreadsheet programs acquired three-dimensional capability; Lotus 1-2-3, Excel, and Quattro Pro are examples. A cell address looks like this: C:E4. The first letter (C) identifies the page. The remainder is the same as a two-dimensional spreadsheet; the second letter (E) identifies the column and the number (4) identifies the row. (In Excel, this would be written "Sheet3!E4.")

Pages can be grouped, i.e., given the same format. This makes it possible, for example, to put the budgets for several divisions on different pages of the same spreadsheet. It is also possible to work on pages independently.

three-tier architecture a database system with a user interface running on a microcomputer, a database engine running on a mainframe

```
1 REM PROGRAM TO DRAW WIRE FRAME IMAGE OF CUBE
2 REM AND ROTATE IT
10 GOSUB 100    'initialize
20 GOSUB 200    'draw cube
30 LOCATE 1,1
40 INPUT "Enter angle to rotate to right:";ANGLERIGHT
50 LOCATE 2,1
60 INPUT "Enter angle to rotate down:";ANGLEDOWN
70 GOSUB 300    'perform rotation
80 GOTO 20      'the program runs as a loop
90              'user will have to interrupt
99 '
100 REM INITIALIZE
110 DIM A(8,3)   'the coordinates of the 8 vertices
120 DIM B(12,2)  'indicates which vertices to connect
130 FOR I=1 TO 8: FOR J=1 TO 3:READ A(I,J):NEXT J: NEXT I
140 DATA 40,40,40,  -40,40,40,  -40,-40,40,  40,-40,40
150 DATA 40,40,-40,  -40,40,-40,  -40,-40,-40,  40,-40,-40
160 FOR I=1 TO 12:FOR J=1 TO 2:READ B(I,J):NEXT J:NEXT I
170 DATA 1,2,  2,3,  3,4,  4,1,  1,5,  2,6
180 DATA 3,7,  4,8,  5,6,  6,7,  7,8,  8,5
190 SCREEN 1 ' set to graphics mode
195 RETURN
199 '
200 REM DRAW CUBE
210 CLS  'clear screen
220 FOR I=1 TO 12
230  X0=120+A(B(I,1),1): Y0=120+A(B(I,1),3)
240  X1=120+A(B(I,2),1): Y1=120+A(B(I,2),3)
250  LINE(X0,Y0)-(X1,Y1)
260 NEXT I
270 RETURN
299 '
300 REM SET UP ROTATION
310 C1=1:C2=2:ANGLE=ANGLERIGHT
320 GOSUB 400    'perform rotation on 1st and 2nd coordinates
330 C1=2:C2=3:ANGLE=ANGLEDOWN
340 GOSUB 400    'perform rotation on 2nd and 3rd coordinates
350 RETURN
399 '
400 REM PERFORM ROTATION
410 ANGLE=3.14159*ANGLE/180    'convert to radians
420 FOR I=1 TO 8
430  X=A(I,C1):Y=A(I,C2)
440  X2=X*COS(ANGLE)+Y*SIN(ANGLE)
450  Y2=Y*COS(ANGLE)-X*SIN(ANGLE)
460  A(I,C1)=X2:A(I,C2)=Y2
470 NEXT I
480 RETURN
```

FIGURE 265. THREE-DIMENSIONAL GRAPHICS IN BASIC

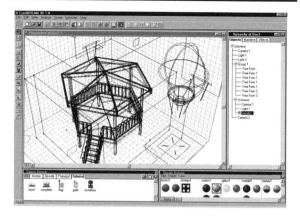

FIGURE 266. THREE-DIMENSIONAL DRAWING PROGRAM

computer or other powerful enterprise-wide computer, and a layer of
MIDDLEWARE that connects these two tiers.

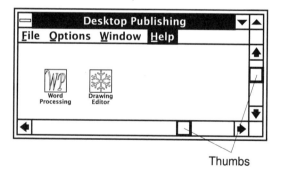

FIGURE 268. THUMBS (ELEVATOR BOXES)

thumb the box on an elevator bar (scroll bar). The position of the thumb
gives a graphical representation of the window's current position in the
document or list. If you are near the top of the document, the thumb is

near the top of the bar; if you are near the bottom of the document, the thumb is near the bottom of the bar. The thumb can be dragged with the mouse to scroll rapidly around the page.

thumbnail (from the artists' term *thumbnail sketch*) a small image of a graphics file displayed in order to help you identify it.

TIA

1. e-mail abbreviation for "**t**hanks **i**n **a**dvance."

2. The **I**nternet **A**dapter, a communications software package developed by Cyberspace Development, Inc., to enable UNIX systems to support SLIP connections.

tickler a program that examines the computer system's date and alerts the user about scheduled events.

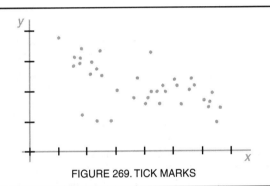

FIGURE 269. TICK MARKS

tick marks small lines that cross the *x*- or *y*-axis to mark the increments of measurement in a graph.

TIFF (**T**ag **I**mage **F**ile **F**ormat) a format for storing bit-mapped images on disk, developed by Aldus, Microsoft, and several other companies. TIFF files can store very large images with millions of colors, using several kinds of data compression. *Compare* PCX; GIF. *See also* BITMAP.

tight type set so closely that the letters almost touch. *See* LETTERSPACING for illustration. *See also* TRACKING; KERNING.

tilde the character ˜. Under UNIX and in many web addresses, the tilde indicates the home directory of a particular user; for example, ˜smith is the home directory of the user named smith.

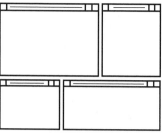

FIGURE 270. TILED WINDOWS

tile

1. to cause windows to divide the screen into sections without overlapping one another (Fig. 270). *Contrast* OVERLAID WINDOWS; CASCADE.

2. to print a large page (larger than your printer can handle) by having the page broken up into a series of regular-sized sheets, which can then be fastened together.

3. to create a pattern with a simple design by repeating it over and over. Many draw and paint programs have a library of tile designs; you can also design your own.

tiled windows windows that divide the screen into sections without overlapping one another. *Contrast* OVERLAID WINDOWS; CASCADE.

timesharing a technique developed in the 1960s for running more than one program on the same computer at the same time, so that, for example, the computer can serve many users at different terminals simultaneously.

Timesharing is based on the idea that a computer spends most of its time waiting for things to happen. Almost all input-output devices (printers, disks, etc.) operate much more slowly than the CPU itself; the extreme case is a terminal or console, where the computer may spend minutes or hours waiting for someone to type something. In a timesharing system, more than one program is loaded into memory at once, and when the computer is unable to proceed with one program, it jumps to another.

In practice, the computer does not stay on one program more than a fraction of a second even if there is nothing to wait for: to do so would prevent other, possibly shorter, programs from being executed. Also, programs that are not executed are frequently "rolled out" of memory (i.e., copied to disk) to make memory space available to programs that are actually running.

Modern operating systems such as UNIX and OS/2 use timesharing to run multiple programs concurrently. *See* MULTITASKING.

Times Roman

a b c d e f g h i j k l m
n o p q r s t u v w x y z
A B C D E F G H I J K L M
N O P Q R S T U V W X Y Z
1 2 3 4 5 6 7 8 9 0 ! @ #

FIGURE 271. TIMES ROMAN

Times Roman a highly legible typeface designed by Stanley Morison in 1931 for *The Times* of London. Times Roman and its many varieties (Times New Roman, Dutch 801, and others) reproduce well at low resolutions, and this probably led to its current popularity as a laser printer font. *See* TYPEFACE.

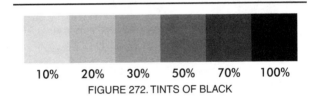

10%   20%   30%   50%   70%   100%

FIGURE 272. TINTS OF BLACK

tint a shade of a color; usually expressed as a percentage of a solid color. *See* Figure 272.

title (web page) descriptive text that defines the title of a web page and displays it in the browser's status bar. *See* WEB PAGE TITLE.

title bar the horizontal bar at the top of a window that contains the application program's icon and name at the left, the name of the open file (if appropriate), and to the right, the trio of window control buttons (MINIMIZE, RESTORE [or full-screen], and close). See Fig. 273. In Windows 95 and its successors, clicking on the application program's icon will pop-up a menu to control the window.

TLA three-letter **a**cronym; three-letter **a**bbreviation. A significant obstacle to progress in the computer industry is the fact that there are only

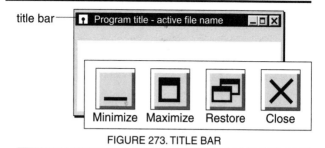

FIGURE 273. TITLE BAR

17,576 TLAs, of which some, such as UGH, do not make good trademarks.

TLD top-level domain.

tn *see* TELNET.

tn3270 *see* TELNET.

TNC *see* PACKET RADIO.

TNX abbreviation for *thanks*, sometimes written TNXE6 or TNX 1E6 to signify "thanks a million" (*see* EXPONENTIAL NOTATION).

toggle to switch something back and forth from one state to another. For instance, in some editors, the Ins key "toggles" insert mode; that is, it turns insert mode on if it is off or off if it is on.

token
   1. the special message that is passed around a TOKEN-RING NETWORK to enable the computers to take turns transmitting.
   2. a basic meaningful unit of a language. For example, the one-line BASIC program

```
10 PRINT "The square root of 2 is ";SQR(2)
```

consists of these tokens:

- The line number 10.
- A space.
- The reserved word PRINT.
- A space.
- The string "The square root of 2 is ".
- A semicolon.
- The function name SQR.
- A left parenthesis.
- The number 2.
- A right parenthesis.

(Some people do not count the spaces as tokens.) Breaking the input into tokens is the first step in processing any computer language.

tokenize to break a character string into the smallest units that are significant in a language (TOKENS, definition 2).

token ring a type of network in which the computers are connected together in a ring. A special message, called the *token,* is passed from one machine to another around the ring, and each machine can transmit only while it is holding the token. IBM markets a token-ring network for the PC family of computers. *See* LOCAL-AREA NETWORK; ARCNET.

toner the black powder that is used by laser printers and photocopy machines to create the image on paper. It consists of tiny particles of easily melted plastic. If you spill toner where it isn't wanted, make sure not to get it hot before cleaning it up.

toner cartridge replaceable assembly in a laser printer that contains the toner (a powdery ink) that will be used to make marks on the paper. Most toner cartridges also contain other parts that are likely to wear out (e.g., the electrophotographic drum), and replacing the cartridge replaces quite a bit of the inner workings of the laser printer. (This contributes to the cost of the toner cartridge.) Some types of toner cartridges are recyclable and refillable; however, the quality of refilled cartridges is not always equal to that of new ones.

tool a specialized version of the mouse cursor which gives the cursor new abilities and properties. For example, in a paint program, the brush tool will have a special shape, size, and color—any pixels touched by the "brush" will change to the brush color.

FIGURE 274. TOOLBOX

toolbox a collection of icons that represent frequently used commands. The toolbox may be displayed across the top or side of the screen or you may be able to relocate it by dragging it with the mouse. The more complicated paint and photopaint programs sometimes have several toolboxes, with similar tools grouped together. *See* DOCK.

top-down programming a technique of programming by defining the overall outlines of the program first and then filling in the details.

The top-down approach is usually the best way to write complicated programs. Detailed decisions are postponed until the requirements of the large program are known; this is better than making the detailed decisions early and then forcing the major program strategy to conform to them. Each part of the program (called a *module*) can be written and tested independently.

topic drift the tendency of the topic of an on-line discussion to shift while the title of the messages remains the same, because everyone is replying to an existing message and therefore automatically keeping the same title. After a while, a THREAD titled "Windows 98 setup" may actually be discussing chili recipes. Topic drift can be particularly amusing when reading a newsgroup frequented by individuals with wide-ranging interests. *See* NEWSGROUP; LURK; THREAD.

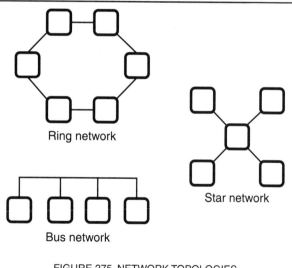

Ring network

Star network

Bus network

FIGURE 275. NETWORK TOPOLOGIES

topology the mathematical study of how points are connected together. If an object is stretched or bent, then its geometric shape changes but its topological properties remain unchanged.

The topology of a computer network is the pattern of connections between the machines in the network. Figure 275 illustrates some common topologies: a ring network, a star network, and a bus network. *See* LOCAL-AREA NETWORK.

tower a computer enclosure that is taller than it is wide. Often a tower will have more space available for add-in cards and extra drives than a conventional enclosure. A tower also has a smaller FOOTPRINT than a horizontal box and can sit either on your desktop beside the monitor or on the floor.

trace

1. (in a draw program) to create a path or outline around the contours of a bitmapped shape. It is necessary to trace bitmaps to convert them into VECTOR GRAPHICS. Tracing can be done by a separate utility program or from within the drawing program.

2. to execute a program step by step, observing the results of each step.

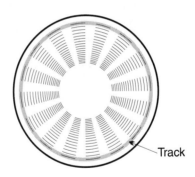

FIGURE 276. TRACK

track

1. one of the concentric circles in which data is recorded on a disk, or one of the parallel strips in which data is recorded on tape.

2. a music selection on a CD-ROM.

3. a portion of a MIDI file that specifies the performance details of a single instrument.

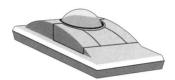

FIGURE 277. TRACKBALL

trackball a computer pointing device similar in function to a mouse. Instead of rolling the mouse around the desktop, the user rotates the ball on the trackball in the direction desired. The trackball unit itself does not move, which is an advantage if there is not enough desktop space to conveniently operate a mouse.

tracking letterspacing (spacing between letters in words). *See* LETTERSPACING for an illustration.

tractor feed a mechanism that uses toothed gears to pull the paper forward in a dot-matrix computer printer. The teeth fit into the feed holes in the side of the paper.

transfer rate the rate at which data is transferred from one place to another; a measure of the performance of disk drives, modems, and other peripheral devices. The transfer rate of a CD-ROM drive is important because the data for video, music, or animation must reach the CPU fast enough to be played back without introducing pauses.

transistor an electronic device that allows a small current in one place to control a larger current in another place; thus, transistors can be used as amplifiers in radio and audio circuits, and as switches in logic gates (*see* NOT GATE; NOR GATE; OR GATE; NAND GATE; AND GATE.) This article deals with bipolar transistors, the most common kind. *See also* FIELD-EFFECT TRANSISTOR.

A bipolar transistor is made by sandwiching a thin layer of one kind of semiconductor material (P-type or N-type) between two layers of the opposite type (N-type or P-type, respectively). Thus, an NPN transistor is a P layer between two N layers; a PNP transistor is the opposite. (*See* SEMICONDUCTOR.) The circuit diagram symbols for NPN and PNP transistors are shown in Figure 278. The middle section of a transistor is called the base, and the other two sections are the emitter and collector.

Figure 279 shows how an NPN transistor works. (A PNP transistor works the same way with all polarities reversed.) The emitter is connected to ground (0 volts) and the collector is connected to +5 volts through some type of load. Electrons try to flow from emitter to collector, but with 0 volts on the base, they can't get through because the base-collector junction is like a reverse-biased diode (*see* DIODE).

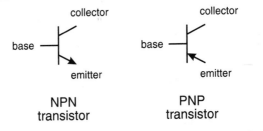

FIGURE 278. TRANSISTORS (CIRCUIT DIAGRAM SYMBOLS)

But if the base were to become full of electrons, it would no longer behave like P-type material, and the base-collector junction would no longer block electron flow. We can get electrons into the base by pulling them in from the emitter. Thus if we apply a positive voltage to the base in order to forward-bias the base-emitter junction, the base-collector junction will become free to conduct. A small flow of electrons through the base controls a much larger flow of electrons through the collector.

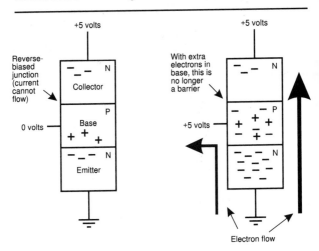

FIGURE 279. TRANSISTOR ACTION

In computers, transistors act as switches. The current flowing through the base controls the current flowing through the collector, turning it on or off under external control. *See* LOGIC CIRCUITS.

transition effect (video editing; presentation software) a method of changing the scene from one view to another. Transition effects can give visual interest to a presentation by introducing an element of motion to the graphics. In video editing, they can help establish a change in location, or indicate the passge of time. There are literally hundreds of transtion effects and the exact terminology varies from program to program. Basically, there are three major types of transition effects:

1. *Dissolve.* Gradually replaces the first image with the second, either superimposing the pictures in mid-transition (like a double exposure) or replacing the image pixel-by-pixel or in larger blocks.

2. *Swipe.* The first image is seemingly wiped off, revealing the second image underneath. Swipes can go from left to right, right to left, up, or down, and the speed and the sharpness of the swipe edge can usually be controlled.

3. *Fade.* The image either darkens to black or lightens to pure white.

It is wise to use transition effects sparingly. Not every editing cut or slide change merits special attention; in fact, overuse of distracting transitions will distract and possibly confuse the audience.

translator
1. a program that exchanges data between application programs. *See also* FILTER; IMPORT; EXPORT.
2. a program that attempts to translate one human language into another. *See* NATURAL LANGUAGE PROCESSING.

transparent
1. lacking visible effect. For instance, if a print-spooling program is transparent, all other software works just as if the print-spooling program were not installed. This is a desirable feature.
2. able to be seen through. Some graphics and paint programs have special features or filters to help you render transparent objects. Of special interest is the ability to adjust the opacity of objects or bitmaps via a sliding scale; the object can be totally opaque to totally transparent with many intermediate gradations. The in-between state where the image is recognizable but can be seen through is called GHOSTING.

transparent GIF a bitmap file whose background color is clear. A transparent GIF will seem to have irregular borders and float above the background.

transposition a common typing error where the order of two keystrokes is reversed. For example "the" may be typed as "hte." A SPELL CHECKER is useful for catching transpositions.

trap the area of overlap allowed between different colors of ink in a color printing job on a printing press. A slight amount of trap will prevent unintentional gaps between the two areas of color. *See* TRAPPING, definition 2.

trap error (in OS/2) an error that arises when a (presumably buggy) program tries to use a memory address that is not allocated to it by the operating system. *See* ILLEGAL OPERATION.

trapping

    1. the act of detecting and responding to events that would ordinarily interrupt the operation of the computer. For instance, some programming languages provide "error trapping," which means that when the program attempts to do something impossible (such as divide by zero or read a file that doesn't exist), control will be transferred to an error-handling routine supplied by the programmer. If no error trapping were provided, the program would simply end with an error message that might puzzle the user. In BASIC, trapping is activated by statements such as ON ERROR. For a Java example, *see* TRY.

    2. the technique of aiding the REGISTRATION of color plates in a printing job by creating slight areas of overlap where two colors meet. The area of the overlap is called TRAP.

    Some software is capable of creating trap automatically (*see* PRE-PRESS; DESKTOP PUBLISHING). At other times, the designer will have to intentionally overlap design elements to ensure full coverage, even with a sight misregistration.

    Trapping is only necessary when preparing CAMERA-READY COPY for a printing press; there are no registration problems when printing directly from your computer to a color printer.

Trash the place where deleted files are stored on the Macintosh, corresponding to the RECYCLE BIN under Windows 95 and its successors. The space occupied by the files does not become available until you empty the Trash. Until then, you can get the files back if you need them.

Traveling Salesman Problem the mathematical problem of finding the shortest route that connects *n* points, given the distances between the points. As far as is known, this problem can be solved only by exhaustive search, which can take a gigantic number of steps. *See* LIMITS OF COMPUTER POWER.

tray (Windows 95 and later) a small area on the screen at the right of the taskbar (*see* Figure 280). The tray holds the system clock display as well as icons for volume control and other device drivers such as printers, video card, and virus checkers.

tree

    1. a data structure similar to a linked list, except that each element carries with it the addresses of two or more other elements, rather than just one. *See* LINKED LIST.

    Trees are a very efficient way of storing items that must be searched for and retrieved quickly. Suppose, for example, that you want to store

FIGURE 280. TRAY (IN WINDOWS 95)

the following names in a computer:

Jones	Voss
Steinfeld	Marino
Alexander	Zhang
Bateman	Rodriguez

The names can be arranged into a tree by using the following two-step procedure:

1. Use the first name on the list as the root of the tree.
2. To find where to put each subsequent name, start at the root of the tree. If the name you are dealing with precedes the root name alphabetically, follow the left pointer; otherwise follow the right pointer. Proceed in this way until you come to an empty pointer; attach the new name to it.

The result is the tree shown in Figure 281. Step 2 in the procedure above can be used to locate names already in the tree in a minimum of steps (in this case, no more than four steps even though there are eight names in the list). The algorithm that results is not quite as good as a binary search, but it is much better than having to work through the whole list. Furthermore, as with linked lists, new nodes can be added at any time without requiring that existing nodes be moved.

2. a branching structure in which information is stored: for example, a system of directories and subdirectories (*see* DIRECTORY) or a branching diagram of a web site.

trigonometric functions the mathematical functions that relate an angle to the lengths of the sides of a right triangle (Figure 282), defined thus:

$$\sin \theta = \frac{\text{length of opposite side}}{\text{length of hypotenuse}}$$

$$\cos \theta = \frac{\text{length of adjacent side}}{\text{length of hypotenuse}}$$

$$\tan \theta = \frac{\text{length of opposite side}}{\text{length of adjacent side}} = \frac{\sin \theta}{\cos \theta}$$

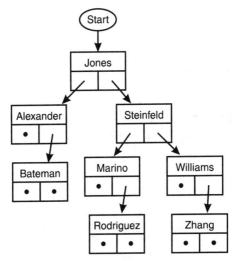

FIGURE 281. TREE (FOR BINARY SEARCH)

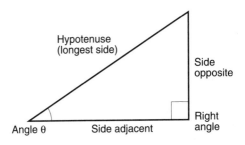

FIGURE 282. TRIANGLE FOR DEFINING
TRIGONOMETRIC FUNCTIONS

If θ is small, $\sin\theta \approx \tan\theta \approx \theta$ (measured in radians).

    See also ARC SINE; ARC COSINE; ARC TANGENT; ATN; SIN; COS; TAN.

Trojan horse a computer program with a hidden destructive function, such as erasing the disks on a specified date. Trojan horses are often distributed as counterfeit "new" versions of shareware products.

    Knowingly distributing a destructive computer program is a crime under common law and under specific laws of various states. *See also* VIRUS.

troll a message that is posted (in a newsgroup, etc.) solely in order to stir up as many replies as possible. Trolls often contain deliberate misinformation or insults. Naturally, the person doing the trolling looks foolish, but some of them don't mind. (From *troll,* a fishing term.)

TrueType font an outline font format (originally developed in 1991 by Apple as a competing format to PostScript fonts). TrueType fonts are sets of mathematical descriptions of the letterforms as B-spline curves. What this means in practical terms is that it is possible to SCALE or size the type to practically any point size. (*See* VECTOR GRAPHICS.) A common competing type format is Adobe's Type 1 font format.

    There is a slight difference in the TrueType formats for Macintosh and PC platforms; conversion utilities can convert one to the other.

Trumatch a color matching and calibration system developed and distributed by Trumatch, Inc., New York, New York. Web address: http://www.trumatch.com.

truncation the act of cutting off part of something; specifically:

    1. dropping digits of a number that are to the right of the decimal point. For example, truncating 6.45 gives 6, and truncating 737.984 gives 737. In Pascal this operation is symbolized by trunc; in BASIC, by INT; in Java, by floor. *Contrast* ROUNDING, which is finding the nearest whole number (such as 738 for 737.984).

    2. cutting off part of an image or a printed word when not enough space is available to print it.

try a Java programming command that marks an operation that may fail. A block of code is surrounded by try if it might cause an EXCEPTION (an error condition) for which the programmer wishes to specify an action. For example:

```
try {theURL = new URL(urlbase,n0);
     /*put additional statements in try block here*/
     }
  catch (MalformedURLException e) {
     System.out.println("Bad URL: "+theURL);
                                   }
```

    The code within the try block will attempt to locate the specified URL. If successful, the program will proceed with the additional statements in the `try` block; if the URL is not valid, then it will execute the `catch` block (which displays a message for the user).

The advantage of this approach is that it saves the programmer from having to write separate `if-then` statements for each possible error that can occur. Instead, any error that arises in the `try` block can be processed by the `catch` block later on. This makes programs easier to read because the code for handling exceptional situations is clearly separated from the code for normal situations.

TSO (**T**ime **S**haring **O**ption) the part of OS/360 and related IBM operating systems that supports timesharing terminals. TSO commands correspond to the various statements in JCL; for example, the `allocate` command corresponds to the JCL DD statement. *See* JCL.

TSR **t**erminate and **s**tay **r**esident. *See* MEMORY-RESIDENT PROGRAM.

TTFN e-mail abbreviation for "**t**a **t**a (i.e., goodbye) **f**or **n**ow."

TTL (**T**ransistor-**T**ransistor **L**ogic) a type of integrated circuit that operates at very high speeds and requires relatively large amounts of power at an accurately regulated voltage (5 volts). Early microcomputers used TTL devices for input-output and control functions; newer ones are switching to CMOS circuitry (*see* CMOS). TTL integrated circuits are recognizable because their type numbers contain "74" or "74LS" followed by two or three digits (e.g., SN74LS02N).

TTL monochrome monitor the type of monitor used with the original IBM monochrome display adapter (MDA) in the early 1980s. *See* MONITOR.

TTYL e-mail abbreviation for "**t**alk **t**o **y**ou **l**ater."

tune to improve the performance of a system by adjusting numerical parameters such as the size of the swap file, the time delays allowed for certain operations, and the like.

tunnel a private, secure link between two distant places that connects two local-area networks. For example, a company with two main offices may establish a tunnel between them using dial-up modems, leased telephone lines, or a secure (encrypted) connection over the Internet.

turbo the higher-speed mode on a computer that offers a choice of clock speeds. (Originally from *turbocharger,* a device for increasing the power of an automobile engine.)

Turbo C++ a compiler for the C and C++ languages similar in design to Turbo Pascal and produced by the same company, Borland International, for the same software environments (DOS and Windows). It supersedes an earlier product, Turbo C, and is accompanied by a more elaborate compiler package, Borland C++, which is marketed mainly to professional programmers. *See* TURBO PASCAL; BORLAND INTERNATIONAL; C; C++.

Turbo Pascal an extremely popular Pascal compiler introduced by Borland International in 1984, contributing greatly to the popularity of Pascal on microcomputers.

The Turbo Pascal language is close to the ISO standard (*see* ISO) but does not include the predefined procedures `get` and `put`, nor is the behavior of `read`, `eof`, and `eoln` entirely standard. Many extensions to the language have been added, including "typed constants" (which are actually variables initialized at compile time), additional ways of using pointers, and predefined procedures for screen control, graphics, and operating system services. Later versions include extensions for object-oriented programming. *See also* DELPHI.

Turing machine an imaginary machine conceived by Alan Turing in the 1930s to help identify the kinds of problems that are potentially solvable by machines.

The machine is a kind of simple computer. It consists of a long string of paper tape and a machine through which the tape can be fed. The machine can do four things: it can move the tape one space, it can place a mark on a space, it can erase a mark, or it can halt. Turing's thesis states that this simple machine can solve any problem that can be expressed as an algorithm (if it has an unlimited supply of paper tape). As you might imagine, in practice it would be difficult to give instructions to a Turing machine so that it could solve a particular problem. The Turing machine is important theoretically, however, because it provides an indication of what kinds of problems computers can solve and what kinds they can never solve.

Turing test a test proposed by Alan Turing in 1950 to determine whether machines have achieved human-like intelligence. According to the Turing test, a machine is intelligent if, under certain specified conditions, it is indistinguishable from a human when you carry on a conversation with it by teletype. For a critique *see* ELIZA; ARTIFICIAL INTELLIGENCE.

turnkey system a computer system that is ready to perform a particular task with no further preparation ("just turn the key and it does it"). A turnkey system is sold as a complete package from a single vendor. By contrast, most computer systems are assembled step-by-step by users who obtain hardware and software from various suppliers.

turtle a pointer that moves around the screen leaving a trail as it goes and that is used to draw pictures in LOGO and related computer languages. Originally, the turtle was a small robot that rolled around on a large piece of paper, drawing a line.

Turtle graphics is a form of vector graphics. The turtle cannot be told to go to a particular position; it can only be told to turn through a particular angle and go a particular distance. *See* VECTOR GRAPHICS. For an example of turtle graphics programming, *see* LOGO.

TÜV (Technischer Überwachungs-Verein, "technical supervision union") a German organization that certifies that electronic equipment meets applicable safety standards and complies with government regulations.

TWAIN a protocol for delivering graphical images from a scanning or imaging device to application software. The name is said to stand for "**t**echnology **w**ithout **a**n **i**nteresting **n**ame."

    TWAIN strives to reduce the number of device drivers needed by providing a standard communication format. For more information about TWAIN, see `http://www.twain.org`.

twiddle *(slang)* to make small changes in settings.

twisted pair a pair of unshielded wires twisted together, providing a cheap and relatively noise-free way to transmit signals. The two wires carry equal and opposite signals. Any electrical noise that they pick up will be the same (rather than opposite) in the two wires, and the circuitry on the receiving end can be designed to ignore it. *Contrast* COAXIAL CABLE.

type
    1. letters printed or displayed by a computer. *See* TYPEFACE.
    2. a kind of data item, such as integers, floating-point numbers, character strings, pointers, etc. *See* DATA STRUCTURES and entries for particular programming languages.
    3. (in DOS and other operating systems) the command that causes the contents of a text file to be displayed. For example:

```
type letter.txt
```

causes the file LETTER.TXT to be displayed on the screen. The equivalent UNIX command is `cat`.

Type 1 font an outline font format developed by Adobe Systems. Type 1 fonts are sets of mathematical descriptions of the letterforms as BÉZIER splines. In practical terms this means that it is possible to SCALE or size the type to practically any point size. (*See* VECTOR GRAPHICS.) TRUETYPE fonts are a competing format to Type 1 fonts.

typeface a particular design of lettering, in a consistent weight and style. Most of the typefaces used on computer printers today fall into the following categories (see Fig. 283):

    1. *Roman type, proportionally spaced, with serifs.* This kind of type originated with the stone engravers of ancient Rome. "Proportionally spaced" means that different letters are different widths (e.g., *M* is wider than *I*); serifs are the marks at the ends of the strokes (e.g., the horizontal marks at the top and bottom of *I*). Times Roman is a popular roman typeface; it was designed by Stanley Morison for the London *Times*. Palatino is a newer roman typeface designed by Hermann Zapf and based on ancient Roman inscriptions.

Times Roman
ABCDEF abcdefghijklmnopqrstuvwxyz
1234567890 @#$%&*().,:;!?

Palatino
ABCDEF abcdefghijklmnopqrstuvwxyz
1234567890 @#$%&*().,:;!?

Helvetica
ABCDEF abcdefghijklmnopqrstuvwxyz
1234567890 @#$%&*().,:;!?

Courier
ABCDEF abcdefghijklmnopqrstuvwxyz
1234567890 @#$%&*().,:;!?

Zapf Chancery
ABCDEF abcdefghijklmnopqrstuvwxyz
1234567890 @#$%&().,:;!?*

FIGURE 283. TYPEFACES

Roman type is the most readable kind of type and is used for the text of most books. Blocks of roman type should never be underlined; use *italics* instead (or **boldface** in some situations). Underlining text on typewriters was originally a substitute for italics.

Roman type usually includes some characters that are not on a typewriter, such as the dash (—) and distinct opening and closing quotation marks (" "). Be sure to use these where appropriate. (*See* TYPESETTING MISTAKES.)

2. *Sans-serif type, proportionally spaced.* A popular typeface of this kind is Helvetica. Sans-serif type is better for short captions, posters, or labels, but can be tiring to read for long periods.

3. *Fixed-pitch, typewriter-like typefaces.* Courier and similar fixed-pitch typefaces are used when all characters must be the same width in order to line up properly, such as in computer program listings (see COBOL in this book for an example), financial tables, and documents that were laid out for a fixed-pitch printer.

4. *Novelty typefaces* such as Zapf Chancery. These should be used very sparingly to make dramatic-looking titles or mastheads.

See also FONT; SERIF; PITCH; POINT; DESKTOP PUBLISHING; LEADING.

typesetting mistakes common errors in the use of type on computers, arising because most computer users do not know the practices of the printing industry. The following pointers will help you avoid blunders:

- Notice the differences between typesetting and typing on a typewriter:

    - opening and closing quotation marks are different characters ("like this");

    - a dash (—) is not the same as two hyphens (- -);

    - underlining is rarely used — where you would underline on a typewriter, use italics (or possibly boldface) in type.

- Your type is proportionally spaced; letters are not all the same width. You can't count letter spaces the way you do on a typewriter; you must use other means of aligning. Always align columns with the Tab key, not the space bar.

- Type carefully. Be sure not to hit the space bar more than once between words. It's hard to tell the difference between one space and two spaces by just looking at the screen.

- Don't justify everything. Justified type looks good only when the columns are wide enough. Flush-left type with a ragged right margin is easier to read if the columns are narrow; with narrow columns, justification puts excessive space between words. (*See* JUSTIFICATION; RIVER.)

- Don't use more than one or at most two fonts in a document (italics, boldface, and different sizes count as a single font). Multiple-font documents are almost always ugly. Odd typefaces (such as Old English) are very hard to read.

- Make sure your document is not missing any essential features such as adequate margins or page numbers. If in doubt, find a well-designed document or book and imitate it.

- Use appropriate features of your software. When you type a footnote, use the footnote instruction if there is one, rather than just moving the cursor to the foot of the page. That way, if you change the layout later, the software will probably still handle the footnote correctly.

- Standardize. Don't face each document as an original design problem. Develop a standard format that you like, and stick with it.

- Beware of font substitutions, especially on the Macintosh. For example, don't select New York type if your PostScript printer is going to substitute Times Roman. If you do, you'll get excessive spacing between words.

U

u typewritten representation occasionally used for the Greek letter μ (mu), abbreviation for *micro-* (1/1,000,000). For abbreviations that begin with μ, *see* page 3.

UI (**u**ser **i**nterface) the part of the program that the user sees and interacts with, as opposed to the part of the program that performs its internal processing. For example, Windows 98 programs provide a consistent user interface in terms of the appearance of menus and the way windows behave. *See* GUI; USER INTERFACE.

UL HTML tag that indicates an unnumbered list. For an example, *see* HTML.

U/lc upper and lowercase; MIXED CASE. Also written *c/lc* (caps and lower case). U/lc is the normal method of setting type; *contrast* CAPS.

ULTRIX a proprietary version of UNIX for Digital Equipment Corporation computers. *See* UNIX.

UML (**U**nified **M**odeling **L**anguage) a language used for the visual representation of software systems (and other types of systems). Much of UML was developed at Rational Software, and it was adopted as a standard by the Object Management Group (OMG) in 1997. UML includes standard notation for representing classes and their attributes and associations, and it includes state transition, interaction, component, and deployment diagrams.

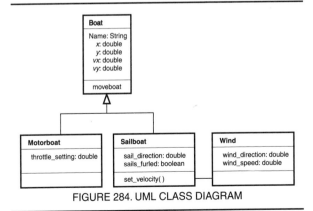

FIGURE 284. UML CLASS DIAGRAM

Figure 284 shows an example of a UML class diagram for a program that keeps track of the movement of boats. Each class is enclosed in a rectangle, with the name of the class at the top. The middle part of the rectangle lists attributes (or variables) for the members of that class.

For example, boats have a name represented as a string, x and y position coordinates and vx and vy velocity components, all of which are double-precision numbers. The bottom part of the class lists the operations (or methods) of that class.

In this example, two specific types of boats (sailboats and motorboats) inherit from the class Boat. Inheritance is indicated by an open arrow. Another class is the wind. The line connecting the wind and sailboat class indicates an interaction between those two classes since the operation that sets the velocity of the sailboat needs to know the wind direction and speed.

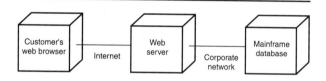

FIGURE 285. UML DEPLOYMENT DIAGRAM

Figure 285 shows an example of a UML deployment diagram for a three-tier system where customers use a browser to connect over the Internet to the web server. The web server is, in turn, connected to the corporate mainframe database.

UML is designed for the development of complicated systems, so a complete design will include many different UML diagrams. UML diagrams can be created by hand or with a specialized software drawing tool.

A summary of UML notation is available at

`www.rational.com/uml/resources/quick/uml_poster.jtmpl.`

UNC (**U**niform **N**aming **C**onvention) the standard way of identifying shared resources (disks, directories, or printers) on Microsoft networks. UNC names have the form

*computer**resource*

or

*computer**resource**path*

For example, if computer `zeta` shares its drive C under the name `cdrive`, then file `c:\MyDoc\letter.doc` on that machine would be accessible through the network as

`\\zeta\cdrive\MyDoc\letter.doc`.

Under Windows 2000, URLs (**U**niform **R**esource **L**ocators) can be used as an alternative to UNC paths. The example just given would be `http://zeta/cdrive/MyDoc/letter.doc` in URL form.

undo a command that allows the computer user to reverse the effects of the most recent operation. If "Undo" is DIMMED (printed in gray), it is not possible for your program to undo a command (perhaps you have performed an intermediate step — or perhaps the most recent command was a complex operation that cannot be undone). For this reason, it is wise to save different versions of the file as you work so that you will have a recent version to REVERT to in case of disaster. *See also* REDO.

undocumented not described in the literature (documentation) provided by the manufacturer of a product.

Some computer programs rely on undocumented features of the machine on which they run. The risk of using undocumented features is that they may not be the same in future versions of the program or machine.

Undocumented features exist for several reasons. Some are accidental omissions from the documentation. Others represent incompletely tested features that will be made reliable and documented in future versions. Still others may be kept secret in order to give the vendor a competitive advantage in making add-on products. *See also* DOCUMENTATION.

unerase *see* RECOVERING ERASED FILES.

ungroup to cause a grouped object to be broken down into its component objects. It is necessary to ungroup to change the attributes of a single object or to change its shape. *See* GROUP, definition 1.

Unicode a system for representing characters using 2 bytes (16 bits), allowing for $2^{16} = 65,536$ different characters (as opposed to the $2^8 = 256$ different characters possible with the ASCII coding system). Unicode provides enough characters to represent all the written languages of the world, including the full writing systems of Chinese and Japanese.

At present, the Unicode standard is not yet complete; Unicode version 2.0 defines 38,885 characters, the first 128 of which are the same as ASCII.

The Java programming language uses Unicode instead of ASCII to represent characters, making it easier to internationalize programs. However, the characters that you will actually see on your machine are limited by the fonts available; you will not normally be able to see all of the Unicode characters even if your computer is executing a Java program. *See also* ASCII; ANSI; CHARACTER SET.

FIGURE 286. UNIFORM FILL

uniform fill the act of filling a graphical object with one solid color or tint, with no gradations. *Contrast* FOUNTAIN FILL.

uninterruptible power supply a power supply that uses batteries to continue providing electricity to a computer for a few minutes in the event of a power failure. This makes it possible to shut down the computer in an orderly way without losing data.

  Usage note: The spelling *uninterruptable* is also widely used. Both spellings, with *-ible* and *-able,* are consistent with the word's Latin etymology.

union a data item that can hold values of more than one type. *See* VARIANT.

universal serial bus *See* USB.

UNIX an operating system, or family of operating systems, developed at Bell Laboratories in the early 1970s as a replacement for an earlier system called *Multics*. UNIX is noteworthy because, although developed by a small team of about four people, it is in many ways superior to operating systems developed by large teams at tremendous expense (e.g., OS/360). The most popular versions of UNIX today are SOLARIS and LINUX.

  The main features of UNIX include the following:

1. *Highly modular, structured design.* The entire system is defined in terms of a relatively small number of subroutines; UNIX can be implemented on any machine by implementing those routines. Furthermore, the operation of the whole system is based on a relatively small number of principles carried through very consistently; there is little arbitrary detail for the user to learn.

2. *Extensibility.* In many operating systems, users can create commands of their own that execute sequences of ordinary commands stored on files. UNIX, however, provides a full-fledged programming language for this purpose (the "shell"), with IF, WHILE, and CASE statements similar to those of Pascal, as well as extensive facilities for string handling.

3. *Input-output redirection.* Any program invoked by a command can be told to take its input from, and/or write its output onto, a file rather than the user's terminal. For example:

```
sort <alpha >beta
```

tells the `sort` program to take its input from `alpha` and write its output onto `beta`. UNIX also supports *pipes,* which allow one program to transmit its output directly into the input of another program. *See* PIPE.

Many UNIX commands, called *filters,* read a file and output a copy of it that has undergone some simple transformation, such as removing repeated lines. Powerful operations can be accomplished by stringing filters together through pipes.

4. *Tree-structured directories.* In all earlier operating systems, a user's files were kept in a single list called a DIRECTORY. In UNIX, however, directories are handled like files and a user can have an unlimited number of them, each of which must be listed in a higher directory until the main ("root") directory is reached. This makes it possible to arrange files into logical groups — for example, to put all files related to a particular project into a single directory. Tree-structured directories are a virtual necessity if one user is to keep track of more than a few dozen files, as is required, for example, on a microcomputer with a hard disk.

The following are some common UNIX commands:

`cc`	Compile a C Program. (*See* C.)
`cp`	Copy a file onto a file or into a directory.
`diff`	Display the differences between two text files.
`grep`	Search a file for lines matching a pattern.
`ls`	List contents of a directory.
`mkdir`	Create a directory.
`lpr`	Print a file.
`rm`	Remove (delete) a file.
`rmdir`	Delete a directory (which must be empty).
`cat`	Copy file from standard input to standard output.
`chmod`	Change file permissions.

See also /DEV; /HOME; /ETC; /USR.

unsharp masking a method of sharpening an image by subtracting from it a blurred copy of itself. This was once done with photographic plates but is more easily done digitally, and most photopaint programs provide an unsharp masking filter. *See also* IMAGE PROCESSING and cross-references there.

uplink
    1. a connection through which signals can be transmitted to a satellite. *Compare* UPLOAD.
    2. a connection from one hub to another hub. *See* HUB.

upload to transmit a file to a central computer from a smaller computer or a computer at a remote location. *See* KERMIT; XMODEM; FTP. *Contrast* DOWNLOAD.

uppercase capital letters, such as A, B, C, as opposed to a, b, c (lower-case) or A, B, C (small caps). The term " uppercase" goes back to the early days of letterpress printing. The metal type was kept in divided drawers called cases; the capital letters were traditionally kept in the upper case, and the small letters in the lower.

UPS

1. *See* UNINTERRUPTIBLE POWER SUPPLY.

2. (United Parcel Service) a major American carrier of packages for mail-order and e-tail businesses. (*See* E-TAIL.) Their web address is www.ups.com.

upward compatibility the situation in which a computer program or accessory works not only on the machine for which it was designed but also on newer models. For instance, programs written for the IBM PC in 1981 will still run (considerably faster) on present-day Pentium machines. Thus we say that the Pentium is upward compatible with the processor in the PC. *Contrast* DOWNWARD COMPATIBILITY.

URL (Uniform Resource Locator, Universal Resource Locator) a way of specifying the location of publicly available information on the Internet, in the form

protocol://*machine*:*port number*/*filename*

Often the port number and/or the filename is unnecessary. For example,

http://csam.uga.edu:80

means 'connect to port 80 of csam.uga.edu using Hypertext Transfer Protocol,' and

ftp://ai.uga.edu/pub/natural.language/Contents

means to download a particular file from ai.uga.edu by File Transfer Protocol. *See also* FTP.

The URL for a World Wide Web site often includes www, as in http://www.spu.edu. Other possible protocols include gopher and telnet. *See* WORLD WIDE WEB; INTERNET; HTTP; BROWSER; GOPHER; TELNET; ABSOLUTE URL; RELATIVE URL; HTML; TILDE.

USB (Universal Serial Bus) a serial bus standard proposed by Intel and other companies in 1997. It provides a data rate of 12 million bits per second, slower than its rival, Firewire (IEEE 1394), but cheaper to implement. USB connections are used to attach personal computers to their keyboards, printers, and other peripherals. USB also delivers electrical power to devices on the bus, and as a result, many peripherals no longer need their own power cords. Because the USB connector is small, full-size USB connectors can be used on laptop and handheld computers. *See also* SERIAL BUS; IEEE 1394.

Usenet

1. a set of thousands of newsgroups (discussion forums) distributed via the Internet (formerly distributed through the Usenet wide-area network). Newsgroups have descriptive names such as `sci.astro.amateur` and are arranged into hierarchies (classifications), of which the main ones are:

`news.` for announcements about Usenet itself;
`comp.` for computer science and technology;
`sci.` for other academic topics (including humanities);
`soc.` for cultural interest groups;
`rec.` for hobbies and sports;
`talk.` for wide-ranging discussions, often heated;
`misc.` for a few topics that don't fit elsewhere;
`alt.` for trial newsgroups and "alternative" topics.

Because the cost of distributing every message is paid by sites all over the world (not just the sender's site), it is extremely important to use each newsgroup only for its intended purpose, and to refrain from posting advertisements or mass solicitations except where they are specifically invited.

Also, before posting a simple question, look for a FAQ file ("frequently asked questions") that may answer it. Many newsgroups have very helpful FAQ files that are posted every two to four weeks. All the available FAQ files are available by anonymous FTP from `rtfm.mit.edu`.

2. a wide-area network for UNIX machines that formerly exchanged files by modem through the UUCP ("UNIX-to-UNIX copy") command. Usenet addresses were of the form

`psuvax!ugacc!aisun1!mcovingt`

which means "user `mcovingt` on machine `aisun1`, which can be reached through `ugacc`, which can be reached through `psuvax`." Usenet has been supplanted by the INTERNET.

user-friendly easy for people to use.

In the days when computers were operated only by specialists, little attention was paid to making programs user-friendly. However, when computers became more popular, it became very important to write programs that could be used easily by nonspecialists.

The most important requirement for making a program user-friendly is that the program should fit the task — that is, it should be suitable for the job it is supposed to do, and should take advantage of what the user already knows about how to do the work. Also necessary are clear, understandable documentation and good on-line help.

Other features that can help make a program user-friendly are menus that clearly list the available choices and command names that are easy to remember. However, a program should not contain so many on-screen explanatory messages that it becomes cumbersome to use for people who have already learned how the program works. *See also* INTUITIVE.

user interface the way a computer program communicates with the person who is using it. There are three important types of user interfaces:

1. *Command languages.* This is a common way of giving instructions to operating systems; for instance, in DOS, OS/2, or VAX/VMS, the user can obtain a list of files by typing the command `dir`. Command languages work well only if they are used constantly so that the user never forgets the commands.

2. *Menus.* The user chooses an item from a displayed list. Menus are ideal for software that is seldom used, but experienced users may find them too slow.

3. *Graphical environments.* The user performs operations by selecting icons (pictures) with a mouse. Environments of this type can be highly productive. For examples, see MACINTOSH; WINDOWS. A drawback is that there is no simple way to describe how something is done; you almost have to see someone else do it. By contrast, commands in a command language can be written down on paper and even embedded in computer programs.

FIGURE 287. U.S. LEGAL- AND U.S. LETTER-SIZED PAPER

U.S. legal the size of paper used for legal documents in the United States, $8\frac{1}{2} \times 14$ inches. *Contrast* U.S. LETTER, EXECUTIVE SIZE. *See also* PAPER SIZES.

U.S. letter the size of paper used for business letters in the United States, $8\frac{1}{2} \times 11$ inches. Elsewhere, ISO size A4 is the nearest equivalent. *Contrast* U.S. LEGAL, EXECUTIVE SIZE. *See also* PAPER SIZES.

/usr in UNIX, a directory that formerly contained users' files (hence the name) and now contains installed software and parts of the operating system. Users' files are now usually stored in subdirectories of /home.

utility a program that assists in the operation of a computer but does not do the main work for which the computer was bought. For instance, programs that compress data or defragment disks are utilities (*see* DATA COMPRESSION; FRAGMENTATION; NORTON UTILITIES). By contrast, word processors, financial programs, engineering programs, and other programs that do actual work for the user are called *application programs.*

UTP (**U**nshielded **T**wisted **P**air) a cable consisting of pairs of wires twisted together and insulated but not provided with a metallic shield. *See* TWISTED PAIR; CATEGORY 5 CABLE. *Contrast* COAXIAL CABLE.

UUCP (**UNIX**-to-**UNIX** **cop**y) a command to transfer files from one computer to another. It has largely been superseded by FTP. *See* FTP. The Usenet network is sometimes called the UUCP network. *See* USENET.

uudecode *see* UUENCODE.

uuencode a UNIX utility program that makes it possible to send binary files through electronic mail systems that only accept text files. A uuencoded file consists of printable characters arranged in lines of reasonable length. The *uudecode* program regenerates the original binary file from it. *See also* BINHEX; BINARY FILE; TEXT FILE.

V

V.21 an ITU-T (formerly CCITT) standard format for 300-baud data communication over phone lines in Europe and Japan. The Bell 103 format is used in the United States for the same purpose. *See* BELL 103A; CCITT.

V.22 an ITU-T (formerly CCITT) standard format for sending 1200-baud data over phone lines designed to carry voice signals. A different format, Bell 212A, is more commonly used in the United States. *See* BELL 212A; CCITT.

V.22 bis an ITU-T (formerly CCITT) worldwide standard format for sending 2400-baud data over telephone lines designed to carry voice signals. (*Bis* is Latin for "a second time" and indicates that this is an extension of standard V.22.) The standard specifies that if the phone line is of low quality, the modem will drop back to 1200 baud in V.22 format. Some 2400-baud modems either do not do this or drop back to Bell 212A format instead. *See* V.22; BELL 212A; CCITT.

V.24 an ITU-T (formerly CCITT) standard for data communication essentially identical to the American RS-232C standard. *See* RS-232; CCITT.

V.29 an ITU-T (formerly CCITT) standard that defines a format for sending 4800-baud and 9600-baud serial data over telephone lines. This format is half-duplex only. *See* CCITT.

V.32 an ITU-T (formerly CCITT) standard format for sending 4800- or 9600-baud data over telephone lines designed to carry voice signals. The modem automatically analyzes the sound quality of the line and adjusts its output as needed. In general, V.32 modems will drop back to 2400 baud (V.22 bis format) or 1200 baud (V.22 or Bell 212A format) when line conditions are poor. *See* CCITT.

V.32 bis an ITU-T (formerly CCITT) standard format for sending data by modem over telephone lines at rates up to 14,400 bits per second; the rate is negotiated by the two modems when the connection is made. (*Bis* is Latin for "a second time" and indicates that this is an extension of standard V.32.)

V.34 an ITU-T (formerly CCITT) standard format for sending data by modem over telephone lines. Rates up to 28,800 bits per second are supported; the rate is negotiated by the two modems when the connection is made and is adjusted during the call as the line quality changes.

V.42 bis an ITU-T (formerly CCITT) standard method for modems to negotiate data compression techniques to be used during communication; an extension of the earlier V.42 standard, which provided a way to negotiate error correction protocols. *See also* MNP.

V.90 an ITU-T (formerly CCITT) standard for sending data by modem over telephone lines at speeds up to 56,600 bits per second (56 kbps). V.90 supersedes two earlier protocols called K56FLEX and X2. The actual transmission speed is adjusted automatically depending on the line quality and can vary during a call.

vaccine a computer program that offers protection from viruses (*see* VIRUS) by making additional checks of the integrity of the operating system. Also known as ANTIVIRUS or VIRUS PROTECTION SOFTWARE. No vaccine can offer complete protection against all viruses.

vacuum tube an electronic component consisting of electrodes placed inside an evacuated glass tube. Vacuum tubes work by using electric and magnetic fields to control the movements of electrons that have been emitted by one of the electrodes.

A CRT (cathode ray tube) television or monitor screen is one example of a vacuum tube. The vacuum tubes originally used in computers performed the same type of functions that semiconductor diodes and transistors perform now. A vacuum tube diode consists of two electrodes: a cathode, which emits electrons, and an anode, or plate, which collects electrons. The diode conducts electricity only when a positive voltage is applied to the cathode. A vacuum tube triode contains an electrode called the grid, located between the cathode and the plate. The flow of electrons from the cathode to the plate is controlled by the electric field of the grid. (Similarly, the current flow from the emitter to the collector in a transistor is controlled by the voltage applied to the base.) Vacuum tube triodes can be used for amplification and logic functions.

The first electronic digital computer, the ENIAC, contained 18,000 vacuum tubes. The disadvantages of vacuum tube computers are that they are very big, they consume a great deal of power, and they generate a lot of heat. Also, it is necessary to constantly replace burned-out tubes. *See* COMPUTERS, HISTORY OF.

value-added reseller someone who buys computers, improves them in some way (e.g., by installing ready-to-use software of a specific type), and then sells them as complete working systems. *See also* TURNKEY SYSTEM.

vampire tap a cable-piercing connector used with thickwire Ethernet (10base-5) coaxial cables. *See* 10BASE-5; COAXIAL CABLE.

vanilla *(slang)* plain, without extra features; for example, one might speak of "vanilla" Windows 95 as opposed to Windows 95 with Active Desktop. This term comes from the widespread misconception that vanilla ice cream is unflavored, a mistake that can only be made if one judges ice cream by its color and not its taste. *See also* FLAVOR.

vaporware software that is announced by a vendor but never actually reaches the market.

var (in Pascal) the keyword that marks variable declarations. In the parameter list of a procedure or function, var means that an item should be passed by address, not by making a copy of it.

VAR *see* VALUE-ADDED RESELLER.

variable a symbol in a programming language that represents a data item, such as a numerical value or a character string, that can change its value during the execution of a program. Programming languages typically require that variable names start with letters. *See also* DATA TYPES; DATA STRUCTURES; ANONYMOUS VARIABLE; SINGLETON VARIABLE.

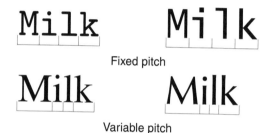

Fixed pitch

Variable pitch

FIGURE 288. VARIABLE VS. FIXED-PITCH TYPE

variable pitch varying width of characters in a typeface; the I for instance will be much narrower than the W. Also called PROPORTIONAL PITCH. *Contrast* FIXED-PITCH TYPE. *See* Fig. 288.

variant (also called *union*) a data type that can take on values corresponding to more than one other type. For example, in Visual Basic, a variable that is declared as Variant can take on values that are integers, floating-point numbers, strings, and a few other types. Internally, a variant is stored as a value plus some additional bits that identify the type of value.

VAX popular line of minicomputers produced by Digital Equipment Corporation since the late 1970s. *See* DIGITAL EQUIPMENT CORPORATION; VAX/VMS.

VAX/VMS the most widely used operating system on Digital Equipment Corporation VAX computers. The command language is similar to DOS. Some important commands are:

`dir`	Display a list of files.
`type xxx`	Display contents of file `xxx` (a text file).
`help`	Invoke the help system.
`@xxxxx`	Execute the commands on file `xxxxx.com`.
`run xxxxx`	Execute the machine language program on file `xxxxx.exe`.

An unusual feature of VAX/VMS is the way it keeps previous versions of files. If you create a file called XXXX.YYY, it will be known as XXXX.YYY;1. If you then edit it, you will create XXX.YYY;2, and XXXX.YYY;1 will still exist. Whenever you do not specify a version number, you will get the latest version of the file. To delete all versions. you must use an asterisk in place of the version number, thus:

```
del xxxx.yyy;*:'
```

The command

```
purge xxxx.yyy
```

will delete all but the latest version of XXXX.YYY.

VBScript a Microsoft product for adding executable commands to a web page using a language based on Visual BASIC. For another example of a web page scripting language, *see* JAVASCRIPT.

VDT **v**ideo **d**isplay **t**erminal, i.e., a computer monitor. *See* MONITOR.

FIGURE 289. VECTOR GRAPHICS DISPLAYED
AS WIREFRAME

vector graphics a method of creating pictures on a computer by telling it to draw lines in particular positions. The lines may be displayed on a screen or plotted on paper. An advantage of vector graphics is that a picture can be enlarged or reduced without loss of sharpness, since the picture is not made of a fixed number of pixels. *Contrast* BIT-MAPPED GRAPHICS. *See also* DRAW PROGRAM; PAINT PROGRAM.

vector processor a computer that can perform an operation on an entire array of numbers in a single step; also known as an *array processor.* Cray supercomputers are vector processors. They have machine instructions that can (for example) add each entry of array A to the corresponding entry of array B and store the result in the corresponding entry of array C. *Contrast* SCALAR PROCESSOR; SUPERSCALAR PROCESSOR.

verifier a program that checks to make sure that a file is truly a Java class file. This is a security feature included to prevent the loading and execution of a class file that may have been tampered with after being created by the Java compiler.

Veronica a database formerly used to search for information via GOPHER; now superseded by World Wide Web search engines.

vertical paper oriented so that it is taller than wide; also called PORTRAIT or TALL orientation.

VESA local bus (VLB) a local bus developed by the Video Electronics Standards Association (VESA) to allow video cards to communicate with the CPU faster than is possible using the regular ISA or EISA bus. VLB uses an additional edge connector in line with the ISA or EISA connector. VLB-equipped computers usually have two or three VLB slots (which can also accept ISA or EISA cards) and several ISA or EISA slots that lack the VLB extension.

V.FAST an interim modem standard that preceded V.34.

V.FC a proprietary modem standard developed by Rockwell before the V.34 standard was released; similar to V.34 but not equivalent to it.

VGA the video system introduced by IBM on the PS/2 computers in 1987 and also available on cards for use in conventional PCs. *VGA* originally stood for **V**ideo **G**ate **A**rray (an ASIC on the PS/2 motherboard) but nowadays is usually interpreted as **V**ideo **G**raphics **A**dapter.

The VGA provides a maximum resolution of 640×480 with 16 colors. It also supports all the video modes of the earlier IBM video adapters (MDA, CGA, and EGA). *See also* SUPER VGA; XGA.

video
1. the signals sent from a computer to its monitor screen.
2. moving pictures displayed on a computer. *See* QUICKTIME; MPEG; DVI.

video adapter *see* VIDEO CARD.

video capture the process of digitizing moving television images and storing them in a computer. Unlike a FRAME GRABBER, a video capture card records moving video, not just still pictures.

video card a plug-in circuit board that enables a computer to display information on a particular type of monitor (screen).

video memory the memory in which a computer keeps track of the present contents of the screen. On the original IBM PC, video memory occupies various locations above 640K, which is why only 640K of memory is available for programs even though the processor can address a full megabyte (1024K).

A fast way to change what is on the screen is to store new values directly into video memory. *See also* SNOW.

viewer a program for viewing graphics files in a particular format. Most WEB BROWSERS can interface to separate viewers that support additional kinds of graphics. By extension, a program for playing sounds is sometimes called a viewer. *See* ACROBAT.

FIGURE 290. A VIGNETTED PORTRAIT

vignette a rounded image with edges that shade gradually into the background. Many photopaint programs have a filter that produces a vignetted effect upon any image.

virtual 8086 mode mode in which a 386, 486, or Pentium microprocessor emulates one or more 8086 (IBM PC-type) microprocessors. This enables it to run the same kinds of programs as in real mode, but with multitasking. *See* REAL MODE; PROTECTED MODE; MICROPROCESSOR; IBM PC; OS/2; WINDOWS.

virtual disk *see* RAM DISK.

virtual machine a computer that does not physically exist, but is simulated by another computer. In IBM's VM/SP operating system, the computer simulates multiple copies of itself. *See also* VIRTUAL 8086 MODE.

A Java applet is run by a Java virtual machine, which is part of a web browser that executes Java bytecode. *See* JVM.

virtual memory a way of extending the effective size of a computer's memory by using a disk file to simulate additional memory space. Typically, the operating system keeps track of which memory addresses actually reside in memory and which ones must be brought in from disk when they are referred to. Virtual storage is divided into units called *pages,* and the operation of bringing in a page from disk is called a *page fault.*

virtual reality the simulation of a person's entire environment (sights, sounds, movements, etc.) by computer. Most commonly this is done by displaying a realistic picture (*see* THREE-DIMENSIONAL GRAPHICS) and allowing the user to manipulate objects by clicking on them with the mouse. *See* VRML.

Truly realistic virtual reality is more a goal than an existing technology, but some computer games achieve a limited kind of realism by having the user wear a special helmet and gloves and/or stand on a special platform.

virtual storage *see* VIRTUAL MEMORY.

virus a computer program that automatically copies itself, thereby "infecting" other disks or programs without the user knowing it, and then plays some kind of trick or disrupts the operation of the computer.

Viruses have existed as academic pranks since the 1960s, but 1987 saw the first malicious viruses, apparently the work of disgruntled programmers trying to sabotage their competition.

The best protection against viruses is to obtain all your software from reliable sources, make regular backup copies of your work, write-protect disks that you boot from and other disks that do not need to be written on, and run virus-detecting software periodically.

Knowingly spreading a computer virus is a crime under common law and under specific laws in various states. *See also* VACCINE; TROJAN HORSE; MACRO VIRUS.

virus protection software a computer program that offers protection from VIRUSES by making additional checks of the integrity of the operating system. No vaccine can offer complete protection against all viruses. Also known as ANTIVIRUS SOFTWARE.

Visicalc the first computer spreadsheet program, developed for the Apple II in the late 1970s by Dan Bricklin and Bob Frankston. *See* SPREAD-SHEET.

Visio a widely used software package for creating business and technical diagrams. Unlike earlier graphics software, Visio recognizes the ways in which symbols interact with their environment. Each symbol, or "SmartShape," can be programmed to behave in specific ways as it is moved or resized. For example, in an electronic circuit diagram, when you stretch the symbol for a resistor, the stretching affects only the connecting lines on the ends; the symbol itself remains the proper shape. Thus, drafting can be done quickly, and Visio helps keep a complex diagram properly connected together as parts of it are rearranged.

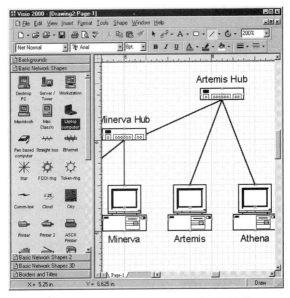

FIGURE 291. VISIO GRAPHICS SOFTWARE

In 2000, Visio Corporation was purchased by Microsoft. Their web
address is www.microsoft.com/office/visio.

vision, computer the use of computers to recognize objects in images
(not just store, retrieve, and manipulate the images themselves). Computer vision is surprisingly difficult to implement. Some of the main
challenges are: *edge detection* (finding the boundaries of objects); *per-
spective* (interpreting a two-dimensional image as three-dimensional);
color constancy (adapting to variations in the color of light, including light reflected from other nearby objects); and *shape constancy*
(recognizing the same shape from different angles).

  Computer vision has found some industrial applications where the
number of objects to be recognized is small and the positioning and light
are constant, such as identifying objects that pass by on an assembly
line and sounding an alarm when one of them is missing or looks
abnormal.

  See also IMAGE PROCESSING.

vision, human the ability to see. Computer displays rely on many
special properties of human vision, among them the following:

1. The eye blends together images that are less than $\frac{1}{30}$ second apart. Most computers redisplay the screen image every $\frac{1}{30}$ second or so, and the human viewer does not see any flicker.

2. Movements that are made in steps lasting $\frac{1}{30}$ second or less appear to be continuous. A moving image is actually a series of still images presented in very rapid succession.

3. Colors can be simulated by mixing other colors. For example, yellow on a computer screen does not contain any yellow light; instead, it is a mixture of red and green light. *See* RGB MONITOR; PLANE; COLOR.

Working with a computer screen can be tiring to the eyes, especially if the display is blurry or glare is a problem, but no permanent harm results. Eyeglasses designed for the proper working distance can make computer work much easier. *See* EYEGLASSES FOR COMPUTER USERS.

vision, machine *see* VISION, COMPUTER.

visit the occurrence of one web browser requesting documents (WEB PAGES) from a site during a short period of time. A single visit to a web site may generate several HITS.

Visual Basic a programming environment marketed by Microsoft for Microsoft Windows. The programmer designs various windows (forms) graphically, then writes procedures to respond to all the menu choices and other actions that are possible on each form. These procedures are written in a very modern dialect of BASIC that looks much like Pascal.

Visual Basic makes it possible to develop practical programs very quickly. The programmer chooses program elements represented by icons, much as in a DRAW PROGRAM, then arranges them on the screen and writes the BASIC code to accompany each element.

Visual Basic implements event-driven programming. There is no "main program" that calls procedures; instead, procedures are called automatically when the appropriate events occur, such as menu choices and mouse movements. In effect, the human user calls the procedures. *See* EVENT-DRIVEN PROGRAMMING.

Visual Basic is only partly object-oriented. Windows, menus, and other input-output mechanisms are objects and have procedures and instance variables associated with them, but the user is not free to define new object classes. *See* OBJECT-ORIENTED PROGRAMMING.

Borland's Delphi is a Pascal-based programming tool inspired by Visual Basic, but it produces considerably faster code.

Visual Studio development environment provided by Microsoft for Visual Basic, Visual C++, and Visual J++ (Java).

VLB *see* VESA LOCAL BUS.

VLSI (**V**ery **L**arge-**S**cale **I**ntegration) the manufacture of integrated circuits (silicon chips) containing 10,000 or more logic gates.

VM *see* VIRTUAL MACHINE; JVM.

VM/CMS *see* CMS; VM/ESA.

VM/ESA (Virtual Machine/Enterprise Systems Architecture) an operating system for large IBM mainframe computers, such as the 370,
3081, and 390, based on the idea of one computer simulating multiple
copies of itself. VM/ESA was formerly known as VM/SP.

There is a straightforward way to make one computer simulate
another; simply program the first (real) computer to recognize the second (virtual) computer's instructions and respond appropriately. If the
real computer is capable of interleaving several tasks, it can even simulate several virtual computers at once. Under VM/ESA, one IBM 370
(or the equivalent) simulates many separate IBM 370s at once. The
user of each virtual 370 can then program it as if he had an entire 370
to himself; the effect is very much like using a large, fast personal
computer that runs IBM 370 software. VM/ESA creates and deletes
virtual machines as users log on and off, keeps the virtual machines
from interfering with each other, and allows them to communicate in
controlled ways.

Most VM/ESA virtual machines run CMS and serve only one user
at a time. (*See* CMS.) However, within a VM/ESA system it is possible to
create a virtual machine that runs MVS (with TSO) and serves dozens
of users at once, just as a real 370 does. This is particularly convenient
for installations that are converting from MVS to VM/ESA and want
to support both at once. (*See* MVS; TSO.)

voice mail messages that are received by telephone, recorded, and
played automatically when the recipient requests them (also by telephone). Voice mail systems are computer-controlled; messages are
saved in digital form.

voice recognition the recognition of spoken words by a computer.
See NATURAL LANGUAGE PROCESSING.

volatile not permanent; erased when turned off. The memory (RAM) of
a computer is volatile; that is, it goes blank when power is removed.
Disks are nonvolatile.

volt the unit of measure of electric potential. If a potential of 1 volt is
applied to a resistance of 1 ohm, then a current of 1 ampere will flow
through the resistance. (*See* OHM'S LAW.)

volume
　　1. an individual diskette, disk, or tape.
　　2. the perceived loudness of a sound. The volume control on a
sound card may be a knob on the card itself, or a setting made in
software, or both.

volume serial number an identifying number assigned to a diskette,
disk, or tape by OS/2, Windows 95 and later, or other operating systems.

Volume serial numbers ensure that the computer will know when the disk or tape in a drive is changed.

Von Neumann architecture a type of computer design in which programs and data are stored in a single kind of memory. *Contrast* HARVARD ARCHITECTURE. *See* COMPUTER ARCHITECTURE.

Von Neumann, John (1903–1957) mathematician who worked on one of the earliest computers and developed the concept of storing programs in memory.

VRAM **v**ideo **r**andom **a**ccess **m**emory; RAM that is specially designed for use in video cards. Commonly, it can be read and written simultaneously so that the generation of the display is not interrupted when the CPU needs to place data in it.

FIGURE 292. VIEWS OF THE VRML EXAMPLE

VRML (**V**irtual **R**eality **M**arkup **L**anguage or **V**irtual **R**eality **M**odeling **L**anguage) a programming language developed by Mark Pesce and Tony Parisi to describe three-dimensional objects for graphical display. A VRML program describes a "world" of virtual objects that a person can walk or fly through. The computer draws the objects as they are seen from a specified position, which can be constantly changing. Objects can respond to mouse clicks.

VRML is still under development. Fig. 293 shows a sample program written in VRML 1.0 (1996). It depicts a sphere and three blocks in front of a large black panel. In the language, a "separator" is an object composed of one or more primitive shapes. Fig. 292 shows this scene as viewed from two different angles with a VRML BROWSER (viewing program). More sophisticated VRML programs can provide very realistic views of scenery and buildings.

```
#VRML V1.0 ascii

Separator {
    Separator {
        # Black panel
        Transform { translation 0 0.1 -0.5 }
        Material { diffuseColor 0 0 0 }
        Cube { width 1.2 height 0.65 depth 0.5 }
            }
    Separator {
        # Ball
        Transform { translation 0 0.2 0 }
        Material { diffuseColor 1 0.7 0.3
                    specularColor 0.3 0 0 }
        Sphere { radius 0.1 }
            }
    Separator {
        # Middle block
        Material { diffuseColor 0.6 0.6 1.0 }
        Cube { width 0.2 height 0.2 depth 0.2 }
            }
    Separator {
        # Block
        Transform { translation 0.3 0 0 }
        Cube { width 0.15 height 0.2 depth 0.2 }
            }
    Separator {
        # Block
        Transform { translation -0.3 0 0 }
        Cube { width 0.15 height 0.2 depth 0.2 }
            }
        }
```

FIGURE 293. SAMPLE VRML PROGRAM

VSN *see* VOLUME SERIAL NUMBER.

VT-100 a computer terminal made by Digital Equipment Corporation that had a major impact on the computer industry in the early 1980s. It provided convenient control codes for positioning the cursor, clearing the screen, and selecting normal, bold, or underlined type (*see* ANSI SCREEN CONTROL). This makes it possible to implement full-screen, personal-computer-like software on an asynchronous terminal. Most personal computers can emulate the VT-100.

VT-101, VT-102, VT-220, VT-320 computer terminals made by Digital Equipment Corporation, upward compatible with the VT-100.

W

W3C *see* WORLD WIDE WEB CONSORTIUM.

WAIS (Wide Area Information Service) a SEARCH ENGINE for the WORLD WIDE WEB developed by Thinking Machines, Inc., and available at some INTERNET sites.

wait state a brief delay introduced when a microprocessor reads data from memory, to allow extra time for the memory chips to respond. Wait states are used when a fast microprocessor is used with relatively slow memory chips. A processor with one wait state on each memory access is typically 10% to 20% slower than the same processor with no (zero) wait states.

wallpaper a picture or pattern displayed as a background in a windowed operating system.

WAN *see* WIDE-AREA NETWORK.

warm boot, warm start the operation of restarting a computer that is already running. *See* BOOT.

FIGURE 294. WARP EFFECT

warp to digitally manipulate an image so that it appears twisted or stretched (Fig. 294).

Warp version 3.0 of OS/2. The term comes from "warp speed," a concept used in science fiction to defy the laws of physics by traveling faster than the speed of light. Version 3.0 runs faster than version 2.1 but is otherwise very similar. The current version of OS/2 is version 4.0.

watch icon appearance of the mouse pointer when the user needs to wait until the computer has completed an operation. It looks like a wristwatch. Macintosh software generally uses the watch icon instead of the Windows hourglass.

watt unit for measuring the rate at which electrical power is being consumed. One watt is equivalent to one joule per second. Wattage depends on both voltage and current, as follows:

$$\text{Watts} = \text{volts} \times \text{amperes}$$

For example, a 5-volt, 10-ampere power supply delivers 50 watts. The amount of AC power going into the power supply is considerably greater, depending on the inefficiency of the supply.

watt-hour the amount of energy consumed by using energy at the rate of one watt for one hour. One watt-hour equals 3,600 joules. In the United States, electricity costs about 10 cents for 1,000 watt-hours (one kilowatt-hour).

WAV the filename extension for digitized sound wave files under Microsoft Windows.

wave file a file containing a digital representation of sound waves. *See* SAMPLING RATE; SOUND CARD; WAV.

wavetable synthesis a technique for synthesizing musical instrument sounds by computer using stored information about the waveforms produced by real instruments. *Contrast* FM SYNTHESIS.

WBASAYC e-mail abbreviation for "write back as soon as you can."

Web the WORLD WIDE WEB.

WEB a programming tool developed by D. E. Knuth to make it easier to create modular programs. WEB is a more abstract form of the Pascal (or, in later versions, C) programming language. The programmer is free to define procedures in any order and write blocks of code to be inserted into larger blocks written later. Heavy use of comments is encouraged and listings are printed elegantly with reserved words in boldface.

web address a string of characters that identifies a file viewable on the WORLD WIDE WEB, such as:

```
http://www.CovingtonInnovations.com/christian.html
```

It specifies a transfer protocol (usually http), the domain address of the site (such as www.CovingtonInnovations.com), and, optionally, a directory path and filename. On some systems, as in Fig. 295, the directory is identified by the character ~ and the account name of a user. *See* URL.

web browser *see* BROWSER.

webcam a digital or video camera whose images are made continuously available to curiosity seekers over the World Wide Web. By using webcams, Web users can view traffic in cities and anything else a webcam owner thinks is interesting.

webcast (**web** broad**cast**) an event intended to be viewed simultaneously by numerous people connecting to the same web site. Webcasts often feature celebrity interviews, open-forum discussions, or product announcements. If too many people "tune in" at the same time, however, the server or network can be overloaded. *Compare* INTERNET RADIO.

webmaster the person who has principal responsibility for maintaining a site on the WORLD WIDE WEB and updating some or all of the WEB PAGES.

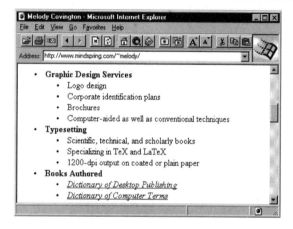

FIGURE 295. A WEB PAGE
(UNDERLINED WORDS ARE LINKS TO OTHER WEB PAGES)

web page a file of information made available for viewing on the WORLD WIDE WEB and seen by the user as a page of information on the screen.

web page design the production of WEB PAGES for others to view. Many web pages are badly designed. Here are some guidelines for designing a good one:

1. Decide on the purpose of your web page. What information do you want to communicate? What's important and what's not?

2. Plan for maintainability. How soon will something have to be changed? Can frequently-changed information be placed in separate files that are easier to update?

3. If you want people to visit your web site repeatedly, put something useful there, such as reference information, links to other sites, or free software.

4. Do not draw attention to the wrong things. The most important part of your message should be the most visually prominent. Unimportant graphics that blink or move can be very annoying.

5. Remember that you do not have a captive audience. People are not going to sit through time-consuming graphics or animations if what they really want could have been delivered more quickly.

6. Remember that some people still use older browsers and even text-only browsers such as Lynx (*see* LYNX). You probably don't want to limit your audience to people who have this month's version of Netscape.

7. Use dark type on a white background for anything the reader may need to print out. Many browsers cannot print out light type on a dark background.

8. Attach links to informative words, not the word "here." Instead of "Click here to learn about our new software," just say "New software."

See HTML.

web page title the descriptive text that appears in the browser's status bar. The web page title is used for the default BOOKMARK label.

web server a computer that is attached to the Internet and contains web pages (HTML files) that can be viewed using a web browser. Every web page resides on a web server somewhere. The web server has to be connected to the Internet continuously, and it runs an HTTP server program such as HTTPD (under UNIX), Microsoft's Internet Information Server or Netscape's Enterprise Server. The web server may also need to run special software (such as a CGI script) in response to a client's request. *See* WORLD WIDE WEB; WEB PAGE.

web site a file or related group of files available on the WORLD WIDE WEB.

Light
Normal
Bold
Extra Bold

FIGURE 296. TYPEFACE WEIGHT

weight the boldness (heaviness) of a style of type. For example, **this is heavy-weight type** and this is ordinary-weight type. Some fonts provide several different weights (light, medium, demibold, bold, and extra bold). See Fig. 296.

weld (drawing program) to join two or more objects so that the resulting single object has the outline of the group of objects. *Contrast* COMBINE; GROUP.

What's This? a Windows 95 and later help feature that helps the user identify unfamiliar icons. To use What's This? simply rest the mouse cursor on the icon; after a few seconds a small label will pop up. *See also* ROLLOVER.

wheel (from "big wheel") a user who has some system administration privileges; on a UNIX system, a user who is a member of the group named `wheels`, reserved for system administrators.

Whetstone a standard benchmark program for testing computer speed. *See* MIPS.

while keyword that defines one kind of loop in Pascal and related programming languages. The loop is executed over and over as long as the condition is true. Here is an example:

```
writeln('How many times?  (0 or more):  ');
readln(n);
i := 1;
WHILE i <= n DO
  BEGIN
    writeln(i);
    i := i + 1
  END;
```

The condition is tested before each pass through the loop; if it is false at the beginning, the loop will never be executed. *Contrast* REPEAT. Here is an example in Java:

```
i=1;
while (i<=10)
  { System.out.println(i);
    i++;
  }
```

whiteboard a simulated panel on which several people can write at the same time, with the results visible to all. Whiteboards are used in CONFERENCING on the Internet.

white noise sound consisting of random oscillations with equal amounts of energy at all frequencies. The effect is a hissing sound, often used in computer sound effects. This is analogous to white light, which is a mixture of all visible wavelengths.

white space characters that, when printed, do not put ink on the paper: spaces, tabs, new-line marks, and form feeds.

wide LANDSCAPE or horizontal orientation. *Contrast* PORTRAIT or TALL.

wide-area network a set of widely separated computers connected together. For example, the worldwide airline reservation system is a wide-area network. The Internet is a set of interconnected wide-area networks. *Contrast* LOCAL-AREA NETWORK.

widow the first line of a paragraph when it appears by itself as the last line of a page. Some word processors automatically adjust page breaks so that there are no widows. *See also* ORPHAN.

wild card a symbol that matches any other symbol. For instance, the DOS command

```
dir ab*.exe
```

means "show me the files whose names begin with ab and end with exe. The symbol * is a wild card and stands for the middle part of the filename, whatever it may be.

wimp *(slang)* cowardly or lazy person.

WIMP interface *(slang)* a user interface using **w**indows, **i**cons, a **m**ouse, and **p**ull-down menus. *See* GRAPHICAL USER INTERFACE.

Win32 the 32-bit core of Windows 95, Windows 98, Windows NT, and Windows 2000. Programs written for Win32 will run under all of these operating systems.

Win32s a subset of Win32 that can be installed as an extension to Windows 3.1, making it possible to run many Windows 95 programs.

Winchester disk any hard disk designed for use in microcomputers. "Winchester" is an early industry code name, not a brand name. *See* HARD DISK.

window an area of the screen set aside for a special purpose. On the Macintosh, in Microsoft Windows, and in other similar operating systems, the screen is divided into windows for different pieces of software. The user can control the size, shape, and positioning of the windows. The *active window* is the one in which you are currently typing.

   Figure 297 shows the main parts of a window in Microsoft Windows 95 and 98. To move the window, place the mouse pointer on the title bar, hold down the left button, and move the mouse. To change the size of the window, do the same thing but with the pointer on the left, right, or bottom border of the window. To close the window, click once on the *close box* (the box with the × symbol) or double-click on the control menu button. (On the Macintosh, there is also a *close box*.) *See also* ICON; SCROLL BAR; MENU BAR; PULL-DOWN MENU; TITLE BAR; MINIMIZE; MAXIMIZE; DIALOG BOX; MESSAGE BOX.

Control
Menu
Button

Window
Control
Buttons

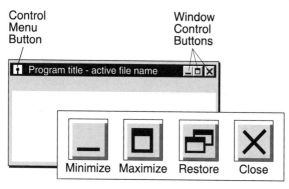

Program title - active file name

Minimize   Maximize   Restore   Close

FIGURE 297. A WINDOW (MICROSOFT WINDOWS)

Windows the name of several graphical operating systems produced by Microsoft Corporation of Redmond, Washington. *See* WINDOWS 3; WINDOWS 95; WINDOWS 98; WINDOWS FOR WORKGROUPS; WINDOWS NT; WINDOWS 2000.

Windows 3 a graphical operating system based on DOS that was widely used on PC-compatible computers in the early 1990s. Versions 1 and 2, released in the 1980s, were less widely used. In 1995, Windows 3 was superseded by WINDOWS 95.

To run Windows 3, the computer must already be running DOS. Windows provides a graphical user interface, extended memory, and multitasking. The screen is divided into windows, and the user uses a mouse to start programs and make menu choices. (*See* WINDOW.) Windows can run not only Windows software (which use the graphical user interface) but also ordinary DOS software. In fact, Windows includes several application programs, including a word processor, a text file editor, a paint program, and a terminal emulator.

Under Windows, screen and printer output is handled by device drivers. Thus, all Windows applications run correctly on whatever screen and printer Windows is configured for. To use a new printer or video card, it is only necessary to reconfigure Windows, not the application software.

Like OS/2, Windows 95, Windows 98, and Windows NT, Windows 3 can use a disk file as swap space to substitute for extra memory. However, Windows 3 relies on cooperation between the programs that run concurrently; each has to yield time to the others, and an improperly written program can stop the machine. OS/2, Windows 95, and Windows NT lack this restriction.

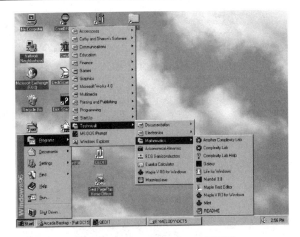

FIGURE 298. WINDOWS 95 MENUS

To run in enhanced mode with multitasking, Windows requires a 386, 486, or Pentium CPU with at least 4 megabytes of memory. In this mode Windows can run several DOS and/or Windows application programs concurrently, each in its own window. The CPU runs in protected mode and virtual 8086 mode. The CPU normally uses 16-bit instructions, but a Windows extension known as Win32s provides 32-bit support for partial compatibility with Windows 95, Windows 98, and Windows NT. *See also* MULTITASKING; OS/2; PROTECTED MODE; VIRTUAL 8086 MODE; DEVICE DRIVER; PIF.

Windows 95 a multitasking graphical operating system released by Microsoft Corporation in 1995. Windows 95 requires a 386, 486, or Pentium CPU with at least 8 megabytes of RAM. Internally, Windows 95 identifies itself as Windows 4.0.

Windows 95 uses the CPU in 32-bit mode, like OS/2 and unlike DOS or Windows 3. As a result, software written for Windows 95 runs faster than comparable 16-bit software. Windows 95 also supports full preemptive multitasking, which allows multiple programs to run at the same time without having to yield time to each other.

Under Windows 95, application software is arranged in a tree-like structure of menus within menus, starting with a START BUTTON that always stays on the screen (Fig. 298). This makes it easy to manage dozens or hundreds of applications on a single machine.

Windows 95 also provides a command prompt like that of DOS, but more powerful. By typing commands or using BAT FILES, the user

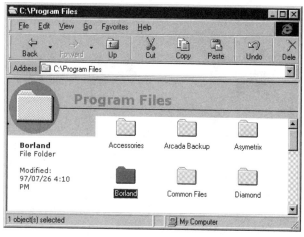

FIGURE 299. WINDOWS 98 USER INTERFACE

can execute not only DOS programs, but also Windows 95 software. Numerous minor enhancements to DOS commands have been implemented.

Windows 95 is compatible with almost all software written for DOS Windows 3, and Windows NT. It will even load and run DOS and Windows 3 device drivers, although its own device drivers should be used if possible, since they are faster. Because of this high level of backward compatibility, Windows 95 is not quite as crash-proof as OS/2 or Windows NT, but it is more reliable than Windows 3.1.

Windows 95 supports LONG FILENAMES, which can contain blanks and other special characters. A filename such as "My Resume" appears as something like MY~RES~1 when accessed from a program written for DOS or an earlier version of Windows.

See also DEVICE DRIVER; WINDOWS 98; WINDOWS 3 and cross-references there.

Windows 98 a revised version of Windows 95 released by Microsoft in 1998, known as Memphis before its release. Internally, Windows 98 identifies itself as Windows 4.1. Windows 95 and 98 are very similar, and they run the same software. Windows 98 adds a modified user interface more closely integrated with web browsing, a new file system (FAT32) that supports hard disks larger than 2 gigabytes, and numerous minor improvements.

Windows 98 SE abbreviation for *Windows 98 Second Edition,* a minor revision of Windows 98 released along with Internet Explorer 5 in 1999.

Windows 9x abbreviation for "Windows 95 and 98."

Windows 2000 an updated version of Windows NT released in February 2000 and intended to supplant both Windows NT 4.0 and Windows 98. Basically, Windows 2000 is Windows NT plus many of the best features of Windows 98, including Windows 98's user interface and easy installation of a wide range of PC software, including PLUG AND PLAY support. *See* WINDOWS 95 and WINDOWS 98 (screen images).

Almost all Windows 3.1, 95, and 98 software will run under Windows 2000. The main source of incompatibility is that the registry works differently and some settings may be lost. However, Windows 2000 is not fully compatible with DOS. Most DOS programs will still run, but software is not allowed as much direct access to the hardware as in Windows 98 nor can 16-bit DOS device drivers be used. Direct hardware access and 16-bit device drivers were a major source of unreliability in Windows 95 and 98.

A special emphasis of Windows 2000 is preventing situations in which the computer would hang or crash. Besides restricting the ability of pieces of software to disrupt the hardware and each other, Windows 2000 incorporates automatic checking of system files and device drivers to recover from damaged disk data.

As in earlier versions of Windows NT, Windows 2000 users are required to log in (which is necessary in any case if the computer is on a network). Files are protected from alteration by unauthorized persons. Like Windows NT 4.0, Windows 2000 supports multiple-CPU computers and is available for the Compaq Alpha microprocessor as well as the Intel Pentium family.

Windows 2000 adds some new UNIX-like features, including mount points (the ability to make a disk drive function as a subdirectory of another disk drive) and full POSIX compliance.

Windows 2K unofficial abbreviation for WINDOWS 2000.

Windows accelerator a graphics card that can move or overlay windows on its own without having the CPU completely redraw each window. *See* SUPER VGA.

Windows CE a Microsoft operating system similar to Windows NT, but much smaller, designed for embedded systems and small handheld computers. The CE in its name may stand for "consumer electronics."

Windows for Workgroups a version of Windows 3.1 that includes network support and some improvements in efficiency compared to earlier versions of Windows. It was the last release of Windows 3 and was superseded by Windows 95.

Windows ME (Millennium Edition) a successor for Windows 98 slated for release in late 2000. The name may be changed slightly before release.

For users upgrading from Windows 98, Windows ME is a less radical change than Windows 2000. The core of the operating system is the same as Windows 98, but features have been added to enhance reliability and ease of use. Windows ME is the last operating system in the series derived from Windows 95.

Windows NT a high-performance multitasking graphical operating system produced by Microsoft Corporation.

Windows NT is the most technically advanced of the Windows operating systems and is the only one that is not built on DOS as a foundation. Internally, Windows NT is more like UNIX, and like UNIX, it includes a security system to prevent programs from manipulating the hardware or operating system without authorization The security system makes Windows NT especially suitable for file servers and computers that are accessed remotely.

Unlike the other Windows operating systems, Windows NT does not require a PC-compatible computer; versions exist for the DEC Alpha and some other CPUs, and they run PC software by emulation.

Windows NT version numbers track those of Windows. Thus, the first version was Windows NT 3.1, corresponding to Windows 3.1. This was quickly followed by version 3.5. Windows NT 4.0 corresponded to Windows 95 and used the same user interface. Starting with version 5.0, Windows NT was renamed Windows 2000. *See* WINDOWS 2000.

Winmodem a modem that relies on a CPU running Microsoft Windows to do part of the signal processing traditionally done by the modem itself. *See* MODEM.

Winsock any of several standardized implementations of SOCKETS for Microsoft Windows. WEB BROWSERS and similar programs use Winsock to provide communication services.

An implementation of Winsock is built into Windows 95. Under Windows 3, the program Trumpet Winsock, by Timothy Tattam, is widely used.

Wintel *(slang)* Windows–Intel, i.e., PC-compatible.

wireframe a drawing displayed in outline form. Displaying a wireframe is much faster than displaying the full image, and details are visible in it that may be obscured in the finished product. Many 3-D and draw programs give you a choice of editing a wireframe image or an image displayed in finished form.

See illustration at VECTOR GRAPHICS. *See also* THREE-DIMENSIONAL GRAPHICS.

wireless communication the transfer of electromagnetic signals from place to place without cables, usually using infrared light or radio waves.

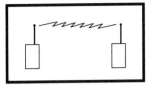 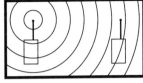

What you want   **What you get**

FIGURE 300. WIRELESS COMMUNICATION

Communication by infrared light is practical only over short distances in unobstructed places with a clear line of sight. For example, infrared light is used by TV remote controls and occasionally to link a keyboard or mouse to a computer. It does not pass through walls.

Radio waves travel freely in all directions and penetrate obstacles. As Fig. 300 shows, every transmitter fills a large area with its signal. Since only a finite range of frequencies is available, transmitters often interfere with each other. Unlicensed transmitters are limited to very low power and short range (*see* PART 15 DEVICE); more powerful transmitters require regulation and licensing. Spread-spectrum technology provides an especially efficient way to share frequencies (*see* SPREAD SPECTRUM).

Radio signals are inherently non-private. There is no physical way to keep them from being received, voluntarily or involuntarily, by receivers other than the intended one. Private information should not be transmitted by radio unless it is encrypted to keep it secret. *See* ENCRYPTION.

wireless LAN a local-area network (LAN) in which computers communicate by radio signals. *See* LAN; PART 15 DEVICE.

wizard

1. a utility that automates certain common tasks in application software. Wizards are useful for setting up frequently used documents or performing tedious tasks. For example, after collecting information from the user about the company name and address, a word processor wizard can construct a letterhead for that company.

Wizards differ from template documents in that they collect specific information from the user and create a unique document that can be used as a template. *See also* SCRIPT.

2. any of various utilities for creating or distributing windowed software. The term *wizard* does not mean anything specific here.

3. an expert computer user; one who is gifted in solving problems or has aquired a vast store of useful knowledge about computers and software.

w/o e-mail abbreviation for "**without**."

WOO a MOO (interactive environment or game) on the World Wide Web. *See* MUD; MOO.

word a group of bits equal in size to one CPU register. The number of bits in a word depends on the type of computer being used. A word on the original IBM PC is 16 bits long; on 386-based machines, 32 bits.

Word Microsoft's word processing program, which is available for both Windows and Macintosh platforms. *See* MICROSOFT.

WordPerfect a popular word processing program available for both IBM PC-compatible and Macintosh computers. It is noted for its ability to handle a wide variety of document formats, including footnotes, legal citations, and foreign language characters.

WordPerfect versions 5.1 and higher have a huge repertoire of special characters, which are printed by switching the printer into graphics mode when necessary. These include full character sets for mathematics, Greek, Russian, Hebrew, and Japanese kana. Special characters are typed by hitting Ctrl-W and clicking on the desired character in the dialog box. WordPerfect was developed by WordPerfect Corporation, Orem, Utah, which is now owned by Corel Corporation.

word processing the process of using a computer to prepare written documents (letters, reports, books, and the like). The boundary between word processing and *desktop publishing* is not sharp, but in general, word processing is the preparation of clearly worded, readable text, and does not include elaborate design or typography.

Word processing makes it easy to change or correct a document and then print it out without introducing new errors. More importantly, word processing lets you turn a rough draft into a finished report with no retyping and no wasted effort. You can start with a rough, fragmentary outline of what you want to say, then fill in the pieces in any convenient order. You don't have to finish page 1 before writing page 2. Many writers find this very convenient; you can get a document almost finished while waiting for information that you will fill in at the last minute, and if you have to produce many similar documents (letters, for instance), each one can be a slightly altered copy of the previous one.

Many word processors include spelling and grammar checkers. Take their advice with a grain of salt; they don't understand English and they don't know what you are trying to say. A spelling checker simply looks up each word in a dictionary and complains if it can't find it; it does not catch substitutions of one correctly spelled word for another, such as *to* for *too*. Grammar checkers catch some common errors, but they also complain about some combinations of words that are not ungrammatical. There is no substitute for careful reading by a human being.

Almost all word processors nowadays have all the features needed for office work and student term papers. Not all of them handle mathematical formulae, chemical symbols, foreign languages, or long footnotes; if you will be typing academic or technical material, choose software that meets your specific needs. The most versatile academic word processor (but definitely not the easiest to use) is TEX, from Stanford University. *See* TEX; LATEX; DESKTOP PUBLISHING; TYPESETTING MISTAKES.

wordspacing The spacing between words. Sometimes called INTERWORD SPACING. *Contrast* LETTERSPACING.

WordStar a word processing program marketed by MicroPro in the 1980s; the first popular word processor for microcomputers. WordStar's editing commands have survived in numerous other pieces of software, including Turbo Pascal. For example, typing Ctrl-Y deletes a line of text and typing Ctrl-K Ctrl-D saves your document file on the disk.

word wrap the process whereby, as you type past the end of a line, the cursor automatically jumps to the next line, rearranging the placement of words as necessary to avoid breaking a word. This is a useful feature when you are using a computer as a word processor because it means that you do not need to hit the return key at the end of each line. It also makes it possible to "even up" the lengths of the lines when material has been added or deleted or margins have been changed.

workaround an improvised method of avoiding a problem, typically by avoiding the use of a defective part of a system. For example, if the Tab key on a keyboard does not work, one possible workaround is to use Ctrl-I instead — on many but not all systems, it transmits the same code.

workgroup
1. a group of people who work together on a single project via a computer network.
2. a group of computers that are treated as a small unit of a larger network.

Workplace Shell the user interface for OS/2 versions 2.1 and up, corresponding to PROGRAM MANAGER in Microsoft Windows.

workstation a powerful microcomputer typically used for scientific and engineering calculations. A workstation typically has more than 32 megabytes of RAM, more than 2 gigabytes of disk capacity, a screen with graphics resolution of at least 800×1000, and a UNIX-like operating system. Examples are the Sun Sparcstation and IBM RS/6000. Some Pentium-based PCs and some of the most powerful Macintoshes fall into the category of workstations. *See* IBM PC; MACINTOSH; SUN WORKSTATIONS; RISC; POWERPC.

World Wide Web (WWW) a loosely organized set of computer sites that publish information that anyone can read via the Internet, mainly using HTTP (Hypertext Transfer Protocol). Each screenful (*page*) of information includes menu choices and highlighted words through which the user can call up further information, either from the same computer or by linking automatically to another computer anywhere in the world. Thus, the information is arranged in a web of tremendous size, and the links are created by the author of each page. *See* INTERNET; HTML; BROWSER; MOSAIC; LYNX.

World Wide Web Consortium a group of member organizations founded in 1994 that works to develop standards and otherwise enhance the World Wide Web. See web address `http://www.w3.org`.

WORM (**w**rite **o**nce, **r**ead **m**any times) a type of optical disk where a computer can save information once, can then read that information, but cannot change it. By contrast, with CD-ROM (**C**ompact **D**isc **R**ead-**O**nly **M**emory), the computer can only read the disk and cannot record any new information on it. *See* CD-ROM.

Congratulations! You're a winner in the very first contest we've ever sponsored! You will get your choice of one of these fine prizes: First Prize—one week in Ghost Town, California! Grand prize—two weeks in Ghost Town, California! Winner pays all transportation costs, gratuities, hotel accommodations, taxes, and $5000 spending money! We provide the rest! Congratulations! You're a winner in the very first contest we've ever sponsored! You will get your choice of one of these fine prizes: First Prize—one week in Ghost Town, California! Grand prize—two weeks in Ghost Town, California! Winner pays all transportation costs, taxes, gratuities, hotel accommodations, and $5000 spending money! We provide the rest! Congratulations! You're a winner in the very first contest we've ever sponsored! You will get your choice of one of these fine prizes: First Prize—one week in Ghost Town, California! Grand prize—two weeks in Ghost Town, California! Winner pays all

FIGURE 301. TEXT WRAPPED AROUND A GRAPHIC

wrap to flow text from one line or column to the next; or to flow text around an illustration. *See also* WORD WRAP.

write to record digital information onto a disk or tape.

write-protect to set a disk or tape so that the computer will not write or erase the data on it. Write-protecting a diskette can keep a computer virus from being copied onto it. However, write-protecting will also block the operation of any software that normally writes on the diskette.

To write-protect a $5\frac{1}{4}$-inch diskette, place an opaque cover on the notch on the side. To write-protect a $3\frac{1}{2}$-inch diskette, slide the movable tab so that the hole is uncovered.

WRT with respect to, with regard to.

WTB e-mail abbreviation for "want to buy."

WWW WORLD WIDE WEB.

WYSIWYG acronym for "what you see is what you get." With a word processing program, this means that the appearance of the screen is supposedly an exact picture of how the document will look when printed.

X

X2 a standard formerly used by 3Com and other modem manufacturers for transmitting data on telephone lines at speeds up to 56,600 bits per second, now superseded by v.90.

X.25 an ITU-T (formerly CCITT) standard protocol that defines a standard way of arranging data in packets. Each packet contains information indicating which computer sent it and which computer should receive it. *See* PACKET. X.25 has been adapted for amateur packet radio, and the adapted version is called AX.25.

X86 abbreviation for 8086/286/386/486, i.e., the series of microprocessors used in all PC-compatible computers, including the Pentium but not the PowerPC. *See* MICROPROCESSOR.

XA *see* CD-ROM XA.

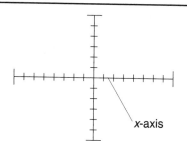

FIGURE 302. X-AXIS

x-axis the horizontal axis in an *x-y* coordinate system.

xcopy a command in DOS, OS/2, Windows 95, and other operating systems for copying groups of files. It works just like copy except that as many files as possible are read into memory before any are written to disk. This is usually faster than using copy. Also, with the /s option, xcopy will copy a directory with all its subdirectories.

XGA (**E**xtended **G**raphics **A**rray) a super VGA card marketed by IBM for the PS/2. The original XGA, introduced in 1991, offered 1024 × 768-pixel images with 256 colors (with the IBM 8514/A monitor) and

640×480 images with $2^{16} = 65{,}536$ colors (with the 8514/A and plain VGA monitors). *See* SUPER VGA.

FIGURE 303. X-HEIGHT

x-height the height of the *body* of the lowercase letterforms (such as the small x of a typeface). Some typefaces make x half as high as X; some make it 40% as high; and some make it 60% as high.

A typeface with a large x-height looks larger than a typeface of the same point size with a small x-height. *See also* FONT, TYPEFACE.

XML (**Ex**tensible **M**arkup **L**anguage) a subset of SGML adopted as a standard by the W3C in 1998. XML is designed to be easier to use than SGML while providing richer features and better implementation of LOGICAL DESIGN than HTML.

In an XML document, the beginning and end of elements of the document are marked with tags, such as `<from>` and `</from>` to mark the beginning and end of the part of a memo that indicates who the memo is from. Note that the notation for tags follows the same format as HTML. However, XML does not define a set of tags as does HTML. Instead, it is extensible because different users can extend the language definition with their own set of tags.

When an XML document uses these tags, a document type definition (DTD) is needed to define the elements. The DTD may be included in the XML document itself, or it may be in a separate document that can be used by all documents in the same document class.

Here is an example of an XML document that we could use to store data about people we might want to recruit for computer jobs in our company (page 542). In this example, the document type definition (DTD) is included at the front of the document.

This example creates a document type called RECRUITLIST, which consists of elements called RECRUITS. Because the DTD contains a plus sign after the declaration of RECRUIT, a document can have one or more recruits. Each RECRUIT can consist of four elements: NAME, ADDRESS, DEGREE, and ACCOMPLISHMENT. Each recruit must have exactly one NAME and one ADDRESS. The asterisk after DEGREE means that a recruit can have zero, one, or more degrees. The element NAME consists of three elements: FIRSTNAME, LASTNAME, and NICKNAME. The question mark after the definition of NICKNAME means that a name may contain zero or one nickname. Following the document type definition, this sample shows two particular recruits.

```xml
<?xml version="1.0" encoding="UTF-8"?>
<!DOCTYPE RECRUITLIST [
<!ELEMENT RECRUITLIST (RECRUIT+)>
<!ELEMENT RECRUIT (NAME,ADDRESS,DEGREE*,ACCOMPLISHMENT+)>
<!ELEMENT NAME (FIRSTNAME,LASTNAME,NICKNAME?)>
<!ELEMENT FIRSTNAME (#PCDATA)>
<!ELEMENT LASTNAME (#PCDATA)>
<!ELEMENT NICKNAME (#PCDATA)>
<!ELEMENT ADDRESS (STREET+,CITY,STATE,ZIP)>
    <!ELEMENT STREET (#PCDATA)>
    <!ELEMENT CITY (#PCDATA)>
    <!ELEMENT STATE (#PCDATA)>
    <!ELEMENT ZIP (#PCDATA)>
  <!ELEMENT DEGREE (SCHOOL, YEAR, TYPE)>
    <!ELEMENT SCHOOL (#PCDATA)>
    <!ELEMENT YEAR (#PCDATA)>
    <!ELEMENT TYPE (#PCDATA)>
  <!ELEMENT ACCOMPLISHMENT (#PCDATA)>
]>

<RECRUITLIST>
<RECRUIT>
<NAME>
    <FIRSTNAME>Bill</FIRSTNAME>
    <LASTNAME> Gates</LASTNAME>
    <NICKNAME> Trey </NICKNAME>
</NAME>
<ADDRESS>
    <STREET>One Microsoft Way</STREET>
    <CITY>Redmond</CITY>
    <STATE>Washington</STATE>
    <ZIP>98052</ZIP>
  </ADDRESS>
  <ACCOMPLISHMENT>Founded Microsoft</ACCOMPLISHMENT>
  <ACCOMPLISHMENT>Completed two years of Harvard
    </ACCOMPLISHMENT>
</RECRUIT>
<RECRUIT>
  <NAME>
    <FIRSTNAME>Donald</FIRSTNAME>
    <LASTNAME>Knuth</LASTNAME>
  </NAME>
  <ADDRESS>
    <STREET>353 Serra Mall</STREET>
    <CITY>Stanford</CITY>
    <STATE>California</STATE>
    <ZIP>94305</ZIP>
  </ADDRESS>
  <DEGREE>
    <SCHOOL>Case Institute of Technology</SCHOOL>
    <YEAR>1960</YEAR>
    <TYPE>B.S.</TYPE>
    </DEGREE>
    <DEGREE>
    <SCHOOL>California Institute of Technology</SCHOOL>
    <YEAR>1963</YEAR>
    <TYPE>Ph.D.</TYPE>
    </DEGREE>
  <ACCOMPLISHMENT>Created TeX</ACCOMPLISHMENT>
  </RECRUIT>
</RECRUITLIST>
```

If we run this document through an XML-validating parser, we can verify that it is a valid XML document. A valid XML document must contain a closing tag for each opening tag, the elements must be correctly nested inside each other, and all of the elements specified in the DTD must be present in the specified sequence. However, the XML parser will not process the data; that must be done with an application designed to work with this type of document. XML is intended for a broad array of applications, including presentation of web documents and storage and transfer of database information. For more information, *see* `www.w3.org/XML`.

XMODEM a protocol for transmitting files from one microcomputer to another and detecting transmission errors if they occur. XMODEM was developed by Ward Christensen and was used extensively by microcomputer hobbyists until more powerful protocols such as ZMODEM were developed. XMODEM will be described here because of its instructive value.

A computer using XMODEM transmits 128-byte blocks of data, each of which is followed by a checksum (a number derived mathematically from the ASCII codes of all the characters in the block). (*See* ASCII; CHECKSUM.) The receiving computer computes a checksum from the characters that it receives. Depending on whether or not this checksum agrees with the checksum transmitted with the data, the receiving computer then either asks for the next block or asks for the same block to be retransmitted.

The technical specifications for XMODEM are as follows:

1. Both computers must be set to transmit and receive 8 data bits per character (instead of the usual 7).

2. The receiving computer starts by transmitting ASCII code 21 once every 10 seconds until transmission begins.

3. Each block transmitted by the transmitting computer consists of the following, in the order named: ASCII code 01; an ASCII character indicating the block (01 for the first block, 02 for the second, etc.); an ASCII character whose code is 255 minus the block number; 128 bytes of data: and, finally, a checksum obtained by adding the ASCII codes for all the characters and taking the sum modulo 256.

4. The receiving computer indicates successful reception by transmitting ASCII 06 or asks for retransmission by transmitting ASCII 21.

YMODEM, ZMODEM and a number of similar protocols have been developed. They provide faster data transfers by using longer packets and allowing transmission of a packet to begin before acknowledgment of the previous packet has been received.

See also KERMIT.

X-OFF, X-ON codes that respectively turn off and on the transmission of data from a computer to a terminal. Many computers are programmed so that if the person at the terminal types Ctrl-S (X-OFF), the computer will stop transmitting until the person types Ctrl-Q (X-ON). This is convenient when the computer is transmitting information too fast for the user to read it. Moreover, when the terminal is actually another computer, X-OFF and X-ON signals can be used to keep information from being transmitted faster than it can be processed.

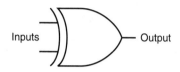

Inputs   Output

FIGURE 304. XOR GATE (LOGIC SYMBOL)

XOR gate (Exclusive-**OR** gate) a logic gate whose output is 1 when one but not both of its inputs is 1, as shown in the table:

Inputs		Output
0	0	0
0	1	1
1	0	1
1	1	0

The XOR function is interesting because if you XOR one bit pattern with another, you get an obscure pattern; but if you XOR that pattern with one of the original patterns, you get the other original pattern. *See* Figure 304. *See also* LOGIC CIRCUITS; COMPUTER ARCHITECTURE.

X server the process that manages the screen, keyboard, and mouse in the X Window System. *See* X WINDOW SYSTEM.

XT the second model of IBM PC, introduced in 1983. The PC XT had eight expansion slots instead of the original five and it included a 10-megabyte hard disk. The microprocessor was a 4.77-MHz 8088 with an 8-bit bus, just as in the original PC.

X terminal a terminal that is actually a small computer capable of running the X Window System. The terminal functions as an X server, managing the screen, keyboard, and mouse, while all other computation is done on the remote computer. *See* X WINDOW SYSTEM.

X Window System ("X Windows" for short) a software package for UNIX systems that allows programs to display text and graphics in windows and respond to a mouse (*see* WINDOW). X Windows software was developed at MIT and is distributed free. Commercial extensions of it have been developed; an example is Open Windows, from Sun Microsystems.

X Windows relies on multitasking. A process called an *X server* manages the screen, keyboard, and mouse; other processes call on the X server when they want to use these devices.

Y

Y2K abbreviation for YEAR 2000 PROBLEM. (K stands for "thousand.")

Y2K compliant unaffected by the YEAR 2000 PROBLEM. Technically, to be Y2K compliant, a piece of software must never print the year as two digits. In practice, however, no problem is caused by printing 2000 as 00 so long as calculations involving the date come out correctly.

Yahoo a popular SEARCH ENGINE for the WORLD WIDE WEB, accessible at http://www.yahoo.com. Yahoo also offers other Internet services.

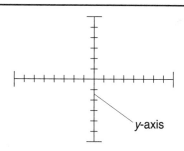

FIGURE 305. Y-AXIS

y-axis the vertical axis in an *x*-*y* coordinate system (Fig. 305).

Year 2000 Problem (Also known as *Y2K Problem*) the problem caused by software that represents the year date as two digits (such as 99 for 1999) and thus does not recognize that 2000 comes after 1999. Instead, the software interprets 00 as 1900. This causes mistakes in calculations that involve the date.

Dates were originally represented as two digits for two reasons. First, in the 1960s, computer memories were very expensive, and even the largest computers' total memory was far smaller than that of a modern PC. Second, data was stored on punched cards, each of which could hold only 80 characters; the two characters saved by omitting "19" could be used for something else.

Some banks dealt with the Year 2000 Problem as early as 1970 when issuing 30-year loans. In 1998 and 1999, computer users were urged to update all software, and there was widespread panic as news media reported that all types of machinery, even microprocessor-controlled car engines and coffee makers, would fail on January 1, 2000. These predictions proved false; problems occurred in only out-of-date accounting software and the like. Nonetheless, much of the updating was necessary or beneficial for other reasons.

Yellow Book the book that originally defined the Philips/Sony standard for recording data on CD-ROMs.

YKYBHTLW abbreviation for "**y**ou **k**now **y**ou've **b**een **h**acking **t**oo **l**ong **w**hen," as in "YKYBHTLW you start to dream in C++." In this expression, *hacking* means "programming," not "attempting computer crime." *See* HACKER.

YMMV e-mail abbreviation for "**y**our **m**ileage **m**ay **v**ary" (i.e., your results may be different).

YMODEM a data transfer protocol similar to XMODEM but using 1024-byte blocks and using cyclical redundancy checks instead of checksums. *See* XMODEM.

yotta- metric prefix meaning $\times 1,000,000,000,000,000,000,000,000$ (10^{24}). *Yotta* is apparently a nonsense word. *See* METRIC PREFIXES.

Z

Z80 an 8-bit microprocessor produced by Zilog, Inc., and used in micro-computers that ran the CP/M operating system in the early 1980s. *See* MICROPROCESSOR.

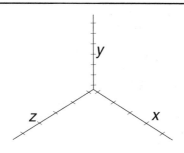

FIGURE 306. Z-AXIS

z-axis the direction toward and away from the viewer in a three-dimensional coordinate system. *Compare* X-AXIS, Y-AXIS.

z-buffer (3D program) an editing buffer that allows the program to keep track of objects that are hidden from view by other objects.

zero wait states *see* WAIT STATE.

zetta- metric prefix meaning $\times 1,000,000,000,000,000,000,000$ (10^{21}). *Zetta* is apparently a nonsense word. *See* METRIC PREFIXES.

ZIF socket (**Z**ero **I**nsertion **F**orce socket) a socket into which an integrated circuit can be inserted without pressure. It has a lever to open up the holes for easy insertion. The lever is then moved to tighten the connectors once the IC is in place.

Zip drive a 100-megabyte removable-cartridge disk drive made by Iomega Corporation of Roy, Utah. Zip drives are often used in the graphic arts to transfer data files that are too large to fit on diskettes. *Compare* BERNOULLI BOX; JAZ DRIVE; EZ DRIVE.

ZIP file a file compressed with PKZIP, a program written by Phil Katz, or with compatible software from other sources. (ZIP files are not related in any way to Iomega Zip drives.)

PKZIP runs on the IBM PC and compatibles and is distributed as shareware. Like its predecessor ARC, PKZIP takes one or more files, compresses them, and stores them in a single file with a name ending in `.zip`. This not only saves space but also makes it easy to keep a group of related files together. The contents of the ZIP file can be unpacked by the program PKUNZIP.

PKZIP also creates "self-extracting" files. These are actually programs that, when run, will unpack themselves into sets of files. Like most executable programs, self-extracting ZIP files have names ending in `.exe`. *See* ARC; DATA COMPRESSION; STUFFIT.

Finally, PKZIP can split a file or group of files across more than one diskette. This is sometimes the only convenient way to transport a file that is too large to fit on a diskette.

ZMODEM a data transmission protocol similar to YMODEM except that it does not wait for each block to be acknowledged before sending the next one; it resends a block only when it receives a NAK. Blocks are 512 bytes long. *See* XMODEM; YMODEM.

FIGURE 307. ZOOM (DEFINITION 1)

zoom

1. to examine a small area of a document closely. The amount of zoom is usually expressed as a percentage and displayed in a status line. To *zoom in* is to increase the magnification; to *zoom out* is to return to normal view (Fig. 307).

FIGURE 308. ZOOM (DEFINITION 2)

2. (animation) to gradually increase the apparent camera focal length during a shot, thus "moving in on" a desired element in the picture frame.

CHARACTERS AND SYMBOLS

Many symbols fall into more than one category. See also ELECTRONIC CIRCUIT SYMBOLS and FLOWCHART for the symbols used in diagrams.

Computer Keyboard Symbols

^	circumflex, hat
~	tilde
`	grave accent
'	upright quotation mark, apostrophe
'	left quotation mark
'	right quotation mark, apostrophe
"	double quotation mark
@	at sign
#	pound sign, crosshatch, octothorpe
$	dollar sign
€	Euro sign
%	percent sign
&	ampersand
+	plus sign
−	minus sign, hyphen
_	underscore mark
=	equal sign
*	asterisk
/	slash
\	backslash
|	vertical bar, pipe
< >	less than/greater than *or* angle brackets
( )	parentheses, round brackets
[ ]	square brackets
{ }	braces, curly brackets
¬	not sign (EBCDIC)

Note: In ASCII, ' is equivalent to ' and ` is equivalent to '.

"Emoticons" used in e-mail

:)	smiling face (happiness, amusement)
:(	frowning face (sadness, disappointment)
−)	tongue in cheek

Commercial and scientific symbols

@	at, price each
#	identifying number *or* pounds (weight)
%	percent (per hundred)
$^0\!/_{00}$	per mil (per thousand)
°	degrees
ℓ	litres (obsolete; use L instead)
Ω	ohms
μ	micro- (millionths)
©	copyright
$	dollars, pesos
¥	yen
£	pounds (currency), lire

English Punctuation

.	period
,	comma
:	colon
;	semicolon
!	exclamation mark
?	question mark
-	hyphen
–	en dash, minus sign
—	em dash
…	ellipsis dots
'	upright single quotation mark, apostrophe
"	upright double quotation mark
'	left single quotation mark
"	left double quotation mark
'	right single quotation mark, apostrophe
"	right double quotation mark
*	asterisk (first footnote)
†	dagger (second footnote)
‡	double dagger (third footnote)
§	section mark
¶	paragraph mark (pilcrow)
•	bullet (to mark list items)

Accents

á	acute accent
a̋	double acute accent
à	grave accent
â	circumflex
ä	umlaut or dieresis
ã	tilde
ā	macron (long vowel mark)
ă	breve (short vowel mark)
č	wedge (hachek)
ç	cedilla

Other Foreign Characters

„ "	German quotation marks
« »	French quotation marks (guillemets)
¿	Spanish inverted question mark
¡	Spanish inverted exclamation mark
ß	German ss (estsett)
Æ æ	AE digraph
Œ œ	OE digraph
Å å	A with circle (Scandinavian)
Ø ø	O with slash (Scandinavian)
Ł ł	Barred L (Polish)
İ i I ı	Dotted and dotless I (Turkish)

Arithmetic and Algebra

$=$	equals
$\neq$	does not equal
$\approx, \doteq$	is approximately equal to
$>$	is greater than
$\geq$	is greater than or equal to
$<$	is less than
$\leq$	is less than or equal to
$+$	addition
$-$	subtraction

Arithmetic and Algebra (continued)

$\times, \cdot$	multiplication
$\div, /$	division
$\sqrt{}$	square root
$\sqrt[n]{}$	nth root
$!$	factorial
$|x|$	absolute value of x
∞	infinity
$\propto$	is proportional to
Δx	change in x
$\int$	integral
∂	partial derivative

Mathematical Logic

$\forall x, (x)$	universal quantifier ("for all x...")
$\exists x$	existential quantifier ("there exists an x...")
$-p, \neg p, \sim p$	negation ("not p")
$p \wedge q, p \& q$	conjunction ("p and q")
$p \vee q$	disjunction ("p or q")
$p \veebar q$	exclusive-or ("p or q but not both")
$p \rightarrow q, p \supset q$	implication ("if p then q")
$p \leftrightarrow q, p \equiv q$	equivalence ("p if and only if q")
$p \vdash q$	from p one can derive q

Set Theory

$\{a, b, c\}$	set whose members are a, b, and c
$\emptyset$	empty set
$\cup$	set union (elements in one or both of two sets)
$\cap$	set intersection (elements shared by two sets)
$\backslash$	set subtraction (elements in one set and not the other)
$\in$	is an element of
$\subset$	is a subset of
$\subseteq$	is a subset of or equals

Greek Alphabet

A	α	alpha	
B	β	beta	
Γ	γ	gamma	
Δ	δ	delta	
E	ϵ	epsilon	(ε in some typefaces)
Z	ζ	zeta	
H	η	eta	
Θ	θ	theta	(ϑ in some typefaces)
I	ι	iota	
K	κ	kappa	
Λ	λ	lambda	
M	μ	mu	
N	ν	nu	
Ξ	ξ	xi	
O	o	omicron	
Π	π	pi	(ϖ in some typefaces)
P	ρ	rho	(ϱ in some typefaces)
Σ	σ	sigma	(ς at ends of words)
T	τ	tau	
Υ	υ	upsilon	
Φ	ϕ	phi	(φ in some typefaces)
X	χ	chi	
Ψ	ψ	psi	
Ω	ω	omega	

Typeset in Adobe Times Roman
with the Y&Y TEX System
using TEX 3.14159 and LATEX2e
under Windows 98
on a 450-MHz
Intel Pentium III processor
by
Melody Covington

Covington Innovations
Athens, Georgia
July 13, 2000

More selected BARRON'S titles: